The Bodhisattva Warriors

The Bodhisattva Warriors

The Origin, Inner Philosophy, History and Symbolism of the
Buddhist Martial Art within India and China

Shifu Nagaboshi Tomio
(Terence Dukes)

SAMUEL WEISER, INC.

York Beach, Maine

First published in 1994 by
Samuel Weiser, Inc.
P. O. Box 612
York Beach, Maine 03910-0612
www.weiserbooks.com

Library of Congress Cataloging-in-Publication Data
Dukes, Terence.
    The Bodhisattva warriors : the origin, inner philosophy, history and
symbolism of the Buddhist martial art within India and China / by Shifu
Nagaboshi Tomio (Terence Dukes).
        p. cm.
    Includes bibliographical references and index.
    1. Kung fu—History. 2. Martial arts—Religious aspects—Buddhism.
3. Buddhism—Doctrines. I. Title.
GV1114.7.D85   1994
294.3'4446—dc20   93-45655

ISBN 0-87728-785-6   CIP
EB

Cover image: The Bodhisattva Acalanatha. This image was seen in 838 by the
Tendai Monk Enchin and is known as the "yellow" form of Acalanatha. The orig-
inal is preserved at the Onjojii Temple in Japan. Copy painted by Ryusen
Miyahara.

Typeset in 10 point Palatino
Printed in the United States of America

09 08 07 06 05 04 03 02 01
12 11 10 9 8 7 6 5 4

The paper used in this publication meets the minimum requirements of the
American National Standard for Information Sciences—Permanence of Paper for
Printed Library Materials Z39.48-1992(R1997).

This work is dedicated to my mother Catherine Ellen Dukes who died suddenly and unexpectedly on November 28th, 1989. Her constant and innumerable acts of kindness, unselfish devotion and compassion to others still inspire those who knew her.

CONTENTS

LIST OF ILLUSTRATIONS X

LIST OF TABLES...XV

ACKNOWLEDGMENTS xvii

INTRODUCTION xix

A NOTE FOR TEACHERS OR STUDENTS OF THE MARTIAL ARTS xxi

BEGINNING THE STUDY 1

THE MANDALA OF ELEMENTS 6

> The natural elements, historical notes. Buddhism's view of self. Elements and symbols. Nature of Mind, its layers and composition. Knowledge of self. Mind in Buddhism, self-discovery, meditation, the schools of Buddhism. Descriptions of consciousness, Chinese approaches, monks and temples, monk's rules and symbols. Symbols of the elements, their origin and development.

THE MANDALA OF HUMAN CHARACTERISTICS 43

> The person as elements, their usage, scriptural precedents. Somatypes in doctrine and scriptures, their basis. The individual described. Paradigm and co-relation. The basis, bases, and types of mandala. Mandala patterning and development. Qualities of mind and body.

THE MANDALA OF SYMBOLISM 56

> History and evolution of the symbols of wisdom. India, China and beyond. Fundamental symbols and their meanings. The Sotoba explained. Colors, shapes and various teachings. Paradigms, the sacred rite. Practices of purification in mind and body, various methods and requirements for this. Self fictions, development of the mandala. Chinese Mikkyo, mandalas explained, their history and types. Personal mandalas. Development of mandalas and their spread. Simultaneous being. Rites and rituals.

THE MANDALA OF EXPERIENCE 93

> Using the body as a basis of spiritual study. Somatypes of man and Buddha. The body mandala, dangers of training, Hatha and Buddhist yogas. Differences of object and evolution in Hindu and Buddhist Yogas. Doctrinal requirements, geographical extension. Attitudes and study, development of philosophy and mysticism. Logic and Nagarjuna, monk and laymen, physical arts. Monasteries in China, their function and duties.

THE MANDALA OF HEALING 117

> Buddhist medicine and healing in principle and practice. Taoist forms of medicine and healing, their differences and interconnections or antagonisms. Historical precedents and practices. India and China compared. Indian healing technique in general. Energy, prana, organic energy, and its centers. Monk healers, their traditions and teachers. Esoteric healing, methods, diagnosis, treatments, related principles, storing energies, reviving the dead. Emergency techniques and methods. Elemental mandalas. Social contexts.

THE MANDALA OF MOVEMENT 153

> The Indian background and Vedic precedents, the Ksatreya and their methods. Weapons and battles. Unarmed combat. Nata, its accounts in literature. Historical contexts and terminology. Vajramukti, Buddhist sutra accounts and records. Ritual mudra. The concept of safety. The Buddha and warriors. Theravada accounts of combative psychology. Sutta accounts. Nagarjuna, Asanga, Shantideva. Development of Vajramukti in India and China. The sacred Nata, its positions and defenses. Interpersonal combat, principles involved in this. The Protectors. Tibet, Buddhist history, doctrines and battles. Monastic soldiers. The mandala and the esoteric masters. Principles and practice. Sthana and Samasthana, schools of practice. Awareness and realization. Pratima. Astadasarahantapani. Hsing and Pratima. Sanchin, its supernatural powers. Death by magic. Esoteric healing and combative methods. The Mahasuklaja, Jetavana, the word "white." Tiger striking. Marma and Nadi. Chinese accounts and events, legends. Development of principles, Marma, Jivat, movement awareness, and meditation practices. Karma and Klesa. The five elemental Nata of energy. The Hsing of five elements. Conditioned confusion, intellectual facades. The Mind of the body. Vital points of the human organism. Clear experience and clearing experiences, inner revolution, dangers, fear, inner aggression. The wordless doctrine. Spiritual and human emulation. The ego, self images, fighting and non-self, ethics. Associated characteristics and symbols. Epilogue.

APPENDICES

APPENDIX 1: THE MAIN CHINESE BUDDHIST DYNASTIES 283

APPENDIX 2: CHRONOLOGY OF THE MAIN BUDDHIST SUTRAS 284

APPENDIX 3: VIEWS OF MIND 285

APPENDIX 4: DEVELOPMENT OF EARLY INDIAN BUDDHIST SECTS 295

APPENDIX 5: BODHIDHARMA, WU TI, AND CHAAN-NA 296

APPENDIX 6: TRANSLATION OF BODHIDHARMA'S CHINESE TEXTS 305

THE SIX GATES (SHAO SHIH LIU MEN) 306

ENTERING THE BUDDHA'S PATH (JU TAO LUN) 309

TREATISE UPON THE BLOODLINE TEACHING OF TRUE DHARMA (*HSIEH MAI LUN*) 318

APPENDIX 7: CHRONOLOGICAL RECORDS OF SCRIPTURES,
              TEACHERS, AND EVENTS DURING THE FIRST
              1000 YEARS OF INDIAN AND CHINESE BUDDHISM 362
APPENDIX 8: PARADIGMS OF THE ESOTERIC MANDALA 391

NOTES AND REFERENCE 393
GLOSSARY 487
INDEX 517
THE MUSHINDOKAI.. 529
ABOUT THE AUTHOR 531

LIST OF ILLUSTRATIONS

Figure 1.   Shakyamuni Buddha making the
mudra of "Teaching the Law" (Dharmacakra)..........4

Figure 2.   Sanskrit—the language of the early scriptures. 8

Figure 3.   Shakyamuni Buddha. 9

Figure 4.   The death of Shakyamuni. 10

Figure 5.   Ancient Chinese map showing navigable
waterways and rivers...............................24

Figure 6.   The Bo Tree at Bodhgaya..........................27

Figure 7.   Monks conduct a
devotional ceremony at the Bo Tree..................27

Figure 8.   Shaving the head...................................28

Figure 9.   Present day ruins of Nalanda University. 29

Figure 10.   "Entering the Mountains." 31

Figure 11.   The empty Chair of the Buddha.....................33

Figure 12.   A popular Buddhist charm of the Theravada school . . . 34

Figure 13.   One of the many forms of the
Buddhist Wheel of Dharma (Dharmacakra). 34

Figure 14.   Worshipping the Stupa. 35

Figure 15.   Carving, said to be of a Cakravartin showing
Vajramukti hand strikes and foot positions. 36

Figure 16.   Traditional chart of medical points. 38

Figure 17.   A rubbing of an engraving showing the harmony
between Taoism, Confucianism, and Buddhism. 39

Figure 18.   A Lamaistic magic charm said to ease
childbirth and given to pregnant women to carry......40

Figure 19.   The Face of Shakyamuni Buddha....................46

Figure 20.   Auspicious markings upon the feet of the Buddha.....47

Figure 21.   Nataraja, the Lord of the Nata. 49

Figure 22.   Different ways to look at somatypes. 54

Figure 23.   Combining the elements
and the qualities (on somatypes). 54

Figure 24.   The hill at Kusinagara marking the place
where Shakyamuni Buddha's body was cremated. 57

Figure 25.   The tower marking the spot where
the Buddha met his former ascetic
colleagues and converted them to the Dharma. 57

Figure 26.   The Bodhisattva Akasagarbha (Womb of Space)......58

Figure 27.   Kukai, one of the Japanese
founders of esoteric Buddhism. 58

Figure 28.   The Bodhisattva Avalokitesvara
              (Chinese: Kuan Yin). 59
Figure 29.   The Bodhisattva Samantabhadra. 60
Figure 30.   The Sanskrit character for the letter "A." 61
Figure 31.   Students practicing Zen meditation.................. 61
Figure 32.   Various Buddhist schools. 62
Figure 33.   One of many forms of Mahavairocana Buddha....... 63
Figure 34.   Mahavairocana Buddha, the primordial Buddha. 64
Figure 35.   The Vajra (Japanese Kongo) symbol of the power
              of enlightenment.................................... 65
Figure 36.   Different forms of Vajra (Kongo) used in
              esoteric rituals..................................... 66
Figure 37.   Ancient Chinese stone carving marking the
              burial place of Hsuan Tsang. 67
Figure 38.   Sotoba gravestone................................. 68
Figure 39.   Sotoba gravestones in the Mount Koya graveyard. 69
Figure 40.   Chinese text of the *Panjo Polomito Hsin Cing*
              (Sanskrit: *Prajna Paramita Hrdaya Sutra*). 72
Figure 41.   A Monk performs an esoteric ritual
              wearing the "Crown of Wisdoms" 74
Figure 42.   Some of the author's Tibetan teachers
              gather for a ceremony at Dharamsala. 78
Figure 43.   An esoteric mandala laid out
              for the performance of a ritual before a shrine........ 80
Figure 44.   Akasagharba Bodhisattva (Matrix of Space). 81
Figure 45.   The fundamental mandala 82
Figure 46.   Esoteric mudras performed in
              secret beneath the long sleeves of a monk's robe. 83
Figure 47.   Grand Abbot Yamada,
              Japanese head of the Tendai Sect. 88
Figure 48.   The animal thrones of the mandala Buddhas
              used in the "Tattvasamgraha" esoteric text. 89
Figure 49.   Maitreya Bodhisattva............................. 90
Figure 50.   Temple mural vividly depicting individual
              characteristics of Arahants and Sages. 97
Figure 51.   Remains of the Monastery of Kusinagara........... 104
Figure 52.   Imperial warriors hunting their enemies. 109
Figure 53.   Imperial soldiers attack the eastern teachers. 114
Figure 54.   A peasant, punished by Taoist judges. 116
Figure 55.   Cover page of the *Nei Ching*. 120
Figure 56.   Taoist long life magic charm....................... 122

Figure 57. Diagram showing acupuncture
points and their individual names................... 124

Figure 58. Chart used in Nyingmapa Buddhism
showing various energy centers of the body.......... 126

Figure 59. Chinese Taoist based text
showing points along the front of the body
at which massage can be usefully applied............ 127

Figure 60. Indian manuscript
showing the Chakras of Hatha Yoga................ 128

Figure 61. Hindu diagram showing
the psychic energy centers of the body.............. 128

Figure 62. The Marmas in the superior extremity............... 130

Figure 63. The Marmas in the head and neck.................. 131

Figure 64. Diagram showing the relative distances
between various vital points of the body.
Also, emergency treatments for a drowned person.... 132

Figure 65. Last page of the introductory
chapter to the *Ch'ien Chin Peng*.................... 133

Figure 66. Buddhist talisman bearing
the image of Avalokitesvara....................... 141

Figure 67. Energy flows within the human body............... 143

Figure 68. A modern chart of the acupuncture points........... 144

Figure 69. A Vedic Deity astride a battle elephant............. 145

Figure 70. Treating or diagnosing the vital points............. 146

Figure 71. A scroll by Chang Sheng Wen
in the Tang period style........................... 148

Figure 72. A Tibetan version of an Indian Talisman............ 150

Figure 73. Two ancient Greek Pancration fighters.............. 156

Figure 74. Temple carving showing
the slaying of a horse by means of a foot strike....... 160

Figure 75. Miniature painting showing a fight between the
Vedic Deities Rama and Sahasrajuna................ 161

Figure 76. The Vedic Deity Yama carrying
a Vajra mace in his right hand..................... 162

Figure 77. The battle of Kurukshetra, mentioned in the Mahabharata, in which Bhima and Durodhana fought...... 164

Figure 78. Jayadratha and Abhimanu fight with
their sacred Bows from their war Chariots........... 165

Figure 79. Two lesser deities fighting....................... 166

Figure 80. Krishna engaged in combat
attempts a throwing technique..................... 167

Figure 81. Siddhartha firing
the winning arrow at a competition................. 168

Figure 82. Vasudeva carries the infant Krishna
across the river Yamuna. 170

Figure 83. Part of the Asoka Pillar bearing
inscriptions in Karosthi script Sanskrit. 172

Figure 84. Nataraja 173

Figure 85. Pages of an ancient Chinese Lotus Sutra. 176

Figure 86. The Four Eyes, or grimaces,
described in the *Gobushinkan*. .179

Figure 87. Illustration of a meditation visualization. 180

Figure 88. A figure from 14th century Japan based upon the
Chinese models. 185

Figure 89. Tung Huang cave statues
of a Bodhisattva and two guardians who
are in "on guard" positions of Chuan Fa.. 186

Figure 90. Tibetan Lamas perform
esoteric Mudras during a ritual. 187

Figure 91. A Vajracchedika Sutra frontispiece.. 189

Figure 92. Wall paintings found at the
Tung Huang Caves in Kiangsu, China.. 194

Figure 93. A page from the *Jogoku Zoshi* (Illustration of Hell). . . .199

Figure 94. Japanese statue of Asanga. (Courtesy of Dr. Wei Tat.).. 200

Figure 95. The Potola Palace of the Dalai Lama. 203

Figure 96. The Gagaku dances of Japan. 206

Figure 97. Rubbings taken from tombstones. 207

Figure 98. The five Buddhas of Kongokai Mahamandala. 210

Figure 99. The four Boddhisattvas surrounding the Buddha
Amoghasiddhi in the Kongokai Mahamandala. 211

Figure 100. Vajrasandhi Bodhisattva. 212

Figure 101. Mahavairocana Buddha. 213

Figure 102. Vajranrita (female Bodhisattva). 214

Figure 103. Pages of Shaolin Temple records. 217

Figure 104. Sotoba towers marking the graves
of monks at the Shaolin temple in Honan, China. 217

Figure 105. Modern Indian Nata dancer. 219

Figure 106. Fudo (Acalaraja with attendants). 228

Figure 107. Bodhidharma. 229

Figure 108. Bodhisattva performing hand movements
from the "Asthimajja Parisuddhi." 230

Figure 109. Restored statues of Arahants
at the Shaolin temple, Honan. 231

Figure 110. Arahants. 232

Figure 111. Nakala, one of the Arahants, with attendants. 233

Figure 112. Gosanze Mio (Trilokavijaya Vidyaraja). 234

Figure 113. Shakyamuni rising from his coffin. 238

Figure 114.   Close-up of figure 92. The figure's left hand is
              clearly held in a knuckle striking position. 240
Figure 115.   Part of one of the historical texts
              prepared by Tibetan Lamas for the author. 244
Figure 116.   A suit of armor unearthed
              by Chinese archaeologists. 245
Figure 117.   The Dalai Lama and the
              Panchen Lama at their first meeting in
              Peking since the Chinese invasion of Tibet. 246
Figure 118.   Vajralasi (female Bodhisattva). 263
Figure 119.   The figure of Mahavairocana Buddha. 264
Figure 120.   Avalokitesvara, the Bodhisattva of Compassion. 268
Figure 121.   Ragaraja, the Bodhisattva
              governing passions and infatuations. 272
Figure 122.   The Bodhisattva Acalaraja with two boy attendants . . 273
Figure 123.   The Bodhisattva Samantabhadra. 274
Figure 124.   Acal Vidyaraja carrying
              the sword which destroys ignorance. 418
Figure 125.   Enryakuji, head temple of the Tendai sect in Japan. . . . 427
Figure 126.   A Tibetan Lama watching
              the practice of Chuan Fa in 1965 443
Figure 127.   The author teaching
              students at a Tibetan Monastery. 443
Figure 128.   A 19th century Taoist forgery of Bodhidharma's
              Astimajja Parisuddhi (Kuzui Chin Ching) and
              a page from a copy of a temple original. 464

LIST OF TABLES

Table 1: Element and Ruling Colors 70
Table 2: Elements and Colors 70
Table 3: Outline of Associated Qualities in the Chinese Tops 73
Table 4: Basic Paradigms of the
Mandala in Southern Chinese Traditions 91
Table 5: Chart of Development and
Nomenclature in the Art of Vajramukti 242
Table 6: Vajramukti Elemental Animal Rulers 273
Table 7: Schools of Teaching 292
Table 8: The Eightfold Nature of Consciousness 292
Table 9: Time and Events 355

ACKNOWLEDGMENTS

A work such as this is really the result of working with many different people. I would like to express my gratitude to everyone who helped, inspired, and advised me during the thirty plus years of study that enabled me to form this book. It has been a privilege to study with my teachers and initiators in both *Chuan Fa* and *Chen Yen*: the Ven Ajari Hsien Tan and Ajari Ryoshu Otomo. The Ryukyuan Otomo and Itosu families, who kept and cared for me in my visits to them. They made it possible for me to meet remarkable men, study rare documents, partake of their native and Buddhist spirituality, and come to know something of the grandeur of their once great nation. Sensei Yasuka, formerly of Okinawa, and Sensei Murakami, of Japan, are both now in Taiwan. I thank my teacher and friend in Oriental Medicine and healing, the late Sensei Shuzo Okada. I thank my guide in Sanskrit, Dr. R. Mishra, and my guide in the Yogacara Sutra, the late Dr. Wei Tat, of Hong Kong. Hikoji Kimura—"Deshi," of Kenwa Mabuni, who spent many hours talking of his experiences. I thank The Mahasthavira Sangharakshita, who perhaps alone in Britain has the diversity and magnanimity of Vasubandhu.

I also thank the following for their various forms of aid, encouragement and advice over the years: Ven Lama L. Gya, Ven Dragpa Dorje (State Oracle of Tibet), Chogyam Trungpa Rinpoche, Ven Candamitto, Sensei M. Oki (for many details and anecdotes concerning his friend Miyagi and others in the Ryukyus and China), T. Hironishi, K. Yamanishi, M. Obata, Z. Shimabukuro, T. Marushima, Shingon Kyoshi, J. Tanaka, Ven Kyudo Roshi (of Ryutakuji), Ven H. Nakamura of Enkakuji, Ven Hyun Ho, Ven Abbess Kuang Wu Li, and Ven J. Myung Soong of Unmunsa Temple (Korea), the family of Ryusen Miyahara (who kindly allowed me to make copies of that great artist's beautiful paintings), Hiroshi Andoh and Koichiro Yoshida of Kosei Publishing (Tokyo) for seeking out and allowing me to use various pictures from *Dharma World*, Morgan Gibson and H. Murakami for use of their poem, Dr. M. L. Gharote of India for his aid on the Kalaripayyat of Kerala and the Marma system, Prof. Lokesh Chandra for his comments upon the "Sword and the Fist," the various national agencies and museums of India, China, and Japan who have assisted in many ways, my persevering proofreader Catherine Bell, and all the instructors and students, both East and West, of the Ryukyu Mushindo Kempo Association and its affiliate groups, who unselfishly serve students and try to make known the path of the Bodhisattva Warriors.

Any and all errors are, of course, entirely my own.

Nagaboshi Tomio
Kongoryuji Temple
Wesak, 1993

Introduction

This work is an account of the origins, history, and influences in the Buddhist art called exclusively *Chuan Fa* by its Chinese practitioners. (This term has been translated into Japanese as *Kempo*.) The art of *Chuan Fa* is what the media often (and incorrectly) calls *Kung Fu*. Proper *Chuan Fa* embodies a tradition from which most of the significant schools of *Karate, Tae Kwon Do, Thai Boxing,* and other "martial arts" have developed their technique. It is also a vision of human potential that is desperately needed in modern times. *Chuan Fa* teachings have directly influenced—and may have, indeed, created—the Japanese art called *Ju Jitsu*, from which *Judo* came, and via this, the art of *Aikido*.

This text covers the first 1,000 years of *Chuan Fa's* development and doctrine as it spread from ancient India into China and beyond. It sets out clearly, and uncompromisingly, the fundamental background and philosophy of the art, and traces its development, influence, and growth. Unlike other books on *Karate* or *Chuan Fa*, the reader will not find this work filled with photographs of physical tricks designed to impress others.

This book is addressed to those who are interested in learning more of the original forms of study within *Chuan Fa*, that is, by including both *Chuan Fa* and the Buddhist teachings equally. There are many who mistakenly believe Buddhism to be a predominantly philosophical teaching that regards physical and spiritual being as incompatible—or even antagonistic—toward each other. The realization of the real basis of the art demonstrates clearly that commercialism and competitiveness are inimical to the teaching and to its teachers. This realization will protect unknowing students from exploitative financial and other manipulation.

A work such as this, which seeks to bring together again realms which should never have been parted, can all too easily fall into over-specialization. I have tried to avoid this and have tried, instead, to present each aspect of practice in terms of its complementary manifestation within the other.

The real *Chuan Fa* is an exploration, study, and discovery of the body through the medium of the mind. It is an exploration of the mind through the medium of the body. Its teaching draws equally upon the practices of the North Chinese Chaan Movement Meditation Tradition, and on the South Chinese Esoteric (*Mi Chiao*) school—both secret traditions rarely known or revealed to the general public, either East or West.

A Note for Teachers
or Students of the Martial Arts

One would think it self-evident that we cannot seriously understand the meaning of the Buddhist Martial Art tradition in China or elsewhere without looking at both its history and the ethical and spiritual philosophy upon which it is based. However most of the currently available "authorative" literature soon demonstrates that it does not explain the subject in the balanced way it deserves. The correct manner to approach such a study requires that we examine both inner and outer levels. It should be non-sectarian and explain central principles. In order to achieve such an approach it is essential that we familiarize ourselves with the most vital prerequisite for such a study—the philosophy from within which *Chuan Fa* developed and grew.

Until we know its background, we can never really come to know our art in a balanced way. The history of the "Dharma Clasped Hand" (*Chuan Fa*) lies so embedded in the Buddhist teaching it cannot truly be separated from it. A balanced study of either reveals their interconnecting influences and we will see that at certain times the two relied upon each other for their continued existence.

That we have to consider a prerequisite study is necessitated by the fact that many works upon Buddhism ignore *Chuan Fa* completely and, more commonly, popular works about *Chuan Fa* or its derivatives, such as *Karate*, also ignore any serious consideration of Buddhism. Unfortunately many works concerning Buddhism have been written by people who have never fully implemented its teaching by becoming monks or nuns. These writers are often unnecessarily academic or over intellectual in their presentations. This has resulted in such works never becoming popularly received or understood. Other, purely academic works concerning the Buddhist sutras (the written teachings of Buddhism) take the form of literal analysis or criticism and consequently do not seem to either understand or convey the practical spiritual message the scriptures were clearly intended to teach. From a Buddhist point of view, they are therefore of limited value. Even worse some authors actually dismiss certain texts as "forgeries" because they may appear (to them) to contain words, paragraphs, dates or references which are anomalous to some other text they regard as more authentic.*

Teachings which many thousands, perhaps millions, of people have studied, teachings that governed peoples' daily lives can never be forgeries—they are spiritual classics. Even if it could be clearly shown that their authorship has been wrongly attributed, their spiritual power remains undiminished. The point of a sutra is not who wrote it

---

*See Note 87 in the reference section.

down but the quality of its content. The word forgery has no meaning in a balanced spiritual training as spiritual insight arises from the depths of our being and nowhere else. A moment of such insight can be worth more than a lifetime's experience. A "middling" teaching by a famous Master may have less value than a brilliant one by an unknown student, and all teaching actually put into practice is superior to a teaching that is not.

A similar, though different, situation exists when we consider works about Karate. Popular works often attempt, by superficialization, to minimize their Buddhist content, and many reputed "Masters" do not even know Buddhism's real significance to their art. Why is this? There seem to be a range of reasons.

1) Disinterest due mainly to a lack of suitable and original research—despite plentiful material for those who know where (or how) to look. Such a reason develops from the insufficiencies present in the arts' instructors—for either not being taught properly in the first place, or lacking a vision of the art which embraces such possibilities. Students studying with such teachers unfortunately, and unknowingly, suffer the same deficit.

2) An inability, perhaps not unexpected, of populist martial arts writers and historians to discern the real from the false. This results either in the continual rehashing of stories and tales that, originally mistaken, are then embellished in ways alien to the spirit of the art or, and even more misleading, their glorification of violent archetypal images of the warrior and his values in general as being the norm.

3) The realization that the real basis of the art demonstrates clearly that both commercialism and certain kinds of competitiveness are inimical to the proper teacher and teaching. Once realized by the public at large such information could be harmful to those whose sources of revenue depend upon their manipulation of the philosophy of the real tradition. This applies in some cases to individuals and in others to schools. It is an indisputable fact that, in some schools which valued such things, no famous founding Master of either China or the Ryukyu Islands ever attained a high grade by means of competition.

4) A lack of available informed Buddhist books in English that acknowledge the significance of the art, often because tentative steps taken by Buddhists to discover more usually had to be through sources of the type mentioned above. This has resulted in a great reluctance to proceed further. Because of this both Buddhism and the art's students lose something.

When people walk into a bookshop—either in the Orient or in the Occident—and look through the popular magazines from the variously named schools of *Karate, Tae Kwon Do,* or the misnamed *Kung Fu,* they may, more often than not, as a student once remarked to me, develop an "immediate raging disinterest" in the subject. Or, perhaps they would just be horrified at the crudity or content, depending upon which magazine they pick up and which weapons manufacturer or competition promoter was advertising within the magazine. Such crass presentations only augment—and do not remedy—our present violent times.

The value of martial arts has been made trivial in martial arts films. These films, although often not meant to be taken seriously, influence newcomers to the art into believing the themes outlined above. For example, when some monks, a Zen Roshi and three Tibetan Lamas were visiting me, they asked to be taken to see some examples of karate. I took them to a national competition organized by a well-known and respected karate organization. They closely watched the various demonstrations and demonstrators. Shortly after the sparring competitions began, three people had been injured and my guests asked me to take them out. On the way home they said they were very glad that teachings of the Chuan Fa tradition had finally come to Britain. There is no need for this unnecessary violence.

There are many good teachers of martial arts around. These teachers are all too often lumped together with the "bad apples" of the field and the results of their work do not come to fruition or are obscured by the actions of others. I regularly receive letters from both well-known teachers and unknown students in the East and West who, disillusioned by their experiences, have ceased to practice in a public club. Often this was because they had asked their teachers about many of the principles outlined in this book and realized that the teachers knew little of the inner spirit of the art they purported to teach. These serious students still search for the reality that they sense exists within a correct form of the Chuan Fa.

This book addresses the problems of philosophy by elucidating some of the most basic principles of Chuan Fa. It will, I trust, furnish serious students with enough material to study in depth, and to protect themselves, and the art, from philosophical and historical exploitation by unscrupulous teachers or organizations.

The "empty hand" martial art has, unfortunately, a surfeit of modern counterfeit teachers, teachings, and organizations and not only in the West. For this reason I have included extensive notes, accounts and references, so you may plan and conduct your own research. I have tried wherever possible to indicate readily available texts. Further explanations of doctrinal tenets are also included in the notes to each translated text. There are many other sources besides those I present here. For those who are unfamiliar with Buddhism or its historical founder, Shakyamuni, I have included a brief outline of his life with the first of the reference notes.

The main text deals with approximately the first 1000 years of *Chuan Fa* development. I have included materials concerning the Indian teacher Bodhidharma, who belongs to the far end of this period. His influence upon *Chuan Fa* is probably the only example of a Buddhist *Chuan Fa* teacher likely to be familiar to a general student of the martial arts. Many students may not be fully informed of his role in China and Tibet, or what he actually taught. The sample of translations and explanations included here will help make this role more clear.

Also included is a chronology of events to enable readers to readily see the overall context of the various periods considered. I have endeavored to supply the basic Sanskrit, Mandarin Chinese and Ryukyuan/Japanese terms for technical points or categories which arise as these are the languages common to both Buddhism and Kempo. The Sanskrit used here follows the meanings used in Stefan Anacker's work upon Vasubandhu, which I regard as the most accurate. However, I have had to supplement this with terms I have been taught orally, and in some cases I have had to approximate or reconstruct a term which, in the original Chinese, has been rendered only phonetically.

I have sought to provide material for beginners and more experienced students. To this end I have included materials at several levels: generally the main theme, elaboration of its implications or background, and the reference notes, which provide very specific details and reference sources. This will make it possible to read the work first at a simple all-inclusive thematic level and again with more specific orientations or special interests in mind. The primary sections of this work are laid out in six different Mandalas, each concerned with a special subject, theme, or pattern of teaching, each fundamental to the art of *Chuan Fa* and embodying a specific spiritual journey. Each journey interacts with the others to form a greater Mandala of totality. *Chuan Fa* is the kinetic expression of this totality.

The study of the origins of Kempo is a fascinating and demanding one, but not without its benefits. It requires the development of a broad understanding of ancient teachings and of one's own nature. The reader may be tempted to think that such a process of study is a purely intellectual, indulgent or solipsistic exercise and irrelevant to training in the art or to the processes of their life. In fact, the study process is fundamental and vital for our modern and increasingly violent age. It is even more relevant now than when it first came into China.

Modern forms of the *Chuan Fa* art—such as karate—have become so fragmented and over-specialized that it is easy to lose sight of the fact that originally their practice was a spiritual, not physical, endeavor that was based upon a religious, not military philosophy. Such fragmentation is unfortunately a common characteristic of our times and involves many levels of our experience. The *Bodhisattva Warriors* is designed to bring the various branches of study back into their original wholistic unity.

Since I began my studies in 1960 I have seen this training method adopted by many social institutions, in drug rehabilitation programs in both the United States and Great Britain, in schools for blind and crippled children in several Eastern Bloc nations, and more recently, in Soviet universities and gymnastic organizations. The study of *Chuan Fa* can help break down the barriers created by a lack of self-understanding which all too often generates fear and results in the mental suffering termed "aggression." Such suffering is a prime concern of real *Chuan Fa* and is one of the reasons its practice and practitioners have always known that it is much more than mere sport.

The Bodhisattva Warriors

BEGINNING

THE STUDY

BEGINNING THE STUDY

In order to begin our study it helps if we can utilize a theme that connects all the different branches of the many teachings which helped develop the art of *Chuan Fa*. What was termed in Buddhism the "Doctrine of Elements" fulfills this need for it deals directly with the fundamentals lying at the heart of our study of mind and body. The Elemental Doctrine was taught by the early monk masters at different levels of understanding according to the needs and abilities of students and, by means of analogy and paradigm, was made to be presented in either very simple or very advanced forms.

When this doctrine was understood by a student it was symbolically represented in special patterns that describe the inter-relationship between its different constituent forces and parts. These patterns were eventually termed *Mandalas* and were expressed in pictures, sound, shapes or movement.

Highly technical and intricate teachings were able to be conveyed in simplified forms through the medium of the Mandala. In later times and in appropriate circumstances, the mandalas could be reconstructed. This form of symbolic and "compressed" teaching was unique to esoteric Buddhism (*Mikkyo*) and enabled the entire doctrine to be transmitted to future generations, even when the teachings were preserved by people who did not always fully understand them.

If you have already practiced a form of martial art, it is likely that you will have been shown, and studied, sets of traditional movement sequences. Although you may have understood these simply as self-defense practices, you will discover that they are kinetic "keys" to open the Elemental "door" to consciousness. This orientation toward understanding the mind, rather than the body, is the real reason they were preserved and passed down through antiquity by generations of Masters.

In order to appreciate such teachings we must first review the ancient doctrines concerning the elements and their relationship to consciousness. From such a review we may begin to see how these teachings influenced and developed the art and practice of *Chuan Fa* and its derivatives, as well as the practitioners themselves. Though it may appear to some to be somewhat dreary or unnecessary, if a student is not familiar with these teachings he or she will never properly understand any proper form of *Chuan Fa*. I have outlined some of the most important themes which directly influenced or affected the early practitioners of *Chuan Fa*. These themes and their concomitant ideas may be entirely new and perhaps unexpected, but I hope that you will be able to see how they each fit together to form the basis of the complete study of *Chuan Fa*.

If we examine a map of a strange place we may get to know the features of the area it covers very well, but such an examination will not convey to us the nature of what it is like to actually be in that place. If we visit that area, our studies with the map will prove useful in that we will have a sense of direction or orientation which helps us to find our way about. People who have not seen such a map will soon get hopelessly lost and waste time and energy needlessly, trying to find the place they want to go. If they do manage to arrive they will be exhausted from their searching.

To most of us, the nature of our mind is a strange and foreign place that we rarely need to examine. If we ever do get "lost" there it is

Figure 1. *Shakyamuni Buddha making the mudra of "Teaching the Law" (dharma-cakra). His two attendants carry flywhisks. (Author's collection.)*

almost impossible to find the way out. Our clinics and hospitals are filled with such travelers. When you lose your way it is also very easy to be misguided by those who, for various reasons, claim to know an exit. We are, in fact, at the mercy of anyone whom we think is familiar with the territory. This position of vulnerability is widespread but often unrealized.

Many years ago the Buddha offered us a teaching that enabled us not only to find our way, but also to see how such a way was actually created. *Chuan Fa* shows that if we can understand this we need never be lost again. When *Chuan Fa* is correctly practiced, it will act as a cathartic force upon the deepest part of our nature. Such a process of "inner cleansing" can only be effectively utilized if we know how to recognize and adapt its principles within our lives. The "self-unmasking" effect of *Chuan Fa* can be explained only in terms of the philosophy that created it. It is not simply a psychological process, or a point of view.

This "unmasking" may make a student acutely aware of his or her deepest fears or apprehensions, and the temptation to run away or escape from the study can be very powerful. This aspect was dealt with very capably within the environment of the monastery where, traditionally, *Chuan Fa* was studied. As it is now possible for people to encounter forms of the teaching outside of a monastery, and thus not have the protection it offers, it is important to understand the Buddhist teachings concerning the basic nature and structure of our consciousness in order to deal either with stresses or phobias that may occur (or be encountered) during the process of unmasking, and to correctly apply the therapeutic meditative practices and methods of concentration that *Chuan Fa* utilizes.

If we do not understand the mind, we will not be able to understand those subjects to which we apply it. Concentration of the mind is not enough, Chuan Fa requires something more. Like a person building a new house, we must learn how to handle the materials of which it is composed. The bricks that form the basic periphery of the structure are expressed in Buddhism as the elements.

THE MANDALA OF ELEMENTS

*Defining the Four Elements
is ever the wise man's resort.
The noble meditator Lion will
make this mighty theme his sport.**

Most westerners have heard of the five elements. They are taught in school as part of the history of chemistry and have been used within the Western Magical Tradition, medieval Alchemy, and in ancient Greek philosophy from the time of Anaxamines (590 B.C.).

The Greek tradition evaluated the elements in a more profound manner than we do in our modern times. To the ancient Greek philosophers the elements described forces which helped create the world as we know it. From Anaxagoras to Plato many systems were suggested within which the elements figured either as creative physical forces or as forms of metaphysical or spiritual agents. The aforementioned Anaxamines produced one of the first theories concerning them in which he suggested that Earth and Water condensed while Fire and Air rarefied.

The ancient Indians also used elements. Many of India's most ancient philosophical and spiritual systems, such as Samkhya, Vedanta, Jainism and Buddhism, contain teachings concerning the elements in their many aspects and from around 1550 B.C. we find them described in the sacred texts and writings.

Within the scriptures of Hinduism the Vedas are very important. The Vedic writings are collections of texts dealing with various themes and concerns and include treatises devoted to magic and healing in addition to more obviously spiritual themes. The Vedas also include the complete collection of writings known as the Upanisads. The Upanisads recount stories of divine and noble personages at the beginning of Indian history. Much of what we call Indian stems from traditions and beliefs first written about in the Upanisads.

Although the European sources regarding the Elements are ancient, those of the Far East are older. It has often been suggested by scholars that much of the elemental teachings found in ancient Europe

---

*Visuddhi Magga XI: V, 117, translated by Nanamoli Bhikku.

were in fact transported there from India or China by Arab traders and merchants. One of the Vedas—called the "Ayur" (*Ayur* = life prolonging) describes a system of healing which classifies things according to their elemental nature and quality. This school of healing still exists and is popular among non-Hindus in India.

In the main, the more practical works contained in the Vedas view elements in their physical sense; that is, as physical substances, and it is in this sense that they are utilized in the Ajur to form medicinal compounds, unguents, plasters and antiseptics.

It is generally accepted that the ancient Indian system of medicine was very advanced. Some of the most ancient Indian archaeological artifacts discovered to date have included complete sets of surgical instruments and tools. The diversity and form of these indicate that the ancient Indians performed intricate surgical operations that included partial and whole trepanation and selective cranial lobotomy. These techniques were not known or used in Europe until many centuries later. Whether such operations were carried out under the auspices of Hinduism is difficult to prove. They may have been performed by the pre-Hindu inhabitants of the Indus river valley (from which we get the term "Hindu").

The Elements are mentioned in the Upanisads (i.e., the Prasna-Upanisad: 4, 6) where they occur in descriptions of the heavenly states. The Satapatha Brahmana (9:1, 6. Verses 16–24) say they were brought into being between the first full and new moons at the creation of the world. [Note 1]

Buddhism,* although Indian in genesis, has different understandings of nearly every Hindu teaching! The same spiritual (Sanskrit) terms in both systems often indicate different and contradictory things, the word "karma" being a prime example [Note 5]. In a text of the Buddhist teacher Vasumitra, as well as in the teachings of the Satyasiddhi school (See Notes 2 & 3) the elements are clearly described as principles rather than substances.

In order to understand both Buddhism's view and its difference from Hinduism concerning themes such as elements, it is necessary to know something of the Buddhist description of the human being, for it is here we can see how Buddhist teachings depart, often radically, from their Hindu counterparts.

From its earliest days, Buddhism was filled with simple, down-to-earth explanations of often highly abstruse and metaphysical principles. Unlike the intricate and often academic Hinduism, Buddhism sought to explain its teaching in as clear a language as possible. The his-

---

*If you know nothing at all of Buddhism or its founder, see Note 1 (p. 393) for a brief outline of its historical origin.

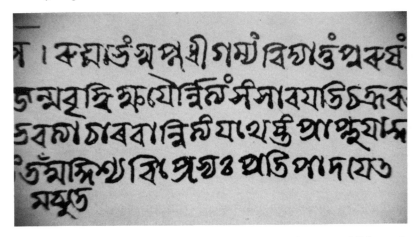

Figure 2. Sanskrit – the language of the early scriptures. (Kongoryuji Library.)

torical Buddha Shakyamuni sought to show a path, a means by which people were able to learn about the true and real nature of their existence utilizing, as far as possible, the language with which they were most familiar. This path was based upon largely heuristic principles. As a result of this orientation, Buddhism adopted many seemingly simple teachings and expanded certain principles to higher and higher levels of understanding. The Buddha directed that the scriptures be rendered into the popular language of any country to which it spread. As a result of this, Buddhism was easily studied by peasant and prince alike, and in many different lands.

Most of us know that human experiences are often far from simple to explain. To make self-understanding easier, there eventually developed a corpus of teaching methods utilizing very simple and experiential principles. Students understand these principles and teachings at many different levels. The Doctrine of Elements was one such teaching, and over the ages, was used to clarify many levels of doctrine [Note 21].

THE EARLY TEACHINGS

Buddhism began around 500 B.C. in Northern India, and spread to the South within a few hundred years. Around the first century it was taken to China and spread outward from there. In Ceylon, a school known as the Theravada eventually rose into prominence, emerging as Ceylon's orthodoxy. It was within this school that the scriptures were committed to writing in the Pali dialect of Sanskrit [see Note 2, last paragraph].

佛尼牟迦釋

Figure 3. *Shakyamuni Buddha (Kongoryuji Library).*

*Figure 4. The death of Shakyamuni. All around his body stand peoples of many differ-
ent types, races and castes. Their robes show that both Indian Arahants and Chinese
Bodhisattvas are depicted. Equally shown are deities and heavenly beings (Ryusen
Miyahara).*

When Muslim invaders slaughtered the Buddhists in Northern
India, these Ceylonese records became an important, and for many
years the only, source of reference. Until the Chinese, Tibetan, and Japanese nations became open to Westerners, these Ceylonese records formed
the main sources for Western researchers to learn of Buddhist doctrine.
In modern times, researchers of Chinese and Tibetan scriptures have
found manuscripts of the teachings taken from Northern India. Many
portions of these Chinese scriptures and their Sanskrit originals are as
old as any present day Ceylonese version. The main form of Buddhism
that arose in China became known as the Mahayana school.

Each of these schools will be discussed in detail.

THE NATURE OF THE SELF

Early Buddhism taught that all within the world is transitory, that it
changes and develops continually. Just as the sea may slowly and gradually wash away a huge mountain until it becomes completely unrecognizable, so human beings alter and change. Buddhism teaches that
the basis for our mind/body knowledge lies in the tendency of the
mind to view its experiences in patterns, and these are called Elements
of Mind.

The Sanskrit word used in early Buddhism to describe these habitual mental patterns is *Skhanda*. It literally means "collections" or "groupings" and is used to describe the various patternings of mental activity that collectively constitute what we loosely term our "Self." The *Skhanda* are the first elements of mind we encounter in our pursuit of wisdom. There are five *Skhanda* enumerated in the ancient scriptures. They are classified as follows:

[1] Form (*Rupa*)
[2] Feelings (*Vedana*)
[3] Perception (*Samjna*)
[4] Mental Volitions (*Samskara*)
[5] Consciousness (*Vijnana*).*

The source of the *Skhanda* is our mind/body complex and its activities furnish us with the "fuel" for our existence.

The first *Skhanda* (Sanskrit *Rupa*) literally indicates "form" or "appearance." This term mainly refers to the particular patterns of mentality engendered when we come into contact with physical objects. How such inner perceptions arise, continue and perpetuate themselves is included within the understanding of what the term *Skhanda* indicates. The Form Skhanda (*Rupa*) represents the mentality engendered when we observe the outer appearances of things. It is composed of mental responses to the five physical elements.

The Feeling Skhanda (*Vedana*) represents the responses of mind when coming into contact with life situations which generate characteristics described as being either pleasant, unpleasant, or neutral. If a situation is pleasant, we wish to continue or extend it. If it is unpleasant, we wish to be away from it, and if it is neutral neither of these responses occur. By these three responses the mental Skhanda of feeling is recognized.

The Perception Skhanda (*Samjna*) represents that aspect of mind which perceives mental and sensorial data, and recognizes or categorizes it into distinctive features—such as color, shape, position, etc. Its repetitive trait enables it to perform the function of memory.

The Volition Skhanda (*Samskara*) represents the trait of consciousness which creates and perpetuates various motivations and impulses of consciousness. It covers all continually maintained motivations (such as love). This Skhanda has a very wide range of applications and often needs to be understood according to its context as it refers to both passive and active creations.

---

*Sanskrit names are italicised.

The Consciousness Skhanda (*Vijnana*) represents the distinctive, collective habit and patternings of those factors of consciousness that perceive and discriminate between fivefold sense data and a purely mental sense. From this sense it creates a fixed locus upon which to base and then project itself.

These five patterns of mental activity make up the totality of the nature of our mind/body experience. Most are present, to a greater or lesser degree, within the others, they exist in a mutually interactive manner, and constitute that which we generally call our mind. In the early Buddhist scriptures very detailed explanations are given for each Skhanda [Note 6].

Because the Skhanda are based upon continually developing phenomena their content and individual patterning changes and adapts to various experiences. Buddhist philosophy concluded that the permanency of Self is an illusory idea that neither reflects reality as it is experienced, or as it ultimately is.

THE ELEMENTS

Make your meditation like the five elements.
(Mahajima Nikkaya I: V 420–425)

Buddhism recognizes two types of element, that which helps form the basis of mind (called *Mano Dhatu*, the basic mental element) and those existing outside of the mind within natural phenomena. These are termed *Maha Bhuta* ("Great Primary").

The Element of Mind, uncreated in a physical form, arises and is experienced from contact with the various elements (*Maha Bhuta*) existing physically within nature. The Element of Mind feeds itself with experiences continuously in order to confirm its existence and to accommodate new impressions as they arise.

The *Maha Bhuta* combine to provide the experiential basis of the Body of Physicality (*Rupa-kaya*) and the *Mano Dhatu* combine to form the Body of Mind (*Mano-kaya*), also called the *Namo* (that which gives names) *kaya*. Let us now deal with each of these two forms of the elements in turn and see how they are presented within the early texts.

Rupa-Kaya and *Maha Bhuta*

The elements of physical existence are perceivable by all beings, even animals recognize and relate to them, though not in the same manner as humans. Elements form the primary basis for our sense of form. It is this very sense of form which is described by the Form Skhanda.

In the scriptures of the Theravada, one of the early Ceylonese schools, five main elements are described by name and other qualities. They are Earth, Water, Fire, Air and Space.

Earth: Characterized by solidity and hardness.

Water: Characterized by fluidity.

Fire: Characterized by heat and/or activity.

Air: Characterized by motion.

Space: Exists only in relation to the above four.

These elements, along with their respective colors (yellow, blue, red, white, and transparent), and other qualities, formed the subject of the most basic meditations used within early Buddhism to uncover the nature of subjective and objective reality [Note 1a].

Buddhism deals with the material elements in several ways. Some texts emphasize their purely physical aspects (i.e., as substances), but others refer more to the mental qualities and principles they are representing. This latter approach is one currently used in the Theravada School, although many of this sect's scriptures outline other approaches.

Such alternative views are not contradictory, they merely highlight aspects of the same thing for different purposes of understanding. Other schools of Buddhism tend to use either or both types of description equally.

Ordinarily we have no need to fully understand the mental (or physical) processes to which we are subject during our lifetime. Without some special event or cause, we may go through life blissfully unaware of them. As a result of this we create and project imperfect and impure understandings into the nature of the phenomena we experience, and, due to this, we experience suffering and discontent. The Buddha's teaching is an attempt to show why and how such a situation arises, and, more positively, how it can be remedied.

Mano-Kaya and *Mano-Dhatu*

While the *Maha Bhuta* intermingle to form the elemental body of corporeality, the elemental "body" of Mind (*Mano-Kaya*) is created by the *Mano-Dhatu* element. The term *Mano-Kaya* signifies that the various mental constituents of which it is composed interlock in a manner similar to bricks in a wall and make up a seemingly solid structure. The various specific mental factors (the "bricks") of which this wall of *Mano* is constituted are called the *Mano-Dhatu*.

The basis of Mind arises from contact with the five physical senses. These in turn arise from contact with their respective physical organs. Though it may seem simple to describe it so, the process involved in the creation of the basis for mentality is, in fact, quite intricate. In order to clarify this process it is approached in various stages and levels. Elements form one of the stages of understanding. The Mind notices the sense produced by each organ, attaches to its object and then creates an interactive response to this attachment. A pattern arises from this activity:

Physical Base	Action to Object	Resultant Sense
Entrance Element	Object Element	Consciousness Element
Indriya dhatu (Skt)	*Visaya dhatu* (Skt)	*Vijnana dhatu* (Skt)
Nose	Smell	Olfactory sense

Ear	Hearing	Auditory sense
Eye	Color	Visual sense
Body	Touch	Tactile sense
Tongue	Taste	Gustatory sense

These gates of experience form the basis for all our sensorial perceptions of the world. To this list is added "Mind," which is regarded as a collective sense in its own right.

Mind Faculty	Mental Event	Mind Consciousness
Mano dhatu (Skt)	*Mano visaya dhatu* (Skt)	*Mano vijnana dhatu* (Skt)

The physical bases form the *Rupa-Kaya* and the three mental bases form the *Namo-* (or *Mano-*) *Kaya*.

It should be noted that although Buddhism traditionally terms the sense of an object *Visaya*, this term really describes the actual object itself as a focus for the senses. The correct term for the actual sense of the object is *alambana*. The eighteen factors *in toto* form the basis for all experience, be it physical or mental, and are called "The Eighteen Elements," "Spheres," or "Gates" of existence. These 18 elements have always been recognized in all forms of Buddhism, and throughout its history, as the basis for a knowledge of ourselves and the world in general [Note 6a].

Building up from these, the Buddhist teaching (*Dharma*) then begins to enumerate the various manners in which the realities generated by these 18 elements may be more fully understood by the student. These concepts of reality are significant for, as a result of them, different manners developed of viewing the "gates" themselves [Note 2].

Mano-Dhatu and *Mano-Vijnana*

In Buddhist teaching *Mano-Dhatu* and *Mano-Vijnana* are used to describe what we usually think of as the Mind. Neither represents the word "mind" as such, and the fundamental Buddhist term for Mind derives from the Sanskrit root *Vij* meaning "to know." From this we can see that from the outset Buddhism regarded the "knowing" of the "knower" as more significant than any personalized form of description.

Consciousness as a subjective experience consists of the totality of its perceptions and knowings. The subject is referred to by the term *Mano* and the "knowing" by the term *Vijnana*. For this reason the experience of Mind is called the Knowing Consciousness (*Mano-Vijnana*). This latter title describes the conditioning faculty we most utilize to form our experiences in life. It contains those processes we are apt to term ourselves. Generally speaking the term *Mano-Dhatu* refers to the elements of consciousness that initiate awareness and the processes of the objective senses, receiving and noting their impressions. It performs the function of organizing sense data into some kind of coherent pattern.

The term *Mano-Vijnana* (or usually simply *Vijnana*) is used when we are considering consciousness as a subjective experience. We use *Mano-Dhatu* when we consider consciousness as a compounded entity in terms of its interaction with the other elements of consciousness. The Theravada texts describe *Mano Vijnana* technically as being that consciousness aspect which performs the three tasks of investigating, determining, and registering impressions of the previous sense organs (previous because *Vijnana* only manifests after the senses have been active in some manner). *Vijnana* is the culmination of this process and forms the last of the 18 factors of our consciousness (see the list on page 14).

Unlike psychology, which attempts to explain the manifestations or traits of a mind based upon a fixed identity, or religion, which places its ultimate source in a divine being, Buddhism addresses directly the central issue of what, where, and how consciousness comes into being. This issue is central to all forms of Buddhism, for it is by perceiving how the mind creates and perpetuates its patterns that we may come to achieve insight into its ultimate nature. The genesis and development of consciousness is often difficult to understand, usually because we begin to try and penetrate it in an unskillful manner, filled with assumptions we are not aware of and which we have never had cause to question.

If we regard the mind as an unchanging feature (or possession), rather like an object we may own, we will often fail to perceive that, unlike an object, the mind alters when we begin to observe its activities. It becomes very difficult, to say the least, to observe something using the thing we are trying to observe! There is a Japanese saying, "The sword which cuts cannot slice itself," emphasizing this fact. Buddhism approaches this difficulty sideways by practicing special meditations. In these meditation practices we are taught to subdue and calm the frenzied process of thought so we may nurture a form of consciousness which is tranquil. Only from such tranquillity can the real process of observation be initiated. During the attempt to achieve this we learn from direct, firsthand experience, how turbulent the mind really is.

We also perceive that Mind is like a dragon which requires constant food. If we withdraw its meals, it gets angry, restless, and upset. Eventually it tries out various strategies designed to bring in meals. However, if we persist, we come to realize that the dragon only exists because of its hunger for the possibility of food. If that possibility dissolves, so does the dragon. One great danger that happens when studying Buddhism is that students consider the various described attributes of the mind as fixed qualities and quantities. When we come across the name of a "part of the mind," we must always recall that what is referred to is not an entity in its own right but a contingent *function* which arises in a moment and will only endure for that moment (See Note 6a, 6b).

Consider, for instance, our faculty of memory. If we have to recall someone's name we do (or cannot do) so almost instinctively. Immediately after we have remembered it, the mind may go on to thinking about something else. We do not have to consciously access and draw out from within us a static function called "Memory" and then subject it to an indexed search, as if the mind was a computer database. Memory comes into being as a faculty as and when we require it. It does not function continually within us but its *potentiality* remains present. While memory is a stationary or "parked" faculty, the Self is not. It must continually regenerate, project, or feed itself by creating patterns which protect it.

◊ ◊ ◊

To summarize, Buddhism describes the consciousness, both in a general manner and as a specific subjective experience. Consciousness as a whole is said to derive its content from the five physical senses, and from these arise their mental reciprocate elements. These form the possibility for individual consciousness to arise. This possibility constitutes the 16th of the 18 mind/body elements. The culmination of these elements constitutes the basis of the 18th element. For this reason the 16th element is called the Elemental Mind, or Mentality Element (*Mano-Dhatu*) and the 18th is called the Knowing Mind (*Vijnana Dhatu*).

The Bite

The bite of the Wooden mouths can make
The body stiff to all intent
When roused is its Earth element,
It might be gripped by such a Snake.

The bite of the Rotten mouths can make
The body stiff to all intent,
When roused is its Water element,
It might be gripped by such a Snake.

The bite of the Fiery mouths can make
The body stiff to all intent
When roused is its Fire element,
It might be gripped by such a Snake.

The bite of the Dagger mouths can make
The body stiff to all intent,
When roused is its Air element,
It might be gripped by such a Snake.*

---

*From The *Visuddhi Magga*: Translated by Nanamoli Bhikku (Kandy, Sri Lanka: Buddhist Publication Society, 1975, Third edition, Ch. XI, v 109). Used by permission.

MIND IN BUDDHISM

> One should think it self-evident that consciousness of
> personal identity presupposes, and therefore cannot
> constitute, personal identity, any more than knowl-
> edge, in any other case, can constitute truth, which it
> presupposes.*

As soon as we try to understand or describe the mind, we will realize
how difficult such a task is. Any meaningful model or form for what
constitutes the most abstract and complex part of our being proves
inadequate, such is the intricacy and diversity of the Mind. It is, however, necessary to begin somewhere! Ancient Buddhist texts use various forms of description, usually based upon a fundamental sectioning
of the activities of consciousness into various processes, sources of stimuli, and/or responses. These were identified as object, source organ,
and subject of consciousness. Unlike psychology, the Buddhist ontology
of consciousness arises from direct experience and in Buddhism we
find out about the Mind's patterns and activities predominantly by
direct, personal, observation.

Through observation we see that consciousness is a nexus of
almost simultaneous activity arising, sometimes independently of stimuli. In order to maintain its position vis-à-vis the outer world, the mind
requires a baseline (or reference point) from which to work, and to this
end forms the "self" to centralize its activities. Like the eye of a tornado,
this center is constantly maintained as a strategically advantageous
position from which to perpetuate (or protect) its future existence and
activities. It is rather like a spinning top painted with the colors of the
spectrum. When it is spun around fast all the colors blend into one
color alone—namely white. The color white is like the "self" of consciousness. It appears to be quite constant and continuous. However
when the spinning top slows down and finally halts, all the different
colors reappear and we realize that the white color was illusory.

Such a "self" cannot easily be comprehended or experienced
except in the most general and vague manner, for it creates a skillful

---

*Bishop Butler, *The works of Joseph Butler*, DCL (Oxford: Clarendon, 1896).

camouflage of sensation and ideation which all but the most experienced would actually believe constitutes its real nature!

The Buddhist philosophy deals with essentials, and before it urges students to rush into belief systems or doctrines, it suggests they first try to understand the experiences of which they are made. Only after such an exploration, and hopefully some discovery, can students know "who" it is who walks the path of spirituality. It is for this reason that Buddhist teachers stress the practice of meditating upon the self nature.

Everyone has a capacity to experience—whether by body, speech, or mind. This capacity qualifies everyone as a potential Buddha, but to attain Enlightenment is not an easy endeavor. It is no wonder that the average person finds it difficult to practice any form of meditation, and finds self-observation even harder. If one succeeds, even to a small degree, the habitual patterns of consciousness will reappear, making it seem very attractive to desist from further attempts. Often the consciousness will attempt to reinforce itself and produce an even greater egocentricity.

To those unfamiliar or inexperienced with Buddhist meditation it may often seem that Buddhism has got it very wrong and that the "self" does indeed permanently exist. It is for this reason that the early teachers highlighted the need to prepare carefully and to examine the nature of the "self."

It is often wise to take note of those who have previously attempted this themselves and learn from their experiences. This is where the tradition proves of practical use. When we consult it, we see it encourages us to practice within a disciplined and controlled mental environment. Only within such an environment can we penetrate the weak spots in the ego defenses or realize just how cleverly it protects its true nature from discovery [Note 2a].

The ego is like a black mouse in a black colored, darkened room. You are seated on a black chair in the center of this room and have a small black torch. Every now and then you hear a noise and flash the torch to see what the noise is, but the mouse hurries away. Your torch beam is very small and you cannot discover the mouse's whereabouts. Only its sounds tell you the mouse is there. As you grow more skillful, your torch beam grows bigger, and the mouse has to run more quickly to escape your beam. Its speed increases and increases as your beam grows. The mouse gnaws your chair and tries in other ways to distract you. If you continue, your beam grows larger and larger until the mouse cannot escape it any longer. Finally, when you have the torch at full beam width, the whole room is bathed in its bright light and the mouse cannot escape it. When this occurs the mouse will evaporate into nothingness.

The early Buddhists practiced self-discovery by means of meditations based upon observation and analysis of the Skhandas. By watching in a non-grasping manner, they succeeded in establishing the veracity of the Buddha's experience within themselves. They could see and know what he taught concerning the Skhandas. We all can experience life in all its turmoils and trials, we know what it is to suffer or to be worried, and it's not difficult to see these conditions within our lives. Because we have no especial "key" to understand the activities of our minds, we often do not know, should we wish to, how to cope with or overcome them.

If we are overwhelmed by our problems we may be advised—or sometimes forced—to resort to a psychologist, who more often than not knows little of what the ancient Greeks referred to as the Psyche or the Logos. Or we might meet up with a psychotherapist who knows even less about the art of the Therapeutae. A favorite technical word used by "the helping profession" in describing the human mentality—namely *alienation*—comes directly from the ancient Greek spiritual term *Alloisus* meaning "one who is separated from his God" [Note 2e]. The sense of separation is an ancient one, but its solution was recognized by the ancients as being spiritual ("psychic") and not psychological.

Happily Buddhist teaching provides us with the "key" mentioned earlier, for it constitutes a measure or rule by means of which we can test out certain mental conditions within ourselves and subject them to meditative disciplines through which we can alter such conditions in a positive and creative manner.

In the early Theravada form of Buddhism, practitioners tended to take a rather static view of meditational practice and pursued themes and methods strictly as described within the scriptures. This orientation highlighted the personal content and experience of consciousness. Practitioners sought to explain and explicate that experience in analytical terms. The danger in maintaining such a pattern is that it's too easy to become rigidly attached to the scriptures themselves while ignoring the living interaction they actually sought to explicate. For example, the "rainy" season meditation retreat arose as a result of the Indian climate where Theravada Buddhism was born. The annual monsoon prevented traveling so the Buddha used this time to practice meditation or other non-missionary activities. In countries which had neither a rainy season, nor an equivalent of the monsoon, many Theravadins continued to practice a "Rains Retreat" even if these areas had little or no rain.

With the rising of Mahayana Buddhism, new, and more adaptable, meditation practices developed which began to stress a more dynamic and functional meditational experience of personal consciousness as part of an interactive process. As foreign religious systems or philosophies were encountered, the Mahayana adapted its practices to include them. They just revamped them into a suitable Buddhist form. Foreign deities were renamed as Buddhist "protectors" and foreign cultural celebrations were re-dedicated to Buddhist values. All of this made the spread of the Mahayana way very successful. Although the outward appearance of the Mahayana adapted to different forms, its intrinsic value and teachings—which were based upon human experience—did not. In this sense the Theravada and Mahayana approaches were identical. The Buddhist emphasis placed upon inner mental exploration was unknown in countries used mainly to prayer but unfamiliar with meditation.

> Afraid of experiencing pain I carefully protect a wound.
> Afraid of being snared between the crushing mountains of the
> hell realm why should I not equally protect my mind?*

Descriptions of Consciousness

One important concern of the early *Chuan Fa* masters was to present their teachings in a manner which accorded with the Buddhist teachings and precepts. To do this they had to present many parts of their inherited tradition in a new manner, especially that which concerned the nature and makeup of Consciousness itself. One important aspect of such a presentation lay in communicating their understanding of the nature of bodily energies. Buddhists were quite familiar with Vedic ideas concerning such energies, but in general regarded these Vedic ideas as, at best, incomplete, and, at worst, mistaken. (We can see examples of such mistaken ideas in the case of the "Tantric" Hindu sexual rituals.)

How one viewed and understood the interconnection between Consciousness and physical being directly determined the ethical and moral nature of physical activities in general, and that of *Chuan Fa* in particular. To practice a physically expressive Buddhist art which also involved a meditative path without incurring criticism from other Buddhists required a systematic and special presentation of its philosophical and other bases. Such a presentation was developed within *Chuan Fa*. All the various schools agree upon the basic Buddhist view that "Mind" is based upon an interaction of physical and mental processes (*Nama-Rupa*). These include the "18 entrances" alluded to previously. Variations later appear concerning the activities of the last of these "entrances," namely those which the Theravadins called "*Mano-Vij-nana*" or some similar term. This term was used to describe the pivotal nexus of the collection of mental/physical stimuli and habitual mental

---

*Shantideva: Bodhicaryavatara (Entering into the Path of Wisdom) Ch. 5: v 20.

patterns (the *Skhanda*) which form Consciousness. In the Theravada system, this represented the final concretization of the individuating experiences then termed "Consciousness."

The generative element of personal Consciousness is to them a quintessential phenomenon of the five (organically) based consciousnesses when aligned with the idea of (personal) permanency. This sense of knowing was called the *Mano Vijnana*. The term *Mano Dhatu* (mental element) was used abstractly to describe the causal factors of Consciousness, itself, rather than any state of consciousness (such as the sense of Self). All experience was held to arise from this mind-body (*Nama Rupa*) interaction, and all the Theravada explanations of experience continually referred to their interaction and mutual dependence.

The Mahayana schools that acknowledged a distinctive mental relationship to body senses also described it in other terms, differentiating between mental activity that receives and organizes sense impressions (the *Mano*) and that which cognized (the *Manas*)—in other words: the mind which "spoke" to the body and the mind which "spoke" to itself. The Theravada did not emphasize such a differentiation and did not use a distinctive term for what was, in the Mahayana, called *Manas*.

It was via the *Manas* that the Mahayana said the Individual Consciousness arose, whereas in Theravada this arose from (*Mano*) Vijnana. In some Mahayana Schools, the terms *Mano* and *Manas* were elaborated until they eventually became the matrix of other types of consciousness. In some schools, both terms were interchangeable. This can be very confusing for newer students reading a range of materials from different schools. It is not helped either by the fact that many key Buddhist terms have been badly translated, oversimplified, or simply not understood by translators. Details of the many understandings of the content of consciousness are outlined in Appendix 3, on page 285, titled "Views of Mind."

Different Approaches to Dharma in China

Buddhism spread into China from very early times. In the first and second centuries A.D. missionary Monks had begun their work, and both Theravada and proto-Mahayana Monks had begun to introduce and practice their different forms of the Dharma [Note 3]. China at this time was already an old civilization complete with strong traditions and teachings. It had already made contact with its Western neighbors, as well as with other Eastern countries, including Japan, establishing its silk trade and many other commercial links. Its society, perhaps copying the Indian, formed four strata—*Shih* (scholar), *Kung* (workers), *Wang* (farmers) and *Shang* (merchants).

The Great Wall repulsed invaders for over 200 years. Porcelain had been invented and advanced mathematics and astronomy were taught in schools. The State examination system subjected everybody to a degree of education. Confucianism reigned at the Imperial Court and

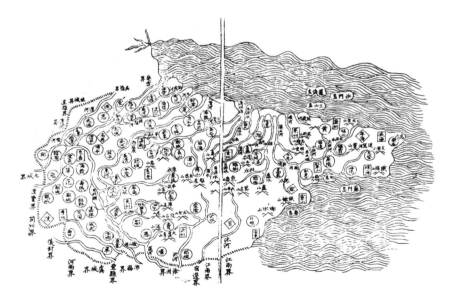

Figure 5. Ancient Chinese map showing navigable waterways and rivers. Maps such as these, if available, were used by travelers to and from India (Kongoryuji Library).

the common people practiced strange shamanistic types of spirituality. The culture that Buddhism found in China was well-established, articulate, and skilled both militarily and technically.

The Chinese strategician Sun Tzu (circa 400–300 B.C.) in his military classic *The Book of War* makes great use of the natural elements in planning battles and attacks. Sun Tzu was one, if not the first, to express tactical concepts in terms of the native Chinese elements commonly understood as being Earth, Wood, Fire, Water and Metal.

Sun Tzu proclaimed, "The only constant thing in battle is change. Like the five elements battle conditions swell and move" [Note 4]. These native elements were not, in fact, elements as either the Vedas described or as Buddhism understood them, though doubtless the ordinary Chinese person thought they were. Examination of the scientific and imperial records of this period shows that they were really descriptions used by scientists and metallurgists to describe the processes of change. This symbolic description of a philosophical concept gained acceptance within China only after Sun Tzu's time and probably because he popularized them. Claims for their greater antiquity are demonstrably spurious [Note 7].

After Sun Tzu, the popular forms of what was termed Taoism adopted his applications of elements and created numerous traditions for them. In fact some of the greatest contributions the so-called Taoists bequeathed to China were really in the materialistic, celestial and technical sciences. Alchemy, astrology, and astrolatry were equally espoused by the Taoists.

During the time that Sun Tzu was active, Buddhism began to spread among the Indian peoples, but it was not until the first century A.D. that Buddhist concepts spread eastward. After this time the Chinese medical arts began to develop, and it was mainly through Buddhism that the Chinese people eventually adopted a different understanding of elements. As Buddhism developed its teachings and practices, various schools formed into sects and what is termed the Mahayana (Great Inclusive Path) orientation developed many adherents. In some ways, the Mahayana doctrine differed so much from the mainstream Ceylonese (Theravada) form that traditions arose which the Ceylonese orthodoxy forbade, such as the open practice of the healing arts [Note 17]. Some Mahayana Sects, called these Ceylonese healers by the pejorative "Hina" Yana (meaning "smaller path"). The more correct term for the present Ceylonese sect is Theravada (Thera = elders; Vada = teaching).

The Mahayana path emphasized the significance of the Bodhisattva over and above that of the Theravada Arahant. Whereas the Theravada Arahants were saintly Monks who had mastered consciousness and gained the meditational insights which lead to the overcoming of all the unskillful mental states and conditions producing rebirth and suffering, the Bodhisattva was someone who dedicated his spiritual studies and attainments primarily to the benefit of others rather than to himself. This seemingly different ideal between the two misled many of the Mahayana devotees to regard the Arahants as being concerned mainly with their own salvation.

It was within China that the Mahayana sects mainly developed and from the second to the sixth century, we find forms of practice and applications unknown to the Theravadins. Prominent among these practices was that of healing. China eventually produced a complete lineage of Monk doctors and healers. These were called *Seng I Shih* and some became very famous in Chinese history. These Mahayana healers used the elements as the basis for their spiritual system of healing and diagnosis. The seeds for this work were already present within the Theravada meditation tradition through one of the earliest meditation practices taught by the Buddha and which concerned itself with mindfulness (Sanskrit: *smriti;* Chinese: *Nien;* Japanese: *Nen*).

The practice of mindfulness took four different forms and dealt with aspects of both the human nature and its relationship toward existence via specific themes. The themes for mindfulness were 1) the body; 2) the emotions; 3) the activities of mind; and 4) the nature of life. The first theme was subdivided into several different categories and aspects.

This primary practice was concerned with the nature and contents of the human body and was called *Kayasmriti*. It required that meditators mentally observe and analyze the structure and content of the internal body. In the scriptures describing this practice, all the body's various organs and components are enumerated and described in great detail. The physical organs are also classified according to their actions and functions. Each part is named and described together with a reminder that they are all impermanent. Another aspect of this first mindfulness meditation was called "Mindfulness of the Elements" (*Dhatusmriti*). Each physical part and activity is classified according to its elemental nature and ruling activity. Prolonged practice of these two meditations would make the practitioners fully aware of the system of correspondences between element and organ held within Buddhism.

It is only a small step further along that path to see illness or physical disorders also described according to their elemental rulership, association and activity [Note 18]. Elemental nomenclature and activity was used to describe the heuristic and anagogic processes vital to preserve health so that initiates could pursue the attainment of spiritual enlightenment.

Immediately after the final enlightenment (*Parinirvana*) of the Buddha, a great convocation took place and his disciples recited anew all

*Figure 6. The Bo Tree at Bodhgaya where
Shakyamuni became enlightened. (Author's
collection.)*

*Figure 7. Monks conduct a devotional ceremony at the Bo Tree in Bodhgaya. The stone
altar-like platform behind them (called the Diamond Seat) marks the very spot where
Shakyamui attained enlightenment. (Courtesy of Kosei Publishing Co., Japan.)*

that he had taught them. From these accounts developed the teachings that eventually constituted the doctrine (*Dharma*) we now call Buddhism. (Actually, there is no word in Buddhism for "Buddhism.") This early form of doctrine remained mostly unchanged (apart from additions) within India for several centuries. (See Chronology.)

Later in India's history, Great Councils were held and during these, all the contemporary versions and accounts of what Shakyamuni Buddha had said were again discussed and agreed upon—or not. By this time there were eighteen nominally different traditions of teaching. (See chart in appendix.)

The school of teaching which eventually developed into the Theravada was taken to Sri Lanka and has remained there. In India, various other schools carried on with a slightly different emphasis or a different practice of Dharma. Some of these found their way into China, Korea, and later into Tibet. The esoteric schools we think of as Tibetan were also present within Sri Lanka from early times, although most traces of these have since disappeared. Though starting in the North, the esoteric teaching seems also to have been popular in southern India and was taken from there to Java, Borneo, Malaysia and beyond [Note 9].

After the Hun and Muslim invasions of the fifth and 12th centuries respectively, Buddhism mostly disappeared from the north of India and was replaced by Hinduism. The teaching universities of Nalanda and

Figure 8. Shaving the head. Part of the ordination procedure for monks. Fo Hsuan Ssu, Taiwan. (Kongoryuji Library.)

Figure 9. Present day ruins of Nalanda University. (Courtesy of Kosei Publishing, Co., Japan.)

Valabhi—where many traditions had their homes—were razed to the ground and their Monks slaughtered. Invaluable manuscripts and historical records were lost forever. All that remained of Buddhist teaching existed only in the lands where it had spread. Thus China and Tibet came to possess many of the oldest accounts of Northern Indian Buddhist doctrine and traditions.

Theravada Views of Mind

> The great physical elements are placed into a position of tranquillity which impedes the production of thoughts.
>
> (E. Conze, *Buddhist Thought in India*,
> London: Allen & Unwin, 1983, p. 114.)

In the Theravada the various forms of confusion received or created by the human consciousness were translated according to the accepted doctrinal "filters." The contents of consciousness were then adjusted and categorized according to their genesis, nature, and inclination. They were positioned within a circle of given teachings and every mental distraction had its own especial therapy.

From the earliest times, the Theravada paid great attention to the workings of consciousness and classified its activities and nature carefully. It took this aspect of the Buddha's teaching very seriously. The Theravada School assumed the image of mind as occupying a central position amid a manifold world of potential sensoria. Mind was like an island perched within a circular sea of sufferings. Although occasionally the island may move around the sea, its intrinsic pattern remains unchanged.

Through the doctrinal understanding of the nature of consciousness, Theravada was able to provide a basis for the development of egoless compassion toward all. It reached out, pulsating from its center, to touch the minds of beings. It drew inward the human world of experiences—the stimulation arrayed at the periphery of the cyclic circle of consciousness that Theravada saw as embracing all humanity. This circularity of awareness, based upon a culture-free quiescence, developed its central inner patterning for future generations. Its Dharma was like a great Sun, radiating out over all who listened; and when quiescent, it acted like a black hole drawing in the troubled, the needy, the suffering, and those who searched for its center of clarity. This center was reflected in the organization and management of the temples and monasteries themselves.

Monastic Traditions

In the Theravada the head teacher occupied his position by virtue of his greater spiritual experience and knowledge. His role as an administrator of a Temple was minimal; he established general guidelines for students but did not rigidly enforce specific disciplines. Specific instruction had to come from within the Order of Monks (the *Sangha*).

The monastic system was open-ended and one could leave it at will without a great fuss being made. We can see this openness described in the early sutra description of how the *Vinaya* (rules for Monks) came into being. Contrary to what one may assume, the monastic rules were not set down beforehand by the Buddha, but were developed from the living experience of the Monks themselves. The sutras describe incidents which brought about specific rules. Many are highly humorous. The Disciple Sugata, for instance, was a monk famous for his psychic powers, and by using them, he had subdued the evil *Naga* spirits who lived in a mango grove and who were terrifying the local people. One day, while going on his alms round in a village named Kosambi, he had accepted many drinks given him by the population. Unknown to him these were all highly alcoholic and by the time he returned to the monastery he was quite drunk. In a short time

Figure 10. "Entering the Mountains." (Painting by author.)

he had fallen senseless on the ground. His fellow monks carried him to the Buddha, who said, "Is this the man who subdued the Nagas with such ease?" The Monks replied, "Yes Lord." The Buddha responded by saying, "Why, he couldn't even subdue a water lizard now!" Thereafter the monks decided to avoid alcohol.

Another tale tells the story of a monk who borrowed another's razor to shave his head. When the monk who owned the razor couldn't find it, he set out to look for it, eventually involving other monks in a mass search of the monastery. The resulting uproar, as monks rushed here and there asking everyone if they had seen the razor, was so great, the Buddha came out and inquired what all the noise was about. When told, he called all the monks together and asked who had it, whereupon the monk who originally borrowed it came forward with it. Because he had been shaving outside he hadn't heard anyone asking for it. After this the monks decided to make the rule about not taking things without prior permission. Each of the precepts in a monk's training came about because of events or experiences like these.

Many followers chose the homeless (*Anagarika*) and temple-less life of forest or mountain dwelling and lived apart from society for great periods in their lives. Although monks did live the solitary life most of them maintained themselves by daily and pre-noon alms rounds. The laity gave them food and other things, and through this a monk could maintain regular and personal contact with followers and society as a whole. It was at these occasions that monks would teach the doctrine and expound its meanings and they provided a means whereby laypeople could increase their knowledge of the Dharma.

As time passed, various sub-circles of teaching and practice developed within the Theravada, and the requirements of study became more intellectually demanding. Scriptural commentaries and other texts had been added to the scriptures and had to be studied in addition to the Sutras (written records of the Buddha's teachings). The transmission of doctrine became increasingly complex to understand and correctly practice, so advisors or guides became necessary. One byproduct of this change was the distance that grew between monks and laity because the monks studied doctrine and the general public did not.

REPRESENTATIONAL ART

One area which remained consistent was religious art. The Buddha had forbidden early followers to make pictures of him after his death (this fact was contrary to the prevalent Hindu practice). As the years passed, it became customary to represent the Buddha by negative symbols which merely suggested rather than stated his presence. The faithful

*Figure 11. The empty chair of the
Buddha. (From the Archaeological
Museum of Amaravati, India.)*

made plaques and painted simple pictures of an empty pair of sandals
or an empty teacher's chair, a sun umbrella with no one beneath it, etc.
These earliest representations of the Buddha showing his presence by
means of suggestions were replaced later by more realistic portraits, but
always these portrayed him simply, looking very much like an ordinary
person. Even though the halo (an ancient oriental invention) was later
added, the features and demeanor of the Buddha were always very
down-to-earth.

In terms of architecture, the elaborate temples we associate with the
Orient were absent from Buddhism at this period. The main architectural symbols used by the monks were the eight-spoked Golden Wheel
(*cakra*) symbolic of the turning of the teaching and the *Stupa* or burial
mound shape, which suggested the burial place of the Buddha. Legend
has it that when the monks asked the Buddha what type of monument
he wished to have built after his death (one should recall that in India a
monument for a monarch and a renowned spiritual teacher were
equally large and elaborate), the Buddha folded one of his monastic
robes into a square and, inverting his begging bowl, placed it on top.
He then told the monks that this should be the shape of his monument.
From that time onwards, this was the traditional basis for the Buddhist
tombstone—a square with a half circle shape above—although later
generations enlarged, extended, and elaborated many of its features.

Pictures and other spiritual symbols were often painted within a
circular border, this representing the 360° significance, relevance, and
value of the Dharma as a protection against the all around susceptibility of the human mind. This was a theme which the Theravadins especially developed.

Figure 12. A popular Buddhist charm of the Theravada school in the form of an eight-spoked Wheel of Dharma Mandala, bearing auspicious signs and talismanic protections in the four cardinal points. (From Thailand.)

Figure 13. One of the many forms of the Buddhist Wheel of Dharma (Dharmacakra). (Author's collection.)

Figure 14. Worshiping the Stupa. (India Museum, Calcutta.)

Later, in other lands, the Indian pristine artistic simplicity underwent elaborate transformation and the simple humanity of Shakyamuni was often replaced by representations of Buddhist attributes and wisdoms endowed with an almost supernatural beauty. The wheel, mentioned earlier, being a very common symbol. In the story of King Asoka (Asokavadana) we can read [Note 70] descriptions of the five different types of righteous monarch, each of whom is known as a "Wheel turning King" (*Cakravartin*). These monarchs are used as symbols of the different types of political power used by rulers to govern. Each is distinguished by their "type" of wheel. One turns an iron wheel, another a copper wheel, etc., up to a golden wheel—and the golden wheel represented the most enlightened and spiritually endowed form of monarchy. These monarchs were often depicted in Chinese and Tibetan Temple murals in highly decorative forms.

The Mahayana tradition developed additional goals to those expressed within the Theravada teachings. One important Mahayana orientation, preserved in many of its schools, lay in the way it regarded the ordinary being. The Mahayana taught that mankind in its very nature was enlightened—not simply in potential, as held by the Ther-

Figure 15. Carving, said to be of a Cakravartin showing Vajramukti hand strikes and foot positions. (Madras Museum, India.)

avada—but in actuality. The goal of enlightenment, according to this teaching, was not something to be attained or moved toward, as such, but was a condition that could be realized within one's being.

Eventually the Mahayana developed teachings that classified themselves as direct paths. These paths were based upon powerful meditational techniques oriented toward an intense inner searching of the human consciousness. These paths were usually considered esoteric because they had to be taught personally within a special environment and, like arrows, were aimed directly toward a target. With the acceptance of esoteric paths of teaching, the earlier forms came to be regarded as "gradual" paths. Another type of description contrasted the two types of practice as straight line or circular. However these basic classifications are not wholly accurate, for even in the circularity of the Theravada doctrinal "pulse," we find a straight path soteriology attempting to ease the sufferings of mankind.

We should not make the error of assuming that the different schools of teachings represented heretical or mutually incompatible teachings, like those we are used to hearing about in the history of the Christian church, for example. All the schools were in agreement as to fundamentals and differences as differences only existed in regard to the training or practice methods employed when instructing monks. Buddhism, as a whole, has always been extremely tolerant of other views within its ranks. This is reflected nowadays in the proliferation of its different forms [Note 16].

Within all schools, human beings are seen as being born bearing the karmic trends of the ages. We are shaped by, and manifest these, according to our level of consciousness. Aspirant Buddhas begin from such a point but, instead of becoming its victim, direct themselves to the ultimate goal lying beyond such burdens. All schools agree about this goal. Ordinary knowledge or education was often a hindrance to realization, for education developed, more often than not, within a materialistic environment that exalted intellectual and logical truth, rather than enlightenment. These principles were aligned with (or formed) particular cultural values and views that generally disapproved of spiritual discovery and all it entailed.

The socio-centric materialist of the Buddha's era has its counterpart in modern times. Bypassing intellect is perhaps difficult to understand in the West, for we are used to learning of things from "authorities" who have become authorities through study and educational discipline. Our Western educational system emulates this structure and even our religious orthodoxy has evolved from it. In Buddhism, knowledge is subservient to wisdom and the approach we take to develop wisdom is different from the one that accumulates information.

Buddhist wisdom is directed toward the attainment of transcendental truth (*Paramarthasatya*), and the means for developing it is found within our minds and bodies. It is not something that is "gained" or possessed by the subject it studies, but is realized within. All knowledge is subject to wisdom and has a subordinate value [Note 68].

The realization of our true nature in the light of the *Paramarthasatya* is the basis of Buddhist endeavor. It was this realization that transformed the former Prince Siddartha into the Buddha. The Four Noble Truths [Note 15a] which he first expounded are so simple and direct that it is difficult to see their spiritual significance. Certainly they are not in any way controversial, and few proponents of other religious systems would even disagree with them. However, their expression began the Buddhist doctrinal system (the *Dharma*) and was to change the face and lives of millions of people in the years to come. The Truths express simple and observable realities upon which rest the basis of self-discovery. Their implications, when followed through, lead directly to the inner heart of the *Dharma*. They provide the strategies necessary to live life fully and clearly.

Our reason for spiritual study should not simply be to overcome problems we encounter, be they practical or psychological, for this is only a reaction (not a response) to life. In resolving to follow the *Dharma*, we are trying to create the basis for an inner clarity and perspective. In the Mahayana such attributes are directed outward toward others in a selfless other-orientation. The root scriptures of all schools

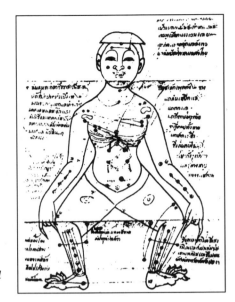

Figure 16. Traditional chart of medical points, Thailand. (Kongoryuji Temple.)

point out that the nature of Self is void. The Self does not lie in the heart, the heart does not lie in the Self. In this Self lies the origin of the World. To try to live life as a Selfless Being is one step on the road toward clarity. The dedication to attempt this path is embodied in the Bodhisattva Vow distinctive to the Mahayana tradition. (Refer to Note 29 of Entering the Path.)

It is unfortunately common to find that many spiritual systems tend to become "clogged up" in their own processes and spiritual forms within a few centuries after their initiation. The original vital spark is replaced by formality and establishmentarianism, honorific titles increase, ceremonial robes become more elaborate and inner value dwindles. At certain later periods in the history of the Chinese Dharma such degenerations did occur. This usually happened when various monastic organizations involved themselves with secular and/or political schemes, or were harboring inhabitants who were political refugees masquerading as monks. These deviations did not affect the development of any major school of teaching for long, however.

A common occurrence within spiritual systems that have lost their vitality is the propensity to discover heretics within their midst and to turn against them with fervor. Throughout its long and diverse history remarkably little of this is found in Chinese Buddhism; instead there arose an increased vitality over the centuries and new institutions and schools proliferated. In this respect, Buddhism was much better off than its later European counterparts as the nature of truth (and, thus,

Figure 17. A rubbing of an engraving showing the harmony between Taoism, Confucianism, and Buddhism. (From the Shaolin Temple, Honan, British Museum, London.)

true doctrine) was never a point of actual contention among the different schools. Their remarkable and extensive inter-acceptance of each other has never been rivaled in other systems of belief. Buddhism was, and is, a tradition of reasonableness and tolerance toward others.

The later trends of thought that developed in Chinese Buddhism did not challenge conditions it regarded as heretical, but were attempts to explicate early teachings in a different manner to the one espoused by traditional schools. Some of the traditional schools seemed, to some contemporary Chinese, a little "long in the tooth" in their presentations.

The growth of Buddhist forms within China was remarkable and diverse, and despite the occasional Taoist inspired purge and prohibition, it re-emerged after such pogroms in even stronger forms, unlike the contemporary Christianity which extirpated the Sabellian, Patripassianism, Docetic and Gnostic doctrines, along with their supporters. The Buddhist equivalents of the fourth century A.D. British monk Pelagius, or the Alexandrian Basilides and Origen, were recognized and acknowledged as making important contributions toward understanding the profundity of the teachings. They were not burned [Note 8]. Such fearless acceptance could only occur within a teaching of supreme confidence, inner stability and maturity.

All Buddhist schools of teaching have an inherent balancing factor—the teaching itself. The *Dharma* acts as a giant gyroscope that maintains its balance despite all attempts to orientate it wrongly in dif-

Figure 18. A Lamaistic magic charm said to ease childbirth and given to pregnant women to carry (Author's collection.)

ferent directions. Any error in understanding the *Dharma* will eventually become apparent if its devotee is sincere and persistent in application of the teachings. This is the *Dharma's* great strength.

What are called the "Three Seals" (*Anatma*—the impermanence of a personal Self; *Annica*—the transitoriness of all things; and *Dukkha*—the dissatisfaction inherent in existence) are principles that are the basis of each school of Buddhism, irrespective of which country or culture it has manifested within.

THE

MANDALA

OF HUMAN

CHARACTERISTICS

THE MANDALA OF
HUMAN CHARACTERISTICS

The auspicious Vajradhara has marvelous open eyes
—his hand rotates the Vajramudra which disperses
like the light of fire.*

One of the practical ways in which the elemental viewpoint played a significant part lay in the assessment of individual character and temperament. Early Buddhism had from the very beginning produced rough and ready guides to character analysis [Note 2b]. These were usually based upon given combinations of mental qualities and/or physiological patterns. Students of the path were loosely classified into various types by their teachers and their practices and meditations were modified to accord with their type. The purpose of this was to enable students to discover the most efficacious method of change suitable for them. These types were not simply concerned with mental characteristics (and thus could not be termed psychological), nor were they purely physical (and thus would not be physiological). They were combinations of both. In modern terminology such a grouping is called a somatype.

Buddhist somatyping concerned the personal (*Pudgala*) characteristics (*Laksana*) of each individual, and the combined term for this practice (*pudgala laksana*) became, in Chinese, the word *Jen Hsiang* (Japanese: *Ninso*). This was one of the earliest Chinese words used to describe what is generally known as the art of Physiognomy. The latter character *Hsiang* was used later in China as a suffix for various technical terms to describe many other forms of the prognosticative arts.

One of the simplest traditional systems grouped people according to their basic mental "stains." These "stains" (*Klesa*) describe the afflicted qualities of consciousness that relate to suffering. The three fundamental forms are greed, ignorance and hatred [Note 2g].

Other combinations of human qualities were also used to form somatypes. In the *Visuddhi Magga* (3: 74), we read of six types of temperament. These are described as being ruled by greed (*Raga*), hatred (*Dosa*), stupidity or dullness (*Moha*), faith (*Saddha*), intelligence (*Buddhi*),

---

*Chapter 7 "Accomplishing Siddhis" of *The Mahavairocana Sutra*.

Figure 19. The Face of Shakyamuni Buddha, Tun Huang caves, China. (Author's collection.)

and rumination or sloth (*Vitakka*). The six types are characterized by posture, physical agility, how they sit, sleep, awaken, and relax, how they hold their facial muscles, their preferred food, etc. These are all described in great detail.

The *greed type* is said to exhibit deceit, tempestuousness, to be always discontented, to love fine clothing and to be fickle.

The *stupidity type* is said to be lazy, to get excited easily, to worry over things, to be always perplexed, to be obstinate and tenacious.

The *hatred type* is said to be angry a great deal, to hold grudges, to act imperiously, to be envious and mean to others.

Another traditional scheme outlines the somatypes into five distinctive patterns and then provides a meditative theme to enable such patterns to be overcome.

Mental Stain	*Remedy*
Greed	Meditations upon the transitory nature of all existent things.
Hatred	Generation of Compassion towards others.
Stupidity	Familiarizing oneself with the principles of causality.

| Selfhood belief | Discriminating between the various components and activities which create consciousness. |
| Confusion | Meditation upon the Breathing process and rhythms. |

Most people would be able to recognize a type using these guidelines. Within both India and China this system (physical appearance, habit patterns, etc.) became very popular.

> In the 3000 fold world all the common multitude,
> Gods, Men, Titans
> Beings in Hell, demons, animals
> All such forms and images
> appear there in his body (the bodhisattva).
> Though not possessed yet of the flawless, mystical, spiritual body,
> yet in his pure ordinary body,
> Every thing is revealed.*

In the early scriptures somatyping is clearly defined as being used to determine spiritual orientations and propensities. There are also precedents for this in the Chinese scriptures. In the Surangama Sutra, we read a story set in a celestial realm, in which five Buddhas describe how each of them, when either an Arahant or Bodhisattva, attained enlightenment via one or other of the five elements. Visvabhi used Earth, Varuna used Water, Ucchumsa used Fire, Dharanimdhara used Air and Akasagarbha used Space.

It is no surprise to find this elemental nomenclature being used in the special arts taken up by the general populace and practiced as a profession of sorts. The Buddha forbade his monks to do this as a means of livelihood, but did not invalidate the system itself. It continued to be applied wherever Buddhism spread, including both China and Japan, where it assumed refined forms and was detailed and researched more fully.

These systems basically indicated a general acceptance of the principle that the mental and physical factors of being should not be regarded as separated from each other, and that understanding one could develop insight into the other. The doctrine of mind/body inseparability was technically termed *Abhisanditakayacitta*—the "dropping away" of "being" from the sense of duality that centered upon the mind and body.

The use of somatypes within Buddhism is straightforward and simple. It enables students to gain a view of themselves outside the

---

*The Lotus Sutra, Ch. 19, pp. 356–357 [Note 2c].

Figure 20. Auspicious markings upon the feet of the Buddha. (Author's collection.)

usual and personal language they may use to describe themselves. It also makes it difficult to present themselves as separate or alienated from either themselves or others, as many of the "others" will share their somatype. In modern times we are not so simple in our nature as the people of medieval India or China, so we expect to find many variations and/or combinations of the "pure" archetypal somatypes that Buddhists used. However, the point of somatyping is to enable us to begin self-diagnosis.

The first somatypes were combinations of a physical and psychological nature. In systems oriented toward the art of healing, more attention was paid to the diagnostic aspects of somatyping mind or body. In systems practicing the warrior arts, greater attention was paid to physical capacities and attributes, and the ability to accurately judge the condition of muscles and tissues by touch, sight, and movement was greatly enhanced and developed in both arts.

Although, no doubt, each of the types of art that utilized somatyping regarded it as an alternative form of self-description, we should not lose sight of the fact that it was, and is, primarily intended to be an aid used by one's teacher to decide what type of meditation best suits the practitioner of Buddhist spirituality. It was from such an impetus alone

Figure 21. Nataraja, the Lord of the Nata, in traditional position. (Author's collection.)

that the art of *Chuan Fa* was developed. In order to understand the many ways in which the various constituents of the range of somatypes were presented, let us now consider some of their distinctive features to see how some of them were studied and memorized by Indian and Chinese students.

The various categories and component energies of the mind/body complex were accorded a ruling element. If we use the five Skhandas they arrange themselves as follows:

Skhanda	*Element*
Form	Earth
Sensation	Water
Perception	Fire
Formation ·	Air
Consciousness	Ether

The order of elements is an ascending demateriality. The order of Skhandas correspondingly represents the progression of mental activity, from simple sensorial stimuli to fully developed concepts. Each element represents the totality of mind/body interactions that can occur in each Skhanda, and collectively represent the whole mind/body complex. They also represent particular individual responses, be they destructive or creative, of the personality pattern within the limits of each Skhanda and are thus denominators of the individual temperament. These can be summarized as follows:

Earth is associated with slowness, regularity and the relationship to detail. It also indicates habitual patterns, reliability and respect for tradition.

Water represents interaction and relationships toward individuals and groups. It describes adaptability and interactive potential. It tends toward over-emotionality, sensuality and/or depression [see Note 1a].

Fire represents activity and creation, expansion and energy, as well as destruction, closedness, and departmentalism.

Air represents abstract concepts and relationships toward them. It describes the thought orientation within an individual, as well as patterns of intellect and ignorance.

Ether symbolizes a quintessential totality of previous patterns and qualities which—plus "Life Energy" (*Jivat*)—represents the possibility of human birth, and the spiritual aspiration or awareness of consciousness itself. It thus serves as a general denominator of consciousness in all its human potential. Ether also describes consciousness bereft of its physical life energy (i.e., not based upon a physical body) and is used to represent spirits, demons, etc.

In the various descriptions of *Mano* and *Manas* (see reference pp. 284-287), the last element developed manifold representation. Ether is the original element of Indian Hindu cosmogeny and represented the innate energy or life power of the universe, which permeated all things. It was adopted thus by the early Buddhists but was soon represented abstractly as the space between the elements of physical existence (*Bhutadhatu* or *Mahabhuta*). Later Chinese Buddhist healers considered it as representing the vivifying physical life energy. In both cases it represented a transcendent force bereft of spatial, temporal, and mental limitations.

The meditation upon the element of Space, in its symbolic form as the "Treasury of the Sky," was accorded the highest value in Buddhism. It is described in the *Gaganaganja Parippccha* (Peking Tripitaka Vol. 33, pp. 1–33) in many different forms and methods of practice. The renowned Buddhist philosopher Vasubandhu exalts its practice and says that this alone makes all the *paramitas* (spiritually perfecting practices) effective. The practice of the Space Meditation, itself, mainly consists of contemplating the infinite expanse of the skies and the development of compassion to an equal extension. It is a simple but potent symbolism of the vastness possible to the human being. As space exists everywhere, so the enlightened compassion of the Buddhist must likewise be unrestricted and ever present. In China its meditation practice is normally called *Kuan Kung* (Japanese: *Kan-Ku*), literally, "to perceive the emptiness." Traditional *Chuan Fa* practice still begins with a ceremonial bow called the *Kuan Kung*, and this practice constitutes a reminder of the original purpose of the art.

The Buddhist elements were also attributed to the sacred mountains of China. Each mountain was ruled by one element that was accorded provenance of a guardian Bodhisattva as follows.

Mountain	Element	Bodhisattva
Chiu hsia	Earth	Ksitigharba
P'u t'o	Water	Avalokitesvara
Omei	Fire	Acalarajah
Wu Tai	Air	Manjusri

Let us now return to the poem "The Bite" extracted from the *Visuddhi Magga* (page 18), to see what it offers us in terms of another type of understanding. This understanding is apart from its literary and poetic value, because it is really a description of elements as an expression of unskillfully minded somatypes. The poem mentions four types of "mouth," namely the "wooden," "rotten," "fiery," and "dagger." The word "mouth" indicates a human way of expression or impression. Each of the different mouths is a symbol for the elements and how people can use what they represent.

The "wooden" means words used in ignorance or in blind repetition. (We still use the word "wooden-headed" in England to denote such a temperament.) This is the Earth element. The "rotten" represents the inevitable decay of the delight in earthly or sensorial pleasures. The word "rotten" can also mean putrefaction and refers especially to the decay and odor of the (beautiful) body when the life force has left it. This is the Water element. The word "fiery" represents those ruled by the heat of anger and hatred which leads to violence and warfare. This is the Fire element. The word "dagger" means those who use cruel or evil words which can pierce the mind. This represents the Air element.

As poisonous insects bite and cling to human flesh so these traits can adhere to our minds and harm us. The incisions these bites make can leave us scarred for a long time afterward. In the same way individual actions and thoughts will either remain with or eventually return to those who initiated them, be they good or ill.

The line in the poem "body stiff to all intent" means two things. The "body stiff" represents elemental stasis. This means that the qualities represented by those elements are held rigidly within a mental pattern or habit. It can also indicate actual physical illness, for the elements represent creative patterns and the renewal processes of the human body. To "hold" such forces "stiff" means to degenerate (i.e., not to produce life or living energies) [Note 18].

"All intent" here means "with inner will" and refers mainly to the vow to attain enlightenment. If one is stiff to such intent, mundane concerns have overcome spiritual aspirations. "When roused" means "in spiritually creative activity" and warns us that it is when we are engaged in doing things for seemingly spiritual reasons that we may—if we are not fully aware—cause more harm than good. This is when the "snake" of the element can strike us most easily.

If we read the poem in this light, we can see that in its few lines an enormous amount of information is given. We may not be aware of this the first time we read it, it is rather like meeting a stranger. It is only after we get into communication with "this stranger" that we discover the many wonderful things he has seen or done. Buddhist literature and symbolism is like this stranger. We have to want to discover it; we have to make the effort to communicate in order to penetrate below the superficial.

The elements are also like strangers. They seem one thing but rapidly become others as we plumb their depths. Another presentation of the elements is given in the esoteric "Dainichikyo" (*Mahavairocana Sutra*) where the elements are allied to the Four Dharma Gifts that one can make to another person. Here they are described as alms (Earth), pleasant speech (Water), useful actions (Fire) and mutual aid (Air).

If we look at these early lists of personal qualities or descriptions, we see that they underwent a gradual process of elaboration and expli-

THE BODHISATTVA WARRIORS / 53

cation. Many of the later descriptions or lists of qualities and characteristics of people amplify ideas already stated (i.e., *Visuddhi Magga* 3).

By comparing the lists already given here we can see that they develop directly from the fundamental three mental afflictions (*Klesa*) of greed, hatred and ignorance. This latter *klesa* is subdivided into various aspects which are then dealt with as if distinct entities.

Three-System	Five-System	Six-System
Greed	Greed	Greed
Hatred	Hatred	Hatred
Ignorance	Ignorance	Stupidity (Ignorance)
	Selfhood Belief Confusion	Faith
		Intelligence
		Sloth

In the Five-System list, *Selfhood Belief* and *Confusion* are two aspects of the quality of *Ignorance*. One (selfhood belief) is oriented toward the inner world, the other (confusion) the outer world. In the Six-System list, we see *Ignorance* presented as pairs of opposites. Intelligence destroys Stupidity (and vice versa). Faith destroys Sloth (and vice versa).

If we compare the later categories of the "Five" and "Six" lists, we see that they interact upon each other, i.e., selfhood belief engenders sloth (especially the spiritual kind), while stupidity engenders confusion.

The qualities of *Faith* and *Intelligence* seem to be simple antidotes for the qualities of stupidity and sloth, as well as corrective forces upon each other, thus avoiding a "one-sided" spiritual development. However when we examine the scriptures more closely, we find that mundane intelligence is similar in nature to hatred, and blind faith is similar to Greed. In the *Visuddhi Magga*, many of the descriptive sections relating to somatypes are followed by lines carrying a warning or cautionary remark describing the result if the previous text is misinterpreted. In this instance the warning notes that as hatred does not wish to possess its object, so neither does intelligence wish to possess wisdom. As greed does not want to let go of that which will eventually harm it, so faith does not let go of the virtues it accrues.

These two qualities—intelligence and faith—are also perhaps the forerunners of a higher and transcendentally unified form described

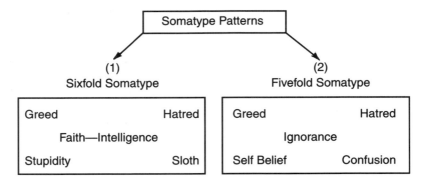

Figure 22. Different ways to look at somatypes.

in Mahayana Buddhism as *Prajna* (compassionate wisdom). If we look even more closely, we see that there are always pairings of active and passive qualities. In both mandalas greed, hatred, faith and intelligence may be both active or passive in nature; sloth and stupidity are passive in basis. Selfhood belief, being passive, is remedied by active, discriminatory, meditations. Confusion, being active, is remedied by passive, mind-stilling, meditation. These interplaying qualities can be

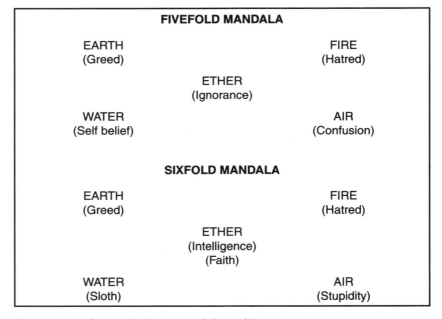

Figure 23. Combining the elements and the qualities or somatypes.

presented in the two patterns shown in figure 22. The sixfold system has its own and optimistic built in remedy while the fivefold system requires additional external meditational remedies.

We can now venture back into the realm of the five elements for, by recognizing the elemental aspects of the human qualities outlined earlier, we can weave both aspects and qualities into a mandala pattern (mandalas are explained later on) and re-present their simultaneous interaction. Mandala patterns are often easier to remember than the lists of words to which they form a mnemonical key. See figure 23.

The Mandala of Symbolism

Find tongues in trees,
books in running waters*

Presenting various points of the *Dharma* in symbolic forms was practiced in all Buddhist schools. It was, perhaps, a natural progression, for symbolism was replacing, or supplementing, human somatypes with universal ones. Studying by means of groups (Sanskrit: *Kalapa*) of qualities or principles was a method employed from the earliest days of Buddhism and is described in the *Visuddhi Magga*: V. 20 as the primary method of insight development (*Naya Vipassana*).

The early Theravada employed many symbols to represent Shakyamuni Buddha. These were true symbols in that they did not seek to represent him directly, but suggested his presence by stating his absence. An empty chair, a sunshade with no one beneath it, a pair of empty sandals—all of these can be found carved or painted in the oldest Theravada temples. Shakyamuni had said that the teaching should be his best memorial and so pictorial representations of this became the natural heir for both imaginative artistic expression and actual memorials of the Buddha's person. We can distinguish several types of representation inspired from different motives. There were some, such as the later Monarch Asoka's, which commemorate events in Shakyamuni's life—where he was born, where he trained in the martial arts, etc., and others, such as the golden Eight-spoked Wheel, which represented the doctrine. These were found everywhere that Buddhism spread.

While the symbols varied a great deal according to who and what was being taught, the principle of symbolism and/or representation remained constant. It was seen as another manifestation of the Buddha's command to "convey the teaching in the language a people knew best." The earliest use of symbols for the different aspects of the Three Jewels (Buddha, Dharma, Sangha) was probably due simply to the fact that often uneducated people were being taught, and thus a simple, picture-book presentation was made of the doctrine. At other times the opposite was true, and to monks these symbols provided "keys" for

---

*Sisya-lekha dharma kavya of Candragomin V. 68 [see Note 4].

Figure 24. This hill at Kusinagara marks the place where Shakyamuni Buddha's body was cremated. (Photo courtesy of Kosei Publishing Co., Japan.)

Figure 25. The tower marking the spot where the Buddha met his former ascetic colleagues and converted them to the Dharma. Sarnath near Benares, India. (Photo courtesy of Kosei Publishing Co., Japan.)

Figure 26. The Bodhisattva Akasagarbha (Womb of Space). He represents the potentiality of all beings to attain enlightenment. His left hand holds an emblem symbolic of the three jewels. (Painting by Ryusen Miyahara.)

Figure 27. Kukai, one of the Japanese founders of esoteric Buddhism. He holds the esoteric vajra (kongo) and rosary (nenju). (Painting by Ryusen Miyahara.)

Figure 28. The Bodhisattva Ava-lokitesvara (Chinese: Kuan Yin). The Bodhisattva of Compassion and the deliverer of the Heart Sutra to Arahant Sariputra. (Painting by Ryusen Miyahara.)

sermon themes. Later the finer points of the doctrine became so abstruse and intellectually demanding that the symbols became a form of shorthand to convey "bundles" of doctrines in an effective manner.

The Japanese master of esoteric teaching, Kobo Daishi (Kukai) often pointed out in his writings that many seemingly straightforward accounts of doctrine were in fact repositories of much higher principles than they appeared to state, and that, providing one had the "key" to understand this, the message could be clearly discerned. He wrote several commentaries upon the Heart Sutra—a favorite scripture of the Japanese that was also used in many non-esoteric schools of teaching—to demonstrate that it clearly contained accounts of principles far beyond what it outwardly appeared to indicate.

So, rather than being a later tradition, the use of symbolic methods of communication is in fact very old. Symbols are perhaps only seen as symbols to certain types of people from certain types of cultures; to others symbols may appear as clear and direct facts. Shakyamuni himself said that there were many doctrines he had not openly taught his students due to them not being necessary at the time. He did not say there were no further doctrines, only that he had not taught them all. If we consider this with the knowledge that the Pali scriptures preserve only one form of the early schools of teaching, the use of different teaching methods, or different ways of communicating the teachings, does not seem unlikely. The school of Chaan Buddhism is said to have evolved from the raising aloft of a flower by Shakyamuni, an act said to have been understood by only one disciple.

The esoteric schools (Chinese: *Mi Ching* or *Pi-Mi*) and traditions of Buddhism developed the use of symbols to a high degree and almost every point or principle of the *Dharma* was, or could be, represented in some form or other. Some of the important scriptures of the school use a form of language which explicitly describes doctrines in symbolism or gives images instead of specifics.

Figure 29. The Bodhisattva Samantabhadra holding the esoteric triple pointed Vajra (Sanko Kongo) and Sphota (Kane) representing the Power and the Word of the esoteric teaching. (Painting by Ryusen Miyahara.)

Figure 30. The Sanskrit character for the letter "A" which is used in esoteric Buddhism to represent the primordial and transcendental body of teachings envisioned as Mahavairocana Buddha. (Kongoryuji Library.)

Figure 31. Zen meditation can be practiced by men or women equally. Here students are members of Rishokoseikai, a prominent Japanese lay Buddhist organization. (Author's collection.)

Symbols cannot easily be understood without some key to unlock them. The esoteric form of teaching emphasized universal rather than purely historical or scriptural contexts and meanings. It may be well at this point to recap Buddhism's general development so we can see how the esoteric (Japanese: *Mikkyo*) path fits.

The various schools of teaching that make up the totality of approaches to Dharma fulfill different needs. The different forms of Mikkyo that developed in Japan reflected the temperaments of the people where it spread. If we take an overview of Buddhist development we see schools oriented toward sutra, principal, faith, mysticism, meditation, and syncretism. I would stress these are not different sects as the term connotes in the West. In the East these are merely different approaches to the same thing. This simplified outline of developments (the schools are discussed further in Notes 2, 3, and 12) shown in figure 32 will help you see the changes.

Like all human developments, the spiritual systematization of Buddhism underwent changes in doctrine in that teachings were explained further or applied to new situations. Some changes were

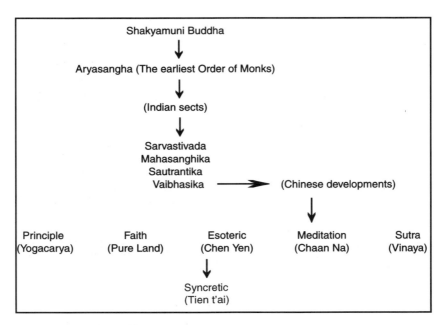

Figure 32. Various Buddhist schools.

merely of emphasis, or they were organizational—i.e., concerning the type and training of monks. Most changes did not cause the rivalry, friction, or sectarian wars so common to other religions. The only distinction of note involved the Esoteric School. This teaching considered itself radically different from the others (which it termed "exoteric") in that it did not rely solely upon the teaching of the earthly Buddha Shakyamuni. Instead, in addition to Shakyamuni's teaching, it incorporated the esoteric Sutras of Mahavairocana Buddha.

One of the most distinctive symbols used in the school of esoteric teachings was the central Buddha figure, itself. Unlike other schools which often used a statue of the earthly, incarnate, Shakyamuni Buddha as the central motif for shrines, Mikkyo schools used the figure of Bud-

Figure 33. One of many forms of Mahavairocana Buddha. (Kongo-ryuji Library.)

*Figure 34. Mahavairocana Bud-
dha, the primordial Buddha.
(Painting by Ryusen Miyahara.)*

dha Mahavairocana (Great Brilliant Shining One). This was a Cosmic
Buddha, one who had never been born as a human, but who was
regarded as the Adi-Buddha principle from which all other Buddhas
emanated. His form within the esoteric temples was quite distinct and
recognizably different from all other schools' representations of Buddhas or Bodhisattvas. It wore a crown and was adorned with jewels
and armor in the style of an Indian Ksatreya warrior king. In China, the
Sanskrit name *Mahavairocana* was translated as *Ta Jih* (Japanese:
Dainichi) meaning "Great Sun." The most common form of Mahavairocana appeared within the esoteric mandala paintings that adorned the
temples.

These mandalas (see Glossary) portrayed the adi-Buddha and his
provenance in all its magnificent glory and radiance and are a distinctive feature of the esoteric temple. The Mandala of Mahavairocana (the
Diamond Realm) was often paired with another describing the realm of
human experiences (the Matrix Realm). Two other well-known symbols
used in the Mikkyo are the Sotoba (Sanskrit: *Stupa*) and the Kongo (Sanskrit: *Vajra*).

UNDERSTANDING FUNDAMENTAL SYMBOLS

The Vajra: Unlike the Hindu triple-pointed form [Note 44] the essential Vajra (thunderbolt) symbol (Chinese: *Ching Kang*, Japanese: *Kongo*) adopted by the Mikkyo sects was a bipolar and five-pointed visible representation of the five elements reflected up and downward, i.e., to the realm of humanity and the realm of enlightenment. Their simultaneous manifestation and interpenetration was demonstrated by the fact that they were joined together in their middle. The hands were often used to represent the Vajra and all the gestures or attitudes which involved a *Vajra* could be substituted by ritual positions of the hand (*mudra*).

The art of *Chuan Fa*, that you will learn about later, used many of these gestures, and we can find many statues representing a Bodhisattva with hands placed in one or more of the positions called a Vajra fist. The five fingers each represent one of the great universal elements and their reflected form was effected by placing the hands together [Note 44].

Whereas woven mandalas came to be imitated and described by the later Arabians as magic carpets, so the Vajra Mudra came to be popularized by 19th century Western stage magicians as "magic passes" of the hands which they used in their tricks before an audience. As with the *Topa*, each symbol shared a part of its being with another, which itself connected with all the others ad infinitum. The Vajra became the symbol of self-unification in both natural and supra-natural realms of endeavor. It was adopted by many non-esoteric forms of Buddhism to represent the self-developed power of infinite truth and reality, a power which dispelled evil and led directly toward Enlightenment. It was for this reason used in ritual exorcism and other evil dispelling ceremonies.

Figure 35. The Vajra (Japanese: Kongo), symbol of the power of enlightenment. (Author's collection).

The Vajra symbolized this coming together of the many forces—mental and physical—within the human being, together with their simultaneous enactments within the world. This was a condition very hard to describe to the laity yet it was a condition they all found themselves within, knowingly or not. The Vajra came to represent the power of spiritual insight and was borne by, or used to decorate many esoteric deities.

The Sotoba: One other consistent symbol found throughout the esoteric traditions is called in Japan the *Sotoba*—the five-tiered pagoda which is a representation of the mystical body of Mahavairocana in the form of the primary elements. It is also known in Japan as the *Gorinto*—the five circles or (wheels). In China it is known as the *To* or in full, *Topa*. (*Topa* is the Chinese way of pronouncing the original Sanskrit name *Stupa*). Its shape is commonly used, in various forms, for Buddhist tombstones all over the Orient.

In the esoteric schools, different meanings were applied to the various component shapes of the *Topa* according to which realm of exis-

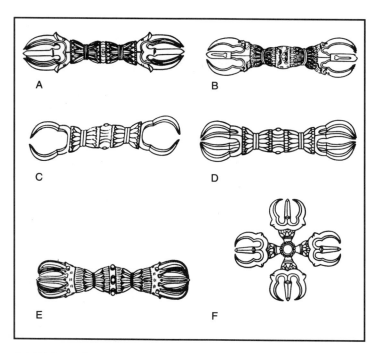

Figure 36. *Different forms of Vajra (Kongo) used in esoteric rituals. The pictures show: a) five prongs; b) three prongs; c) two prongs; d) four prongs; e) nine prongs; and f) crossed Vajra—a sign representing creative spiritual activity. (Author's collection.)*

tence (there are six in Mikkyo) the *Topa* is being considered. Despite these multiple understandings, or later architectural embellishments and ornamentation, all *Topa* have the same basic meanings.

The Topa has five shapes, two are unitary and three are derivatives of the first two. The base is square—this, in the *Sarvastivada* tradition, was said to be the shape of the smallest possible atom of matter. The square represents the element Earth and also the fundamental state of being (in Mikkyo this is interpreted as immaculate wisdom). The next shape is the circle representing Water and perfect vacuity. The next shape—the triangle—is formed from half of the square and represents the element Fire. It is a symbol of perfect activity on behalf of others. The next shape is the half-circle, formed from the previous circle. This is the Air element and represents perfected awareness. Above the Air is the jewel shape. This is formed from half the circle and half the triangle. This corresponds either to the element Ether—in terms of matter—or perfect enlightenment—in terms of consciousness. The jewel shows the synthesis of all the previous constituent factors, both mental and physical, into a transcendental whole.

Because the *Topa* is a manifest shape it is used to describe various qualities and attributes of the "body" of Mahavairocana in both its out-

Figure 37. Ancient Chinese stone carving marking the burial place of Hsuan Tsang, who went to India in search of the scriptures. Note the Sistrum staff, used to worn off animals and the unusual, and the highly functional design of the ruc-sac. (Author's collections.)

ward and inner forms (i.e., manifest and unmanifest). These attributes are usually presented as embodying the two aspects of all teaching, namely their constituents viewed as demonstrating either Dharmic *Ri* (principle) or *Chi* (wisdom).

The *Topa* describes the body of humankind when viewed as inherent Buddhas. The *Topa* was one of the earliest Mikkyo symbols to be imbued with paradigmatic qualities and we can find it used to describe many different aspects of the *Dharma*.

The shape of the earliest *Topa* was composed of just the first two shapes taken from the folded robe of Shakyamuni Buddha with his begging bowl on top (in an inverted position). Thus the square and circle shapes were formed. Later the Buddha pronounced, in contrast to his earlier statement, that in future times only his teaching (*Dharma*) was to be his memorial. The earliest monuments were of this simple "bowl and robe shape" similar to Islamic mosques (although they predate Islam by many centuries). When used as a repository for the bones or other relics of a famous monk, the *Topa* were called *Caitya*. This title usually serves to distinguish between *Topa* intended for practical and symbolic use.

The various colors of the different parts of the *Topa* and other symbols were originally outlined in early Theravada texts (like the *Visuddhi Magga*) where they occur in descriptions of the elements of the *Kasina* (Sanskrit: *Krtsna*), which are colored clay shapes used for meditation practice by monks. Earth is yellow, Water is blue, Fire is red, Air is white and Ether is either black, transparent or gold.

Some later traditions of Northern India and Tibet adapted or changed these colors and very much altered chromatic traditions exist nowadays in Tibet and Japan. Whereas the earliest accounts always mention primary colors, both Tibetan and Japanese sects use combina-

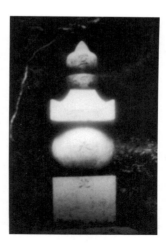

Figure 38. Sotoba gravestone. (Author's collection.)

tions of colors. As the *Topa* is supposed to represent primary and pure qualities, there seems to be no rationale for such innovation. There is always the possibility that originally the colors were copied correctly but that time has aged the minerals and chemical compounds used in ancient Japanese copies. Later generations, not recognizing this fact, simply repainted or copied the transformed colors they found.

In Chinese the various characters used for colors were not always consistent. The character for blue was also used to describe a shade of green and vice versa. However, as stated before, the earliest colors are easily discovered from the Sanskrit original texts. We can see these color changes by comparing different accounts of the element colors as stated within the texts of several Mikkyo masters, as shown in Table 1 on page 70. These traditions are based upon accounts given in the *Mahavairocana Sutra*, the *Tatvasamgraha*, and the *Vajrasekhara Sutra*, all of which were used by the two Acaryas in China, and the *Gorin Hishaku*, a translation of parts of these scriptures concerning the Maha Mandala compiled by Kakuban, a later Japanese Master.

Amoghavajara's account is simpler in form than Subhakarasimha's and includes paradigms of stars, devas and the forces of nature. It echoes a passage in Matreyanatha's work *Abhisamayalankara* (8:v 29) where the elements are accorded the colors yellow, red, white and black, but no blue. Subhakarasimha's work is more doctrinally explicated and has paradigms for doctrines, wisdoms and consciousness. This is the most common source used within Japanese Shingon [see Note 47]. The *Mahavairocana Sutra* contains several accounts of the colors ascribed to the elements and one of these (contained in chapter 8) accords with the account in the *Visuddhi Magga*. It ascribes the color black to the Ether or Space element.

Figure 39. Sotoba gravestones in the Mount Koya graveyard. (Author's collection.)

Table 1. Element and Ruling Colors from Mikkyo texts.

Element	Amoghavajra	Subhakarasimha	Kakuban
Earth	Yellow	Blue	Yellow
Water	Black	White	White
Fire	Red	Red	Red
Air	White	Black	Black
Ether	Blue	Yellow	Blue

Table 2. Elements / Colors from Tibet and the *Visuddhi Magga*.*

Element	Soothill (Tibet)	Canton and *Visuddhi Magga*
Earth	Yellow	Yellow
Water	White (Black)	Blue
Fire	Red	Red
Air	Black (Green)	White
Ether	Azure (Light Blue)	Gold

*In the *Topa*, perfected consciousness was understood as a sixth and unseen element.

   Soothill, in his *Chinese Dictionary* [Note 36] describes the then current (circa 1890) Tibetan usages as follows, while southern Chinese
Chen Yen (esoteric) healing traditions use another, which is in accord
with the *Visudhi Magga* description. See Table 2.
   The earliest colors used for meditation were drawn direct from
nature—for instance, monks would often place new robes in the
Ganges mud to make them unattractive, the robes would then take on
the Ganges' yellow color). The sea was blue, Fire was red, etc. These
same colors are used in the *Maha Vyutpatti* [see Note 4] to describe the
colored rays which were said to emanate from an enlightened one's
body when he used his supernormal powers (*Siddhi*).
   Gold was often chosen as the fifth color because it was the color of
the most precious metal, the Sun, and the Lion—ancient and sacred
symbols for India. The *Maha Vyutpatti* also mentions the color of the
crystal (i.e., transparent) as that used to indicate the unseen and unrep-
resented sixth element of consciousness.

INTER REFERENCING

In the Theravada tradition the various teachings of Shakyamuni were often grouped together for the purposes of study by number and length. Thus we find texts dealing with the "Sayings of 5," or the "Groups of 28," etc. The Sutras themselves are also arranged according to their length. We have the middle length sayings and the shorter length sayings. The Mahayana teachings, on the other hand, were more often than not grouped together by content and theme rather than length or number, and due to this it became easier to notice the connections between types of teachings that dealt with similar themes. If one *Acarya* (Master) described something in one set of terms another Acarya would use a different set. Reading both you could see the pattern or principle behind the teaching itself—how the particular illustration came to be used in the first place.

These patterns became paradigms of meaning and eventually different manifestations of the same principle came to be expressed in terms of their inter-relativity to other principles. Shakyamuni Buddha had often done this himself as an expedient teaching aid when dealing with new converts. He would present something they already knew in a new and Buddhist form. On one occasion, when confronted with a noble Brahmin who had practiced worshiping the Gods of the six directions, he re-presented them as indicating the various types of relationships one generated in the world. The East represented mother and father, the South the teacher. The West was children, the North was Friends. Downward represented servants and Upward, the Brahmins.

Elements were also one of the first items to be used in such a manner. Elemental Paradigms, arranged according to the native Chinese cosmogeny, are even found in the apocryphal *Sutra of Trapusa and Bhalika* [Note 57]. The element for Space was used to describe the unique view of motion in Buddhism. The idea of motion, itself, was in Buddhist teaching never regarded as simple kinesis but a multi-level action involving the mind and all its functions equally. Subtle distinctions were made between the various types of movement in mind and body, body movement alone, and purely mental movement.

In the *Prajnaparamita Sutra* of Nagarjuna, physical motion is considered in four forms according to the Space element. These are 1) the space transversed (*gata*); 2) the spatial direction (*dik*); 3) the actual space

摩訶般若波羅蜜多心經

観自在菩薩行深般若波羅蜜多時照見五
蘊皆空度一切苦厄舎利子色不異空空不
異色色即是空空即是色受想行識亦復如
是舎利子是諸法空相不生不滅不垢不浄
不増不減是故空中無色無受想行識無眼
耳鼻舌身意無色声香味触法無眼界乃至
無意識界無無明亦無無明尽乃至無老死
亦無老死尽無苦集滅道無智亦無得以無
所得故菩提薩埵依般若波羅蜜多故心無
罣礙無罣礙故無有恐怖遠離一切顛倒夢
想究竟涅槃三世諸佛依般若波羅蜜多故
得阿耨多羅三藐三菩提故知般若波羅蜜
多是大神呪是大明呪是無上呪是無等等
呪能除一切苦真実不虚故説般若波羅蜜
多呪即説呪曰

揭諦揭諦波羅揭諦波羅僧揭諦菩提薩婆訶

Figure 40. Chinese text of the Panjo Polomito Hsin Ching (Sanskrit: Prajna Paramita Hrdaya Sutra). It bears the figure of Acalaraja, Chief of the "Five Kings of Light" (Ming Wang) pictured within the Mandala. (Kongoryuji Library.)

being transversed (*gamyamana*); and 4) that space not yet transversed (*agata*).

The elements were allocated to the *Topa* and from this their implications upon other doctrines began to be drawn out and compared. Even the *Topa* symbol, itself, could be considered simply as a structure representing the early Theravada *Kasina* in a vertical form. The natural colors were the primary ones, and these were associated with the basic six senses. From here the various groupings of five- and sixfold qualities or doctrines made interesting patterns of teachings. Aspects of Buddhist medicine and the movement arts developed from recognizing these qualities which became apparent after studying the Topa. See Table 3.

As these various qualities represented the experiences of humanity as a whole, so they simultaneously represented their perfected forms within *Mahavairocana*. Every association made went upward and downward in a pattern. Both *Mahavairocana* and humanity were unified by manifestation within the *Topa*, and all other later symbols reflected this fact. The interconnection found in nature between the elements was likened to the interconnections of the "Chain of Dependent Origination" taught by Shakyamuni as the cause of all things. To view one meant simultaneously to see the other [See chart in Note 59].

The symbols used in Mikkyo that represented Mahavairocana simultaneously represented humanity also. The two were seen as inseparable and as different aspects of the other. Thus in the lowliest person resided a Buddha of glory and majesty. The spiritual communi-

Table 3. Outline of Associated Qualities in the Chinese Topa.

JIVAT ((Sixth Element) Life force dissolving to body		
Topa Shape	Mental aspect Sanskrit	Resultant Skhanda
SQUARE	PANCA INDRIYA (5 Senses)	FORM/BODY
CIRCLE	MANO	FEELING
TRIANGLE	MANAS	PERCEPTUAL ACTIVITY
HALF CIRCLE	CITTA	DISCRIMINATION
MANI (JEWEL)	ALAYA	CONSCIOUSNESS (Identity)
JIVAT (Sixth Element) Life force dissolving from body		

Figure 41. A Monk performs an eso-teric ritual wearing the "Crown of Wisdoms," Mushindoroku. *(Kon-goryuji Temple.)*

cation between human beings was actually a communication with the Adi-Buddha. In the Mikkyo tradition the Masters (Chinese: *Achali*; Japanese: *Ajari*) developed this kind of communication with their disci-ples. Such was the vision the esoteric teachings conveyed to its follow-ers. One could realize that wisdom which goes beyond all boundaries. This was the highest form of communication that could occur. It meant that Mahavairocana was within oneself and to realize this, one needed to establish a communication with him. If this could be achieved, and the Mahavairocana within could be realized, the radical transformation called "enlightenment" would occur and the dichotomy of experience and sufferings which characterize this existence would disappear never to return.

SIMULTANEOUS BEING AND THE RITE

The Sky and the palm of his hand are the same to his
Mind.*

The Principle of Simultaneous Being was inherent in every Buddhist
reference to multi-level consciousness. *The Avamtamsaka Sutra*
expressed this principle clearly in its illustration of Indra's net (*Indra-jala*) [Note 8a]. Schools that appreciated this, such as the Tien T'ai and
Hua Yen, likewise included references to it within their doctrine. While
such teachings were difficult for laymen to properly appreciate, another
manifestation of simultaneity, namely reflection, could be.

Although the Principle of Simultaneity came first, reflection was its
humanized face and all higher studies indicate this. For practical, rather
than doctrinal reasons, various titles and symbols of reflection became
common to many schools as a didactic or phronesic aid to study. Those
who could not understand the principle thought of it simply as indicating symbols, that is, a representation (in another form) of a finite thing.
One can find references to symbols understood in such a manner in
many popular Buddhist traditions.

The interpenetration of all things conferred great possibilities for
teaching, as they could show or hide a principle, depending on who
and how they were viewed or taught. One thing could be many other
things, in the same way that a woman may be simultaneously a wife,
mother, friend, sister and daughter.

Within the esoteric schools, the principle of reflection was utilized
in many forms, but the practice of esoteric ritual was its most obvious
manifestation. It is esoteric Buddhism's unique contribution toward
self-understanding [Note 67]. In general the rituals of the esoteric (Chinese: *Mi Chiao*; Japanese: *Mikkyo*) path take two common forms, namely
those appealing to higher forces and those associated with rituals of
self-purification. These two are the most commonly performed.

Self-purification practices and rites, known as *Visuddhikriya* (Japanese: *Shugyo*; Chinese: *Hsiu Hsing*), express the various manners in
which we can directly experience the essence of self-vacuity. Shugyo

---

*From the *Avadana sataka* [Note 4].

demonstrates the basis for that experience in symbolic activity, either directly or subtly [Note 81].

Although it is often called a "purifying" practice, it is not meant to cleanse us from sins even if occasionally it may resemble the Christian bodily mortifications practiced by its monks. The Chinese and Japanese terms for this practice come from the Sanskrit root *Kri* which indicates a spiritual activity of both body and mind. From this root comes also the Buddhist term *Karma*. The term *Kriya* is used in modern (Hindu) Hatha Yoga to describe bodily purification practices. Theravada Buddhism used mainly the Pali term *Vodana* or *Visuddhi* to describe such activity.

Many of the methods and techniques of Shugyo are based in nature and reflect the outdoor life—bathing in ice cold streams is a good example. (Modern esoteric students living in the cities are taught to pour bowls of cold water over the body while standing on the balcony of the apartment house—if they have a balcony!) In present day Japanese Tendai esotericism (Japanese: *Taimitsu*) there is a Shugyo of long distance running in the snowy mountains (the distances and times for performing these far exceed the requirements for some Olympic records) [Note 49].

The practice of special forms of *Chuan Fa* (which is described later) was another important Shugyo method used in China. However, not all forms of Shugyo involve only the physical body. We should remember that our reasons for spiritual study are not simply to overcome past guilts, problems in our lives, or to gain power. Such goals would be a reaction—not a response—to our suffering.

The aim of Shugyo is to try to create an inner clarity and perspective, and to do this it often directs much of its attention toward the physical body and the conditions that affect its functioning and usage. Through the Shugyo we are brought directly into contact with the various attributes of our physical and mental existence, and because they confront the forces of nature we can have no verbal debate or argument with it. There is simply a direct body and mind inter-dialoguing.

The root scriptures all point out that the nature of Self is void of all permanency. This Self does not lie in the heart; the heart does not lie in this Self. In the nexus of activity which creates this very Self lies the origin of the world and the possibility of attaining enlightenment. Shugyo is a creative and balanced step toward affirming and acknowledging this potential. In days gone by, many of the practical aspects involved in the performance of Shugyo were part and parcel of everyday life, so the practice of Shugyo is in many ways a return to the simple life patterns of the past. This, in itself, often effects astounding medical cures (even nowadays lay people practice Shugyo in an attempt to cure a serious or "incurable" disease) [Note 80].

There is little difference between the practice of some methods of Shugyo and the performance of certain other rites. All physically based Shugyo have rites associated with them and often the rituals involve various physical actions, although some rituals are only performed mentally. It is often difficult to distinguish between them, but, in general, a rite requires more ritual than physical activity. If it has predominantly physical requirements it is more likely to be a Shugyo.

The two expressions of ritualized practice attempt to enact the highest condition of humankind within mind and body. Ritual is seen as a dramatic expression of a spiritual principle in action. However one should not regard esoteric rituals in the same way as one would a non-Buddhist ritual. Unlike the theistic systems of belief, Buddhist ritual was simply a multi-dimensional acknowledgment of the human capacity and possibility. It did not base itself upon appeals to an external force for its validity, value, or efficacy.

Ritual is, in fact, an invocation of the inner Buddha Wisdom by means of emulation and discipline which required its participant to try to experience existence as if actually a Buddha. The traditional discipline involved in its correct performance is filled with precise requirements, and pre-requirements, as to the time, place, condition, materials, words, breathing patterns, ways of directing the mind, etc. These requirements were as painstaking and detailed as the Theravada monastic code of conduct (*Vinaya*) and many of the traditional rites took hundreds of days (or longer) to complete.

Thus performed the rite became an act of total meditative endeavor and in the Mikkyo schools no difference was seen between the performance of the rite and the practice of meditation.

> In a clean and pure spot, erecting his altar
> he anoints himself with oil,
> Having bathed away uncleanliness
> he puts on a new clean robe,
> clean within and without
>
> Calmly seated on the Law throne
> he teaches as he is questioned.

(Myohorengekyo; Ch.14, p.277)

The rite should be seen as an assertion that this body and this mind are inextricably linked together and that activities of one continually affect the other. If one uses the body in a destructive manner, the mind likewise disintegrates itself.

Conversely the practice of mental purification cannot take place without a similar activity occurring within the body. As one purges

Figure 42. Some of the author's Tibetan teachers gather for a ceremony at Dharamsala, India.

impure thoughts, so the imbalanced body is purified simultaneously. These actions have to be performed mindfully and knowledgeably to be of any effect. In esoteric Buddhism the ritual is the means and the method by which this takes place.

One of the primary contrasts seen by both monks and laymen alike in their performance of ritual is its aftereffect. The difference between the inner world of the temple and the outer mundane world is enormous and apparent. From this primary dualism arises the wish to overcome such dualism, to make each the other so that there exists no distinction between either. This wish is synonymous with the aspiration to attain Buddhahood, for the condition of enlightenment and the human condition are not to be separated or distinguished from each other by anything, any situation or any state of consciousness.

In Buddhism, knowledge in any form is subservient to transcendental wisdom. Values, which arise from knowledge, are similarly subservient to wisdom. If we could overcome the tendency to confer fixed values upon things the separateness between them would disappear. We could begin to regard things as they actually are. Actual physical representations of this dualism (between perfected and mundane life) were unnecessary to Buddhism. Whereas the mundane was all too obvious from one's own experience, representations of the exalted states are rare in one's daily life. The experience of even one moment of an exalted meditative state led one to aspire to greater heights and served as a reminder of what could be. Such experiences are often encountered within the practice of the Shugyo, but we need to know how to interpret or perceive them properly.

The delusive quality of our "own" experiences is one of the first things we may become aware of when we begin to seriously practice any method of self-purification. This is why in many Buddhist scriptures our world is likened to a dream or a momentary image which fades away. Suffering consists of taking the fictions we create, about ourselves and others, as if they were facts. (This theme is covered later in some detail within the notes to the *Hsieh Mai Lun*.)

THE ARISING OF THE MANDALA

The experience of fragmented mental conditions or inner environments naturally leads aspirants to desire wholeness and completeness, and the spiritual path which suggested these qualities must contain teachings or presentations explainable in experiential terms. Long ago, the Buddha recognized that it is not the world which requires understanding but our own nature. There are no mysteries except those of an unclear mind.

In order to portray such undividedness, the early Acaryas used symbols of unificatory wisdom, dividing them into parts that could be perceived by the laity in a way that was both understandable and practicable within their day-to-day life patterns. The primary source for this was the "Three Jewels," the figurative term used to describe the Buddha, His teaching and the community of monks or followers of the

Figure 43. An esoteric mandala laid out for the performance of a ritual before a shrine. (Author's collection.)

*Figure 44. Akasagharba Bod-
hisattva (Matrix of Space). His
right hand makes the Varamudra
while his left holds the symbol of
the Three Jewels. Painting by
Ryusen Miyahara, Kongoryuji
Temple.*

teaching. While the Buddha symbol, itself, was inviolate, aspects of the
teaching and community were not.

A practice developed to graphically present the various facets of
life in terms of contrasting views of life experience. The bad monk was
contrasted with the good monk, the false teaching with the real teaching, etc. This re-presentation of the creative and destructive aspects of
a situation was depicted in the shape of the primary form of matter.
This is the square, the four-sided symbol of manifestation. When using
the basic square pattern as a schematic plan of contrasting qualities, a
central point was usually added to represent the solution to this graphically portrayed multi-ism.

Thus, the mandala came into being and its nature was, from the
first, shown as an interactive spiritual device. These were, perhaps, the
summit of symbolic presentation and are now found painted, drawn, or
woven in silk and hung upon temple walls for use as teaching aids.
They form pictures of Dharmic principles and are usually intricate, and
vividly chromatic in form.

In this fundamental mandala pattern, the Three Jewels [Note 2f]
have become five interactive principles. See figure 45 on page 82. The

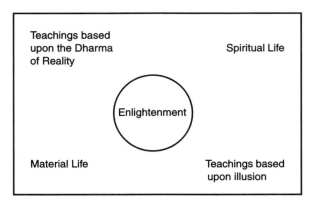

Figure 45. The fundamental mandala.

next step was to represent them as, and within, the five elements. As we have seen previously, this was done both horizontally and centrifugally, one-dimensionally in the drawn mandala, and in three physical dimensions in the form of the *Topa*, although, of course, this latter form was not so portable as a drawn or painted mandala.

There were other interconnections drawn between the pattern of the five and the three. The triangle of the *Topa* could represent the Three Jewels in their soteriological activity, the four corners of the square could represent the Four Noble Truths. The circle represented the infinity of total and perfect wisdom attained by a Buddha, or the cycle of dependent origination; the half-circle represented the two levels of worldly (*Laukika*) and transcendental (*Paramartha*) truth (*Satya*) [Note 68].

The fivefold pattern added to the three made the Eightfold Path, etc. All these aids made it easy to use symbols in missionary activities, particularly in a new and large country such as China. It is then no surprise that these tools were eagerly taken up by monks and used to explain the "law." They are still found all over China in the form of monuments, pagodas or temple paintings.

Such usage of "skillful means" (Sanskrit: *Upaya*; Japanese: *Hoben*) [Note 45] did not indicate a degeneration of understanding, as is sometimes alleged in the more conservative schools of tradition, but rather showed the opposite—a vitality and freshness easily adapted to the different needs of an alien environment. Upaya were developed, particularly in the Mahayana tradition, as one of the methods shown by Shakyamuni and other Buddhas for experiencing the truth of the teachings and thus knowing its reality for themselves. There are many Upaya methods and these are developed according to what is most appropriate for each student, and many are intended only as provi-

Figure 46. Many estoeric mudras were performed in secret beneath the long sleeves of a monks
robe. These can be clearly seen in
this illustration. (Kongoryuji
Library.)

sional techniques or methods of practice. They may consist of mental or physical techniques equally, and are all oriented toward the attainment of a calm, experientially based form of wisdom.

In order to go beyond dualism it is necessary to understand it, and the use of symbols to gain understanding is vital, for it permits manifestation and an examination of realities in recognizable forms. This helps the student in the drama of self-discovery and transcendence. It is difficult to maintain an inner reticence of expression concerning one's understanding, or perceptions of the Dharma, if one has to express or manifest such perception to others. The lure of alienation was circumvented by an emphasis laid upon both spiritual self, and selfless expression, within the Mahayana as a group and within the Mikkyo in particular (though not every school of the Mikkyo tradition knew or possessed formal expressive manifestation practices) [Notes 51, 58, 73, 79].

DEVELOPMENT OF THE MANDALAS

Both the earliest and the latest schools of Buddhism were familiar with the principle of relativity in its humanized and spiritual aspects. Long before Einstein, Buddhism had realized its consequences in terms of mental development and the often habitual nature of its experience. In order to overcome these habits it is necessary to acknowledge and emphasize their existence; one way of doing this is to present them pictorially. This practice of artistically expressing the inner and outer realms of experience gave birth to the mandala.

The mandala became a teaching device which graphically showed an array of the potential forces for good which existed within each individual. These would be used by the wandering Acaryas to teach or explain the status quo both of the experiential and individualized world and of the perfect, universalized, Buddha realms. The Acarya of southern Chinese Mikkyo sought to represent these potential complexities of mind within the mandala in as clear a manner as possible. To this end they used designs unlike some of the intricate Northern Chinese traditions, which often simply portrayed the contents of a scripture, or else were purely decorative works. In such a re-representation they were reaffirming the inner basis of the significance of mandala as a manifest reflection of the perfect experience of Mahavairocana Buddha and humankind. This looking backward in order to go forward is a typically Chinese trait.

It is not uncommon to find in books of esoteric Buddhism the statement that the mandalas exist in four distinct forms. These are usually given as the Dharma, Samaya, Karma, and Maha Mandala forms. This latter form is the most significant. In the esoteric teachings, the Maha mandala describes an iconographic representation of Mahavairocana Buddha in his totality. The other three are said to be but different aspects of this main one.

The Samaya mandala is formed from representations of symbolic objects, such as the thunderbolt or lotus flower, etc., each of which is said to represent a specific manifestation of the vow of Buddha to aid us toward enlightenment. The Buddhas in other types of mandala often hold these objects in their hands. The Dharma mandala is usually formed from graphic representations of the voice of a Buddha, and is composed of "seeds" presented as being letters of the Sanskrit alphabet—each of which symbolizes a word or term describing the various generative forces by means of which enlightenment is obtained.

The last form, Karma mandala, originally described sculptural and/or other creative representations of the Buddha's wisdom. This form was never fully introduced into Japan, but is found in other nations, particularly those with long-lasting and active connections to China. However this is not the whole story; the four categories outlined are, like the elements, partial aspects of the all-embracing unity which Mahavairocana embodies, and which is portrayed in the Maha mandala.

These four forms mentioned, and all other mandalas can be understood through the four elements and vice versa. In order to understand this better we must look anew at what actually constitutes a Mandala. Unfortunately, there have been very few works devoted to the explanation of mandalas as spiritual forces, with the result that, except for those interested in art history, they have remained colorful symbols of religiosity. The few materials that have been written about them have usually been highly complex, analytical works done by historical-doctrinal scholars and of interest only to a very specialized group. The result of such presentations has been that very few, even if members of an esoteric Buddhist school, actually understand the use of a mandala as a personal, interactive spiritual guide. Even the main esoteric sects in Japan tend to carefully guard knowledge concerning them from non-orientals. Although, historically speaking, mandalas usually consist of painted pictures (what are called Genzu mandala in Japanese) this is merely a practical convention.

First and foremost a correct mandala is a representation of the unity between the Buddha and mankind; it describes an interpenetration of the human condition and wisdom which is complete. Implicit in this concept lies the fact that all people are inherently Buddhas themselves and can, with proper training, realize this in their lifetime. A Maha mandala always represents a perfect and balanced representation of a realm of existence, that is, its "up" is the same as its "down," etc. The symmetry of wisdom is, in Buddhism, complete, all-embracing and perfect. No matter in what manner one considers or explains this fact, it remains constant.

Originally in China, and probably also in India, there was only one mandala (a Maha mandala) used in esoteric Buddhism, but as time passed some Acaryas found it convenient to reflect aspects of it which related to conditions found within the human world (i.e., negative forms such as the passions, ignorance, etc.) and arrange them into a sub-mandala relating to the ordinary world of experience [Note 43].

The original Maha mandala described the realm of complete and perfect enlightenment, the "thunderbolt" realm (Japanese: *Kongokai*) [see note 26], and its "reflection" represented the world of complete experience, commonly called the "matrix" realm (Japanese: *Taizokai*). These two contain (and represent within them) all that can, or must be known or experienced by humankind in the quest for enlightenment. They are not two different mandalas; one is simply an aspect of the other.

The *Chuan Fa Mikkyo Acaryas* tended to view the physical body and mind complex as a matrix mandala and therefore paid little attention to its purely iconographic representation common in later esoteric sects. This manner of representing the matrix mandala as a physical embodiment was a didactic method and designed to aid esoteric students in assimilating their studies of the Maha mandala. It also made it possible to utilize the mandala in teaching the laity as they were perfectly familiar with the human passions represented within an experiential mandala they actually inhabited, while they may not have been so knowledgeable of the Buddha wisdoms portrayed in the Maha mandala.

The Dharma, Karma and Samaya mandala forms are all representations of different aspects of the all-embracing (Maha) wisdom of Mahavairocana Buddha. The Samaya represents the personal relationship a student maintains toward the source of wisdom. The Karma represents the activities the student engages in to realize this wisdom. The Dharma represents the unavoidable voice of truth and reality awaiting realization by the student following the path. Each of these aspects is non-discriminatory and can embrace many different endeavors and undertakings. They are by no means limited to the traditional representations made of them in iconography.

Creating a mandala need not be an exclusively artistic endeavor as is often thought. Each of us creates a mandala by our own spiritual activities. Whether we choose to see and/or acknowledge it as such is entirely up to us. If we are taking instruction, our mandala will be outlined for us by our teacher. Our task is not then to create but to perceive the totality of our being within it. From this we become aware of an interrelationship toward the mandala which has always existed but has -not been recognized before. The most important thing about the pictographic mandala is that its observer realizes he or she is part of it and that his or her prescience before it confers "life" upon it. All activity of esoteric students takes place within a periphery determined by their own personal mandala.

This periphery is as large or as small as the students' understanding, accomplishments, and mental karma permits. If students have some understanding of the possibilities accessible to them, they will aspire higher and higher toward that pinnacle and their faith is limited only by their capacity to understand. The question of "free will" does not arise for Buddhists, for each is regarded as free to choose to participate in the process of his or her own personal evolution. While this choice is free, the quality of that choice is determined solely by the physical and mental clarity and purity of the individual at the time of the choice.

Each qualifies the other continually. From the Buddhist viewpoint, the highest aspiration possible is to attain enlightenment after all others have been aided to that same point. Such an aspiration constitutes the Bodhisattva's Vow to the World, and how this is put into action delineates the circle of the mandala. Some people are complicated and create intricate goals and aims. Others are simple and envisage things in basic, fundamental patterns only. For each there will be a way of perceiving a mandala that is totally appropriate. Despite the wide variety of personal (and therefore limited) choice and possibility, everyone lies somewhere within the Vajra (thunderbolt realm) mandala and that point is simultaneously reflected into the matrix mandala. In *Chuan Fa*—of which you will read later—the constituent forces of the Maha mandala were expressed equally in sequences of color, gestures, and movements.

The main Japanese sects of Mikkyo [Note 46] use a system of mandala designs based mainly upon an interpretation of the lineage teachings of the two masters who are credited with introducing, on a systematic scale, the esoteric teachings of India into China—Shan Wu Wei (Sanskrit: *Subhakarasimha*) and Pu Kung Chin Kang (Sanskrit: *Amoghavajra*). These two masters are said to have based their explanations of mandala iconography upon the descriptions given to Nagarjuna and recounted in the *Mahavairocana Sutra* (Japanese: *Dainichikyo*), and a section of the *Vajrasekhara* (thunderbolt crown) *Sutra* (Japanese: *Kongochoyugakyo*) known as the *Tattvasamgraha* ("Collection of the Essences"). There are at least four different forms of the Vajra World mandala (Japanese: *Kongokai Mandara*).

1) The "Nine Assemblies Mandala" used in the Japanese Shingon sect is a combination of nine different mandalas in one. Each part describes a particular aspect or interaction of Mahavairocana. This form was brought from China by Kukai, the founder of the Japanese form of Chen Yen esoteric Buddhism. In Japan, it was known mainly by the title of the "Perfected Body" Mandala.

2) The "Mandala of Eighty-one Bhagavats" was brought back by Ennin of the Tendai sect. This consists of what in the Shingon form of Nine Assemblies is the central illustration only.

3) The form exhibited in the manuscript titled the *Gobushinkan* (Five Sections Mind Meditation). This is said to be the form taught by the Indian master Subhakarasimha. It was brought to Japan by the Tendai

Figure 47. Grand Abbot Yamada, Japanese head of the Tendai Sect. (Author's collection.)

monk Enchin, who was the nephew of Kukai. In this form, the Buddhas and Bodhisattvas sit upon thrones formed from various animals, whereas in the others they sit only upon lotuses.

4) Tibetan forms: these generally correspond with the first two types described above except that some use squares to delineate the central part of the Maha mandala, whereas the others use circles (see also Note 84b).

The *Jogenshinjoshakkyumokuroku* (Taisho, Vol. 2157 [see Note 84b]) records that in A.D. 742 Silamegha, the monarch of Sri Lanka, gave a collection of the "Eighteen Assemblies" of the *Vajrasekharayoga Sutra* (Japanese: *Kongochoyuga kyo*) to Amoghavajra. On his return to China in 746 he began to translate this, but only succeeded in completing the first section of the first assembly before his death. He also compiled a short treatise upon it called in Japanese the *Juhachieshiki* (Synopsis of the Eighteen Assemblies, Taisho, 18 No. 869 [see Note 84b]). For many years this was the only explanation relating to it available to Japanese monks. Later, around the ninth century, Danapala and Dharmabhadra translated the 1st, 6th and 15th Assemblies. The text of the *Juhachieshiki* was not brought into Japan until 1073, when the monk Jojin brought back a copy he had obtained from the Inkyo Temple in China.

All the mandala used in Japanese Mikkyo were brought back from China by either Kobo Daishi of the Shingon sect, Dengyo Daishi of the Tendai sect or their respective students. These vary in some respects

Figure 48. The animal thrones of the mandala Buddhas used in the "Tattvasamgraha" esoteric text. The forms of the Buddhas are also different from those described in the Mahavairocana Sutra. *(Author's collection.)*

because they are based upon different versions of the Sutras and many of the Sutra descriptions used to create mandalas or their symbols conveyed different teachings. The descriptive symbolism also reflected the teaching traditions of both the time and the backgrounds of the Acarya. However, knowing that the Maha mandala always reflects unity, we can usually see the symmetry in descriptions of them and thus differentiate between aspects and their source.

In Japan the tradition of mandala representation and explanation lies firmly established in the works of the founders of the various sects, particularly in the case of Kobo Daishi's School. While in Japan there were perhaps political or socio-historical reasons for the extremely hierarchical nature this school developed, the esoteric sects in China (the *Mi Tsung*; Japanese: *Mi-Shu*) had set no precedent for this as, on the whole, they never felt a need to develop a central and dynamic teacher figure within their ranks. Instead, they produced the wandering Acaryas. These teachers could clarify and make explicit to individuals personally the inherited iconographic tradition and show both what was and what was not essential.

Although later times produced semi-permanent institutions of Mikkyo Buddhism, its essential dynamic always remained with the solitary and wandering practitioner of a manner and nature similar to the questing of the last incarnate Buddha Shakyamuni. It is for this reason that one often comes across the statement that the Chinese Mikkyo "died out" after the time of Kobo Daishi. What this means is that there appeared to be no organized, centralized administrative group of temples practicing or propagating the esoteric path subsequent to the return of the various Japanese patriarchs to their homeland.

When one examines the records of the Japanese monks who traveled to China in order to study the esoteric teachings after the time of both Dengyo and Kobo Daishi, there are plenty of teachers and temples fully functioning. Not only this, but various forms of the Mikkyo had also appeared in Tibet and were rapidly growing larger and larger. These later spread to Mongolia and re-entered China later from the north. All of which make it quite clear that the Mikkyo tradition continued to be firmly established and practiced within the wandering Acarya tradition. By its very nature such a continuity was difficult to discern from the "outside" and was not amenable to being included in the later historical accounts of foreign countries. Such Chinese sect continuity—despite some Japanese accounts—existed long after the time of the Kobo and Dengyo Daishis.

The later proliferation of mandala as artistic creations within other non-Mikkyo schools, demonstrated clearly this lack of understanding of what the real and esoteric purpose of mandalas was intended to be. There are certain conventions in the creation of mandalas and these are observed in those esoteric schools which understand the interactive significance of mandalas. It is in the observance of these artistic, and other,

Figure 49. Maitreya Bodhisattva. He will become the next Buddha of this world. His right hand makes the Varamudra (Segan In). Above the lotus held by the left hand can be seen a representation of the stupa. (Painting by Ryusen Miyahara.)

Table 4. Basic Paradigms of the Mandala in Southern Chinese Tradition.

Mandala Form	Element	Wisdom	Bodhisattva Vow	Unskillful Craving
MAHA (All Body)	Earth	All Embracing	To follow the Buddha's path	Craving for possessions
SAMAYA (Symbols)	Water	All Reflecting	To save all beings	Craving for sensations
KARMA (Creations)	Fire	All Accomplishing	To end all suffering	Craving for power
DHARMA ("Seed" sounds)	Air	All Discriminating	To study the Buddha's teaching	Craving for knowledge
THE OBSERVER*	Ether	Void Realization	To attain enlightenment	Craving for extinction

*This latter form is never represented pictorially.

conventions that one is able to recognize an esoteric (one with "spirit") mandala from a purely artistic creation.

While a mandala cannot be wrong, it only has spiritual significance if it is understood and interacted with as a living force, but there can be mandalas which have lost their "life" because they play no dynamic and active part in the spiritual development of those who try to study their intricacies and meanings.

The very act of painting or creating a mandala was considered to be a valid part of the esoteric meditative process and as such also had its own disciplines, meditations, and penances connected to it. The creation of the mandala was divided into five parts or stages, each according to an elemental ruler. Table 4 on page 91 shows how this works. Note that some Japanese traditions reverse the wisdoms of Earth and Water and other qualities.

Earth: Gathering the materials and prerequisites;

Water: Preparing them;

Fire: Forming and completing the embellishments;

Air: Blessing and dedicating them;

Ether: Conferring "life" upon it.

THE

MANDALA

OF

EXPERIENCE

THE MANDALA OF EXPERIENCE

Dhamma Kayenapassati
"He sees the Dharma with his body."*

In traditional schools of mind/body spirituality the human body is viewed in at least three distinct manners. These are often classified as follows:

a) The body as a source of experience;
b) The body as a metaphysical representation;
c) The body as in penultimate enlightenment.

As a "source of experience," the body indicates the ordinary mind-body intercommunication common in day-to-day life. This body is subject to disease, decay, old age, as well as happiness, joy or pain. The "metaphysical representation" of the body means viewing it as if it was a mandala; that is, as a patterned matrix and symbol of fluctuating energies and forces which, if understood correctly, can transform or transcendentalize one's being. This body does not age or decay for it does not depend on its physical coordinate. It is used as a source of spiritual knowledge. The body as "penultimate enlightenment" indicates a stage of advanced spirituality in which the body is known and used like clothing; it is put on and off at will without any interruption of consciousness.

Most of us labor in view "*a*"; here mere existence is a heavy burden. In "*b*" we may understand the burden and bear it wisely. In "*c*" the burden and body have been totally transformed. If we do not have a spiritual path or teachers, it is very difficult to overcome the limitations of the first condition. Only by actively seeking out such a teacher and earnestly wanting to learn can we begin to come face to face with our true nature. Not seeking a teacher is like running away from one we already have.

In spiritual matters there are no easy stages, for if we are not actively treading the path, mundane life will approach and draw us

---

*Dhammapada, V. 259.

away from it. Existence, itself, will subject us to so many pressures or temptations that only a single-minded attempt to overcome such things will suffice. If we can recognize the connection between mind and body we can also see that it is better to begin any study with both these "wings" in their optimum condition.

If we can attain a detached balance between our daily patterns of physical and mental activities, one in which neither interferes with or weakens the other (i.e., by illness or stress), we reach a stage where the body calms itself. This stage sets the scene for our understanding of mind. By learning of the factors which make up our mind and of their true nature we can begin to improve and eventually master a great deal of its negativity. It is such negativity which perpetuates the great sufferings of life as expressed in the Four Noble Truths [Note 34].

For this reason Buddhist teachings concerning suffering go to great depth, and to properly understand its nature is regarded as the beginning of wisdom. Avoiding extremes and maintaining the highest attunement enables us to gain access to levels of mind previously unconsidered. Such access can completely transform us. The maintenance of an attunement to wisdom is very important. It is first developed by endeavoring to follow the voluntary restraints of the mind and body—the "training to refrain" of the basic Buddhist precepts. Through practicing to create a positive absence of errors we may come to know the positive presence of wisdom. In Buddhism this wisdom adopts many forms but each has the same flavor.

SOMATYPES

It was mentioned earlier, in the Mandala of Human Characteristics, how people were classified into groups according to their mental "stains" (*Klesa*). These groupings were equally applicable to monks. Much of the individual training and future orientation of esoteric monk students would be based upon the assessment the master made of their character and temperament. As in the lists outlined within the *Abhidharmakosa* and other scriptures, the students' personal meditations and devotions would be shown by the teacher and directed in type and duration toward those parts of the consciousness where balance or stability was needed. Later the students would learn of these groups and realize why the training had taken the turns and directions it had done.

We should at this point also remind ourselves that awareness of the Somatypes in China was not simply a form of character analysis but a way of providing a future "baseline" for students to work from so

Figure 50. Temple mural which vividly depicts individual characteristics of Arahants and Sages. Shown are (from left to right) Buddhamitra, Punyayasas, Kapilamala, and Aryadeva. (From Sonan Temple, Patriarchal Hall, Sunch'on Province, Korea.)

they could eventually clarify their views about themselves. By learning to relate to both physical and mental patternings the monks developed awareness about their own natures, and also learned that mind
and body should not be considered as separate entities in any endeavor
and that due allowance must be made for both bases of experience.
These precedents eventually created the basis for a distinctly Buddhist
system of Medicine.

The highest Somatype was naturally the Buddha, himself, and to
this end his various distinguishing characteristics and physical features were noted. Many of these were supernatural (i.e., they could
only be seen by Bodhisattvas), others were visible to all. The psychological descriptions of the Buddha were simply elucidations of
enlightenment, itself, and both types of characteristics served as
models for the perfect, universal and completely awakened one. Elements were also considered both directly and indirectly in these
descriptions. This latter type of description appeared in accounts of
miracles performed by the Buddha. In order to achieve these it was
necessary to have mastered the inner forces which control the outer
elements.

Although played down a great deal in all Buddhist scriptures,
some of the Buddha Shakyamuni's achievements in this field were
truly remarkable. Even in the Theravada scriptures we find an account
of what is called the "Yamaka Patihariya," where the Buddha made
water appear in streams from the top half of his body while simultaneously causing flames to appear from the bottom half. There are also
accounts of him walking upon the surface of lakes. Such events were
considered normal to a Buddha and consequently were not used in
later scriptures to prove his status or attainments.

The arising of a view in which models of perfection were described
by an elemental nomenclature was a prominent feature within the esoteric schools. It is within these schools that we find the first true
somatypes described. Because somatyping was intended for spiritual
purposes, its development took a distinctly religious form; its presence
was obvious within the field of the Buddhist meditative arts.
Somatypes were later expanded to include secular temperamental
types, thus allowing the system to be applied to lay persons who were
mentally disturbed, confused, or physically ill. These innovations were
significant for they revealed an existential approach to society and its
problems. Although Taoism had many teachings designed to attain a
long, and often sensorial life, the Buddhist systems stressed life's quality and spiritual content rather than length. The eventual amalgam of
Chinese culture and Buddhist healing traditions incorporated most of
the better features of native China but re-presented them on a new
basis. This re-presentation included physical movement therapies,

some forms of which had been practiced in China long before Taoism was systematized. These took form as various types of Buddhist transformative yoga.

In India an amalgam of spiritual and military arts had been part and parcel of the nation's spirituality (which is why the young Shakyamuni was partly raised as a warrior king), whereas the China of that period had no real spiritual precedent for such an orientation. Indian missionaries sought common points of traditional experience which they could point out to possible Chinese converts as factors confirming their expertise in fields they were both familiar with. Two arts especially appropriate as cultural bridges were those of healing and *vajramukti* (combat) for these were seen as mandalas embodying patterns of the universal totality of wisdom. It was within these arts, along with their subsidiaries, that the elemental descriptions and meanings were described, developed, and extended in practicable ways. Both these arts are considered later.

THE BODY MANDALA

To early mankind the first and most personal mandala was the physical body and, after that, the natural phenomena of the universe. With the right viewpoint (Sanskrit: *Samyakdristi*) the body can reveal all things. The ancient Chinese had no indigenous equivalent to the mandala of early Buddhism. In later China (notably within the Buddhist Tang Dynasty) the practice of astrolatry had evolved into astrology and this eventually began to relate certain of the constellations to parts of the human body and develop an interactive symbolism between them. Both Indian Hinduism and Buddhism had by this time vast, ancient and subtle traditions of mandala meanings.

Hinduism developed its concepts of mandala in a very different way. They emphasized purely physical aspects or reflections. These attitudes culminated in what were called the *Sahaja* or *Maha Sukkha* (Great Bliss) Yogas, which were oriented toward sexual practices. These practices (termed Tantric Yogas) were far removed from the Buddhist traditions, but were responsible for many later Buddhist teachers regarding all forms of physical training with suspicion.

DANGERS OF TRAINING

One danger recognized as inherent in all physically manifestable trainings is that certain training can evoke powerful emotional responses. It is easy to grow attached or overly dependent on their perhaps vivifying results. In many non-spiritual physical arts practitioners may get attached to their own, and others, supposed virtues or attributes. Such an attitude closes the door of the path.

It is necessary to respect our physical being and take care of it, but also to feel neither love nor hate toward it. It is sufficient to understand it fully and correctly. Such equanimity toward the body is simply a form of the ego un-doing "Heart oriented toward Enlightenment" (Bodhicitta). This heart is the first thing we need to arouse if we are seeking to liberate ourselves from any of the many sufferings inherent within our existence, be it physical or not.

Without this will, this "Buddha Heart," it is not possible to begin the spiritual path or find the strength to persevere in its trainings. To aspire toward knowing our bodies both as a metaphysical force and as a nexus of paradigmatic energies enables us to understand something of its true place in the pattern of life.

> When a man so much as changes a step
> or breathes out or in
> so the motives of such acts be only
> the hearing or teaching of the good Law.
>
> —*Siksa Sammuccaya, v 42*

From such understandings the genuine arts of interpreting the body derive. Medicine in its diagnostic form, and cosmobiology both grew from this view. The medical prognostics of cheirology developed from physiognomy and, if one has the heart, can be a great source of knowledge. The body can become a great mandala of discovery and wisdom.

> I declare to you that within this fathom-long Body lies the
> origin and the ending of the whole Universe
>
> —The Buddha, *Anguttara Nikaya 2:46*

Hatha and Buddhist Yogas

The ancient Indian systems of spirituality were wide in range and content, embracing many different areas of human endeavor and thought. One of these areas, the path of Yoga (unification) included a branch termed Hatha [Note 8b]. Lying within the fold of Hinduism, this path concerned itself with using the body as a means of actively worshipping the Deity. However, this principle—namely using the body as a spiritual text—was one which Buddhism also encompassed. Although Yoga as a term was included in the accounts of teachings available in pre-Buddhistic times, there is no real evidence for the practice of its Hatha form in the popular manner we are familiar with in the West. The odd statue or two in what is now called a yoga pose is not sufficient to show that such poses were being practiced as part of a Hatha Yoga system, as is often claimed. Many of the movements used within Hatha Yoga were in fact drawn from everyday life situations and activities.

What distinguishes a yoga position from an ordinary day-to-day pose is the attitude one takes toward such poses. We can perhaps see from this that a yogic position exists within the intentional awareness of the practitioner, rather than within any specific bodily position assumed. It is this factor—intentional awareness—that distinguishes a person practicing or performing a yoga position from someone who is not. The main resource text of Hatha Yoga, namely the *Yoga Aphorisms of Patanjali*, was written down after Buddhism had developed in India, so it will probably never be known for certain which form preceded the other, Hindu or Buddhist.

While Hindu Yoga is well known in the West, particularly in its Hatha form, the Buddhist forms are not. Very few of the Buddhist texts are known or have been translated. Some are not appreciated for what they are. Often they were dismissed by scholars in favor of more "religious" or philosophical teachings. On the whole very few of the vast amount of Buddhist scriptures have been translated into Western languages. A similar situation also exists with those Buddhist scriptures concerned with healing or medicine.

There is a great difference between the orientations of the Hindu and Buddhist physical Yoga systems. In the Yoga of Hinduism, students aim ultimately to attain union of their Self with Brahma—an all-pervading God force. Buddhism regards this aim as mistaken because there is no such a thing as a permanent self. It cannot be therefore unified with anything at all (except its own mental creations). The Buddha himself once said that there could be no such thing as an enlightenment purely through physical movements and it was probably the Hindu Hatha Yoga that he had in mind when he said this.

Unfortunately because watered-down versions of the original yoga are now popular simply as aids to losing weight or keeping fit, many people have a mistaken idea as to what it really involves. In India the practitioners of the real yoga fully understand the place of its Hatha branch as being one of the "Eight Limbs" of their Hindu spiritual discipline, aimed at union with the Godhead. They practice it according to this orientation. This is often done simultaneously with other forms of yogic practice. The yogins search for the Infinite is serious and as complete as its scope. Few Westerners practice yoga like this, or perceive its intrinsic holiness of purpose. Even fewer actively change their religion of birth and renounce their families, goods, and other inner inherited values, as the traditional search for the Infinite requires.

Buddhist Yoga, in common with all other Buddhist practices, confines itself to those areas conducive to understanding the process of self and other creation and dissolution, in both mind and body, as a prelude to the attainment of enlightenment. The Buddhist way includes meditative explorations and disciplines, philosophical investigations/observations, and applications leading to a unification of these various types of understanding within the experiential capacities of the individual. This whole endeavor is known as yoga and describes a unification, not with a God, but with that Wisdom of complete Enlightenment (*Parinirvana*) which is found and realized within one's consciousness. Buddhism uses the term yoga in its most ancient and literal sense rather than simply as a synonym for physical practices as it is commonly, and mistakenly, understood in the West. One should bear this in mind when coming across references to Buddhist Yoga.

The manner in which one begins the task of attaining enlightenment is the basis for differences between the various schools of Buddhist thought and practice. Some emphasize understanding, others meditation. The path of unification within a Buddhist Yoga predominantly uses the category of experiential capacity as its field of activity. This is not simply how one experiences things but how one's illusory Self creates and perpetuates itself within the inner and outer world of human experience. By observing that process in action we may come to experience it differently. It is not considered sufficient to blame life events upon others, or upon one's destiny.

The mind is certain to enact the results of its current consciousness as long as it does not realize its true content and nature. Ignorance produces habitual patterns of perpetuating suffering. All too often what is called one's destiny simply means living as a victim of the results of one's experiences, together with the concomitant mental patterning they create, without understanding their real nature or significance. The way beyond such destiny is a way beyond the ordinary understanding of the self. Some of these mistaken views of the self have been summarized as follows:

> So he clings firmly to his body and believes its Form is part of the Ego; Perceiving Mind embracing all countries everywhere he believes that their Form is within his Ego; Perceiving Forms created to follow his Ego; he believes that Ego exists apart from such Form; Perceiving Ego continuing to exist in the flow of Samskaras he believes it is within Form (*Leng Yen Ching, Surangama Sutra*)

In order to walk this path it is necessary to prepare ourselves and therefore to study the Buddha's teaching concerning these processes so that one is familiar with the various stages, layers, and possible pitfalls of obfuscation that we all unfortunately carry within us. Long ago the Buddha said that it is not that he argues with the world but the world which argues with him. That which requires understanding is not outside our own nature, it is that nature. There are no mysteries except the unclear consciousness itself.

For some this is very difficult to perceive, particularly those who are reticent, shy, or reclusive, who tend to seek solutions to their problems outside of themselves. The essential nature of an integrated canonical and experiential endeavor means fully encompassing within one's nature, and without restriction, the whole potential of life in all its breadth and depth. Such life is not restricted to the human realm alone but extends out to embrace other realms of existence which lie beyond the human. In Buddhism the human realm is seen as the most fortunate of all possible realms [Note 8c], for only within this can one attain enlightenment. The field of Buddhist Yoga attempts to achieve such a goal.

Both Hindu and Buddhist traditions preserve early records of teachings concerning spiritual and physical syntheses. In each the physical forms of their respective founders (Vishnu and Buddha) are said to have walked seven steps at birth, proclaiming their wisdom. Hindu Bodily Yoga was systemized soon after the Buddha's teaching began to spread and was in contrast to the early Buddhistic forms involving Mudra and other ritualized movements in both the exoteric and esoteric schools.

Both traditions have physical requirements of an active and passive nature. Hindu Hatha (bodily) Yoga has static positions (*asana*) used to still the body and mind. It also, later, put these asana into simple sequences. Active yoga can be considered as these sequences, though temple dances are the real heirs to the Hindu kinetic spirituality. In esoteric Buddhism the kinetic manifestation of meditation was perfected in both the forms of healing technique and the practice of movement training, such as *Chuan Fa*.

Because of the Muslim invasion and the subsequent killing or destruction of the most important Buddhist temples, many early records of Buddhist kinetic practices appear lost. Only the southern part of India remained relatively unscathed by this invasion, and it was here that one of the early 18 schools, the Theravada, was preserved and remains to this day.

Some Northern monks must have fled southward, carrying with them their traditions, when this invasion took place. Historically and doctrinally, however, little seems to remain of their influence. The earliest teachers of the esoteric traditions came to China from southern, not northern, India and one famous esoteric teacher, Nagarjuna, was born there. Because of the later predominant Theravadic influence within Sri Lanka little was recorded of esoteric schools. We have no real literal account of the construction of the enormous Mandala Temple of Borobodur in the Malaysian Islands. The construction of this esoteric edifice

Figure 51. Remains of the Monastery at Kusinagara. The tower at the back commemorates the Buddha's disciple Ananda and is said to be where his ashes were buried. (Courtesy of Kosei Publishing Co., Japan.)

must have taken many years and required vast resources and faith, comparable perhaps to the construction of the huge cathedrals of medieval Europe or the building of the pyramids. The Esoteric School must have had enormous influence in this area of the world, but we can find no consistent account or trace of it in the Theravada records.

The Maghadan Sanskrit which the Buddha and his disciples spoke was, in Sri Lanka, replaced by Pali, a dialect of Sanskrit. In this language—with a few important exceptions—most of the earliest Indian Buddhist records were made and preserved [See Note 34g]. The Theravada records do contain material concerning the physical body, however. Its structure, psychological and physiological interfaces, and its subtle rhythms, were all concerns of its Buddhist meditational tradition. The body was analyzed, and its activities described in great detail. We can read in the *Abhidharmakosa 8* of how, in the developing stages of the Brahmavihara meditations, the practitioner suspends the act of breathing. The *Mahavastu* also mentions this in its description of the space filling Samadhi (*Asphanaka*) [Note 36,k].

Despite such accounts there are only minimal descriptions of the body considered in its kinetic aspects. The Theravadin texts describe the four positions (i.e., walking, sitting, standing and lying) as a valid basis for spiritual observances and this is expressed in the tradition of walking meditation, performed no doubt for health reasons as much as anything else. Sitting meditation is quite common but there is little else. Even the *mudras* are quite simple, usually being related directly to some historical aspect of Shakyamuni's teaching in order to exemplify or explain its meanings.

In contrast Tibetan Buddhism, which preserved many of the teachings lost to India because of the Muslim wars, contains many complex, esoteric *mudras* and ritual dances. Here is one living and continuous tradition possessing at least some of the teachings current at the time of the invasion. Tibet was the land where "body wisdom" acquired a special and eminent value culminating in its unique practices of Tantric Buddhism.

As stated previously, only China and Tibet continued actively the esoteric doctrines of Buddhism's early phases. Despite differences in the Hindu and Buddhist teachings concerning the nature of Selfhood, each accorded the physical body a special place in spirituality. If the teachings of Hindu Yoga could be said to stress the passive, invocative aspect of holiness, the Buddhist form should be considered as an active, evocational form. In both there is consensus that when mindfully stilled and truly known, the body can become the instrument of holiness itself. In Buddhist understanding, the blending of both static and kinetic movement was acknowledged as an important basis of mental and physical holiness [Note 36p].

GEOGRAPHICAL CONSIDERATIONS

No doubt some of the Mahayana emphasis on the virtues of acquiring "body wisdom" had a simple practical basis. Theravadin monks were forbidden to wear more than their three permitted robes. This ruling was kept strictly by the Theravada School. One result of this was that Theravada monks could not easily survive long journeys in or to countries with subzero temperatures. Due to this Theravadin missions to Tibet or other mountainous regions proved nigh on impossible and few were mounted over the years. The old and venerable mission chiefs of the type sent to spread the teachings in foreign lands often proved the least able to climb mountains or survive harsh winters. The Mahayana monks simply donned extra robes and went into such colder and inhospitable environments undeterred. If one looks at a map of the Orient, the only areas readily accessible from India by foot, and bereft of mountains, are Burma, Thailand and beyond.

These countries have always been Theravadin areas of missionary work. China has several mountain ranges between it and India. Not until after the first century A.D. did monks penetrate these and other geographic obstacles, often only after the discovery and utilization of Arab traders' land or sea routes.

The Mahayana missions were peopled by persons both willing and able to be away from their homelands. They had to be capable of striking bargains and maintaining their safety with foreign sea captains (and crews). If this could be achieved they then had to be able to survive the usually long journeys if and when safe landing had been made. Such activity required a certain type of attitude and confidence. Fortunately for the Chinese, this courageous traveling was characteristic of the valiant bold and (probably younger) Mahayana adherents with faith in heart and warm protective outer robes! One recognition of this basic physical requirement developed within Tibet. This was the practice of *tumo*, the yoga of "inner fire" [Note 8d].

Tumo is a required practice in the oldest Tibetan school of Buddhism—the *Nyingma-Pa*—and is clearly a relic of the early Buddhist yoga practices of India. While later Buddhist schools in Tibet bypassed tumo practice in favor of other studies, similar traditions had already gone to China and been developed and refined to high degrees of expertise. Monasteries in high and cold places were common in China and many sects based their head temples in such locales. The Wu Tai (Five Peaks) range was famous for its many monasteries. It is significant that many of the sects positioned in these mountain locations were also the ones who developed the widest range of healing and medical practices.

THE DEVELOPMENT OF MONKS
AND MONASTERIES IN CHINA

After a period of gradual assimilation of the habits and needs of the Chinese people, new forms of doctrinal and temple arrangement arose. This latter feature was no doubt modeled upon the existent social patterning to which all Chinese activities were subject [Note 10]. The Chinese authorities took great pains to ensure that all foreigners (i.e., monk missionaries) within their country fell in with the existent systems of social order. This pattern was hierarchical. The Emperor stood first under Heaven and was considered its sole representative. His officers and soldiers stood below the Emperor and served him. The population was subject to both of these powers and ultimately, through them, to the Emperor himself.

In a similar manner the Chinese patterned their conduct toward their temple masters. A new model was arising, one based not upon a passive circularity, as sometimes befell the Theravada, but instead upon an intense and direct line. Monks served their teachers as the ministers served the Imperial Court, and the daily life of a monk became creatively organized and channeled. The attainment of enlightenment was seen not only as an individual's wish but as a task requiring also great discipline and subservience to one's teachers.

Unlike those in Sri Lanka, a far greater proportion of the Chinese monks resided in temples for the major part of their lives and the forest tradition was espoused by only a small number of practitioners. Another difference, although seemingly small but in fact far reaching in implication, lay in the different form of ordination espoused by the Chinese Mahayana. Chinese schools began to use the Bodhisattva ordination rather than the Bhikku (monk) ceremony. This ordination stated that its recipient vowed to attain the condition of Bodhisattva, rather than the Arahant of the Theravada tradition, and conferred upon its recipient a status that was neither exclusively monastic nor lay [Note 36 q].

Many renowned teachers in China had taken this kind of ordination and never were monks in the Theravadin sense of the word. The Mahayana recognized that a central commitment to the Buddha's path was the characteristic of a Buddhist and that formal ritualism was not so relevant. Instead of vowing to keep the traditional major and minor Monk Precepts (and thus live a life strictly apart from society, and its conventions) the Bodhisattva ordinee also vowed to renounce his attainment of enlightenment until all other beings could also be brought to the same stage. The Bodhisattva did not see this vow as being only applicable to monks. It could be practiced both within and without the temples. The vow was a statement of total sacrifice and devotion to others and placed spiritual welfare on equal footing to that of the devotee. In the Theravada model the difference between monk and laity was that one was "inside" and the other outside the circle of teaching.

In China this circle was turned upon its edge and its borders compressed. The teacher was at the top of a vertical line, the students were at the bottom. The Mahayana saw itself as an arrow which entered the "bull's-eye" of the Theravada target and went straight to the heart of the doctrine. This pattern was seen by some, not only as a favorable cultural assimilation to Chinese tradition, but also as the antidote to the potentially solipsistic Theravada emphasis upon doctrinal mastery.

In the vertical system all began from the same position (the bottom) and worked their way upward. One ascended higher in the majority of cases not by doctrinal accomplishments but by virtue of one's labor for others. One attained enlightenment only as a culmination of effort upon many different levels. It was not even strictly necessary to enter the monkhood in order to do this [Note 11].

The vertical approach was not necessarily maintained as a definite move against the earlier form of teaching; it simply developed naturally from within the modifications which were needed for the Chinese people. Throughout much of its development, Chinese temples continually hosted Indian, and other teachers of the "circular" path. Nor was this vertical approach patriarchal in a negative sense. Indian Hinduism had inherited the "guru" class and caste of teachers, but Buddhism was a great force in sweeping this away by reinstating the essential and optimum spiritual possibilities available to all classes of people.

The Chinese had never possessed a role model such as the guru and, although certain types of pre-Buddhist sages existed, they were predominantly solitary teachers. (Gurus were socially oriented and lived close to their students, or vice versa). Many Chinese master teachers eventually came to occupy a role similar in status to that of the guru, but, of course, bereft of any caste or class implications. Such a position was not of an exclusively authoritarian nature, it more often than not meant that students developed a father-like relationship with their teacher. He represented their spiritual father. Whereas the tradition of living with one's master to study secular subjects was known in China (as also did trade and other craft apprentices in medieval England) such domiciles were often arranged by the families of the student and often for commercial reasons. They were thus not always due to the student's own volition, even if for his social or other benefit, nor could a student study a subject above his own social class or caste. One of the distinctive factors common to all forms of the Dharma, in both India and China, was that it offered an equal opportunity to all people irrespective of origin.

The choice to study and live with a master who had accepted you was, in the case of Buddhism, open to all. It was also the master who bore eventual responsibility for the temple itself, and considering the Chinese tendency toward rebellion and revolution it was often not a safe vocation [See Note 10].

As the students of the path grew wiser so did the following of the path itself. One could find the same principle being taught in many different ways within China at any given time [Note 16]. Schools and styles waxed and waned but one development that was to prove highly significant and which affected, either directly or indirectly, all subsequent traditions lay in the arising of the "Self and Dharma Vacuity" schools such as the Yogacara [Note 12].

This vacuity embodied one of the most significant doctrines of the Chinese masters and developed from the realization that in their intrinsic nature all people were essentially Buddhas already. This suggested that the Buddha nature and the human nature were not different [Note

Figure 52. Imperial warriors hunting their enemies. (Woodblock print from one of the sections in the Mushindoroku.) *(Author's collection.)*

11]. As a direct result of this thinking, emphasis began to be placed upon teachings concerned with how one understood and experienced this inner vacuity of Selfhood. This principle was not intrinsically original and could be found in previous teachings or scriptures. What was different was the emphasis placed upon this aspect of the Dharma and the subsequent re-orientation of various forms of training. The task was thus not to attain enlightenment but to realize it.

From this concept a whole range of new practices developed and schools arose which held to the principle of voidness in Dharma and self as a central doctrine. Buddhists refused to indulge in intricate arguments or debate concerning points of doctrine they considered fruitless, and they acted as critics of those which did. As Buddhahood was infinite, so too was the inner nexus of being. To realize vacuity was synonymous with attaining Buddhahood. One could not speak of the condition of Buddhahood—it was beyond all predication. Among the schools which espoused this teaching were the Yogacara and Madhyamika. These, and their derivative lineage schools, collectively came to be known as *Sunyavada* (Path of Inner Emptiness) traditions.

After the Sunyavada Schools, no real innovatory teaching arose in China. From this point onward in the history of the Dharma, subsequent schools attempted to synthesize or explicate previously existing points of doctrine or to re-present them in a different manner. Some of these re-presentations led the Dharma practitioners into what were, for them, new fields of endeavor [Note 13].

As even more time passed, various teachers arose from within, or without, the Sangha to attempt reforms, criticisms, or a "return to the source." This had occurred within Sri Lankan Buddhism early in its history, but had been held in check by the "establishment" monastic authorities with the aid of the monarchy of the time. As a result of this, the Theravada School became the central authority of the doctrine.

In China criticisms of current doctrine by individual masters were not, as was often the case with European Christianity, due simply to corrupt practices or heresy, but more because some of the sects developed static attitudes or a spiritual complacency and had in fact lost their dynamic impetus toward Self-penetration. In China, Nagarjuna, one of the great teachers in the doctrine of vacuity, had performed a "back to the roots" task amid the more intellectually oriented sects of his day. Nagarjuna used intellectual dogma to invalidate itself and, by various processes of argument and debate, tried to direct his contemporaries' endeavors toward self-insight, rather than a sterile, abstracted reasoning. He himself was an intellectual and perfectly capable of confronting the most advanced teachers of his day, yet he was also and simultaneously a mystic oriented far beyond the usual and materialistic intellectual goals [Note 36p].

Nagarjuna translated many texts dealing with themes and teachings which pointed out the inevitable stasis inherent in purely academic philosophy and emphasized the positive qualities of the "wisdom which goes beyond" all predication. To this end Nagarjuna wrote many treatises and commentaries upon commonly held errors in understanding or interpreting the existent texts and Sutras. He also translated Indian Sutras into Chinese, the *Prajna Paramita Sutras* being the most renowned of these. This Sutra is an example of the manner in which a logic-free being perceives and expresses the nature of the world. That is without mathematics, philosophies, relativity, truths or proofs. The refined logic of demonstrating validity by principles of contradiction is rendered meaningless and impotent by the *Prajna Paramita* because the basis upon which logical systems are founded (the subject) is both challenged and rendered otiose. He created the basis for a type of anti-logic and demonstrated that while purely Buddhistic logic could be an attempt to convey the rationality of the Dharma in as effective a manner as possible, it was not intended to show the truth of it.

Prior to Nagarjuna many teachers had been disposed toward dry intellectual systems of analysis. The popular reaction to this style caused the arising of the doctrines of faith. These tried to surpass the intellect by drawing attention to the emotional aspects of the human being often overlooked in the search for wisdom. The assertion of pure faith is itself a statement bypassing the intellect.

Nagarjuna's contemporaries, such as his student Aryadeva and the Indian teacher Lokasema, also translated and expounded Sutras describing similar metaphysical realities, and because of the nature and content of their work we can deduce that they must have felt there was a need for them among the contemporary Buddhist scholarship. The works they translated were often Sutras which expounded metaphysical rather than logical truths, and recounted teachings by Buddhas other than the historical Shakyamuni. That such texts were chosen for translation is significant for their "flavor" stood in great contrast to the standard Abhidharma (Explanations of the Dharma) of the day. These choices were perhaps subtle suggestions not only that their type of content was needed most at that time but also that they had an equal validity to the teachings of the Abhidharma [See Note 2].

Two centuries after Nagarjuna, the philosopher Vasubandhu gave new form to this Abhiharma teaching. After writing the definitive account of it (the *Abhidharmakosa*) he was converted to the Mahayana teaching and his revised wisdom was embodied in a school called the Yogacara. Many of his revisions of Abhidharma terminology were subtle and often misunderstood by later commentators. However, the main import of his teaching was to extend the possibilities of knowledge to the extreme limits, and in the course of this he supplemented Nagarjuna's teachings with a concept of three forms of truth, and in such a manner as to make its meaning more understandable and practicable.

One thing that strikes any casual observer of Buddhist history is the vast diversity of its teachings. Over the ages many different schools of teaching flourished, waned and then reappeared in a revised form centuries later. New types of teaching arose to meet changing particular forms of meditation. Others stressed the performance of rituals. The rise of the different schools more often than not reflected the current needs of the society within which the teaching was being transmitted.

One of the Mahayana's significant doctrinal emphases lay in the assertion that the spirit of Buddhist teachings can be followed equally well outside the monastic path. In contrast to the earlier schools, which kept within the limits of received and literally expressed teachings, the Mahayana outlook embraced practices which would, from the outside, not normally be regarded as either particularly spiritual or religious. The anti-nomianism or autarchism of later schools in which meditation was prominent, such as Chaan, resulted in an especially Mahayanic interest in secular arts as vehicles of spiritual expression and insight. It was as if no area or thing could be held back from the field of spiritual potential available to the Mahayana practitioners.

Secular arts were transformed into spiritual practices or exercises in various ways and we can see the results of such influence, in both lay and monastic Buddhism, within the architecture and literature of China, Japan, and other Asian nations. Other popular arts, crafts, practices and skills were also transformed into spiritual expressions of the teaching. Not all arts were suitable or were chosen to become vehicles for this process but those that did were subjected to a spiritualization that changed their nature radically. Later practitioners of these transformed arts became masters of their time. The sweeper/cleaner monks became the creators of the Chinese sand gardens. From the humble temple gardeners came the masters of flower arrangement so popular still in Japan. In many artistic fields, craftsmen forsook personal expression in order to embrace a more universal and selfless form.

The Physical arts underwent selective and radical Buddhist transformation. These included the development of special forms of healing, physical therapeutics, natural medicines and certain types of unarmed self-defense. This latter was particularly used by Buddhists because of their belief in non-violence. All weapons were regarded as incipiently aggressive and monks were forbidden to manufacture, produce, repair, possess, or admire any weapon whatsoever [Note 20].

While monks were forbidden to watch actual battles or armies engaged in training, the warrior tradition of China was a fact of life. So replete is China's history with revolution, insurrection, protest and suppression that most peasants knew of, or were conscripted into, an army at some time in their lives. Many movements of the populace were designed to evade such conscriptions but there were so many long-standing conflicts that few managed to escape enforced conscription. Even the lowliest peasants usually knew the rudiments of self-preservative techniques.

The nature of warfare gives its participants ample opportunity to ponder the value of life and death. Within the many and often painful experiences of those engaged in battle conditions, insights into the nature of human experience and destiny manifest. Occasionally people join an army to discover themselves more fully as a form of self-imposed test of their nature. Most soldiers were involved in the art of war because they were ambitious or wanted to prove that they were courageous. After Buddhism the innovation of what we could term "insight-provoking" situations developed a different ethos among warriors. The art of warriorhood widened its scope to include those seeking a purely spiritual progression.

In order to understand some of the significance of this development we need to look briefly at the role of the monasteries within China and their influences upon society. The power base in China rested mainly with the Emperor and his military officers. Through an extremely well-ordered chain of command and a large number of advisors in various subjects, the Imperial Court was able to maintain control and exercise restraints over the whole of its vast empire. When the reigning Emperors espoused Buddhism, the influence of monks was added to the existent band of advisors at court. These representatives of the current spiritual force were able to exert influence in various beneficial ways for the well-being of the monasteries. This included gaining Imperial approval for the appointment of abbots or the freedom to appoint other types of officials without Imperial approval. These appointments sometimes meant the release of obligations to pay state taxes and often brought the religious advisors into conflict with those concerned with the nation's finances and national budget. In times of prosperity this meant little, but in times of drought or famine, when money had to be conserved or raised, the lands of the monasteries often accounted for considerable loss of revenue to the throne.

Increasing pressure was brought upon subsequent Emperors to force monasteries and monks to pay taxes as others did. The Taoist advisors, who were notorious for their opposition to Buddhism throughout most of China's history, were often the most vociferous of these who sought to impose such obligations. Whereas in other countries such situations may have resulted in open conflict, in China the Buddhist representatives succeeded in creating an alternative and complementary system of social obligation which supplemented the Impe-

Figure 53. Imperial soldiers attack the eastern teachers. The highly mobile nature of the army is depicted here. (Kongoryuji Temple.)

rial. Monasteries agreed to protect the people who lived upon their land, or who served their interests in other ways, by arranging for grains and other foodstuffs to be stored within their buildings. Along with these, medicines and other things were saved.

In times of distress the monastic cellars were opened for the benefit of the local populace and the Emperor was relieved of social obligation (and costs) in the areas where monasteries lay. As monasteries increased in number and spread around the nation, the resultant social services from them grew and grew.

The monk communities also invented systems of common land ownership and food storage/sharing over 1300 years before the rise of Marxism. This enabled the local communities to have a grain "bank" for times of famine. Such systems were very popular but, surprisingly, were not copied by the Imperial leaders during the periods when Buddhism was forcefully suppressed. When tracts of land were presented to monasteries by grateful patrons or the Imperial Court, the people who lived upon them became technically their property also. The monks shared the land with the inhabitants, granting them ownership "in perpetua" providing they contribute a portion of their produce toward the upkeep of the monastery itself. The grateful peasants usually gave more than was required and this became the origin of what were termed "the inexhaustible cellars" of food. Peasants also collected herbs to be made into medicines and other similar goods of use to the community as a whole. At one period the monasteries became alternative banks for the peasants' savings. Monks were more trustworthy than the city-based monetary establishments. These social innovations abounded in many of China's various forms of Buddhism. Some later developing sects occasionally maintained principles which were politically, not spiritually, oriented and seem to have been founded not as the result of wise study but because of social circumstance and condition. These secularized groups by and large were a minority and their influence confined to the capital.

Buddhism has, of course, absolutely no political views concerning anything, and this fact was exemplified in the (successful) arguments that eminent country-based monks used before the Chinese Emperors to justify why Buddhist monks refused to pay taxes or bow to the Imperial processions. Some of these debates were very well known and much quoted in later Chinese Buddhist accounts. One third century court Taoist successfully used an argument that Buddhist monks were like women, being docile and useless to the Emperor, but this was turned around by a later monk to opposite effect by the following argument. Those that follow the Dharma, they said, were like wives who sit silently by their husbands and serve him while he does the business of the day, pays his taxes, or entertains his friends. The wife would not prominence herself at such occasions, but would support her husband in the background. So it is with the Dharma followers. They, like a wife, do not pay taxes, are not required for military service, and do not seek fame or fortune at the expense of the State. The monk supports not a husband, but, instead and only, the spiritual needs of the nation and its people. They bow only to the Buddha because he is the head of Heaven and its laws, while the Emperor is the head of Earth and its laws. The monk respects the Emperor but places Heaven above him as the wife bows to her husband and places him above her. The wife has no say in her husband's business as the monk has no say in the nation's politics. From the Imperial point of view, people whose lives were secure and healthy were potential recruits for his armies and, as the throne took credit for all social benefits, the well-being of an Emperor's subjects vastly increased his prestige and their loyalty.

Whether Buddhist or Taoist advisors ruled at court had a direct bearing as to what form of martial art training was espoused by the populace. After the initial period of assimilation we can see that Buddhism began to become increasingly independent of the Imperial Court. Through such independence it was able to preserve itself irrespective of political or financial maneuvers at the Chinese capital and

Figure 54. A peasant, punished by Taoist judges with the wearing of a Cangue, implores a monk to aid him. (Illustrated from the Mushindoroku.*) (Kongoryuji Temple.)*

also to establish the basis of perpetuating the doctrine of inward peace and stillness [Note 15].

One of the most important forms of mental therapy developed within Buddhism was healing the violent and unrestrained aspects of human nature. Shakyamuni is recorded as having stopped one great battle between his own clan of the Sakyas and their opponents the Kaliyas. Until its Buddhist era (roughly coinciding with the Tang Dynasty), China had never known such a peacefulness. This orientation was, and is, a unique distinction of the Buddhist philosophy. Unlike other systems, Buddhism seeks to enact its peaceful teachings within the lives of its own followers and urges them to express and practice, as far as is possible, its implications within their daily lives. The expertise which developed from understanding the Buddhist scriptures did not result in military crusades or vengeance killings such as later became common within the various forms of Christianity, Islam or Judaism. Instead we find a growing and all-permeating influence of peacefulness and tranquillity in all the Buddhist nations which only ended when that influence was forcibly extinguished.

THE

MANDALA

OF HEALING

THE MANDALA OF HEALING

Concepts of healing held a profound importance in the daily lives and spiritual work of the early Buddhist monks, according to the ancient texts of the Pali canon. The prevention or proper treatment of illness held (and continues to hold) a great importance for the Buddhist monk. For those fully intent in achieving enlightenment, knowledge of how to prevent or cure serious illness was of utmost importance.*

We might at this point say to ourselves, "What has the art of healing to do with the subjects we have been discussing so far?" In truth the two have always been so intimately connected it is very hard to discuss one without some reference to the other. From earliest times, and in most countries, the various arts of healing have been the almost exclusive prerogative of spiritual and medical teachers. Suffering and death have concerned both disciplines equally. Although not so obvious in the West, the link between healing and religion is ancient. In England the first public hospitals were founded by religious orders and the medieval period created the Knights Hospitallers, a devout group of warriors dedicated to the practice of healing the sick. England, especially, has an old tradition of using natural medicines and herbal remedies. European traditions have their equivalents in the orient. Here we will look at *Tao Yi* (Taoist healing) and *Seng Yi* (Buddhist healing).

We should compare some of the principles of the Indian and Chinese systems of healing and medicine and consider a little of their vast histories. The two systems, although superficially similar, were in fact historically quite different in genesis and orientation. The Chinese native system derives its theory mainly from the classical medical compilation and reference called the *Huang Ti Nei Ching* ("The Yellow Emperor's Book of Internal Medicine"). This text, nominally Taoist, contains remnants of ancient pre-Taoist principles. According to the record of the Han Dynasty (Han Shu), it was part of a set of medical treatises that included the *I Ching* (Classics of Medicine), *Ching Fang*

---

*Raoul Birnbaum, *The Healing Buddha* [Note 17].

Figure 55. Cover page of the Nei Ching. *(Kongoryuji Temple.)*

(Collection of Prescriptions), *Fang Chung* (assorted texts mainly on hygiene), and *Shen Hsien* (Methods and Prescriptions for Immortality). Apart from the *Nei Ching*, all these ancient texts are lost. Within the *Nei Ching* the bodily organs and their activities are allocated various rulers symbolized by descriptions of various processes of change, called the five activities. These activities are often wrongly interpreted as elements [Note 29].

Despite its using a metaphysically oriented vocabulary, Taoism viewed the body in a very mechanical and functional manner, describing its activities and regulators in much the same way as a mechanic would an engine. The body has its predominant organs acting much like the various parts of a motor. It has its fuel, which must be present in the right places at the right time, as well as circulating properly. This fuel is termed the body's energy (*Chi*). The appearance of the body and its organs also has significance. If an organ or part is mis-shapen it will not function correctly. Functionality is a key factor to the whole Taoist approach to healing and this emphasis reflects accurately the primary concerns of the courtly art of Taoist State Medicine at the time the *Nei Ching* was written.

Taoism was only organized and systematized in the first and second centuries A.D. (perhaps as a result of the introduction of Buddhism and a consequent fear on the part of the Taoist elite that its sources of power or finance might be threatened). Bearing this in mind, we can see that what is most ancient and original within the *Nei Ching* is, in fact, its pre-Taoist folk medicine content.

We can easily see other evidence of changes from an earlier system of elements if we examine the elements used in ancient texts, such as the divinatory *I Ching* (Book of Changes). In the Book of Changes we find a complete system of elements along with their paradigms, most of which fail to correspond with those natural forces of change presented in the *Nei Ching*. These I Ching elements, being older than the *Nei Ching*, are closer in meaning to the elements of the Indian systems.

It is recorded that the introduction of the Five Element Theory, as used in the *Nei Ching*, is credited to Tsou Yen. As he lived around 305–240 B.C., the elemental system within the I Ching must have been used prior to this period.

While the *Nei Ching* is filled with physiological inaccuracies, there are many sections that demonstrate unique discoveries. It is, for instance, the first work in China to suggest the circulation of the blood within the body. It also classifies bodily organs and their processes into active and passive aspects and functions. (The yin and yang symptomology was only innovated by Chang Chung Ching around A.D. 160.) Unfortunately the early Taoist healers and magicians hijacked many of these real discoveries and for several centuries proceeded to add or overlay them with various metaphysical and idiosyncratic doctrines. As a result, the development of useful healing techniques was slowed for several centuries.

Such retardation was not restricted to medicine alone but spread to many other parts of Chinese society. The elaborate courtly rituals and observances devised by the Taoists far exceeded those required by the simple precepts of Lao Tze and Kung Fu Tzu (Confucius) as outlined in the *Book of Rites*. In other countries courtly or public rituals occurred only occasionally or seasonally. In China they were a daily event. As time went by, more and more were added until an Emperor spent a great deal of time involved in their performance. Important decisions or statements were often held up for months because of the backlog of state affairs created by such ritual requirements.

These rites were detailed precisely and exhaustively in their requirements. A good example occurs in the Chinese classical text written by Lu Pu Wei (d. 230 B.C.) called the *Lu Chih Ch'un Ch'iu* (Spring and Autumn Annals). This has an elaborate description of how the Emperor must act and conduct himself during the different periods of the year. What he should wear, where he should face when entering a building, how the courtiers should be clothed, and in what colors etc., etc.

So powerful was the influence of the Taoist doctors and philosophers within the Imperial Court that care of the Emperor's health was totally in their hands. They arranged and supervised all treatments, as well as providing and administering their patent medicines. Several Chinese Emperors, acting on their advice, were systematically poisoned and subsequently died as a result of taking their "long life" medicines composed of mercury, mercury oxides, or other lethal substances. It was for such reasons that the arrival of Buddhist medicine from India was warmly greeted by the native Chinese.

Not all Taoist doctors were charlatans or eager to gain the attention or political favor of the Imperial Court through the monopoly and practice of the art of medicine, but a great number of them were. One of China's greatest doctors, Hua To (also called Yuan Hua), was certainly

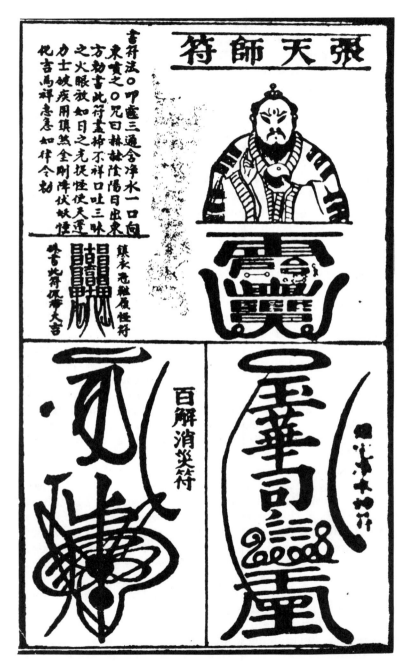

Figure 56. Taoist long life magic charm. (Kongoryuji Temple.)

an exception to this trend. He lived during the first century and innovated many surgical and physiotherapeutic techniques centuries in advance of his time. He used many Buddhist medical traditions. Some accounts say he later became a monk and carried on his profession. He is also credited with introducing a series of remedial movements and exercises for the public called the Five Animals Play (*Wu Chin Hi*). Such a name indicates his familiarity with the Indian Vajramukti training and this title seems based directly upon the five animals of the mandala.

Not until the Tang Dynasty did other systems of medicine and medical theory gain Imperial approval and Taoist and Buddhist doctors work together for the benefit of the people. It was at this time that the *Tso-chuan* was written. This is the oldest Chinese medical text.

Sun Ssu Miao, one of the greatest Chinese physicians (circa 600–682) wrote about the Indian element system and showed his own approval and use of this technique. In his text *Chien chin yao fang* (Prescriptions Worth a Thousand Pieces of Gold), he points out that to be a good healer one must study the medical texts of Buddhism. Although nominally a Taoist, his interest in Buddhism was very great, and his Taoist contemporaries nicknamed him the "new Vimalakirti" [See Note 11].

In contrast to the native Chinese system, Indian medicine began with and continued within a metaphysical basis. Its practical aspects flow out from this directly (unlike the Taoist system which is exactly the reverse). The most influential set of writings within India are the Vedas. These are tentatively dated around 1500 B.C. and are sets of spiritual documents dealing with what was later termed the Hindu philosophy. Not all parts of the Vedas date from this early time.

Veda is a collective noun for four different manuscripts, namely the Rig, Sama, Yajur and Atharva Vedas. This latter, the Atharva, consists of teachings concerning two types of healing (*ayur*). One is concerned with healing through the use of charms and spells, the other with drugs and other medicinal substances. It identifies illness as coming from three causes, namely wind, dryness or water (Atharva Veda 1, 12:3). This differs from the now standard Hindu medical classification of illness by qualities (*guna*) of which three are identified [See Note 3]. All these Vedas are pre-Hindu in essence and contain details of happenings pertaining to the very birth of Indian civilization.

The Atharva Veda was added to and compiled in different formats and collections by various doctors and healers over the ages. Consequently it contains diverse and divergent material about health and is an important source of Indian history.

The Indian ideas concerning medicine were systematized from 600 B.C. onward into different schools and traditions. These schools usu-

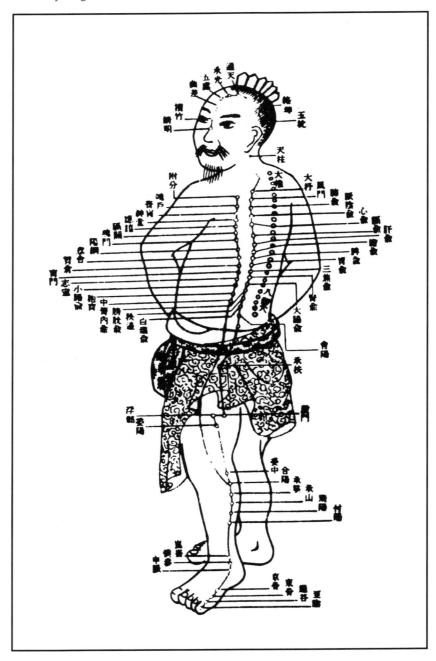

Figure 57. Diagram showing acupuncture points and their individual names. (Kongoryuji Temple.)

ally based their viewpoints (and thus from a medical point of view, their diagnostic methods) on the extant philosophical schools, i.e., Samkhya, Vaishesika, Mimamsa, Vedanta, Nyasa, Yoga, etc. [refer to Note 2]. These varied, often widely, in their views upon certain points concerning the nature and intrinsic structure of both humanity and the Gods.

Of all these schools, the Yoga (unification) was the most generally practiced and has the most derivative forms. From earliest times, the title "Yoga" was used to describe spiritual practices in general and does not always refer to the physical practices used within the Hatha (Sun-Moon) form. The Hatha Yoga developed after Buddhism and its systemizer, the sage Patanjali, codified its main teachings into his "Yoga Sutra." The Hatha form concerns itself with the human body as a means of spiritual experience. It is a school which provided many later accounts of the healing arts in both its theoretical aspect and in actual practice over a long period of time, although some of its methods were taken from, or based directly upon the Buddhist precedents. After the Pali canon of Buddhist texts was committed to writing (circa third centruy A.D.) the term was used as a synonym for a "bond" or "fetter" to spirituality [Note 8b]. Not until the Lankavatara Sutra do we find the term yogi used as a description for the Bodhisattva Yoga.

Around the 12th century A.D. two famous Hindu physicians, Susruta and Charaka, drew together most of the current schools of healing and medicine and established a coherent and standardized system which included the teachings contained in ancient Buddhist and Vedic texts. Much of this ancient system continues in present times and, being based upon these original systems, shows Indian medicine as the oldest continuous medical system in the world. Within Indian medical theory, we find the genuine elements of nature and therapies intimately connected with them (i.e., poultices made from leaves or various types of earth and clay). These are administered initially to restore elemental, not energic, balance [See Notes 18, 30].

Indian medicine also possesses a theory of energy, often expressed within the schools of Hatha Yoga philosophy. It is called *prana*. Although it is often equated with the Chinese *chi* by Western alternative medical practitioners, there is a basic difference between the Chinese *chi* and the Indian *prana* which is often unrealized.

The Sanskrit word *prana* refers primarily and directly to the breath. In Hatha Yoga the breath is regarded as a part of the natural processes on a par with the wind. Breath must flow and be of good quality in order to maintain life. The depth and regularity of breathing must normally attune to the demands made upon the body. If this is not so, and the body continually overtaxes the breath, the personal "energy store" of the body is used up, and an accelerated form of internal and exter-

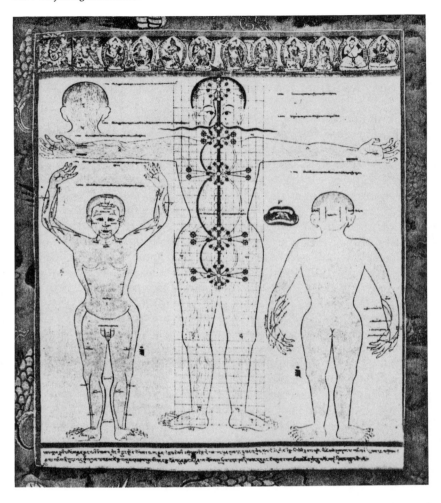

Figure 58. Chart used in Nyingmapa Buddhism showing various energy centers of the body. (Author's collection.)

nal aging ensues. This will cause various parts or functions of the body to deteriorate rapidly, and in such a case, medicine can only mollify the symptom, not cure the cause.

Such an idea is intimately linked with the philosophical stance of the Vedas. Within these it is taught that the life of every living thing is measured in terms of the number of breaths it takes from birth until death. In such scriptures these numbers are enumerated carefully for every living creature. This philosophy possesses a distinctive and pan-cosmic view of time and life spans, stemming from an ancient

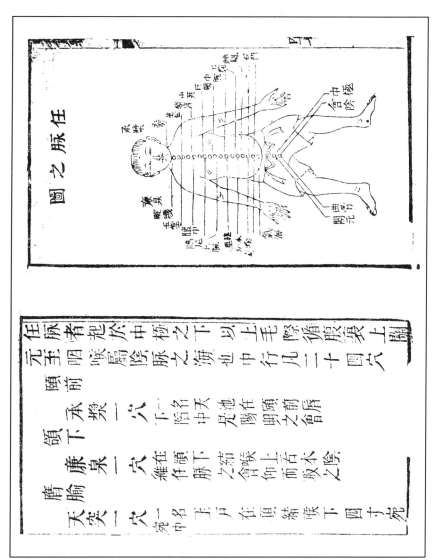

Figure 59. Chinese Taoist based text showing points along the front of the body at which massage can be usefully applied. The text (left) names and describes these points. (Kongoryuji Temple.)

Figure 60. Indian manuscript showing the Chakras of Hatha Yoga. The Sanskrit character atop the head is the mantric sound "Aum" amid the Thousand Petalled Lotus Chakra. (Kongoryuji Temple.)

theory of creation cycles (*Kalpa*). Life is viewed as part of a plan of events ordained by the spiritual forces ruling humanity. In Taoism, the Chinese character for *chi*, used to portray the vital force of the body, developed from ideographs indicating steam or vapor [Note 53]. Though it represented a subtle force which permeates the natural world and the human organism it was not correlated exclusively with the breath.

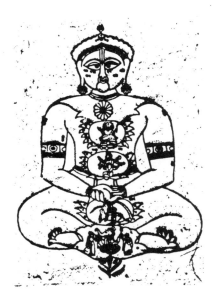

Figure 61. Hindu diagram showing the psychic energy centers of the body. A divinity is represented at each. (Kongoryuji Temple.)

Like a river, *chi* flows through and around the physical organism, in channels termed meridians, activating, regulating and balancing bodily activities. If missing or blocked, the *chi* will build up or overflow, causing interference with the energies of another bodily function and this, in turn, will lead eventually to a deterioration in the workings of that organ. Such interference can also come about as a result of physical or psychological injury.

As each organ and bodily process has its own distinctive pattern, direction, and form of Energy utilization, overflows interfere with the natural homeostasis of the body's functioning. Illness (energy imbalance) is the result of this state [Note 18]. This imbalance can, in the Chinese system, be corrected and attuned to a higher degree. Such an approach is predominantly practical and intent upon optimizing the functional aspects of being. It does not rely upon, nor have recourse to doctrines concerning the creator(s) of the world or any specifically spiritual teachings. Nor does it require adherence to them.

In the Indian spiritual system of medicine the breath (*prana*) is also said to flow through the body. It passes through certain channels called *nadis* (lit: rivers, channels or streams) which eventually join into psychic centers or zones termed *chakras* (wheels). There are said to be seven of these chakras positioned in a central position vertically through the body. These are connected by three main, intercommunicative *nadis* (called the *Ida, Pingala* and *Susumna*). Each chakra is credited with governing a certain type of spiritual wisdom.

Energizing these chakras by exerting control of the *prana* flow within, or toward them, is said to enhance or develop spiritual insight. *Prana*, when used in this manner, is transmuted into an energy form called *kundalini*. There is a whole branch of yogic philosophy and practice associated with this theme.

In addition to the chakra zones permeated by *prana* there are also *marma*. This Sanskrit term describes various specific points within the body at which the basic life force (*jivat*) can be influenced [Note 54]. This can be done by medicines, potions, massage, or movements. *Jivat* is, in fact, the nearest to what the Chinese call *chi*, but in the Indian system it is simply regarded as an all-pervading life essence and is not, within the yoga schools, presented as being patterned in such specific circuits as is the Chinese *chi* [Note 33]. While the *prana* does circulate in channels, these are much simpler in pattern than the Chinese energy meridians. Within the Indian system, the science of *prana* is related primarily toward personal spiritual awareness rather than healing. In both Hinduism and Buddhism a disinterest in the subject of spiritual development is seen as the real cause of all suffering, including the kind of suffering experienced as ill health.

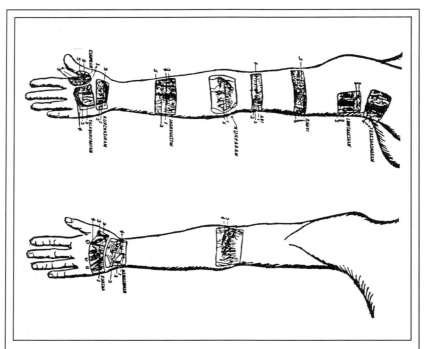

Kshipram
1. Tendon of adductor pollicis
2. Arteria princeps pollicis
3. Digital branch of median nerve
4. Tendon of deep portion of flexor pollicis brevis
5. First dorsal interosseous muscle

Talahrudayam
1. Adductor pollicis muscle
2. Superficial volar arch
3. Interossei muscles
4. Lumbricals

Kurcha
1. Tendon of extensor digitorum communis
2. Radial artery
3. Tendon of extensor pollicis longus
4. Tendon of extensor indicis proprius
5. Dorsal metacarpal branches of radial artery

Kurchasiram
1. Ulnar artery

2. Median nerve
3. Transverse carpal ligament

Manibandham
1. Radio-ulnar ligament
2. Ulnar collateral ligament
3. Radio carpal ligament
4. Radial collateral ligament

Indravasthi
1. Median nerve
2. Flexor digitorum sublimis muscle
3. Radial artery
4. Pronator teres muscle
5. Flexor carpi radialis muscle

Kurparam
1. Radial collateral ligament
2. & 3. Ulnar collateral ligament
4. Annular ligament

Ani
1. Median nerve
2. Ulnar nerve
3. Arteria profunda brachii
4. Biceps brachii muscle

Bahvi
1. Brachial artery with its venae comites
2. Median nerve
3. Radial nerve
4. Ulnar nerve
5. Biceps brachii muscle
NB; Bahvi corresponds to Urvi in the inferior extremity.

Lohithaksham
1. Pectoralis major muscle
2. Pectoralis minor muscle
3. Brachial artery with its venae comites
4. Median nerve
5. Ulnar nerve

Kakshadharam
1. Axillary artery and vein
2. Medial head of the median nerve
3. Ulnar nerve
4. Tendon of pectoralis minor

Figure 62. The Marmas in the superior extremity. (From the collection of Dr. M. L. Gharote.)

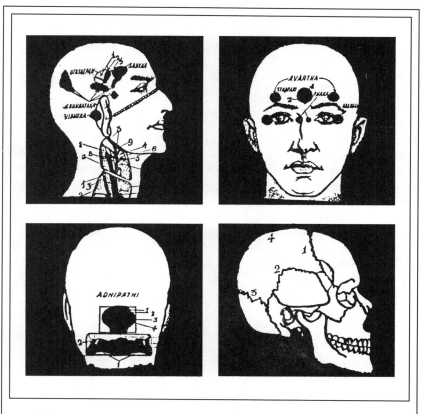

Neelamanya
1. Internal jugular vein
2. Common carotid artery
3. Glossopharyngeal nerve
4. Hypoglossal nerve
5. Lingual artery
6. Stylohyoid muscle
7. Lingual vein
8. Internal carotid artery
9. External carotid artery

Mathruka
1. Phrenic nerve
2. Vagus nerve
3. Internal jugular vein
4. Common carotid artery
5. Subclavian vein
6. Subclavian artery
7. Sternothyroideus muscle
8. External jugular vein

Krikatika
1. Atlas

2. and 2a. Lateral atlanto-
   occipital ligaments
3. Occiput bone
4. Posterior atlanto-occipital
   membrane

Sankha
1. The thinnest portion of the
   temporal bone.

Utkshepam
1. Temporalis muscle
2. Frontal branch of the
   superficial temporal artery
3. Zygomatico-temporal
   nerve

Sthapani
1. Emissary vein emerging
   from the foramen caecum
   joining the superior sagittal sinus
2. Cristagalli exposed

Seemantha
1. Frontal suture (one)
2. Parietal sutures (two, one
   on either side)
3. Lambdoid suture (one)
4. Sagittal suture (one)

Srungataka
1. Visuo-sensory center
2. Visuo-psychic
3. for hearing
4. for taste and smell
5. for speech (Broca's)

Adhipathi
Dorsal view:
1. Middle peduncle of the
   cerebellum
2. Superior peduncle of the
   cerebellum
3. Medulla oblongata
4. Inferior peduncle

Figure 63. The Marmas in the head and neck. (From the collection of Dr. M. L. Gharote.)

BUDDHIST MEDICINE

One of the ways the Buddhist monks sought to create a basis for the development of an inner and outer mind/body balance within their Chinese students lay in the practice of healing and preventative medicine. This practice was not based on the native Taoist ideas concerning health they encountered, but on their own Indian precedents. Even in the older Theravada forms of the scriptures, we can read of the different forms of illness and the types of people associated with them, of nursing or visiting the sick, and of the relationships between doctors and nurses themselves [Note 30a]. These practices fulfilled the requirements laid out in the Sutra of the Emerald Light of the Master of Medicine (*Bhaisajaguru-vaidryaprabha*; Chinese: *Yao Shi Ching*; Japanese:

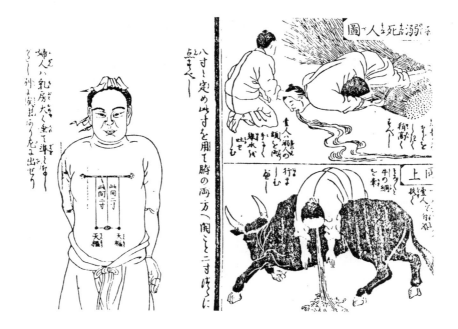

Figure 64. Left: diagram shows the relative distances between various vital points of the body. Right: emergency treatments for a drowned person. (From the Kokeisai Kyuho *of Gentoku Tamba, Japan.) (Author's collection.)*

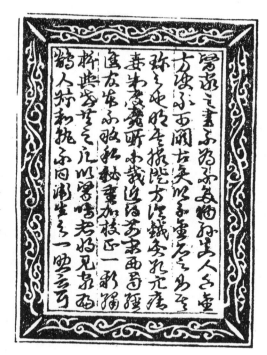

Figure 65. Last page of the introductory chapter to the Ch'ien Chin Peng *(Senkinho) "Prescriptions worth a thousand gold pieces" of Sun Szu Miao, which incorporates current Buddhist techniques of treatment and diagnosis according to the Elements,* A.D. *652. (Page taken from a Japanese facsimile circa* A.D. *1752. (Kongoryuji Temple.)*

Yakushikyo). This Buddha together with Manjusri (Chinese: *Wen Shu*; Japanese: *Monju*), the Buddha of Wisdom and Learning, were patrons of healing in Buddhism [Note 78].

The early scriptures, particularly of the Sarvastivada School, also had certain ideas concerning subtle bodily energies. One of these is called *prasada*. This term, which literally means balance or tranquillity, was used to describe the most subtle physical matter derived from the perfectly balanced five elements. It was said to be non-resistant (*apratigaha*) and mentally translucent (*accha*) to the subjective consciousness. The total bodily elemental equilibrium was termed *Rupaprasada*, and this was the basis for the sense organs themselves. It was the different elemental proportions within the *prasada* that were responsible for the various colors and shapes of things.

Different schools of teaching dealt with *prasada* in various ways but it is clear that *prasada* is one of the terms describing the Buddhist equivalent of the Hindu *prana* and the Taoist *chi* during the first few centuries of Chinese Buddhist medicine. It was understood in a far deeper manner than either of the latter two systems for it was recognized as the result of the complex interplay between mind and matter taught within Buddhism and could only be understood through such studies. In contrast, both *chi* and *prana*, although subtle in their natural condition and effects, were considered as physically based energies alone. *Prasada*, in the Sarvastivada School, was said to exist throughout life and even if one had a limb amputated its *prasada* remained in place unchanged until the subject's death, at which point it is said to slowly disintegrate. It was this idea of *prasada*, or something very like it, which probably formed the basis for what later Chuan Fa monks called the ether element. We will return to this theme later.

PHYSICAL LANGUAGE

In order to properly appreciate the various understandings of the physical body within Buddhism, its *Chuan Fa* or its healing systems, we need to know something more of the supportive philosophy it employed, particularly when these have reference to our considerations of its history and development. A great deal was known concerning the body as an anatomical unit and there was also an existing Vedic tradition of anatomical description and nomenclature; however, for Buddhists this was inadequate, and, as many Buddhist terms differed widely in their usage from their Vedic counterparts, a new terminological vocabulary needed to be devised.

Buddhism's early classification of our experience of existence into *nama* and *rupa* (name and form) served adequately to highlight the distinctive features of both, however the term *Rupakaya* as a descriptor of the body was intended to be used mainly for analytical meditations or presentations in regard to understanding the nature of physical and mental existence itself. As both physical and mental life is made up of many different factors, both *nama* and *rupa* actually described a multiplicity of forces and events, and were not in themselves precise enough for medical purposes. Shakyamuni Buddha, himself, freely admitted that he had not taught all there was to know, but rather only those things necessary for spiritual development. Due to this, there were many areas of study, along with their associated terminologies, which were not included or only barely outlined in the earliest teachings of the monks.

As the years passed and different conditions and needs arose, different forms of description and/or explanation of teachings were utilized. Slowly and steadily Buddhist monk healers began innovating terms and descriptions of their own.

One very basic to their system was *Kayaka*. This singular Sanskrit term was used within the Buddhist healing arts to reference the body and its associated organic functions. We are familiar already with the Sanskrit term *kaya*, indicating a grouping of physical or non-physical objects. This word was used, in combination with other terms, to indicate an associated assemblage of some kind. We find it in words such as *Dharmakaya* (Body of the Law) or *Dhatukaya* (the totality of elements), etc. *Kayaka*, however, was one of many medical terms not often encountered in purely religious references, and refers to the physical body simply as a physical entity. Its usage was probably innovated by the Buddha's doctor monk Jivaka or one of his disciples. Jivaka's name, itself, is of interest here, for it clearly indicates his status and literally means "He who is characterized by his capacity to install life" (*jiva* = life-giving). It is really a general title for a doctor, rather than a personal name.

I have alluded already, in chart A of the "Mandala of Elements," to the tripartite description of mind/body interaction envisaged in the Buddhist healing tradition and knowing what these three forms indicate is of great importance to understanding the role of the physical arts within Buddhism. Each describes a distinctive form of inter-communication which conveys "information" relevant, in various degrees, to the existence of the physical body. They can be summarized simply as the intercommunication (I term it a "language") between body and body (i.e., itself), body to mind, and mind to body.

BODY LANGUAGES

As we have seen, early Buddhism gave great and detailed attention to describing the mental states and their relationship to and with the physical body, particularly with regard to the sense impressions. This form of description entailed utilizing the "mind to body" language, and is found, consciously used, within descriptions of the meditations centered around using the breathing cycle as an object of mental regulation, and also within the analytical meditations upon death, in which the various states of a corpse's physical decomposition were observed and related to the doctrines of insubstantiality (Anitya). Such methods did not, however, need to concern themselves with any other aspects of the living physical being in the manner required for the purposes of preventative medicine and healing.

"Body to mind" language was also dealt with peripherally in explanations or interpretations of the results of internal body states or conditions which, when forming the objects of observation, gave rise to texts describing the different temperaments of students.

Despite these, such partial descriptions of bodily and mental interaction were inadequate for medical purposes, and other forms of presenting such interaction were largely unknown or ignored outside of those persons especially concerned with them and their effects. It is for this reason we find the truly Buddhist arts of healing only described within those monastic traditions, especially the Chinese, familiar with *Chuan Fa* practice or the physical arts in general, and those Buddhist traditions, such as the Esoteric schools (Chinese: *Mi Tsung*), which did not ignore the role of the physical being in spiritual endeavors.

It was probably around this period of development that the nearest thing to an acknowledgment of a physical basis for the Consciousness came to be developed in the Theravada (*Sarvastivada*) School. Here Consciousness was regarded as being situated, or arising from, the heart organ (Pali: *Hadaya vatthu*). This tradition, though not mentioned specifically in the Theravada canonical scriptures or Abhidhamma, appears in many commentarial references and is certainly still generally accepted among present-day Theravadins. For them the heart formed the organ which, in common with the other sense organs, was found in the schemata of the "18 Entrances" covered earlier.

There are instances of other monasteries and sects using adaptations of the native Chinese Taoist inspired practices, but these usually consisted of very basic applications, or simple herbal remedies, which were probably known in India anyway, and we should not lose sight of the fact that many of the Buddhist techniques, because they were so dangerous if misapplied, were deliberately kept secret.

THE DOCTRINE OF PHYSICAL AND MENTAL ENERGY

The various means of understanding the process of growth form the tools of the healer's diagnostic art and skills, and the various exponents of these arts gave rise to the diverse forms of Buddhist healing science. The concept of the body to body "consciousness" is essential in understanding the nature of the physical generative and homeostatic forces at work within the physical being, indeed it is *the* fact of physical life. Without it there is no possibility of life at all.

In Buddhist medical Sanskrit, the bodily life force principle (*Utpadajiva Srotasiddhanta*, Chinese: *I Sheng lau Li*; Japanese: *Ishoryu Ri*, or *Kikatsuryu Ri*) is described as being a *Kayakajiva santanikrotkarsa* (bodily life energy serial event). We can understand better what this term indicates if we consider it as describing an integral physical tactician, protecting and renewing the various processes of the body as and when it is required, at any or all levels, regulating or prompting organic and cellular growth.

Both Buddhism and Hinduism represent bodily energy in various forms, sometimes portraying it as a force, a person, or a deity. Others viewed it as if a component part, working in unison with others and flowing out to initiate or regulate the internal workings of the physical being as well as providing "prompts" toward consciousness.

This latter attribute is perhaps most easily recognized in the sensation of physical pain. This is a state arising directly from an organic action which transmits its state around the body until it is, in turn, "picked up" and passed into the basic consciousness. From here it is then perceived, responded to, and acted upon. Without the first, the second, and subsequent, phases would not occur. Without continual life force renewal the organs would not function.

Buddhism utilizes the associative tendencies of the consciousness and their interplay with the physical body to highlight the constituents of the processes involved in such a way as to enable a practitioner to understand, modify and enhance their quality. This orientation is geared primarily toward the practice of meditation and the purification of the mental series. In healing a different orientation is required, one which acknowledges the mental forces at work, but one that tries also to understand more about the physical factors involved. Such an orientation needs to know how the body "talks" to itself as well as how it "talks" to the consciousness.

Usually the body talks to itself in its own language and does not need to refer to any other. However, when its language fails to be understood, or if it becomes overwhelmed, it sends out messages in a body to mind language which are picked up and understood by the consciousness series. This is what occurs in instances of pain, and other circumstances, in which an alteration to the bodily series of activities is needed.

In Buddhist *Chuan Fa* (*Kempo*), this type of language is termed in general a *Kayaka Manas*—a bodily form of consciousness. This could be defined as a bodily state or condition which, upon arising, has the capacity to take as one of its objects the production of a mental response. Like the mental *manas*, it carries and is subject to those factors (both past and present) arising from causes and effects, and manifests, in physical forms, the patternings of each. The patterns of our chromosome inheritance are a simple example of this. In purely experiential terms that which we call "instinct"—which is, properly speaking, an initiating process not founded upon any conscious volition or activity—is also an example of the *Kayaka manas* at work.

This tactical awareness is termed in Sanskrit *Prasada*, a term we met earlier in discussing its *Sarvastivada* usage. The significance of this term (which literally means something like "sensitivity") within the practice of medicine is rarely recognized among those who primarily concern themselves with descriptions of the process of consciousness. As we are perhaps realizing, there is far more to these ancient terms than may be first suspected.

THE SPIRITUAL ROLES AND
FUNCTIONING OF *KAYAKAJIVA*

We may now ask ourselves, "What spiritual purpose, role, or function does the *Kayakajiva* serve?" Obviously life itself depends upon its existence, and illness of the body acts as a debilitating or obsessive factor to the consciousness. The less consciousness has to interplay with the *Kayakajiva*, the more it can concern itself with its inner spiritual progress. An important role of *Kayakajiva* is to perform its task efficiently and successfully by receiving, responding, and renewing our physical being where necessary and thus requiring minimal usage of its other languages which involve consciousness. When this does occur, consciousness has full freedom to consider its goals and is not hindered in any manner.

The force (Sanskrit: *Vibhutva*) of physical growth continues until its renewal capacity is exhausted and then, usually slowly, diminishes until physical death. A perfectly functioning life energy vibrates and radiates its energy outward in a manner similar to what we may encounter in healthy pregnant women. The best healers possess such a quality. I think also it is this *Jiva* which was the basis for what was seen as a "halo" around holy persons.

We should not assume that such a perfectly functioning *Jiva* (if such a state could be achieved) confers with it some form of physical power or strength. There is no direct connection between physical prowess and *Jiva*. It may arise within a physically strong person, but it is not dependent upon such a condition. Physical strength, itself, is only a relative condition anyway. A fully functioning *Jiva* is an inner quality of balance and harmony.

Bodily *Jiva* normally fluctuates according to current mental or physical capacities and available potential. It is subject to influences from both equally. If it were possible from birth to preserve its quality unaltered in any manner, our life quality would be subject only to our inherited factors, and we would probably have great limitations in adapting to any external environment or influence outside the range of our inheritance. Fortunately this is not possible, and so it is possible to overcome and learn from the challenges, limitations, or imbalances we encounter as and when they occur in our life path.

In traditional Buddhist manner, the life energy is said to be composed of the four elements (*Mahabhuta*) in an integral form, which itself forms a fifth. In the healing tradition this element is termed ether. Each of the elements has provenance over different bodily aspects, as well as acting in specific combinations of predominancies toward other general areas.

In *Chuan Fa* tradition, the *Kayakajiva* is held to be a physical counterpart to what is known as the *Alaya* or "storing" consciousness, for, like the *Alaya*, the bodily *Jiva* carries the "seeds" of its own patterning within it, which it continually modifies and develops according to current patterns and habits. In Buddhist teaching the forces acting to create these seeds stretch back before our present lifetime and persist beyond our present one.

Many Buddhists were familiar with the extensive knowledge of surgery common to Indian medicine and this aided them both in spreading the teachings and in their practice of diagnosis and therapy. Surgical technique was almost unknown within China prior to the arrival of Buddhism and, due to this, contemporary concepts of how the body worked and interacted were based upon strange combinations of fact and fiction.

Jivaka—a direct disciple and the doctor of the Buddha—was the father of Indian pediatrics and in partnership with another famous Disciple of the Buddha—Mahakasyapa—is credited with several definitive treatises on medicine and surgery. The skill of this pair is attested to within early Hindu works on surgery, but is only mentioned tangentially within the Theravada Buddhist scriptures, a fact which suggests some editing of these scriptures has taken place [See Notes 30, 56].

The renowned Buddhist teacher Nagarjuna is said to have translated at least two traditional works dealing with healing and medicines in the first centuries of our era. A section of his *Maha-Prajnaparamita Sutra* is quoted by the Chinese monk I Tsing in his commentary upon the *Mahavairocana Sutra* (Taisho 39, pp. 606–609) in which he describes the five winds (Chinese: *Wu Fung*; Japanese: *Gofu*). This description enables us to see that the breath Hatha Yoga termed *prana* is in fact forming only part of a wider system known in Buddhism. These winds or airs are said to contain the vigor of the physical body and are named according to their zones of influence. *Udana* is situated in the upper body and controls the head, hands, arms and upper throat. *Prana* is situated in the heart; *Apana* is in the abdomen, *Samana* at the navel and *Vyana* permeates the rest of the body.

The second century A.D. esoteric master Srimitra is also said to have effected miraculous and spectacular cures. Even the art of obstetrics was described by Vasubandhu in his *Abhidharmakosa*. Many later monks also taught and practiced the healing arts. These skills were a practical necessity, as monasteries were often a long way away from any organized social health system (if any existed at all) and would be called upon both by their own inhabitants and the local populace to deal with all manner of injury and illness.

It was probably from within the fold of the traditional Indian healing arts practiced by the monks that the specific preventative therapies involving physical movements and sequences were developed. These movement sequences, which were the forerunners of the modern arts of corrective physiotherapy, therapeutic massage, and remedial joint manipulation, were later taken into China and elsewhere [Note 23].

The Buddhist systems were not simple clones or adaptations of the Hindu Vedic system. Buddhist healers developed some techniques quite distinct and individual to them. Some of this was due to the fact that they had a different set of references to develop ideas and practices from (i.e., the Sutras). In the *Anguttara Nikaya 4*, and the *Sivaka Sutra 36:21a*, we see that the suffering which produces illness is said to have eight main causes: namely bile, phlegm, a mixture of both, irregular or imbalanced lifestyle, imbalanced weather, injury and karma. All of these are very interesting categories for they reflect some areas of the most modern medical research. These categories reflect the primary concern of the Buddhist doctor, namely relieving suffering, and relieving its cause. In cases of spiritual sickness this order was in fact reversed.

Imbalanced weather is an interesting category; not many realize that the European word temperament, found in several old European language roots, means "weather." It seems, as is often the case, that the oriental medieval peoples recognized far more subtle influences upon our health balance than is done nowadays. Temperamental illness is usually classed as being psychological nowadays. See, for instance, the way the French attribute certain mental imbalances to the "mistral" winds and acknowledge this in their common law.

This category also indicated illness caused by or due to the seasons. G. G. Luce, the pioneering researcher in the U.S.A., produced some very interesting research data indicating very fundamental health disorders such as heart disease, epilepsy, metabolic disorders, etc., being due to the body's response to light—both in their natural or artificial forms. Such illness accords with the changes in light due to the various seasons, weather patterns, and local environment. When she first announced her findings many disbelieved her conclusions. Now science has had to think again as the importance and significance of her work is being finally acknowledged [See Note 21a].

It was only within China, over 1000 years ago, that remedial sunbathing was prescribed as a medicine, particularly for those working predominantly in the darkness or actually underground (as in the case of miners). Some of the Buddhist methods do seem a little bizarre to our "enlightened" times. There is, for instance, a whole tradition of painting

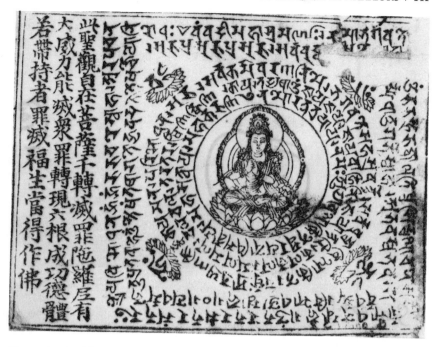

Figure 66. Buddhist talisman bearing the image of Avalokitesvara and surrounded by Sanskrit mantras of protection. Tung Huang caves, Kiangsu, China. (Kongoryuji Temple.)

esoteric charms or Buddha pictures upon certain points or places on the body. (This practice may have been the foundation for the more recent art of permanent tattooing!) Although this seems simply superstitious, recent research done in China shows that many of the paints used were composed of powerful herbs or minerals which, if taken orally, would rapidly kill their recipient. However, when placed upon the skin as a paint they are absorbed more slowly and acted very effectively for a long period. Such a therapeutic method is still being researched in modern times. In 1989, Japanese laboratories announced the invention of a very modern, battery-powered, microprocessed and self-timing hypodermic syringe designed to gradually dispense a medicinal compound in exactly the same manner. The difference in cost between the two methods can be imagined.

Painted charms or talismans (Chinese: *shu*) were used in a wide range of applications, particularly those written with inks made from various combinations of minerals or healing herb compounds. Often parts of the charms were used in different ways (e.g., they had sections which were to be eaten or chewed and functioned like modern day tablets, depending on the type of paper used for them), so the healing substances would circulate slowly around the body. Opiate anaesthetics and sedatives were administered in this way by Buddhist healers. Other types of charms were used as bandages and wrapped directly onto open wounds, sores, or infected tissue. These acted just like modern adhesive plasters. Many persons unfamiliar with such traditions did not realize just what they were and dismissed them as superstitious hocus pocus.

The earliest healing practice concerned itself with the injuries suffered by warriors in battle. Treatment of injured warriors also offered good opportunities to further anatomical and practical knowledge of the body. In all armies the training and provision of good field surgeons gives confidence to the combat troops and every war leader tries to obtain and train the best available. As pointed out earlier the Chinese were often embroiled in various internal conflicts until Buddhism became a major influence in the country. Such conflicts often broke out between the various rulers of different regions of the nation. The refugees of such conflicts often sought sanctuary and medical aid at the monasteries.

Military officers who experienced aid from the monasteries often returned to these "fields of inexhaustible compassion" and ended their days peacefully as monks, helping the temple and composing their memoirs. Rendering aid helped Indian missionary monks become familiar with the distinctive principles and practices of Chinese warriorhood. The skills developed in treating injuries distinctive to the Ksatreya were eagerly integrated into the healing repertoires of the Chinese military. The most notable of these being the art of surgery [See Notes 30, 55]. It was probably among the Ksatreya doctors that the adjustable bone splint was invented. This orthopedic device, made from wood and string, allows a fractured bone or joint to be set firmly in a variety of different positions, which can then be altered as the bone itself heals. The limb, when set in this device, can be kept fully mobile. In simple fractures of the leg or arm, the patient can walk or grasp normally immediately after it is put on. Although now seemingly forgotten in India, the Chinese have improved this design even further and produced very light bamboo forms which have wooden screw adjusters on the individual splint components themselves. By means of these, compound fractures can be reset in place by tightening the various joint sections individually as required.

In 1970, the Chinese Medical Association published a five year study on this which showed that joints treated with this device—rather than the conventional plaster of Paris immobilization—healed in up to a third of the time. Despite this study, Western hospitalized patients are still treated to the plaster of Paris method.

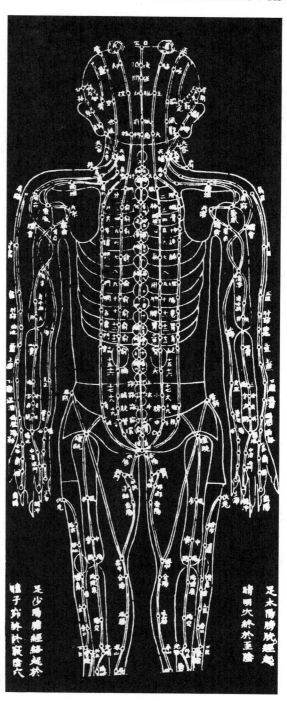

Figure 67. Energy flows within the human body. It is these points that the Chuan Fa practitioner can alter by means of either massage or blows. (Kongoryuji Temple.)

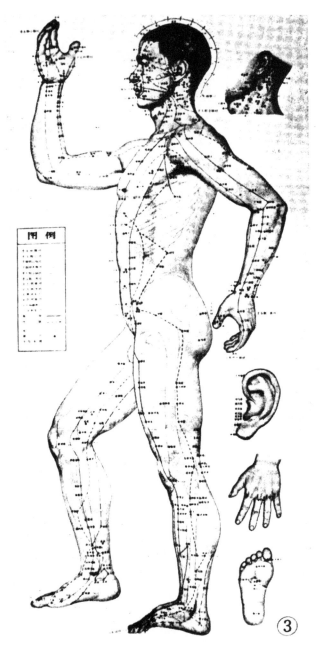

Figure 68. A modern chart of the acupuncture points. (Chinese Medical Association, Kongoryuji Temple.)

In modern day acupuncture lore, there is recounted a legend that the discovery of the vital bodily points began within India as a result of combative research studies undertaken by the Indian Ksatreya warriors in order to discover the vital (and deadly) points of the body which could be struck during hand-to-hand encounters. It is said that they experimented upon prisoners by piercing their bodies with the iron and stone "needle" daggers (called either *Suci, Vasi* or *Sulan*), common to their infantry and foot soldiers, in order to determine these points. The use of these daggers is preserved and reflected in the ninth chapter of the esoteric *Mahavairocana Sutra* which contains the images and mantras of Bodhisattvas of the "Thunderbolt Suci" and of the "Thunderbolt Fists."

This Chinese legend reflects and complements the traditional Indian account of its origins, where it is said that in the aftermath of battles it was noticed that sometimes therapeutic effects arose from superficial arrow or dagger wounds incurred by the Ksatreya in battle. By associating the sudden cures these particular wounds seemed to induce based on the point of the body where the wounds occurred, various doctors were inspired to begin experimentation, with both solid and hollow needles, upon their own and others' bodies, in order to discover both the points and areas of therapeutic value and any others at which energy could be generated or dispersed. These points were recognized as special zones of the body where vital energies were amenable to being changed or altered by external influences or techniques such as finger pressure or manipulation.

These changes of energy were not only possible at the physical level but equally at what we usually term the psychological level. Using these methods it is possible to induce a psychological change in a subject. Such techniques, so long scoffed at by Western medical ortho-

Figure 69. A Vedic Deity astride a battle elephant. He carries several Suci daggers. (Kongoryuji Temple.)

doxy, have developed new significance and meaning in recent times because the West has improved its understanding of the hormonal and other systems that affect the human organism. The East has always acknowledged the inseparable link of mind and body together with their interactive life support systems, and that one can be affected, approached, or cured, via another.

Although therapies and diagnostic techniques directed toward this link are ancient within Buddhist healing, it was only in modern times that people like Wilhelm Reich, originator of bioenergetic therapy, rediscovered some of its principles [Note 56b].

Chuan Fa, the Buddhist martial art, preserved many Ksatreya techniques in their original forms. It calls the skill of vital point energy alteration *Tien Hsueh Fa* (Japanese: *Tenketsuho*) and reasserts it as a purely therapeutic technique, to be used as an alternative to the needle therapy of acupuncture. The trained hands and fingers of a *Chuan Fa* exponent were as capable of manipulating the vital points in a patient's body as an ordinary doctor's metal needles. The Chinese *Chuan Fa* exponents who acted as battle surgeons were in a better position to gather specific knowledge and expertise of both anatomy and the healing art than ordinary doctors who could only develop such experience in general, and who were for many years forbidden by successive Imperial proscriptions to dissect bodies for purposes of study.

The monks who practiced *Chuan Fa* were often the sole preservers of the Ksatreya art of *Avasavidya*, called in Chinese *Huo Ming* or *Huo Fa*. This was a special practice of applying emergency first aid techniques

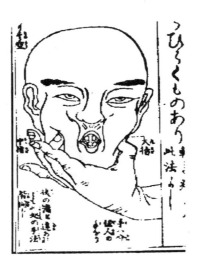

Figure 70. Treating or diagnosing the vital points. An illustration from Kokesai Kyuho *of Gentoku Tamba, which was based upon Chinese monastic texts. Many of the martial art forms in Okinawa and Japan copied their revival techniques from this work. (Kongoryuji Temple.)*

in order to revive someone newly dead. It consisted of blows and special screams performed to and at the patient both before and after revival. In *Chuan Fa* it was a necessity, as its advanced practice of experimental techniques involving striking or pressing the vital points of the body could easily result in a student's accidental and sudden death. Esoterically it was said that the screams and cries used either drove the departing spirit back into the patient's body or made it difficult for it to leave.

These methods were not only mystical but also involved techniques only recently acknowledged by orthodox medicine [See Notes 64, 66]. For example, direct heart massage and mouth-to-mouth resuscitation were ancient techniques of the *Huo Ming*. I myself demonstrated both these techniques to doctors in the early 1960s long before they were generally known in Europe.

Traces of these techniques were taken to Japan for we can find accounts in such works as the ancient *Ishinpo* [Note 66].

> Fearlessness and Reviving are synonymous terms in Buddhism.
>
> —Acarya Shan Wu Wei
> *Commentary upon the Mahavairocanasutra*

The repertoire of monastic healers was wide-reaching and involved many esoteric techniques. Charms and talismans dedicated to the healing Buddhas were often written out for patients and carried by them or they were painted upon the vital points in colors compounded from special herbal healing mixtures. Mantras—sacred chants—were also used as therapeutic aids. Sometimes these were very apt; when, for instance, they were prescribed for patients suffering from asthma or other respiratory disorders.

Chih I, the sixth century founder of Tien T'ai Buddhism, drawing on the ancient precedents, taught his students many methods of health preservation including diagnosing illness by the elements and the "Six Healing Breaths" technique. In his text *T'ing meng Chih Kuan Lun* (Japanese: *Jomon Kiken Ron*), we read how monks and lay people were taught to regulate and balance their diet, clothing, hygiene, movement and sleep. Another text gives the following advice to prepare for meditation:

> Sit in the Lotus position, make saliva in your mouth
> and swirl it around three times.
> Visualize energy going into the belly and lower parts of your body.
>
> Now pucker your lips and shout "Ho!" loudly to clear the lungs.
> then close the mouth and breathe quietly in through the nose.

Chant the sounds for the inner organs;
HU for the spleen, SZU for the lungs, HSI for the stomach,
CHUI for the kidneys.
Repeat each of the sounds six times so as to make 36 sounds in all.
Thus purify the lungs.

Dietary therapies [Note 79] as well as therapeutic meditation exercises all formed part of the rich tapestry of Buddhist healing in ancient China [Notes 66, 78]. Herbal medicine was a refined art and the Indian trained monks used plants initially unknown to the Chinese. When after a few generations the two traditions of India and China began to blend and interact, the resultant system and fund of experience formed a body of teaching oriented toward healing a person's mind, body and spirit equally and this concept still exists.

Much of the inner teaching concerning the principles of medical technique was preserved in the mandalas and the texts associated with

Figure 71. A scroll by Chang Sheng Wen in the Tang period style. The colophon (top right) shows it is dedicated to both Shakyamuni and the healing Buddha Yao Shih. At the bottom right are six guardian spirits each representing one of the human senses (Kongoryuji Library).

them, although many of these teachings came directly from the earliest times. If, for instance, you look at the charts contained in Note 6c you can find lists of the "Six Tastes," the "Four Odors," etc. These terms were used in medical diagnosis to formulate the creative or destructive aspects of the elements. A patient may exhibit a certain skin color (see the colors chart) or complain about a body sensation (see the charts following Note 6c, and for greater detail, see Note 56).

Each of the attributes identified with the elements represents both physical and mental phenomena and can be used to diagnose and identify the elemental basis of health disorders. Conversely it also tells one of the therapeutic methods within which the cure lies. The various attributes are interchangeable. This means that a particular elemental symptom of health disorder will have a corresponding resonance in all the other areas of the elements. For instance, a disorder of earth element may exhibit itself within the appetite, posture, visual ability, skin color, movement pattern, sense of smell, or any other of the six senses described in the charts of Note 6 (page 405–6). In addition to these external symptoms there will also be inner, mental symptoms. In many cases these may simply be extra worries concerning the illness itself but more subtle effects are also noted. The ability to recall certain types of events may be impaired, the short (or long) term memory may be affected; how one communicates to oneself and thinks about things will also be affected. Such symptoms can only be elicited by conversing with a suitably relaxed patient and the monk healers were very gifted at this type of healing conversation (Chinese: Yi Yen).

The five element system of nomenclature enabled monk healers to make basic medical decisions concerning health even if they were not experts. It was a distinct advantage of the element system that it could be learned and applied so readily and, if followed properly, would not cause serious harm to a patient even if a drastically wrong diagnosis was made.

Monk healers became skilled by learning and memorizing the paradigmatic meanings of the elemental mandala and sought to incorporate more and more factors into their medical judgment. They often ventured into areas of study previously unknown or unthought of in earlier traditions and made startling discoveries concerning the body and its workings. (See appendix of Mandala paradigms.)

The advantage of Buddhist medicine was that a physical diagnostic skill alone was not deemed good enough for a healer. All therapies had to include psychological and spiritual components as well, and an apparent cure without these components was regarded as shortsighted, imbalanced and doomed eventually to fail. It is because of such views that Buddhism created the very first techniques for treating the psychologically disturbed. While other cultural traditions often incar-

Figure 72. A Tibetan version of an Indian talisman believed to frighten away demons and popularly called a Lion's Head Protector (Sanskrit: Simhamukkhapala). It bears the letters of the Sanskrit alphabet used to write down the mantras. The lion's three eyes show mastery over the three times (past, present, and future) and the skulls used as decoration represent specific evils which he has vanquished (author's collection).

cerated the "mad," monks engaged in therapeutic encounters with them.

Much of the Chinese Buddhist esoteric therapy can only be understood through knowledge of the mandala and its meanings, for the mandala enabled monks to assess subtle and peripheral factors in illness which were unknown to Taoists or the Chinese folk tradition. Equivalent representations of the hormonal activity and lymph flow were both known to the Buddhist elemental doctors but this knowledge was not widespread.

While the effects of mandala-based healing methods could sometimes produce spectacular results in patients, its principles and techniques were restricted to practitioners of the esoteric path (Chinese: *Mi Chiao*; Japanese: *Mikkyo*) as the very nature of its mystical principles encouraged research into the subtle and paradigmatic phenomena of spirituality. It was very common however, both in ancient and modern *Chuan Fa* (Japanese: *Kempo*) to practice medicine and healing for the benefit of the local community. We can find examples of this ethos even in comparatively recent times.

Canton was a Southern Chinese area long connected with Buddhist *Chuan Fa*, and a strong stand was taken by its socially minded Kempo masters against the opium trade foolishly sanctioned by the British colonial government. They initiated various societies and organizations against its usage and propagation. Taoists also were involved in this anti-opium movement, which unfortunately for the Chinese, led to the famous Boxer Wars and the eventual secession of Hong Kong to England as a reparation for the damage caused by the uprising [Note 23a].

We should also not lose sight of the fact that monks were not allowed to practice the art of healing for material benefit and so, as in modern times, formed an alternative medical system for most other doctors often would only treat patients who could afford to pay. This was one of the reasons there was so much opposition to Buddhism and Buddhist cultural arts at the Imperial Court.

By teaching and actively encouraging compassion Buddhists were able to identify with those who suffered. They saw another's pain as their own. This Bodhisattva attitude was the prime cause for the development of the Buddhist system of healing and medicine. This theme of healing, in its more specific relationships to the practice of *Chuan Fa*, is discussed in depth in the next section.

THE

MANDALA

OF

MOVEMENT

THE MANDALA OF MOVEMENT

Put mind in body and body in mind
(*Samyutta Nikaya* 283–284).

Now we need to look at the Indian background. India is a mysterious land, steeped in history, with a civilization stretching back far in time. It was from India, around 2000 B.C., that the first Indo-Aryans began their journey toward the European continent to found the tribes that later grew into what we now call the civilized world. If we take a very brief overview of the first 8000 years of India's development it would look something like this:

8000–4000 B.C.—Earliest trace of organized communities in western India;

4000–3000 B.C.—Earliest trace of organized communities in eastern India;

2500–1600 B.C.—The Harappan civilization;

1600–1000 B.C.—Time of the Rig Veda and Samhitas;

1000–600 B.C.—Time of the later Vedas, Brahmanas, and the early Upanisads;

600–400 B.C.—The Epic stories describing previous times;

550 B.C.—The Buddha;

400–0 B.C.—The Suttas and Nikayas, etc.

Much of India's history is still in a process of discovery as archaeological excavations continue. Facts and figures are continually being revised concerning both its past and its peoples. Some of the most recent discoveries have pushed back even further the time civilization began there.

When we come to consider the various influences and sources of the Buddhist movement arts, it is toward India we must turn to look. Here, in the land which gave birth to some of the greatest spiritual teachers mankind has known, we find civilizations and cultures as old as our recorded time. By 1000 B.C. iron and other metals were being used both for weapons and household implements. Gandhara, the area where the Buddha came from, is one of the earliest places in which iron was found.

It is perhaps surprising to discover that, far from being in a primitive condition, ancient India was highly civilized, possessing a refined culture far more advanced than any other land of that time. Long before the arising of Greece or Imperial Rome, India could boast of sophisticated city states, institutionalized monarchies with large standing armies, a refined and balanced medical system, all based within a tolerant and influential religio/philosophical system.

Within such a society we would expect to discover a foreign neighbor threatening to invade such a land and take its riches, but this was not so. Warfare in those days was more often than not a small, usually localized affair between close neighbors or relatives rather than with foreign invaders. Indeed, there were no foreigners close or advanced enough to invade ancient India. Even its neighbor China only began to organize large armies around 500 B.C. and not until 400 B.C. did the Chinese learn to utilize iron. The Chinese Cavalry, created around 320 B.C. was a primitive force in comparison to its Indian equivalent.

Apart from archaeological discoveries, much of what we know of India's history has come to us through accounts in the sacred books known as the Vedas and their associated literature. These Indian scriptures tell us of the interchanges between Gods and mortals, and mortals between themselves. They recount the trials and tribulations of the earliest inhabitants of India and were intended to be used not only as religious or historical references, but also as sources for self-discovery, personal philosophy, and as practical moral guides. This moral guidance extended into the military sphere and one finds spiritual treatises of many types considering the ethics of warfare, and through such

Figure 73. Two ancient Greek Pancration fighters assume positions ready to kick or strike each other. (Ashmolean Museum, Oxford, England.)

themes, trying to ascertain and establish the real "leitmotiv" of life and death both within nature and warriorhood itself. Unlike the Prussian master tactician Clausewitz, or his Chinese equivalent, Sun Tzu, these spiritual texts go beyond mere dualisms such as "victor" and "vanquished," or "friend" and "foe" to reach conclusions that clearly establish the spiritual potential of both war and warriorhood. With the coming of Shakyamuni Buddha and his teachings, further refinements and clarifications were made to these principles until they reached their summit within an integrated system of non-violent strategies and techniques possessing a rare beauty and power.

THE RISE OF THE KSATREYA

Prior to and during the life of the Buddha various principles were embodied within the warrior caste known as the *Ksatreya* (Japanese: *Setsuri*). This title—stemming from the Sanskrit root *Ksetr* meaning "power," described an elite force of usually royal or noble-born warriors, who were trained from infancy in a wide variety of military and martial arts, both armed and unarmed. In China, the *Ksatreya* were considered to have descended from the deity *Ping Wang* (Japanese: *Byo O*), the "Lord of those who keep things calm." Though the title *Ksatreya* was originally a general term used to signify all nobles, in the Rig Veda it is always connected with royal or divine authority. The classical word *Rajanga* (a member or "limb" of a royal family) was synonymous with that of *Ksatreya*.

In the early Indian religion the central deities Indra and Agni represent, among other things, the principle of power, and their warriors—the *Ksatreya*—considered themselves "sons" of both deities and the principles they symbolized. Not simply concerned with developing physical prowess or a mindless violence, the *Ksatreya* undertook the study of literature, history, religion, esoterica, and philosophy in all their forms. These studies were termed "light" (*vidya*) and the Chandyoga Upanishad speaks of the *Ksatreya Vidya*. Only when all these and kindred arts were mastered, and such mastery had been publicly demonstrated in open competitions and tests, could monks don the robe and armor of a fully qualified *Ksatreya*. This they considered their destiny and purpose in life. In the *Mausala Parva* of the epic tale titled *The Mahabarata*, a *Ksatreya* mother reminds her children that the great occasion for which a *Ksatreya* mother bears a son is for him to be victorious in battle—even if it means death.

Becoming a *Ksatreya* was not simply an intellectual exercise. They were expected, if required, to fight in the forefront of any battle, and they maintained throughout their history the principle of "righteous conquest" (*Dharmavijaya*). Unlike the European interpretation of this term, the *Ksatreya* understood this principle to mean the righting of wrongs or injustices they encountered, irrespective of who committed them. This principle of *Dharmavijaya* was considered a universal one and binding upon all *Ksatreya* without exception.

Doubtless in the very earliest days of India the *Ksatreya* were much less sophisticated, but as civilization developed and the city states emerged, their ethical and philosophical orientation advanced considerably. The growth of the *Ksatreya* coincided with the stability of Indian society in general and, as we have seen, this began very early in the history of the world. If we peruse a selection of quotations from *The Mahabarata* (the story of the Barata clan) concerning the ethics and conduct of the noble warrior, we can see the high degree of humanity espoused by the *Ksatreya* caste.

A *Ksatreya* should only fight equals in battle.

A *Ksatreya* may not strike a Monarch.

Those who attack by the use of words should only be fought with words.

In battle a *Ksatreya* should not strike a *Ksatreya* who is confiding in another, is unprepared, or is panic stricken.

One should only strike after giving due notice.

One fighting another person should not be attacked.

A *Ksatreya* should not strike one who is tired, weeping, unwilling to fight, who is ill, or who cries surrender.

A *Ksatreya* should defend even an enemy who has surrendered with folded hands.

In war, civilians are to be allowed to continue their life unhindered.

Temples and places of worship are not to be touched.

A *Ksatreya's* duty is to fight a just war in order to right a wrong.

If a *Ksatreya* turns away from such a fight he reaps only sin.

To die of disease at home is sin for a *Ksatreya*.

A *Ksatreya* should never strike a Brahmana (priest) for by doing so he attacks his own source.

As entry into the *Ksatreya* ranks was usually the result of birthright, the lowly workers (*Vaisya*) could never join them, but instead there existed a sophisticated army of the people with its own elites and hierarchies. Lacking the classical training in the arts and literature of the *Ksatreya*, this people's (*Vis*) army (*Balam*) was more akin to the military forces of our immediate modern past.

There were, for instance, the *Nasatya*, an independent class of warriors whose duty was to safeguard the provisions of treaties between warring factions, and, if necessary, slay any army which broke them.

They acted as an ancient "United Nations Peace-Force" to keep kings and people in order. Military commanders were called *Senani*—a name reminiscent of the Japanese term *Sensei* which describes a similar status. The foot soldiers were called *patti* (a "walker") reminiscent of the Latin "pedestrian" meaning the same. The *patti* could rise through the ranks to become a member of the *Asibhandhakaputta*. These were a community of foot soldiers trained as shock troops. *Gramani* were local village leaders of mercenary bands who came from the ranks of the common people (*visah*). A *senani* would command many hundreds of *Gramani* bands in a battle.

Life was not, however, all glorious battle and honor. There were the injured as well as the injurers. In the Rig Veda we read one warrior's lament:

> The ribs that compass me give me pain and trouble me like rival wives. Indigent nakedness and exhaustion press me sore; My mind is fluttering like a bird's. As Rats eat Weaver's threads so cares are consuming me (Rig Veda, 10: 33, 2–3).

By Buddha's time, all military forces were highly organized into the classical four divisions, reminiscent of the esoteric elements used within Hinduism. These military divisions comprised chariots (*rathakaya*), ele-

Figure 74. Temple carving showing the slaying of a horse by means of a foot strike. (From the author's collection.)

phants (*hastakaya*), horse cavalry (*asvakaya*), and foot soldiers (*pattikaya*).
Each of these had their own specialized tactics for warfare. Fighting
had become an important profession and armies were a regular institu-
tion.

A comparison can be drawn between the *Ksatreya* and their code,
and that adopted by the later European (Christian) knights. Each possessed a strict code of ethics, chivalrous conduct, and organized into
clans, families, or groups, and dedicated themselves and their art to a
spiritual goal. The Japanese *samurai* also had similar traits to the
Ksatreya. Their battle practices and techniques are often so close to that
of the *Ksatreya* that we must assume the former came from the latter,
perhaps via China. The traditions of sacred Swords, of honorable self-
sacrifice, and service to one's Lord are all found first in India.

The fighting armories, methods, and techniques used in battle
were familiar to all Indians of the time. They learned about war in their
holy books, or, if they were unlucky, they saw war tactics in action. The
Rig Veda attests, for the first time in the history of humankind, to the
use of infantry flags as signaling devices, bows, spears, tactical battle

*Figure 75. Miniature painting showing a fight between the Vedic Deities Rama and
Sahasrajuna. The figure on the right holds a hand striker which may well be an early
form of the Vajra. A blocking movement is shown by the stereoscopic portrayal of his
right arm. (Kongoryuji Temple.)*

formations, armor, poison arrows, axes, daggers, slingshots and lances. Cries and screams were used to frighten the enemy both individually and en masse. There were many types of battle horns and trumpets.

One of the most famous weapons used in battle was the *vajra*. In later Buddhism, especially the esoteric kind, this was understood to represent the thunderbolt, and was interpreted as a symbol for the power of various types of wisdom. In the Rig Veda, however, where the symbol is originally encountered, *vajra* usually signifies a mace or war hammer.

The Rig Veda has the word *vidyut* for thunderbolt and lightning, but this latter term is only associated with *Parjanya*, the rain god of the Vedas. Indra is called *Vajrahasta* (Thunderbolt Hands) but never *Vidyuthasta* (Lightning Hands). In the Rig Veda, the *Vajra* is described as "whirling about in different directions in the brightness of the Sunlight." As thunderbolts rarely exist simultaneously with sunlight, *vajra* here can be seen to describe a weapon rather than a thunderbolt. The Veda further says *vajra* is a fatal weapon made of a metal called *Ayas* (perhaps iron) and, like the hammer of the Norse deity Thor, was forged by Tvastr, the divine smithy.

It has a notched surface, a hundred or thousand edges/spikes. It is firmly held in Indra's hands. It is *Sthavira* (stable) and *Dgarnasi* (durable) (*Rig Veda VIII*, note 55).

Figure 76. The Vedic Deity Yama carrying a Vajra mace in his right hand. (Kongoryuji Temple.)

Some of the mechanical weapons of the popular armies were horrific, complex, technical devices for reaping destruction. *The Mahabarata* describes a weapon called the *cakra*. This was a sharp iron discus thrown at opponents. In the scriptures it was the main weapon of Krisna. He cut off the head of Suspala with it in one throw.

The *Sataghni* (hundred killer) was a column of wood, with wheels at each end, covered in sharp spikes. It was hurled at approaching armies of footsoldiers or rolled down from a castle's walls onto the enemy below.

A smaller version, covered in sharp needle projections, was hurled from slingshots or by hand at charging opponents. The earliest form of anti-personnel grenades were created from cows' horns filled with burning oil, which were hurled at soldiers and chariots. Other versions filled with pepper were used to break up enemy horse charges.

In the Rig Veda we also read of the *yantra*, a defense weapon used in forts, etc. The term describes an apparatus such as a ballista or mechanized slingshot and used to hurl bombs, stones, arrows, and oil at the enemy. Spears were called *sakti* and came in many different forms, some tipped with poison. It is interesting to see how many of the titles for weaponry became incorporated into religious terminology at later dates. *Yantra*, *sakti*, *vajra* and *cakra* now have very different meanings within Hindu and Buddhist spirituality.

To the *Ksatreya*, however, the bow was a favorite and noble weapon which they trained with until high degrees of perfection were reached. Whereas the footsoldier's use of the bow and arrow was simply to swamp an enemy soldier's attack with arrows and kill as many as possible in the shortest amount of time, the *Ksatreya* used expertise toward specific targets. We can read in the scriptures of the use of the *nalika*, a hollow iron arrow which penetrated so deeply they could knock down a charging elephant. Arjuna is said to have fired one which sunk into an elephant's body up to its feathers.

The *ksurapra* and *ardhacandra* were circular and crescent-shaped razor-sharp arrowheads used to cut off opponents' heads, or the limbs of horses. (Similar types were used by the ancient Romans.) The expertise of the *Ksatreya* is such that one named Ekalavya is said to have shot seven arrows into a dog's mouth while it was barking before it had time to close it. (It was said that the dog was not seriously hurt but could bark no more.) Arjuna is said to have shot twelve arrows into the open end of a cow's horn while it was swung to and fro from a rope. We can see from such accounts that the Bow was regarded as a special, almost sacred, weapon. It was removed from a warrior's right hand as the last act of his funeral rite. Unlike the mass destruction devices of the People's Army, the bow was used by the *Ksatreya* only in battles against other *Ksatreyas*.

Figure 77. The battle of Kurukshetra, mentioned in the Mahabharata, in which Bhima and Durodhana fought. Here the various weaponry of the Ksatreya is clearly seen. (Victoria & Albert Museum, London.)

Figure 78. Jayadratha and Abhimanu fight with their sacred Bows from their war Chariots. (Temple carving at Ahichchatra [Uttar Pradesh] India.)

The scriptures abound with their feats of archery which became the subject for many legends and epic stories. All the paraphernalia of archery, the bowstring, the armguards, quivers, etc., were eulogized in hymns and verse throughout the sacred literature. Arjuna, a warrior hero of the Bhagavad Gita, being ambidextrous (*savyasacin*) could shoot one equally well from either hand. One significant, although perhaps not unexpected, result of having sophisticated human destruction devices, lay in the carnage they caused. The scenes after a battle were often more horrific than the fight itself. It was such scenes that turned the Monarch Asoka away from warfare toward Buddhism.

UNARMED FIGHTING

Fighting without weapons was a specialty of the *Ksatreya* and footsoldier alike. For the *Ksatreya* it was simply part and parcel of their all around training, but for the lowly peasant it was essential. Often peasants who joined a professional military force had little money for either weapons or armor. We read in the Vedas of men unable to afford armor who bound their heads with turbans called *Usnisa* to protect themselves from sword and axe blows.

Fighting on foot for a *Ksatreya* was necessary in case he was unseated from his chariot or horse and found himself without weapons. Although the high ethical code of the *Ksatreya* forbid anyone but another *Ksatreya* from attacking him, doubtless such morals were not always observed, and when faced with an unscrupulous opponent, the *Ksatreya* needed to be able to defend himself, and developed, therefore, a very effective form of hand-to-hand combat that combined techniques of wrestling, throws, and hand strikes. Tactics of movement and

Figure 79. Two lesser deities fighting. The unarmed combatant has performed a flying kick to his opponents thighs. (Lucknow State Museum, India.)

evasion were formulated that were later passed on to successive generations. This skill was called *Vajramukti*, a name meaning "thunderbolt closed—or clasped—hands."

This title, *Vajramukti*, used both by the Brahmins and the early *Ksatreyas* to describe their art, has several possible origins. One is that it referred to the usage of the hands in a manner as powerful as the *vajra maces* of traditional warfare. Alternatively, the word *vajra* actually referred to the weapon of Indra and indicated the speed, power, and divine-like origin of the art.

The thunderbolt, we should recall, was the favorite weapon of the deity, Indra. Such an interpretation would have appealed to the more religious *Ksatreya* warriors for it implied a divine approval of their practice, especially if they were called upon to fight infidels.

Vajramukti was practiced in peacetime by means of regular physical training sessions and these utilized sequences of attack and defense technically termed in Sanskrit *nata* [Note 36h]. As the *Ksatreya* practiced both armed and unarmed, we know that unarmed forms of *nata* would also have been taught to them by their *acaryas* (masters). Over a long period of time most of the possible and useful combinations of attack/defense would have been recognized, preserved, and included into their *nata* trainings.

As the years went by and combat experience increased, the *Ksatreya* developed more balanced, all inclusive, methods of practice which eventually evolved into predetermined, set patterns of practice movements, each emphasizing different principles and practices, etc. The *nata* were differentiated according to their value and technical emphasis.

The tactical necessities of warfare also modified training in the *nata*. Irrespective of the disposition of their enemies, some *Ksatreya* groups fought more with their elephant troops, others with their footsoldiers close by. The four divisions of the traditional Indian armies each required a different type of interaction for the *Ksatreya* and these provided an impetus to adapt aspects of the *nata* training to suit the battle environment. For instance, in the midst of an elephant brigade, great care had to be taken not to be trampled; in the midst of the close hand-to-hand struggle favored by footsoldier battalions, more care had to be taken to protect one's flanks, etc. To account for these different requirements, certain types of movement sequences were practiced more often than others. Often *Vajramukti* training would be altered to accord with the type of battle or opponents the practitioners would be most likely to meet on the battlefield.

From this impetus, various types of *nata* developed. These were eventually given different names, names which often distinguished the emphasis they placed upon different types of movement or maneuver. It was perhaps by means of the *nata* that the trainee *Ksatreya* first came into contact with the discipline which formed the basis of the self-control expected and required of their status.

Figure 80. Krishna engaged in combat attempts a throwing technique. (Lucknow State Museum, India.)

From time immemorial, one of the *Ksatreya* titles for their monarchs, and later of many other nations, was that of "Lion" (Sanskrit: *Simha*), the King of Beasts. Together with the associated title of "Sun" (Sanskrit: *Surya*), the two terms loom large in the Oriental and royal (Sanskrit: *Rajah*) repertoire of personal names. Many Indian monarchs, and also teachers of esoteric Buddhism, had a name containing the word "Lion" (even now the animal features on Indian postage stamps). Shakyamuni Buddha was said to pronounce his teachings with the "Lion's Roar" (*Simhanada*. Japanese: *Shiku*) of the Shakya clan—an indirect reference to the *Ksatreya* fighting cries, for the particle *nada* also means a warrior's scream or howl of battle. This was said to be able to "freeze birds in midflight, halt fish in midstroke and utterly subdue elephants." The *Anguttara Nikaya* (V 32–36) associates such a cry with the "Ten Powers" of a Bodhisattva. Shakyamuni's Grandfather was named Simhahanu ("A Lion of Reliability," Chinese: *Shih li*; Japanese: *Shiri*). Generally the inclusion of the epithet "Lion" within a name or title is a good sign that the person bearing it was both of a *Ksatreya* lineage (Sanskrit: *Gotra*) and, as such, had been trained, or was familiar with, the art of *Vajramukti*.

The warrior traditions of India then were well-established in the *Ksatreya* environment that Shakyamuni was born into. The early records concerning Shakyamuni's childhood clearly recount his practice of the martial arts. When 7 years old, the teachers Arata, Kalama, and Rudrakarama began instructing him in the *Pancavidya* (Five Arts) of the *Ksatreya* and Kshantideva is said to have instructed him in the physical arts, which included grappling, boxing, gymnastics and weaponry. According to the Chinese accounts of his youth recounted in the *Lalitavistara*, when he was 10 years old he hurled an elephant some distance with such power that the depression made by its falling body

Figure 81. Siddhartha, prior to becoming a Buddha, excelled at many martial arts. Here he is shown firing the winning arrow at a competition. (Painting in the grotto temple of Dambulla at Matal, Ceylon.)

was named *Hastatigarta* (elephant ditch) and was used afterward as a water channel by local villagers. He is also said to have fired arrows with such power that one of them hit a rock and opened an artesian spring, thereafter named the *Sarakupa* (arrow well).

There is no doubt that the young Shakyamuni was highly trained and skilled in all the warrior arts as befitted his status of son and heir to the reigning monarch. He was fully "body aware," and his keenness and perseverance in practicing the physical mortifications associated with the traditional development of spirituality also tends to demonstrate this fact.

As all *Ksatreya* were considered to be of royal status, their practice and trainings (*Pratipatti* and *Siksa*) of the *Vajramukti* and its *nata* practices were called the "Lion's Play, Art, or Skill" (*Simhavikridita*). This epithet eventually became the general name for all the structured *Vajramukti* sequences. The *Ksatreya* warriors who practiced these sequences were called *Simhanata*, "those who practice the lion's art movements." This was the origin of the sequences introduced into China and later developed into the considerably shortened but famous "Lion Dance" of Chinese New Year festivals.

The *Ksatreya* kept their *nata* trainings to themselves as part of their own elite training method but, as such things cannot be hidden from a mass of people among whom one is often fighting for one's life, many of the techniques were copied and adapted by the enlisted army. Such adaptations developed later into another school of practice which came to be called the "Striking Tiger" School, perhaps in an unconscious mimicry of the *Ksatreya* "Lion."

Tiger striking, which is explained more fully later on, was practiced by both the common soldier and the *Ksatreya* equally, although it is highly likely that its techniques were in fact developed by the *Ksatreya* doctors primarily for emergency first aid purposes. Like all medicine, it could both cure or kill depending upon how it was applied.

The inner teachings of *Vajramukti*, and its *nata*, were always considered to be highly secret and only to be taught to persons of high moral character. It was usually only practiced by the upper echelons of Indian *Ksatreya* society and was transmitted orally from master (*acarya*) to disciple (*sisya*) over the generations.

Combative techniques had many precedents within Hindu religious literature. *The Mahabarata* describes the god Krishna as a great fighter. *The Salya Parva* describes a fight between two of its heroes named Bhima and Duryodhana and mentions them using maneuvers such as *Kausika* (jumping up and down), *Yamaka* (turns to right and left), *Gomutraka* (zigzag movement). Such sequences of tactical movement were technically called "mandalas."

Figure 82. Vasudeva carries the infant Krishna across the river Yamuna. Two Ksatreya guards protect him, one of whom nervously looks backward for assailants. (Temple at Amritpur [Karnataka District], India. From author's collection.)

Bhima is also described having a marathon unarmed fight with Jarasandha involving such techniques. He whirls Jarasandha around one hundred times above his head and throws him to the ground, killing him. Later Bhima defeats a *Yaksa* by breaking him in half with a "bow and arrow" hold.

In the *Bhagavad Gita*, a title meaning "Song of the One Who is Dear to Us," there is an account of a warrior king named Arjuna who, on the eve of an important battle, has great doubts about participating in it, and almost decides to surrender. Suddenly the God Krishna appears to him and they begin a long dialogue in which Krishna reminds him, among other things, about divine morality and the ethics of warfare. Their discussion ranges over many themes, and Arjuna is concerned with the amount of killing which will take place.

In fact, Arjuna assumes an attitude which is consonant with the Buddhist. Krishna however, by emphasizing specifically Hindu virtues such as predestination, duty to one's God etc., persuades him to go through with it. *The Gita* is filled with praises for the warrior and the duty to engage in war. Arjuna is told, "it is his nature to fight" (*prakritis tvam niyoksyati*), that everyone is born to act (*karma karayate*) helplessly (*avasah*) by the impulses of nature (*prtakrtijaih*). He is told to "Remember me and fight" (*mamanusmara yuddha ca*), that his actions have been predetermined by the past (*pubbe kata hetu*).

Although *The Gita* does stress the duty of the warrior both to fight without cruelty and to protect others unselfishly, much of this ethic concerning warfare is at variance to other paths within Hindu teachings, such as that of the *Jnana marga* (Way of Wisdom). It is clear, at least according to *The Gita*, that the *Ksatreya* was placed under strong obligations toward his monarch and the state, irrespective of what he individually may have believed.

Unlike the Chinese, to whom winning a battle was most important, the Indians interwove life and death with spiritual destinies and maintained a very high degree of ethical conduct. We should also recall that to the ancient *Ksatreya* monarchs, *how* the battle was won, and the motives for fighting it, were at least as important as winning. Ancient China had no equivalent attitudes to Arjuna's. Its oldest book on warfare (the *Sun Tzu*) is a masterpiece of cunning, trickery, and tactical exploitation of the enemy.

HISTORICAL CONTEXT

We must now look briefly at the historical development of India in order to appreciate the social environment into which the *nata* emerged. After this we will consider the *nata* further, for it was their sequences which were taken by monks into China and developed into a native form which, in turn, gave rise to many of the Buddhist physical meditation arts.

Buddhism has a long and extensive influence within India, its teachings spreading far into China, Malaysia, and westward into Iran, Turkey, and beyond. Indian history can be classified into four great historical periods in which monarchs governed their realms according to Buddhist ethics and precepts. We can assume that in all of their monarchical regions the cultured arts of Buddhism were all well known.

The first great period came under the King Asoka (circa 269–232 B.C.). His was a time of great cultural expansion, peacefulness, and sin-

Figure 83. Part of the Asoka Pillar bearing inscriptions in Karosthi script Sanskrit. (Courtesy Kosei Publishing Co., Japan.)

cerity. Asoka, a warrior monarch sickened at the mass slaughters he had encountered in his many battles, became a devout Buddhist and commenced an enlightened reign in which the execution of people and the slaying of animals was forbidden. Later in his life, and in pursuit of Buddhist principles, he became a wandering beggar after giving away all his property and power.

Next came the Kushan Dynasty (first century B.C. to fifth century A.D.). During this time, regular contact was maintained as far west as Rome and the Middle East, and as far east as China and Malaya [Note 34g]. This was followed by the Gupta Dynasty (fourth to seventh century A.D.). One of its monarchs, Harsha, revitalized the Sanskrit language and Indian cultural arts. He sponsored sculptures, temples, art, drama, and Buddhist *nata* in all their forms. It is only from this dynasty that the Hindu *nata* can be dated. Lastly, the Pala Dynasty arose (around A.D. 750) until it was extinguished by the Muslim invasions.

In ancient Hinduism, *nata* was acknowledged as a spiritual study and conferred a ruling deity, Nataraja, representing the awakening of wisdom through physical and mental concentration. However, after the Muslim invasion of India and its brutal destruction of Buddhist and Hindu culture and religion, the *Ksatreya* art of *nata* was dispersed and many of its teachers slain. Due to these invasions, subsequent traditions of *nata* which arose within Hindu India drew inspiration from sources such as the southern Indian (*Dravidian*) folk dance and developed very

Figure 84. Nataraja. The Lord of the Nata, in traditional position. (Author's collection.)

different orientations from its original form. These different sources resulted in the *nata* becoming a popular performance art of mime and dance, reflecting mainly the myths and legends of the Hindu religious past, rather than the energetic, body-oriented form of the *Kasatreya* spiritual warrior training. It is only in these *Dravidian* areas of India that indigenous martial arts, under the name of *Kalari* exist nowadays.

When Buddhism came to influence India (circa 500 B.C.), the Deity Nataraja was converted to become one of the four protectors of Buddhism, and was renamed *Nar(y)ayana Deva* (Chinese: *Na Lo Yen Tien*). He is said to be a protector of the Eastern hemisphere of the mandala.

The Muslim invasions and subsequent slaughter of Buddhist monks and nuns caused many to flee into Southern India, China, and elsewhere. Because of this, much of what we know concerning *nata* within Indian Buddhism comes to us via Chinese tradition and Buddhist writing. Refugees carried with them living knowledge, not only of Buddhist spiritual teaching, but also of its cultural arts and skillful means of teaching. The Gupta and Pala Dynasty *nata* would have been among these, and doubtless continued to be developed by subsequent Buddhist Masters [Note 34a].

In the countries to which the Buddhist *nata* were taken, particularly Thailand, Korea, and Malaysia, we find evidence of various unarmed martial arts, which were (or are) still practiced with *nata* movement patterns and techniques, even though Buddhism, itself, has been largely forgotten or replaced by other teachings. It is not difficult to recognize their connection with the Buddhist *nata* if one knows something of them.

In *The White Lotus Sutra* (*Saddharma Pundarika Sutra*; Japanese: *Myoho Renge Kyo*) [Note 2c], whose extant text dates from around the second century A.D. (and thus is coincident with the Kushan Dynasty), we can read in Section 14 of the practice of *nata*. It occurs in the Sutra within a context bidding the Bodhisattva-Mahasattva to "avoid all contact with evil or cruel persons who brutally practice sports and the arts of boxing, wrestling, and *nata*."

Although modern Sanskritists usually present the term *nata* as one describing the Indian classical art of representing events and characters in the Hindu scriptures by means of highly stylized dance, mime, and acting, this is not the meaning of the term as evidenced within the Buddhist Sutras. The term *nata* in Mahayana Buddhism described "body nourishing movement sequences" of "a demanding nature," performed by one who was "vigorous and determined." It referred not to a spectator-oriented activity of entertainment or pleasure (as were the Hindu *nata*) but to the practice of warriors. Even popular Buddhist dictionaries often mistranslate this term through borrowing from modern Sanskrit (i.e., Hindu) reference texts [Notes 36m, 37].

In the Sutra passage, four classes of people are enumerated, namely those who practice brutal sport, those who practice boxing, those who practice wrestling and those who practice *nata*. After this particular reference, the Sutra then goes on to enumerate other classes of people who all keep, catch and then kill living animals. It highlights the fact that all those enumerated are concerned with the taking of life, be it human or otherwise. It would seem therefore highly unlikely that in the midst of such a list there is placed a term meant to indicate actors, dancers or mime artistes! The Sanskrit word *natavajra* (thunderbolt *nata*) was a colloquial Buddhist term of this period for someone who was strong, "manly," and "physically stable" [Note 36b,c].

We also find the term *nata* in other Theravada and Mahayana texts such as the *Asokavadana* (Story of King Asoka) and also the *Gilgit Manuscript* (3;Part 3) of the *Mulasarvastivada Vinaya* (Rules for Monks). This tells a story in which Shakyamuni Buddha, while traveling in the Surasana country, predicts that on a particular wooded hill he can see there will be a monastery built by two brothers whose names will be Nata and Bhata, and that this monastery will become very famous and be known as the Natabhata.

In the Chinese edition of the Sanskrit original, the term *nata* is represented by the two phonetic characters which attempt to convey, in the Chinese language, the original sound of the Sanskrit term. Such transliterations, rather than translations, of Sanskrit are always difficult to "reverse interpret," as phonetics are capable of a wide range of possible meanings.

A common error made in interpreting these Chinese characters for *nata* is to apply the relatively modern Hindu religious explanation of the term as being the one used by ancient Buddhists. Such interpretation is not surprising if one does not know of the *Ksatreya* traditions or their technical meanings of the word.

Another possible explanation of the Chinese characters used in the *Saddharma Pundarika* and sometimes in other scriptures, is that they represent not only the word *nata* but another, closely related term, *narya*. The phonetic characters used to represent the word *narya* were also used to equally represent the sounds of the Sanskrit words pronounced as *Na Ra, Na Lo, Na Rya*, or *Na La* [Note 36b,c]. Since *nata* and *narya* were written with identical characters in Chinese, they were pronounced in the same way, and there is no definite way to distinguish between them [Note 36, l].

The term *narya* describes—apart from its Hindu religious usage as both the name of a deity and the name of the first human created by Brahma which here is inappropriate—"a strong and vigorous man," or, "one who can stand firmly against others" [Note 36b]. *Narya* was also occasionally used to represent both the formal movement practices

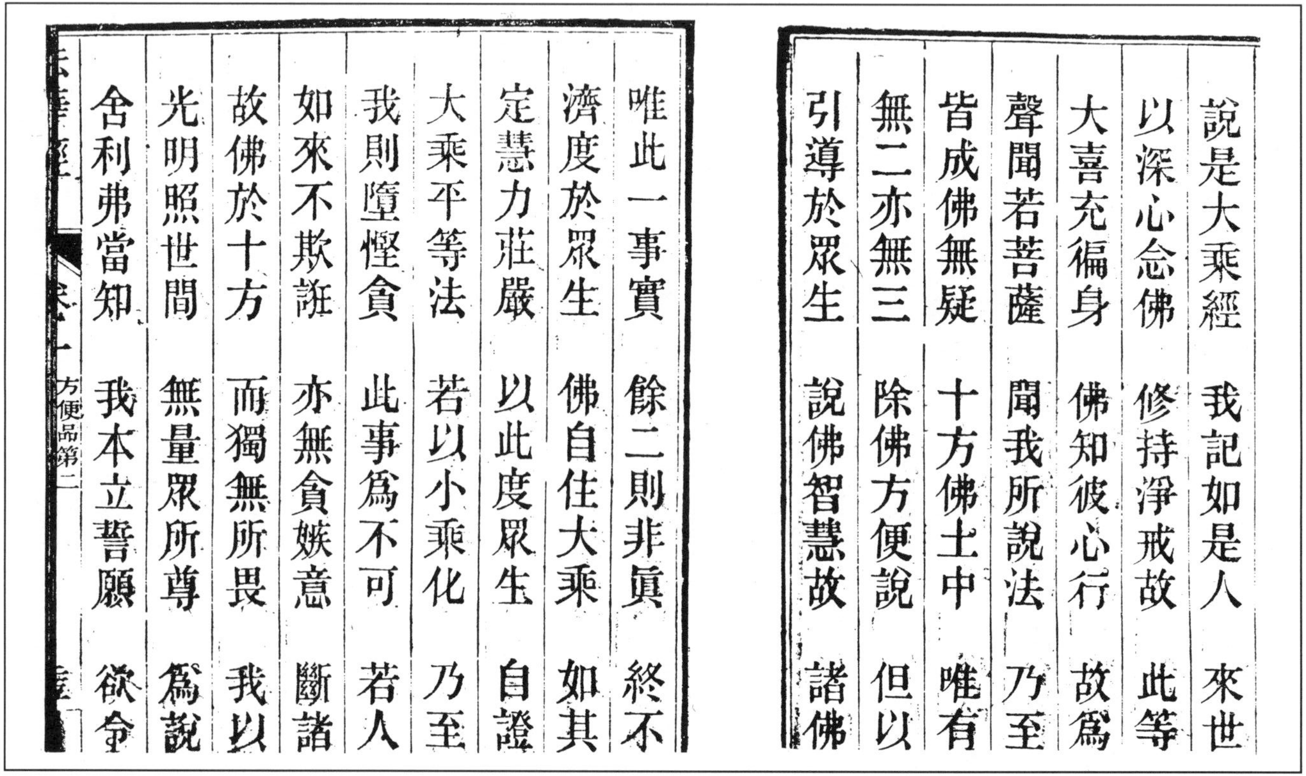

（妙法蓮華經 方便品第二）

說是大乘經　我記如是人　來世成佛道　以深心念佛　修持淨戒故　此等聞得佛　大喜充徧身　佛知彼心行　故為說大乘　聲聞若菩薩　聞我所說法　乃至於一偈　皆成佛無疑　十方佛土中　唯有一乘法　無二亦無三　除佛方便說　但以假名字　引導於眾生　說佛智慧故　諸佛出於世

唯此一事實　餘二則非真　終不以小乘　濟度於眾生　佛自住大乘　如其所得法　定慧力莊嚴　以此度眾生　自證無上道　大乘平等法　若以小乘化　乃至於一人　我則墮慳貪　此事為不可　若人信歸佛　如來不欺誑　亦無貪嫉意　斷諸法中惡　故佛於十方　而獨無所畏　我以相嚴身　光明照世間　無量眾所尊　為說實相印　舍利弗當知　我本立誓願　欲令一切眾

方便品第二

Figure 85. Pages of an ancient Chinese Lotus Sutra. (Kongoryuji Temple.)

of the *Ksatreya* warriors of India and the unarmed art, itself. The *Saddharma Pundarika Sutra* usage clearly refers to one who practices "manly heroic movements" (*narya*). What is also clearly evident in this Sutra passage is that the art of *nata/narya* is distinguished from the art of boxing, i.e., the common peoples' practice of fist fighting. Such ambilocutory terminology is inevitable when a sophisticated language such as Sanskrit is rendered into Chinese by means of phonetics.

The *Lotus Sutra* is an early import into China, coming in around the second century. It was not until later that editions of the scriptures were made which actually translated the meanings of the Sanskrit terms into their approximate Chinese equivalents. It is also not surprising to find such technical terms preserved within Sutras, for the strict caste system of India, although not approved of by all Buddhists, was still linguistically acknowledged and recorded in Buddhist writings.

We can see this from the caste titles of people who came and spoke with the Buddha, as all of the Hindu caste terminologies were recorded as they were encountered by the various disciples. If the *Ksatreya* art was known in the Buddhas time as *nata* or *narya*, it would be recorded as such. Our little puzzle lies not with the Sanskrit meaning, but with the Chinese presentation of the term. Whatever way we translate the term (*nata* or *narya*) a common theme of physical vigor (and not sport or pleasure) pervades both.

In the *Si Yu Ki*, an account of the Indian travels of the Monk Fa Hsien, he mentions meeting a *Narasimha* (*Naryasimha*). This title represented the leaders of areas of India who were clearly not of royal descent but rather like localized *maharajhas*. They commanded large mercenary armies and from this we can see that both the title particles *simha* and *narya* persisted within India even as late as his travels (circa 629 A.D.).

Vajadhara has the power of Narayana, he has the Power of Mahanarayana (*Mahavairocana Sutra*, Ch.1) [Note 84b].

In another paragraph of the *Saddharma Pundarika Sutra*, we can also read of men performing what is represented in Chinese characters as the arts of *Shang-Cha* and *Shang-Po*. These two are also Romanized as *Hsiang-Cha* and *Hsiang Pu* [Note 38]. In Chinese *Hsiang* means either "mutual, characteristics, aspects or interchange." It was used in Chinese Buddhist literature to represent the Buddhist Sanskrit term *Laksana*, or *Nimmita*, both meaning "characteristic," or "distinctive signs."

The term *cha* is a native Chinese one. In manuscripts of the Sutra it is often found represented by an over-simplified character form which stems from the Chinese term *chiao* meaning, in one way of writing it, "connection(s)" or, in another way of writing, "exchanging," "associating," "crossing," "inter-secting or -acting," or "handing over" [See Note 36b].

All of these latter terms mostly refer to actions performed with, or through, the hands. The Sanskrit terms for what *Hsiang Cha* implies here mean something else again, but more of that elsewhere.

In Japanese, *Hsiang Cha* is pronounced *Bo Ko*. *Hsiang Po* means "distinctive (or adhering) grasping" and refers to grappling or wrestling. It is a much more common Chinese term and is pronounced in modern Japanese as *sumo*—a famous form of wrestling which many do not realize comes from China [Note 34e]. Japanese *sumo* still preserves many ancient Chinese practices and rituals identical to the *nata* and its derivatives (e.g., *sumo* bouts are held within a circular area). There is also a ritualistic bowing ceremony common to both.

As a matter of interest the suffix, *po* derives from the ancient Chinese character meaning "one in authority," or "one permitted to strike you." It stems from the Sanskrit root for "father" (*pitra*) [Note 36c]. From this Sanskrit root, we get the Latin *pater*. The Japanese character for *fu* (father) is a simplified form descending from the Chinese *po*. This ancient reference from the *Rengekyo* is just one of many found throughout Buddhist literature, and which are often not fully appreciated by either martial art researchers or religious scholars.

Due to the passing away of the *nata/narya* tradition, later Buddhist schools, while preserving many of the physically oriented (but statically performed) meditation exercises and some terminology of *nata/narya*, were unable to fully appreciate their significance as kinetic Buddhist practices [Notes 2d, 37]. Representations of Buddhist *nata* movements and positions are preserved pictorially in the mandalas of esoteric Buddhism, usually in a form of the Vajramukti or Vajrasandhi Bodhisattva (Chinese: *Chinkang Chuan Pusa*) holding his hands in the "*vajra* closed hands on guard" position. These form part of the mandala quarter ruled by the Amoghasiddhi Buddha (Chinese: *Pu Kung Cheng Tzu*; Japanese: *Fukujoju*).

Fukujoju is the embodiment of the wisdom of enlightened, all-encompassing and discriminating mental and physical activity (Sanskrit: *Krytyanusthanajnana*). Simultaneously, this reveals and liberates knowledge of the physical training required for its generation and demonstration (*Paravikriditasikksa*). This latter particularly applies to that insight wisdom required to make decisions and judgments.

The whole art of tactical encounter (Chinese: *Hsien Hsiu*; Japanese: *Senjitsu*) used within Vajramukti emanates from this aspect of wisdom. Whereas in ordinary fighting arts *Senjutsu* indicates an art of strategy and counterattack, within the fold of Buddhism it described skill in acts of non-harmful defense toward one's opponent.

The art of defensive blocking naturally arose from within this practice. We can see examples of such tactics echoed in the earliest Chinese accounts. The commentary upon the *Prajnaparamita* of Nagarjuna

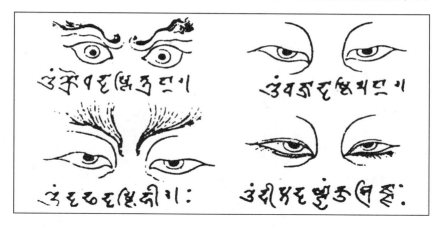

Figure 86. The Four Eyes, or grimaces, described in the Gobushinkan. (Author's Collection.)

describes five types of eyes which are, in fact, postures of the face assumed in order to convey an impression to evil forces (which category includes humanity). Such bodily postures are termed in Sanskrit *Vijnaptikayakrita*, a word which is described as indicating, "a non-verbal or bodily communication by means of a sign, gesture or other form of intimation." It is utilized in daily life happenings (e.g., a secretary answers the phone to hear someone say he wishes to talk to her boss. When she looks up at her boss he frowns at her, and understanding the significance of such a frown, she tells her caller her boss is not available at that moment). Familiarity with the many patterns of *Vijnaptikayakrita* was an important skill to any warrior, as it enabled him to "read" the intentions of a possible opponent prior to any action on his part.

After its adoption by Buddhism, the indigenous *Ksatreya* system of unarmed self-defense known already by the Sanskrit title *Vajramukti* was, in Buddhist circles, renamed Bodhisattva Vajramukti (Chinese: *Pu Sa Chin Kang Chuan*). This indicated the thunderbolt-like art (Sanskrit: *vajra*) which served to integrate mind, speech and body equally by means of the clasped hand art (*mukti*) for the benefit of all others [Note 34b].

Esoteric Buddhism (Chinese: *Mi Chiao*, or *Pi Mi*) in India and China especially concentrated upon attaining a balance of calm and wisdom between the three experiential areas through which Mahavairocana Buddha (the most important Buddha in the Mikkyo path) communicated the ultimate truth. These three areas are considered to be mind, body, and speech. The "body" aspect concerned itself with *Mudra* (Chinese: *yin*). This word loosely indicates the symbolic, ritualized, hand gestures, reflecting the degrees, powers, and aspects of spiritual attainment.

Figure 87. Illustration of a meditation visualization depicting Shakyamuni surrounded by different Bodhisattvas, each of whom forms a distinctive hand mudra. To the front, surrounded by flames, is Acala Vidyaraja, one of the five "Kings of Light" whose fire burns away passion. The rope he holds in his left hand binds and restrains the passions and his sword cuts away ignorance. (Author's collection.)

What are practiced as sanctified gestures in modern Japanese esoteric Buddhism are in fact often static forms of the components of *Vajramukti nata* sequences [Note 21].

> Make a Fist with the right hand. Hold it in such a way as to strike out. This is the Mudra of confrontation (*Abhimukkha*) (*Mahavairocana Sutra*. Ch.9)

We can see that the hands themselves were regarded at several levels of symbolic interpretation. Their static forms took shape within the mudra, which represented quiescent, eternal, and unlimited qualities of the Buddha's enlightened wisdom. Their dynamic form (which included the whole body) manifested within the sequences of the *Vajramukti nata*. These *nata* expressed the active, creative practice of the insights available to humankind when they approached total enlightenment.

There is sometimes confusion with the title *Vajramukti* because as well as describing the Hindu and Buddhist defensive arts, in the sixth and seventh centuries it was also used occasionally to describe the path of esoteric Buddhism in general. However, although written with identical Roman characters, the two titles have different Chinese characters and mean different things. Despite this, there are still some instances when monks refer to the art in either of the ways.

The suffix *mukti* (Pali: *mukkha*), when used as a description of a state of consciousness, properly means "spiritual liberation." It stems from the same Sanskrit root as the term *moksha*, which is also used to describe a form of spiritual liberation in both Buddhism and Hinduism.

In the Bodhisattva Vajramukti art, the successor of *nata*, the suffix *mukti* means "clasped hand." A chart will perhaps make this more clear.

Sanskrit	Chinese	Japanese	English
Vajramukti	*Ching Kang Chuan*	*Kongoken*	Clasped Hand of the Thunderbolt
Vajramukti	*Ching Kang Chieh*	*Kongogedatsu*	Liberating Thunderbolt

In the esoteric mandalas, deities representing both of these spiritual aspects, and their associated skills, have always been clearly represented. The title *Vajramukti* indicates the early connections of the art with Esoteric Buddhist teachings, as the prefix *vajra* was common among its followers as a designator of an *Acarya* lineage tradition, and we can find many esoteric texts, rituals, and teachings prefixed by the word *vajra*. This usage was not, however, exclusive to purely esoteric Buddhism, for we can find this prefix also used by the Chaan, Tien T'ai and other schools within China which recognized the principles of, but were not exclusively devoted to esoteric, integrative Buddhism.

In addition to the *mukti* suffix, other Sanskrit words, such as *Dharma* (teachings), *pala* (protector), *pani*, *kara* and *hasta*, meaning "hands", *sandhi*, and *khataka*, both meaning "closed fist," were also and equally used.

In general Sanskrit terms describing hands (*pani*, *sandhi*, *hasta*, or *kara*) in a Buddhist title usually indicated that the hands they referred to were intended to be understood as representative symbols for some aspect of enlightened creative wisdom. Thus these terms (*hasta*, etc.) referred to the hand(s) as a source or representative of a spiritually based skill or power.

Buddhist records at other times referred directly to the physical hands and we can find Bodhisattvas bearing names such as *Vajrapani* (Hands of the Thunderbolt) and *Vajradhara* (he who holds the Thunderbolt) included in the esoteric Buddhist mandalas found in China, Tibet, and Japan. Parts of these names were also used as epithets of certain famous Chinese monk warriors. In both the Tibetan and Mongolian artistic traditions, many Bodhisattvas are depicted in combat positions and poses of hand and limb.

In the early scriptures [e.g., *Mahajima Nikaya* 2:78–105] there is a direct reference to features and skills of the hands in an account of the bandit named Angulimala. The name *Angulimala* means "finger" (*anguli*), "rosary," or, "neck garland" (*mala*). It is told how he, after killing and robbing his victims, would cut off their fingers and string them upon a necklace he wore. Everyone feared him and avoided the forest he lived within.

When the Buddha proposed to visit a certain town, the road he intended to use went directly through the forest in which Angulimala lay in wait for his victims. The Buddha's hosts warned him about this but the Buddha was undeterred. Presently, after he had spotted him, Angulimala attempted to attack the Buddha. The resulting events are extremely amusing. After the Buddha converts Angulimala he takes him back as a companion to the village he had just departed, but no one recognizes Buddha's companion as the reformed murderer. In the midst of the subsequent feast the Buddha suddenly announces that his companion, whom everyone had assumed was another monk and with whom they had spoken to and offered food, etc., is Angulimala. The result of this announcement is that all the guests at the meal halt in mid-sentence or mouthful and, with screams, flee from the room. The Buddha had to work hard to persuade them all to return.

This story was later re-presented in an allegorical manner, explaining that the fingers represent the "body" (*anga*) of the various spiritual attainments the Bodhisattva must earn to generate enlightenment. Their being cut off and strung on a necklace represents the failure to practice and attain the "limbs" (Sanskrit: *anga*) of enlightenment [Note 31]. Thus it can be seen that all of us wear an *angulimala* of some type during our own lives. The figure of Angulimala, himself, represents the craving for the mundane world, along with all its values, materialistic attractions, and distractions.

The hand as a symbolic designator was used very early on in Buddhist and Vedic literature, perhaps because its digits were convenient symbols of the Five Elements of Nature (*Mahabhuta*) and the hands themselves of the Two Truths (*Dvasatya*) [see Notes 21, 44, 68].

Your own Body is the Thunderbolt—Firm and Indestructible.

Shan Wu Wei
quoting the *Vajrasekharasutra*
(*Kongochokyo*, Ch. 1).

THE TITLES VAJRAMUKTI AND CHUAN FA

The Tang Chinese equivalent for the title *Vajramukti, Chuan Fa* (Japanese: *Kempo*) was a nominal approximation used by monks for that section of the Buddhist Vajramukti art concerned with ritualized movement practices which contained the principles of health preservation, weaponless self-defense and meditative insight.

The term *Chuan Fa* was commonly used from the Tang Dynasty onward by many to represent in general these aspects of the Vajramukti practices which missionary monks imported from India. Much later it was exported to offshore islands such as Taiwan and the Ryukyus, where the title was pronounced *Kempo* [See Note 61]. This is the name it was known by to the Ryukyuan/Japanese, some of whom were its very last recipients.

The actual Tang Chinese character particle *chuan* (meaning "closed or clasped hand") used to represent the Sanskrit term *mukti* was chosen not because of its historical roots within the *Ksatreya's* India—which may not at that time have been fully known by all—but instead, or also, because it occurs in a recorded and relevant incident [Note 48] within the life of Shakyamuni Buddha.

Fearful that the Buddha might die without teaching some vital important principle, one of his disciples asked him if there was any other teaching he had not so far shown them. The Buddha replied by taking up a handful of leaves from the ground and asking the disciple whether these leaves in his hand were greater in number than the leaves upon the trees in the forest they were in. When the disciple replied that there were more leaves upon the trees than those in his hand, the Buddha said so it was with his teaching. What he had shown his disciples was compared to the leaves in his hand. What he could have taught he compared to the leaves upon the trees in the forest.

The Buddha then said he did not have the *clasped hand* (Chinese: *chuan shou*) of the teacher, but rather he had the *open hand* (Chinese: *kai shou*) of a Buddha [Note 50]. Though there were many doctrines, he had concerned himself only with what was most important for those around him to attain enlightenment.

Thus, the term "clasped hand" used here (*chuan*) was thought to be appropriate to describe the Vajramukti method, as its mastery was considered an esoteric and difficult to understand lineage practice, taught only by a few masters to even fewer students. By comparison the ordinary (exoteric) teaching of the Buddha was an "open-handed teaching" (Chinese: *kai shou fa*).

The word *chuan* is etymologically related to the ideograph used to describe a manuscript text (also pronounced *chuan*) but using slightly different characters. We often find accounts of the Chinese Buddhist Sutras existing in two or more *chuan* for it is a term identifying a document which, having been written upon manuscript paper is rolled up or folded, for protection and storage. This "turning inward to protect" action of the paper is what is meant by the title *chuan* for a written work. The ideograph for clasped hand (*chuan*) also describes this same type of action in the fingers.

The suffix *fa* was the Chinese transliteration of the Sanskrit term *dharma* (teachings of the Buddha). Such a suffix was commonly used throughout Chinese Buddhism to represent not just the teachings themselves but all the arts, crafts, and practices associated with them. Thus it also could also mean techniques, methods, or manners of practice, i.e., it could be used, as a suffix, to represent a particular sect.

While China later developed many localized names or terms for schools or later traditions of *Chuan Fa*, the essential meaning and nature of the art conveyed in this title was unchanged. If we "reverse translate" the meaning of *Chuan Fa* back into Sanskrit we see that it literally means *Dharmamukti* ("closed hand of the Dharma"). In the matrix and womb mandalas of esoteric Buddhism, both the Buddha and Bodhisattva representing the skills and practices of this art are depicted.

Figure 88. A figure from 14th century Japan based upon the Chinese models. Note how the left hand position has been simplified into a fist. This was common to later times as the techniques of Chuan Fa were forgotten—or, as in the case of Japan—never introduced. (Freer Gallery of Art in the Smithsonian Museum, Washington, DC.)

There are, of course, other, and more well known, representations of these forces and powers such as *Vajrasattva* (Essence of the Thunderbolt), *Vajrapani* (He of the Thunderbolt Hands) and *Vajradhara* (He Who Grasps the Thunderbolt) [See Note 56].

We should be always aware that Buddhist Chinese is often very different from both the modern and the classical (Taoist or Confucian) forms of the language in its understanding or perception of what certain characters mean or imply. It is for this reason that special dictionaries of Buddhist Chinese terms need to be used for study or research.

> To those who must be saved he appears as a Diamond-holding God and preaches them the Law (*Myohorengekyo* Ch. 25).

Many a Buddhist temple possesses statues of the *Dharmapalas* (Chinese: *Fa Huo*; Japanese: *Hogo*), idealized portrayals of the Protectors of the Doctrine. These are often found flanking its entrance door or on either side of the main altars of important shrines and esoteric temples. They are usually depicted in the form of the two Vajra Kings (Chinese: *Ching Kang Wang*; Japanese: *Kongo-O*) and in Japan are named *Mishaku* (*Red*

Figure 89. Tung Huang cave statues of a Bodhisattva (left) and two guardians (right) who are in "on guard" positions of Chuan Fa. (China News Agency.)

Kongo) and *Naraen* (*Narayana Kongo*), the latter being, as we learned previously, the synonym used in India for practitioners of the Vajramukti.

These are usually portrayed assuming the classical defense stances of *Chuan Fa* and performing tactically significant *mudras* (ritual gestures) with their hands. Their forearms are often held in the traditional protective positions (Japanese: *Kamae*). Not many people realize that the praying position (Sanskrit: *Anjali*) with hands joined before the chest, is an ancient Vajramukti based defensive position.

Statuary records for us, in a highly visible form, that active aspect of Buddhist practice which recognizes no dichotomy between movement and stillness in either body or mind. It is for this reason that images are found presented pictorially in the karma (activity) mandala of esoteric Buddhism. They highlight the unique esoteric understandings of motion itself. The actual positions they take, be it within a manuscript or a statue, are always accurate even down to subtle details such as the positions or angles of finger phalanges, i.e., they are not drawn from simply the mason's imagination, and to those familiar with the art, are obviously reflecting something actually witnessed by their creators. It is this statuary that traces the earliest *Chuan Fa* positions and gestures so they can be clearly recognized today. The hand mudras were the initial starting point of the *Chuan Fa* art and at later times were expanded and explained at several levels.

Figure 90. Tibetan Lamas perform esoteric Mudras during a ritual. (Kongoryuji Temple.)

RITUAL GESTURES

The fundamental pair of symbolic gestures (*mudras*) used in the Vajra-mukti showed the giving of fearlessness (Sanskrit: *Abhya Mudra*; Chinese: *Shi Wu Wei Yin*) and the Fulfilling, Bestowing or Receiving of the Vow (Sanskrit: *Vara* or *Dana Mudra*; Chinese: *Shih Yuan Yin*). The mudra of Fearlessness (Japanese: *Semmui-In*) is formed by the upright right hand held with the palm toward the front and with fingers extended forward and downward. It represents a mental condition in which that which experiences fear no longer exists. It was a prime choice to represent the principles of warriorhood or martial arts. However, in order that this fearlessness should not be mistaken as simply representing the mundane bravery of the battlefield, it was always shown simultaneously with the Varamudra.

The Varamudra (Japanese: *Segan-In*) is formed by the left hand, which is held, palm upward at the height of the waist with fingers extended. It symbolizes both the Buddha's promise to aid beings seeking to develop enlightenment and the Bodhisattvas' binding vow to continually dedicate themselves to such an ideal. Both these *mudras* were commonly depicted in the earliest Indian and Chinese statues of the Shakyamuni Buddha, and the versions described above are the oldest and simplest forms of their representation. Later dynasties often showed the forefinger and thumb held touching or holding numerous other adornments, such as bowls and sistrums. In Japanese Mikkyo the combined *mudras* were termed collectively the *Segan-Semmui In*.

The *Semmui In* was the basic position for the circular defensive movement (Sanskrit: *Parivrttapala*; Chinese: *Hui Hu*) upon which all *Chuan Fa* motion is based. When the *mudra* was "drawn" in a circular motion before the body, all and every attack against one's body was harmlessly redirected away from it. The *Semmui In* represents the ultimate and unselfish form of defense, the *Segan In* describes its object.

Figure 91. This Vajracchedika Sutra frontispiece, the oldest printed book in the world, shows a guardian deity (bottom right) taking up a Vajramukti combat position. (British Museum, London.)

Together they form a summary of the Buddhist *Chuan Fa* attitude toward the idea of multilevel safety and protection. It is well at this point to consider the idea of safety itself.

> The five great elements have vibrations;
> Each of the ten worlds has its language;
> The six kinds of objects are expressive symbols;
> The Dharmakaya Buddha is the Reality.

SAFETY

Unlike the modern military world, Buddhism has unique ideas of what security or safety is. Buddhism considers all things to be ultimately subject to the law of dependent origination (Sanskrit: *Pratitya Samut-pada*; Japanese: *Juni-innen*) and thus in a state of continual change and development. The concept of a secure, unchanging condition in any form is therefore rejected as an unrealistic and extreme view, and the idea of "safety" or a personal refuge from this state is regarded as impossible. Actions to protect something or someone from any undesired change, even if apparently successful at one moment, will be eventually undone or changed at some other time. The motivation to protect oneself in the way we usually understand this act, is not found in real *Chuan Fa*.

One may now naturally ask, "Why then does the Buddhist *Chuan Fa* apparently teach and practice defensive actions and movement?" As in so many Oriental things, appearances are often deceptive. Verse 34ff of Shantideva's *Siksa Sammuccaya* [see Note 4] reads, ". . . with a bodily practice directed by the impulse of renunciation, one relinquishes all acquisitiveness. . . . Thus we must duly preserve the self even if sacrificed to others," and a little later, ". . . O Sariputra, one must preserve one's self when one intends to preserve others."

Chuan Fa teaches that while personal defense is ultimately pointless, the opportunity to help or teach others exists continually. If, in the face of aggression, one can avert harm to oneself or others, an opportunity to teach the aggressor is created. We can see an example of this in the Jataka story concerning "Prince Five Weapons" in which a forest demon, despite his great power, is ultimately defeated by a young prince. The Buddha's encounter with the murderer Angulimala mentioned previously also demonstrates the futility of the "first attack is the best" mentality.

Shakyamuni Buddha thwarted several attacks on his own life made by his cousin and fellow Ksatreya Devadatta. In one case he halted a maddened elephant by means of the *Abhaya Mudra* mentioned previously.

The desire to help others, even from their own expressions of ignorance or hatred, can be expressed by means of action which also negates the desired effects of such ignorance or hatred. Such activities also create a potential environment for learning the teaching (*Karmavarsita Dharmak-sana*) [Note 56a]. This is not too difficult a situation to envisage. If person "A" were determined to hurt another (person "B") and attacked "B" again and again, and yet each and every one of these attacks proved futile and was averted in some manner, "A" would get very frustrated and eventually fearful as he began to realize that "B," whom he perhaps thought would be easily overcome, seems unaffected by the most powerful attacks. It may dawn upon "A" that if "B" could avert his attacks so easily what would "B's" counter-attacks be like? Could they be stopped? In such a situation "A" may have second thoughts or regrets concerning his actions and try, maybe desperately, to amend the situation so that he would not be the subject of such an envisaged counterattack.

Both very early and later accounts record that it was often as a result of such situations that many of the *Chuan Fa Acaryas* recruited their students. Skillful defense is a subject of *Chuan Fa* defensive movement, but it is not the object of it. We can read in Asvaghosa's *Bodhisattvabhumi Sastra* that the Bodhisattva must be fully prepared to give up body, life force and possessions in pursuit of enlightenment. The *Siksa Samuuccaya* (v37) confirms this when it states of the person committed to enlightenment ". . . there is no bodily activity in which he does not venture out of respect for his masters and teachers."

To be able to give to others a freedom from fear is one of the meanings of the *Abhaya Mudra*. To take on the unlimited responsibility of doing so is a meaning of the *Vara Mudra*. We can find vestiges of this exalted spiritual ideal even in the more modern and "sportified" partializations of *Kempo* (*Chuan Fa*) teachings such as Japanese *Aikido* and *Judo*. In their traditional sparring terminology, both of these arts still refer to attackers or defenders as givers and receivers. These terms stem from the Chinese words originally describing the *mudras* of the *giving* of fearlessness and the *receiving* of the vow.

Many examples of *Chuan Fa* technique and their practitioners exist in the scriptures. The *Buddha Jataka* [Note 35f] is a text recounting stories of the Buddha's previous lives, which he sometimes spoke of in order to get across some point he wished to explain more clearly. The tale called "Prince Five Weapons" mentioned previously, vividly describes techniques of armed and unarmed attack and defense common to the *Ksatreya* of the day, which anyone familiar with *Chuan Fa* would instantly recognize.

In the *Bushogyosan* (a Japanese translation of the "Life Stories and Acts of the Buddha") [Note 35g] we can read of the Buddha's cousin Devadatta engaging in strength trials and contests with his brother Ananda. Shakyamuni Buddha was of course born into the warrior caste, and would have been fully familiar with all the contemporary armed and unarmed combative arts. The *Lalita Vistara* (Account of the

Buddha's Relaxing Activities) details his prowess in many of these [Note 36g].

In the earliest existing catalog of the Chinese collection of the Teachings (Sanskrit: *Tripitaka*) there are sutras listed as being of the Theravada traditions with such names as the *Rasistrapala pariprikkha* ("Sutra of the Meeting with the Bodhisattvas Who Protect a Country," Chinese: *Huo Kuo Pusa Hui*). This was translated by Gnanagupta in the Sui Dynasty (589–618). In the list concerning the *Ratnakuta* section, another is called *Guyhapada Vajra balasvamin pariprikkha*, (Meeting with the Vajra Strong Teacher Named Secret Word," Chinese: *Mi Tsi Chin Kang Li Shi Hui*). This latter term in Chinese, *Li shi*, could also represent the *Licchavi*, the *Ksatreyas* who formed the republic of Vaisali and were among the earliest followers of Shakyamuni. Some later catalogs rename the sutra simply as the *Guyhapada Malla Sutra* and translate the word *malla* as meaning a "wrestler," perhaps in imitation of a Ceylonese sutra of that name. However, this is incorrect, as the characters used quite clearly indicate the first meaning. The Ceylonese sutra concerns a King of the people who lived in Kusinagara or Purva, who was known as *Mallas*.

One Indian translator of the Yogacara philosopher Vasubandhu's texts into Chinese named Vimoksaprajna (Chinese: *P'i Mu Chih Hsien*) is mentioned in the Chinese text of the *Kai Yuan Shih Chiao Lu* [Note 39] of Chih Sheng. In this, he says that Vimoksaprajna came from the land of Wei Chang (*Uddiyana*) and was of a *Ksatreya* family descended from the Shakya clan. He further mentions that in ancient times the Indian King Pi Liu Li (Virudhaka) destroyed the city of Kapilavastu, and massacred the Shakyans, whereupon four Sons of Shakya (i.e., monks) resisted him by raising an army which succeeded in driving Virudhaka away. When the four Shakya sons returned to the city, the inhabitants refused to allow them in saying that they (the Shakyas) were followers of the religious life who had vowed never to resist violence and that the four sons had violated this principle. Cast out from their home, the four each wandered to different regions. Such was their fame that each was asked to become a monarch in the land he settled in. The *Kai Yuan* says that at the present time (circa 720) the Kings of Wu Chuan (Uddiyana) and Fan Yen (Bamyan) are their descendants and that Vimoksaprajna belonged to their family.

This story of combatant monks is also mentioned in the *Sarvastivada Vinaya* (Taisho 24) and the *Ekottaragama* (Taisho 2), as well as the Chinese translation of Dharmatrata's *Undanamarga* (Chinese: *C'hu Yao Ching*, Taisho 4). These latter give slightly different versions of the story [Note 34 I].

In the biography of Emperor Asoka (the *A Yu Chuan*) translated by Fa Ch'uan in A.D. 300, we find listed the 32 sacred places worthy of worship at which Asoka built a memorial stupa. These include both the training hall at which the youthful Shakyamuni studied the martial arts, and the place where he practiced them. We can also read in the *Life of the Buddha*, by Spence Hardy (and used by J. Legge in his translation of Fa Hsien's A.D. 399–414 Diary) of an occasion when Devadatta slays an elephant in one blow of his fist.

Mahayana Buddhism, especially the esoteric school (Chinese: *Mi-Chiao*; Japanese: *Mikkyo*), fully utilized the imagery of the martial arts to inspire the general populace. Its espousal of art, literature, and physical activities represented not an inevitable "degeneration" of "pure" Buddhism as is often alleged by some, but instead is a return to the living imagery and principles of the Pala and Gupta Dynasty Buddhism, with its promotion of cultured arts which have been transformed into spiritual endeavors and expressions, and/or such endeavors expressed as physical arts.

In China, the title *Dharmapala* mentioned earlier also described certain classes of warrior-trained monks whose duty it was to guard the holy relics, the treasures of shrines and occasionally teachers of the Dharma, from robbers [See references in Note 14]. Various titles for these protectors exist, the most common Chinese one apart from *Fa-Hu* (Sanskrit: *Dharmapala*) and *Seng Hu* (Sanskrit: *Sanghapala*), being *Seng-Ping* (Japanese: *So-Hei*) literally meaning a "monastic leveler," or "peacebringer." The Seng-Ping name for their Buddhist protective art was *Chuan Fa* (Japanese: *Kempo*) [Note 60].

Figure 92. Wall paintings found at the Tung Huang caves in Kiangsu, China. These show many deities and Arahants in Chuan Fa positions and stances. This picture dates from A.D. 530. (Author's collection.)

Such protectors were not only active in this physical realm, but also in other dimensions of being. Their prayers and intercessory rites were especially sought after by the relatives of those who were thought to have been particularly bad during their lives, as it was believed these people would be consigned to a terrible Hell realm in which they would be made to suffer. This belief also extended such a destiny to animals. One should not be misled by, or over-simplify titles like *Seng Ping* in relation to Buddhism.

The monks did not advocate the life of a military warrior, indeed the arts of *nata* mentioned in the *Renge kyo* (*Saddharma Pundarika*) occur in a context describing the types of skills forbidden to the Great Being (*Mahasattva*) and the text specifically mentions *brutal Shang Cha*. The practices of brutality are naturally discouraged in Buddhism, along with the attitudes conducive to it and, as in the quotation below, brutal "sport" is not only the prerogative of human beings.

Kumbhanda demons crouch on the earth and mould into it; sometimes springing from the ground a foot or two high, wandering to and fro, giving full rein to their sport, seizing dogs by the legs and striking them so they lose their voices [Kumbhandas are demons with enormous scrotums] (*Myohorengekyo, 1*).

Nevertheless Shakyamuni is not recorded as ever having demanded contemporary army leaders or kings to actually disband their forces or desist from recruiting them. Indeed, one who is "in the service of a king" is forbidden to enter the monastic order [See Refs in Note 14, 36e]. This is not a rule of disapproval as is sometimes thought; it is more a recognition of the demands of duty and a definitive statement that "national" service and "wisdom" service are not to be confused.

The monk was, however, certainly a spiritual warrior and the "battle" he engaged in was that between his higher and lower nature. Its "field" was within the monk's mind, speech and body. It was a "Triple Level Conflict" (Chinese: *Sanchin*) and this battle could sometimes be more ferocious than the ordinary form, for it could last many years or even lifetimes.

I see Buddha sons who abiding in the power of perseverance though men of utmost arrogance hate, abuse and beat them are able to endure all of these (*Myohorengekyo*, Ch. 1, p. 1).

Although probably common at the time, explicit accounts of the valiant arts in the literature of the Theravada School of Buddhism are rare. This is probably due to the Muslim destruction of north Indian literature alluded to earlier, and also that the Theravada tradition is, although well preserved in Sri Lanka nowadays, but one of the eighteen early sects of Indian Buddhism. It was probably within these other and Northern schools that the cultural *narya-nata vajramukti* were maintained.

Chuan Fa's elemental principles and its usage of a realistic sense of "time moments" [see Note 12] from which developed its art of tactics, indicate the Sarvastivada School as the most likely candidate to have transmitted, or at least influenced, the *Chuan Fa* metaphysical doctrines in China.

Despite the paucity of references (the early *Jataka* are not considered canonical in the Theravada School) there are many points of Dharma which deal directly with the mental and physical processes relevant to *narya/nata*, or *Chuan Fa*, in the Theravada Pali texts.

The *Dhamma Sangari* (circa 300 B.C.) contains many sayings concerning the physical and mental controls common to the warrior, such as those describing which events are beneficial and answers . . . "a tranquillity of body, a lightness in body, a tranquillity in consciousness, a lightness in consciousness," and continues to pair both mind and body in a similar manner including "pleasantness" and "fitness." The integral quality of mind/body relation is obviously acknowledged although, it should be noted, few Abhidharma lists include the category of "fear." In the Pali dialect used by the Theravada, awareness of fear or terror is objectively oriented and called *Bhayaupatthana*, being identified as the third of the "eight kinds of knowledge of the path." After it comes *Adinavauppassana*, awareness of danger/misery.

The category of the subjective state of fear occurs rarely as an important term. Such rarity is significant, for it reflects a caution exercised in dealing with the subject of emotionally charged situations as an ongoing experience. The Theravada preferred to view these conditions only as composites of the various states of consciousness in a somewhat abstract manner. One danger with such an approach lay in dealing with the laity, who could easily view such approaches as unsympathetic to what they saw as their "real" experiences of suffering. This abstracted quality of communication grew common in the later Theravada. The subjective state of fear occurs, and is discussed, many times in the Mahayana references and texts, in a more outwardly sympathetic manner. (This is discussed in detail later.)

Actions of the body in general occur in many meditation texts. In the *Karma-Siddhi—Prakrana* they are called *Kayakrita karma* and are classified in Pali as being performed ". . . after willing (*Cettapiyita*) after mental association (*Manottsamprayukta*) with effort (*Prayoga*) with dharma (*Dharmacaritta*) with performance (*Karitra*)." This latter term was used to describe the public demonstration of *narya/nata*. The above texts by Vasubandhu, preserved in Chinese translation, represent principles of the early Indian teaching. In the *Visuddhi Magga*, the great compendium of explanations of the doctrine compiled by the Theravadin Buddhaghosa, there are plenty of references to physically based meditation themes which are still practiced within modern *Chuan Fa*. The "mindfulness of breathing" (*Anupassanasati*) the "contemplation of the five ways of moving" (*Iryapatha*) and others, all serve to demonstrate that the Theravada tradition, even if not completely representing the whole of Indian Buddhist practices, certainly retained the mind-body relationship nexus elaborated more fully in other schools.

In the *Brahmajala Sutta* [See Note 35], the very first work of the Theravada Canon, we find described various views concerning the Dharma. One of its sixty-two cases contains an exposition of what it calls the "Lion's play" method (Pali: *Sihavikkilitanya*; Chinese: *Shih Yu Hsu Hsiu Hsing*, or *Shih Yu Hsu*; Japanese: *Shih yushu shugyo*, and *Shi Yushu*) [Note 34d]. This term occurs, in several forms, within Chinese descriptions of the Vajramukti art as being the name of one of its seminal schools and has been discussed elsewhere.

The particular chapter of the Sutta (Sanskrit: *Sutra*) here is concerned with responses to one's body, uncontrollable anger, inner resentment and other similar conditions. It summarizes the mindfulness practices relating to the body needed by both mundane and spiritual warriors. It seems particularly apt for present day *Chuan Fa* and this scripture is possibly a survivor of the earliest traditional lore of the *nata* training. The Mahayana, in all its component schools, contains more direct references to the involvement of bodily actions in the expression of Dharma. We can find a whole meditation practice devoted to a "Lion Play" Samadhi in the first century A.D. text of the *Catasahasrika Prajna Paramita Sutra*.

Shakyamuni Buddha dealt with many warriors and warrior kings in his spiritual teachings, although this is not often realized by those who study the Sutras. Some interesting accounts are told in his encounters with King Prasenadi of Kosala, a seasoned warrior monarch well acquainted with the necessities involved in maintaining his lands and title.

In their encounters we can see traces of the military training, discipline, and practice of their time. In the *Samyutta Nikaya,1*, the Buddha asks Prasenadi whether in wartime he would employ an untrained, unpracticed and undrilled Ksatreya youth (*khattiya kumaro*; Sanskrit: *Ksatreya kumara*) as a warrior. Prasenadi says he wouldn't. The Buddha then asks if he would accept such a one as a laborer or worker. Prasenadi replies no again. The Buddha then asks if he would accept such a youth if he were trained, skilled, expert, and practiced? To which Prasenadi replies, yes. So it is with monks, says the Buddha: they must be taught and trained in a similar disciplined manner.

By the time of the Buddha, armies were highly organized and disciplined in both battle and ethical conduct. The fourfold army division is shown in the *Vinaya* (section 4) when Prasenadi defeats Ahjatasattu, for it is said he confiscated the latter's elephants, horses, chariots and infantry (*yodhika, balagga, senabyuha, anikadasana*). Practice fights were also still being organized. The army is said to have practiced in full battle array and monks were expressly forbidden to observe such activities in their code of practice (*Vinaya*).

The *Vinaya* also refers to arrow-throwers (*srahatyha*). The *Abhaya Rajakumara Sutta* of the *Mahajima Nikaya* tells of Shakyamuni Buddha referring to the skillful charioteer and of how a monk must train his mind as the charioteer trains his horses. He describes how in battle one warrior may lose heart at the sight of the cloud of dust preceding an army, another when he sees the enemy's banner raised high, a third feels fear at the cries and shouts of the enemy, and a fourth in the actual battle itself. Here the Buddha is summarizing the responses of the four elemental temperaments.

Another similar instance occurs in the Chinese text of the *Surangama Sutra* in a comparison drawn between the discipline of a monk's training and that involved in training a horse for warfare. The mythology prevalent among warriors is evident in another tale. The same *Nikaya* (section 4:308) describes the Buddha meeting a *Yoddhajiva Gamani*, a title describing the non-*Ksatreyan* head of a village community of mercenaries. He tells the Buddha of his belief that he will be reborn into a Heaven realm filled with sensual devas only if he dies fighting in battle. The Buddha tells him he is mistaken, and warns and cautions him that such a warrior after death goes only to a painful Hell realm or else is reborn as an animal.

The Buddha could see that good warriors, be they *Ksatreya* or not, are essentially alone and solitary in their nature, and that sometimes, even if only in rare moments, they realize this and feel fear.

It was by such tales that the Buddha tried to direct the orientation of the warrior away from battle and toward spirituality. The persistency of the Buddha's stand on the virtue of non-harming abounds throughout his life. The accounts in the *Anguttara Nikaya (5:289)* condemn even Hunters to the suffering Hell realms for their actions.

Many scriptures concern themselves with attitudes or practices descriptive of both pure Buddhist teaching and Kempo practice. Some are well known, others little seen. The *Bodhicaryavatara* of Shantideva [Note 35b], although a relatively late writing (fifth century A.D.), summarizes most of their common maxims. Chapter 7, the "Perfection of

Figure 93. A page from the Jigoku Zoshi *(Illustration of Hell). This picture shows the fate of monks who have mistreated animals during their lifetime. (Seattle Art Museum, Washington.)*

Strength" (*Viryaparamita*) is especially relevant for warriors, as it concerns the themes of hatred, the enemy, conquerors, and victory.

It was probably recognition of the fact that those engaged in battle often (whether willingly or not) experience a heightened awareness of the transitory nature of life and death that prompted some teachers of Buddhism to include conflict as one of the potential areas for spiritual development and progression. The implications of this condition are considered later on.

The *Bodhicaryavatara* elucidates and expounds the *Paramita* (perfecting practices) of a Bodhisattva [See ref's in Note 35]. Its treatment and exposition of the *Paramita* echoes that found originally in the *Brahmajala Sutra* mentioned earlier. In this earlier sutra we find an account of both the *Paramita* and the Bodhisattvas in their Theravada form (many are under the impressions that *Paramitas* and Bodhisattvas are of Mahayana origination) [Note 13a].

Shantideva's predecessor Nagarjuna (second century A.D.) was the impetus behind the Madhyamika and Vijnaptimatra (Yogacara) Schools of doctrine. Both these schools contributed maxims within which the esoteric (*Mikkyo*) *Chen-Yen* and *Chaan* sects arose. As these latter two were directly involved in formulating the Chinese principles expounded in both *Chuan Fa* and its subsequent derivatives, the study

Figure 94. Japanese statue of Asanga.
(Courtesy of Dr. Wei Tat.)

of Buddhist texts connected with them, or of their schools' students, is of relevance in understanding *Chuan Fa* philosophy. Indeed, one cannot understand *Chuan Fa* principles, be they of exoteric or esoteric form, without such study. The works by Vasubandhu especially are highly relevant to the art of *Chuan Fa* [Note 32].

The *Suvarnaprabhasa Sutra* (10, p.114) has an interesting, and provocative discussion of the various *Paramitas* (spiritually perfecting practices) and how they should or should not be applied in one's life. It describes particularly various forms of ignorance which permit harm to come to others by means of one's own personal inaction. This description extends to the meditative sphere and includes the ignorance "which permits one to enjoy the bliss of meditative conditions but which prohibit one from compassionate action towards others." The *Suvarnaprabhasa* also draws attention to the particular ignorance that engenders the activity of non-activity (i.e., which allows a condition or situation to continue, because of one's own inaction). We find similar sentiments echoed in the seventh century by Shantideva: "although one may be powerless to act when experiencing the restrictions of fear and agitation despite this if an act of charity (*dana*) is required the conventional precepts may be overlooked" (Ch. 5, v42) *Bodhicaryavatara*.

Asanga in his *Bodhisattvabhumi* (10, p. 25–129) says that in some cases the application of *Paramitas* should be ignored or "suspended."

He describes the *Paramita* relating to compassion and shows that in certain cases it should not be applied by the Bodhisattva, as to do so may allow more suffering to be visited upon people. He gives an example of tolerating a monarch who is continually torturing his subjects. Asanga goes on to say it may be necessary to topple such a monarch and his government—even by violent means if required—in order to alleviate the suffering of others [Note 69]. This may refer to the "Body of Compassionate Anger" (known as the *Adesana cakrakaya*) mentioned in the *Vajrausnisa Sutra* (*Kongochokyo*).

Queen Srimala echoes this active attitude in the ninth vow of the *Srimalasimhanada Sutra* [see Notes 35, 70a] when she says, "When I see persons with sinful occupations, such as dealing in pigs and those who violate the doctrine or discipline proclaimed by the Thathagata, I shall not take it lightly. . . . I shall destroy what should be destroyed and foster what should be fostered" [Note 36h].

Such concepts are mentioned only rarely in Buddhist scriptures but far from advocating simple revolutionary activity, they indicate a vision and familiarity with the Bodhisattva's power of purposeful but egoless, compassionate action. That is, the ability to cause creative change without generating *Klesa* [Note 62].

> Although one may be powerless to act when experiencing the restrictions of fear and agitation, despite this if an act of charity (*dana*) is required, the conventional precepts may be overlooked (Ch. 5, v42, *Bodhicaryavatara* [Entering into the Path of Wisdom] by Shantideva).

DEVELOPMENT OF THE CHINESE VAJRAYANA

The Bodhisattva has a strong body and large limbs. He can protect others and ward off attacks (*Astahasrika Prajnaparamitasutra*, 20,v371–373).

Chuan Fa bases many of its most important tenets upon teachings and experiences outlined in the early scriptures and was probably formalized long before their committal to writing. Although the present day form of the Theravada School includes many principles and terms common to *Chuan Fa*, other early schools must also have played a significant part in its development, because its philosophy of tactical encounter (*Hsien Hsiu*) includes methods of tactical assessment and judgment based upon teachings known only to have existed within the Sarvastivada and Vaibhasya Schools of Buddhism.

It is likely that Northern India (where these schools are recorded to have flourished) was the birthplace of *Chuan Fa's* systematization. Other schools, such as the Yogacara (and its offshoot, Cha'an Na) also gave birth to traditions of self-understanding which contributed toward *Chuan Fa* meditation practices.

Chuan Fa seems also to have been practiced in Southern India and Ceylon but, as it was considered a secret art, it was not studied by all Buddhist monks. This was probably due mostly to the lack of qualified Indian teachers (*acaryas*) and also, because of the dangers inherent in its being misunderstood, the reticence of *acaryas* in general to teach any but the few students they personally select.

From its earliest inception within India, the Bodhisattva Vajramukti was regarded as a powerful and potentially dangerous cathartic physical practice. Because it dealt directly with the liberation and channeling of primitive energies and instincts within mankind, a teacher powerful in both body and mind was necessary to convey its principles and guide its students. These cautions were carried over into China and the resultant *Chuan Fa* (*Kempo*) was likewise taught only to monks or devout Buddhists of a suitable disposition. Such cautions as existed both in India and China were often justified.

Buddhist schools which dealt with these powerful energies were in general called *Vajrayana* (Thunderbolt Path) Schools. These took many forms, one well-known one being introduced into Tibet by Pad-

Figure 95. The Potola Palace of the Dalai Lama. (Author's collection.)

masambhava (the "Lotus born") in the eighth century. It is he who is credited with introducing the Indian *nata* sequences into Tibet which, in various forms, are still performed as "Lama dances." The most renowned of these is the *Padmasambhava Drag dmar*. In general, such sequences are known in Tibet as *Cham* dance. These sequences were codified within the text called *Rolme Tenchoe* and said to be based upon the second century *Natyasastra* of Bharatanatyam.

It is often said that the King of Udiyana, Indrabhuti (678–717), Padmasambhava's father, founded the Vajrayana, but this is unlikely, as esoteric Buddhism in general, and the title of Vajrayana, was already widely known in both India and China. Indrabhuti's form of Vajrayana Buddhism used images and symbols which included representation of female deities and powers, unlike the Chinese or other esoteric schools. Such forms of the Vajrayana are usually termed "tantric," a word loosely meaning "integrated" or "connecting," and rarely applied to the Chinese esoteric branch or its derivatives.

Another classification used to distinguish them is to term the Tibetan female Vajrayana a "left-handed" tantra and the Chinese male Vajrayana a "right-handed" form. The Tibetan tantric followers also used non-canonical collections of religious writings, which they termed "tantras." In Tibet, these often supplanted the Sutras as sources of doctrine. To distinguish between these different types of esoteric teachings (Chinese: *Mi Chiao*; Japanese: *Mikkyo*) modern scholars differentiate between right and left handed *Mikkyo* and the "pure" and "mixed" *Mikkyo*. Pure *Mikkyo* keeps to the tenets formulated by its lineage teachers, while the mixed incorporates tenets from many other sources. Esoteric sects can thus be formed of all the various combinations of these. Non-Buddhist (i.e., Hindu) esoteric teachings can thus be classified as a "left-handed tantra," of the "mixed" type.

One branch of the "left-handed" Vajrayana, called the *Sahaja-yana*, may have been relevant to the history of Kempo as it included disciplines oriented to the attainment of a condition termed the "Thunderbolt Body" (*Vajrakaya*). To this end it utilized physical movements and sequences termed *Kayagita* (singing with the body).

It is said, however, that the aim of this school was to realize voidness by means of what was symbolically designated *Mahasukha* (Great Bliss) in one's body and mind. Popular in the Bengal region of India, it become influenced by Hindu Tantrism and rapidly degenerated into a teaching of depravity advocating *Maithuna* (ritual sexual intercourse) and other titillations. It soon lost its significance as a Buddhist school and was eventually ignored. Due to this we have very little information concerning its overall physical practices and trainings.

Not all Vajrayana Schools were degenerate, and some brilliant philosophers emerged from its ranks. Tibetan Vajrayana is mainly of the type initiated by Padmasambhava, and still exists there in the Nyingma-Pa sect. It may be this school's influence which has preserved the Lama dances and movements within Tibetan Buddhism as a whole. [See Note 73]. The Lamaistic form of Buddhism, together with its physical practices, was also taken to Mongolia and had some influence upon that Nation's physical arts. In China the Vajrayana (translated as *Ching Kang Cheng*; Japanese: *Kongojo*) was not associated with, or influenced by the *Sahajayana*.

It is difficult to determine precisely when Vajramukti teachings first permeated China or into which specific forms it developed. Unfortunately the many internal turmoils China subsequently suffered have meant that no consistent record of their battle history or Indian innovations in this military sphere was ever made by a common and continuous source.

Within China the various military divisions and commanders of a losing side were often ruthlessly executed and their belongings burned or looted by the victors. It is difficult to find a progressive and continuous account of military methods or styles of training and strategy in any one section of the Chinese army.

While China has many accounts of its great battles and great individuals, most of these were made by disparate tribes or dynasties whose concern was mainly their own particular people, locales and times. We cannot find one single secular group who continued throughout the various dynasties recording such matters unscathed. This is reflected in the fact that the present Chinese army uses quite modern texts for its training theory, or else has recourse to the works of ancients such as Sun Tzu (600–700 B.C.?). It uses little that was written between these two times.

The continuity we do find is, as is often the case, within religious groups. Both Buddhist, and, much later, Muslim groups, continued through Chinese history more or less unscathed. Within certain monastic records and accounts we find mention of practices and events in the life of the nation and populace. This is especially so when we encounter converts who, prior to becoming monks, were military leaders or officers, for these often spent their time writing memoirs that recorded events and occurrences happening around them.

To win in victory a hundred battles is not the height of skill;
To subdue an enemy without fighting I call the highest skill.

—Sun Tzu: *The Book of War*, 3;3

Many forms of martial arts existed in China before the arrival of Buddhism. These are known non-specifically as *Wu Shu* (military arts). Most of these were the prerogative of the ruling classes and involved the use of weaponry. There was such a range of peoples and cultures comprising the Chinese nation that it comes as no surprise to discover that many of the inhabitants had their own distinctive and localized forms of practice.

One of the oldest known to the non-military public was an art called *Go Ti Ta* (Japanese: *Kaku shoku uchi*). This was a primitive form of sparring in which the combatants donned deer antlers and attacked each other with them. Its invention is credited to Chi Yu who is said to have lived around 2000 B.C. The Manchurians (Mongolians) were especially fond of this and some of its techniques are preserved still in their traditional folk dances and wrestling. In the northern parts of China we find Han Dynasty descriptions and rock carvings of unarmed combat between man and bulls. This sport—which seems more fair than the modern Spanish version—was known as *Chiao Ti Tsi* (Japanese: *Kojishi*). In the scenes depicted, combatants are taking up classical *Vajramukti Chuan Fa* sparring positions quite unlike any Taoist equivalent.

In 108 B.C. the Han Emperor Wu staged a demonstration of this art as part of his dynastic celebrations. It is said to have begun around 473 B.C. in the Warring States period. Extant stone carvings depicting its practice date from around 250 B.C., so it is certainly ancient. Another similar event is recorded by Mei Ching of the Han Dynasty, where he describes a *Chuan Fa* proponent fighting barehanded with a tiger and a bull simultaneously.

Figure 96. The Gagaku dances of Japan contain many movements derived from the Indian Nata and the Chinese Chuan Fa. (Courtesy of Kosei Publishing Co., Japan.)

Many techniques of both armed and unarmed hand-to-hand combat are also outlined in the *Book of Han* (*Han Shu*) by Pan Kuo (A.D. 32–92). Here the local form of unarmed combat is termed *Chi chi hsiu* (Japanese: *Gigekishu*). This name means "Skillful striking (with the) hand." The various methods employed are described, and, in the Chinese manuscript, shown in outline drawings. There are other sections upon strategy, charioteering, tactics, and the use of natural forces in battle which all seem drawn from the Indian methods.

One can see a great difference already between the ethics espoused by the ordinary Chinese soldier and the Buddhist doctrines of this period. The early monk missionaries had to contend with a highly sophisticated and military society in which might counted more than right and respect was gained by skill in battle rather than any other qualities. Despite this, the Indian teacher Kasyapa Matanga began to translate scriptures into Chinese and by the year A.D. 50 both the *Sutra of 42 Sections*, and the *White Lotus Sutra* were in circulation. According to traditional and reliable temple accounts, there were several seminal methods of unarmed combat training which came into China from the second to the eighth centuries A.D. All of these came from India and thus stemmed directly or indirectly from the martial traditions of the Indian nobility, that is, the *Vajramukti* method.

While there are very few actual accounts of *Vajramukti* as a separate and distinct art at this early time, we can see its traces in accounts of local festivals or celebrations, where the names of certain of its Nata and other practices are mentioned as being performed. Much can be learned from the records, attitudes, and relevant doctrines concerning the contemporary Buddhist schools, particularly the scriptures of the Vaibhasika, Sarvastivada, and Yogacara (Vijnaptimatra) derivative traditions.

The earliest method of *Vajramukti* known in China was, as has been shown, the classical Ksatreya *Lion's Skill* (Sanskrit: *Simhasiksa*, or *Simhavikridita*). This was directly brought in by the monks and was to prove an extremely important and influential Indian school, responsible for many later derivative forms of unarmed combat in China. Once in China it was initially known simply by a phonetic representation of its Sanskrit or Pali titles in characters (pronounced in Chinese as either *Seng Cha Shih Sha*, or *Shing Cha Sha*) [Note 37b]. As was to prove common in later times, this title was transliterated so it conveyed the sense of the original Sanskrit meaning more readily to the native Chinese. This later and more correct title being *Shih Yu Hsu Hsiu Hsing* ("lion's skillful practice").

Within a few centuries it had acquired the prefix "Eastern" and was known in some areas as the "Eastern Lion's Art/Practice" (*Purvasimhasiksa*, Chinese: *Tung Shih Hsiu Hsing*) and also the "Eastern Lion's Art Closed Hand" (Chinese: *Tung Shih Yu Hsu Chuan*). This prefix "Eastern" may refer to the *Purvasaila Sangharama*, whose title means "the Eastern Mountain." It was at this mountain that one of the five sub-sects of the Mahasanghika arose. Equally it could refer to the Buddhist monasteries of Vikramasila or Nalanda of Dhanakataka in eastern

Figure 97. Rubbings taken from tombstones in Nanyang region of Henan, China depicting barehanded defensive techniques of the Han period, 206–210 B.C., shows two opponents who are attacking simultaneously from both sides. (Nanyang Museum, Henan, China.)

India at which the *Vajramukti* and other physical arts are reported, by I Tsing and others, as having been practiced during the second to eighth centuries [Note 36n, 55]. Such a prefix would have distinguished between the oldest bases of the art and the forms which were practiced at Chinese monasteries bearing a similar name or title to their Indian counterparts [Note 70b].

Another method known to have been introduced was "Tiger Striking." This was the name given to a specialized technique of *Vajramukti* concerned with manipulating, or causing changes within, the body's vital points. This name was retained unaltered in China and simply transliterated into the native tongue as *Po Fu*, or *Po Hu*. It was said to have been used by Kuo Chi Yi (Japanese: *Koku Kyu Ki*) of the Hou Han Dynasty (25–220) and to have been incorporated into a system later named *Chang Shou Men* (Japanese: *Cho Te Mon*). This title means "extending hands" and was a reference to Yi's ability to be able to defend himself from persons standing a long distance away. It was said he could "extend" the "power" of his hands and disarm people long before they could close in on him. This ability was an advanced technique of the *Po Fu* method.

At a much later time, when the esoteric teachings were well advanced, the *Po Fu* technique was still present in the teachings of Sze Hung Pei (Japanese: *Shikubei*) of the Tang Dynasty. His method of teaching also involved extensive usage of mudras as feinting maneuvers which totally confused would-be attackers. So good was his method that it was called the teaching of "Up down pretend Mudras" (Japanese: *Jotoka shakushuin*).

A rich, and usually untapped, source of information regarding the principles and development of *Chuan Fa* lies in the monastic records, both literal and oral, which were preserved within the various sects and whose teachings were passed down through the ages to successive generations of students. It was here that many of the most important inner developments of *Chuan Fa* took place.

This passage of knowledge, both in general and ritualistic forms (Japanese: *Denpo*) still continues in our modern times as teachers fulfill their obligations and duties to their lineages.

Whirling fire becomes a square and a circle as the hand moves. many changes are made according to our will; One eternal sound "A" turns into many others, expressing innumerable Buddha truths.*

---

*Translated by Morgan Gibson and H. Murakami in *Tantric Poetry of Kukai, Japan's Buddhist Saint*. Thailand: Mahachulalongkorn Buddhist University, 1982.

THE MANDALAS

Many teachings lie enshrined within the mandala illustrations mentioned earlier. These express the teachings in a symbolic form. Many
mandalas, together with their ritual liturgies, are still preserved in Chinese and Japanese temples. In addition, there are accounts, drawings,
and descriptions of other mandalas made or studied by traveling
monks during the sixth and seventh centuries

Accounts of the Vajradhatu Mahamandala are significant to the
art of *Chuan Fa*, for its Northern quarter is that traditionally ruling
Vajramukti. Its tutelary Buddha Amoghasiddhi (Japanese: *Fukujoju*;
Chinese: *Pu Kung*) is the embodiment of the Buddha wisdom concerning enlightened activity and creation. He is surrounded by four Maha-
Bodhisattvas, each of whom holds his arms in classical and dynamic
Vajramukti poses of both mystical expression and physical defensive
readiness called by Japanese, in the former view, an *In* (Sanskrit: *mudra*)
or in the latter a *Kamae* (Sanskrit: *Hastasthana*).

These positions and gestures are described in the second part of
the *Vajrasekharasutra* (*Kongochokyo*) [See Note 84a]. The *Juhachieshiki* of
Amoghavajra describes this second part as containing the rituals for
initiating disciples, which includes "various sounds and Thunderbolt
dancing." He describes these as "Whirling dance," "Facing (confrontation) dance," "lesser dance," and "knowledge dance," and these seem
to be descriptions of different *Chuan Fa Nata* (*Hsing*).

Each of the Maha-Bodhisattvas embody the perfecting qualities of
Mahavairocana's wisdom and are named (in Sanskrit) *Vajrakarma*,
Vajrayaksa, *Vajraraksa*, and *Vajrasandhi*. In Japanese mandalas *Vajraraksa*
(Thunderbolt protector) sits to the right of Amoghasiddhi. His hands
are raised above his head and clasped together.

Vajrayaksa sits to the left of Amoghasiddhi, his hands forming fists
which are raised to his heart with wrists slightly bent. Vajrakarma sits
in front of Amoghasiddhi, his hands raised to chest level and in fists
with the first knuckles protruding. In contemporary *Chuan Fa* (Japanese: *Kempo*) the same hand position is termed in Japanese the *Ipponken*,
and is considered an extremely dangerous bodily weapon utilized for
defense.

Vajrasandhi sits behind Amoghasiddhi. His hands are held parallel to each other in fists and in front of the chest. The identical position is found in the *Sanchin Hsing* of *Chuan Fa*. All of these hand
gestures are amplifications of the meanings implicit in the one gesture,
made by Mahavairocana, who sits in the center of the mandala, termed
the *Jnanamusti'*(Japanese: *Chiken-In*), or "Knowledge Fist Mudra,"
which itself is formed by a combination of the *Ipponken* gesture just
mentioned and a *Chuan Fa* "One Finger Spearhand" position. This

Figure 98. The five Buddhas of Kongokai Mahamandala. At the top is Akshobyha, to the right Ratnasambhava, at the bottom Amitabha, at the left Amoghasiddhi, and Mahavairocana is in the center. (Author's collection.)

was the Buddhist representation of the *Suci* dagger weapons of the Ksatreya.

Vajrasandhi Bodhisattva embodies the highest and last of the sixteen stages to perfection, each of which is represented by the groups of four Bodhisattvas surrounding each of the four other mandala Buddhas.

At the thirteenth stage perfection of bodily activities is obtained; at

Figure 99. *Vajrasandhi Bodhisattva (middle right—north). Sits behind Amoghasiddhi and represents the last of the sixteen stages to perfection. His fist expresses the Paramita of exertion (Virya) in benefiting other beings and bringing them toward enlightenment. The hands are held in the "on guard" position. Vajrakarma Bodhisattva (middle left—south). Embodies skillful action in protecting sentient beings and in making offerings to Buddhas. He sits to the east of Amoghasiddhi and makes the mudra of Jujikongo (crossed Vajras), which is still used in Chuan Fa as a defensive technique. Vajraraksa Bodhisattva (top—West). Sits to the right of Amoghasiddhi and embodies Compassion in the Paramita of energy (Virya). He protects the student from lethargy and wastefulness. Vajrayaksa Bodhisattva (Bottom—East). Sits to the left of Amoghasiddhi and symbolizes the skillful means employed in conquering obstacles to the path. He represents the terrifying aspect of wisdom used sometimes to convert those unamenable to pacific methods. (Author's collection.)*

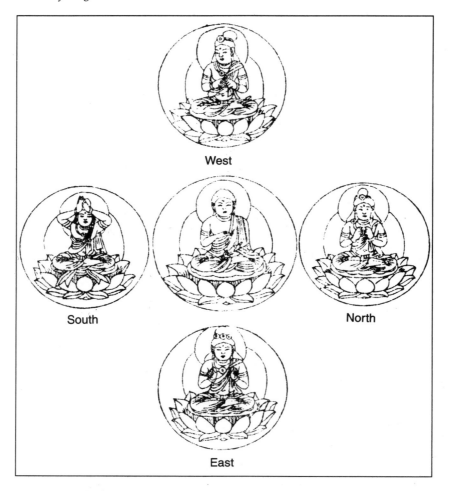

Figure 100. The four Bodhisattvas surrounding the Buddha Amoghasiddhi in the Kongokai Mahamandala. (Author's collection.)

the fourteenth laziness is overcome by the adoption of the perfect practice of strenuous exertion, and at the fifteenth all evil or demonic forces are completely subjugated and expelled. In the sixteenth and last stage the practitioners mind, body and speech merge with those of Mahavairocana Buddha.

In addition to the Maha Bodhisattvas, two of the other sets of four Bodhisattvas presented in the mandala are termed the "Inner offering Bodhisattvas" (Japanese: *Naikuyo*) because they lie closest in the man-

Figure 101. Mahavairocana Buddha. The primordial Buddha of all Buddhas. (Painting by Ryusen Miyahara.)

Figure 102. Vajranrita Bodhisattva. Symbol of heroic movements and energy. The same hand position is still used in the ritual "Ping An Hsing" of Chuan Fa. (Author's collection.)

dala to Mahavairocana and are within the "Circle of Thunderbolts" surrounding him. The other group of four are termed the "Outer offering Bodhisattvas" (Japanese: *Gekuyo*).

One of these inner offering Bodhisattvas is named Vajranrita (Japanese: *Kongobu*). He represents the Paramita of heroic energy. The Sanskrit term *Nrita* signifies "dance" or "ritualized movement," but equally means "manliness," or "virility" in much the same way as the term *Narya* discussed earlier in this text.

Vajranrita personifies the knowledge of skills (Japanese: *Zengyochi*) and is called "Master of the Samadhi of the dance of the Divine Powers" (Japanese: *Jinzu buge sammaji*) [Note 85]. This is said to "remove the darkness of ignorance to attain the liberation of being able to roam at will through the many realms of existence."

The hand position of this Bodhisattva is one with the forearm extended to the front with the palm downward and the right arm bent across the chest, again with palm downward. It is called the *Funnu Ken In* ("Fist of Wrathful Anger"). This identical position occurs in the most ancient classical *Chuan Fa Hsings*, where it represents both a blocking maneuver and a part of a breathing meditation sequence.

The *Shokyo* section of the *Mikkyo Daijiten* [Note 26a], an important Japanese source dictionary and reference of esoteric teaching, says that attaining the *Kaji* (ritual empowerment) of Kongobu Bodhisattva confers the "Body of Instantaneity" and immediately enables the practitioner to reach the "unconditioned realms" of wisdom.

Amoghavajra, one of the *acaryas* who introduced esoteric Buddhism into China, seems very familiar with the practice of the movement arts, and refers often to the dynamic aspects and sequences of ritual movement in the *Mahavairocana Sutra*. It is recorded that in A.D. 750 he went to live in a military camp for five years and both taught and initiated its commanders and officers into the esoteric methods.

This no doubt gave a fresh vitality and impetus to the esoteric Buddhist principles of *Chuan Fa*. Fei Hsu's biography of him records that his sponsor, the Emperor Su Tsung, ordered the construction of a temple within the imperial palace expressly for the purpose of celebrating the esoteric Rites.

It was in this temple that in 761 Tai Tsung, under Amoghavajra's guidance, staged a great mandala ritual. It appears that each of the Emperor's immediate advisors took on the role of their tutelary deities, his bodyguards taking the place of Thunderbolt Bodhisattva protectors (*Kongo Shin O*) and every member of the court was involved [Note 84c].

Amoghavajra seems to have held this ritual as part of a series of practices designed to familiarize those around him with the esoteric principles and practices, and also perhaps for him (or the Emperor), to learn something more of the character of those around him by ensuring they participated in this "experiential enactment" of the Thunderbolt World. We can be certain that the Vajra Bodhisattvas of Amoghasiddhi were represented and that their arts and skills were performed here. This whole event seems to echo a statement of the Roman poet Virgil in the *Aeneid, 1, 405*: "Vera incessa potuit dea" ("The true Goddess was known by her gait").

It was from this period onward that *Chuan Fa* began to emphasize a dual practice of both the Yogacara/*Chaan* Meditation and the *Mikkyo* teachings, an emphasis which persists into present times. (Many, not knowing its history, still believe *Chuan Fa* or its derivatives are based exclusively upon *Chaan*) [Note 26a].

After some time it probably occurred to the monk teachers that the all-pervasiveness of military ideology in Chinese society could be re-oriented into more useful and creative realms. To this end they began to look to their own national precedents for a bridge between the Chinese and Indian military cultures. From this train of thought developed the socialized teaching and transmission of the principles of Buddhist *Vajramukti* under its newer Chinese title of *Chuan Fa*.

After it had been openly shown in China, *Chuan Fa*'s value was recognized and adopted by the native population, but they often, by overemphasizing its physical value to individuals, lowered its universal and spiritual value. Even in those days there were people who believed that a "tough" person had to have a physique resembling a gorilla. They could not see how meditation might generate students who were both finer warriors and people. Such native developments were not, of course, what the monk teachers taught or would have wished [Note 38b].

There are many tales in China's *Chuan Fa* history of people who tried to study with a master but were refused permission because they were considered unsuitable. In these tales, rejected students are often said to have spied secretly upon the monks when they were training. By these means they learned some of the physical techniques or movements used in *Chuan Fa*. Newly developing Taoism also plagiarized *Chuan Fa's* physical techniques and, ignoring its spirituality, created "new" systems of their own martial arts. By such surreptitious and presumptuous methods, non-Buddhists often came to learn *Chuan Fa* techniques bereft of their spiritual teachings, and cursed successive generations by popularizing this travesty [Note 52c, 38b].

It was probably these same secular people—often political refugees or fugitives from justice or debt—who later comprised the monastic "armies" said to have fought in pitched battles for various Emperors. Certainly no monk would have knowingly taught *Chuan Fa* without its spiritual basis, and no *Chuan Fa* teachings were recorded in books or manuscripts accessible to outsiders at this time [See Notes 14, 24]. However we must not forget that there were instances of proper *Chuan Fa* monks (termed *Seng Ping*) [Note 60] resisting warring troops. In such cases, it is often noted that the monks drove away invaders without resorting to the use of any manufactured weapons.

There is a very old story told of a Shaolin monastic cook named Wu I (of the Han Dynasty) who encountered a native Taoist army called the "Yellow Turbans" intent upon putting into action an Imperial proscription against Buddhist temples by burning them down and slaughtering the inhabitants. Wu I apparently seized a Buddhist sistrum (a ritual staff adorned with bells used to warn animals of a monk's approach) from the temple, and defended himself from all attacks. Such was the expertise in his movements, he eventually caused the whole terrified group to flee.

Later a school of quarterstaff fighting—the Shaolin Wu I Method— was named after him. However, the sistrum is not a quarterstaff, and no Buddhist monk is permitted to carry, train with or use, weapons of any kind in battle. It naturally follows from this that there can be therefore no real monk or Buddhist school of armed fighting.

The Tang Shaolin monastery, one of the original homes of the real *Vajramukti* had, within two generations of Bodhidharma's residency, moved to the south, but we can still surprisingly read of schools started by persons claiming to have been monks who trained there many hundreds of years later. Even China had (and has) its opportunist pretenders.

The modern Chinese government has created a restored Shaolin Monastery originally for use in a film set. It is now possible to buy a tour to go there and enter training courses in martial arts designed for foreigners. In common with certain schools found in the island of Okinawa, the course ends with an award of a Masters Certificate. The

Figure 103. Pages of the Shaolin Temple records. (Author's collection.)

Figure 104. Sotoba towers marking the graves of monks at the Shaolin temple in Honan, China. (Author's collection.)

monk trainers who wander around conspicuously in their robes are state appointed officials.

Although modern books concerning *Chuan Fa, karate,* or its derivatives do not draw out—or deliberately ignore—its spiritual implications, some serious works acknowledge the Buddhist spiritual origins of this art [See Ref's in Notes 20 and 25].

What is the Mind in fetters?
It is the inclination to remain immobile with the two legs.

—*Mahavairocana Sutra* Ch.1

THE INNER MEANING OF THE NATA

Historically speaking, *Vajramukti* was practiced in two forms—which we could call the "early" and the "later" forms of practice. The earlier was practiced within India prior to the arrival of Buddhism and was predominantly Vedic in spiritual impetus. The later was the form developed by the Buddhist priesthood. This of course was Buddhist in spiritual orientation and was generally called by the monks the "Bodhisattva Vajramujkti" to distinguish it from the earlier Hindu School. The early form—which persisted even during the Buddha's lifetime—utilized the weaponry common to the Vedic tradition, but the latter Buddhist form did not. All forms of weaponry have always been forbidden to all Buddhist monks [See Note 20].

From these beginnings the Bodhisattva Vajramukti developed and grew into a coherent, recognizable and communicable practice.

Figure 105. Modern Indian Nata dancer. The movements of Chuan Fa are still clearly visible. (Author's collection.)

Although the *nata* possessed tactical explanation, it was not this aspect which had resulted in them being adopted by monks, but more the results of these aspects within the minds of people. They had noticed that some warriors, when engaging in the trainings, experienced the movements as if they were actually occurring (i.e., they were engaged in a real battle). In fact, the best trainers encouraged their students to do this and "act out" the situation knowing that this brought forth the best physical results.

The monks reasoned that a corresponding mental determination must also be present and that such intensity could be put to far greater use within the practice of spirituality. Building upon this, the monk masters began to transform and develop the *Ksatreya Vajramukti* into something very different from its original Hindu goals.

Unlike the practice for armed battle, the Hindu Ksatreya are mentioned as pursuing in the Buddhist *Samyutta Nikaya*, the unarmed Bodhisattva Vajramukti defense sequences (*nata*) came to be initially performed as health giving exercises (*Agadakayasiksa*) which prepared and balanced the body and mind relationship required for the esoteric trainings. They were practiced in sequential rhythms, usually out of doors, and often to the beat of a drum [Note 74].

These sequences and rhythms drawn from the *Vajramukti Nata* formed the foundation for the esoteric systems of therapeutic practice later developed in China and known as Vajra Yogas (Chinese: *Ching Kang Yui Chia*) [See Note 17]. Regular practice of the training sequences indirectly built up bodily stamina as well as skills in the techniques involved, and through these practices the physical degeneration, so common to the monks who spent many hours studying or meditating, was alleviated.

The traditional combinations of the component sequences and their movements were called *pratima*, one of several Sanskrit terms meaning "shape," or "apparent form," and suggesting both an inner and outer significance or expression. While the *nata* proper were complete, long and subtle traditional sequences embodying many layers of meaning and interpretation, the *pratima* were shorter, condensed sequences, usually concerned with specific point(s) of the teachings. By their very nature, they embodied the principle of a progressive accumulation of wisdom, each acting as a preparatory stage for the next. Sometimes the *pratima* sequences were extracted directly from a *nata* and taught progressively as a simpler means of learning a long *nata*.

The movements comprising the early *pratima* were not only simple battle sequences, or self defense movements, but also included techniques incorporated by the monk masters from various Buddhist Yogas and medical teachings. These were designed to work upon a student's mind, body, and breath equally, and to channel them into specific patterns of simultaneous interaction.

Each *pratima* expressed a particular physical or psychological pattern and orientation. Such orientations were often not revealed to their practitioners when they were first taught the *pratima* for, if practiced correctly, it would reveal itself within the student's mind, initiating certain problems or queries which, by virtue of their arousal, would inform the teacher that the *pratima* was being practiced correctly. As the exact sequences were only taught orally and personally from a master to his student, the *pratima* could not be compared to other physical trainings for battle, or to simple health gymnastics; they were understood from the very outset as being an integral form of dynamic mudra (Chinese: *Hsing Yin*; Japanese: *Gyo In*).

STHANA

The central and interior purpose of the *pratima* lay in their ability to enable students to reveal and recognize their *sthana*. This term, *sthana*, represented the totality of a student's perceived and acknowledged mental "stance" or concurrent position in regard to their self-understanding. It represented their public "face" to the world, which was held and maintained with mental rigidity and, occasionally, an intense fierceness. *Sthana* was also a term applied to describe an individual's physical condition and health balance [Note 85a].

The method of introducing a student to the practices and what was actually practiced depended on the master's assessment of the nature of both the physical and mental forms of *sthana*. If the student had formerly been a warrior, the *pratima* were probably presented as if defensive techniques. If not, then the movements would be presented as either mudras for ritual purposes, mudras for meditation, or as a therapeutic practice, in whatever manner considered most appropriate by the master. Thus we can see that initially what one student may have understood at any moment as being a defensive movement, another may have understood as a doctrinal expression. Because the kinetic possibilities of both therapeutic and defensive movement were of limited number, and the doctrinal meaning and explanation of mudras were limitless, eventually all who continued with the training would have come to recognize the movements as embodying the profound meanings of mudra.

By applying the various meditative practices students' revelation of the personal *sthana* entailed direct confrontation with the totality of previous unskillful mental conditions (*klesa*).

The strong are able to ignore death and suffering whilst in the midst of violent combat. The extreme sufferings and pain caused by many arrows or spears is not as great as the suffer-

ing caused by one's own faults (Ch. 4:17, *Bodhicaryavatara*
("Entering into the Path of Wisdom") by Shantideva).

Again and again students would return to recollect previous errors,
misunderstandings, sorrowful experiences, etc., until they could see
their part in their creation. They would come to be aware of the particular techniques of self-deception they employed—both in dealing with
the world at large and with themselves. Such self-deceits manifested
equally in the physical realms of being. How students took care of their
health reflected their *sthana* toward their bodies.

In the mind/body encounters of defense, self-deceit due to *sthana*
meant the creation of blind spots in defensive movements, ways of performing techniques which ensured injury to oneself. If a particular
sthana meant habitual concentration upon a certain part of an assail-
ant's body, it ensured that his movements in another part would not be
observed. In turn this meant a dangerous blow could be received. It is
not difficult, even for a newcomer to *Chuan Fa*, to see how a practitioner
whose mental condition adopts a *sthana* which predominates in fearful
or guilt-filled states can create a mental desire (or obsession) to be punished for "wrongs," and consequent upon this perform movements—
alone or with others—in such a way as to ensure personal bodily injury.

A person who continually maintains these mental conditions (or
any others) during day-to-day life can be seen as possessing a very
rigid *sthana*. Such unaware mental patterns and drives are revealed and
uncovered through the meditative examination of the *sthana*. Until this
process is fully engaged in, the student can not perform the trainings in
the correct manner. Once this position of initial self-awareness has been
correctly attained and acknowledged, the student is in a position to
gain a wider perspective of the potential inner forces previously
unavailable. The student would then seek to penetrate and understand
the deeper "strata" of the mind/body interplay and being he experienced as his "own."

> If exercise is not interrupted and goes on to the purification of
> Mind, it will make what is immature become mature and the
> supernatural powers will be attained (*Mahavairocana Sutra.*
> Ch.11)

SAMASTHANA

The process through which the student became fully aware of the
causal forces involved in the creation of (and clinging to) their *sthana*,
lay in a form of self-awareness training called a *Samasthana* (Chinese:

Hsing I; Japanese: *Shin I*) [Note 86]. This term, which literally means a "configuration" or "distinctive collective patterning or shape," was used in the Vajramukti tradition to depict a series of practices designed to blend, intermingle and then dissolve all the various faces (*Sthana*) worn by the practitioner. Such a blending was seen as the antidote to the rigid mental and/or physical demarcations employed in the maintenance of a *Sthana.*

Samasthana practices were performed in many different ways and toward many different forms of "self-fiction," but in each case it indicated the development of a dissolving awareness regarding a "position" held by the student. The basis of this position was then acknowledged, and a series of practices were engaged in that were designed to overcome it. These fixed "positions" may be mental or physical in nature (or combinations of either), and the *Samasthana* sought to overturn them at source. The word, and what it represented, was also applied to the process of both healing or therapeutic endeavors (where the *Sthana* was the "face" or "form" of illness and *Samasthana* was the manner of therapy). In the case of mental illness, the process and goal indicated by the term *Samasthana* was doubly appropriate.

In *Chuan Fa,* the goal of *Samasthana* was to attain a complete mastery over all the active processes that gave rise to the various forms of suffering engendered, experienced, and perpetuated, often unknowingly, by the practitioner. Dynamic *Samasthana,* a concept unique to *Chuan Fa,* manifested within the *pratima* and required the practitioner to develop a special and continuous awareness of both the inner and outer mental and physical generative activities as they actually manifested during the practice. At its simplest level, the performance of *pratima* involved creating an internal mental drama within which students visualized, and then warded off, various kinds of armed and unarmed attacks. Later these attacks would also be visualized along with the appropriate emotional responses also being involved. Students would try to create an awareness of both their own and the attacker's mental and emotional state during the sequences. Not only would they "see" the movement, they would also mentally "feel" the intensity and hatred involved in its creation. By meditatively observing the mental relationship to such experiences students could develop a direct awareness of the nature and content of their personal *sthana.*

> Having overcome impure forms of the Self one should create instead the priceless likeness of the Conqueror's Jewel. Seize firmly that essence which is the aspiration to Enlightenment (Ch.1:10 *Bodhicaryavatara* [Entering into the Path of Wisdom], by Shantideva).

Repeated psychodramas took many different forms and manifestations, and eventually created all the mental patterns of the "real" thing. There arose a form of vicarious knowledge within which body and mind "saw" each other clearly. These methods were known within Buddhism as "skillful means" (*upaya*). Each of the *pratima* movement sequences had special visualizations connected to its performance, and their mental reflections were observed in a meditative manner.

As mentioned previously, certain of these reflections could be predetermined by the teacher because of the *pratima* he chose to teach and explain to the student. The most important *pratima* were accorded an elemental "ruler," and practice of all the elemental forms equally ensured that the whole range of mental and emotional conditions they paradigmatically represented would have to be fully experienced [Notes 86a, 89].

As the mental and physical practice deepened and was continually repeated, certain insights into both the meaning of the movement itself—and into its mental correspondences—manifested. From such insights students gradually perceived more of their own personal nature and causal patterns. As these insights accumulated, and if they were correctly perceived and interpreted under guidance, students steadily became freed from their deep substrata (*laksya*) of influence. Such a condition was very difficult to achieve fully, demanding total concentration, as ordinarily each of the factors concerned (mind or body) was, in itself, sufficiently powerful to occupy the attention in its own right [Note 86b]. Students' attitudes of concentration in this practice are expressed in chapter 1: verse 12 of the *Manjusrinama sangiti* as:

Mahabalo Rddhibalopeto, Mahavego Mahajava
Mahadhiko, Mahasakhyo, Mahabalaparakrama.

With great Power, great impetus and speed.
Majestic, powerful, renowned and thrusting forwards
    with great power.

However, if it could be properly achieved, it enabled practitioners to determine (and extend to its fullest) the awareness potential of his or her individual mind/body complex to new and greater levels. It was similar in significance to both the *Theravada Vipassana* (insight) and *Samatha* (calming) meditation methods, but unlike them, its method of development involved an active and dynamic process of mind and body which, in some forms, could equally involve other beings.

Practice of the *pratima* continued unceasingly until its physical requirements were perfected, a stage which could only be achieved when its mental reflex was equally mastered. At this point a new *pratima* would be shown, one which required a different form of physical and meditational ability. Through such progressive practices, students would gradually balance out the elements of both mind and body and hopefully eliminate the various unskillful conditions of either. In doing this, students used and, more importantly, reoriented the very components which previously had been the cause of mental or physical suffering. An ancient Buddhist saying expresses this principle as "turning poison into medicine."

> Those who receive blows upon their chest conquer their enemies. They are victorious Heroes. Others are only slayers of the dead (*Bodhicaryavatara* 5:v20).

Pratima performed in such a manner as to aid the development of *Samasthana* were called in Chinese *hsing* (Japanese: *Kata*) and this word, or its literal equivalents, is still used in modern times within many of the martial arts of China and Japan, although within them its original significance is not often understood. Many modern texts of Buddhism present the Sanskrit term *Rupa* to represent the apparent forms or shapes of things in general, but this term does not adequately convey the subtleties of Buddhist terminology in regard to such descriptions, nor the particular connotations implied in certain of its descriptive terms. While the term *rupa* described the type of external appearances in things, *Samasthana* conveyed the idea of various cohesive principles themselves, which result in an appearance or shape. This may, or may not, include the creation of a *rupa*. We can make the shape of a circle with our hands and this can be seen, but we can also think its shape and this cannot [Note 74b].

What was taught by the *Samasthana* was a multilevel process in that students first came to understand more of what already existed (i.e., their *Sthana*), and then they engaged in penetrative meditative and physical practices in order to truly determine the causal forces in all their manifestations (i.e., the *Samasthana*). Viewed simply, the kinetic *pratima* enacted and expressed the practitioner's *Sthana*, while the successful results of *Samasthana* were expressed in the *nata*, which themselves were regarded as models of perfection which could only be performed perfectly when the mind/body dichotomy had ceased to exert its influence. *Samasthana* application aimed to develop not only a complete, dynamic and contemporaneous experiential awareness of mind and body (*Anubhakayacitta smriti*), but equally an awareness of a dynamic, non-temporal stillness.

The *Pratima* thus became the expression of a dynamic stillness and a stilled dynamic. Through such realization the highest mental liberation in, and of, mind and body could be attained, This exalted principle could only be found in the traditions of the Chinese esoteric schools but its principle underlay many of the Yogacara doctrines and Sutras.

This realization could seem to have both tactical and spiritual advantages, for it enabled its possessor to act in a completely liberated manner, without fear or psychological barriers. It could be viewed as potentially dangerous in the wrong hands, but it could not really be dangerous because this attainment was not a possessed "thing," but a manifestation of a gradual process of self-unfolding and liberation which, in its journey, transformed its bearer.

This transformation was the real significance of the *Sthana* and *Samasthana* principles in the art of *Chuan Fa* and the real goal of the kinetic sequences. This method was especial to *Chuan Fa*, which often sought, through skillful methods, to present the teachings in a form understandable to both the warrior class and ordinary people. *Chuan Fa* embodied harmonized teaching and training which could serve as either self-defense, healing, psychological revelation, vivifying exercise, or a spiritual path, and could act as a catalyst to people who would normally not be interested in spiritual principles or other training. Human existence was the common denominator, though its condition and qualities vary greatly. The practitioner proceeds as we are told in chapter 5, 10 of the *Manjusrinama sangiti*.

> Mahadhyanasamadhistho Mahaprajnasariradhrk
> Mahabalo Mahopaya Pranidhijnanasagara

> Dwelling in the Samadhi of deepest concentration and great Wisdom, with body of great Insight and great Power, with skillful methods and bearing the Vow like the Ocean of Wisdom.

SCHOOLS

Various teachers devised different ways of teaching or performing the *Nata* or *Pratima* sequences, some practiced them faster and faster, others mixed fast and slow rhythms together. Different emphases were adapted for different kinds of students. These differences did not constitute variant "schools" of teaching, for "schools" were only distinguished by their teacher or monastery rather than by what they practiced. All the teaching groups possessed a *Gotra* (spiritual lineage) and *Kula* (spiritual family) but this was incidental. As far as Buddhism was concerned there were no such things as "schools" of practice, for all equally followed the received dharma (teachings) and no monk would be foolish enough to pretend he had "invented" a method superior (i.e., different or altered) to that of a Buddha [Note 74d].

In general Buddhist terminology relating to *Chuan Fa* emphasizes principles rather than specifics, and describes its practices in terms of attitudes or motivations, rather than precise constituents. This is what we would expect, for the central issue in a living teaching must always be the attainment of its highest ideal (the dharma). It is not until much later that we find retrospective accounts of the environment conducive to these principles or descriptions of their practices. In such accounts reference is often made to texts which no longer exist. We also find incomplete quotations that only cite the title or the authors' names.

DEVELOPMENT OF VAJRAMUKTI

The Holy Masters, the Lions expounding the Sutra, mystic and supreme (*Saddharma Pundarika Sutra*)

Astadasarahantapani

A central practice of the Buddhist Lion Play School lay in its *nata* and forms (Sanskrit: *pratima*). The most important *nata* in India was called, according to the Chinese accounts, the "18 Subduings" (*Astadasajacan*) or "18 Victors" (*Astadasavijaya*). These names seem to reflect the doctrine of the 18 Paramitas and the 18 Voidnesses of Wisdom developed

Figure 106. Fudo (Acalaraja) with attendants. One of the manifestations of Great Wisdom. With the rope he binds all evil and with the sword he cuts off the heads of Greed, Aversion and Ignorance. (Painting by Ryusen Miyahara, Kongoryuji Temple.)

Figure 107. Bodhidharma. Chinese painting. (Kongoryuji Temple.)

within Chinese Buddhism by the Yogacara School of Vasubandhu, although there are similar groupings of 18 spiritual realities in many earlier traditions.

The 18 Subduings is usually said to have been introduced into China by the Indian teacher Bodhidharma [Note 14, 39]. He was sent, perhaps as a missionary to succeed Bodhiruci, by his Sarvastivada-trained teacher Prajnatara, but its practice must have preceded him as its constituent principles were already long known to Chinese Buddhists. Bodhidharma taught various Vajramukti health exercises and sequences of the Ksatreya *nata* to the monks of the Shaolin Monastery in the Sung mountains of northern China, a temple originally founded by Emperor Hsiao Wen for the Sarvastivada monk Bhadra. It is recorded that these mountain temples had been in the Sung range since 381.

Bodhidharma, in true Mahayana spirit, was moved to pity when he saw the terrible physical condition of the monks who had practiced the long term meditation retreats. Likening them to the young Shakyamuni—who almost died from such ascesis—he informed the monks that he would teach their "bodies and minds" the Buddha's dharma. To this end he taught them one complete *nata* and two *pratima* of the

Bodhisattva Vajramukti, namely the aforementioned *Astadasajacan*, which is a kinetic emulation of the 18 levels of *prajna* wisdom achieved by means of ritual mudra sequences. The *Asthimajja Parisuddhi*—a Buddhist movement and respiratory yoga for tissue regeneration, catharsis, and karmic recognition—and the *Snavasjala-nidana-vijnapti*—a special and cathartic physical discipline of psychic energy purification through mantra and meditation. These last two teachings have Chinese titles taken from lines in the *Vajrasamadhi Sutra* of Nagarjuna [Notes 74c].

The sequences, and the philosophy they express, formed the origin of all the spiritually oriented medical practices, diagnostics, therapies and meditative arts used within the genuine *Chuan Fa* today. The school of health-maintaining exercises and movement meditation subsequently founded upon these sequences was based upon a phronesic extension of the *Sarvastivada/Vaibhasika Vijnapti* Doctrine (from which derived *Chuan Fa's* philosophy of tactical encounter) blended with the Yogacara theory of existence (from which came *Chuan Fa's* perception of the Self and of Consciousness).

Figure 108. Bodhisattva performing hand movements from the "Asthimajja Parisuddhi." Tung Huang caves, China. (British Museum, London.)

Figure 109. Restored statues of Arahants at the Shaolin Temple, Honan. (Author's collection.)

As was common in China, the "subduings" developed a new title and were called the *Shipalohanshou*, the "18 Hand Moves of the Arahants" (Sanskrit: *Astadasarahantapani*). Whether this was an original Chinese name or one taken direct from Sanskrit we cannot tell but the very title "Arahant" is an ancient Buddhist Sanskrit term derived from the word *Arihan* (Chinese: *Lohan*) literally meaning "those who subdue, or attain victory over foes" [Note 38a]. Many contemporary Chinese and Korean temples possess Arahant halls where stand lifelike statues of the original 18 Arahants. Some of these are many hundreds of years old and the Arahants portrayed can be recognized from appearance and dress, for they represent many different races and cultures.

This *Hsing* was composed of eighteen classical sets of mudra (ritual symbolic gestures) each of which were combined with respiratory patterns, steps, muscle flexations and specific meditation themes. It was the most important Buddhist *nata / Hsing* introduced into China and was, in the five element system, associated directly with the quintessential element held to contain the "seed" of all Vajramukti practices. It was from this early period that such *Hsings* were taught as containing three levels of understanding and meaning (Sanskrit: *Trisatyabhumi*), each relating to the mind, body and speech analysis common in both the esoteric (Chinese: *Mi Chiao*) tradition and exoteric schools.

Figure 110. Arahants. (Ryusen Miyahara.)

Figure 111. Nakala, one of the Arahants, with attendants. (Painting by Ryusen Miyahara, Kongoryuji Temple.)

By the sixth century, the *Hsing* had developed a shorter name based upon an abbreviation of its Sanskrit titles. The original *Astadasajacan* and *Trisatyabhumi* were integrated and shortened into *Trican* (Triple Battle) and this Sanskrit term was transliterated into Chinese as *Sanchin* or sometimes *Sanchan*, meaning the same, and was understood as indicating the battle of mind, body, and speech undertaken by the trainee esoteric monks. This name has persisted into modern times [Note 88].

The predominant way of placing the body in this *Hsing* (its *kayasthana*) is termed the Sanchin stance. This is distinct from many other forms of body posture used for defensive purposes. When wearing the monk's robe, it is the only stance completely invisible to an observer. It is thus non-aggressive in appearance. It is the only stance taken directly from the outer shape of the *vajra* (thunderbolt) and physically embodies its triangulation of physical and mental harmony and balance. In the stance the body is segmented into five elemental levels, each being composed of three equal degrees of torsion. In toto these form three complete "jewel" shapes representing the Buddha, Dharma and Sangha [Note 36C].

Figure 112. Gosanze Mio (Trilokavijaya Vidyaraja). "He who has conquered the three worlds experienced through Desire, Form, or the Formless." The hand position is a form of the "Turning of the Wheel of the Law" Mudra common in Tibet. (Seventh century, Toji, Kyoto, Japan. Author's collection.)

By balancing the tripartite torsion, both in the outer muscles and the inner organs, a composite pattern of physical power is maintained in which the body, although totally stilled, is capable of instantaneous response to external conditions. It is also the only stance to and from which a monk can immediately stand or sit in the crossed-legged meditation position. In the *Sanchin Hsing* the arms are placed in the mudra of the Vajramukti Bodhisattva portrayed in the Kongokai Maha Mandala and this whole position is known as the *Trilokavijayakayasthana* (the position of one who has subdued the three realms of existence). This in turn represents the supreme and non-ignorant manner of dealing with situations perceived as dangerous or life-threatening.

Ritualized practice of the *Sanchin* took place after an elemental mandala of nine squares had been drawn on the ground. This Karma (activity) Mandala form represented the elements at each of its cardinal points and, as the student went through the steps and sequences, he or she symbolically re-enacted a cathartic rebirth into the world of human beings which began and ended at the central element of ether (or vital energy). Such practices enabled a student to truly say they had been "walking" on water, fire or air and the expression "walking a mandala" (*mandalapada*) came from this practice. It is referred to indirectly in descriptions within the *Kongochokyo* [See Note 83] where the initiate is told to "walk with diamond steps from one part of the mandala to another." The phrase "diamond steps" refers to a series of eight movements and turns in the *Sanchin* stance which, when performed, cause the body to trace the eight sections of the *kongokai* (thunderbolt) mandala on the ground and in the process also define its central (ninth) area. The *Manjusrinama sangiti* (Ch. 9 V,3) describes a similar ritual enactment in the following terms:

> Bahudandasataksepa
> Padanilsapanartana
> Sroimac chatabhuyabhago
> gaganabhoganartana.

> Moving the arms like a hundred clubs
> and walking with thudding steps
> the one of glory flexes his arms
> like the expanse of the Sky.

SUPERNATURAL POWERS

One of the *Sanchin Hsing*'s renowned Vajramukti techniques was called in India the *Iksana Vidya*. This term described the mystical art (Sanskrit: *Vidya*) of being able to determine and/or direct another person's thoughts or intentions (Sanskrit: *Iksana*). Examples of the *Iksana* methods are shown in the tale of the sage Mahakatyana contained in Kumaralita's treatise titled the *Kalapananmamdatika*. In this tale the sage is told by King Pradyota (whom he is visiting) that his student Sarana, son of the King of Uddiyana, has been sleeping with the King's wife. The

King, despite Sarana's protests of innocence, imprisons Sarana and has him beaten severely.

Sarana subsequently emplores Mahakatyana to release him from his monastic vows in order that he may get his father to raise an army against Pradyota. Mahakatyana advises Sarana not to engage in a planned battle but Sarana states his intention to ignore his advice. Through his mental powers, Mahakatyana causes a vision to arise in Sarana's mind while he is asleep. In this vision he is defeated in battle and taken prisoner under miserable and pitiful conditions. Then he is led away to be executed. On the way Sarana encounters Mahakatyana and begs his forgiveness. This vision eventually persuades Sarana not to seek revenge.

Another and similar account is contained in the Theravada *Samyutta Nikaya* (Vol.1, Chapter 11:227), Buddhaghosa's *Sarahappakasini*, and other *Mahayana Sutras*. This is the story of Vemacitra, King of the Asuras. The King announces his intention to come and pay his respects to a group of forest dwelling sages. When he arrives before them, instead of being humbly dressed and bringing the traditional gifts and offerings, he is arrayed in all his royal robes and weapons. The sages realize this is a mark of his secret arrogance and a sign that they should fear for their lives in the future.

After he leaves, and in order to dissuade him from harming them, they vanish from their huts, reappear before him and ask him to give them a pledge for their safety. Vemacitra, as they suspected, tells them that he gives only terror to others. They decide to give him a demonstration of the superiority of their powers and predict that he will never be free from fear from that moment forth. They then vanish from his sight. Vemacitra ignores their words but shortly after this event begins to have troubled sleep and worries consume him. He suspects plots against him everywhere and, within a short time, becomes frightened of even his own shadow, seeing it as if the shadow of an assassin.

The ability to disturb the consciousness of another person by such supernormal methods is a faculty readily accepted in all forms of Buddhism and was spoken of in the *Vimsatika Karika* of Vasubandhu, who used these two stories as examples of both its efficacy and its scriptural precedents. However this was a dangerous technique in that it incurred a far greater karmic responsibility on the part of its initiator than someone who resorts to merely physical violence or acts of revenge. While someone may be able to endure physical pain or verbal abuse with perseverance, the disruption of another's consciousness prohibits all forms of equanimity whatsoever.

In Buddhism the motivations and volitions governing a physical action are considered at least equal, and sometimes more, than the actual act itself. An act of violence held in the mind can sometimes be more harmful than its physical expression.

> Even in sorrow the enlightened ought not to disturb inner tranquillity because he is fighting with the passions and, in warfare, pain is trivial (*Bodhicaryavatara* 5:v.19).

Much of the descriptive language used within the ancient accounts of *Chuan Fa* is highly colorful or symbolic in content. This was often done deliberately to hide its significance from those who were not students of *Chuan Fa*. The elemental colors, especially, crop up again and again in presentations of *Chuan Fa* descriptions. In Buddhist explanations of *nata* movement sequences (and arts which developed from them) a special significance is placed upon the color white as a prefix to the name of important techniques or sequences.

USAGE OF THE TERM "WHITE"

The term "white" used in these and other titles was common in Buddhist practice and seems to have been understood as being synonymous in meaning with "good" or "without impurity." It occurs in many descriptions of Buddhist activities [Note 90]. Another reason for choosing the term "white" is perhaps explained by the Chinese scripture's descriptions of the death of the Shakyamuni Buddha. Within them it is said that when he died all the Sala trees in the grove around him flowered out of season and their "white blossoms" fell around his resting place. In the Chinese scriptures the leaves of these trees are described as "turning white like the wings of a Heron." I Tsing mentions this legend in his diary [Note 55].

The *Jetavana* (Grove of Victory) in which the Buddha chose to leave this realm was, prior to his renaming it, known as the "White Heron Grove" (Sanskrit: *Suklahavarsa*; Chinese: *Pal Hao Lin*; Japanese: *Hakukakurin*) which probably explains the association made between leaves and wings in the Chinese accounts. (Modern day Japan still preserves the Chinese custom of taking a white heron made of folded paper to a sick person's bedside in the belief that it will aid recovery.)

The esoteric master Nagarjuna is said to have received part of the *Prajna Paramita Sutras* while at a "White Heron lake" (Chinese: *Pa Hao Chia*) in Rejagraha, India. The use of the word "white" in a Buddhist title often indirectly refers to this grove, in the sense that it implies something perfect has been achieved within an activity. A short form of this Chinese name, *Pai Lin* (White Grove; Japanese: *Hakurin*) became a common synonym for a monastic dwelling. The popular title of the Shao Lin Szu (a monastery later famed for its traditions of *Chuan Fa*) is

Figure 113. Shakyamuni rising from his coffin. This picture with Chinese style fig-ures echoes a legend that Shakyamuni rose once before he died to greet the spirit of his mother, who had just arrived. The protecting deities are shown in red on the right. (Ryusen Miyahara.)

but a shortened form of the fuller title *Shao Pai Lin,* a small white (leaved) grove and refers to the Jetvana grove.

In Chinese transliteration *Jetvana* became *Chin Lin* (Japanese: *Chin,* or *Sho-Rin*). It may be relevant that one of the sects within the Indian Sarvastivada School was also called the Jetavana. The term "white" was later also adopted by temples devoted to chanting the White Lotus Sutra (*Saddharma Pundarika*). We can see that it was an extremely common title with a variety of explanations. All or part of these nomenclatures were used in later schools developing from the Shipalo-hanshu.

Another Trican technique was the *Maha Suklaja,* a title literally meaning "Great White Shattering" (= destruction). This term described an esoteric technique which hyperactivated the intrinsic energy within parts of an attacker's body, causing them to vibrate and disrupt the workings of the major internal organs. One result of this was an instant unconsciousness and—if the technique was continued—death. It was practiced by placing the hands in a special mudra and chanting certain sacred syllables continuously.

A less powerful form of this technique, known simply as *Suklaja,* was used in "Tiger striking," a practice I will describe later. These techniques may seem violent, but really consist of extracted parts of the Buddhist science of healing. The *Mahasuklaja* is intended to be used against physical illnesses such as physical tumors and cancers, or the expulsion of foreign bodies (such as arrowheads, etc.). We can compare these techniques with ones used in native Indian Tantra, such as what was called in Chinese the *Chu Pan Chu* (Japanese: *Kuhanku*). This term described an Indian method for cursing and causing the death of someone by means of the *Vetali* method. The *Vetali* practice involved exhuming a freshly buried corpse and chanting ritual incantations over it. This was a technique used by those inclined to magic or witchcraft. The name *Vetali* was translated in Chinese as meaning "those who half-open the door" and this apparently refers to the door of life and death. It seems very similar in nature to the Haitian Voodoo belief in Zombies.

The Sanskrit name *Mahasuklaja* was rendered into Chinese as *Pa She* and this word was used in China to refer to both the healing art and the *Vajramukti* techniques of disarming and rendering someone harmless without resorting to weaponry or violent means. Its practice method was called the *Suklavijaya* (Chinese: *Pa*, or *P'ai*, *Chin*), a name which literally means the "White Victory" [See ref. in Note 36c]. Several other esoteric techniques were credited to the *Trican Nata* and its correct performance was considered highly advanced and difficult to master [Note 89]. These mysteriously termed techniques were some of the secret methods of the Bodhisattva Vajramukti transmitted to China by the monks.

VYAGHRAJA: TIGER STRIKING

Although part of the Lion Play, Tiger Striking (Sanskrit: *Vyaghraja*) became a practice of the non-Ksatreya Indian warriors and was oriented toward developing battleground combat efficacy, it was probably originally practiced as a battle art by those who could not afford to purchase adequate weapons but nevertheless needed to defend themselves. Compared to the Vajramukti proper, it consisted of very simple and direct movements and, in popular usage, seems to have possessed little of the exalted spiritual philosophy so heavily emphasized within the Ksatreya caste. According to accounts, Tiger Striking consisted mainly of developing efficacy in administering fast handblows which were directed toward the neural centers of an opponent's body and/or its psychic energy structure. It used the hands and fingers rather like the armed warrior used a sword and club.

It seems highly likely that the title *Vyaghraja* described the art developed and used by Indian doctors (perhaps Jivaka, the Buddha's physician) for healing purposes. According to temple healing theory, the human body was animated by its vital energy or life force (Chinese: *Sheng Lai Li*; Japanese: *Seirairyoku*; Sanskrit: *Jivasantanikratkarsa*). This

Figure 114. Close-up of figure 92. The figure's left hand is clearly held in a knuckle striking position. The right hand performs a blocking technique. (Author's collection.)

circulated around and through the body like blood. Such a force corresponded to what in India was called *jivat* (see Notes 53 regarding *Chi*, 54, 17). The "veins" and patterns this energy took when it circulated within the body were termed in Sanskrit *nadi* and its strongest flow was within the "pith" or bone marrow. Some accounts held that it was actually generated from within this. From here it radiated out, or directly flowed into specific parts of the body. In this case, where it did so was its most vulnerable point, and it was to such places that therapists and warriors directed their attention.

We can see the suggestion of "flowing" (Japanese: *ryu*; Chinese: *lai*) existed even up until the seventh century because the diary of the Chinese pilgrim I Tsing, who went to India in search of the teachings, mentions a river called Naganadi (dragon flow). This title was an alternative title for *Sheng lai li* and was possibly used in this case because the river embodied a healing spa or spring.

The entrance and exit points in the body at which *jivat* was accessible to external influence were known in India as *marma*, meaning "vulnerable," or "vitality" points (Chinese: *Chiu So*; Japanese: *Kyusho*). The *marma* could be manipulated, in various manners, to alter the rate, presence, or direction of the *jivat* flow within the *nadi*. Such points are referred to by Queen Srimala in chapter 2, Section C of the *Srimalasimhanada Sutra* when she vows (among other things) to physically strike opponents of the dharma on such vital points [Note 36 h].

As we saw previously, it was an old tradition in India that *marma* and other vital points had been discovered by battle surgeons noticing that warriors who had been slightly injured by enemy arrows or daggers often experienced miraculous cures to ailments they had previously suffered from. The *marma* could also be used to halt or expel *jivat* completely and this art of arresting the *jivat* seems to have formed the effective basis of Tiger Striking. Because this teaching used the doctrine of elements, it seems highly likely that it stems from a Sarvastivada lineage of Northern India.

Building on their rapidly developing knowledge, the ancient doctors developed charts of the *marma* points and included them in the various massage (*udvartana*) techniques common to ancient Indian medicine. We have records of ancient texts relating to these being translated by the Buddhist monk Nagarjuna in the years A.D. 100–200 (see chronology, Table 5 on page 242.) In A.D. 148 the famous Indian Buddhist missionary An Shih Kuo had translated texts on respiratory exercises and unexpected causes of death. These works were translated later into the Arabic language by visiting merchants and helped form significant sections of the later Arabian treatises upon the healing and diagnostic arts. Such texts had earlier been taken to Greece and further by the invading Alexandrian armies.

While we cannot say for certain that the Chinese developed their ideas about acupuncture points directly from India, it does seem an obvious extension of the Vajramukti teachings. In the earliest Chinese medical text we have dates from around 540 B.C. although Chinese medicine must have existed as a general folk system long before that.

The famous Doctor Hua To (second to third century A.D.) is known to have used acupuncture to heal. It was also at this time that the Chinese used imported Indian herbs as anesthetics and antiseptics during their medical treatment. Many Indian Buddhist missionaries entered China then, bringing all their knowledge and skills. We should recall that for many years China's Confucian ethics had forbidden the dissection of bodies and due to this, there was a great lack of surgical knowledge. Any major surgery was therefore very hazardous. To those native surgeons eager to learn more, the Buddhist monk healers must have seemed like a gift from heaven.

It was at this time and probably through these missionaries that the Lion Play and Tiger Striking methods first entered China. This is reflected in the rise of the "extending hands" teaching of Kuo Chi Yi mentioned previously. The defensive nature of the practice is high-

Table 5. Development and Nomenclature in the Art of Vajramukti.

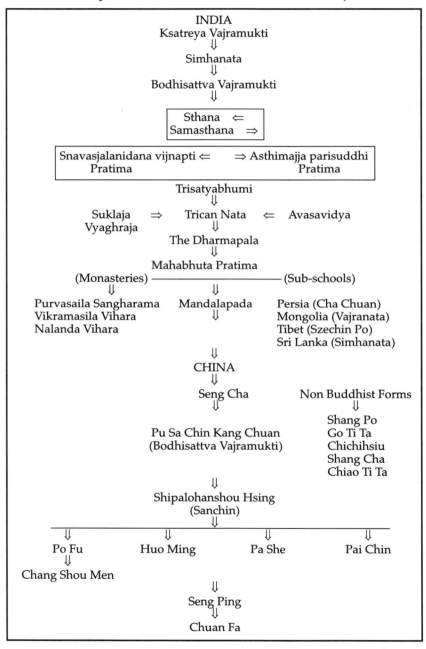

INDIA
Ksatreya Vajramukti
⇓
Simhanata
⇓
Bodhisattva Vajramukti
⇓

Sthana ⇐
Samasthana ⇒

Snavasjalanidana vijnapti ⇐   ⇒ Asthimajja parisuddhi
Pratima   Pratima

Trisatyabhumi
⇓
Suklaja   ⇒   Trican Nata   ⇐   Avasavidya
Vyaghraja   ⇓
The Dharmapala
⇓
Mahabhuta Pratima
(Monasteries) ——————————— (Sub-schools)
⇓   ⇓
Purvasaila Sangharama   Mandalapada   Persia (Cha Chuan)
Vikramasila Vihara   ⇓   Mongolia (Vajranata)
Nalanda Vihara   Tibet (Szechin Po)
                                                     Sri Lanka (Simhanata)

⇓
CHINA
⇓
Seng Cha   Non Buddhist Forms
⇓   ⇓
                                     Shang Po
Pu Sa Chin Kang Chuan   Go Ti Ta
(Bodhisattva Vajramukti)   Chichihsiu
                                     Shang Cha
                                     Chiao Ti Ta

⇓
Shipalohanshou Hsing
(Sanchin)
⇓
⇓   ⇓   ⇓   ⇓
Po Fu   Huo Ming   Pa She   Pai Chin
⇓
Chang Shou Men

⇓
Seng Ping
⇓
Chuan Fa

lighted in an account of a Master called Tung Chuan (literally, "Eastern clasped hand," (Japanese: *Token*) [see Note 37b].

During the time of Emperor Ni Wan Ti of the Liang Dynasty (535–551) he was recorded as being able to overcome and disarm any armed person who attacked him using only his bare hands. This account was recorded within twenty years of Bodhidharma's death. Certainly for the 500 years prior its second-century inception and after the time of the Chou Emperor Chi Chi Wang, the Chinese National Army had made great technological and tactical strides, inventing the crossbow along the way, but as yet they had no form of subtle combat training. The Indian Vajramukti would have fulfilled this need exactly and at the right moment for the current Chinese military needs, as at this very time they were desperately battling against an invasion by the Huns in the North, who were threatening to sweep down across the country, and who used battle techniques quite unknown in China. In such conditions generals are apt to seize upon any techniques they encounter that can help.

Later, in the tenth century, even Emperor Sung Tai Jo is said to have mastered the "extending hand" system of Kuo Chi Yi and recommended its practice to his army. He is said to have mastered this defensive art in order to aid his people to defend themselves from the invading armies of the north. It was also possible that by the eighth century the Huns themselves had learned something of the Vajramukti techniques from visiting Tibetan traders and explorers.

Another early Indian school of practice is known to us only as a "Monastic Body protecting form" called in Sanskrit equally *Bhikshu Angapala* (monk's limb protection), *Bhikshu Rakshana* (monk defense), or *Prajapala vidya* (method for defense of the state's subjects) but little else can be discovered concerning its practices. We can see an echo of the *Angapala* in the name of the *Surangama Sutra* for this title was translated by Kumarajiva in the fourth century as meaning "He of the heroic (*sura*) limbs (*anga*)."

These arts developed in those northeastern parts of India most concerned with the Sarvastivada form ("all is as it is" teaching) of Buddhist Doctrine and we must assume that they were part of that sect's interpretation of the Bodhisattva Vajramukti principles. They may have been the source for the still prevalent Szechinpo Lama dances. The technical term *Prajapala* was certainly known in Tibet [See Notes 72m, 73].

In addition to the Indian and North Chinese accounts there is a legend, preserved in both the Ryukyuan *Kempo Hishu*, the *Itosushi*, and other Japanese manuscripts, that the technique of Vyaghraja in *Chuan Fa* developed from teachings contained in a manuscript account brought from India, via a Tibetan monastery, into China which

རྱ་ཆེན་སྤྱོང་ཕྱུག་མད་པོ་དང་རྒྱ་ལ་ལྔ་མ་ཆེ་ཤེས་གསུམ་རེད། དེ་བཞིན་ལ་གླུ་བདག

ཆེན་རེར་པོ་ཆེ་ཞེས་པ་ས་སྐྱེའི་ཚོ་ལ་ལུགས་ཏུ་དྲུག་འཁྲིད་དང་། གསུམ་པ

རེན་པོ་ཆེ་ཞེས་པ་བཀའ་བརྒྱུད་ཚོས་ལུགས་ཏེ་དྲུག་འཁྲིད་དང་། བདུན་

འཛོམས་རེར་པོ་ཆེ་ཞེས་ནང་མཐི་ཚོས་ལུགས་ཏུ་དྲུག་འཁྲིད་རེད།

ཚོས་ལུགས་ལ་དེ་ཉིད་དགོནེ་བ་ལ་ཡང་མང་ལ་ལགས་ཡོད་ལུགས་ཡོད

པ་རེད། ~ སྐྱབས་མགོན་དུ་ལའི་བླ་མ་ཚོག་ཉི་ས་སྐྱ་དགོ

ལུགས། བཀའ་བརྒྱུད། རྙིང་ལ་བཞ་ས་ཏེ་ཚོས་ཆོན་མ་མཐུན་གྱི

ཡོད་ཀྱང་གཙོ་བོ་ནི་དགོ་ལུགས་པའི་ཚོས་གཞན་གི་ཡོད་པ་རེད།

ཆེན་ཀྱང་ཁོན་ཉི་ད་ཚོ་ཟོད་མི་ཟམ་ཚད་དི་བླ་མ་རེད་ལ་རྒྱལ་པོ…

ཡང་རེད། མེར་འཛུས་དགག་ག་སུམ་དང་། བཟོས་ལྷུན་པོ…

ཞེས་པའི་དགེ་ལུགས་པའི་དགོན་པ་ཆེན་པོ་དེ་ཚོའི་ནང་དུ་ཚོས་ཀྱི་སྤྱོབ་སྤྱོང

ལ་ལུགས་མ་ཁྱད་བོད་ཚོལ་ཁ་གསུམ་ཏེ་མི་དང་། ཏེ་རྒྱལ་རྒྱ་ཟག་སོ

པོ། ཟ་ལ་པོ། རྒྱ་གར། ལ་དྭགས། འབྲུག འབྲས་ལྗོངས། འཛར་

པབ་སོགས་འཛོམ་སྐྱིད་ནང་པའི་ཕྱུལ་སྟེ་མང་པོ་ནས་ཆེས་ཏེ་སྤྱོབ་སྤྱོང

ཐུས་ཏེ་རང་ཕྱུལ་ནང་དུ་གོན་པ་གསར་འཛུགས་དང་། བླ་ལ་སྤྲུ་པ་གས

བཟུག་མད་པོ་བྱས་ཡོད་པ་རེད། དཀོ་བོད་ཀྱི་དགོན་པ་ད་གོ་ལུགས

རྙིང་ལ་བཀའ་བརྒྱུད་ས་སྐྱུ་བཞ་ས་ཀྱི་ཆེ་ཆུང་ཆད་ལའི་དགོ་འདྲུས

ཆེའི་གསོ་ལ་ཆས་འཚོ་བ་མདང་ཆེ་བ་ནི་བོད་ག་ཟུང་དགས་ལྲ་ཕོ་བྲང་ལ

རབ་འཛས་རྒྱུ་དུ་གཟང་གི་ཡོད་ལ་རེད། དེ་བི་ཕོག་བོད་མི་རྣམས་ཚོ་ལ

དང་པ་ཆེ་དུག་མ་སོད་ཏུང་། ཚོ་ᆖ་ལས་ཚེ་འདི་དང་སྤོ་ལ་ག་ཉིས

ཆར་ཏྱེ་ཆེ་ད་དུ་བསྟིན་ཀྱར་གསོ་ལ་ཆ་ས་འདུ་ལ་མཁན་ན་རྒྱུན་ཆད

མེད་པ་ཡོད་ཏེ་ཡོད་པ་མ་རད། དགེ་འདུན་སོ་སོའི་ཕྱུད་ལ་ཁང

རས་ཀྱང་ས་མ་སྤྲུན་ག་ཆེད་དགགས་རྣན་ན་བཟང་དང་། ཁ་ལ་ལག་ཟས

པོ་བསྐྱར་གྱི་ཡོད་པ་རེད། ད་དང་ཡང་ཕྱུལ་ཁ་གསས་སྟོ་དགོན

དགོན་རྣས་དང་ལྲ་ལ་བོ་ཏྱི་རྒྱལ་བར་ཆེན་མཚན་རད་མི་ཏ་རང་དུ

recorded the hand-to-hand combat held between two deities. Their names are given phonetically as *Ka-shi-ma* and *Ka-chu-ri*. The account is said to describe their movements and practices and says they used these techniques to "control and restrain their followers." The manuscript is usually named in Japanese Ju Jitsu schools as the *Ta-ka-no-kabi*. I was even told this story while sitting by a mountainside of the Motobu peninsula of Okinawa with an old Karate master.

Here we have a fascinating record of a living tradition passed down from generation to generation among people who don't really understand its constituents, but who nevertheless still retain accurate elements of an earlier Chinese tradition. The word *Taka no Kabi*, literally meaning "the giving and receiving of the high(er) places" (Chinese: *Kao Cha Li*), actually represents the Sanskrit term *Devaloka dana adana*, meaning "The heavenly realm of those who give and those who receive," a meaning almost the same. The names *Kashimi* and *Kachuri* probably represent Chinese transliterations of the Sanskrit Buddhist term *Ksatre(ya) ksetra*. This means "the place—or land—of the Ksatreya." It is both a synonym for the land of India and a place where warriors train and exercise control [Note 76].

Figure 116. A suit of armor unearthed by Chinese archaeologists in the mountains bordering Tibet and preserved in the intense cold. Second to third century A.D. (Chinese Historical Agency.)

The whole name seems likely to represent a literal Sarvastivada source originally called something like the *Devaloka danadana Ksatreya ksetra*, and which, if the tradition is accurate, passed from the Vikramasila monastery of India, for it was to here the Tibetans mainly came to be taught Buddhist teachings [Note 72]. It may be a coincidence, but the area in India which contained the most Sarvastivada/Mahasanghika monasteries was named "Danakataka," a word which can be translated fancifully as the "gift of the closed hand." One further, as yet unnamed, method of the Vajramukti was said to have arrived in Southern China via Sri Lanka, but this awaits further research.

One point to recall in considering the history of *Chuan Fa* is the attitude of those who hold a reactive view regarding its origin, i.e., that it is an offensive art, perfected by those in need of defense or protection. A reactive art predominantly arises when the external conditions require it and ceases when those conditions are not met. If this were actually true we would expect to find that in times of warfare its practice would be more plentiful and in peacetime its practice would decline. In fact the very opposite proves true, the most obvious

Figure 117. The Dalai Lama and the Panchen Lama at their first meeting in Peking since the Chinese invasion of Tibet. (Author's collection.)

example being the Tang Dynasty of China. This era, predominantly a Buddhist one, was remarkable for its peacefulness and yet it is within it that *Chuan Fa* was most developed and practiced. There was obviously no tactical reason for this, and it is quite clear that it was the spiritual and therapeutic aspects of practice which made it most popular, and it is a responsive, rather than reactive, attitude toward *Chuan Fa* which ensured its continuance. Though aspects of *Chuan Fa* can be applied to external conditions it is not dependent upon them and it will arise even if they do not.

MASTERING THE MOVEMENT OF BODY AND MIND

Initially the study of movement patterns involved in the Vajramukti practices was mastered by learning the spiritually oriented *pratima* and *nata*, which were termed in China, *Hsing*. These movement patterns balanced and stabilized both bodily metabolism and muscular co-ordination, with the result that the physical being became healthy and energized. All of these physical practices were subjected to subsequent meditational observation in which students would examine what had arisen within their minds during the practices and their responses to such stimuli.

In order to enable us to overcome mental and spiritual imperfections, the Buddha taught what are called the "Four Foundations of Mindfulness" meditations. These are a progressive series of four meditations which are concerned with the development of a balanced, quiescent and ultimately realistic experience of mind called *smriti* (Chinese: *nien*; Japanese: *nen*). The four stages of this practice successively concern the body, feelings, mind, and mental objects. The basis of this teaching is laid out in the *Mahavagga* along with other forms of physical mindfulness. Movement awareness, a derivative of the first stage of practice, is described in the *Digha Nikaya* (2:94–5).

In China the first theme of the four stages, namely the mindfulness of the body, assumed an important position in the practices used for developing insight into the elemental and physical aspects of things. This practice consisted of a mindful observance of each constituent part of the body (what we could call its earth aspect) and then a recollection of the elemental principle it embodied (its air aspect). It was then recollected that these components did not constitute the "I" of their possessor (the fire aspect), but were shared by all beings (the water aspect). In the Theravada scriptures outlining this practice, each and every part of the body is described in detail, the result of which was to enable the practitioner to forge a new and more perceptive mental awareness and relationship to those parts of his or her being instinctively regarded as "his or her" most personal possessions. By becoming conscious of the most basic interplay of mind and body involved in the process of forming the idea of "self" ownership, the practitioner was beginning to develop an increased awareness of the autonomy of being.

Using one's imaginative faculty, take apart this leather bellows. With a knife of Wisdom cut the flesh from one's bones. Then, having taken apart one's bones and having gazed upon their very marrow, ask yourself, "Where is its essence?" (Chapter 5.V62–63 *Bodhicaryavatara* [Entering into the Path of Wisdom] by Shantideva).

This practice formed the precursor to the concept of a "body of mindfulness." To the monk this "body" was an idealized image of perfected being, a metaphysical body of the Buddha within, with which one aspired to communicate, whereas to the ordinary warrior, such autonomy over the body indicated only a superior and tactical battle psychology. Eventually the two differing orientations blended, and were used as tools to manifest another body—that of embodied mindfulness. This body represented the perfected harmony between the four wisdoms of the Mandala Buddhas (see *Mandala*) and the perfected human condition of existence.

Through such practices as mindfulness, practitioners were brought face to face with a greater experience of the nature and motivations they carried within their bodies and minds. The greater the amount of "self hiding" people engaged in, the greater the eventual revelation. The Hsing (*pratima*) demonstrated that interpretation of mind/body experience (*kayacittanubhu*) took three forms—the mentally created (*parikalpita*), the inter-dependent (*paratantra*) and the ultimate (*parinispanna*). The first two forms were conducive of suffering because they gave rise to, or reinforced, a dualistic and delusive interpretation of experiences. They did this by helping to create subtle conditioning impulses, known as "perfumes" (*vasana*), which in turn affected the patternings of the *klesa* in one's consciousness.

Vasana, once set into activity and if unchecked, carried on through life (and beyond) restructuring and orienting our responses and ways of being in various ways. As a result, the manner in which one understood things was often narrowed or warped. This in turn created the basis for specific mental karmas and the sufferings they initiated.

KARMIC ACTIVITY

The subsequent re-examination of self occupied a very important position in the training and could not be omitted. This practice can only be studied and understood within the proper environment—both physically and mentally. The factors involved in the generation of negative karma patterning became significant in order to understand how one actually generated wrong views concerning violence. This was very important for those who had entered the training from the military.

To be karmically generative (and thus retributive), the Sarvasti-vada and other sects taught that there are five factors whose presence is necessary for a retributive karmic activity (*karmaphala*; Chinese: *yeh hua*; Japanese: *joge*) to take place. Such activity is initiated even if the action is completed only mentally, for in such a case a mental karma is created. These factors are as follows: object (*vastu*), intention (*samjna*), effort (*prayoga*), mental stain (*klesa*) and accomplishment (*nispati*). This latter factor is an attitude of relief, satisfaction, or gladness at the event being completed. Vasubandhu and others also showed that the act of insti-gating another person to commit a violent act equally created a karma for the instigator.

In any act of violence, the higher the intensity with which the act is carried out, the greater the internal effect to the executor. Thus, in an act of violence there will be the *klesa* of hatred, which helps create the atti-tude necessary for the act, the person (object) of it, the intention/moti-vation to do it, seizing an opportunity and carrying it out, followed by the sense of satisfaction or relief when it has been done. These factors can be elementally co-ordinated thus:

> Earth: object
> Water: intention
> Fire: act
> Air: mental satisfaction
> Space/Ether: *klesa*

The *klesa* present can equally be a combination of factors, i.e., in the case in question, if the act is motivated by envy, the *klesa* of hatred will be present; the longing to do the act will be the *klesa* of greed; and belief that the act itself will change the situation will stem from delu-sion. It can be seen that in some cases an act which is thought about, nurtured and dwelt upon, but not actually carried out, can create more harmful patterns than a brief unplanned action. Similarly, an act of death caused unintentionally will likewise not carry the causal factors mentioned.

We can see that the various *klesa* involved here act as conditioning factors of consciousness and are themselves composed of the various forms of mental karma and *dukkha* (sufferings). These in turn arise and are dependent upon the various individual *samskaras* created or main-tained by the individual during life. *Klesa* form the predominant theme in creating the pattern of consciousness, itself, and it is from this pattern that we develop attitudes and desires that induce suffering in oneself and others.

This suffering can take many forms but common areas for their manifestation are concerned with the following:

Earth: Physical appetites
Water: Compulsive pleasures
Fire: Repetitive or fixed patterns of mind
Air: Negativizing attitudes
Ether: Self centeredness

Because these subtle principles were central to the practice, it is vital to have an overseeing master (*Upadhaya*; Chinese: *Sifu*; Japanese: *Shifu*) to both set up the environment around the practitioners correctly and to amend or correct errors in performance or understanding. According to the *Mahavagga* scripture, these teachers should be served faithfully for a minimum of ten years and, according to the *Siksasammucaya*, never willfully or prematurely abandoned [Note 36i].

> For those who are fortunate enough to be able to exert themselves, even if only out of fear of being punished, mindfulness is more easily generated by living with one's Master (Chapter 5;v.30 *Bodhicaryavatara* [Entering into the Path of Wisdom], by Shantideva).

Lacking a proper master, there is always the danger of developing mistaken understandings unknowingly, or "lapses" into the expression of brutal impulses or drives in practices such as sparring. It is easy to become carried away. It is for this reason that a full understanding of what is involved, and one's concurrent motivations, must be approached and examined before any spiritual practice of *Chuan Fa* can fruitfully commence.

This is where the elemental symbols proved extremely useful for, by forming a practical and progressive view of the basic structure to the training, they enabled the sometimes complex patterns of consciousness involved to be approached and penetrated more easily, forming a "ruler" by which practitioners could orient their progression, modify its results, and reorient them where necessary.

MAHABHUTA NATA

Elements served both as dynamic and static representations of the mental and physical experiences undergone by the trainee and served to illuminate the physical patterns and helped clarify various confusions experienced by students in the course of training and application. In *Chuan Fa* an important method, serving as a reminder of the various levels and types of practice required, lay in those *nata* which especially concerned themselves with emulating the principles of the five elements. According to ancient tradition, these *nata* were known in Sanskrit by the term *Mahabhuta Nata* (Five Great Elements *Nata*) and were always found divided into their practice stages or sections, each of which was termed its *pratima* and concerned one of the elements.

Various sets of pentamerous *pratima* existed, the most often mentioned being called *Pancadravya* (Five Natures) or *Pancatattva* (Five Essences). The name *Pancadravya* was favored by the Vaibhasika sect which taught that the *Mahabhuta* possessed a distinctive essence. Vasubandhu argued many times with this sect's teachers, saying that *dravya* was incorrect as it gave a notion of permanence to that which was intrinsically impermanent.

In early Buddhist Chinese, the *Mahabhuta Nata* and its component *pratima* were called *Wu Tai Hsing* (Japanese: *Godaigyo*), a term literally meaning the "five great elemental forms." Around the fourth and fifth centuries, we find the name *Ping Hsing* (Japanese: *Byogyo*) being used for the five *pratima* of the *Mahabhuta Nata*. This title literally means the "leveling or balancing elements" and is doubly apt in describing the *pratima*, for the particle *Ping* is also the earliest Chinese title for *Ping Wang*—the legendary founder of the Indian Ksatreya caste. *Ping* was probably one of the literal equivalents for the Sanskrit term *Prasada*, and *Wu Tai Hsing* the equivalent for *Rupaprasada*, mentioned previously in the healing section of this work. In the esoteric traditions it is said that the *Wu Tai Hsing* formed an important part of the early trainings in *Chuan Fa*, for both meditative skill and as a form of auto-physiotherapeutic healing.

The five elemental parts of the *pratima* each deal with the various paradigms of human nature in all their manifestations, and call into being the subliminal forces which they represent—be they psychological or physical. The *pratima* are performed in preset sequences and stages, each relating to the especial element it governed. By attempting to perfect the practice of each of these components, *Chuan Fa* practitioners travel through the many layers of their being, exposing it to their gaze both physically and mentally. This practice was accompanied by meditations, doctrinal studies and other practices associated with the particular realm of influence each element was viewed as dominating. This series of *Hsing* seems to have been preserved in China for many years, but in the Tang dynasty was renamed the *Ping An* (Peaceful Equanimity) *Hsing*.

Later Monks "reverse translated" this title back into Sanskrit as *Samashanti* (non-differentiating peace), a name which is not inappropriate. These early descriptions occur long before the Taoist boxing traditions and practices called either "five elements," "five forms," or "five activities fist." These systems are often claimed to be the "originals" of other Taoist pentamerous sequences of boxing or self-defense.

We can see traces of the *Ping* title particle in the *Ping Kuan* meditation of the Tien T'ai sect, which describes it as a meditation concerned with merging the phenomenal and noumenal realms of existence. In the esoteric sect, this meditation was said to be synonymous to the Equalizing Wisdom (*Samatajnana*) of the Mandala Buddha Akshobhya (Japanese: *Ashuku*). The *Ping Kuan* was always associated closely with the practice of the *Kuan Kung* Meditation common to *Chuan Fa* (see the mandala of human characteristics). A much later Ryukuan student of *Chuan Fa* named Itosu (Chinese: *Su Chow*) mentions studying a set of *Ping An Hsing* under the Chinese esoteric monk Li Tsun San (Japanese: Rijunsan) in the late 1800's. [See references in Notes 14, 72e, 25, 20a, b, e, g, f.] From the Tang Dynasty onward, Buddhist terminology commonly used the particle *Ping* to represent the Sanskrit prefix *Sama* (together with, unified or conjoined) or the word *Samata* (characterized by joining or unification). Both these terms indicate a condition of calming, blending with—or into—tranquil or equanimitous mind and were used to describe certain types of meditation practice. This condition of unification is often the very opposite to that usually experienced by the ordinary consciousness, which is all too often affected or confused by life experiences.

CONDITIONED CONFUSION

Physical or mental confusion arises from the often attractive but delusive nature of experience which serves to produce mistaken understandings of the inner and outer situations in life. The relationships between different stages and moments of being are not clearly understood and occur haphazardly, disturbing their proper pattern, rather like a record being played at the wrong speed and with a needle that "jumps." The result is that life experiences serve to create stress or a sense of unfulfillment. This creates tension within the physical organism, and illness of both a static and dynamic nature is the result.

The elements serve as a measure of the natural, universal order and balance of things through which the "temperature" of the times can be taken. This "order" of things was already spoken of by the Shakyamuni Buddha when he taught the doctrine of the "chain" of dependent origination (*pratitya Samutpada*). This is a presentation of the linked patterns in the arising of our conscious experience and through which we can come to see more clearly the things we create that are conducive to suffering. [See Note 59 references.]

A great part of the early training of monks lay in trying to recognize patterns and, by this knowledge, to eventually dissolve their "power" of automatic association and perceptive fictions. Mental confusion, in fact, arose only because we experience things without realizing their place in this chain of events and seek to connect various facets of our experience in disordered or mistaken ways.

Some may reason a psychological theory of synchronicity from "events" in "time," when what is actually occurring is that the subject has, at some moment, become mindfully aware of a culminating pattern(s) of activity based firmly upon the causal forces of dependent origination. Moments of mindfulness are themselves dependent upon the mental karmic patterns of the individual concerned, and they happen unexpectedly. If one is cognizant of the conditioned genesis doctrine taught by the Buddha (the subsidiary effect to the meditative perfection of mindfulness), what is considered coincidence to one who is unmindful of the pattern of creation within consciousness is simple occurrence to one who is. The full perception of mental moments (Sanskrit: *Ksana*) was a theme Vasubandhu elucidated, for it is in their nature that the patterns of mind are given birth and form. The practice of meditation is the elucidation of moments [Note 100].

Because most of us lack the ability to prophesy the events of our own consciousness moments, we are truly, as Kukai once noted, "floundering in the Ocean of Sufferings." A similar situation occurs in physical terms when we attempt to perfect elementally balanced patterns of movement (such as were shown in the Hsing based upon the *pratima* or *nata*). The discord and absence of rhythm and harmony can become all too apparent to the newer *Chuan Fa* practitioner.

Even though we may convince ourselves that our minds are clear (or in control), the pattern of our movements will reveal the opposite. The intellectual facade is quickly penetrated by the demands of a kinetic presentation. The fourth century A.D. Buddhist scholar Vasubandhu laid out much of the philosophical basis upon which the interpretation of *Chuan Fa's* ethical principles rests, and a study of these—outlined in his *Yogacara Sutra, Madhyanta Vibhaga Bhasya*, or the *Karma Siddhi Prakarana* and other works—are necessary to fully understand *Chuan Fa's* heuristic basis [See Note 3].

Vasubandhu's teaching clearly eliminates many modern arguments used to legitimize, permit or justify the use of personal violence "in special circumstances" [see Note 62]. He distinguishes many of the pseudo justifications for action, including those based upon direct apprehension (*upalabdhisama*, i.e., "He did this to me," "I saw it with my own eyes."). The pseudo justification of alternative choices (*Vikalpasama*, i.e., "I had no choice, to do anything else would be worse") and pseudo justifications based upon unwarranted extension of a principle (*Atiprasangasama*, i.e., "This is what it's really all about," "This is my own/new version according to my experience," or "There is already precedent for this").

Vasubandhu had already sounded the death knell to any claim that competitive or sport arts have a Buddhist basis.

True to the principle of the five elements and their ascending order, students encounter the various facets of study in different stages. In terms of the basic *Chuan Fa* trainings, the strengthenings, stabilizings and stamina practices were ruled by the earth element. Physical fluidity and adaptability were ruled by water. Power and speed were ruled by fire; tactics by air. Earth governed the stances; water the blocking techniques, fire the exchange of techniques, and air the breathing methods. Each of these general fields possessed more subtle aspects. Special practice was done in accordance with the seasons; for example Spring, being "ruled" by water, required emphasis upon the blocks. Winter, "ruled" by earth required stances to be perfected.

These classifications were annotated in great detail by various generations of masters as they sought to associate each practice and principle with another and thus see their place within the great Mandala of existence.

When first learning to practice the *nata* or *pratima*, the *Chuan Fa* students concentrated initially upon their physical sequences and rhythms. They learned to integrate their breathing patterns with the movements and eventually to simultaneously perform special concentration exercises. They practiced both alone and with others to perfect their exterior coordination and control. If and when this could be accomplished, the various explanations (*Prakasita*) of the movements were shown. These were presented as sequences expressing the interconnected movements and principles of the five elements at many different levels, only one of which (water) concerned self-defense techniques.

Such explanatory stages could take a long time as they included many different bodily and mental healing (or diagnostic arts and techniques), together with more mystical studies. After this the symbolic attributes of the component movements were shown—that is, the ritual gestures (*mudras*). Their names and principles had to be memorized and these were integrated into subsequent performance of the *nata*, which by this stage was becoming more intricate. From this point, they entered into the "field of experience" (*anubhugocara*) in which all the principles were translated into experiential conditions and mental situations within the practitioner. The practice thus became more internalized and static.

This was an important transition point for students, for from this point on they could no longer hide faults, fears, or wrong motivations. Those who had undertaken to study *Chuan Fa* for selfish reasons were weeded out; their own attitude filled them with fear. It meant approaching the inner temple.

The aim of this point was to directly try and overcome the three *klesas* (mental imperfections) present within students. Such practices began to orient students to new levels of clear experience (*visuddhianubhu*; Japanese: *Shinyukai*) This latter stage varied in its requirements and depended a great deal upon the method and abilities of the teacher as to what precise form it took. It also had its own special difficulties. When practicing "outer" sparring students had simple and instantaneous response to mistakes; i.e., if a defensive block was inadequate, a blow was received. Here the responses were more subtle. Both instantaneous bodily response (*kayakritaphala*; Japanese: *shingyoge*; Chinese: *hsinhsinghua*) and mental responses (*vijnanaphala*; Japanese: *shikige*; Chinese: *shih yen*) arose and had to be dealt with equally—or often simultaneously.

Students were often subject to inner reversals or doubts and could feel strongly alienated (*ekayati*) as the lower levels of consciousness attempted to withdraw from encroaching changes. Many students would feel like giving up and running away instead of using the arising fears (*bhaya*) as a basis for self-examination.

As Stefan Anacker (opus cit) has clearly recognized, Vasubandhu points out in his *Madhanta Vibhanga Bhasya* [Separation of the Middle from the Extremes] that a potent cause of the ego's reinforcement lies in its keen sense of susceptibility to harm (*dausthulya*; Chinese: *huan yi*; Japanese: *kan-I*). If the "person" lacked such a sense, it could experience itself only as a plurality of forces rather than as a complete entity. Due to this susceptibility, there arises an increased sense of unity whenever danger threatens any part of the plurality of forces making up the ego. The ego recognizes that harm to one part of its being could affect other parts equally and perhaps result in its extinction.

Vasubandhu says that in the situation of danger there arises an "intensified interdependence of (mental) events."

> When all who are close turn upon us as enemies remember, this is the Wheel of Sharp Weapons turning upon us from wrongs we have done before (*37 Practices of the Buddha's Sons*, by Thogs-med Tzang Po V 28).

It is often a subtle intimation of *dausthulya* which prompts a student into studying "self"-defense in the martial arts. Vasubandhu's observation occurs in the *Bhasya* in the section relating to the eradication of mental distractedness that occurs after meditation practice.

The condition of post-meditation experiences, or mental moments, is given special attention by Vasubandhu. This condition is described by him as being specially vulnerable to the production of mental tendencies serving to create counter patterns of consciousness inimical to the goals of meditation itself. These tendencies are characterized by him as being especially liable to produce the following mental effects or conditions: "Emergence; gliding to sense objects; relishing the meditative state; slackness or excitement regarding this state; deliberate intentions regarding its experiences; a sense of "I" within mental attention."

Each of these conditions is examined, described fully and commented upon, so as to show their causes, dangers, and effects upon an incomplete or unsettled meditation practice. We can also see that the increased "sense of being" created by *dausthulya* can, itself, become a potent object of craving. For those whose sense of existence is already dulled by the *klesas*, an increasingly vivid sense of their existence can seem to be highly desirable. One result of such a craving is fanaticism, a condition in which the individual seems to have "found" his or her "self." Those who dedicate themselves to the practice of aggression or to destructive forces, or powers within which they "feel more alive" are victims of *dausthulya*.

Vasubandhu noted also that the Perfection of Tranquillity was the "antidote to *dausthulya*" and that this tranquillity was "a skill in mind and body."

Despite the arousal of negative attitudes or inclinations, all through this time the *Chuan Fa* student would be continually practicing the *hsing*, developing a higher awareness of the essential nature of his existence and creatively applying the insight of meditation to his difficulties in an effort to overcome any innate imperfections. Such practice was distinctive of *Chuan Fa* in China and truly esoteric to outsiders, for it appeared as something entirely different from what it actually was, constituting a powerful path, worthy of the cautions the ancient masters placed around its study and practice.

> If the self is to be protected it ought not to be concerned with its protection (Ch. 8: V173, *Bodhicaryavatara* [Entering into the Path of Wisdom], by Shantideva).

BODY MIND

One category of consciousness often bypassed in mainstream Buddhism was that developed within the physical body itself and known abstractly in *Chuan Fa* as a *Kayaka Manas* (Chinese: *shen hsin*; Japanese: *Taishin*). Normally the *manas* of consciousness arises from the threefold pattern of an object, the perception of the object, and a corresponding consciousness for such a perception (as found in the "18 entrances" format).

The "consciousness" of the body (i.e., that the body itself produces) does not accord with this tripartite genesis of *manas*. Lacking such genesis it cannot, in its own right, create a specific rising of the *manas* consciousness. Neither can such a consciousness possess the *manas'* attribute of being able to develop awareness independent of an objective source. It does, however, possess some features in common with *manas*.

The body can serve as an underlying support for the rising of *manas* in that its particular pattern of bodily homeostasis (*kayakrita santana*) can act either as a filter or as a prompting base for certain forms of consciousness, and by such means impart a special tendency or orientative patterning to the subsequent functioning of consciousness. We can easily understand how, for instance a damaged eye can give rise to a visual *manas* which is impaired and cause an object to be mistaken for something it isn't. It isn't so easy to understand how one's muscles "remember" a pattern of movements.

The explanation of more subtle experiences, such as this, was of crucial importance in the development of *Chuan Fa's* philosophical view and was a subject of debate among many famous Buddhist sages and sects, each of whom usually had slightly different explanations. All explanations for a body "consciousness" came under the careful scrutiny of Vasubandhu, for he perceived many of them as either flawed, incomplete, or inconsistent. Vasubandhu was one of those people who could pose a question of such subtle simplicity that it could not be easily answered [Note 96].

He was especially concerned with explanations which suggested, or depended upon, qualities imbued with any form of permanence, for he saw this as a form of "self" projected into the physical being of the body. All and any explanations that involved or implied teachings like the Vaibhasika sect's suggestion of an independent bodily *dravya* (nature), he rejected as mistaken. Vasubandhu did not deny that instances of events like "muscle memory" occurred, only that the current explanations for it were not, as yet, fully consistent. Many other contemporary descriptions of consciousness were also rejected by Vasubandhu as incomplete, although certain of them, such as ones like the "muscle memory," he accepted but modified their meanings or explanations [Note 97].

The *Kayaka manas* mentioned earlier are the physical *manas* of the body communicating with itself in response to the *kayakrita santana* of the individual. It is this *manas* which both retains the muscle memory phenomena and sends prompts to the ordinary consciousness. The influence of these physical prompts or filters exerts or extends its effect upon consciousness by modifying the particular mental or the physical *manas* of the moment.

The subsequent mental *manas* rising from this are not attributes *of* the body, but are instead a result of its prompts. At a very simple level, we may think of the "Philosopher's toothache" as an example of such a physically generated *manas*. The patterns of bodily homeostasis may be latent while its activity, long recognized in Buddhism, is expressed within modern scientific ideas such as that of genetic coding [Note 94].

Chuan Fa had also long maintained the idea of a bodily consciousness, an embodied mind (*kayaka citta*) [Note 92], long before it was formally expressed in philosophical ways. This consciousness gives added meaning to the significance of *nata* practice, for we can see that the patterns and sequences they engender can be remembered by the body and they serve (either actively or passively), to modify subsequent patterns of consciousness [Note 99].

It is in such a way that *Chuan Fa* asserts that the awakening of certain aspects of consciousness can be brought about by means of symbolic physical enactments. By observing the results it becomes possible to discern the causes. This fact was of great importance to all connected with the arts of the physical body—healers or spiritual warriors—and underlay many of the principles of diagnostic and therapeutic practices used in Buddhism [Note 95].

The association of certain of the *nata* with specific mental states and qualities indicates that their sequences and patterns were recognized as being capable of providing the necessary body memory stimuli for those mental states.

At any moment our consciousness is the sum total of all its previous states of consciousness and similarly at any moment our physical body represents the sum total of its previous conditions. Specific physical patterns of the present, whether gross or subtle, represent specific totalities of former conditions, which themselves are always preceded or modified by their particular body memories. As has been mentioned previously, consciousness often works in patterns of repetition and it is by such patterning that consciousness creates its various distinctive features and qualities. By recycling its own imperfections, they are both modified to accord with changes in present conditions or environments and confirmed in their existence. It is in such a manner that repetitive (i.e., seasonally based) illness occurs. Perhaps it is also one of the unsuspected factors of inherited genetic disease.

Chuan Fa shows that by immersing oneself both physically and mentally within a creative pattern of mind/body inter-activity one is planting seeds for the future, and that even if their fruits are not immediately visible or discernible, their results will be. There can thus be no such a thing as a wasted action or a meaningless thought.

REVOLUTION IN MIND AND CREATIVE ACTION

Even in motion a visible object is subject to transformation.
Its own inertia can rotate.

—Kukai: *Shoji jisso gi*

The condition or state of being able to initiate *klesa*-less compassionate activity is at the very heart of the application of the Bodhisattva Vajra-mukti. We saw earlier how this principle had been discussed by Asanga—the brother of Vasubandhu—in his *Bodhisattvabhumi* [Stages of the Bodhisattva] scripture.

These activities are not simply good deeds, but are ways of being (*bhavapatha*) generated and maintained without attachment to their goals or processes. They act first upon one's nature and from it radiate outward to others. Compassionate action itself is a dynamic quality emphasized by the Mahayana Schools of Buddhism, and is developed in many different ways.

In regard to *Chuan Fa*, which concerns itself with the physical body and its perfected skillful activities (Sanskrit: *Satyakriya*; Japanese: *Shingyo*), there are several dangers unique to it. One of these, common to many specialized mental or physical arts (particularly in modern times), is that it easily becomes obsessive. One's mind can become so preoccupied with the intricacies of physical training or the principles of its application that its spiritual practices are excluded or overlooked. This is true of all physical arts in general, but it is more so of *Chuan Fa* in particular, for it has an especially intense nature, often requiring complete mind and body concentration. With an over-development of sophisticated and often specious physical abilities (*kayasamartha*), practitioners can all too easily develop an attraction to its products or become objects of admiration by others. Accepting such a position places one in danger of forgetting the goals of the practice itself.

If these obstacles can be overcome and the intrinsic spiritual principles upheld continually, the physical practices begin to transform one's body and mind. When the training is successfully followed, the metabolic equilibrium developed through the physical practices results in a calmness of mind which, when coupled with the physical power of the body, creates a special condition of vibrant purity akin to that attained in the *Kriya* practices already mentioned. The practices are oriented not to make a perfect warrior, but to act in this cathartic (*Visuddhi*) manner at all the levels of being.

Sometimes a glimpse of this realization appears to the student during the *pratima* trainings and many of these are specially designed to coax this awareness out from where it usually hides. If such a "breakthrough" occurs, its effects can sometimes be traumatic to unprepared people, for it can appear as if their lives are in danger of collapse and students may not be fully prepared for the arising of the new types of experience and awareness of life it manifests. New experiences can seem sudden and overwhelming. Practitioners may realize just how wasteful they have been. They may feel guilty or ashamed. Because these feelings seem powerful, students' minds attempt to experience in the "old" manner, for by doing this new experiences can be kept under control and rendered meaningless.

As the condition of *dausthalya* arises, it may seem as if one is standing on the edge of a cliff knowing one must step forward into space. The logical mind says "Beware!" but an inner knowledge says, "Do not worry—there is nothing to fear." The whole inner world may seem to be at a crisis point. One voice comes from the ego, the other from something that seems only an aspiration and unclear. This total condition has many other names within Buddhism but they all indicate much the same thing. Such powerful and experiential condition of a transforming consciousness is called in Buddhist Sanskrit *Paravritti* [Note 91]. *Paravritti Vijnana* (Japanese: *Henge shiki*) is mentioned within the *Lankavatarasutra* of the Yogacara School.

It indicates a fundamental transformation, evolution, or "turning about" of the mind within itself, so that it becomes something experientially different from before. The patterns of consciousness previously sufficient have been challenged by the developing experiences and threaten to overwhelm its negativities. The Christian mystic St. John of the Cross called part of a perhaps similar condition the "dark night of the Soul."

It was not uncommon for students to abandon their training altogether at the threshold of this point, even though this experience is one of the aims of training itself. Some would even try to escape its consequences and immerse themselves even more strongly in the material world: they get married, produce a child, emigrate, etc., in order to avoid seeing the true Self as it truly is. Of course, it is impossible to escape from one's Self, but it is possible to ignore or drown it for a while in other concerns.

It is for this reason that the merit of dedicating one's training and studies totally for the benefit of others (i.e., the Bodhisattva Vow) is so strongly emphasized to students. To ignore one's inner evolution may seem easier at certain times, but the Vow shows that it is also an extreme and self-centered indulgence.

Subhuti: "Lord, how does the Bodhisattva who, stable in his Perfect practice of Morality, acquire the Perfection of Vigour?"

The Lord: "The Bodhisattva does not relax his physical and mental vigor; He is determined to rescue all beings from Samsara and establish them in the Deathless element" (Chapter 62, "The Supreme Attainment," in *The Large Sutra on Perfect Wisdom* (based on the translation by E. Conze).

Paravritti is closely allied to another experience known in Sanskrit as *Abhisanditakayacitta*. This term, used to indicate the "inseparability of body and mind," literally means "body / mind dissolving." It was a teaching used and often spoken of by Bodhidharma, the patriarch of Chinese Chaan meditation.

In *Chuan Fa*, this condition can be experienced at different levels, each more refined than the last, and many of the traditional formal sequences of movement (Chinese: *Hsing*) are designed to set the stage for this experience. It forms part of the cause, process, and effect of *Paravritti* and establishes it.

It is by perfecting such body / mind interaction and capacity within a spiritual and purifying environment that the art of *Chuan Fa* achieves its goals; namely by transforming body, one is freed from body. By transforming mind, one is freed from mind. The *Srimalasimhanada Sutra* calls this "exchanging one's body for that of the Buddhas."

The resultant mental condition of this path is termed in Sanskrit *Nairatmyacitta* a Non-Self being (Chinese: *Wu Hsin*; Japanese: *Mushin*). It is this "being" that the greatest Buddhist philosophers (such as Nagarjuna, Vasubandhu, and Amoghavajra) sought to communicate to their students in their various ways.

Figure 118. Vajralasi (female Bodhisattva). Found within the section of Aksobhya Buddha, she embodies the joy which arises from taking the vow to enlightenment. The fists are held with foreknuckles extended at the waist and represent the firmness of the vow. (Author's collection.)

INNER AGGRESSION

Master of Mysteries what is the Combatant Mind?

The Master: It is to have the tendency to decide by "yes" or "no"   —(*Mahavairocana Sutra*, Ch.1).

One of the great problems encountered by both enquiring martial artists, and people who have no experience of them at all, lies in explaining why there is a *Chuan Fa* practice of sparring. People often tend to make judgments concerning this practice as if they fully understand it and then react to their own misunderstanding by labeling the practice and its practitioners as aggressive, non-Buddhist, or violent. This has resulted in

Figure 119. The figure of Maha-vairocana Buddha. (Ryusen Miyahara.)

many misconceptions concerning some of the martial arts (although we should bear in mind that some modernized and competitive forms fully deserve the criticism they receive). Many people who believe that they are peaceful in temperament or nonaggressive in outlook are, in reality, not so at all. Many successfully mask the very opposite condition and live tightly controlling such responses. Shielding themselves with a high degree of expertise, they fool themselves, and others, for a long time by pretending such aggressive tendencies don't exist in themselves. In certain situations these people can emerge as more physically violent or vicious than an outwardly aggressive person. We can see evidence of this in accounts of incidents which take place during wartime [Note 101].

Experienced teachers of the ordinary martial arts are often familiar with people who, beginning to train as if they were mice, end up becoming raging bulls. Such experiences, although they may prove personally refreshing, in that they sometimes, and temporarily, release pent-up energies and mental frustrations, are not sufficient for *Chuan Fa*. That violence needs to be dealt with, both in oneself and others. Even in the time of the Shakyamuni Buddha it is evidenced in the first section of the early *Mahajima Nikaya* which deals with how Buddhists should respond to being beaten and injured. It was Shakyamuni himself who is quoted as saying, "It is the world that quarrels with the Buddha not the Buddha with the world" (*Samyutta Nikaya* 3:94).

Chuan Fa deals practically with this situation and teaches that what is really required is to dissolve the situation through which such inner violence is produced so that it never arises. The various releases from it are then never required. Furthermore, the process of dissolution, itself, could serve as an aid to the development of wisdom. Such an approach conserves energy and increases peacefulness.

> How many Enemies, measurelessness as the Sky
> will I be able to destroy?
> Yet when the Thought of Anger is destroyed
> so are all Enemies.

(*Bodhicaryavatara*, of Shantideva. Ch. 5: V 12)

Inner violence also evidences itself within meditation practice and proves a difficult barrier for the development of inner tranquillity.

Such barriers have occurred within people all through our history and serve to make the training and practices of a monk more difficult. Recognizing this, the ancient masters created various skillful methods to deal with this problem and one of these lay in practice of the *Chuan Fa nata*. In order to understand this development, let us first look more closely at the situation it seeks to explicate.

Early Buddhist teachers realized that the essential nature of the confrontational experience lies primarily within the practitioner's consciousness, and this is where Chuan Fa should direct its attention. While the ego is very experienced at self-deceit, and can readily convince itself that it is peaceful and free from hatred, an individual's life experiences often demonstrate the reverse. Any person who has suffered frustration, envy, hatred, jealousy, fear, stress, or worry will know this. The Buddhist writer Edward Conze has mentioned attending certain meditation classes designed to generate compassion, and observing participants leaving the building and stepping over the prone body of a tramp lying unconscious outside.

Such events are not unique to any country, and it is toward the attitudes that can produce these situations that Buddhist teachers in many lands and times have addressed their attention. Both Bodhidharma, whose sayings are translated later, and Vasubandhu, who outlined so much of the *Chuan Fa* principles, were directly concerned with the practice and application of the teachings which lead away from mental suffering in all its forms. Though each addressed a different type of audience, the thread running though their teachings can be clearly seen to be the same. They are both concerned with how people see themselves and what they subsequently make or create from such a seeing.

THE WORDLESS DOCTRINE

How people see themselves—and whether or not what they actually see represents any form of truth—is a central theme of the Buddhist teachings regarding self-awareness. There are many approaches to such awareness and the *Chaan (Zen)* teaching is one very well known in our modern times. It is distinctive because it is said to arise from a "direct pointing" to one's Mind. In an account given within the *Ching Te Chuan Teng Lu* (see Note 39) it is said that Shakyamuni had assembled his monks for a lecture but that few of them had been able to understand its inner meanings, they all sat there pondering what it was they were supposed to be understanding. After what seemed an embarassingly long period of waiting, Shakyamuni, who knew well how puzzled his monks were, stood up, picked up and held aloft a flower. The monks were even more confused by such an action. Suddenly one of the elder disciples named Maha Kasyapa stood, and looking directly at Shakyamuni, burst into a great smile. At that point, it is said, Shakyamuni Buddha knew that Maha Kasyapa alone had understood his words.

This incident is often used within accounts of the *Chaan* teachings as its first instance of what it later termed "direct transmission" of the teaching—a "transmission" it claims to be unique to its method of teaching. It is from this instance that Chaan is said to be based upon a

"Transmission" (Chinese: *Pieh Chuan*; Japanese: *Betsuden*) outside of the Scriptures (Chinese: *Wai Chiao*; Japanese: *Gaikyo*). The actual nature of such transmission is never discussed or explained and is really a mystery to *Chaan* students who often regard it as some force or power passed between a Master and his student. Such a view is obviously not strictly in line with the Buddhist doctrine, but lacking any alternative explanation within *Chaan*, it is one students are forced to conclude. From another viewpoint, this incident, if in fact it actually occurred at all, is quite capable of explanation. We saw in the previous section about "Body Mind," how physical actions are quite capable of giving rise to certain states of an observer's *manas* and that *manas* can take very specific forms of manifestation. Both the practice of *nata* and also that of the art of healing depend upon such a possibility. Bearing this in mind, it is not at all mystifying or puzzling that any physical action of Shakyamuni Buddha should prove capable of initiating understanding within his students, providing they are aware of such possibility (as were the students of *Chuan Fa*). To those who are not—and this often includes many modern students of the *Chaan* (*Zen*) teachings—explaining the nature or actual content of such an account must be very difficult.

We can contrast such a direct transmission with that form of teaching used within the Esoteric (*Mikkyo*) Schools of teaching called *Kuden*. This is usually explained as being the oral transmission made by a Master to his direct pupil which explains or conveys the inner nature (or realities) of the teachings studied. It is the *Kuden* which is said to confirm a teaching within a student, and without it, a student is never considered to have understood completely what has been taught. The similarity of meaning between *Kuden* and "direct" transmission (*Betsuden*) can be seen in that both are said to be essential for the final "polish" to mastery of a teaching. In both traditions, *Kuden* and *Betsuden* can arise within many different situations or forms. This similarity is not coincidental, for both the Esoteric and the *Chaan* Schools are based upon the principles of Vasubandhu's *Yogacara School* of teaching and neither can really be understood without some understanding of its teachings.

Both of these schools show that the various ways in which we perpetuate sufferings of all kinds arise from the manner in which we understand our experiences, and to do this we need to know clearly how—and from where—they arise. Ordinarily, we believe that our experiences arise only from the external events we create or witness. However, on closer examination we discover that the mental stance we take actually influences, in ways both obvious and subtle, what it is that we actually see or do. To realize the full extent of this pre-activity of our ordinary consciousness, we need to place ourselves in a suitable situation. Such a situation arises voluntarily in our practice of meditation. It also arises in conditions of great stress or danger, when things that we hold dear can

Figure 120. Avalokitesvara, the Bodhisattva of Compassion. (Painting by Ryusen Miyahara.)

seem threatened. In such inner environments, the workings and extent of the content of our consciousness can appear directly and with a vividness we do not usually experience. As such conditions occur due to external dangers, we usually forget them when those dangers are overcome; however, it is this experience of consciousness that both Bodhidharma and Vasubandhu continually remind us of, for it is within it that we may perceive great insights into the real nature of our consciousness. Such situations, being totalities of multiple forces and influences, do not easily lend themselves to simple literal or verbal description, but there is a way in which some features of those forces and influences can be reproduced. This way takes form in the art of emulation.

EMULATING THE PERFECTED

To the Greeks, the body was an instrument for worshiping the Gods, and many cultural arts reflected this attitude. The original Olympic games were not competitions, but acts of worshiping the Gods by emulating their prowess. It was for this reason that the greatest prize was a garland of laurel leaves—a symbolic Crown of Apollo. From such religious orientations, the concept of calisthenics (beauty and strength conjoined) arose; beauty for the Greeks being a spiritual attribute.

Many aspects of Greek spiritual culture, especially the theatre, were echoed in the Chinese practices of *Chuan Fa*. The ancient Greeks perfected the art of drama; part of its expertise lay in the practice of mimesis [Note 83]. This involved actors taking on the "being" of a Divinity and expressing his or her ideas and words as they had been recorded in their legends. Such an art was far removed from our modern "mime," being based upon a philosophy that acknowledged the close interaction between the Gods and humankind. We find a similar theme used in the philosophy of *Chuan Fa*.

In order to help circumvent the ego's power for self-deceit, particularly in the area of expressed aggression, *Chuan Fa* drew directly from the past experience of the Indian Vajramukti masters and taught the *shugyo* of emulative conduct, a re-enacted situational encounter (*pratyanubhavati avastha*; Japanese: *gen u*; Chinese: *kuan-yu*) based upon the confrontational situation (Sanskrit: *abhimukkya avastha*; Chinese: *mien hsien*; Japanese: *mensen*) between two persons [Note 82]. By means of this students could be brought to confront and realize the patterns and self-images developed from their dependence upon self-generated delusions (*parilkalpita*) or those created/projected by others (*paratantra*). This realization helped them realize the contents of their personal *sthana*.

Self-revelation arose particularly within the practice of self-defense techniques, for it was within this form of encounter that a skillful master could help create a vivid, arising sense and fear of impending death within students. This was, in fact, similar in nature to the self-generated responses encouraged within the earliest schools of Buddhism in its practice of meditating before a decomposing corpse or upon the theme of one's own personal death (*maranasmriti*).

The actual defensive techniques utilized in *Chuan Fa* sparring arose from studying the applications of the movements within the various *hsing* as simple movements rather than just symbols (i.e., *mudras*). This extension constituted a spiritual path of action (*karmapatha*; Chinese: *yeh hsing*; Japanese: *gyo do*) distinctive of *Chuan Fa*.

"O Master of Mysteries, what is the Mind of Ritual movement?"

The Master: It is to wish to ascend and manifest a miracle.

(*Mahavairocana Sutra*, Ch.1)

Situational encounters were practiced and repeated again and again (*abhiksnam*). By means of mutual sparring, the true nature of the endeavor and endeavorer was recognized, understood, and hopefully transcended by its practitioner. This was the real goal of what outsiders often see as "fighting" practice. It was a method of integrative, non-verbal and experiential effects that fully involved the five basic elemental factors of body (earth), emotions (water), movements, actions (fire), thoughts (air) and energies (ether), as well as their paradigms.

This situational encounter also took place within the practice of the *hsing*, only in this case the "opponent" was one's sense of self. In this battle the opponent was one's *sthana* and it was the revelation and realization of its nature which constituted the "victory" over it. One danger inherent in such solitary practice (even if practicing in a group, one's realization was solitary) was that of self-deception. It could be all too easy to create another, more subtle, *sthana* to replace the first [Note 102].

We can see self-deceptions in those who know only the basic physical forms of *hsing*. Because they view the *hsing* simply as physical techniques, they seek to perfect this aspect and accumulate knowledge of many different ones. In such a view, one who knows more is one who knows more, and such people imagine "they" are progressing. The same situation exists in those who continually enter commercial sparring competitions, such as are held in modern day karate. The champions go on and on fighting at different competitions until they become too injured or too old to continue. The compulsion to exchange the old self of a contender for the "new" Self of a champion is very strong and rooted in self-misunderstanding.

It was for such reasons that the early masters of the *Ping An hsing* laid down that each of its five parts should be studied for at least three years before learning the next. Thus it would take a minimum of fifteen years study to begin to understand the whole sequence fully and correctly, and such an emphasis is still maintained in modern *Chuan Fa*. Only one who was seriously committed to something far greater than mere fame could persevere in such a training [Note 103].

To circumvent the errors of inner deception, an "external" mani-festation of insight was deemed necessary by the *Chuan Fa* masters, and took the form of the (spiritual) situational encounter. Unlike ordinary life events (which also involve the elements of experience) both meth-ods (*Hsing* and encounter) were initiated with a mindful preparation and spiritual motivation.

The revelatory and transmutative power inherent in these encoun-ters derived from their ability to extend experiential awareness of situ-ational encounters (*Anubhavati avastha*). This "situation" was an environment composed of commonplace components, but which was "charged" with different meanings and required a form of response dif-ferent from the ordinary.

The efficacy of such a situation lay in the fact that it was directly comprehended and its results immediately experienced (*Yugapad anubhu*) without any different conditions being able to be created by the experiencers.

Lacking external supports, the practitioners' responses must pro-ceed directly from the essence of their being and will therefore reflect the real nature of that being. Any fears and apprehensions present within practitioners rise to the fore and their manifestations are instantly expressed and recognizable by both self and others. These manifestations are later examined and re-examined in a meditative manner.

By emphasizing an examination of responsive mental activities, *Chuan Fa* pointed its finger directly at their experiencers. Rather than positing an enemy "out there," students discovered one already in their midst. It was through practice of the *Chuan Fa Hsing* and its principles that this "enemy" was rendered harmless and yoked into useful ser-vice.

This kind of battle could be dangerous for it required participants to engage in a combat bereft of evil intentions and with minds free of the three *klesa* of greed, ignorance, and hatred. In such a battle, the teacher (*Upadhya*; Japanese: *Shifu*) played a vital part, for it was he who directed and guided the training and practice according to his experi-ence and knowledge, and a special bond of experience was developed between master and pupils.

The fist is the bringing together of the Mind, Body, Speech Thunderbolt (Amoghavajra, in *Mandara no Kenkyu* [Note 84a]).

One of the most significant Chinese developments lay in realizing the value of relating or attributing various features and results of the *Vajara-mukti Pratima* and *Samasthana* to the mandala. This practice, which was an ancient one, enabled esoteric monks to present teachings in a chro-

*Figure 121. Ragaraja, the Bo-
dhisattva governing passions and
infatuations. He holds the triple
Vajra, representing the adept's
mind, body and speech. (Ryusen
Miyahara.)*

matic or pictorial form to students and thus emphasize the universality
of the principles involved. When students looked at the sky they saw
its color, which in turn reminded them of Ratnasambhava—the Buddha whose color in the mandala was the same as the sky. Both external
sensorial and internal mental conditions were associated in this manner.
These patterns of associative characteristics were successful in conveying both esoteric teachings and *Chuan Fa* movements, sequences, and
attitudes of Vajramukti, and various teachers used this principle in
many different ways. Their being adaptable to any environment meant
that, although there was the possibility for a great diversity in presentation, the basic principles remained constant. [See Note 59.]

The knowledge of All Knowledge is analogous to the Five
Elements (*Mahavairocana Sutra.* Chapter 1).

Some teachers, particularly from the eighth century onward, used animals portrayed in the various thrones distinctive of each of the mandala Buddhas iconography as descriptors of the elemental categories,
principles, and values. Each of these animals represented a quality of its
ruling Buddha wisdom and expressed its dynamic aspect.

Figure 122. The Bodhisattva Acalaraja with two boy attendants. He holds the rope to bind evil and the sword which cuts off the heads of the three Klesa. (Ryusen Miyahara.)

These animals were drawn from original Vajramukti mythology and are fully consonant with the elemental philosophy. See Table 6. They were not, as some believe, innovated especially for esoteric teaching methods.

Because the esoteric Buddhist schools made such use of animal symbols in their mandala pictures, commonly by means of portraying a Buddha seated upon an animal "throne," that is, a chair the base of which is supported by a row of animals, some thought of them as exclusively religious symbols representing universal values of the Bud-

Table 6. Vajramukti Elemental Animal Rulers.

SANSKRIT BUDDHA NAME	JAPANESE BUDDHA NAME	THRONE	ELEMENT
Akshobyha	Ashuku	Elephant	Earth
Ratnasambhava	Hosho	Horse	Water
Amitabha	Amida	Peacock	Fire
Amoghasiddhi	Fukujoju	Garuda*	Air
Mahavairocana	Dainichi	Lion	Space

*A Garuda was a mythical bird which had the power to search out dragons and destroy them. It was the only bird which could do so.

dhist world view. Such portrayals can be seen in the texts listed in Note 84. However, as we have already seen, both animals and elements were also utilized as metaphors for human qualities in both allegorical parables and monastic character analysis. In *Chuan Fa* such metaphors assumed a much more significant importance for they represented and guided the type of physical training and *Hsing* a teacher would set his students. As a simple example of this, we can say that if a student was excessively lethargic in spirit he would be termed an "elephant" type. Such types would then be taught "tiger" meditations, which often involved ascetic practices aimed at the student realizing and highlighting both the causes, and the remedies to, such an elephantine spirit. In addition to performing these, he would study the spiritual knowledge associated with the Buddha "ruling" the tiger, which in this case is the Buddha of infinite light—Amitabha. The element Earth would be meditatively stressed by visualizing it in its dynamic forms, such as occurs in earthquakes or within volcanoes. All such practices and teaching methods could be seen as being represented within a mandala, but few could understand this aspect of the symbolism.

These presentations were misunderstood by non-Buddhists as being somehow indicative of, or associated with, the actual physical

Figure 123. The Bodhisattva Samantabhadra. He sits on the Elephant Throne of Royalty and Lordship. (Ryusen Miyahara.)

performances of the animals portrayed. It was often thought, for instance, that the tiger symbol, used in Chinese schools as a substitute for the peacock, simply showed that one had to attack and move in a tiger-like manner, etc. Plagiarism by martial artists who based their art upon Taoist, rather than Buddhist, philosophy was often responsible for such errors and misunderstandings and was encouraged by various state officials seeking to discredit Buddhism in order to reinstate Taoist values and professions back into the mainstream of Chinese life. Such plagiarism continues even in modern times. Such mistakes by non-initiates were successful in keeping *Chuan Fa* knowledge out of their hands for many years [Note 74d, 75].

As the years passed, the mandala became an increasingly important method of transmitting the inner spirit of the teachings [See Note 59]. This inner spirit was the most important gift of *Chuan Fa* as it constituted the Buddhist contribution toward overcoming mankind's inadequacies, aggression, and destructive tendencies.

> They tear the body, they enter the Avici hell. For the sake of all there they do all that can be done. Even one who has done the greatest injury is to be treated with kindness (*Bodhicarayavatara* 6; V121).

REVIEW AND SUMMARY

We have come a long way in our journey through the history and development of *Chuan Fa*, and it is useful now to summarize some of the most significant principles we have covered in that journey. In such a way we will refresh our minds as to what, how, and why they developed, and what this entailed. By reminding ourselves of *Chuan Fa's* history and teachings we can avoid becoming confused or mistaken as to its fundamental principles and goals.

We have seen how ancient India had developed a highly sophisticated and intricate system of warfare and that its warrior caste (known as the Ksatreya) had developed special methods of physical training in line with their Vedic spiritual and military ideals. With the arrival of Buddhism these ideals were further developed and extended until they formed a distinct and separate view unique to Buddhism alone, and one whose implications were later extended to related fields, such as medicine and healing. The resultant blend of Buddhist spirituality and Indian military trainings took form within the art that came to be known as *Chuan Fa*. We learned how teachers, such as the Yogacara Master Vasubandhu, had developed Buddhist doctrines which provided the basis for its practice, and that in its later growth *Chuan Fa* masters openly incorporated important but often neglected themes relating to bodily arts and activities, particularly that of ritual gesture (*mudra*), whose significance had only been briefly alluded to in the early Buddhist scriptures.

We saw how, when the early monk teachers went to China and beyond, they introduced many new teachings, including those relating to physical disciplines and healing arts, and that in this process they adopted and adapted many native beliefs but improved and extended them into new and relevant fields of endeavor. In this the teachers of esoteric Buddhism (the *Acaryas*) were most prominent. We learned how, although familiar with their own native schools of combative technique, the apparent efficacy of the physical techniques of *Chuan Fa* naturally appealed to the prevailing military classes, who probably viewed it initially as a useful and health means of preserving health and "letting off steam." Its military and combative possibilities must have been obvious and of great appeal, but realizing this, the monk *Acaryas* were selective about what and whom they taught [Note 51].

We learned of the esoteric *Acaryas* influence in the social movements of the Tang Dynasty during which many Buddhist Emperors, perhaps emulating the Indian Buddhist Monarch Asoka [Note 70], opened their prisons and forbade capital punishment, as in the case of Leung Wu Ti (see the section on Bodhidharma). We saw how the military class who enforced such rulings were influenced by them, so that as China's Buddhist learning developed, their tactical role became more one of defense, concerned more with occasional foreign invaders than, as had been common before, internal rebellions among their own people.

We saw how the Mahayana Buddhist philosophy completed *Chuan Fa's* philosophical and practical development into an art combining spiritual and psychological evolution. Within this development the use of symbolic metaphors based upon the natural elements played a significant part, forming a bridge between the expression of potentially abstract spiritual teachings and the mundane and physical requirements of the times. Using the doctrine of elements as an heuristic model, its Indian Masters had adapted the various foreign teachings and beliefs they encountered into Buddhist intermediary and hermeneutical (translative) forms which were more easily understood by the Chinese.

We saw how the Earth element was used to represent the practice of bodily purification, energy alignments, and the physical principles used in *Chuan Fa's* practice. The Water element represented the social orientation and motivations for practice, particularly in the field of healing. Fire represented the practice and application of the movement sequences called *pratima* and *nata*. Air represented the respiratory training, studies, and meditations toward which all the physical practices were oriented and refined. The fifth element, known at different times as either Ether, Space or basic Consciousness, itself, was used to represent the quintessence of all the practices, being a simultaneous presentation of the spiritual and physical ways of being. At the spiritual level, Ether indicated a condition of perfected, non-dualistic, balanced, and aware Consciousness, replete with abilities and attainments, poised at the very edge of the ultimate attainment, namely that of supreme Enlightenment. At the physical level, Ether portrayed a stable, pure, balanced, and vibrant physical organism filled with a powerful and therapeutic energy which could be passed on to others as required at various manners and levels.

We learned how such a view of Energy differed greatly from that of the Chinese Taoists or Animists, whose basic views tended to reinforce attachment to the physical body by over emphasizing the significance and value of physical attainments in a manner similar to the Hindu Yoga Fakirs. We saw that *Chuan Fa* regarded such attachment as a serious error, and to overcome such structured restrictions described the various expressions of the perfected physical/mental organism as being multi-level and interdependent symbols for the transcendent Wisdom of Perfect Enlightenment [See Note 59].

Chuan Fa described such multi-level understanding in many ways and forms, and such descriptions had taken a final and structured form within the pictorial mandala. This was used to present a picture of the mind/body doctrine in its entirety, and accorded with the Chinese temperament which initially could only understand Buddhism within a Taoist inspired "heaven and earth" framework. This use of symbols and art came to be the foremost representation of the integration of mind and body, and was perfected within the esoteric schools of Buddhism.

Despite the many ways in which one could undergo realization of the significance of the various types of mandala, and the many different presentations made of this significance, the principle of integration, itself, remained identical, and could be found within every form of mandala. For *Chuan Fa* the interconnecting spiritual forces arrayed in the mandala described not only the patterns of *Chuan Fa* physical movements, but also what constituted the moment, itself.

An acknowledgment and practical expression of this interconnection of the intrinsic homogeneity between mental and physical acts lay in the different movement sequences (*Hsings*) introduced by monks such as Bodhidharma and Hua To as part of their meditation method. Later the different *Hsing* were shown as equally being representations of particular problems or misunderstandings enacted within living consciousness, and that certain of these *Hsings* were used to bring this fact to one's attention, often in a dramatic manner. One advantage of such a meditation method is that while it is easy to be either verbally or self-deceptive, it is very difficult to be kinetically so.

We have seen that *Chuan Fa* regarded these patterns of the mind/body interaction as a most important means of realizing the true nature and condition of both the sense of individuality and its multiple projections, and that how an informed perception of such mind/body patterns, be they expressed in doctrinal or kinetic forms, revealed the particular, and usually unknown, dialogue maintained by individuals through which they perpetuate various forms of suffering. In showing this, the monks had laid the basis for a form of kinetic therapy based upon principles existing within the earliest forms of Buddhism but which had lain unsuspected or unrevealed until the advent of the Mahayana Schools of teaching. By revealing such principles the monk masters also showed the means to attain a total freedom from such suffering.

Finally we learned how, many years later, these mind/body teachings were to slowly spread out to China's neighboring lands including Korea, Taiwan, and the islands named by the Chinese Lu-chiu. (Japanese: Ryukyu) [See Notes 61, 71] and that although many such schools changed, adapted, or deliberately omitted, certain vital parts of the teachings, there still remain some, usually private, groups maintaining the ancient truths of the Bodhisattva warriors [See Note 71]. What was revolutionary in the art of *Chuan Fa* was that it extended the peripheries of endeavor required for the development of a fully balanced sense of spiritual being. Such an extension of physical and spiritual boundaries outlined specific practices of a cathartic and therapeutic nature which, when applied to mind and body, enabled a student to fully perceive, attain, and understand how to strengthen and balance their process of spiritual evolution. A significant tenet of this being that a skilled practitioner could equally express such a balance in different dimensions of being (Note 107).

As its philosophy was expressed by and within special physical actions, and these actions in turn were expressed by and within its philosophical doctrines, the principles of both the *Chaan* "wordless" doctrine and the *Chen Yen* esoteric doctrine became integrated back into their original unity. This theme, itself portrayed in all esoteric schools as the Maha (greatest) Mandala, was actively presented in the ritualized movement sequences of *mudra* and experienced only through the active application of its constituent spiritual principles.

Chuan Fa used the wordless strategy of direct interpersonal encounter to teach the words of personal self-encounter. It uses the "words" of personal self-encountering to understand the wordless doctrine of interpersonal encounter. Ultimately it sought to encounter the infinity known as perfect and complete Enlightenment.

With this development the Monk Acaryas had completed their initial task, and, with India as its Father, China its Mother, the rest of the world became its children.

APPENDICES

Appendix 1

THE MAIN CHINESE BUDDHIST DYNASTIES

2852–2204 B.C.	Three and Five Emperors	(Southern & Northern Dynasties)	
2205–1766 B.C.	Hui	A.D. 420–457	Sun
1766–1122 B.C.	Yin	A.D. 479–502	Shi
1122–256 B.C.	Chu	A.D. 502–557	Liang
221–206 B.C.	Chin	A.D. 557–589	Kan
A.D. 201–8	Western Han	(Northern Dynasties)	
A.D. 25–220	Eastern Han	A.D. 386–534	Wei
		A.D. 535–557	Western Wei
(Three Kingdoms)		A.D. 534–550	Eastern Wei
A.D. 221–263	Shu Han	A.D. 550–567	Northern Shi
A.D. 221–265	Wei	A.D. 557–581	Northern Ken
A.D. 222–280	Southern Wu	A.D. 589–618	Sui
A.D. 265–316	West Tsin	A.D. 618–907	Tang
A.D. 302–376	Olden Lian		
A.D. 317–420	Chin	(Five Dynasties)	
A.D. 352–394	Olden Chin	A.D. 907–923	Later Liang
A.D. 384–417	Late Chin	A.D. 923–936	Later Tang
A.D. 385–431	Western Chin	A.D. 936–947	Later Chin
A.D. 393–439	Northern Lian	A.D. 947–951	Later Han
		A.D. 951–960	Later Chu
		A.D. 960–1127	Later Sung

Appendix 2

Chronology of the Main Buddhist Sects and Scriptures

SECT NAME (CHINESE)	SUTRA USED (SANSKRIT)	FOUNDER	APPROXIMATE YEAR	YEAR FIRST TRANSLATED
Pi Tan	Abhidharma	Sanghadeva	c. 383	42
San Lun	Madhyamika	Seng Chao	c. 384	384
Lu Tsung	Vinaya	Hui Kang	c. 402	150
Ch'eng Shih	Sattyasiddhi	Kumarajiva	c. 417	250
Nieh P'an	Nirvana	Dharmaraksha	c. 423	180
Ching T'u	Sukhavati	Tan Luan	c. 476	286
Ti Lung	Dasabhumi	Bodhiruci	c. 500	100
Cha'an Na	Lankavatara	Bodhidharma	c. 502	414
Tien Tai	Pundarika	Chih I	c. 531	286
Chu She	Abhidharma	Paramartha	c. 563	383
She Lun	Samparigraha	Paramartha	c. 563	410
Fa Hsiang	Vijnaptimatrata	Hsuen Tsang	c. 596	596
Hua Yen	Avatamsaka	Fa Tsang	c. 643	410
Chen Yen	Tattvasamgraha	Vajrabodhi	c. 720	720
	Mahavairocana	Shan Wu Wei	c. 725	725

Appendix 3

VIEWS OF MIND

We are now going to consider the various ideas concerning how the consciousness is constituted. Although it may be complex for some, it is very important to understand how the different schools viewed such principles, for it was their differences which determined the manner in which they studied and the themes of their meditation practices. As *Chuan Fa* and all its philosophy arose from such meditative insights, we need to be quite clear about what was taught and understood when it arose. The purpose of this appendix is to outline such precedents, and in particular those precedents concerning descriptions of consciousness which were termed *Mano* and *Manas*.

If we look at both early and later accounts of *Manas* and *Mano* as they occur within the different schools of Buddhist teaching, we can easily see the varied ways in which they were presented, both then and now. From the earliest times, newer and extra categories were added to the basic and traditional lists of the constituent factors of consciousness as subsequent generations of students sought to explain more. Often these categories carefully detailed aspects, functionings, and orientations of consciousness which had not been specifically elaborated or catered for in the early teachings. In *Chuan Fa* sometimes very different explanatory ideas arose in order to explain its rationale and ethic.

The results of the process of development can be seen when we compare the accounts of Sarvastivada (Theravada) and Mahayana texts concerning very basic ways of explaining consciousness. We can consider some of these now.

The Sarvastivada (of which the modern Theravada is a doctrinal offshoot) did not distinguish as a special function what is termed *Manas* in the Mahayana. Instead they concerned themselves with describing the *Manodhatu* (mental element) and the *Mano*, which is its result. There are many and varied definitions of these. Here is a summary of some:

MANO DHATU
One of the 18 elements. The term does not apply to the whole of consciousness, but designates only that special element of consciousness which at first, at the beginning of the process of sense perception, performs the function of advertence to the sense object. (*Buddhist Dictionary*, Nyantiloka. Ceylon: Frewin & Co. 1972, p. 96.)

MANOVINNANADHATU (Sanskrit: *Manovijnana dhatu*)
Describes that consciousness element which investigates, determines, and registers impressions of the five previous sense organs and is syn-

onymous with *Vinnana* (consciousness of mind) and *Citta* (state of consciousness). NB: *Vinnana* is the Pali form of the Sanskrit term *Vijnana*.

Attention, the Mind, reflection.

Psychological term of the *Skhandas*, or one of the seven mental factors (*Cetasikas*) that are inseparably associated with all states of consciousness.

Mind's first confrontation with an object. There are two classes of consciousness: (1) adverts (*avajjana*) at the sense "door"; (b) adverts at the mind "door."

Generally—methodical attention, wise reflection. (*Buddhist Dictionary*, Nyantiloka. Ceylon: Frewin & Co. 1972, p. 95.

The next category considered by the Sarvastivada School was that of *Mano*. Here are some views concerning this:

MANO
. . . the 6th centre of consciousness in Yogacara Buddhism. . . . the sense centre of mind/consciousness which collects and receives the 5 sense perceptions. (*Shingon Buddhism*, M. Kiyota. Los Angeles/Tokyo: Buddhist Book Int'l., 1978, pp. 168, 169.)

"Mind" is, in the Abhidhamma, used as a synonym of *Vinnana* (consciousness) and *Citta* (state of consciousness, mind). According to the Commentary to the Visuddhi Magga, it sometimes means sub-consciousness (bhavanga-sota) (*Buddhist Dictionary*, Nyantiloka. Ceylon: Frewin & Co. 1972, p. 96.)

(Note: In Sarvastivada/Theravada teachings *Mano* is described predominantly in combination with other factors, i.e., mind-entrances, mind element, mind consciousness element, mind karma, etc. All of these categories and descriptions are mainly used to describe the formative *process* of consciousness rather than its content.)

From these early views we come next into the Mahayana's equal emphasis upon the content, rather than process, of consciousness. This, as we said earlier, is termed *Manas*, and has been described as follows:

MANAS
. . . A sensory consciousness serving as a direct antecedent condition (*samanta pratyaya*) for a mental consciousness. . . . Such sensory consciousnesses are by necessity absent during the attainment of mental

"cessation" since they are always concomitant with *Vedana*, i.e., motivating dispositions (According to Vasubandhu in the *Abhidharmakosa* V. 2: para: 62 a–b).

Physical consciousness (as in the preceding 4 forms) does not condition what it sees, it acts only as a substratum. . . . Any consciousness serving as a condition for the 6th consciousness and which gives rise to sensory data. . . . Asanga introduces Manas as the 7th consciousness, and says it carries the sense of Ego, in the "Mahayana Samgraha." This is also occasionally used by Vasubandhu (7 *Works of Vasubandhu*, S. Anacker. Delhi: Motilal Banarsidass, 1984, pp. 143, 60, 61).

Manas . . . has the character of cogitation or intellection (V 5, p. lxxv). . . . always has self delusion, self belief, (self) conceit, (self) love. Ceases to exist at Arahatship. . . . is different from Citta (the 8th consciousness) and the first 6 consciousnesses. . . . continually relies upon the *Bijas* (seeds) and *Alaya* (store). . . . is supported by the senses but independent of them. They depend on it for manifestation (*Cheng Wei Shi Lun* of Hsuan Tsang Vol. 3, chapter 2).

. . . active mind. Thinking, measuring "mind" in its widest sense. . . . quality of consciousness. Thought, Idea, Will, but in Buddhism—the faculty of Thought (*Dictionary of Chinese Buddhist Terms*, Houdous & Soothill. Taipei: Cheng Wen Co. 1970, pp. 149b, 400).

. . . The Mind. 6th faculty conditioning man as an intelligent and moral being. . . . one of the Nidanas (causes of existence) (*Sanscrit & Chinese Dictionary*, W. Eitel. Tokyo: Sankusha, 1904, pp. 193, 197).

. . . The 7th level of consciousness in Yogacara Buddhism. . . . value judging level of consciousness. Stems from the 6th level (Mano vijnana) (*Shingon Buddhism*, M. Kiyota. Los Angeles / Tokyo: Buddhist Book Int'l., 1978, p. 169, 46).

The subjective part of our mind viewed as a receptive faculty is represented by one element called, indiscriminately, *Citta, Vijnana,* or *Manas.* It represents pure consciousness or pure sensation without any content. Its content is placed in the objective part which contains the definite sensation (*sparca*) feelings (*vedana*) ideas (*samjna*) volition (*cetana*) and various other mental phenomena up to the number of 45 separate elements. (*The Central Conception of Buddhism*, Th. Stcherbatsky. Delhi: Motilal Banarsidass, 1988, p. 15.)

In descriptions of *Manas* it was Vasubandhu who proved to be the most innovative, for under his teaching its meaning was extended to indicate a state of pre-consciousness somewhat similar to what in modern philosophy is termed "apperception." We can see that such an understanding existed in a basic form even in the earliest teachings but was never fully developed. This is because its object was "bodily" consciousness (Sanskrit: *Kayakamanas*) and such themes were treated very warily in those forms of Buddhism which had little experience of the use of physical training as meditative endeavors.

All the above descriptions are based upon the pattern of mentality generation shown in the diagram that follows.

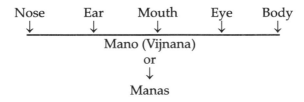

These last two categories (*Mano* = *Vijnana* and *Manas*) are the ones most likely to be interchanged within the different schools. It is here that confusion can arise concerning them and their status. This difference reflects the various opinions as to whether, in spiritual studies, one should emphasize mental activities alone as constituting consciousness, or whether one should regard the mental faculty in its totality as more significant. Such orientations produced different schools of teaching and training both in India and China.

In addition to the *Mano* = *Manas* nomenclature, the Mahayana developed and extended use of the Sanskrit term *Citta* (heart or mind) to describe the mind. Let us now look at this important term. Soothill describes Chinese usage of the term for mind as consisting of three parts called as follows in Chinese (Japanese in parens):

Hsin (*shin*)	*Yi* (*I*)	*Hsiang* (*shiki*)
Mind	Thought	Perception

The term *Citta* gained great predominance within China, and later Japan, becoming almost the standard popular Mahayana word for mind. The emphasis upon this term probably came about as a result of the Pure Land Schools of teaching in China, for these stressed a personal and emotional commitment toward Buddhism, and the term *Citta* was highly appropriate, for in popular Chinese this word was understood to mean "heart." This emphasis still exists and many modern schools speak of the standard précis of the *Prajna Paramita Sutra* as being the "Heart Sutra." As mentioned before, all this can be very confusing to the newcomer to Buddhist texts, but essentially, *Citta, Mano* and *Manas* all refer to different aspects of what we experience as the "mind." Here is an overview of its many descriptions.

CITTA

Derived from *Citi*—to think; that which is aware of an object. *Citta, Ceta, Cittapada, Nama, Mana, Vinnana* are all synonyms. . . . In the Abhidhamma no distinction is made between Mind and Consciousness. (Quoted from She Zan Aung *Compendium of Philosophy*); see *Citta* in *Manual of Abhidhamma*, Narada Thera. Kandy, Sri Lanka: Buddhist Publication Society, 1968.)

. . . When so called being is being divided into two constituent parts *Nama* (mind) is used. . . . When so called being is being divided into 5 *Skhanda, Vinnana* is used. . . . Citta is invariably employed whilst referring to different classes of Consciousness.

Cetana and *Citta* both derive from *Citi* = to think; *Citta*. . . . root = discerned (*Vinnana*); *Cetana*. . . . co-ordination and accumulation of mental states associated with itself and object of Consciousness.

. . . regarding the seat of Consciousness . . . Contemporary accounts say the *Citta* is the seat of Consciousness but the Buddha himself did not teach or commit himself to either a mental or physical base. (*Manual of Abhidhamma*, Narada Thera. Kandy, Sri Lanka: Buddhist Publication Society, 1968, p. 9.)

Citta is a simple descriptive Buddhist term for Mind. (*Shingon Buddhism*, M. Kiyota. Los Angeles / Tokyo: Buddhist Book Int'l., 1978, p. 162.)

CITTA(s) . . . can be derived from their *Citrava* (variety) [p. 79, Note 23]; or *CITRA* (manifold) [p. 31]; or (2) from *CINOTI* (to accumulate). This is the meaning utilised in descriptions of the *Alaya Vijnana* [p. 80].

. . . according to Vaibhasika and Mahasisaka theory in each Consciousness (of the six) to be so named must represent an object of consciousness (*Visaya*) and an aspect (*Laksana*) . . . through which it is recognised [p. 80 Note 25].

CITTA . . . is defined in the *Dhatukaya* of Vasumitra as concomitants of Consciousness. Mind "things"—in general "thoughts" [p. 145]. (From *7 Works of Vasubandhu*, S. Anacker. Delhi: Motilal Banarsidass, 1984.)

In Japanese *Citta* is translated by the word *Shin*. This is defined as "Mind, Will, Heart, or Meaning." (*New Dictionary of Japanese-English*, Tokyo: Kenkyusha Co., 1974.)

Integrating the Meanings

Many of these diverse descriptions arose because the key texts in which they first occurred were encountered only in the form of translations from Sanskrit into another language, and different nations and peoples understand or express experiences in different ways. We can have a rough overall idea of what is meant by the terms *Mano, Manas,* or *Citta* simply by reading the above variants, but in order to make more sense of these descriptions, which still confuse some people, we must be a little more precise. The following definitions, based upon the views of Vasubandhu, may help:

> The Sanskrit term *Citta* describes a fully formed moment-event of the "mental" consciousness, in its totality, at any one point of its existence. As such, it is a term describing consciousness as a state, viewed out of its dynamic continuum (*Asantana*).
>
> When Consciousness is termed *Manas,* what is being indicated is any form of consciousness arising from any of the five physical senses, which immediately and subsequently gives rise to a fully formed conscious moment event (*Citta*). It is necessary to distinguish between these two because, whereas all *Manas* gives rise to *Citta,* not all *Cittas* give rise to *Manas.* For instance, consciousness on the verge of attaining the meditative state of "freedom from all cognitions and feeling" (*Nirodha samapati*) gives rise to nothing at all—this very state being characterized by the absence of such activities.
>
> The term *Manas* emphasizes consciousness in its dynamic, sequential continuity of moment events (*Santanikotkarsa*). Vasubandhu in his *Vimsatika Karika* and *Madhyanta Vibhaga* [See Note 3] describes an additional, extended meaning for *Manas,* namely as a reflector (*Cinta*) of its own activity. Vasubandhu's brother, Asanga, saw this "looping back" repetitive activity as responsible for the sense of persistent individuality (*Pudgalabhava*) experienced as the "Self." Whereas *Manas* usually gives rise to moment events of wide diversity, in Asanga's sense it becomes temporarily fixated upon its own dualistic processes of auto-referencing (*Atmabhava*). We should not confuse this activity with the "Reflective Wisdom" (*Adarsajnana*), which is a non-dualistic attribute of the Buddhas.
>
>   This activity of *Manas* may give rise to a *Citta* whose only object is its own re-enforcement. Some Yogacara followers regarded this action to be so important that they viewed it as

another form of Consciousness in its own right, and added it to the list of six basic consciousnesses to form a seventh or later an eighth. In the Japanese form of Shingon Buddhism, this self-reflecting attribute was credited also to the Buddha Dainichi, and debate concerning its nature and meaning was responsible for the arising of new schools of Shingon in Japan.

In order to make the above a little clearer I have set out all the basic components in Table 7 on page 292. One should not see the factors in Table 7 as Consciousness "levels" but simply as common factors to all Consciousness, most of which occur in a sequence either from physical to mental bases, and from there to Consciousness, or in reverse. Table 7 covers the various schools and contrasts their individual nomenclatures concerning *Manas* and *Mano*. *Hosso* is the Japanese name for the Dharmalaksana School of teaching, which itself was a Japanese version of the earlier Yogacara School of Vasubandhu; *Kusha* is the Japanese name of the Sarvastivada Abhidharma teaching. *Mikkyo* includes Japanese Shingon and Tendai. (A chart of these schools and their historical evolution is given in Appendix.)

I have also included in this chart the category of *Alaya* consciousness not yet mentioned. This advanced term was used by the early Yogacara School, and some others, to describe a deep aspect of consciousness acting as if a repository for those patternings of mind which underlay our usual Consciousness, and acting as an impersonal and inaccessible modifier of all mind/body activity. Previous schools of teaching had their own special terms to describe such states although these did not always correspond exactly to what the Yogacara meant by this title. The Theravada School called its equivalent the *Tanmatra* or *Bhavangasrota* (stream of consciousness). The Mahasanghika School termed it *Mulavijnana* (root consciousness) and the Mahasisaka termed it *Asamsaraskhanda* (the collection beyond the birth and death process). Alternative or equivalent terms for the same category are shown where appropriate.

Previously we have seen how the different senses can produce eighteen different bases of activity which are then reflected on and into different kinds and levels of mind or body. These reflections are then collected together and give rise to the idea of an experiencer of them. From this idea the concept of a permanent "self" arises [Note 6c]. If we now combine the previously described factors, we can produce a synthetic chart of how the majority of schools viewed the basis for the mind/body matrix of consciousness. This is outlined in Table 8 on page 293.

We should recall that any such analysis of the mental constituents is merely a Buddhist therapeutic antidote for the dis-ease of habitual

Table 7. Schools of Teaching.

PHYSICAL BASES	Theravada	Kusha	Yogacara	Hosso	Madhyamika	Mikkyo
(Rupakalapa)						
1) Nose	✓	✓	✓	✓	✓	✓
2) Ear	✓	✓	✓	✓	✓	✓
3) Eye	✓	✓	✓	✓	✓	✓
4) Tongue	✓	✓	✓	✓	✓	✓
5) Body	✓	✓	✓	✓	✓	✓
BODY TO MIND Jivitakalapa*						
6) Mind + Body	Nama-Rupa	Mano	Mano	Mano	—	Mano
MIND TO BODY Manodhatu						
MIND BASES (Manoayatana)	Citta	Citta	Citta	Hrydaya	Sunya/Citta	Citta
7)	Manovijnana	Caitasika	Manas	Manas	—	Manas
NON-PERSONAL						
8)	Bhavangasrota	—	Alaya	Alaya	—	Alaya
9)	—	—		Amala	—	—

*This word means the "Life Principle Group"—the *élan vitale* without which physical life cannot arise. It here describes all the physical activities or energies required to maintain life. These are not necessarily accessible to consciousness.

Table 8. The Eightfold Nature of Consciousness.*

RUNNING THROUGH ALL LIVING BEINGS IS JIVAT (LIFE FORCE ENERGY)			
Eightfold Nature	Element	Skhanda Name	Predominant Characteristic
1	Earth	Rupa	Materiality
2	Water	Vedana	Sensation (Three Forms)
3	Fire	Samjna	Perception
4	Air	Samskara	Volition
5	Space	Vijnana	Consciousness (Three Aspects)
	↓		↓
		↓	
6		MANO	
(Basic mental integer for body and mind connection and ordering sense data and instinct) ↓			
7		MANAS	
(Discriminating/evaluating Self producing Consciousness) This is the "Mind" we utilize in "our" day-to-day life. ↓			
8		ALAYA	
"Root Store" Consciousness			

*Number 1–7 form *Citta* = any moment of Consciousness—all its constituents.

self-belief patterning from which arises the suffering of humanity. It is not, in itself, a technique or approach intended as a statement of an ultimate "truth." When the "disease" has been alleviated a dis-attachment to the process of cure must also take place. It is true of all doctrines that when they achieve their goal they become irrelevant, being only a skillful means to an end. In Buddhism, they are likened to a boat which carries you on a journey across a river. When you reach the other side, the boat is discarded and the journey continued.

The journey of discovering our minds is a new one for many. It is strange territory and we need all the maps and help we can get. By establishing a method to uncover such help, one which has been tried and tested by many millions of people in different countries and cultures, the Buddhist teaching gave to the world the possibility of a true, liberating, and liberated autonomy of being, free from fears and neurosis.

The extension of this life liberating principle into the field of the human body, via *Chuan Fa*, opened up a door for those who may have previously considered themselves "beyond the pale" of any spiritual virtue, but who nevertheless experienced the pains and sufferings of life and death identically to others.

(NB: A more detailed analysis of common orientations and functionings of the personal "mind" is given in the sections commentating upon Bodhidharma's *Hsieh Mai Lun*.)

Appendix 4

Development of the
Early Indian Buddhist Sects

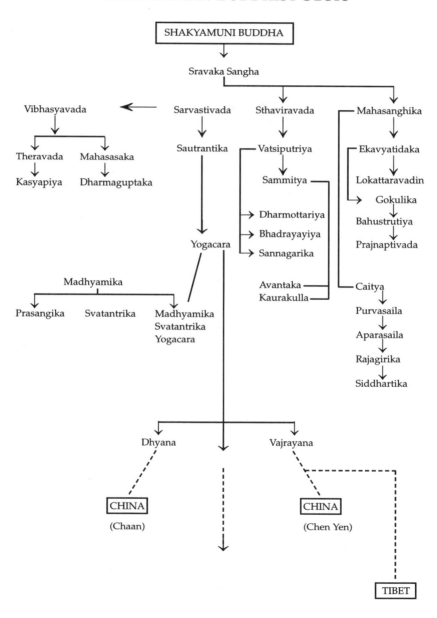

Appendix 5

BODHIDHARMA, WU TI AND CHAAN-NA

Nine years facing the Wall.
listening to the Ants scream
Vastness
No Holiness

(Numbers in brackets refer to references in the Notes section.)

It is truly said that any account of *Dhyana* (*Chaan Na*) is but a record of moments. *Chaan* is one of the most difficult types of Buddhism to comprehend, for its nature is fleeting and not easily expressible. For those interested in the historical or sectarian developments of the *Chaan Na* approach, the subject is well covered in a literary and poetic sense by R. H. Blythe, and, succinctly, by Junjiro Takakasu [Note 40].

One of the most enigmatic figures in Chinese Buddhist history is Bodhidharma. In China, his Sanskrit Buddhist name was Pu Tai Ta Mo, but this was shortened to Tamo. Many Zen sects in Japan regard him as one of their patriarchs, while some Buddhist schools ignore him completely. Chinese followers of Chaan came to regard Bodhidharma as quintessentially Chinese and yet he was clearly an Indian. In common with Japan (where his name was transliterated into Bo-Dai-Daru-Ma = *Daruma* and *Chaan Na* into *Zen*) the Chinese made Bodhidharma the subject of art, poetry and handicrafts.

Because our knowledge of Bodhidharma has been mostly limited to the accounts preserved in Japan, he seems to appear suddenly in Chinese Buddhist history, with few obvious precedents, emphasizing a teaching of the *Dhyana* (*Chaan-Na*) meditation method and approach. (*Chaan-Na* is simply the native Chinese way of pronouncing the Buddhist Sanskrit term *Dhyana*, which means "meditation"). Meditation was, of course, already known and practiced in China by many already well-established Buddhist schools.

In common with many other traditions, comparatively little is really known about him, save for the strange stories told of his sayings and pronouncements. Even his name is subject to speculation and appears in some texts in several different forms. There are many oral accounts of Bodhidharma and his teaching. Some have been written down and preserved in temple libraries. Others are found within the Japanese Imperial Collections. Japan has copies or summaries of many of the texts that were available at the time the various collections of scriptures were formed or added to, but as time progresses, it has become evident that there are many others.

As newer texts are discovered concerning Bodhidharma and his teaching, the picture some popular writers have given us—of his being a "legendary" figure—is rapidly receding, and as we gain more factual knowledge of the Buddhist doctrines of that period and of his historical precedents, he can be seen in a far more balanced manner, as one of the many missionaries who left India for the Eastern Kingdoms [See Note 39, Precedents].

The *Hsieh Mai Lun* included here formed part of the tradition of the Northern School of Chaan. Its teaching contains subtleties and doctrine not usually associated with the teachings of patriarchs like Hui Neng, and makes Dogen's assertion (in the Shizen Biku section of the *Shobogenzo*) that the Platform Sutra is a forgery seem quite possible.

The sects founded upon Bodhidharma's teachings which, in the past we have been led to believe were quite uniform and continuous, are now revealed as far more diverse and intricate in their ramifications and sub-branches than was previously suspected. Whereas it had been all too common for many orthodox Japanese Zen sects to ignore completely other Dhyana systems which stemmed from the same Indian / Chinese sources as their own, and also to ignore completely the differences in the various accounts of the Zen lineages as if they had no meaning, it is now possible for modern researchers to discover some of the original rich tapestry of diversity which has, in fact, always characterized the various forms of Chinese Buddhism.

We now have accounts of his teachings, sayings, and followers within China, Korea, and Tibet, and details of the many, previously unknown, teachers who followed after him [See Note 42], including those who followed the esoteric teaching simultaneously to that of pure Dhyana. Bodhidharma's methods and attitudes appear to emphasize a unique variation of the non-verbal but didactic insight training peculiar to the Madhyamika and Yogacara (Mind only) schools philosophy of Nagarjuna and Vasubandhu.

It also has points in common with the Dharmalaksana teaching (the Japanese Hosso sect) as well as the Abhidharma philosophical tradition [see Note 28], and it can be clearly seen that each of these schools contributed and affected what we know of Bodhidharma's approach and method of communication. He is said to have described the Supreme Void as: "A grain of millet seed in the beak of a golden Cockerel."

Hakuin, a famous Japanese Zen artist, once described Bodhidharma as "a divine blue eyed virtuoso with a purple beard." He also summarized his life in the following verse:

Reaching the forest peaks of Bear's Ear he amused himself
playing a holeless iron flute.

Finding its sounds unable to split men's bowels he carved out
his own flesh and blood and handed it around.*

This may all sound very gory and violent to delicate Buddhist ears but is
a typical Zen manner of expressing Bodhidharma's life events. Let's
now consider some of these life events and their environment according to a summary of the various received accounts.

According to legend, Bodhidharma was said to be the son of the King
of Kancipura (Chinese: *Hsiang-chih*; Japanese: *Koshi*) in Southern India. In
some accounts he is named Bodhitara, and in others, Tarabodhi [Note
42c]. The times before Bodhidharma's birth were active ones in both India
and China. India was in a state of panic as Hun invaders entered from
the North and roamed the country looting and pillaging. Bodhidharma
was born in the middle of this invasion and must have grown up surrounded by activity—both political and military. His childhood memories
must have helped convince him of the transitory nature of existence.

If he was indeed a royal prince he would have been educated and
trained fully in the military arts in order to succeed his father during
this dangerous period of history. Something, however, happened during this time. In the midst of all these military strategies and activities,
and despite his education in statecraft, he encountered the Buddha's
teaching. A radical change occurred within him. Renouncing his inheritance, he enrolled for classes under the famous teacher Prajnatara and
from that time forth studied the Buddhist doctrines of Existential Reality (*Sarvastivada*).

Many teachers of the Abhidharma (the early Buddhist philosophy
and metaphysics) had gone to China at this time, and its teaching was
finding a growing acceptance among Chinese circles, but even at that time
China was the subject of internal wars. Some of these wars, no doubt were
inspired by the presence of the invaders in India whom, the western Chinese feared, would sooner or later turn their attention toward them.

The Vijnaptimatra (Mind Only) School was being studied by many
Chinese and its growing popularity had created a need for translations
of the older texts. Due to this, and because of the civil unrest, many
Indian teachers were journeying to China, and the next fifty years saw

---

*Spearman, *Hakuin's Zen of Daruma*, Journal of Mushindo Studies, Vol. 3, No. 1. London, January, 1964.
In this poem the "forest peaks" and "Bear's Ear" refer to the Shaolin Temple's environment. "Amused"
indicates Bodhidharma's informed but antinomian approach. The "holeless" flute cannot make a
sound, thus Bodhidharma's teaching is in the silence of meditation. The "iron" probably refers to the
"Iron Tower" of Nagarjuna, from which he is said to have received the teaching—both exo- and esoteric—from Vajrasattva Bodhisattva. Because its "sound" is the voice of the Void, it is difficult to understand in one's "source mind" because it is obscured by the *Klesa*. The "bowels" serve the same function
to the body that the mind can to the *Klesa*. The reference to "flesh" is explained in the last paragraph of
Note 39.

them establishing themselves and teaching growing numbers of native Chinese as well as several Japanese visiting monks. Chinese monks were also themselves translating Buddhist Sanskrit texts, and it can be seen from this that the Chinese had already developed great doctrinal expertise. It cannot therefore truly be said, as is sometimes stated, that Bodhidharma left for China in order to introduce Buddhism—it was already well established and to a high degree.

According to most accounts, Bodhidharma was sent to China by his teacher Prajnatara, perhaps to aid or succeed his famous contemporary, Bodhiruci. Prajnatara was a master of the Sarvastivada sect teachings. This was one of the proto-Mahayana schools which emerged from the Theravada. It taught distinctive ideas concerning the nature of reality and differed from the mainstream doctrine over such questions as the nature of the elements, what did, and did not, constitute karmic activity, and other interesting questions. It seems a healthy precedent for one such as Bodhidharma to have emerged from.

Arriving in A.D. 520 or thereabouts, he was summoned to an audience with the reigning Emperor—Wu Ti—of the Leung Dynasty at Nanking. Certain writers, even ones regarded as knowledgeable, have expressed opinions that this story of Bodhidharma's meeting with Wu Ti is "apocryphal" or "unlikely." In my view this simply demonstrates their lack of knowledge concerning either of them.

The balance of probability—drawn from what is actually recorded of Wu Ti's character and his method of ruling—show that in fact, if Bodhidharma was around, he is highly likely to have summoned Bodhidharma to a meeting, rather than Bodhidharma having to seek one with him. Wu Ti was an enlightened ruler who brought about many changes both in the nation and in the relationships a monarch had with his subjects. Devoutly Buddhist, he sought out teachers and invited them to preach at his personal court—not simply as a political or socially inspired gesture as could sometimes occur—but in a sincere effort to discover the Truth.

Wu Ti was an unusual person, who conducted himself more like one of his subjects than a monarch. His reign was characterized by his increasing liberality and open-handed form of government. Because of his devotion to Buddhism, he undertook many social improvement schemes, pardoned all criminals he considered over-sentenced, and forbade the death penalty. He suffered opposition in this from his Taoist and other advisors, but such was his zeal that within a few years of his coming to power, most criminals were excused any severe punishment, and the jails were steadily emptied of their prisoners. To those incarcerated, it must have seemed like a dream come true.

Despite numerous and vociferous objections from his ministers—whom he often dismissed if he discovered them involved in any form of corruption—he continued such policies for many years. One unfortunate (and perhaps foreseeable) result of his philanthropic actions was that the number of crimes increased and people began to be afraid to venture outside their homes. Knowing his reluctance to execute or imprison anyone, crimes, criminals and murders multiplied throughout his reign.

Naturally the Taoists continued to oppose what they saw as social madness on his part, but, if one considers Wu Ti as trying to emulate the Indian Buddhist monarch Asoka, he was simply being true to his beliefs. On May 2, 504 he issued the following edict:

> Although Lao Tzu and Kung Fu Tsu (Confucius) were disciples of the Buddha the outer manifestation of their doctrines is not correct since they are restricted to only what is good in worldly terms.*

In such statements he demonstrated both his allegiance to Buddhism and his view of the Taoist and Confucian elite which he had inherited upon coming to power. Wu Ti invited many Buddhist monks to serve as his intimate advisors and thus deliberately alienated those antagonistic to Buddhism. Under Wu Ti's reign the oldest existing catalogue of the Buddhist scriptures was collected.

One remarkable facet of his government was his open court. He permitted anyone who wished to visit him, and peasant or prince alike could attend his meetings as equals, and he dispensed completely with the elaborate rituals and court etiquettes so beloved by his predecessors. This was a truly revolutionary act and his court was flooded with people requesting audiences and favors at every session.

On one famous occasion the monk Chi Tsang sat upon the imperial throne and when Wu Ti arrived to hold court he asked him to vacate it. Chi Tsang refused and responded saying, "Where I am, the Dharma is." Wu Ti allowed him to stay there throughout the day. On another occasion a monk refused to come to his feet to greet Wu Ti—one of the few simple acts of respect Wu Ti permitted—Wu Ti did nothing to censure him.

His devoutness can be seen when he came across a golden statue of the Buddha which had been originally found in 376 at Chian Lin. It bore an inscription saying it had been made by the Emperor Asoka himself. Wu Ti, greatly moved by this, had it brought to his capital with great pomp and ceremony and installed it personally in the Chang Sha monastery as an offering.†

---

*Recorded in *She Shih Li Lao Tao Fa Chao*, this is contained in the *Kuang hung ming* (Taisho 2059) Section 8, v 140:1.
†Recorded in the *Tao Seng Chuan* during its description of the life of the monk Tan I, and also in the *Kuang Hung Ming* (Taisho 2059) Section 15, v 202:2.

One account of the initial meeting between Bodhdidharma and Wu Ti says that when Wu Ti enquired of the merit he had earned for all his good deeds, Bodhidharma informed him that he had accrued none whatsoever. This puzzled Wu Ti who had at that time no previous experience of the Chaan attitudes and ways of communicating that so characterized the person of Bodhidharma. As Wu Ti was plainly a devotional and expressive Buddhist, he was neither impressed by nor temperamentally disposed toward the iconoclastic autonomy and simplicity of the pure Dhyana method. Perhaps not surprisingly Bodhidharma was unable to convince the Emperor of the value of his method of teaching.

Knowing he would have no Imperial patronage, Bodhidharma set out for Loyang, a great Buddhist center of the day, crossing the Yang-Tse river "on a leaf" as the legend says, but in reality upon one of the leaf-shaped ferryboats which still ply their trade nowadays. He then went to the Sung Mountains and climbed Bear's Ear Peak (Hsiun Erh Shang) of Mount Wu Tai (Five Peaks) until he reached the Shao Lin (Little Forest) Monastery which had been built next to the Five Nipple Peak by Emperor Hsiao Wen for the Theravada missionary Bhadra. There he lived and remained in a small cave for nine years meditating, according to legend "facing the wall"—a reference to the "Emperor's Table," a steep mountainside cliff-face of the Shao Shi range. The Shao Lin Temple had been deliberately built opposite to it (see Note 14).

It is while he was here that he is said to have introduced the Indian Buddhist health-giving exercises and remedial therapeutic movement sequences that later formed the basis for many martial arts [see Notes 14, 42]. Though he was never recorded as becoming the master of the monastery, his influence seems to have been considerable, and it is his teaching alone which history associates with the temple. Tradition states that his main successor was an ex-Confucian scholar named Hui K'o, and that one snowy night he stood outside Bodhidharma's cell and sliced off his own arm to convince Bodhidharma of his sincerity in wishing to study with him.*

---

*Some authors cast doubt upon this event, quoting an account which says he lost his arm later on in a conflict with some robbers. Anyone familiar with Bodhidharma's writings would recognize this story as a reference to Bodhidharma's *Kuan Hsin Lun* sastra, and in particular the chapter titled "Seeing the Six Thieves Correctly." In this scripture he describes how six robbers are continually stealing things from us, and in particular our perception of truth. They are also continually at work poisoning us with the "Three Evils."

Hui K'o "lost" his arm to the "robbers" because he was perhaps too emotionally intense in his wish to study with Bodhidharma. In a manner somewhat resembling the early Gnostic Christian genius Origen, he was simply over-zealous. This whole saying seems to be a retrospection of Hui Ko himself. The robbers are the senses, the three evils are the *Klesas* greed, hatred, and ignorance. This may also explain the alleged poisoning of Bodhidharma.

The *Zengaku Yokan** quotes a scriptural account in which it is said that sometime after the nine years he called his four disciples together and asked each to express their attainments. They each then replied in a manner suitable to demonstrate their understanding of the Dharma. When they had each spoken, Bodhidharma quoted Nagarjuna saying to one, "You have my skin." To the next he said, "You have my flesh." To another he said, "You have my bones." To the last (Hui Ko) he said, "You have my marrow." In this manner, Bodhidharma is said to have chosen his successor [see the last reference in Note 39]. When Bodhidharma died (some accounts say that he was poisoned, see Note 42c), his ashes were interred in the grove on the Bear's Ear Peak.

Because it seemed so different to what they already had been taught, the Chinese mind was eager to know from where the Chaan Na method arose, and to satisfy this need a "lineage" of Patriarchs was devised. According to some accounts there were 24 Patriarchs while others held there were 27 or 28 [see Note 39].

Bodhidharma's meditation is said to use two approaches, both of which he is said to have taught. One approach, later termed *Thathagata* meditation, was based upon four meditation themes, each of which were divided into three aspects or levels. These themes were methods practiced within the oldest Indian Buddhist teachings, and showed a path of gradual, steady progression and application.[†] The other method, later termed "Patriarchal meditation" by the southern Chinese sects, described the method used by the later teacher Hui Neng. This was a teaching of "sudden" progression and enlightenment. In the south of China this method grew popular, and it was also popular in Japan, where it was taken up by the Samurai Warrior Caste for its tactical, psychological benefits.

The "gradual path" meditation method is called the Northern school while the sudden realization method is known as the Southern School. In reality, there is little difference between them, and both names came after Hui Neng. A contemporary of Bodhidharma, Shen Hsiu, was the master of the Northern method. Shen Hsiu's school is the one in which Dengyo Daishi—the founder of Tien Tai Buddhism in Japan—studied, and certain forms of its techniques are still included within both the Japanese Tendai teachings and the Chinese Mikkyo sects.[‡]

---

*Published by Segawa Shobu, Japan, 1907.

†These methods should not be confused with accounts of Bodhidharma's teaching presented under other titles.

‡The Tendai School synthesizes both active and passive forms of meditation in a manner similar to the Chinese esoteric schools. It recognizes four types (as opposed to themes) of meditations. Two of these involve physical activity and two are passive. This part of its tradition seems to be based directly upon Bodhidharma's teachings. Refer also to Note 2d.

The effect of Chaan in China immediately after Bodhidharma was minimal. It was overshadowed for many years by other emerging schools of teaching. Bodhidharma and his immediate contemporaries formed part of the movement which grew from Vasubandhu's doctrine of "Mind Only" in China, and its doctrine proved highly influential in the development of many later schools. Bodhidharma is said to have bequeathed to his students several written manuscripts of the doctrine, including the Lankavatara Sutra. This Sutra is highly important to the development of "Mind Only" (*Wei Shih*) doctrine. Even if they did not adopt it into their own teaching, the various schools could not ignore its effects upon their spiritual life and polemics. (See also the Appendix and Notes concerning Bodhidharma.)

There were many other lineages of Chaan Na teachers within China, whether founded by, or credited to a Patriarch or not. Korean Zen (*Son*) is older than the Japanese form, and has a wide range of schools. It often embraces distinctly Chinese approaches not taken to Japan. Due to its close proximity to China, Korea had access to scriptures and teachings bypassed by the Japanese sects. Buddhist teaching and Buddha images were, in fact, introduced to Japan from Korea.

A very famous Chaan Na mystic and poet, Han Shan (1546–1637), once wrote the following, which is recorded in the *Han Shan Meng Yu Chi*:

> When Bodhidharma came to the West he set up only the doctrine of Transmission of mind and used the four books of the Lankavatara Sutra to seal it. . . . Therefore the Patriarchal and the Thathagata teaching are one (and the same) teaching.*

This clearly shows and reasserts that Bodhidharma's teaching did not ignore literal studies (as is often claimed), but more that he encouraged a nonattached relationship to external sources of knowledge.

Many of Bodhidharma's oral teachings are preserved in China, Tibet, and Korea—although few are regarded as canonical in the orthodox Zen of Japan, which is actually based upon the "sudden" School [Note 42a,b]. Because we in the West have been exposed to so many accounts of this type of teaching, I include here representative translations of the alternative and Northern School tradition. One, "The Six Gates," presents a description of path and levels of the Tathagatha

---

*We have no other account of a Lankavatara sutra "in four books" save for that used by Tao Yin at a later date. Most other authorities quote more books than this (see Note 42). If this is the same, it must have been an early Chinese edition, as such texts tend to accrue commentaries or additional translator's notes over the years, and gradually increase in number of volumes to contain their entirety.

method, and another, "Entering the Path," describes the manner in which we set about practicing it.

On the whole, the literal expressions of the Southern (sudden) School are distinctively enigmatic. Consider, for instance, this (deadly serious) episode from the tenth section of the *Cheng Teng Lu* concerning a student's interview with Master Tzu He Li Tsung (800–880) [Note 42]:

> At Lake Shi there is a Dog.
> Superior people get his head.
> Mediocre people get his heart.
> Inferior persons get his legs.
> (answer me quickly)
> If you hesitate your life is lost!

> The monk asked, "What about the Dog?"

> "Woof, Woof," barked Tzu He.

Appendix 6

TRANSLATION OF BODHIDHARMA'S CHINESE TEXTS

The Six Gates
(Shao Shih Liu Men)
[A small peripheral (teaching)
concerning the six entrances of human experience]

Entering the Buddha's Path
(Ju Tao Lun)
[A fragment of a Teaching by Bodhidharma,
with Explanatory Notes, from Section 30, *Cheng Teng Lu*]

Treatise Upon the Bloodline Teaching of True Dharma
(Hsieh Mai Lun)
An excerpt from Bodhidharma's *Wu Hsing Lun*
(The Collection of Treatises upon No-Mindedness)
[An explanation and study of the meanings of the Hsieh Mai Lun;
recollecting our terms of experience; Time, Ego and the process of
awakening; Timelessness; Unreal experience.]

THE SIX GATES

Shao Shih Liu Men

(A small peripheral (teaching) concerning
the six entrances of human experience)[1]

Bodhidharma said:

If a sentient being continually develops the roots of good Karma, the Nirmanakaya Buddha will manifest.[2]

If he develops Wisdom, the Sambhogakaya will manifest.[3]

If he develops non-doing, the Dharmakaya will manifest.[4]

In the Nirmanakaya, a Buddha soars throughout the ten directions and adapts to all circumstances encountered in order to save human beings.[5]

In the Sambhogakaya, Shakyamuni came across the snowy mountains, overcame evils, cultivated the good and attained the Path.[6]

In the Dharmakaya, Buddha remains in tranquillity and unchanging, without speaking or teaching.[7]

From the view of Ultimate Principle no Buddha exists.[8]

The idea of the Triple Body came into being merely to accommodate the differences in people's intelligence.[9]

Those of lower intelligence enjoy wealth and possessions. They see the Nirmanakaya.

Those of middling intelligence engaged in attempting to overcome their passions see only the Sambhogakaya.

Those of higher intelligence engage in trying to realize Enlightenment. They deludedly see only the Dharmakaya.

Those of the highest intelligence direct their Light inward and illuminate their inner natures and attain a state of perfect tranquillity.[10]

With minds perfectly clear they are real Buddhas, for they have attained insight without involving their confused mentality. They realize that the Three Bodies, and all other things, cannot be grasped nor expounded upon.

Is this not what the Sutras say when they preach?

Buddhas do not preach Dharma, nor save sentient beings, nor realize Enlightenment?

Notes

1. *Shao Shi Liu Men* is often translated as meaning "The Little House with Six Gates," however, in some Chinese and Korean versions, the character for "house" (*Shih*) does not occur. Instead there is an ancient character meaning something like "range," "extent," or "periphery." We can therefore alternatively translate the title as stated.

2, 3, 4. The *Sambhoga*,[2] *Nirmana*,[3] and *Dharmakaya*,[4] mentioned here constitute what is termed in Buddhism the "Three (*Tri*) Bodies (*Kaya*)" of a Buddha. The last two *kaya* are known in the Theravada School but the first is a Mahayana development. The Three Bodies doctrine is a method of representing the manifestation or form utilized by a Buddha in order to communicate with his followers at their different levels of understanding.

The *Nirmanakaya*[3] represents the human form taken by a Buddha—in our case this is usually understood as indicating the figure of Shakyamuni, the historical Buddha. The *Sambhogakaya* represents the body of a Buddha as seen by more spiritually advanced beings, such as Bodhisattvas. This body represents a manifestation of some of the fruits of spiritual advancement and possesses a wider range of possibilities and attributes than the *Nirmanakaya*. The *Dharmakaya*[4] represents the Buddha as embodying the ultimate principle of the Law itself.

These paragraphs outline the three levels at which a student can perceive or follow the teachings. They also make a connection between the cause and effect of the different approaches made by students when they develop the wish to understand the Dharma.

Nirmanakaya is contrasted with the phrase "roots of good karma." This means conducting one's spiritual life in accordance with the precepts and rules of self-restraint.

Sambhogakaya is contrasted with the phrase "wisdom" and refers to those who study the scriptures and develop knowledge of the doctrines.

Dharmakaya is contrasted with the phrase "nondoing" and refers to those who practice both meditation and spiritual activities bereft of unskillful motivations or restrictive goals.

Although originally devised in order to simplify and explain certain aspects of communication within Buddhism, some sects developed elaborate and extended philosophies concerning the *Trikaya*, and it is probably due to this that Bodhidharma is addressing the theme in this quotation.

5. The three paragraphs (footnoted as 5,6,7) elaborate the approaches given in paragraphs 2 through 4 and represent the different conceptions that followers of the Law have concerning the figure of a Buddha.

In 5 Buddhahood is perceived as a multilevel principle of manifestation existing in all and every level or form necessary in order to liberate sentient beings. This is a universal multidimensional Buddha which includes, but is not restricted to, the historical

Shakyamuni. This is a Buddha who has attained enlightenment because of his great compassion.

6. Here we have a Buddha figure as was often portrayed in China and Tibet—one who heroically strives to lead others and who has undergone great hardships and trials in order to win enlightenment. "Coming across the snowy mountains" implies the physical arrival of the teachings in China from India, both in the form of the monk missionaries— who cared enough about China to bring it—and of the Buddha images which inspired the early emperors to support it. This is a Buddha who has become like a Chinese for the Chinese and acts as a counterpoise to the universal Buddha of the previous paragraph.

7. This is a Buddha of the ultimate Void, bereft of manifestation, quiescent, and beyond time.

8. Here we have the first revolutionary statement of Bodhidharma himself, an extra "fourth principle" designed to explode the first three, for here he is saying to his students that, in the end, no figure or representation of a Buddha has any value whatsoever, and that it is pointless to create any image or view of a person or thing in order to attain a condition created in the first place by the unskillful and suffering mind. Even the view expressed in (7) is simply a view, and one's imagination, no matter how great, inspired, or vivid, should never be confused with the reality of the Wisdom of the Void.

9. How does such confusion arise? The next few paragraphs explain that the idea of *Trikaya* was devised in order to aid people (i.e., as an expedient means) attain understanding. It does not have any value in itself. Furthermore he shows that a great barrier to the development of real understanding is the creation of pseudo goals which we come to regard as actually having value.

He then couples the idea of intelligence with simple but enslaving characteristics of worldly life namely, wealth and possessions, passions and enlightenment. Instead of the indigenous Chinese respect for learning, he is here characterizing it on a level with possessions and passions.

Due to the tainted understanding of the ordinary mind, these characteristics are mistakenly seen as being the actual goals that worldly people have to overcome or attain in order to be "spiritual." This enables them to maintain a fixed idea of what is and what is not truly a spiritual value. It is such fixity that Bodhidharma is addressing directly. Even a view of the *Dharmakaya*—not a usual concern of the worldly—but here stated so as to apply to monks, is said to be less than enough, and merely substantiates a position taken by the "higher" intelligence. Bodhidharma says that having the *Dharmakaya* as a goal category is "deluded."

10. Bodhidharma now reasserts his fourth principle again, and proceeds to describe the correct orientation for seekers of enlightenment. This is, he says, simply recognizing the real content of our own minds as it existentially is, with nothing added or taken away. Only when we recognize what is can we begin to deal with it properly; anything less than this is illusion built upon delusion.

ENTERING THE BUDDHA'S PATH

A fragment of a teaching by Bodhidharma,
with explanatory notes, from
Section 30, *Cheng Teng Lu*

Bodhidharma said:

There are said to be many different ways in which one can enter the Path of the Buddhas, but essentially there are only two types of entrance.[1]

One is termed the "Entering by Dharmic Principle,"[2] the other "Entering by Means of Dharmic Activity."[3]

Entering by means of Principle indicates experiencing the Dharma through application and study of its teachings.

By this means we come to realize our essential source nature.[4] This essential Nature usually lies hidden because of the Klesa.[5]

If someone takes up the practice of Pi Kuan[6] he realizes there is no Self nor Other, nor can anyone or thing be distinguished from each other.[7]

Such realization frees one from the necessity of communicating exclusively through words and speech.[8]

In a silent contemplation[9] one is in direct contact with the Dharma Principle itself, serene and beyond the creation of Klesas.[10]

Thus is the "Entering the Buddha's Path by Dharmic Principle."

"Entering by Means of Dharmic Activity" indicates observance of the "Four Skillful Actions." This category embraces all other forms of activity.

What are they?

1) To abandon generation of Hatred by discovering its causes.

2) To accord with the higher Karma.

3) To abandon the creation of Unskillful Desires.

4) To live according to the Dharma teaching.[11]

What does the first Dharmic Activity indicate?

One disciplining himself in the Path, when finding himself in hardship, should recall that in numerous other existences he has experienced many other forms of suffering and trial.

Throughout such lives he has acted unskillfully or unknowingly and generated the "Three Evil Roots" (Greed, Ignorance, Hatred) which lead to suffering.

Even if no evil deeds have been done in this present lifetime, the effects of past deeds will surely come to fruit in the present life. No one can predict what or when that will be. Knowing this, one must be prepared for all things at all times and accept, in knowledge, what is experienced.[12]

In the Sutras we can read of how such events are generated and also that it is by penetrating our inner Wisdom we come to directly know their real causes.[13]

If and when such a realization is experienced, a follower of the Buddha's path will accord with the Dharma Wisdom and be able to turn hatreds into various skillful means of spiritual advancement.[14]

This is what abandoning Hatred really means.

What does the second stanza show?

To "accord with higher Karma" reiterates the Dharmic teaching that there is no permanent "Self." All experiences undergone are likewise impermanent, transitory, and the intermingling of the forces and patterns of Past and Present. Consequently they are always liable to change or reverse themselves.

At one time you may receive riches, at another time you may be a beggar. According to the causal Karmic force present within the moment so will the amount of gain or loss waver, fading only when that causal force is exhausted.

The source Mind in its own nature knows neither the increase nor decrease of Karmic forces. The winds of Pain or Pleasure do not blow across it nor disturb it.[15]

Accepting all experiences without complaint, and in silence, is termed "Being in accord with Karma."[16]

The third stanza teaches that the generation of Desires is inseparable from mental confusion. These incline our attention to one thing after another, generating an unending and constant succession of dispersion and craving. Those who act with Wisdom, however, recognize this and practice meditations upon the Uncreated.[17]

When the Mind can rest within this, the Body can move around in a desireless accordance with Dharma.[18]

All things are ultimately empty of permanence and therefore nothing permanent is worthy of desire. Even within the virtue[19] of Knowledge (Light) there lies the vice of Ignorance (Darkness).[20]

The Triple Realm of existence[21] we are within is like a burning house.[22]

The possibility of human birth also possesses the possibility of human suffering, and one enmeshed within life finds it difficult to know peace.[23]

Those possessing the Highest Wisdom do not create ignorant desire but dwell in calmness.[24]

The Sutras say that wherever there is Craving there is also Pain. If you cease from the first the second vanishes.[25]

To accord with the Dharma Teaching reminds us that the Dharma itself is founded upon the teaching of Emptiness.[26]

Because of this, those that live in accordance with this principle do not create sufferings or ignorance. Liberated from a belief in a permanent self, their Minds are not stained with the "Three Poisons,"[27] nor do they generate a desire for Self.

Understanding this the Wise naturally live according to the Dharma principle.

They may practice charitable acts, offering their bodies, their property or even their lives without regret or reticence[28] but as they understand fully the threefold Emptiness of Being, they are beyond partiality or attachments.

It is only because of their desire to liberate suffering beings[29] that they take form among them, but they are not attached to this form. The Wise perform the "Six Perfect Practices"[30] in order to rise above confusion, yet ultimately they know there is no Mind[31] to get confused.

Thus is the living "in accordance with the Dharma" teaching.

Notes

1. The term "entering" used here was, in China, taken from the Pali word *Sotapanna* (stream enterer) indicating "one who has entered the stream leading beyond suffering." *Sotapanna* is a Buddhist term used in the earliest Theravada tradition to describe the first stage of progress toward enlightenment. This idea of "entering" also occurs in another Chinese Buddhist technical term *men*, meaning the doorway to a temple. This was one of the first words used in Chinese Buddhism to describe a sect or distinctive school/method of teaching. The concept of different attitudes toward identical practices occurs in the oldest Theravada texts where they are often described as varying forms of *vimutti* (deliverance) and classified as either deliverance by mind or deliverance by wisdom.

2. "Principle" (*Li*) is a native term adopted by both the Chinese exoteric and esoteric schools in an attempt to present Buddhist teachings in a native form or manner, making them more likely to be readily understood. The term was used mainly in combination with "wisdom" (*chih*), and the pair were said to represent the two aspects of the Dharma. The essence of this pair of terms is represented in the two mandalas of Taizokai and Kongokai. Bodhidharma is here reinterpreting its Confucian meaning (within which it was a stand-alone term) to make it instead represent a phronesic summary of practice.

3. Dharmic Activity—a form of "right effort"—represents the Sanskrit term *carya* (meaning "purposeful spiritual actions" as in *acarya*). The Chinese transliteration being *hsing* (Japanese: *gyo*). This term, *hsing*, was used, in combination with others, to specifically describe various forms of ascetic undertakings performed to purify one's thoughts, speech and body.

4. The term "nature" as used here first appears in the teachings of the Mahayanic Yogacara School, where it approximated the earlier Sanskrit *bhava* (beingness). This term does not indicate "temperament" or an individualized characteristic which, in essence, is an unknowing mental tendency to prolong, adhere to, or expand the various experiences of selfhood. Instead, it represents the *Bodhicitta*, the Buddha heart, said to live within us all and whose awakening develops the wish for enlightenment. In the Mahayanic Schools such a heart is regarded as the real source nature of humanity, for it confers the potential orientation to achieve enlightenment in this very lifetime.

5. *Klesa* is a Sanskrit term used to indicate various unwholesome mental traits, such as greed, hatred, delusion, conceit, etc. Usually ten are defined.

6. The term literally means "wall insight," and refers to the development of a meditative practice oriented to pierce through the "wall" of ignorance. Its mention in the scriptures (if the term has been accurately copied and preserved in the manuscript) is quite unique to this account of Bodhidharma, and occurs nowhere else in Buddhist literature before or afterward. According to certain temple traditions, at the Shaolin Temple and directly opposite Bear's Ear Peak, where Bodhidharma meditated, there rises a steep precipice, part of the Sung mountain range. This was known to the local monks as the "wall" and was used by them as a locus of sight to minimize distractions. It should be noted that Bodhidharma practiced an insight (*kuan*) meditation and not a dhyana (zen)

form here. An important and central meditative practice of the Tien Ta'i School was called *Shi Kuan*. This term, *kuan*, is seen by some as representing the earlier Theravada meditation practice of the Vipassana-Samatha method [see Note 28 at the end of this book].

7. The concept that all things continually intermingle until a condition is reached in which differentiation is impossible was popularized in the *Hua Yen* (flower garland) *Sutra*. This does not simply mean all things are mixed up, but more that as one approaches enlightenment the common bonds of craving and its consequent suffering which bind us to the wheel of karma are clearly recognized and acknowledged by the practitioner. There is no longer the possibility for self-deceit. "No self" refers to the basic Buddhist teaching of *Anatta*—that there exists no unchanging, permanently existing entity that could be termed our "self" or "soul."

8. This is a comment upon the practice among monks of Dharmic debate and logic argument, a tradition common to many schools as a means of improving one's ability. It was taken, by some, as an indicator of one's actual spiritual achievements. Often this would not be so, a monk who could argue skillfully was not always suited to be a teacher nor necessarily spiritual. Bodhidharma is distinguishing between those who have such skills and those who truly are spiritualized through their actual practice of the Dharma.

9. See the previous note regarding speech in general. Silent Contemplation is probably a remark directed toward the followers of the then increasingly popular Pure Land School who practiced and encouraged everyone to worship by chanting.

10. This idea of going "beyond *klesa*" (see Note 5) presents us with a picture of the form of approach to practice taken up by the schools of that time. On one side we have the schools of steady and gradual progression in the spiritual path, an image and pattern preserved especially by the Theravada School. In contrast to this, other schools, especially the esoteric, propounded an approach of "direct leaping" into enlightenment. Also there were the schools stressing faith, such as the *Omito Fu* (Japanese: *Amida*). Each of these had their own unique attitude toward what constituted spiritual progression, and not all agreed as to what this was. Serenity (Sanskrit: *uppekha*) is a quality developed at the second level of the traditional "four stages" of meditation (see Note 21:2).

11. These four actions clearly echo the Four Wisdoms of the Mandala Buddhas, namely:

The Wisdom of Equalizing Penetrative Insight—which seems indicated in the first activity. This dissolves the basis upon which hatred forms by neutralizing the fundamental standpoint from which it is generated.

The Wisdom of Reflective Penetrative Insight—which seems to refer to the second activity. This enables an insightful perception to avoid the development of negative responses which tend to the creation of those unskillful mental conditions through which suffering is perpetuated.

The Wisdom of Creative Penetrative Insight—which refers to the third activity and enables one to bypass the causal forces of sensorial or delusive delight through the positive application of Dharmic principles and endeavors toward others.

The Wisdom of Discriminative Penetrative Insight—which refers to the fourth activity, and relates to the inner decisions and judgments made in the course of spiritual life toward one's own inner or outer conditions.

These four wisdoms were utilized only within the esoteric schools and shows the familiarity of Bodhidharma with this terminology and tradition. The Chinese term used for activity (*hsing*; Japanese: *gyo*) was also used to describe the associated active practices involved in spiritual training—particularly that of "self" purification or healing. It was also used to transliterate the Sanskrit terms for the physical elements, time or periods of change, and the skillful means (Sanskrit: *upaya*) of the Bodhisattvas (see Notes 3, 14).

12. The idea that in order to be exhausted individual Karma must be received and experienced in exactly the same form that it was originally generated is a concept not in complete accord with all the early scriptures. It is shown in several instances that external (physical) karmic retributions are not always experienced in the same form as they were generated. In the *Mahajima Nikaya 2* (and also the *Theragatha 866* onward) there is an account of the ex-professional murderer Angulimala. He was taught by the Buddha that because certain injuries Angulimala received (in an incident described earlier in the Sutra) since he had been converted to Buddhism had been borne by him without complaint or desire for retaliation, his past karmic debts—though originally of a much greater and more serious form—had been rendered null and void. The implication being that Angulimala had been granted, or earned, a form of "compressed" Karma extirpation.

The teaching that all human events are totally subject to the action of Karma is not a Buddhist but a Jain teaching. It was used by them to validate their teachings of extreme passivity and acquiescence to world events. Buddhism, on the other hand, demonstrated a dynamic and active spirituality in which one creatively prepares the conditions for enlightenment. The *Sivaka Sutta* was expressly preached to clarify this point. It was the later espousal of such a fatalistic view of Karma which led to the gradual disintegration of spirituality within Hindu and Jain India. This teaching here by Bodhidharma is, I think, meant to refer to an inner perception and transcendence of one's imperfect mental conditions and experiences and not—as it may appear—a comment upon external conduct or actions.

13. This "real cause" means the chain of dependent origination (*pratitya samutpada*) according to whose pattern all things come into being or manifestation, exist for a while, and then pass away to reform again.

14. This is a reference to the *upaya* or "skillful means"—a Mahayanic innovation which figured prominently in all Chinese sects and schools of exposition. It referred to the practice of incorporating or utilizing practices, things, situations, objects, or experiences as a means of conveying the dharmic realities to students. It is primarily a didactic rather than doctrinal precept, although later an extensive philosophical framework explaining it was developed within China. In esoteric Buddhism, *upaya* is termed "the art of changing poison into medicine."

15. That the "source mind" or principle is said to exist—almost as if a separate entity—may seem surprising to one not familiar with Buddhist teachings. However, this is not an innovation. The idea is propounded in the 15th chapter of the *Lotus Sutra* (Japanese: *Myohorenge Kyo*) which speaks of an "Eternal Buddha." While previously the dharma had mostly been written of as an abstract, but dynamic, reminder of the purpose of Shakyamuni's teachings, here in the Lotus Sutra, the teaching became embodied as a recognizable, distinct, and named entity. Such a docetic tendency originated first within the Indian *Mahasanghika* from whence it spread, probably via the Sarvastivadins, into China as early as the second century A.D.

In the esoteric schools, a Primordial Buddha (*Mahavairocana*) is spoken of but is not regarded, or related to, in the same manner as this Buddha of the Lotus Sutra. The source inspiration for the statement here is probably the Dharmalaksana sect teaching of the eight consciousnesses. In this scheme the eighth level, called the *Alayavijnana* (storehouse consciousness), is held to exist continually—but it is not personalized in any manner. As Bodhidharma was trained in the Yogacara School—a direct descendant of the Dharmalaksana—the *Alaya* is probably what he refers to here when he speaks of something "beyond the creation of *klesa*."

16. This is, perhaps deliberately, a very externalized and simplified presentation of the Buddhist teaching concerning one's attitude toward Karma. It seems oriented toward

the Chinese concern with practicalities rather than abstractions, and perhaps represents a teaching delivered by Bodhidharma at the early stages of his mission to newer students (see also footnote 12 above).

17. A description of the mental conditions as "confusions" is found in the *Sutta Nipata 730*. "Uncreated" (*wu hsing*), or more precisely, the Sanskrit *abhava*, means without developing new, old or fresh cravings, and refers to the practice of meditation in which one views the arisings of consciousness without either attachment or any preset theme of meditation. In general such a meditation is termed "bare perception," or "just sitting." In this text, the term is used to represent *abhava* but as a specific quality (*abhava* is a general term). "Uncreated" means the innate, inexpressible Wisdom of Enlightenment realized by all Buddhas.

18. This refers to a section in Bodhidharma's *Hsieh Mai Lun* scripture which concerns mind/body interaction and movement, and constitutes one of the doctrinal bases for therapeutic and other body movement systems used by the monks of China.

19. The term "virtue" (*te*) is a particularly Chinese innovation and was taken from the Classical literature (i.e., the *Tao Te Ching*, etc.). In China virtue was viewed as a commodity which could be conferred or earned in various manners. It was not an exclusively human quality. In Buddhism there is no exact equivalent to such a secular idea, but what were classed as being beneficial Karmic patterns came to be regarded as an equivalent to the native "virtue." This is the sense in which Bodhidharma utilizes this term. "Vice" simply means the absence of "virtue."

20. The reference to light and darkness probably comes from the *Sutta Nipata 3:21* (The Sutra of Light and Darkness), which describes the various types of people and their spiritual evolution and destiny, depending on their degree of knowledge or ignorance of spiritual truths. The various combinations of people who are getting better, and others who are getting worse are described in terms of passing from light into darkness, or vice versa. An important point of the Sutra is that people's condition is continually changing and that what was once seen as a beneficial state transforms into a detrimental one at a later time. In fact, one of the beneficial conditions described therein is birth as a "wealthy warrior." We see in Bodhidharma's words the teaching that nothing is completely perfect—even though it may appear to be so at any one moment.

Within religious India, "light" also represented the *vidya* (supernormal knowledge or practice) utilized by Hindu and Buddhist mystics alike at various times to aid them in meditation or healing. In the secular sense, *vidya* was used to describe the required educative studies and arts, such as grammar, mathematics, etc., required of the high-born castes.

21. Buddhist doctrine holds that all knowledge of our existence, and thus our experiences derived from it, arises through various actions of our minds or body exclusively. The fundamental meditation tradition of Buddhism maintains that persons can liberate themselves from the limitations or sufferings of mind or body by practicing meditation based upon 1) the form of the primary elements or their direct and different manifestations (such as their color), 2) four stages of formlessness beyond these, and 3) a further condition which was beyond either of the previous two. This classification left its mark within Buddhism in the form of the teaching concerning the Triple Realm of Existence.

In early Buddhism meditation traditions fell into two forms, one being the development of discriminating insight, the other method concerned what is contained within the following explanation of the term "triple realm." All meditation practices were to be preceded by generation of the pre-meditative experiences. These are described as being:

A) Joy and happiness in the practice itself accompanied by contemplation and reflection.

B) Inner calm and oneness of heart, and joy and happiness arising from concentration.

C) Happiness arising from physical well-being accompanied by equanimity and mindfulness.

D) Equanimity and awareness only.

The term "triple realm," found in the *Mahajima Nikaya 3*, and *Dhigha Nikaya 3*, refers to a tripartite strata of existence within which we all exist. They are described in the scriptures as follows:

1) The realm of objects of desire (*Kamadhatu*); This is said to refer to an experiential level containing the world of our everyday experience and predominantly consisting of things we identify through our minds (*nama*) and things we experience through our bodies (*rupa*).

2) The realm of visible forms not creating desire (*Rupadhatu*); This is said to refer to an experiential level corresponding to the condition which could be attained by meditation practice upon the elements and their various manifestations or colors, i.e., the *kasina*.

3) The realm devoid of visible forms. (*Arupadhatu*). This refers to an experiential level corresponding to the condition which could be attained by meditation on the four immeasurable spheres. These are:

The sphere of infinite space;
The sphere of infinite perception;
The sphere of nothingness;
The sphere of neither perception nor non-perception.

According to one's spiritual development we can be reborn in and of these three realms (*Kamadhatu, Rupadhata, Arupadhatu*).

22. The reference to the "burning house" comes from the parable in The Lotus Sutra (*Saddharmapundarika*), Chapter 3.

23. "Peace" here (*ping hsin*) means an "untroubled mind."

24. i.e., have reached the *Dhyana* stages outlined in Note 21 supra.

25. This comes from the Four Noble Truths pronounced by Shakyamuni.

26. Although this obviously refers to the *Anatta* doctrine, the teaching of emptiness was perfected within the Yogacara School teachings within which Bodhidharma was schooled. The Lankavatara Sutra which he handed to his disciples was a fundamental scripture of this school.

27. These are greed, hatred, and ignorance; or alternatively, desire, aversion, and confusion.

28. Self-immolation was not unknown either in China nor within Buddhism itself. At least one direct student with Shakyamuni ended his life by his own hand, as also Nagarjuna is said to have. The Buddha, himself, told of giving his body and life to a starving tiger at one time in order for her to feed her cubs. However these were not cases of simple suicide, as the persons concerned were of a special and spiritual level of consciousness before, during, and after their actions. Some Chinese sects certainly went in for bodily mortifications, such as burning the skull, or other parts of the body, with incense, etc., but on the whole such practices were regarded as extreme.

29. This is a reference to the four Great Bodhisattva Vows innovated by the Mahayana. They are:

Although the number of sentient beings is countless I shall not attain Enlightenment until every one of them has equally reached this stage.

Although the capacity and depth of human suffering is without count I shall not attain to the supreme Enlightenment until I have brought all others to the same stage.

Although the depth and range of the teaching has no end point I shall study it without respite.

Although the way of the Buddhas is without limitation I shall follow it.

30. The Six Spiritually Perfecting Practices (*paramita*) are: generosity, morality, patience, vigor, concentration, and meditation (*dana, sila, ksanti, virya, dhyana, prajna*).

31. "No Mind" (*wu hsin*; Sanskrit: *nairatmyacitta*) "Non-Mind" (*pu hsin*; Sanskrit: *acittaka*), "Empty Mind" (*kung hsin*; Sanskrit: *sunyatacitta*), are all synonymous terms for a condition in which the consciousness is perfectly free from creations, fictions, desires, hatreds and ignorance. Bodhidharma deals with this condition as a spiritual and physical principle in its own right within his text titled the *Wu Hsin Lun* (Treatise upon No-Mindedness).

THE *HSIEH MAI LUN* OF BODHIDHARMA

Most of what Westerners know concerning Bodhidharma comes from studying the many English language translations of Japanese Zen texts, some of which leave much to be desired. Many popular translations are often simply paraphrasings of other texts, based on partial, simplified, or westernized accounts.

We should always recall that what Bodhidharma studied with his Sarvastivada teacher, Prajnatara, was not the sole basis for his teachings. The Sarvastivada School taught various doctrines, many of which were based upon an acceptance of a provisional or apparent reality whereas, leaving aside the connection of Bodhidharma with the Yogacara based *Lankavatara Sutra*, Bodhidharma expresses a view only compatible with the Yogacara teachings of total non-substantially and "nowness."

The sayings of Bodhidharma only make sense if we recognize them as being based directly on the Yogacara Consciousness Only concepts expounded by Vasubandhu, which taught that the ultimate reality lay in a non-reality of all perception. It was ultimate reality which concerned both Vasubandhu and Bodhidharma. Apart from refuting errors within other sect's views and theories of consciousness, Vasubandhu also paid great attention to the post-meditative state of consciousness, for it is here he saw the immediate pre-meditative conditions of consciousness reasserting themselves anew. This was an activity where the contents of consciousness quickly seized upon the insights generated within the meditative activity and re-translated them into something other than their original condition.

Vasubandhu saw in this activity a mimesis of the conditions surrounding birth into the world—in fact, as a rebirth of the consciousness itself, complete with all its pre-configured patterns and restricted abilities. By asserting such an emphasis, Vasubandhu is not explaining the reality perceived by consciousness, but rather highlighting one of the bases for understanding its real origins and condition. Both Bodhidharma and Vasubandhu initially studied and practiced the Sarvastivada concepts of reality, but progressed them into newer and more complete realms of description and analysis. Both eventually reached a point where descriptions themselves were rendered irrelevant altogether, because the basis upon which they were perceived was dissolved. The obstructed view which recognized a "Self" had been replaced by direct perception of a "self" which had no fixed basis and no real permanent locus of activity. It did not ultimately exist at all in the manner it was normally thought to.

It was at such a point that the "wordless" doctrine became cogent and the only possible expressive response to what was perceived both physically and mentally. Such a wordless doctrine did not develop simply to assert that the self did not exist at all, but that its existence was transitory and illusion-engendering in nature, and that the way in which it was viewed was the very same way that suffering was created.

Both Vasubandhu and Bodhidharma showed that this view was not especial to the "Self" and that it was the view, itself, that produced and perpetuated the patterns of suffering. *How* this view was formed, and the various locations it was applied to—be they physical or mental—was the basis of much of both Vasubandhu's writings and Bodhidharma's sayings. Such a process demonstrated by Vasubandhu showed that one has to master certain doctrines and themes completely in order to liberate oneself from them. It is not the case that one can simply ignore having views or replace them with substitutes or teachings based on pure faith; they will cause effects irrespectively.

This had great and paradigmatic implications in the study of *Chuan Fa* (and is expressed in various forms within its writings and traditions) for this process suggests that the acquisition of real power—be it physical, mental, or spiritual—arises only after its concomitant requirements had been fully mastered and understood, and that the subsequent response of such a complete mastery can only end in its resultant abilities or powers being rejected.

To place this into a *Chuan Fa* context, it teaches that only by becoming very effective in understanding the principles and practices of the art of combat can one truly be capable of never engaging in combat. Only in situations which you could truly alter do you possess the ability to *not* alter them. We can see such a principle in situations requiring someone to engage, perhaps unwillingly, in acts of violence (i.e., in wartime). Those who, filled with fear, wish not to fight, do not hold the same position as those who could fight, but choose instead not to. Nor are those who could fight, but possibly not win, compared with those who could fight and could definitely win. Though all may produce the same apparent response to the situation, each is actually very different in nature. Both Vasubandhu and Bodhidharma show that to uncover the way of discerning the differences between such conditions is to uncover also the basis for the causes of all sufferings and, simultaneously, the attainment of the ultimate wisdom.

Bodhidharma Meditation Method

The meditation method shown by Bodhidharma should not be thought of as being simply of another sect of Buddhism, one that can be studied from within the depths of an armchair. It is more an approach to life for students of all forms of Buddhism. Because it grew within seminal periods of Chinese Buddhism it embodies many principles common to all of them, and thus all schools have within them somewhere an equivalent strand of teaching. Its message lies in the wordless communication between the Buddha mind and the ordinary human mind, and in this process all written descriptions or portrayals of it are irrelevant.

There is a great difference between modern presentations of meditation practices gleaned from a study of extant texts, and the real records of teachings made by monks who have been recipients of the empowered oral doctrine, taught them by a living representative of a tradition. In the Mikkyo sects, this latter practice is called *Kuden*, or *Denbo*. Within Buddhism such oral-based teaching methods are held to be more reliable and accurate than literal renderings.

In this text we have a clear account of such verbal teachings of Bodhidharma. I hope that readers can use this account for the reason it was originally designed; that is, as a prelude to the actual practice of "self insighting."

About the Text

In the *Hsieh Mai Lun* we do not have a record intended to be mass distributed as if a book or literary work, but rather personal, and probably private, accounts of students queries to their teacher. It was created, most likely secretly, as an "aide mémoire" for the students' personal use. Such aids are known in China as *Yen Li* and in Japan as *Goroku* (sayings) and form a unique category of spiritual literature unaccounted for within the earliest canonical divisions of the sacred records.

The various teachings preserved in this account reflect a wide range of students' enquiries and some ask very basic questions, while others enquire of more subtle points and nuances—not all of which are easily recognizable on a first reading. Some of the queries are merely preludes to longer teachings and are probably interpolated accounts from other occasions added later in order to explain a point or principle involved in the original query.

Unlike many of Bodhidharma's other recorded sayings, much of his teaching delivered here is quite descriptive and precise, paying attention to correcting the understanding of the student(s) and reiterating important points. The fifth part of the manuscript called "Movement is the source of No Mindedness" forms one of the important bases for *Chuan Fa* philosophy, for it outlines the inseparability of mental and physical events.

Within it much emphasis is placed upon the unity of mind and body, and the inseparability of Buddhahood to the human mind. It is this emphasis, and its explanation, that has so much relevance for those who practice the martial arts. The remarkable passages concerning the nature of body and mind are almost mystical in their wording.

Some of the accounts are teachings obviously delivered privately to a single student while others appear to refer to a small group of students. In many sections of the manuscript, the student is asking sensible questions, but Bodhidharma is replying supra-logically in order that the student may realize that even asking a serious question is already missing the point. The understanding that Bodhidharma is suggesting is one without any basis that can be posited, named, or used in any manner amenable to the fixed mind and its value judgments.

What is easy to miss in such accounts is the intensity and earnestness of the participants. A student monk may have waited for some weeks to enter into such an interview, and it may be his only chance for some time to engage the teacher in a direct communication concerning his own particular studies or problems. Living at a time where there was no electricity, television, radio, or any similar distraction, the student monk approached his studies with a sincerity and devotion difficult to comprehend. The teacher-student relationship became extremely important and each was highly sensitive to the other's words and actions.

While reading this, or similar dialogues, it helps to sit back and visualize the time, environment, and intensity surrounding the events and endeavor to get into the "feel" of the situation. With such an attitude, we can perceive different meanings in the words and expressions used within the accounts. Over a period of time it is possible to understand them in a completely different manner from the initial impression gained at first reading. Sections of the text can be read and meditated upon. Indeed, some portions are very suitable for such an endeavor.

The accounts presented are sections of the complete text and are based upon a translation and representation of texts in two different Chinese works—the *Tamo Chaan Ching* (An Account of the Meditation Methods Used by Bodhidharma), which is a Chinese manuscript of Bodhidharma's teaching presented to me by the Ajari Senda of Okinawa in traditional Chinese *Chuan* (manuscript rolls) along with the *Tamo Hsieh Mai Lun* (Treatises on the Teachings of the Buddha's Blood Lineage), a work preserved in several Chinese and Korean monasteries and recently rediscovered in modern archaeological excavations of the Tun Huang Cave Temples. I have also compared these with several other different Chinese language versions from Korea. As these works cover the same ground and contain some different orderings and renderings of certain parts, I have endeavored to integrate the meanings of all the versions into this one work.

All translation from Chinese into English is difficult, for often the medieval Chinese originals bear little or no punctuation. Couple this with the fact that Chinese does not have a direct way of showing either time sense or whether a Chinese character means the singular, plural, or something else, and we may see the problems involved in any translation! All through this work I have had to extensively consult dictionaries of medieval Chinese in the Kongoryuji Library as many of the characters are no longer used in either modern Chinese or Japanese. Some have very different meanings in our modern times.

Bracketed numbers in the text refer to additional explanatory notes, appendices and references concerning Bodhidharma that will be found at the end of the text. The dotted lines across the text indicate where my original manuscript rolls end and the next one begins.

In many old sutras, each of the Chaan patriarchs is said to have handed on the doctrine to his successor with a short saying or poem symbolic of the conferring master's understanding. Such significant verses were used by subsequent masters as meditation themes. In the *Tamo Chaan Ching*, mentioned earlier, this verse (*gatha*) of Bodhidharma is placed at the head of the manuscript. The "five petals" it refers to are symbols for the five elements.

TRANSMISSION GATHA OF BODHIDHARMA
TO THE SECOND PATRIARCH HUI K'E

I arrived in this country
To liberate suffering beings by teaching the Dharma
A single Flower opens five petals
Its fruit will be self-realized.

THE *HSIEH MAI LUN*

(Treatises on the Blood Lineage of True Dharma)

Manuscript Part One

THE MIND KNOWS ITS OWN SOURCE

Pronouncement Theme

> **Even though the triple world[1] has given birth to many chaotic events, all of them will be concluded in the attainment of singlemindedness.**

> **Buddhas of past and future have conveyed the mind-to-mind teaching without depending on written words.**

Student: If we do not depend upon any written word, with what and how must we conceive the mind?

Bodhidharma: If I had no Mind how could I reply? If you also had no Mind how could you ask? Making your request is mind in you; when I reply, that is Mind within me.

From the ancient, beginningless moments and through all the different times and places, the mind tries to cut through time and reject changes. In its heart the mind knows that it is its own source of awakening.

It has been said that mind, in itself, is the original Buddha, for without it no one could seek the different forms of Buddha.

It is impossible to either find or aspire toward the Buddha's Nirvana outside of the mind.

Our self nature seems real and precious to us. In truth it is already neither cause nor effect. It is simply the effect of its own causes.

Self has its own mind. This mind, in itself, is intrinsically Buddha. This mind is that which is already brightly shining and serene.

If, lacking experience, we say that there could be a Buddha or Buddha Wisdom outside of the mind, where could such a Buddha or Bodhi (Wisdom) be? Can empty space be held?

Empty space is just a name, it has no mental aspects, form, or size. It is impossible to either hold it or to drop it.

Seeking Buddhahood outside of this mind would be like trying to hold such empty space.

Since Buddha is a product of one's mind, how can it be possible to seek Buddha outside of the mind? Former and later Buddhas have said:

> **Mind exists in the Buddha.**
> **Buddha exists in the Mind,**
> **Only the mind is Buddha,**
> **Only Buddha is the mind.**

If Mind exists outside then Buddha is not;
If Buddha exists outside then Mind is not.

If Buddha did exist outside of the Mind, where could it be? If Buddha does not exist outside of the Mind, from where did it arise?

Not able to understand the original source of true Mind, false opinions and reasonings arise and our inexperienced nature misleads itself.

We become empty of life, blind to its truth. This is how we become unfree beings.

Buddhahood is the opposite of this condition, and free of all deception. Confused beings think and do not realize or understand the fact that one's mind is already Buddha.

If you see Buddha is just your mind, do not seek Buddha outside of it. Buddha cannot be liberated by Buddha.

Buddha cannot be realized if sought with the mind. Such a seeking would suggest that Buddha is outside of it. This view is caused only by not knowing that Buddha and your own Mind are identical.

Being Buddha already, do not worship Buddhas. Buddha being your mind, do not constantly recall thoughts of Buddhas.

Buddha, in itself, cannot read the sutras. Buddha, in itself, cannot uphold the monastic precepts. Buddha, in itself, does not have something to maintain or violate. Buddha, in itself, does not cause the good or the bad.

If you truly seek Buddha, you must simply see the self nature which is Buddha. Without seeing self nature, no matter how well you are mindful of Buddhas, read the Sutras, bow in ceremonies, or uphold the precepts, still no benefit will result.

Being mindful of the Buddhas will promise you a happy next life. Reading the Sutras may make you wise or knowledgeable. Upholding the precepts will let you be born in heaven. Aiding others will create a prosperous future time but, Buddha cannot be seen simply by doing any of these if you still do not know yourself clearly.

You should awaken to the essence of life and death by finding and meeting a Master who already has attained the great awakening and can liberate you.

One cannot be called Master if he has not yet seen self nature. Even if he has studied all twelve sections of the Sutras, he would still, without fail, fall into the sea of life, death and the Triple World's karmic cycle. He would still be without freedom from great sufferings.

Once there was a monk named Sho Sung. Although he had mastered all twelve sections[2] of the Sutra volumes, he had not seen self nature, and thus, he could not be freed from his karmic chain.

People today, by studying the thirty-five source commentaries on the Sutras, believe they can become masters of the Law or even enlightened! How mistaken they are.

Without understanding one's mind, memorizing countless passages of writing is useless. Without self-insight Buddha does not appear.

Enlightenment comes without reliance upon materials or things.

Buddhahood is developing such a nature within oneself, without doing or creating anything extra. Without seeing one's self nature, no matter how hard you look, whether by day or night, it will prove impossible to find Buddhahood.

From its beginning, Buddhahood is void of particular characteristics. Even though we may say there is "originally not a thing to be attained," if you do not yet understand this, you must open your heart to find and meet a Master who will liberate you.

Life and death is a great mystery. Do not spend your life in vain. Deceiving yourself does not help you in any way.

Even if one owns a mountain of jewels, or has many followers and devotees, these things in themselves can only be seen while the eyes are alive.

When eyes are dead can you still see them?

Therefore it is obvious that anything we do is but a fleeting apparition and as tangible as a dream or a ghost.

Unless you quickly find a teacher, you will waste your life meaninglessly. Everyone already has Buddha nature, but unless you rely on your teacher's help, no one can acknowledge and sanction your understanding.

That is why it is almost impossible to attain great understanding without a teacher.

One who, by his karmic[3] privilege has already attained the level of understanding, does not have to go find a teacher. Although everyone has a Buddha nature from before birth, if there is just a tiny trace of misunderstanding remaining, he must go and meet with the teacher who will open and cultivate his understanding.

If one understands perfectly, he may be different from ordinary beings and not have to learn.

But, if, still, he cannot make a clear distinction between black and white, or pretending to be a master, then discusses or teaches the Dharma, he will humiliate the Buddha and destroy Dharma.

Such a one's teaching, no matter now flowingly spoken, is the talk of evil spirits not Buddhas. The leader of such speech-makers is a devil and his followers are evil spirits. Without a doubt, they will fall into a dark sea of life and death under such instructions.

Only the people who have not seen the self nature talk about Buddha nonsensically and become the creators of great sin.

By self-deception they lead people toward the realm of evil spirits.

If one is able to speak about the twelve sections of sutra volumes perfectly, yet still does not see the self nature, then an evil spirit is speaking and producing his offspring. If understanding is not crystal clear, how can one avoid life and death?

Recognizing the self nature is Buddha, not recognizing the self nature is incarnate being.

If you believe Buddha nature can be attained by separating from the incarnate being's nature, where then could the Buddha be?

The nature of incarnate being is the Buddha nature. Buddha does not exist outside of the self nature. Buddha is this self nature.

Without this self nature, Buddha cannot be attained.

Without this Buddha, the self nature cannot be attained.

Manuscript Part 2

ORIGINAL MIND IS ALWAYS APPEARING

A student asked: Is it possible to become Buddha without seeing the self nature, if one endeavors in the perfect practices of chanting, reading sutras, upholding precepts, and exercising a great discipline?

Bodhidharma: It is impossible.

The student asks: Why is it impossible?

Bodhidharma: If one says there is some form of Dharma to be attained, be it a large or small attainment, then this Dharma is of the form of doing, a Dharma of cause and effects, a Dharma of the necessity of inevitable result and of karmic result.

Since these dharmas cannot avoid the life-and-death situation, at what point within them could the way of Buddha be attained?

To attain Buddha, one must truly see the self nature. Without seeing the self nature, speaking of the cycles of cause and effect, or any of the other points, is holding a non-Buddhist Dharma.

Buddha, himself, cannot enact such a Dharma, a Buddha is beyond Karma and is without the bases of cause-and-effect.

As soon as one says there is a Dharma to be attained, whether old or new, then he is actually humiliating the Buddha. How can such a person attain Buddhahood?

Clinging also to views such as internal or integrating mind, one functioning, one opinion, even one idea, results in no room being left for Buddhahood.

Buddhahood has nothing to maintain nor violate. Mind nature is originally void.

There is neither a pure Dharma nor an impure Dharma. Nothing to be practiced, nothing to be attained—no causes nor effects.

Buddhas neither maintain nor discard the precepts, neither practice the good nor cause the bad, they neither endeavor nor are languid. Buddha enacts the true transcendental stillness.

As soon as you raise the thought of mind biding somewhere or attaching to something, there is no longer room for Buddha.

If a Buddha is called a Buddha, he ceases to be the Buddha. Do not even raise a thought of "Buddha."

If you do not try to be aware of this at all times and places, original mind cannot be grasped or recognized.

If one continuously raises a thought of non-doingness[4] without seeing the self nature, one is simply a great sinner of great ignorance. Dwelling in blank-minded emptiness, blinded like a drunken man, such a person cannot distinguish the good from the bad.

If you want to practice the non doing Dharma, see and recognize the self nature first, then you will attain a calmness and freedom. Before seeing the self nature, there is no place to enlighten and no place to attain.

Someone who ignores the truth of cause and effect, while creating many kinds of bad karma or who says that, "everything is originally empty," or, "there is nothing wrong even if I do some bad things," without fail such a person will enter the Exitless and Lightless Hell for an eternity, without a hope of escaping,

A wise one would not create this kind of thought.

The student asks: If, as is taught, original mind continually exists in every distinction and every movement, why is it not apparent when the physical body is unbalanced?[5]

Bodhidharma: Original mind is always appearing in front of you, only you do not see it.

The student asks: If the mind is already there when I look, what is the reason I cannot see it?

Bodhidharma: Have you ever dreamed?

The student replies: Yes, I have.

Bodhidharma: When you had a dream, was that your own body?

The student replies: It was not different from it.

Bodhidharma: When you are talking, distinguishing, and moving in this dream are you different from, or the same as, your self?

The student replies: It is not different.

Bodhidharma: If it is already not different, then this very body, as it is, is your original Dharma body. This Dharma body, itself, is your original mind.

Mind, from the beginningless beginning, is not different from that which it is at this very moment.

It has never been born, nor has it died, never perished, never increased, never decreased, never been impure nor holy. It has never been good, never been bad, has never come, has never gone, was never right, never wrong, never taken a man's form, never been a woman's. Never been a monk, never been a layman, never been old, never been young, neither a saint, nor an ordinary being, not Buddha, nor an incarnate human being.

Mind has had nothing to attain, nothing to practice. It has no cause, no effect, no energy, no form.

It is like empty space, it cannot be held nor can it be dropped. Mountains, rivers, even the Great Wall[6] cannot obstruct it.

Whether entering or leaving, coming or going, it is equally free to cross over the ocean of the life and death and the mountains of the Five Skandhas.[7] No form of karma can imprison this Dharma body.

Such a mind is hard to see because it is deep-rooted. Mind is not the same as physical material. Mind is the Buddha.

Everyone wishes to understand, yet, already you are in the midst of a bright light.

You may move your arms and body in as many directions as the sands of the Ganges River, yet, when asked what Mind is, there is silence, like the thoughts of a wooden man (puppet).[8]

Feelings and sensations are central to the experience of self so why cannot the consciousness be directly known?

Buddha said,

> **"All beings are confused and produce their future Karma, falling into the ocean of life and death they are trying to escape it; instead they fall back into it. Why? because the self nature was not yet seen."**

If incarnate beings are not confused, why does one offer empty silence when questioned? How can anyone not know who is in the center of their being?

Even though the words spoken by all the Enlightened ones were correct, still they are not understood.

Therefore, you should know that it is difficult to comprehend the mind. Buddha is the only one who has accomplished this. No one in the human or heavenly realms has done this.

When the Mind is understood, clearly by the bright compassionate Wisdom, it is known as the Dharma Nature or Liberation. Birth and Death cannot grasp or cut into it.

Because such an insight cannot be seized or grasped, even by the Dharma, it is also called the Great Monarch of Self Insight Buddha. Sometimes it is known as "The One Beyond Thought" and at other times, "The Sage-like Body." Sometimes it is called "The Master of Life and Death"; sometimes "The Great Sage and Holy Man."

All differentiations and particularizations are not separated from the mind in itself. The mind has immeasurable size and its function is limitless.

Using the eye, it perceives its shape; using the ear, it hears sounds, with the nose it smells odors, and with the tongue knows taste, and from such movements and turnings forms the idea of self.

In one cut, slice time from its middle and destroy the way of words and speech, along with thought and its resting place.

It is our mind.

In the past, it was said the Buddha's form was without limit, his Compassionate Wisdom also.

One must regain and restore this infinite form within our mind of Self.

Conscious mind is that which discerns everything, but since mind is formless wisdom and limitless, all its functioning and movements are also its wisdom.

Thereafter, it was said Buddha's form is uncountable; likewise his wisdom.

Again I repeat that all acts by the four great elements[9] or forms of being constitute the basis for the afflicted body subject to Birth and Death.

The Dharma body, being without birth, has no fixed nature and, as such, abides nowhere.

This is the reason why the Tathagata's[10] Dharma body is unchanging and continuous.

A Sutra says:

**"The source of Birth and Death lies in the nature of our Being.
This very Being is the source of Buddha nature."**

Mahakasyapa[11] freely achieved a realization of the true nature of the self. Again I say to you, at its very roots Buddha Mind is the original nature of the self and totally freed from distinctions or particularizations.

This Buddha's mind, the former Buddha's mind and the later Buddha's mind, are all the same mind.

There is no need to search outside of it.

The confused, suffering and unrealizing being does not realize his mind is a Buddha. He turns and searches outside of it to find it. Whether by day or night, he may be continually mindful of the Buddha, or practice paying reverence to the Buddha.

Where is this Buddha? Do not produce such a view, just know that in one's nature, there lies a vastness of Buddhahood.

There is no other Buddha outside of this mind.

A Sutra says:

**Whenever thoughts or being arise, all will be delusory.
Wherever being is, there is Buddha.**

Since the mind in itself is this Buddha, do not show reverence to Buddha again. Being as it is is already the Buddha.

Even if a Buddha or Bodhisattva were suddenly to appear, you must never regard them as being holy. Since Mind at its source is void of such forms, any such manifestations or apparitions will tend to captivate you. Such evil spirits will lead you into a corrupted way.

It is clear that such phantoms are raised by the mind. There is therefore no need to show reverence toward them.

One who shows reverence toward the bodies of spirits knows nothing.

One who does know will not show respect. If you show them respect you will be used by them. You can only solve such a situation by becoming a Buddha.

I am explaining this to liberate students from such corruption. While the source nature is intrinsically elevated and reverent, the discovery of innate being is sometimes inseparable from apparitions.

Cut out such apparitions from your mind's responses. It is the nature of the world to produce such things. Cut away these clingings.

It is a most important thing to realize that all Buddhas, in their original self nature, do not possess images.

If some extraordinary outer visions appear, do not try to attach to them, nor be afraid of them or raise doubts within yourself. Since mind in itself is already clear shining oneness, where else could that image be?

Furthermore, do not make high the thought of respect to Heaven, Dragon, Yaksas, Celestial Beings or Monarchs, Sakra or the Brahma King. Neither be afraid of them. Your mind is originally void and serene.[12]

All appearance is but a delusory image, do not follow or try to grasp such images. Try instead to see with the Buddha eye.

By making high the thought of Buddha or Dharma, or the thought of respect toward Buddha or Bodhisattvas, you are chained to the wheel of Birth and Death.

If you want to understand clearly, recognize your nature from its very center, as it truly is—a collection of tendencies and habits.

That is the reason the Sutra says,

"Whatever appears to be manifest, as a whole, is delusory."

There is no defined reality, neither does illusion have a defined characteristic. It is called the Dharma of Transitoriness.

Avoid grasping forms and you will be at once with the truth.

This is why the Sutra says,

"Slicing off from all mental aspects is the Buddha."

Manuscript Part 3

IN A DREAM IT IS VERY DARK

Student: Why do we not gain virtue by visiting holy places?

Bodhidharma: Through magical powers, evil spirits such as the Demon Kings, Devils, and Asuras, etc., can disguise themselves to appear as Buddhas and Bodhisattvas. They are not Buddhas although they may appear to be. Since Buddha is your mind, do not bow to any aspect representing him.

Buddhahood is supreme self-awakening, according to the different roots and different types of being within each person's mind.

Sometimes it blinks its eye, sometimes it raises its eyebrows, sometimes it moves its hands, and sometimes takes strides with its legs. All these movements are the nature of self-awakening.

The nature of Buddhahood is the mind. The Mind is Buddha. Buddha is the Way, and the Way is the Buddha.

This word, "Buddha," is not comprehensible by beings bound to the wheel of birth and death. However, a sutra says that,

"Seeing the original self nature is Buddha."

If the original self nature is not seen, then Buddha cannot be.

Even though one can discuss a thousand sutras and even more sastras, as long as the self nature is not seen, one is still an ordinary being and does not know the Dharma of a Buddha.

The utmost truth is profound and impenetrable, not easily understood by spoken words and impossible to know just by sutra.

If original self nature is seen, it matters not whether one is knowledgeable of words or letters. The nature of reality, which is from the beginning perfect and clear, cannot be tainted.

Seeing self nature, one is immediately the Buddha. Although each and every word can be fulfilled in the mind of the wise, the essence of wisdom is ultimately void and unattainable by means of the named or the spoken.

How could wisdom possibly be attained by the twelve sections of the sutras on their own?

Truth is, at its origin, already apprehended clearly. It needs no practice or attainment. Truth is neither the sound nor the color and is too profound to be seen.

The warmth or coolness of water can be known only to the one who drinks. Now, do not try to talk to others about this. Only the Tathagata knows fully what truly is. Those bound firmly to the wheel of birth and death have no way of realizing this. Ordinary beings, because of their narrowed views, are attached to what appears. They do not know that their mind is brilliant, void and secure.

Therefore, if one attaches to phenomena of a transitory Dharma, he suffers and naturally becomes a non-Buddhist.

If you fully understood that all Dharma arises from the mind, then you would not develop any attachments, for, as soon as one attaches, no thing can be known.

If self nature is seen, the Twelve Sections of the Sutras[3] become unnecessary and the many thousands of Sastras[13] serve only to explain the mind as it is experienced.

When understanding occurs immediately, the word "dependent teaching" is rendered useless, and it is seen that the ultimate truth is wordless.

Teaching by word is only illusory language. Truth does not give itself names. Whatever is named is illusory.

In a dream, you may perceive wonderful houses or palaces, sometimes herds of elephants, or horses, trees, forests, lakes and other things.

Do not, even in thought, become captivated by such sights. You should be very careful because such images are the offspring of delusion.

At to the final moments of your life, if you have not chased outer appearances, all bewilderment will be cut off.

If you then give rise to illusory thoughts, you will immediately be captured and led by them.

The body of Dharma inherent in all beings is so pure that it has no sense perception; only by confusion does one become unknowing and unawakened.

By illusory cause and effect, one becomes captured and attached. Finally one is not free.

It is never too late to awaken original mind and body. By realizing this you will be free of habitual contamination.

Sometimes the Buddhas take the form of sages, come into this realm, and join in ordinary activities, disguising themselves by means of many different appearances.

They do this to assist beings bound to the wheel of birth and death. No kind of karma can, however, hinder them.

Because they are sages, they are free to progress or regress at will.

If they possess the power of great virtue, developed from times long past, even heaven and hell can not interrupt them and the different karmas comply with their requirements.

Ordinary beings are called ordinary beings because they are confused, while the sages shine bright both inwardly and outwardly.

[End of manuscript roll]

If you lack confidence, do not be overcome by it, lest you will fall into the sea of birth and death. There even regret cannot help.

Poverty and suffering arise from delusion. Realize the mind and awaken it constantly, for if one practices without attaching to the thought of performance, he will immediately enter a realm of Buddha vision.

Even one who has initially awakened the mind, may still not be tranquil and might see supernatural visions in a dream. Even so, he should not chase them or lack confidence in the path.

He should realize that everything was made significant by a mind which is not outside. At that time, when the remaining habitual karmic patterns and potentials have faded away, and the self nature is fully disclosed, you may see a light brighter than sunshine coming toward you.

If you have this kind of experience, it will play an important part in developing awakening. Such experiences are unique to each individual and cannot be eclipsed by another person.

Sometimes while you are walking, stopping, sitting or lying down in the quiet forest, you might perceive a very large or very small silent light. Do not talk about it to anyone and do not attach to it. It might be the light from your self nature.

Sometimes when you are walking, stopping, sitting, or lying down at night, you may perceive a brightness as brilliant as lightning.

Do not be surprised by this for it may be a sign that your self nature is becoming clearer.

Sometimes the moon and stars appear clearly in your dreams. This also may also be a sign that your self-mind is liberating from phenomenal objectivity. You should not speak of such things to anyone, as it is only your own experience.

If, in a dream, it is very dark, as if you were traveling in the middle of the night, you will know that your lack of mental confidence has created a thick wall of which you should be carefully aware.

When one has seen original and self nature, there is no need to understand sutras, or to recite the names of Buddhas, or engage in a wide range of studies in order to develop understanding. Such endeavors, rather than giving you benefit, may darken your spirit.

Various forms of written teachings were set down to point out the mind clearly to us. When the mind is seen, the written teaching is no longer useful.

If, as an ordinary being, you want to co-exist with the wise, you should rely only upon your karmic inheritance and, for the rest of your lifetime, nourish the spirit in accordance with your own ability.

The farther away you are from the truth, the more the hateful and pleasurable states will arise. There is also self-deception.

The sage, being free within birth and death, comes and goes; sometimes hiding, sometimes revealing things.

He is always unpredictable. No single karma can interrupt him for he prevails over ignorant spirits.

When beings bound to the wheel of birth and death see the original self nature, their remaining habitual potentiality totally dissolves, until, finally, their spirit is no longer dark.

If you truly want to know the Buddha's path, do not attach to a single Dharma teaching. Instead, rest from karmic activities and nourish the spirit.

When the remainder of your karmic potentiality dissolves, your spirit will be brightened. Finally, you will have no thing to study.

Since they do not know the Dharma, the understanding of those outside it is not compatible with reality. No matter how hard they may try to become wiser, they will move in a counter motion to the awakened views.

In spite of chanting the Buddha's name or reading the sutras with great effort, their darkened spirits and self nature cannot escape karmic result.

Being liberated from the karmic bases of necessity, the Enlightened One has no need to perform activities. How could such a one have something additional to do?

What are you going to do after eagerly looking for fame and fortune?

Only those who have not recognized the true nature of the self read sutras and chant the names of Buddhas.

Such persons believe that practices of long duration, chanting six times a day, sitting for long periods without lying down, or wide learning is the Dharma.

Such beings are bound more tightly to the wheel of birth and death and are actually humiliating the teachings.

All the Buddhas of the three times have emphasized the necessity of seeing the nature of Self. The greatest sin is to ignore this seeing while ignorantly claiming to have attained the ultimate truth.

Among the great disciples of Buddha's time, Ananda was the most knowledgeable and experienced. The Buddha once reprimanded him, saying,

"Let all Great Listeners and Outsiders try to become knowledgeless."

The attainment of Knowledge by numerous words leads to the Dharma of cause and effect. The natural Karmic cycle of beings, bound to the wheel of birth and death cannot avoid them. In such a condition they act against the Buddha Dharma.

All those bound to the wheel of birth and death humiliate the Buddha, and even taking their life would not be a fault.

A sutra says,

"Since they have never awakened the faithful mind, it would not be a sin to kill an evil doer who cuts the root of the good."

One who has awakened to the faithful mind is abiding within the level of Buddha. Not seeing the self nature, you must continually be mindful of not humiliating the wise. Self-deception is of no benefit.

The good and the bad are already distinct, for Heaven and Hell are crystal clear, right in front of your eyes.

Even though they have fallen into a dark hell caused by not having awakened a mind of faith, the unwise can neither understand nor notice it. Why?

Because their Karma has arisen strongly, the faithless, like a blind one, cannot recognize their condition. Even if placed in the sunshine the unwise ones are so.

At this moment they are being born as animal, at that moment, as one of the various unknown creatures, sometimes among poor and lower class beings, sometimes elsewhere. They cannot determine where or what they wish to be.

They want to exist, but cannot; they want not to exist, but must. Even though they are in such suffering every moment, when they are questioned directly, they will reply saying:

My pleasure at the present time is
No different from being in heaven.

Therefore we see it is easy for beings bound to the wheel of birth and death to not notice or understand their present condition. Instead, they describe it as being to their ultimate satisfaction. They are like this because of their stored karma.

By realizing that the mind is Buddha, anyone can attain Buddhahood, irrespective of whether one shaves the head and beard or not.

However, if the self nature is not seen, not even a shaven-headed monk could help you.

Manuscript Part 4

COINCIDING WITH THE PHYSICAL BODY

Student: One who has a wife and children or many worldly goods has not yet overcome sensual desire. Can such a person attain Buddhahood?

Bodhidharma: Previously I have deliberately spoken only concerning seeing one's real nature rather than desires.

If one truly recognizes the self nature, other desires become nought, and there is nothing to be concerned about or to attach oneself to.

Though one may still have remaining and potential desires, these would not be disruptive.

Student: Why is that?

Bodhidharma: The source of the nature of beings is clear and bright, and, although buried deep within the physical body and bearing the Five Skhandas, this nature is fundamentally pure and shining. It cannot be stained.

This body of Dharma, from its beginning, does not possess senses nor has hunger or thirst. It has no cold or heat. Nor does it suffer from diseases nor sickness. It is not holy nor desired. It belongs to no sect. It has no sickness nor pleasure, no good or bad. It is not longer nor short in size, nor is it strong or weakened. From its beginning it was empty of activities and seeking. Though coinciding with the ordinary body, which produces all the physical ailments of life, it cannot be misled concerning it.

If mind can recognize this Dharma Body, the Wheel of the Dharma can be turned in one easy movement, as if you possessed magical powers and abilities, and the self nature will be seen as void.

The inexperienced Mind immediately becomes wise, and, capable of deep meditation, it will master the world of distractions.

However, if this freedom is not attained, it is this world which will turn you, and you will not be able to stop turning instead the Wheel of cause and effect.

One who knows the self nature knows all and can dwell wherever he wishes and be free of obstructions. When self nature is recognized as it really is, even a person who kills animals will become a Buddha.

Student: A slaughterer regularly takes the life of animals, how is it possible for them to attain Buddhahood?

Bodhidharma: When you look, simply try to see the self nature and not only resultant Karma.

Although one who sees the self nature is creating Karma, still he is different from one who is confused.

All the different varieties of Karma can not imprison him.

From the beginningless beginning, those who have not truly seen the self nature have been falling into a hell.

Because of their Karma, they are still turning the wheel of birth and death.

If one's real nature were awakened, karmic power would wane and disappear.

Without seeing the self nature, chanting and prayer will not prevent you from causes and their effects. Killing is, compared to this, of no great concern. If one, by seeing self nature, totally eliminated the confused doubt, even killing live creatures would not be disruptive to him.

Twenty-eight patriarchs from India before me have transmitted the seal of Mind. My coming to this country (China) is to point out Sudden Enlightenment, which is the Dharma that Mind is Buddha.

I am not speaking of simply practicing the precepts, arduous practices, exorcisms, making rain, ascetic practices, the magical ways of entering the fire and water, standing on the wheel of sharp weapons, the eating of only one meal a day, or sitting for long periods of time without sleeping.

Those who practice such are all outsiders, dependent upon a dharma of performance.

Your Mind is the Buddha's Mind as long as you fully see the connection of each and every action and moment.

All the Buddhas of the three times have taught a Dharma of transmitting the Mind and nothing else.

By seeing the Mind, without knowing a single letter of the language Buddhahood can be attained.

[End of manuscript roll]

Work hard upon seeing one's self nature even if the physical body becomes as ashes for, without truly knowing the self nature, Buddhahood cannot be attained.

Buddhahood is called Dharma Body or Buddha Mind.

Such a Mind is without structured concepts. It has no Destiny. It possesses no muscle or bones. It has a nature like empty space; it cannot be grasped.

It has no time, nor is it bound by the material world. Non-Buddhists could not understand its true nature. Only "he who has moved to here," or "he who has gone to there" (*Tathagata*)[10] can know Mind's unified continuity, unlike those borne into the suffering of being without the light of awakening.

Manuscript Part 5

MOVEMENT IS THE SOURCE OF NO MINDEDNESS

This Mind should not be viewed as separated from the Four Elements of the physical body.

Its Instantaneous Emptiness is the ability to correctly interconnect this Dharma body with the Wisdom of Emptiness.

Such interconnection exists naturally within such diverse things as the grasses, trees or rooftiles.

The Body, itself, does not possess feeling and sensation. How can it then come to move?

The unskilled and inexperienced Mind moves easily to extremes: speaking, doing, seeing, hearing, feeling and experiencing its senses; it mistakenly understands their functions as being its mind.

There is also movement, which is not such simple body movement, but, instead, of a kind which immediately fulfills the task of the mind itself.

This movement of the senses is viewed as a natural completion of the mind's function.

This type of mind is outwardly oriented toward the world.

The Non-Mindedness of Total Clarity (*Wu Hsin*) is synonymous with Buddha Mind.[14]

This Mind lies outside of all concepts of movement:

> Movement is not this Mind
> Mind is not this movement
>
> Movement is the source of No-Mindedness
> Mind is the source of Non-movement
>
> Movement is not separated from Mind
> Mind is not separated from movement.

Non-Mindedness can separate that which inclines to separate. Non-Mindedness can move that which inclines to movement.

Correct functioning Mind uses its functions just as functions.

Correct movement Mind uses movement just as movement.

The Instantaneous Mind uses itself simply as a function. As soon as it uses movement just as movement, there is no function and no movement.

Using the idea of separation is the source of emptiness. Emptiness is the source of Non-movement.

Movement and its usage together make up the mind, but Mind's source is empty.

Therefore the sutra describes

"Movement without a place to move."

By day and night it goes and comes, yet it has never gone and has never come. This is the movement of Mind, itself, and of what that Mind is.

Day and night it sees, yet it has never seen, laughed, yet has never laughed.

Listened, yet has never listened. It knows all, yet has no knowledge. Happy, yet has never been happy.

Walked around, yet it has never moved. Found a home, yet has never had a home.

This is the reason the sutra says,

"Word and utterance is for all time severed.
Thought and its abiding place are also annihilated."

Seeing, hearing, feeling, and knowing are themselves completely serene. How possibly can anger, pleasure, itching, and suffering be different from the original self? No matter how hard you look for them, you will find them nowhere.

Therefore the sutra says,

"Bad karmic elements will result in suffering,
and good karmic elements will result in happiness."[15]

Anger results in conditions like hell; happiness results in being born to a heaven. If you see the empty nature of anger and happiness without having attachment, then you will immediately be free from karmic power.

Again, if one has not seen the self nature, no matter how well one teaches and speaks of the sutras and sastras, it would not be of help.

Although it requires endless discussion to explain all the necessities, nevertheless, I have here simply represented what is wrong and right, although details are still not adequate.

Notes

1. "Triple World" is the Buddhist term used to describe the realms of sense, physical form, and the unmanifest. See Note 21d of "Entering the Buddha's Path."

2. The twelve divisions of the teachings are:

Vyakaruna: predictions concerning the disciples.
Sutra: the sacred words of the Buddha Shakyamuni.
Geye: the repeated chants.
Gatha: the verses.
Udana: impromptu discourses.
Nidana: reasonings.
Dvadanba: fables.
Itivrttaka: accounts of former things and times.
Jataka: accounts of the previous lives of Shakyamuni.
Vaipulya: assorted later sayings.
Adbhutadharma: unprecedented lessons / lectures.
Uradesa: dogmas.

3. Refer to Note 5 in the main Notes section.

4. The phrases in the next four paragraphs are references to schools of contemporary teaching in China:

Non-doingness = Taoist teachings of *Wu Wei*;
Originally Empty = Taoist "Universal Void" School;
Do bad things = Taoist and Shamanist sexual practices.

"Exitless Hell" refers especially to a hell for those who taught that by means of magical practices one could escape the consequences of evil actions.

"Lightless Hell" refers especially to those who taught that special native forms of esoteric practices enabled a person to attain control of certain types of Wisdom (symbolized by the word "Light").

5. The character for this can also mean "in ill health" or "unbalanced (physical) energies."

6. The Great Wall of China had only been commenced some 250 years before and its construction was still proceeding.

7. The "Ocean of life and death" refers to the Wheel of Karma which modifies—the cycle of coming to be and passing away (*Samsara*) to which we are all bound. (See Note 6 in the main Notes section.)
The Skhandas are the five senses of sight, sound, touch, taste, and smell together with their reciprocate mental activities. In Buddhism they form the basis for all physical experiences.

8. This reference to a "puppet" is repeated in the sixth century *Bodhicaryavatara* of Shantideva at Ch. 5, V 61, where it alludes to the practice of mindfulness of the body and the practice of regarding one's body as if a useless wooden puppet.

9. The elements refer to those of the Indian tradition, namely fire, water, earth and air. In Buddhism these are synonyms for many different physical and mental activities.

10. "*Tathagata*" is a Sanskrit word usually understood as meaning "one who has come (or gone)," and was used as an epithet of the Shakyamuni Buddha. However, with regard to the Buddha, it does not simply describe his arrival and departure, but also indicates the process of coming to be, being, the "presence," and its passing away. In regard to unenlightened beings, the term can be used to describe the kinetic pattern of movement.

11. *Mahakasyapa* is a Sanskrit word meaning "Great Turtle" and was the name of one of the eminent disciples of the Buddha who was credited with being the first to understand the principle of wordless communication.

12. This idea of "respect to heaven" refers especially to the Chinese school of Confucianism which stressed reverence to Family, Emperor and Heaven as a binding duty.

13. *Shastras* are collections of writings usually commentating upon or explaining a doctrine or teaching more fully.

14. Contrary to what one may first think, both these conditions, being transitory, are causes of suffering. The next verse confirms this.

15. This unusual phrase occurs in the *Mahavairocana Sutra* Ch. 29, concerning the "Explanation of the Formless Samadhi," and shows Bodhidharma's familiarity with esoteric teaching.

THE *HSIEH MAI LUN*

An explanation and study of its advanced meanings.

(NB: Numbers in square brackets refer to the footnotes to the text itself.)

Bodhidharma's teaching was written down some time after A.D. 529. We know this due to the comments he makes concerning various types of Buddhist practice (such as chanting, or belief in the Pure Land) which did not arise in China until after 529. In that year Bodhiruci translated the *Sukhavati Sutra*. This dealt extensively with the practices of chanting the Buddha's name and belief in the Pure Land teachings. Bodhidharma's words try to show us how we should form our views concerning personal enlightenment. He says, over and over again, that this view is "No View."

"No View" is not a new view, nor is it an alternative view of things as they stood at that time within Chinese Buddhism. "No view" means a view developed free from the law of cause and effect, one arrived at through genuine free choice—that is, a choice made from the Buddha mind Bodhidharma insists is inherent within us all.

Now, we may say to ourselves, "all life is the result of the law of cause and effect and therefore any viewpoint concerning any matter is subject to it," or, looked at another way, "all views and realization are a result or aspect of cause and effect." We cannot, therefore, hope to arrive at some definite rendering or explanation of our experience of the world which is not a product of that world or of our mind's part in its processes.

What is it, then, that Bodhidharma is trying to show? This is not a question with a simple or fixed answer. Bodhidharma's treatise is a remedy for perplexity. It tries, by means of suggestion, to inspire students to realize that the only correct view is one that is "non-abiding," one free from the fixity of being subject to the law of cause and effect.

It cannot, therefore, be regarded simply as a personal opinion. This "view" acknowledges that all experience is, at least, a secondhand effect and that "secondhandism" is a fact of every part of our experiential lives.

This "dream" of life, which materializes when living secondhand experience is, in Chaan, broken by direct realization. The point of the teaching is to show, exemplify, and encapsulate a relationship to the world which is primarily concerned with aiding others. Bodhidharma points out that in order to make this effective, it must begin from a real beginning, namely that of self-understanding, instead of the usual waking sleep bereft of spirituality we all too frequently dwell within.

Often our spiritual life is like that of a boy who never wants to get out of bed in order to go to school. His mother, being over-kindly, always brings him up a cup of tea, and he then leisurely prepares himself, eats his breakfast, and arrives late to school every day. The boy's father, tired of both his son's bad school reports and complaints from his teachers, decides to deal with the problem himself, and (like the Chaan teacher) begins to go daily up to his son's bedroom to pull him from the bed onto the floor. The boy doesn't like this, and after enduring it for a few weeks, begins to rise early and ready himself, just to deny his father the pleasure of pulling him out. The result is that from then on the boy gets to school early!

The sleep of life is a deadly serious addiction. It is not simply pleasure or leisure. All too often our "sleep" can cause, either actively or inactively, great suffering to others. We occasionally need someone to pull us out of the bed. Bodhidharma is such a person, he has strong arms.

Meditation is a Buddhist therapy for the illness of ineffective self-approachment. One of the ways we begin treatment is to directly ask ourselves, "Who goes in and Who comes out of this journey through life? What does this journey consist of?"

The "Way" of awakening is "real" and filled with vitality. It is not a self (or other) projection of hopes and wishes, fears or dreams. The way to see self (and Self) directly, is to first recognize its "clothes" and then see it naked. It is also transchronological—which is why it is of contemporary interest. Apart from professional academics, few other ancient Chinese practices concern people nowadays.

From its very beginning, Buddhism dealt with the experiences of everyday life and demonstrated a practical experiential teaching which could be utilized by all. It taught how, by simple analysis and meditation, the intricate functionings of the mind could be recognized, mastered, and calmed. From such a position of calmness, insight could develop. As it grew and spread to other lands, Buddhism underwent changes and adaptations. Different forms of teaching arose and the meditation repertoire grew considerably. Despite the diversity of its teachings, the central point of its concern, namely self-understanding, always remained the same. Within China, it was common for all the various schools to share and practice each other's meditation traditions. Later scholastic divisions, such as the division of meditation practice into a Northern and Southern school, were unknown and meaningless.

Methods such as Bodhidharma's are especially relevant today because our society embodies and replicates the illnesses that meditation, in some of its aspects, was especially designed to cure. Originally, within China, these illnesses were of a far simpler nature than nowadays, however the treatment is just as effective. An accurate diagnosis will help cure diseases great or small, if it is an accurate diagnosis.

The cure for this illness is not prescription of a set medicine or obedience to a corpus of rules and regulations, it merely lies in recognizing the true cause and nature of the illness. The Chaan approach deals in direct spiritual awakening and realization, and here realization means making REAL the experience of the Buddha within ourselves.

The *Hsieh Mai Lun* also suggests how one is to view this realization, what views consist of and presuppose, and what such a task actually entails. In Bodhdidharma's text, he also describes visions and images which may occur to the student involved in such a task and offers advice as to what they indicate.

How and what it is to SEE, and what can, and cannot, be expressed is a perennial problem of mankind's. Philosophy is a direct result of the desire to express clearly certain experiences. Unfortunately ordinary (academic) philosophy has developed a method of expressing its language which places it far beyond the capabilities of the people it should be intended to assist. Due to this, there have arisen "linguistic" philosophers who consider it their duty to clarify what their contemporaries say or mean.

In Bodhidharma's India, there were many such sophisticated philosophers, in both Buddhism and Hinduism, who would have been more than a match for our modern philosophical "greats." Bodhidharma is not concerned with any of these problems; to him the way is clear and any obfuscation is simply a creation of our samsaric tendencies and inclinations. The precise structure of problems is irrelevant, their causes are all important. Bodhidharma would have been very familiar with both the Sarvastivada methods of analytical logic and analysis and their opposite, the Sautrantika School. He would have studied both himself while a young monk. Bodhidharma's response was to go to China.

The dynamic approach to self-understanding is portrayed, in Buddhist language and literature, in phrases such as "going to meet the Buddha" or "attaining the path." These and many other terms are used to describe the beginning of that inner process whereby the individual recognizes and acknowledges the transitory nature of his or her personal self.

The development of a relationship toward this transitory nature of self requires much re-orientation, for it alters many of the values we ordinarily and unquestionably take for granted. We must forge a relationship with both the old samsaric [see Note 7, p. 345] self and the new Buddha self (Self). The progression of this relationship is portrayed in a Chinese Chen Yen sect pictograph thus:

Chinese Term	English Translation
Wo	self
wo-nai-Wo	self in Self
Wo-nai-wo	Self in self
wo-ju-Wo	self enters Self
Wo-ju-Wo	Self enters self
Wu Wo	Non self
Wu	*

Each "self" enters its counterpart and establishes a communicatory interchange. Eventually they blend into each other to form one whole and, in turn, this "whole" blends into the Void of being.

This image is one remarkably close to that of modern psychology, with its concepts of "self-fragmentation" and descriptive ideas of its processes, such as "integrating" various layers of the "self." In this pictograph, "self" refers to the mind of suffering humanity succumbing to the Five Skhandas and unable or unwilling to free itself from the creation of Karmas (Notes 7, p. 345, and Main Reference Notes 5, 6). "Self" is synonymous with Bodhidharma's "Buddha Mind," "Mind from its beginning," or "Original Mind."

In the *Hsieh Mai Lun*, Bodhidharma speaks of the folly of holding ideas such as that of "integration," and this eclipse of the self by Voidness is reminiscent of a saying by Oscar Wilde. One of Wilde's definitions of true beauty was that an object which had this quality would be invisible—because it lacked imperfections. What he meant by this was that things usually categorized as beautiful possessed features which were not harmonious. That is why they were noticed. Using this analogy, we could view the eclipse of self by the Void as the self's attainment of its true beauty and harmony.

Changing or altering the way in which we view or experience our "self" can lead to startling discoveries, things which, in their nature, are not surprising, but which we have never noticed before. The modern media are skilled in presenting us with images of what they think we should become, or what we should possess. Some of us may actually believe their advertising. The media attempts to pander and reinforce our egos; the media image is that we are the most pleasant, most beautiful, most refined or most skilled "person" we have ever met. It is, of course, a sham.

The realization that what we accept without question to be "ourself" can be mistaken in its desires, or that which we look upon as our personal choice isn't; that our "self" can be directed by forces we are unaware of, or that the cause of much of our suffering lies in simple self-ignorance is not so surprising. If given the time to consider it, most people can readily understand and accept that we are influenced a great deal in our allegedly "free" choices. The various media may present views of things upon which we base important opinions and each of these views effects an individual's freedom of choice, whether consciously or subliminally.

Many fail to perceive that if we apply the same principle to self-knowledge, a similar result is noticed. Whereas we may be familiar with the workings of advertising, or other aspects of materialism, and even have consciously developed an almost automatic immunity toward it, when it comes to self-knowledge, we have no teacher or "rule" to guide us. People often have a conception of their nature which is quite primitive. Westerners think they are more developed than so-called tribespeoples, but in fact tribespeople often possess a much greater fund and tradition of self-knowledge than the modern "civilized" city dweller.

In part, this is a reflection of the fact that, although we live in an advanced technological world, our ideas concerning the nature of spiritual life (if we have such ideas at all) are often drawn from the simple religious traditions we grew up within, and that the majority of such traditions rarely concerned themselves with the form of spiritual autonomy common to Buddhism. They were, instead, mainly concerned with subservience to a primitive God of judgment, partiality, and power. From such traditions arose our views of what we "really" are, and, directly stemming from this, what we should become.

Nations such as the Romans or Vikings had many different Gods and were more fortunate in their divine relationships. Their Gods gave them personal recognition, autonomy, and a guaranteed place in a Heaven. They also recognized the authority of women. The few brave Christian sects which gave similar eminence to the female were quickly eradicated by the established orthodoxies of their day. The Romans, in fact, innovated the term "Atheist" (meaning one who lived without the *Gods*) to describe Christians and Jews—whom, because of their "atheism" were considered uncivilized and barbarous in nature. As with many other non-Christian terms, it was afterward appropriated by the emergent Christian Church, reversed in its meaning and applied to "heretics."

It is from such precedents that the majority of Europeans have drawn their inspiration concerning their own individual paths to knowledge and spirituality. One result of this is that we still cling to the dream that we have a real or permanent self, that this "real" self is free from any influence, and that only "we" (or our Gods) know our "real" being. This myth of a natural self-knowledge has been responsible for much suffering and ignorance in the world, inflicted upon others as well as upon self.

In Buddhism, ignorance takes many different forms and that concerned with the self is regarded as a a particularly active force. Self-ignorance does not merely indicate not knowing about the self, but also describes an active disinclination and evasion of self-discovery. Seen thus, ignorance concerning the self cannot be justified simply by stating, "I don't know about it." This usually means one didn't try to find out, or were too involved in selfish desires to bother.

At the time of our physical death, one's self becomes an overpowering concern, but by then we are not usually in a position to do anything useful about it. If we grow interested in self-discovery, statements of self-justification or righteous indignation concerning our state of self-ignorance come under close scrutiny as we burrow in deeper toward the center of our being. Even though it can become uncomfortable to see how we live our lives, or at whose expense many of our habitual patterns are perpetuated, it is important we do so. It is only by such means that we can begin to develop a sense of a greater responsibility toward ourselves and the world at large. Such a sense is one of the blessings given to us by Buddhism.

In this text Bodhidharma gives us hope, for he tells us that within the lowest, most destructive and evil person lies a Buddha awaiting unfoldment, and that all we need to realize this is the will to begin the process. This will is termed in Buddhism "The Bodhisattva Heart" and, although it is not specifically mentioned as such throughout Bodhidharma's text, its essence pervades every line.

RECOLLECTING OUR TERMS OF EXPERIENCE

As pointed out earlier, one of the difficulties we encounter when coming to study some of the principles of Buddhism stems from the fact that we rarely understand our own mental language well enough to fully understand what certain Buddhist terms actually refer to with respect to our own day-to-day experiences. I am sure that many of us know, personally or otherwise, of someone who has continually repeated a pattern of mistakes. He or she may have attempted something many times, learned absolutely nothing from the process, and have been forced to blindly go on and on until the solution or resolve dawns. In some activities this is, in fact, the only way any progress can be made by some individuals. Intelligence, as such, is not a decisive factor here, for some endeavors require an instinctive or illogical knowledge.

The blind clinging to patterns of conduct is one of the characteristics of the unenlightened, and it is a feature which Buddhism addresses directly, characterizing it as a distinctive human and samsaric trend. I have innovated an analogy—"The Dog Syndrome"—to describe this process of blind adherence to patterns, and most often use it to illustrate people who, after seeking advice and being told how to resolve certain problems, insist on ignoring all and any advice they have been given. These people all too often will then blame everyone, except themselves, for what ensues.

This is the Dog syndrome scenario.

You come across a dog who is slowly dying through lack of water. When you find this dog, you take it to a brimming pond which, all the time, lay but a short distance away from the dying dog, but which, for his own reasons, he didn't notice. However, when you put his nose close to the water, he totally refuses to drink. No matter what you say or how you plead with him, he insists on crawling away, lying down and calmly awaiting death. You then are faced with a choice as to whether to try to save the dog's life or, by ignoring his condition, to collude and participate in its suicide. If you decide it is worth attempting to save the dog's life, you drag it again to the water and put his nose in it. This you repeat many times. When he still refuses each time to drink, you take a large stick and beat him. You repeat this again and again, each time putting the dog's nose into the water. Eventually the dog's fear of being hurt exceeds its desire to commit suicide, and it will begin, albeit slowly at first, to lap up the water. Once it realizes how beneficial it is, he will begin to lap it up even faster and wonder how he could have not seen it before. In a short time he recovers, grows healthy and becomes your faithful friend for life!

People are often like such dogs. All too often, the solution to their real problems lies clearly within their own hands but they cannot, or will not, see it. One of the differences between human beings and animals is our greatly enhanced ability to learn from our "experience." This means we do not have to suffer pain to know certain things are painful (in the same way we do not have to drink poison to know it will kill us). It should thus be, at least in theory, only necessary to undergo a painful situation once to be able to overcome repeating it in the future. We have ample capacity to never recreate a destructive or painful chain of events for ourselves or others, as our knowledge endows us with a capacity for reasonable foresight. If this is not our present situation, we resemble the dog more than we resemble the human.

When we come to observe such patternings within ourselves, or even discuss them with others (our teachers for instance), we are usually hampered by an inability to describe just what it is that we "experience." We are not helped in the task of clarifying self-experience by our use of language itself. When we come to apply ourselves to discovering more about our intimate nature, we usually find our linguistic capabilities inadequate. This isn't surprising; few of us have been trained in any form of psychology or use its vocabulary. Even if we have, we soon discover that its vocabulary also proves inadequate or misleading.

We usually have to re-learn certain terms of our own language in order to make distinctions between things we assumed we knew well. This is quite common when we are involved in trying to understand words or terms in another language—especially if that language is full of distinctions and meanings outside of the normal use of our native language. It is not so common when we have to apply the relearning to the language of our "self." It is, however, necessary, for, to many of us, our internal self's workings and patterns are indeed foreign lands and language.

For this reason we must distinguish what experience is, and what it isn't, before we can begin to consider any changes to be made in our personal patterns of mental or physical experience. The Buddhist "language" is designed for just this purpose.

Because Buddhism describes fully the range of human experiences both mundane and spiritual, it possesses a wide range of technical terms to describe them in all their subtleties. Somewhere within its vast vocabulary lies exactly the right word we need to describe our endeavor along with the resultant mental states or capacities we became aware of as a result of that endeavor.

Many of the technical words of Buddhist Sanskrit possess some specific or general equivalent in the English language. I say this with some reservation, as many of the useful terms in English are in fact drawn from ancient Greek! However this is not a coincidence, for both the Greek and Slavic languages descended in part from Sanskrit and possess still a very similar grammar and declension. There is a saying in England, "The Greeks have a word for it," and in this case, as many others, it is perfectly true.

The ancient Greeks made a clear distinction between the different use of recollective knowledge (for that is what we most often mean when we speak of our "experience"). They spoke of *syneidesis*—which describes the consciousness of and judgment with regard to past activities—and its opposite, *synteresis*. This is consciousness of, and judgment with regard to future activities. Experience was not considered by them as containing within its realm any more than two of the three distinct time periods—namely past, present, and future, a factor which is evidenced in Homer's *Iliad*, and the classical and syneidetic drama *Klytemnestra* of Aeschylus, as also in many other ancient Greek dramas and sagas.

As the future is an abstract concept, we cannot truly experience things in advance of their occurrence. In the case of synteresis, we are not talking of experience at all, but an anticipation of a condition of our consciousness which may modify, in advance, decisions regarding our future activities. Syneidesis concerns the past, and is what we mean when we speak of past experiences, i.e., based upon our retrospective memory of events or happenings.

In addition to these two words, the Greeks used *synesis* to describe the consciousness of, and judgment with regard to, the actual content of current events or situations, irrespective of their outward presentation, appearance or demonstration. *Synesis* was achieved by uniting the resultant knowledge attained by the usage of either *syneidesis* or *synteresis* and thus established the personal base from which to form correct conclusions or knowledge concerning personal events and decisions.

While these three words describe accurately the component factors of what we would (unknowingly) describe as experience or our experiences, and although synesis integrates two of these three factors, what is really required is one single term for a state of consciousness which describes all three times, along with their various aspects and qualities. A term which serves to describe an integrative and conscious act of consolidative, judgmental recollection concerned with the quality of content but unrooted in any specific. Such a word would render more accurately what we intend to mean when we use the Latin derivative "experience."

There is such a word and it is used in such a sense so far only within Buddhism. The Sanskrit Buddhist term for recollection, concurrent awareness or transchronological knowledge of things is *Smriti* (Chinese: *Nien*; Japanese: *Nen*). This is usually translated simply as "Mindfulness" but, unlike the Greek term *synesis*, takes into account all time periods involving judgment and other factors which modify the nature of consciousness (see Table 9).

Table 9. Time and Events.

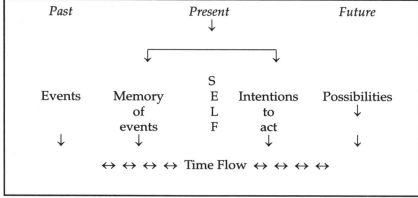

The term *Smriti* ideally indicates Mind completely permeated with enlightened awareness, and it is such a condition which Bodhidharma describes and refers to in the *Hsieh Mai Lun* as the real condition of the human being. It is, he says, "Source Mind." This source is a synonym for total and complete Enlightenment.

Whereas the Greek terms mentioned above concerned what are in essence events within the psychology of the individual, Buddhist terms begin by extending the borders of what is considered to be the "individual," viewing it in its Enlightened and Universal context. Such a context is beyond the range of earthly time altogether, and stretches the meaning of what is meant by "individual" toward the infinite, until its protective boundaries of ego, personality, feelings, individualisms, self, or divine spirit, can no longer be discerned, and indeed, no longer have any meaning relevant to the "individual" whatsoever. In Buddhism the experience of self is oriented to become synonymous with what is termed "the experience of the Great Void" (Chinese: *Tai Kung*, or *Tai Wu*), or "Timelessness."

Time, Ego and the Process of Awakening

Because consciousness is continuous, the effects of past moments carry themselves forward into future moments, as if "seeds" (Sanskrit: *Bija*) posited in memory. Such seeds are not distinct entities or "levels" of consciousness, but descriptors of those multiple, varied and significant mental "moments" which "in toto" make up the transitory, ever-flowing patternings of the moments of consciousness.

The nature of these moments is continually oriented according to the adopted and adapting Self maintained by their creator, and they are subject to its created limitations. According to Vasubandhu, such seeds can dynamically interact upon each other to form new seeds. One important function of seeds lies in their efficient re-inforcement and incessant re-creation of the sense of ego (which is what recalls them). Such activity may be either active or latent, intensive or extensive in effects.

The Samskaric functional aspect of consciousness called "memory" arranges the recall of past mental events, ordering and selecting them according to the predominant mental traits held in consciousness at the moment of recall. Pure memory, being but an abstract function of consciousness, in itself is neither good nor bad, although the motivations which prompt it may be either. The process of memory is an important means for the ego to reinforce its activities, because ego must posit itself somewhere. It cannot exist in a void and has to create a stable "center" for itself. Without such a center, ego cannot assert either its own existence or that of others. By continually recalling itself, it reinforces its validity.

This is why ego rapidly associates itself with other conditions, be they emotional or intellectual in nature, and makes "friends" with conditions, overtones, or responses from all sources. Ego will also embrace contradictory conditions, for it is within conflict that its existence is strengthened. This activity or recall acts as an efficient barrier to the development of an awareness of the innate Buddha Wisdom.

The Buddha aspect of consciousness associates itself with nothing at all, but if aligned for long enough with "concreting" sources of consciousness (i.e., persons or situations) is always in danger of taking on some of their qualities. When such a process occurs, consciousness is described as being stained, perfumed, or colored by such an approximating activity, as it has added to its store of experiences by adopting something outside of its own intrinsic state. It rapidly loses sight of its original pristine condition (its "original mind") and may even forget it entirely.

This "colored" consciousness forms the basis (and provides the power) for the idea of "person" to emerge, along with all its associated conditions, thoughts, and feelings toward the external world. We do not even have to work very hard to create such a basis, for it typifies the world into which we are born and the society in which we grow up. Its reinforcement is the method employed by those afraid of being considered as not "normal." From such a position and its concurrent activity, the Wheel of Suffering is turned and perpetuated.

To restore consciousness to its original, uncolored, condition requires us to clearly perceive its original nature. We must return it to its purest condition and quality. For this reason, the Buddha has taught the meditational medicine of "watching without involvement." This practice helps create a counter cycle of consciousness working to slow down the accumulation of suffering and conflict created by the cyclic and repetitive condition of self-ignorance.

Eventually this practice can result in a "balance" point being achieved between the two cycles of Wisdom-creation and Self-creation. The Wheel of Suffering slows down, stops turning and rests upon its central balance point. Then the central balance point is dissolved.

In voidness there is no up or down, no high or low. The Wheel has no "where" to fall to. It simply ceases to be. This condition Bodhidharma also calls the "Original," or "Timeless Buddha Mind."

Timelessness

Time is not a true sense; there are some who speak of it as if it were. It is an abstract concept colored in various ways and degrees by our personal and societal patterns of consciousness. Abstracts often appear to be purely speculative and usually are; but in Buddhism certain of them are conferred positive and creative qualities or powers that influence the ego (e.g., the Void). Within Buddhism, the traditional description of this power is conveyed by negation, which describes attributes of enlightened mind by stating what they are not. What it is is thus "filled in" by the thinker's pattern of consciousness and colored according to the individual's disposition. A misunderstood negation can easily become a basis for NOT seeing the abstract at all. Instead, the "colored" consciousness creates its own pretty pattern and presents a pseudo goal of its own, choosing to entertain and delight the unwary consciousness into insensitivity.

The sense of time (departmentalization, separation, or fragmentation of the now) is essential for the "colored" consciousness to maintain its condition. It is one of the separations (from the absolute) most amenable to conflicts, and the ego enforcing conditions of consciousness.

Both karma and time are dependent upon consciousness and, like it, are cyclic in essence and pattern. Therefore Bodhidharma in the *Hsieh Mai Lun* uses timelessness as a synonym for "nowness." However, nowness must not become an idea in itself, nor must it be desired. Such a condition would lead to the very fixation and positing within time that the *Hsieh Mai Lun* teaching seeks to overcome. Nowness can only be considered as an "open-ended" description, without any undue association to any specific quality being made by the subject. We simply watch it.

In Buddhist "watching" meditation, the activities of consciousness are returned again and again to their source, creating a cycle of mental activity centered within itself. If this cycle can be maintained, the ego consciousness can no longer easily seek outward for its sustenance and renewal. Instead, it is forced to turn inward upon itself and make its own qualities and essences the fuel for its renewal or regeneration. Like a cork afloat in the Sea of Samsara (see Note 7 on page 345), the Ego consciousness sometimes sinks from one's view to arise again another time. Although it may seem to disappear, again and again it re-emerges in a different location.

If nothing is added to or taken away from this recycling action, the mind's hungry samsaric agitation is increasingly slowed down until it has to pause. It then begins to lose its power to draw in the external stimuli which permit it to create illusion and fascination. At this point of pausing, the true inner color of consciousness may emerge naked— ostensibly in an attempt to reassert itself and reinforce its own impulses in order to retain its locus within consciousness. If its "food" is not forthcoming (and if one perseveres), it exhausts the fuel of its own internal activities. It is at such a point that insight into its fundamental nature may arise. A moment of such insight can be worth a lifetime of experience.

The practice of "just watching" (termed either *Kuan Hsin* or *Kuan Ting*) formed an important basis for the development of the Chaan method in China, but came, in other lands, to represent actual sects of Buddhist teaching devoted to its practice. It is worthwhile remembering that no single Buddhist practice can ever form the basis for a sect. To elaborate concerning the theme of "false experience," this is one of the realms that Bodhidharma's training is especially oriented to clarify; i.e., what is and what is not personal experience. Clarification is vital here, because all too often people are unable to make clear distinctions between personal experiences which are real and those which are not.

Unreal Experience

To many people the things—the mental or physical events they create or are part of—are classified as experiences simply because they have become aware of their occurrence. Such a classification of mental or physical events in which they have played a part, or become conscious of, is made irrespective of whether they fully know who or what it is that actually experiences such events or whether such events have actually been "experienced" at all.

Most people are unable to distinguish between false and real experience. We assume that both forms are the same. We need to examine this concept. The word "experience" comes from two Latin particles meaning "out of," or "from," and "attempting or trying." The term indicates a form of knowledge that arises from the process of striving to achieve some goal or endeavor. It does not merely describe information obtained from the recollection of events in our personal past; for example, "In the end I put it all down to experience." Experiential knowledge (what our "experience" develops from) can only really be called experience if it develops from, refers to, or describes a process of attempting to achieve something. The emphasis is both on the attempting and the attemptor.

It also follows that whether or not we achieve our intended goal or activity, the process of engaging in the attempt does not necessarily mean that we are any wiser from the endeavor. It is an assumption implicit in our use of the word that we will be, but this is an assumption. It is quite possible to engage in some activity for many years and yet understand nothing at all about or from it. We must also be able to make a distinction between the process of engaging in the attempt and actually processing it.

There may arise occasions when we need to use knowledge gained from endeavors which were not actually experienced (in the proper sense of the word as described above) at the time of their execution. In such a situation we may be unable to act or understand what we did. We are, in effect, imprisoned by our lack of experiential knowledge, although we may be totally unaware of this at the moment of the engagement. This inability is also tied in with our unspoken assumption that knowledge relating directly to the self or coming from the self is experientially based. That is we "know" our selves better than anyone else. This assumption is what we are considering here and, as we shall see, is usually quite false.

We tend to use very general terms to communicate our experiences to self or others. If we need to specifically describe or use the knowledge gained from what occurred during or after an activity, such generalizations are often inadequate. Because people speak in such general terms, the classification of experience is made irrespective of whether they know who it is that actually experiences their experience.

To many of us "self-knowledge" means being able to give an account (to ourselves or others) of our reasons or motives for doing something. We must be clear that describing feelings, motives, or actions is not self-knowledge! It is not surprising that when we try to uncover self-knowledge within ourselves using our day-to-day methods of reasoning instead of awareness, we are left with frustration and, worse still, we are none the wiser from the attempt.

A basic definition of false and real experience is as follows:

False experience is formed in the Mind by participating in events (both mental or physical) without full awareness of their origins in the chain of cause and effect;

Real experience is formed in the Mind by participating in events (both mental or physical) with full awareness of their origins in the chain of cause and effect.

The implications of this statement are far-reaching for once we have the capability to describe experience and non-experience to ourselves, we can begin to distinguish and understand both forms. Until then we are ever at risk, believing we have and use our "free" will to make our own personal decisions about the various facets of our lives, when in fact we are simply dwelling within our own personal Dog Syndrome and growing accustomed to our experiential inabilities.

False experience generates an alienation from the source of being, and serves to make unclear and unusable the real significance and consequence of perceptual or conceptual activity. Due to this we seem unable to learn anything from life and it forever serves to disappoint us. It also serves to fortify the habitual patterns of samsaric self-punishment we often generate. These in turn increase our sense of self and its importance. We personalize and individualize our life patterns to such an extent that it becomes natural not to consider others before ourselves. Materialism is the result and all the cultural or social negativities which ensue from it.

The early—perhaps spiritual—goals we set ourselves may seem unattainable at times, but so do many worthwhile and unselfish things. We need to seriously consider the quality and patterns of our judgment and strive to see how these patterns underlie, influence, and alter our being within daily life situations.

What Tibetan Buddhists term "the coming face-to-face with reality" usually occurs only at the moment of death. Then we have no choice. Bodhidharma—through his teaching—presents us with an alternative—and we do not have to die to achieve this clarity. He says, "Look into the Oneness and you will become its source."

Appendix 7

Chronological Records of Scriptures, Teachers, and Events During the First 1000 Years of Indian and Chinese Buddhism

This chronology has been researched from many different historical, archeological and doctrinal texts and sources within the library of the Kongoryuji Temple. In some of these references the various dates assigned vary by around 100 years—particularly in the case of Vasubandhu and his contemporaries. Despite this, the various relative years between teachers and teachings usually remain constant. The number (2),(3), etc., after a name or title indicates that this is a second or third reference to a name, usually at a later date than the first reference. This may, or may not be, the same person or source indicated in the first reference number and is due to the inclusion of information from many different sources, some of which use different methods of calculating Chinese dates and chronologies. Alternative dates for various persons or events are also given in brackets. All dates are approximate. Canonical works of the Mahayana are in italic.

Many, but not all, early translations of the Sutras were, in fact, only partial, and later teachers completed the task. This is why certain Sutras are mentioned as being translated several times.

500 B.C. (ca.)   The Enlightenment of Shakyamuni Buddha.

483 B.C.   The Sravakas and other disciples recount the Teachings at Rajagaha.

383 B.C.   The second Buddhist Council at Vasali where the liberal and conservative students separate into their various schools. The Aryasthaviravada School.

350 B.C.   Sautrantika School.

340 B.C.   Mahasangika School from which comes the Sthaviravadin School from which come the Pudgalavadin, Vibhasyavadin, Theravada, Kasyapiya, Mahisasaka, Dharmaguptaka. From the Mahasanghika (by a different lineage) stem the schools of Ekavyahariuka, Lokataravadin, Gokulika, Bahustrutiya and Prajnaptivadin. Schools. Caitya—from which come the Purvasalla, Aparasrilas, Rajagirika, and Siddhathika Schools.

327 B.C. Alexander the Great invades India.

322 B.C. Chandragupta founds the Mauryan Empire.

300 B.C. The oldest existing record—literal or inscriptual—of India, Asokas' *Rock Edits* (some sections are carved in an inscriptual style called *Asses Lip* (*Kharoshthi*) only practiced by Aramaic scribes.

280 B.C. Vatsiputriya School (until A.D. 1–200) from which came the Sammitya (100 B.C.), Dharmottariyas, Chadroyaniyas and Sannagarika Schools.

247 B.C. Third Council at Pataliputra.

246 B.C. Mahinda brings Buddhism to Sri Lanka.

240 B.C. King Asoka [reigned 269–237] The two Pitakas are enlarged to include the Abhidharma, henceforth the three scriptures are termed the *Tripitaka* (Three Baskets [holding the writings]). In this collection are included the *Asthagrantah* (eight books) and Katyani's *Jnana Prasthana* (Source of Knowledge).
Sarvastivada School.
A Greek monk, Yossa Dhammarakkhita, is mentioned as being ordained and sent to teach in northwest India.

217 B.C. Li Fong and 17 other Arahants arrive in China. They are imprisoned but by means of a "miracle" escape.

215 B.C. The Great Wall of China is begun by Ch'in Shih Huang Ti.

200 B.C. Sthaviravada leaves the Mahasangika.
Nagasena (who was taught by Dhammarakkhita) debates with the Greek King Menander who later issues coins bearing the image of the Buddha.

150 B.C. (ca.) Period of the three great Chinese doctors: Chang Chung Ching, Hua To, and Shun Yu Yi.

145 B.C. Szu Ma Chien writes a history of China but omits mentioning Buddhist events, etc.

122 B.C. The Silk Road.

Buddhila—a Sarvastivada monk.
Mahasanghika extent.

115 B.C.   The Burma Road.

100 B.C.   Erection of the great Stupa at Sanchi.
The *Ratnaguna Samcayagatha*—a summary of the *Prajna Paramita* is written down. This includes the oldest literal reference to Bodhisattva, Mahasattva, and Bodhiyana.

102 B.C.   Silk trade developed between China and Europe.

78–6 B.C.   Liu Hsiang writes the *Pieh Lu*, a dynastic record. His son, Liu Hsin, later writes another, the *Ch'i-lueh*.

60 B.C. (ca.)   *Astahasrika Prajnaparamita Sutra*.

25 B.C.   The *Tripitaka* is written down for the first time in Ceylon.

23 B.C.   The first record in Japan of a combative bout taking place. This being won by a Sukune who was later adopted by Sumo followers as their Patron saint.

2 B.C.   The *San Kuo Shih*, a Chinese historical text, records the oral transmission of Buddhism from the Scythian teacher Yi Tsun to Ching Lu.
Consecration of the Mahastupa erected by King Dutthagamani of Ceylon.

A.D. 1   Vasumitra of the Sarvastivada tradition.

A.D. 4   The Dipavamsa (Ceylon).

A.D. 5   Avantaka and Kaurukulla Schools derive from Sammitya.

A.D. 6   First Civil Service examinations in China.

A.D. 22   Chinese capital moved to Loyang.

A.D. 25–220   Han Dynasty translation of the *Ne Shan Kuan Ku Ching* (concerning meditation upon the inner body).

A.D. 32   In the *Book of Han* Pan Kuo (ca. 32–92) mentions the practice of exorcism and "practicing with one's hands."

A.D. 41   King Kaniska 1 reigns in India.

A.D. 50   *Sutra of 42 Sections* first translated into Chinese by
              Kasyapa Matanga. Kuo Ku Yi records a school of *Chuan
              Fa* called the Chi Chi Hsiu (Japanese: *Gigekishu*).

A.D. 50   *Saddharma Pundarika Sutra* (The Lotus of the Wonderful
              Law).
              The period of the Ajanta Caves.

A.D. 65   First record of a Buddhist city-dwelling lay community
              within China (Shantung).
              Monks at Suchow in Chinagsu province.

A.D. 78   King Kanishka accedes and issues coins bearing the Bud-
              dha's image (Alt. date is 128–167).
              Abhidharma Vibhasasastra, a commentary upon the
              Jnanaprashtana of Katyaniputra, recording many previ-
              ous Buddhist doctrinal schools is compiled. Asvaghosa
              (lit. "horse voice") is said to have participated in this.
              The Pali scriptures are written down.
              The *Hsi Ching Fu* of Chang Heng (78–190) of Loyang men-
              tions the Buddhist communities and monks there.

A.D. 80–104   King Gautamiputra.
(ca.)

A.D. 93   P'eng Chang writes first detailed description of a Bud-
              dhist monastery in Kiangsu, China.

A.D. 100   Asvagosha (2. Alt. date is 405) writes down the *Bud-
              dhacarita, Saundaramamananda, Mahayanasrtottapadana* (the
              first Sutra to specifically mention the existence of the
              Trikaya) and the *Sariputraprakaram. Dasabhumika Sastra*
              and *Sukhavati Sutra* extant.
              Council of the Sarvastivadins under King Kanishka (Alt.
              date).

A.D. 100–   Nagarjuna writes *Vigravyavartani* (Refutation of Argu-
200 (ca.)   ment), *Ratnavali, Mahayanavimsaka,* and a commentary on
              the larger *Prajna Paramita*. He also adds a commentary to
              the *Susrutasalya Tantra*, a work on healing and surgery.
              His commentary, termed the *Uttara Tantra*, mentions
              other works on healing by Jivaka and Kasyapa (*Kaumara
              Tantra*) and one by Kasyapa alone (*Kasyapa Samhita*).

A.D. 119 (ca.) King Kaniska (2).

A.D. 126–144 The *Tao Ping Ching*, a Taoist text of Kung Chung, criticizes Buddhist teaching.

A.D. 128 The *Abhidhammavissudhiprakrana* is translated. This includes mention of the four bodies of a Buddha and the three conditions of "own being" utilized by the Mikkyo sects.

A.D. 148 An Shih Kao (a Parthian) comes to Loyang, collates the *Dharmapada* (said to have been written down previously by Bhadanta Dharmatrata) and translates it into Chinese. He later translates the *An Pan Shou I Ching* (Sutra concerning respiratory exercises and meditations), the *Chiu Heng Ching* (Sutra on the nine unexpected causes of Death) and the *Samadhiraja* (Candrapradipa) *Sutra*.

A.D. 150 First traces of Tara known, *Vimalakirti Sutra, Sandhinirmocana Sutra* extant.
Aryadeva writes *Prasanampada* (Clear Words).
A 400 foot high stupa is erected at Peshawar to enshrine relics of the Buddha.
Translation by Chi Lu Chia Chan (Lokasema ?) of the *Ratnagunasamcaya gatha*.

A.D. 152 Translation into Chinese of the *Dharmaguptaka Vinaya* rules by K'uang Seng Kai.

A.D. 150–189 The Kanberi (Ajanta) cave temples are built. These contain carvings bearing invocations to Avalokitesvara for protection as well as decorations featuring couples making love.

A.D. 166 *Sutra of 42 Sections* and *Vajracchedikasutra* extant.
An envoy of Marcus Aurelius Antonius arrives in southern China.

A.D. 167 Chih Chan translates the *Prajnaparamita* at Loyang.
Nagarjuna (circa 150–250).

A.D. 168–179 Lokasema arrives in China and translates into Chinese the *Surangama Sutra. Pratyutpannasamadhisutra*, and parts of Asvaghosa's *Astahasrika Prajna Paramita Sutra*.

A.D. 178–184   *Kasyapa Parivarta Sutra* extant.

A.D. 180   *Srimaladevisimhanda Sutra* extant (This may be the original of Gunabhadra's 436 text).

A.D. 180–200   *Prajna Paramita* literature commonly circulated.

A.D. 200–
300 (ca.)   It becomes the custom to give monks a name particle indicating their country of origin. *Parthia* (An-Hsi) has prefix *An*. *Scythia* (Yueh-Chi) has *Chih*. *India* (Tien-Chu) has *Chu*. *Sogdia* (Kang-Chou) has *Kang*.

Nagarjuna(2), a pupil of Rahulabhadra at Nalanda. He also studied the Sarvastivada teachings under Rahula. He later writes *Madhyamika Sastra* and *Dvasvara Sastra*.

Lokasema translates the *Pratyutpanna Samadhi Sutra* into Chinese.

Purna writes the *Mahavibhasa Sutra* a commentary on the Jnana Prasthana = Vaibhasika School. It includes views by Ghosaka, Buddhadeva, Vasumitra and Bhadanta Dharmatrata.

Aryadeva (Nagajuna's pupil) writes *Satasastra*, and *Catuhsataka*.

A.D. 223–253   Chi Chien translates into Chinese the *Puspakuta Dharani Sutra, Amitamukha Guhyahara Sutra, Vimalakirti Sutra, Sukhavati Sutra*, and rewrites the *Dharmapada* of Vighnas. He is the first Chinese to write and compose Buddhist hymns.

Wei Chi Nan and Chu Lan Yuan translate collections of texts and publish them under the title *Fa Chu Chung*.

A.D. 226   Dharmaraksha (d 317) from Tun Huang arrives at the Pa Ma Temple. He translates 175 texts.

A.D. 230   Chu Fa Lang (an Indian monk) translates the *Matanga Sutra* containing mantras.

A.D. 232–338   Fo T'u Teng. Esoteric Master in N. China. He teaches Tao An.

Dharmakala translates the *Pratimoksa* (Rules) of the Mahasanghika School while residing at the Pa Ma (White Horse) Temple (Szu) in Loyang. Sanghavarman is also there.

The *Wei Shih* of Ch'en Shu contains the first known biography of the famous healer Hua To.

A.D. 239   Aryasimha (a Kashmiri teacher), the last of the Tien T'ai (Japanese: *Tendai*) Indian Patriarchs and the "Great grandteacher" of Bodhidharma.

A.D. 246   A monk named Ananda is recorded as having donated a Stupa to the monastery of Nagarajunakonda in south-eastern India.

A.D. 250   Kang Seng translates the *Karmavacara* of the Dharmagup-taka School. He also establishes a Pa Ma Temple in Nanking to enshrine a relic of the Buddha.
The *Mou Tze Li Huo Lun*, a Mo-ist text, mentions Buddhist ideas and temples.

A.D. 250–350 Hanivarman (of the Sautrantikas) writes *Satyasiddhi*.
Chinese travelers in Japan.
The *Abhidharmasara* of Dharmasri is translated into Chinese.

A.D. 254   The *Kie Mo*, a Dharmagutaka work, is translated by T'an Tai.

A.D. 260   Chi Shih Tsing brings the *Prajnaparamita* to China from India. This event is recorded in the *Fan Kuo Pan Jo Ching*. Probable year of Srimitra's birth.

A.D. 265–316 Translation of the *Fo Shuan Fo Chih Shan Ching*, concerning the Buddha's teachings on how all the Buddhas maintain their bodily order and health.

A.D. 276   Sun Chao (300–386) writes the *Tao Hsien Lun* and *Yu Tao Lun* (336–377).
Wang Tan (Army Commander) and Wang Tao (Prime Minister) become monks.

A.D. 280–312 *Abhiniskramarana Sutra* translated into Chinese (Dharmaguptaka).

A.D. 281–340 Ko Hung, a Chinese alchemist and healer, renowned for popularizing various methods of health preservation still in use today, such as *Tao Yin* (breathing exercises) and *Fu She* (dietary enrichment of the blood). These were probably based upon current Buddhist treatises.

Moksala translates into Chinese the *Pancavimsati Astahasrika Prajna Paramita Sutra*.

A.D. 286–313 First translation of the *Saddharmapundarika Sutra* by Dharmaraksa of Tun Huang caves (ca. 230–308). With Chu lu Yen (an Indian) he translates esoteric texts, the *Virmalakirtinirdesasutra*, the *Sugaranagaguraja Sutra*, *Sukhavativyuha*, *Lalitavistara*, *Yogacarabhumisastra* (of Sangharaksha), the *Prajnaparamita in 2500 lines*, the *Paramarthasamvritisatyanirdesa* and many other sutras and sastras.

A.D. 286–374 Chu Tao Chien acts as advisor to the Chin Emperors.

A.D. 290 (ca.) Yen Fou T'sao (a convert of An Shih Kuo) writes the *Sha Mi Shih Hui*, a text for trainee monks concerning the Ten Principles and rules.

A.D. 300 *Lankavatara Sutra, Vajra Sutra* (*Ching Kang Ching*) extant.
Susruta is a famous doctor in India.
Monkhood is permitted in China.
First translation of the *Asokavadana* (*A-Yu-Wang-Chuan*) by Fa Ch'uan (Taisho 2042).

A.D. 304–442 Hui Yen promotes the practice of Dhyana as fundamental to all Buddhists.
Maitreyanatha.

A.D. 306 The Buddhist doctor Jivaka arrives in China from India and visits Loyang. He introduced Indian medicine and methods of healing.

A.D. 308–442 Buddhabhadra translates the *Tamo Ta Lo Chaan Ching* (Darumtarazen-Kyo).

A.D. 310 Buddhajhanga—a miracle worker and follower of esoteric dharmas—arrives at Loyang.

A.D. 311 From this year until 316 there is a transition of scholar monks from northern Buddhist centers at Loyang and Chang An, which have been captured by the Hsiung Nu (Huns) into Chien K'ang near Nanking in southern China. Nan Hai (Canton) and Ton Kin (in Vietnam) become more important.

A.D. 312–385   Tao-An collects and writes commentaries upon works concerned with the practice of Dhyana to promote its practice by monks. He creates the first cross-indexed and verified catalog of the existing scriptures (known as the *An Lu*) and invites Kumarajiva (see 343) to come and teach the Sarvastivada Vinaya in China.

A.D. 314   The monk Chi Tao Lin (a.k.a. *Chih Tan*) retranslates the Taoist term *Li* (Universal Principle) as indicating the Wisdom of Prajna. He successfully converts Taoists by using analogies and parallels between Buddhist and Taoist texts and founds a tradition of such a teaching method within China.

A.D. 316–396   Earliest date given to Vasubandhu and Asanga.

A.D. 320   Chandragupta 1 founds the Gupta Dynasty which lasts until circa 470.

A.D. 328   The *Hou Han Chi* of Yuan Hung mentions the Buddhist concepts of rebirth.

A.D. 330   Yu Fa K'ai (d 397) the disciple of Jivaka, a renowned healer monk treats the Emperor.

A.D. 334   Hui Yuan (d 416).

A.D. 340 (399)   Fa Hsien travels to India. He returns in 414 via Ceylon and Java [Alt. dates are 319–414). His account of the journey is called *Fo Kuo Ki*.

A.D. 343   Srimitra dies. He wrote / translated the *Kuan Ting Ching* (*Kanjokyo*), a summary in 12 parts of occult teachings, exorcisms, medical therapies and divination methods.

A.D. 343–413   Kumarajiva, a Kashmiri pupil of Rahulabhadra, Saraha, Buddhayasa, Buddhabatta and Bandhudhatta. (The latter name could be an alternative translation of the former or possibly of Vasubandhu.) In 384 he goes to Ku tsung (China) and in 401 is summoned to Chang An. He translates many important works, among them the *Dvadhasasamukkha Sastra, Vimalakirti Nirdesa Sastra, Surangama Sutra, Dasabhumi Sutra, Mahaprajna Paramita Sutra*, plus a commentary, *Vajrachedhika*, and the *Sata Sastra* of Deva,

which is completed in 405. His main pupils were Seng Chao (383–414), Tao Sheng (d 434), Seng Jui, Hui Yuan and Tao An.
Early cave paintings at Tun Huang.

A.D. 347   *Vajrasamadhi Sutra* is translated.

A.D. 348   Sramana Wu Chin predicts the outcomes of battles and is retained by the Hun Emperor as an advisor. (There are many internal battles taking place over the next 40 years.)

A.D. 350   Hui Yuan founds the Sukhavati School at the Ting Lung temple.

A.D. 356–412   Dharmatrata translated the *Udanavarga* (*Ch'u Yao Ching*). The Ting Lin Hsia Temple is built on Mount Chung.

A.D. 364   Kumarajiva (now converted to the Mahayana by Sulvasuma) tries to convert his old teacher Bhandudhatta. He tells him the parable which was probably the basis for the European folk story of "The Emperor's New Clothes."

A.D. 365   Chu Fa Kuang (327–402) heals many followers of Buddhism with mantras and dharanis.

A.D. 366   Lo Tsun begins to dig caves at Tun Huang.

A.D. 367–368   Gunavarman.

A.D. 371   Emperor Chien Wen utilizes the services of a Buddhist monk to exorcise the influence of an "Evil Star" from his kingdom.

A.D. 372   Buddhism spreads to Korea.

A.D. 383–390   Many Sarvastivada monks come to China including Dharmaphasa, Dharmanandin, Kumarabodhi, Sanghabuti and Sanghadeva. The latter translates the *Abhidharmakosa* (*Pi t'an*) and *Vasumitra Sutra* into Chinese. Translation of the *Sarvasti Abhidharma Pitaka* by Gautama Sanghadeva. They introduce usage of the *Sarvastivada Vinaya* for monks.

A.D. 384–414   Seng Chao. Founder of San Lun (Sanron) Madhyamika, student of Kumarajiva.

Dharmanada, Ming Chih and Hui Sang translate the *Ekottaragama Sutra*.
Sanghadeva translates the *Jnanaprasthana*.
Po Nien (383–413) writes commentary on the *Bodhisattvabhumi*.

North Liang Dynasty: 387–439

A.D. 391 *Abhidharmahrydaya* and *Dharmapada* translated into Chinese by Dharmotara.
Abhidharmakosa translated into Chinese by Dharmatrata (2). An alternative date for this translation is 414.
Sanghadeva arrives in Hsun Yang.

A.D. 397 Translation of the *Vajrasamadhi Sutra* (North Liang Dynasty 357–439).

A.D. 400 Kumarajiva (ca. 344–414) teaches Tao Shen, Tan Chi, Seng Lang (end of the old Sanron line).
A Kashmiran Sarvastivada monk predicts events with such accuracy that he is retained as an advisor by Meng Hsun.
Bodhisattvabhumi Sastra of Asanga extant in Chinese.
Saptasatika extant.
Dharmaguptaka Vinaya introduced into Iran.

A.D. 402 Hui Kuang founds the Lu Tsung (Vinaya School). A pupil of Kumarajiva Sangharaksha translates the *T'sao-Chaan San Mei Ching* which includes a description of how to judge the character of pupils.
Kumarajiva translates the *Vimalakirti Sutra* until 412. He also translates the *Karunikaraja Prajna Paramita Sutra* (completed on Feb. 1, 406), the *Vajracheddhika Sutra, Benevolent Kings' Sutra*, the *Sarvastivada Vinaya*, in conjunction with Dharmaruci, and the *Chaan Pi-yao Ching* (Secrets of Dhyana) at Chang-An.
Hui Yuan (Hui Kang?) stages the first public monastic recitation of the *Amida Sutra* and founds a "White Lotus Society" (*Pa Lien Hui*).

A.D. 406 Second translation of the prose sections of the *Saddharma Pundarika Sutra* and the *Dhasabhumika*, by Kumarajiva.

A.D. 409   *Madhyamikasastra* and *Satasastra* translated by Kumarajiva (alternative date for Kumarajiva is 359–429).

A.D. 410   Buddhabhadra (d 439), Sarvastivada pupil of Buddhadeva [2], and / or Buddhasena arrives in China. He translates the *Avatamsaka Sutra* at Chang-An. (An alt. date is 406). He strongly emphasizes the importance of Dhyana practice for all monks.

A.D. 410–500   Alternative date for Asanga (elder brother of Vasubandhu and initiator of the Yogacara School). He writes *Mahayana Samparigraha, Yogacarabhumisastra,* and translates the *Mahaparinirvana Sutra.*
Fa Hsien is in India.

A.D. 412–413   Dharmaksena arrives in China and translates the medical sections of the *Suvarnaprabhasa Sutra,* and the *Mahaparinirvana Sutra.* He becomes an advisor to Emperor Meng Hsiun and a miracle worker. When Meng Hsiun ignores his advice concerning the outcome of an important battle, he loses all his kingdom.

A.D. 414–431   Dharmaraksha (2) arrives in China and translates the other sections of the *Suvarnaprabhasa, Chin Kuang Ming Ching,* and the *Lankavatara Sutra (Leng Yen Ching).*
Fa Hsien arrives back in China (2).

A.D. 415   Founding of Nalanda monastery by Sakraditya (Kumaragupta 1?). Subsequent monarchs built additions in the four cardinal points, eventually reclassifying it as a *Mahavihara.*

A.D. 417   *Dvasvara Sastra* and *Satyasiddhi Sastra* (Cheng Shih) translated by Kumarajiva (Sautrantika School).
Fa Hsien translates the *Mahaparinirvana Sutra* at Chien K'ang (417–418).
Death of Hui Yuan (Sept. 2) at Lu Shan.

A.D. 420   Sanghabhadra (Vaibhasika) student of *Sai chien ti lo.* He writes *Nyanusara* and *Samaya Pradipika.*
Dharmaraksa translates the *Nieh Pan Ching (Nirvana Sutra).*
The great Stupa at Sanchi (India) is erected.

A.D. 420–500 Vasubandhu (studied with Dharmatrata and Buddhamitra of Sarvastivada / Vaibhasika Schools), Maranatha of the Sautrantika School, Jayati of the Dhyana methods. He writes *Abhidharmakosa Karika* and *Abhidharmakosa Sastra*. An alternative date for Vasubandhus' birth is 316. He was the teacher of Gunaprabha, Gunamati Sthirimati and possibly Dignaga.
Buddhaghosa.

A.D. 426 Dharmotara writes *Samyukti Abhidharma Hridaya*. *Samyuktiabhidharmakosa* written by Dharmatrata and Buddhapalita.

A.D. 430 Buddhamitra translates the "Meditation upon the element Water" in the *Wu Men Chaan Ching* (Japanese: *Mumon Zenkyo*).
Ryukoji temple (Chinese: *Lung Ka'o Szu*) is founded.

A.D. 431 Gunavarman in Nanking.
Buddhism in Java, Sumatra, Borneo and Burma.

A.D. 433 Sanghavarman arrives in China.

A.D. 435–436 Gunabhadra (420–479) and Buddhayasas translate the *Srimaladevisimhanda, Prakaranapada* of Sthavira Vasumitra (2), and the *Lankavatara Sutra* (*Ryogabattarahokyo*).
Death of Tao Sheng.

A.D. 443 Translation of the *Leng Yen Pao Ching* (Lankavatara Jewel) by Gunabhadra. This was probably the version used by Bodhidharma.

A.D. 450 Division of Madhyamika / Yogacara into the *Prasangika* (reductio ad absurdum) under Buddhapalita and *Svatantrika* (direct reasoning) under Bhaviveka.
Dignaga, founder of the Nyaya system of Buddhist formal Logic (*Hetuvidya*) writes *Pindartha, Nayayamukkha, Nyayapravesa*, and *Nyayasammuccaya*.
Sthirimati writes *Madhayantavibhaga Sutra*.
Cagotra.
The Yun King rock caves and shrines are first built in Shansi.

A.D. 452–522 Chih Tsang and Seng Nien conclude that the Sarvastivada is a Mahayana school.

A.D. 453 Ceylonese monks bring Buddha images to the Emperor.

A.D. 462 Tan Tao translates texts describing the construction and usage of mandalas.

A.D. 475 The Roman Empire falls and contact with India is broken.

A.D. 476–524 *Fa Yuan Ling Chuan* and *Wei Shih Chih* written by K'uei Chi. Tan Luan founder of Ching T'u Tsung (Pure Land School).

A.D. 484 The White Huns invade Northern India to slaughter and destroy.

A.D. 486 Birth of Hui K'e (pupil of Bodhidharma). Died 593.

A.D. 489–580 Fa Shang, teacher of the southern T'u Lun school.

A.D. 492–5 Gunavyddhi in China.

A.D. 493–564 Shan Hui born, a contemporary of Bodhidharma with many Zen-like sayings and teachings. His life is recorded in the *Ch'uan Teng Lu*.

A.D. 495 First inscription at the Lung Men caves.

A.D. 499–529 Paramartha.

A.D. 500 Srimitra translates esoteric texts into Chinese.
Internal wars disrupt the life of China for the next 25-plus years.
Prajnatara, heir of Punyamitra.

A.D. 502–557 Liang Dynasty. Liang Wu Ti (502–549).
Prominent Satyasiddhi sect students are Fa Yun, Chih Tsang, Seng Ming, Chi-I, Chi Tsang and Ching Ying.
Gautama Sanghadeva and Ku Fu Nien translate the *Asta Grantha*.

A.D. 507–581 Fa Lang studied under Hsiuen Tsang, who teaches Chi Tsang, who teaches E-Kwan (visiting from Japan), who teaches Chizo, who introduces the Satyasiddhi sect teachings into Japan.

A.D. 508–512(537) Bodhiruci (of Northern India) in Loyang (China). His pupil Tao Ch'ung founded the northern Ti Lun School. He translates the *Lankavatara Sutra* in 513, *Nyuryogakyo* and later 38 other sutras including various esoteric writings including the "Talismanic Wheel," *Dharani Sutra*.

A.D. 512 (alt. 506) Sanghabhadra (2) Chinese: *Seng ch'ieh p'o lo*. He translates the *Asokarajavadanasutra* (*A Yu Wang Ching*).

A.D. 514–577 Hiu Szu, teacher of Chih I, at the Ta Su Temple.

A.D. 515 Building of the Yung Ning Temple.
Savikranta-vikrami-pariprrcha extant.
Emperor Wu builds the K'ai Shan Temple.

A.D. 517 Narendrayasas (517–589), translated the *Srigupta Sutra*.

A.D. 518 Sung Yun arrives at Gandhara sent as an envoy by the Empress of Wei.
Manjusri Parippcha-Sutra translated into Chinese by Sanghapala.

A.D. 520 A debate is held between Buddhists and Taoists at Loyang.

A.D. 521 Bodhidharma (470–534), after studying with Prajnatara in India travels to China and introduces Chaan meditations (Liang Dynasty). The Chinese call him P'u Tai Ta Mo (the Chinese transliteration of his Sanskrit name). In Southern China he is known as *Dot Mor*.
The Tung T'ai Temple begins to be built and is completed in 527.

A.D. 523 Hui Yuan.

A.D. 529 *Sukhavati Sutra* and *Dasabhumi Sastra* (Ti Lun) translated into Chinese by Bodhiruci, Ratnamati, and Buddhasanta. Ratnamati's pupil Hui Kang founded the Southern school of Ti Lun.
Year in which Bodhidharma said he was leaving China (refer to the *Kao Seng Chuan*). He leaves his disciples Hui

K'e, Tao Fu, Tao Yu, and Nun Tsing Chih as his Chinese successors.

A.D. 531   Translation into Chinese by Buddhasanta (d 589) of the *Mahayanasamparigraha* by Asanga (2).

A.D. 531   Chi-I (2), Tien T'ai (Tendai) School. He was also known
(538)–597   as Chi Che Shih and founded the Kuo Ching Temple. Studied with Ting Kuan and taught Hui Pan and twenty others. Chi I taught moving and static meditation practices (*Jogyo Sammai*).

A.D. 535   In his foreword to the *Classics of Literature* Emperor Ni Wan-Ti records that Tung Chuan (Japanese: *Token*) could overcome opponents with his bare hands.

A.D. 541   Translation of Vasubandhu's *Karmasiddhiprakarana* (Chinese: *Yeh ch'eng chiu lun*; Japanese: *Seishin no Jogoron*).

A.D. 547   *Loyang Chia Lan Chi* written down by Yang Hsuan Chi, the earliest record of Bodhidharma's presence in China.

A.D. 548–557 Paramartha (499–569) = Chi Chen Ti—an alternative date is circa 710—founder of the *Shih Lun* Sect. At Valabhi Buddhist University (India) studying under Grand Abbot Silabhadra, then aged 102 (106). Also at Valabhi were Sthirimati (2) and Gunamati of the Dharmalaksana doctrine. Jina writes the *Hetuvidya Sastra*.

A.D. 549–623 Chi Tsang (2), teacher of San Lun Tsung (Madhyamika).

A.D. 549–626 Huang Tsang (Alt. 564–596/602–664).

A.D. 550–557 Hui Wen (Taimitsu).

A.D. 550 (ca.) Dharmabodhi translates the *Nirvana Sutra* of Vasubandhu.
Around this time Jnanagupta translates the *Amoghapasa Sutra*.

A.D. 552   Christian missionaries in China smuggle out silkworms.

A.D. 557   Paramartha to China from Valabhi University after study-
ing Sarvastivadin doctrine under Buddhatrata. *Abhidhar-
makosa, Surangama* and *Trimsiksa* later translated into
Chinese by him.
The Han Dynasty (557–589) records of Nanking tell of the
translation of the *Mahaparinirvana Sutra* by a Tamo Pu Tai
(Dharmabodhi). A reference to this is found in the later
Kai Yen Lu and the *Nien Tien Lu.*
Chih I (f: of Tien Tai) becomes a student of Paramartha.
He translates the *Sroddhapada Sutra.*

A.D. 561–632 Kuan Ting was taught the *Jogyosammai* (*Dynana-
caryasamadhi*) by Chih I.
Chi Chung, a Buddhist monk doctor arrives in Japan
bringing medical texts.
Buddhism spreads to Sumatra.
Sthirimati.

A.D. 563   *Mahayana Samparigraha* and *Vijnaptimatra* (Consciousness
only).
Abhidharmakosa and *Trimsiksa* translated into Chinese by
Paramartha (alt. date is 546).

A.D. 564   Death of Shan Hui (Fu Ta Shih), in Japan known as Zenne
Daishi.

A.D. 580   Birth of Tao Hsin (Chaan Na). He dies in 651.

A.D. 581   Sun Szu Miao (d 682). One of the greatest Chinese doctors, he studied and synthesized the elements of Buddhist
medicine with indigenous Chinese systems. He was the
first to use hydrotherapy, anesthesia, and advanced surgical techniques.

A.D. 589–618 Sui Dynasty Emperor Wen Ti (581–604) grants funds for
the founding of the Ching Ling Ssu and Ta Hsing Ssu Esoteric Temples at Chang An.

A.D. 590   Emperor Wan Ti writes a letter to Tien Tai master Chih I,
declaring his love for Buddhism and his wish to expand
the number of monks and monasteries.

A.D. 596   (Alt. 602–664) Hsuen Tsang (2) translates the *Fa Hsiang*
(*Dharmalaksana*) and the *Wei Shih Shi Chih* (*Vijnaptimatra*).

A.D. 596–647 Tao Hsuan, a student of Hsuan Tsang, wrote the *Dharmagupta Vinaya*.

A.D. 600 (ca.) Hui Ying, a Madyamika monk.

A.D. 600 Fa Lang (2) teaches Chi Tsang (549–623).
Dignaga (2) student of Vasubandhu.
The Hua Yen School begins.
Formation of the Jetavaniya sect in India.

A.D. 601 Dharmagupta (whose patron was Hsuan Chien) and Jnanagupta revise the Gathas of the *Saddharma Pundarika Sutra* of Kumarajiva and translate the *Amoghapasasutra*.

A.D. 600–650 Nagarjuna (2), master of the Vajrayana (Ching Kang Cheng), in Chinese called "Lung Shou."
Hui Ying, a pupil of Nagarjuna. writes notations to his works.

A.D. 600–700 Yuan Tsang writes *Vijnaptimatratasiddhi*.

A.D. 601 Birth of Hung Jen (Chaan-Na). He dies in 674.

A.D. 602 The famous Doctor Sun Szu Miao mentions using the Indian five elements in his medical system.
Wang Shuo in his "Account of the Miracles Happening by Relic Shrines," Section 17, v223:2, records the miraculous appearance of a White Heron at a Buddhist shrine.

A.D. 605–706 Shen Hsiu (Northern Zen Patriarch).

A.D. 605 Southern Zen of Hui-Ko.

A.D. 606 Seng Tsang dies (author of the *Hymn to Meditation*).

A.D. 607 Horyuji (Japan) developed as a hospital and shrine center (the oldest surviving wooden building in the world).

A.D. 608 E Nichi and Fu Ku In arrive in China from Japan to study medicine. They return in 613.

A.D. 617 Birth of Sron-btsan (Tibet), the monarch who introduced Buddhism.

A.D. 618   Birth of Hui Neng (d 713).

A.D. 618–907   Tang Dynasty

A.D. 625   The first *Ise* (Japan) shrine is built. (It is demolished and rebuilt every 20 years.)

A.D. 627   Prahhakaramitra, a translator, arrives in Chang-An. He dies in 633.

A.D. 629–30   Hsuan Tsang (3) studies with Silabhadra (2) at Nalanda. At Nalanda are Dharmapala (alt. dates 437–507), Agotra, Nanda (who also taught Hsuen Tsang), and Jayasena, who writes an account of his travels (the *Si Yu Ki*). Jinamitra (Chinese: *Sheng Pei*; Japanese: *Shotomo*).

A.D. 632–682   K'uei Chi is a student of Hsuan Tsang (Dharmalaksana School).

A.D. 634   Traditional date of birth of En no Gyoju, the founder of Japan's Shugendo Mountain esoteric Buddhists.

A.D. 635–770   Dharmapala (alt. dates are 437–507), a pupil of Dignaga, teacher of Silabhadra, whose nephew is Buddhabhadra (of Yogacara School).
                Tai Tsung receives missionaries from the West. Persian fire-worshippers are driven out by Muslims and settle in India.

A.D. 637–735   Subhakarasimha (Shan-Wu-Wei) ex-king of Orissa, Master of Esoteric Buddhism (Mi-Ching), studies under Abbot Dharmapala at Nalanda University with Dharmagupta.
                I Ching studies at Nalanda and meets Wu Hsing (d. 674).

A.D. 637   The *Tao Seng Ka* (rules governing monks) adopted. They are forbidden to read or study books upon military arts and crafts.
                The Lu Tsung (Vinaya) sect formed.

A.D. 638–713   Persian refugees settle in China.
                Persia appeals to China for aid against the invading Muslims.

A.D. 641–642 Gyogi (607–748) becomes student of Dosho in Japan.
Buddhism comes into Tibet.
Srong tsen gampo (Tibet).

A.D. 643–712 *Avamtamsaka Sutra* translated into Chinese by Fa Tsang
Dharmakirti (alt. ca. 620).
The *Mahavairocanasutra, Vajrausnisasutra,* and the explanation of one-eighteenth of its contents (the *Tatvasamgraha*) are in use at Nalanda University.

A.D. 645–664 Hsuan Tsang (660–663) translates the *Vijnaptimatra* of
Dharmapala after returning from India. He also translates
the *Mahayana Samparigraha, Dharmaskhanda, Sangitiparayaya,* and *Vijnanakaya.* He brings esoteric texts into
China after having studied with Jinaprabha.
Tao Hsuan composes the *Hsu Kao Seng Chuan (Kosoden),* a
record of Chaan masters in China.

A.D. 650 *Madhyamakavatara* extant.
Hsuan tsang translates the *Bhaisajayaguru-vaiduryaprabhasa-Tathagatapurvapranidhana Sutra* (The Master of Healing).
Candrakirti and Candragomin.
First Buddhist Temple in Tibet.

A.D. 652 Sikshananda (652–700) to China from India; translates the
Avatamsaka Sutra (Hua Yen Ching) and the *Sraddhotapada
Sutra* (Awakening of Faith).

A.D. 653 Dosho to China to study under Hsuan Tsang and K'uei
Chi (Yogacara).

A.D. 654 Chitatsu, student of Chitsu, who was student of Hsuen
Tsang, brings *Abhidharmakosa (Kusharon)* to Japan.

A.D. 658 Emperor Tai Tsung brings together Li Jung (a Taoist healer)
and I Pao (a Buddhist monastic doctor) to debate and
prove their medical systems.

A.D. 664 Translation by Tao Hsuan of the *Nien Tien Lu (Nentenroku)*
and *Kai Yen Lu.* He also creates a great catalog of all extant
Buddhist works titled the *Tai Tang Nei Tien Lu.*

A.D. 655 Punyodhara introduces esoteric texts into China.
Empress Wu ascends the Throne of China.

A.D. 659   Hsuan Tsang translates the *Prakaranapada*.

A.D. 663–723 Vajrabodhi (Chin Kang Chih) esoteric Master, studies at Nalanda (Vinaya, Madhyamika, under Santabodhi); logic (under Dharmakirti); Yogacara, Vijnaptimatra and Madhyanta Vibhaga under Jinabhadra at Kapilavastu; Vajrasekhara under Nagabodhi in Southern India.

A.D. 668   Tao Shih writes the *Fo Yuan Chiu Lien*, which records Buddhist events in ancient Chinese history.

A.D. 670–762 Shen Hui He writes a critique of the Hui Neng schools of Chaan.

A.D. 673   Dosho returns to Japan from India.

A.D. 678   King Indrabhuti (the father of Padmasambhava) writes the *Jnanasiddhi* and *Kurukuslasadharma*.

A.D. 679   Suryaprabhasa travels to China from India and teaches Hsien Shou (Abhidharma School).

A.D. 680   Divakara (613–689) brings the *Gandha Vyuha* to Japan from India.

A.D. 683–727 I Hsing (alt. 635–713), a pupil of Subhakarasimha and Vajrabodhi. As a former Taoist, he studied Chaan, Tien Tai and Vinaya forms prior to meeting Vajrabodhi. He eventually writes a famous account of his travels to India called the *Nan Hai Kiei Na Fa Chuan*.
Budhiruci is first invited to China.

A.D. 688   Li Chen dies, a prince of Yueh and eighth son of Emperor T'ai Tsung, who committed suicide this year.

A.D. 689   Divaprajna in China, brings the Ti Lun teachings.
Shantideva.
Emperor Wu Chao reigns 690–704.

A.D. 691–700 Shantideva writes down and translates into Chinese the *Bodhicaryavatara*, the *Awakening of Faith in the Mahayana* (*Mahayana Srottapada*) and the *Siksa Samuccaya*.
Bodhiruci (2) of Southern India brings the *Amoghapasasutra* to Loyang (683).

Siksananda translates the *Sraddotpada Sastra* and the *Buddhabhasita Dasabhadra Karmamarga Sutra.*

A.D. 693   The *Amoghapasa Sutra* is translated for the second time. Dharmaruci translates the *Ratnamegha Sutra (Pao Yu Ching)*. Buddhatara translates the *Daihoko engaku shutara ryogi kyo* (Perfect Enlightenment Sutra).

A.D. 695   Empress Wu Tse T'ien (ca. 674–705) sponsors the production of a Catalog of the scriptures.

A.D. 700   Chi Chou is a student of K'uei Chi, a contemporary of Buddhapalita and Bhaviveka.
I Tsing retranslates the medical sections of the *Suvarnaprabhasa Sutra*, originally done in 414.
Sikshanada translates the *Lankavatara Sutra*, but by Imperial Order his work is revised by Fu Li and Mi To Shan before it is published. *Jinamitra* (Chinese: *Sheng Pei*; Japanese: *Shotomo*) writes down the *Sarvastivada Vinaya Samgraha* at Nalanda. Reputed to be a Chuan Fa practitioner.

A.D. 703   Chikan and Chiho return to Japan from China and teach GyoYen (a pupil of Gyogi).

A.D. 705–770   Amoghavajra (Pu Kung Chin Kang) 705–743, pupil of Vajrabodhi. At death of his teacher (723/741) he visited Ceylon and studied Vajrasekhara Yoga and *Mahavairocanagarbhakosa* under Samantabhadra. Was teacher to three successive Chinese Emperors and translates some 110 texts. Chung Tsung ascends the throne; he reigns for five years.

A.D. 706   Death of Shen Hsiu (Northern Chaan) Emperor Chung Tsung assists Bodhiruci (2) in translating sutras and acts as copyist to him.
Sze Hung Pei (Japanese: *Shikubei*) creates the *Jotokashaku* method of Chuan Fa in China.

A.D. 707   Emperor Chung Tsung renames the main temples in each area, "Lung Hsin Szu" (Buddhist) and "Lung Hsin Kuan" (Taoist). He honors Chaan master Hui-An, a successor to Hui Neng with a purple robe. Many Vinaya masters were also honored this year.
Srimata, an esoteric master.

A.D. 710   Tao Hsuan, a Chinese Chaan master comes to Japan (Nara). His pupil is Gyoho.
Muslim invasions lead Kashgar regions to seek aid from China for resistance. This was refused.

A.D. 715   Subhakarasimha (Shan Wu Wei) [637–735] esoteric master and a student of Dharmagupota of Nalanda, arrives at Ch'ang-An (China) via Tibet, accompanied by I Ching and is welcomed by Emperor Hsuan Tsang [685–762]. Taught I Lin, who taught Shun Hsiao, who taught Saicho (founder of Tendai and the Taimitsu in Japan). Saicho studied Chaan with Gyoho, Hsiu Jan, Tao Sui and Chan Jan [717–782].

A.D. 717   Shan Wu Weu translates the *Mahavairocana Sutra*, assisted by I Tsing.

A.D. 719–720 Vajrabodhi (d 741) another former pupil of Dharmagupta at Nalanda, arrives in Canton (719) after a one year stay in Ceylon, and travels on to Loyang (720). He translates the *Vajrasekhara Sutra* (*Tattvasamgraha*). Accompanied by a 14 year old Amoghavajra. I Tsing writes a definitive commentary on the *Mahavairocana Sutra* called *Ta Ching Su*, in which he clearly recognizes and describes the differences between the Theravada and Mahayana Schools.
Buddhism spreads to Thailand.

A.D. 721   Manicintana (Pao szu wei) dies. He was an esoteric master from Kashmir.

A.D. 723   Vajrabodhi translates the *Lueh chu nien sung ching*.

A.D. 728   Traditional year for the founding of the Todaiji Temple (Japan).
P'ei Tsun erects an inscribed plaque at the Shaolin Temple on Mount Sung.

A.D. 729   Laksminkara, a teacher of the Sahajiya, writes the *Advayasiddhi*.

A.D. 730   The *K'ai yuan shih chiao lu*, a catalog of the Scriptures, is completed.

A.D. 732   Shen Hui (d 762), a disciple of Hui Neng, challenges the legitimacy of the Northern School of Chaan at a public meeting held in Hua t'ai (Hopei). He is responsible for popularizing Chaan teachings among the military there. One of his main criticisms is that the Northern Patriarch Shen Hsiu was appointed teacher to an Emperor (but see 745).

A.D. 735   Bodhisena to China; he teaches *Avatamsaka Sutra*.

A.D. 736   Gembo (student of Chi Chou, who studied under K'uei Chi) returned to Japan in 735.

A.D. 740   Shen Hsiang of Simla (Korea) to Japan.

A.D. 741–746 Amoghavajra in Ceylon to collect more texts.

A.D. 745   Shen Hui invited to teach at Loyang to preach the doctrines of Hui Neng.

A.D. 746–805 Hui Ko (746–805) student of Hsuan Ch'ao (student of Shan Wu Wei and of Amoghavajra). In 804 he teaches Kukai (founder of Shingon in Japan) for three months. I Ming is the succeeding esoteric Master in China.

A.D. 747   Boroboudur (Mandala Temple) built.
Padmasambhava enters Tibet.
The giant Buddha at Nara (Japan).
The main esoteric temples of Chang An are the "Ta Hsing Szu" (in the southeastern sector) and Lung Hsin Szu (in the southern sector). Both were founded by Emperor Wen of the Sui Dynasty.

A.D. 589–618 Amoghavajra goes to live in Ho Hsi among the military leaders whom he teaches and initiates into the Mi Chiao path.
The Japanese Emperor Shomu orders that wrestling and other combative arts should be included in the public demonstrations connected with the annual "Five Grains" celebration.

A.D. 751   Gagaku masks are made to commemorate the inauguration of the Great Buddha in Japan (174 still survive).
Chinese paper-makers captured by the Arabs at Samarkand.
Founding of the Samye monastery in Tibet.

A.D. 753   Liang Su characterizes Chaan teachers as immoral and corrupt in their understanding of Buddhism. He declares them to be heretics.
Shen Hui exiled to I Yang in Honan.

A.D. 754   Kanjin (687–763), a Chinese doctor monk comes to Japan (Todaiji-Nara). His pupil is Eiei. In 756, Empress Komyo presents him with the medicine store of her recently dead husband.

A.D. 755   The An Lu Shan rebellion begins. This is fought mainly around Chang An and Loyang. It destroys many manuscripts and temples and is responsible for undermining the scholastic traditions of Buddhism then prevalent.
The practice of selling Ordination Certificates is officially approved as a means of earning government revenue.

A.D. 756   The Caliph of Baghdad sends military aid to Hsuan Tsung to help crush the revolt.
Su Tsung ascends the throne until 762. In August he re-enters Chang An and frees Amoghavajra from rebels.

A.D. 759   The first Vajranaga Temple (Ching Kang Lung Szu) is founded in China.
Foundation of the Toshodaiji (Japan).

A.D. 760   Santirakshita writes *Tattvasamgraha* (Collection of Truth). His pupil is Haribhadra.
Muslim Arabs begin an invasion of central Asia.

A.D. 761   Dramatic rites celebrated in the Lin Te Hall of the Imperial Palace by order of the Emperor. Courtiers are said (according to one account) to have been made to dress up as Vajra Devas, etc., and "worship" bodyguards who were dressed as Bodhisattvas. (This seems to be an "outsiders" report of an esoteric rite.)

A.D. 765   The Emperor writes a preface to Amoghavajra's translation of the "Benevolent Kings Sutra."

A.D. 767   Birth of Saicho (Dengyo Daishi).
Dharmapala(3) at Nalanda University.

Haribhadra—his pupil is Sarahapada (2) who teaches Savarapada, who taught Lui-Pada—reckoned to be the first of the Sahajaya teaching lineage.

A.D. 770   King Dharmapala (Pala Dynasty) ruled 770–815.

A.D. 774   Birth of Kukai (Kobo Daishi) June 15th.
Circa this period, King Dharmapala builds the Vikramasila University.
Gopala builds the Odantapuri Buddhist Academy.

A.D. 778   Birth of Joshu, a Chaan teacher (d 897).

A.D. 779   The "Awakening of Faith" brought to Japan from China by Kaimin of the Yakushiji.
The Ch'a Ching, the world's first handbook concerning tea is produced.

A.D. 785   Saicho founds the Enyrakuji Temple.

A.D. 789   Siladhana translates the Dhasabumika into Chinese.

A.D. 793   Kamalashila (student of Santirakshita) writes Bhavanakarama.

A.D. 796   Emperor Te Tsung issues edict appointing Shen Hui the 7th Patriarch of Chaan.

A.D. 800   Candrakirti formalizes the Madhyamika logical system.
Haribhadra writes the Abhisamayalankaraloka. He teaches Sarahapada.
Buddhism in Cambodia.
Prajna arrives in Chang An. He translates the Avatamsaka Sutra into Chinese and is accompanied by Munisri (d 816) of Nalanda.

A.D. 801–806 Ancho, a Japanese monk, writes the Churonryuki, a work upon the Madhyamika carika and commentary of Chi Tsang.

A.D. 805   Emperor Hsien Tsung presented with a copy of the Hsin Ti Kuan Ching, an esoteric text, by the King of Ceylon.
The Manjusrimalakalpa Sutra is hand-copied by a monk at Gaura in northern Bengal.

Saicho (Dengyo Daishi) returns to Japan and founds Tendai School. He performs the first esoteric rites held within Japan and creates a center on Mt. Heiei.

A.D. 806   Kukai (Kobo Daishi) returns to Japan after having been away for thirty months in China. While there he studied Sanskrit with Prajna and Manusri, poetry, crafts and calligraphy and esoteric Mikkyo with Hui Ko, a pupil of Hsuan Cho, a pupil of Shan Wu Wei.

A.D. 810   King Devapala (ca. 810–845) donates the "income of five villages" for the founding and preservation of a Buddhist Library and sutra copyings at the Nalanda universities.

A.D. 814   Enchin (814–891) nephew of Kukai. He travels to China in 853 to study with Fa Ch'uan. He returns to Japan in 858 bringing many ancient forms of the mandala, etc.

A.D. 822   Death of Saicho, who taught Enchin (814–891).

A.D. 835   Death of Kukai (21st day of the third month) at Mount Koya.

A.D. 838   Jogyo (?-866) travels to China, studies at the Ch'i Ling Szu under Wen Chen, learns the *Taigensuishiki* (rite for subduing enemy armies).
Engyo (799–852) to China, studies with I Chen at the Ching Ling Szu, returns in 839 to found the Reigan-Ji Temple.
Enin (799–864) to China; remains until 847.

A.D. 842   Eiun (798–869) travels to the Ch'ing Lung Szu (China). He studies the Ryobu Mandara with Achali I-Chuan.
Shuei (809–884) travels to China. He studies with Fa Ch'uan of the Hsuan Fa Szu, and returns to Japan in 865.

A.D. 843+   Anti-Buddhist period in China. By 850 it had, in major areas, been replaced by Islam.
Devapala builds the Somapuri Buddhist University in India around this period.

A.D. 847   Eiun returns to Japan and founds the Anjo-In monastery.

A.D. 858   Enchin (Chisho Daishi) of the Taimitsu, and a disciple of
Gishin, brings the illustrations of the *Vajrasekhara Sutra* to
Japan from China. He was taught by Fa Ch'uan of the
Ching Ling Szu and by Liang Hsu of the K'ai Yuan Szu
in 858. Enchin was head of the Onjoji ((Mii Temple) and
principal of the Tendai Jimon sect. He received Taizokai,
Kongokai and Soshitsuji initiations in China, and
regarded the esoteric (Mikkyo) sects as being higher in
merit than any Lotus ones.
Emperor Buntoku orders his two sons to engage in barehanded fighting in order to decide who was to succeed
him. The victorious son, Koreshito, became the new
Emperor Seiwa.

A.D. 868   Chinese production, on May 11th, of the oldest printed
book in the world, *The Diamond Sutra.* (A copy open to
view is in the British Museum.)
Death of An-E Abbot of Enryakuji (Japan).
Annen (841–915) studies Taizokai in China with Dokai,
Sanskrit with Cho I, the head of Gangoji (884) and
founder of the Godai In Temple on Mt. Hiei. He taught
Enryo and Hen Jo. He regarded the exo- and esoteric
teachings as being of identical value. He encourages use
of the *Fan Wang Ching*'s Sammaya precepts in monasteries.

A.D. 900   *Abhidharma Sangaha*, by Anurnuddha.
By Imperial Order a great encyclopedia of all existing
knowledge is compiled, *T'ai P'ing Yu Lan.* It is completed
in 904.
Lang Dharma begins a persecution of Buddhism in Tibet.
Danapala retranslates the *Astahasrika Prajna Paramita
Sutra* done by Lokasema.

A.D. 907   The end of the Tang Dynasty. Until 960, there is civil war
(The Five Dynasties Period).

A.D. 911–983 Minamoto no Shitagau produced a dictionary of Chinese
medical terms entitled the *Wamyo Sho.*

A.D. 912–995 Tamba Yasuyori, a Buddhist doctor/writer wrote the *Ish-
inho,* an account of the Buddhist four elements in medicine.

A.D. 935   The Khitans (from Siberia) invade China from the north.

A.D. 938   The Khitans desert their old capital in China and set up a
              new one which is later called Peking.

A.D. 942–   Genshin (Tendai) popularized the concept of "Tariki"
1047   (other power) Amidism.

A.D. 950   Sung Dynasty. Translation of the *Shizenmonkuki*, of Chi-
              Ko, a record of the oral accounts of the transmission of the
              Chaan doctrines according to the Tendai masters.
              Emperor Sung Taso is nominated as a master of the Chi
              Chuan (Japanese: *Kiken*) Chuan Fa School.
              Birth of Dipankara Srijana.

A.D. 972–983 The first printed collection of the complete *Tripitaka* in the
              Chinese language is produced and circulated.

A.D. 980   Atisa (980–1052) who taught in Tibet.

A.D. 986   Sabuktigin of Ghazni (Afghanistan) invades India and is
              opposed by the Jaipul ruler of Kangra. He holds them at
              bay until 1001 when he is defeated and taken prisoner.
              The Moslems sweep into India destroying everything and
              killing all monks be they Buddhist or Hindu.

Appendix 8

PARADIGMS OF THE ESOTERIC MANDALA

Ruling Elements				
Earth	Water	Fire	Air	Ether

PARADIGMS OF THE PHYSICAL REALM

Senses				
Touch	Taste	Sight	Hear/smell	All mind/body

Digits				
Middle	Index	Ring	Small	Thumb
Sensing	Feeling	Doing	Knowing	Wisdom

5 Feelings				
Pleasure	Sorrow	Pain	Joy	Liberation

5 Ignoble Desires				
Property	Sex	Power	Fame	Sleep

The Body (in general)				
Solid Organs			Hollow Organs	Life Force
Bone	Blood	Muscle	Nerve	Brain
Stillness	Flexibility	Power	Respiration	Vital energies
Solidity	Adaptability	Creativity	Study	Integration

5 Working Organs				
Anus	Mouth	Sex organs	Hands	Energy

Healing Methods				
Dietary	Massage	Manipulation	Respiration	Energy
Environment	Companions	& Movement	Understanding	Blessing

Causes of Health Imbalance				
Locale	Nutriments	Season	Mind	Karma

PARADIGMS OF BUDDHIST DOCTRINE

Unskillful States of Mind				
Greed	Jealousy	Anger	Pride	Delusion

4 Right Efforts			
Destroy the unwholesome	Develop the wholesome	Prevent the unwholesome	Maintain and increase it

Dharma Gifts				
Goods	Cooperation	Beneficial conduct	Kind speech	Dharma
Mudra		Mantra		Mandala
Sutra		Sila		Samadhi
Studies	Faith	Activity	Thought	Meditations

Realms of Existences				
Animals	Titans	Gandarvas	Yaksha	Devas

4 Sources of Mindfulness			
Body	Feelings	Mental object	Mental state

4 Wisdoms				
All Inclusive	Reflecting	Performing	Discerning All Transcending	

5 Skandas				
Form	Feeling	Activity	Perceiving	Consciousness

Objects of Consciousness				
Body	Body/Mind	Mind	All C'ness	Enlightenment

5 Spiritual Faculties				
Mindfulness	Confidence (trust)	Energy	Concentration	Wisdom

5 Body Types				
Dhatukaya	Manokaya	Manaskaya	Cittakaya	Alaya

5 Offerings to Shrines				
Foods	Unguents	Candles	Incense	Mind

The 5 Teachers				
Sutras	Sastras	Vinaya	Abhidharma	Meditation

The 5 Kinds of Fear & Loss in Students				
(losing) Life	Home	Reputation	Mind	Themselves
(fear of) Livelihood	Loved Ones	Arousing anger in others	Addressing an assembly	Being possessed

Deadly Sins				
Trying to kill: a Buddha	Mother	Father	Arahant	Causing disunity

Chuan Fa Hsing				
Chungking	Tsaifa	Shengyenchin	Shengsan	Sanchin

Chinese Rulers of Samashanti Nata				
Tortoise	Horse	Tiger	Heron	Dragon

Indian Rulers of Samashanti				
Elephant	Snake	Lion	Peacock	Garuda

Ryukyu Chuan Fa Techniques/Artifices/Movements (and Japanese terms)

Stance	Blocks	Thrusts	Breathing	Strikes
Foot	Leg	Eye	Arm	Mind
Press	Sweep	Push/Pull	Hook/Circle	Immobilize
Kiba	Kokutsu	Zenkutsu	Tsuruashi	Sanchin
Teisho	Haito	Ippon-nukite	Shuto	Senjitsu
Tettsui	Hiraken	Uraken	Empi	Ipponken
Still/drop	Back step	Forward	Up/Side step	Paralyze
Kihon	Kata	Kumite	Kokyu	Katsu
Yoi I	Sen	Go no Sen	Sen no Sen	Mushin

Chuan Fa Principles				
Fun (Fixity)	Hen (Fluidity)	Yu (Courage)	Senjitsu (Tactic)	Semmui (None Fear)

NOTES AND REFERENCES

These notes supplement the main text and cover details and sources not indicated there. In many cases they contain the essential explanations of the general principles or practices outlined in the text. Where relevant, I have indicated the origin or source of the respective teaching principles or practices, and these can be followed up by students engaged in individual research via their local libraries or Buddhist groups. Some resources are, however, quite unique, and were available to myself only because of special circumstances at the time. In such cases and where possible I have tried to indicate alternative sources.

To the "ordinary" student of the martial art, some of this information may seem quite overwhelming; however, it is fundamental and basic to the art, and serves perhaps to show just how little is generally known or taught by many modern so-called "Masters."

A BRIEF SUMMARY OF BUDDHISM AND ITS FOUNDER

Around 500 years before Christianity had emerged into the world, an Indian Prince named Gautama Siddhartha of the Sakya clan of Maghadi in northern India decided to renounce his rightful heritage and become a monk. Leaving his newborn son Rahula and his beautiful wife Yasodhara, he set out to learn firsthand from the greatest teachers of his time. After studying for some years with all these teachers, and practicing their various meditation methods, philosophical systems, and Yoga practices, he became convinced that their teachings were inadequate.

Determined to discover the higher reality, he sat under a Banyan tree and vowed not to arise until he had attained Enlightenment. According to tradition, he endured many different kinds of temptation and mental assault, but finally he realized that condition beyond life and death termed Enlightenment (Nirvana)—the awakening to the ultimate reality. Henceforth he was a Buddha—an "awakened one." After his Enlightenment, he converted many, including his former teachers, his son and cousins, and taught unceasingly for some forty-five years until he chose to attain the complete Enlightenment and leave this realm of existence (the *Parinirvana*).

His doctrine (Dharma) was expressed in the form of "The Four Noble Truths" which explain the origin of suffering. The last of these includes the "Noble Eightfold Path" which, together with the precepts of self restraint, forms the moral code to which all Buddhist endeavors aspire. Many aspects of his teaching surpassed the limitations of the contemporary belief systems, including its rebuttal of the Caste System, and were considered radically new. After the *Parinirvana*, his sayings and teachings were recounted and memorized by his disciples until, some hundred years after this, they were committed to writing. The teachings spread to many of the countries around India and developed many different forms of practice and application. Despite this, they all conform to the fundamental Buddhist moral code and philosophy.

Buddhist teaching is unusual for a "religion" in that it does not require belief in a God—but it does not deny God or Gods. It cannot, therefore, be classified as atheistic. It does not assert that after death the Soul goes to an eternal Heaven—so it cannot be classified as an Eternalist teaching. It does not hold that this is the only, or the most important, life available, nor does it teach a doctrine of inescapable karma, such as is found within Hinduism. Instead it has a view and teaching of human spiritual potential which exceeds all and any boundaries we care to place upon it—yet it is an intensely practical and practicable system oriented toward the here and now.

It emphasizes the development of a spirit of peacefulness and unlimited compassion for others which is open to all, irrespective of social position, caste, race or life situation. It is also a system of total self-responsibility, and holds that all our thoughts and actions come from us and return to us in various forms throughout existence, but it is not fatalistic nor does it encourage blind belief.

The doctrine shows that through the practice of meditation, we can become aware of the true nature of the mental patterns which induce suffering to ourselves and others. It stresses the practice of such self-examination in many different and clear forms.

Note 1: Buddhist references: *Visuddhi Magga*: 11.2;15.17; *Samyutta Nikaya*: 14; *Mahajima Nikaya*: 115; *Dhamma Vibhanga*: 2; *Prakaranapada of Vasyumitra*; Hindu references: *Prasna-Upanisad*; *Sathaphata-Brahmana*; See also the references in Notes 1a, 55, 56.

Note 1A: The methods for examining and analyzing the elements of the body (*Dhatu Vavatthana*, in Pali) are described fully in the *Visuddhi Magga*:11.1–2, 27–39, 93, (V. 37, 84, 92). 12:1–3. 14: 42–61. Detail can also be found within the *Digha Nikaya* 10 (in general); and in greater detail within the *Mahajima Nikaya*: 28, 62 and 140. (All the *Nikayas*, etc., are published by the Pali Text Society, London, 1975.)

The "Dhamma Sangini" and "Dhamma Vibhanga" sections of the *Abhidhamma Pitaka* contain the earliest description of the Theravada view of elements as material qualities rather than substances. The "Dhamma Sangini" is contained in *Guide to the Abhidhamma Pitaka* by Nyanatiloka (Ceylon: Buddhist Publication Society, 1983).

Pali Names of the Elements:	Theravada Principle:
EARTH: Pathavi = PUTH	to expand/extend (extension) hardness and softness
WATER: Apo = PAY AP	to grow/increase to arrive cohesion, fluidity and contraction
FIRE: Tejas = TIJ	to sharpen/mature vitality and maturity due to this It also contains Cold (= null Tejo)
AIR: Vayu = VAY	to move/vibrate pressure, motion

SPACE: There are at least four possible explanations of this word: 1) In Ceylon it is: $AKASA = A + KAS$ = to plough = space; 2) In Sanskrit it is: $= A + KAS$ = to view/recognize; 3) L. Saydaw states: $= KAS$ to shine/appear; 4) Its third interpretation is a feature arising from a relation between—and dependent upon—material objects (Rupa). Explanations are as given in *A Manual of Abhidhamma* by Narada Thera (Ceylon: Buddhist Publication Society, 1956).

NB: According to the Theravada school, one can only touch Earth, Air, or Fire, but not Water, as this represents the quality of cohesion; e.g., in "touching" Water, the cold felt is Fire (i.e., its absence). Its softness or texture is Earth; its pressure is Air. Such a definition suggests Water is only an inferred physical category. The Sarvastivada sect disagreed with such definitions, ascribing elements more positive values. A full discussion of this question (from the Madhyamika view) is given in the text of Note 2a.

Note 2: Although all the Buddhist schools agreed upon the basic factors enumerated, by no means did all the schools agree about certain other aspects. There were many and lively interpretations of various parts of the schemata outlined. Much discussion and debate took place concerning the status of the Mind Consciousness mentioned in the list and also concerning the status of the "Form" Skhanda itself. Edward Conze outlines these well in the work cited in Note 3. Here are some of the viewpoints concerning the Form Skhanda as perceived within the various schools and as described within the *Cheng Wei Shih Lun*. In the Sarvastivada School there were held to be two forms (Rupa) of matter namely the solid and resistant (*Rupapratigraha*) and the non-resistant (*Apratigraha*). This latter was of two types—voice and body. That of body was termed *Kayavijnapti* and that of voice *Vagvijnapti*. Both of these were understood to mean a state of consciously indicating or suggesting something to others by means of one's voice or indirect actions. (What in the army is termed "dumb insolence "could be said to be an enactment of a form of *Kayavijnapti!*) *Vijnapti* literally means a subtle intimation, suggestion, or communication of some bodily form, the *Vajramukti Nata*—of which you will read later—can also be seen as manifestations of *Kayavijnapti*.

In the *Abhidharmakosa*, we read that the Vaibhasika School used these two latter terms but added a third called *Avijnaptirupa*. This term described bodily or vocal activity which indicates nothing to an observer. In other words, acts or intimations which are karmically neutral.

The Theravada School agreed about body and mind acts, but did not accept anything but these two. In this school *Avijnapti* refers only to unmanifest, latent mental karma.

The Sammitya School held that *Kayavijnapti* was ultimately real activity and constituted an actual expression in bodily activity and movements.

The Darsatantika School held *Kayavijnapti* to be a "special" rupa bereft of color or form (both color and form can intimate things to others) and produced not by body, but only by the mind.

The Tirthantika School (who were Jain Saints) held that both *Kaya-* and *Vag- Vijnapti* were ultimately real in themselves.

The Satyasiddhi School reduced all matter to molecules and then to nothingness (void). It held that all elements are temporary in nature. This school utilized the sutras of Prajnaparamita, Saddharma Pundarika, and the Nirvana.

The Dharmalaksana School said that the consciousness which acknowledged the Rupaskhanda (*Manovijnana*) was separate in its nature from the others. This school held that consciousness was extant upon eight levels or forms and included a sense center (*Mano*), a thought center (*Manas*) and an integrative center (*Hridaya*). This school also held that there were classes of beings who could never attain Enlightenment.

Some 200 years after the Buddha's Enlightenment, debate still continued upon different aspects and their definitions. Buddhadeva held that the Samskara Skhanda didn't really exist in its own right, and that it should be considered as part of the Vijnana. Bhadanta Dharmatrata said that Vijnana and Samskara are forms of mental volition. Such differences as the above still persist through the various derivative schools into modern times. We can see, for instance, that the Dalai Lama on page 38 of his book (see Note 3) mentions *Avijnaptirupa* as an eleventh constituent of *Rupa*. This posits him firmly in the Vaibhasika camp.

The informative commentary to this book written by the Ven. Bhikku Khantipalo (of the Theravada school) refers to a work by Conze which in turn describes the *Avijnaptirupa* as being something totally different in nature to the Vaibhasika meaning outlined in the *Cheng Wei Shi Lun*. Such are the burdens Buddhist scholars have to bear! This whole problem—namely misunderstanding and / or misrepresenting even fundamental Buddhist terminology—is dealt with comprehensively within Anacker's work on Vasubandhu.

The doctrines of each of the early schools is discussed in great detail within *Buddhist Sects in India* by N. Dutt. (Calcutta: Firma KLM, 1970). Details of the Sarvastivada view of elements are outlined within *The Central Philosophy of Buddhism*, by T. Sterbatsky. (Delhi: Banarsidass, 1988 reprint). This contains also a translation of the fifth chapter of Vasubandhu's *Abhidhamma Kosa* although the terminological explanations given should be modified according to Anacker's text.

Sangharakshita in his *The Eternal Legacy* (London: Tharpa Publications. 1987) also notes several salient points in his remarks upon what actually constitutes an authentic or original Buddhist language and what the Pali language really was.

Note 2a: A good presentation of both the different teachings held by the early Buddhist schools and the various notions of the Self can be found within *Nagarjuna's Philosophy*, by K. Venkata Ramanan. (Tokyo and Boston: Charles E. Tuttle, 1966; republished 1978 by Motilal Banarsidass). The many works by Edward Conze upon the schools of teaching are all highly recommended.

Note 2b: The *Abhidhamma Pitaka* contains a section entitled "Puggala Pannatti" (Description of Individuals) but this mainly concerns itself with enumerating the qualities to be found in the various types of Noble Disciple and not so much individual characteristics of personality, etc. It does contain some interesting examples of the categories of people who could and could not become good teachers, etc.

Note 2c: *Myo Ho Renge Kyo* (The Sutra of the White Lotus). Translated by B. Kato and rearranged by W. Schiffer & W. Soothill. (Tokyo: Rishokoseikai, 1971).

Note 2d: At a later date the Tien Ta'i School of China re-introduced many of the kinetic meditation practices which were based around what was termed in the Theravada Schools the "pratyutpanna (pro-longed) Samadhi." These were regularly practiced in the temples. We can find ample evidence of the "perpetually moving meditations" (Japanese: *Jogyo Sammai*) in many forms which were later introduced into Japan under the auspices of the Tendai Taimitsu sects. When such practices were used, it was always in combination with a static form (Japanese: *Joza Samadhi*). The classical tradition of these forms divided them into three stages: Static (*Za*), half-moving half-sitting (*Hangyo Hanza*) and continually moving (*Gyo*). These were taught by the Tien Ta'i Master Chih I, the founder of the Tien T'ai system as early as 550 A.D. and were recorded by Huan Ting as being performed from the period 570–630 onward. The Tien Ta'i dates are contemporary to those of Bodhidharma—another practitioner of movement meditation.

Note 2e: See *Alienation: The Concept and its Reception*, N. Rotenstreich. (Leiden: E. J. Brill, 1990). *Therapeutae*: To the ancient Greeks, the profession of doctor or healer was as much a spiritual calling as it was a physical one, and the healing profession reached its peak in the teachings of the Therapeutae (from which our term "therapy" comes). This was a sect totally devoted to the integrated practice of medicine. Their practitioners and healers were naturally also Priests. Therapeutae lived strict semi-monastic lives and were not permitted to take payment for their services, a factor reflected in the wording of the Hippocratic Oath, a fact conveniently forgotten by modern medical organizations. All healing had to be done in accordance and harmony with the Gods, and it was therefore impossible to be a healer if one was an Atheist or lived a non-spiritual life. They also practiced various therapies called "Temple Sleep," a practice involving overnight residence at a temple during which the Gods could speak to the patients (and vice versa), offering solutions to their problems. This was a form of meditational self-observance, visualization and communication which was also common in ancient India, where it was called *Nidra*.

Psycho-therapy: Buddhism has long stressed the importance of what is called a "spiritual friend" (Sanskrit: *Kalyana Mitra*). This is someone who has no vested interest in another, but a genuine concern for their well-being at all levels. It is a fact that the many who resort to psychotherapy often simply have no one else they can talk with or to about their apparent problems. They are forced to pay someone else to fulfill the role of the Kalyana Mitra. This is more an indictment of the values of our society and its inhabitants in general, than a revelation concerning the nature of our mental being—as some believe Freud's writings to show. While Freud could not have qualified in any form of ancient Greek or Indian healing, at least Jung had the good sense to plagiarize some Buddhist traditions, even if he failed to realize their full significance or recognize the value of applying their spiritual teachings.

Note 2f: The "Three Jewels" are the Buddha, his Teaching (the Dharma) and the Order of Monks (the Sangha).

Note 2g: In Buddhism there are various overall terms used to describe the kinds of mental unwholesomeness and afflictions which serve as hindrances to spiritual insight. Such terms usually fall into two forms dealing with 1) specific mental negativities which have a common theme by means of which they manifest and are recognized; and 2) generalized forms of obstruction which act as filters for other types of mental activity, whether obstructive to insight or not. The term *Klesa* describes a quality of this second category and thus may manifest within other, more specific mental negativities, also acting as an underlying substratum for them. Because of this, the various components usually termed as *Klesa* are found in other lists of mental negativities.

In the Theravada teachings, the *Klesa* are seen as acting in ten particular ways, each of which serves to cloud consciousness by aiding the overall development of 1) greed, 2) ill will; 3) delusion; 4) conceit; 5) speculative views; 6) skeptical doubt; 7) mental torpor; 8) restlessness; 9) shamelessness; and 10) lack of moral dread. These ten are found in the *Dharmasangini 1229*, and enumerated within the *Vibhanga 12* (see Note 1a). No specific classification of them is found within the Theravada suttas. In addition to the *Klesa* there are also found the *Nivarana* or "mental obstructions." These are classified as being: 1) sensual desire; 2) ill will; 3) sloth and torpor; 4) restlessness and scruples; and 5) skeptical doubt.

The Mahayana predominances the first three of the above *Klesa* list (ignorance, greed, and hatred) and usually means these three when referring to *Klesa*. Such a generalized usage re-emphasizes their non-specific, overall influence upon consciousness. It was by restating more accurately the meanings of such Buddhist terms, that the great Yogacara philosopher Vasubandhu elucidated and overcame many errors which had crept into the contemporary Theravada teachings.

There are a wide range of karmic causal forces or motivations particular to what makes up the individual, all of which, being intrinsically afflicted, tend to give rise to various forms of suffering and anguish which summarize their overall "root" or predominant impetus dynamic. The *Klesa* modify the goals and qualities of all mental and physical activity in ways both subtle and obvious. The human being inherits a distinctive individual pattern of physical *Klesa* through the previous physical patterns of his parents. He also inherits an individual mental pattern through his own previous mental conditions and activities. As the human consciousness incessantly changes and modifies its contents, so the *Klesa* patterning is likewise continually altering and adapting to new conditions to provide a dynamic basis of modifying characteristics for future accumulated patternings. These patternings manifest within the specific states and orientations of our consciousness, acting like a filter to its perceptions and activities.

They are therefore pre-conscious patterns in their efficacy and cannot be a subject of observation for they are effective at each moment of consciousness, being continually succeeded by fresh ones. Due to this they are only seen in retrospect and usually in the form of a memory of their resultant effects. This is why teachers like Vasubandhu placed such a great emphasis upon perceiving the real nature of each "mind moment," for it is the only moment that can be seen. The results of consciousness affect the physical being equally and similarly create patterns reflecting mental conditions, particularly in conditions of worry, stress, pain or happiness. As with the consciousness, some of these patterns are obvious, others are subtle. The result of all this activity is to provide the basis for the mental and physical *Sthana*.

Note 3: The early Buddhist schools quickly enumerated distinctions between things as complete entities and things as compounds. Of the two, the basis which forms the entities (the mind) is seen as the substantiator for the compounds. In Buddhism this substantiator itself is recognized only as a compound of its own creation and thus possessing no lasting permanence. This view stands in great contrast to that of the non-Buddhist spiritual scriptures in which many qualities and entities, be they human or celestial, are held to be permanent and unchanging in essence, and are usually found only in connection with explanation of the origins of the world, etc. The traditional view of elements in such accounts has only one category of description, namely that which, in Buddhism, would be termed the physical qualities or *Maha Bhuta* aspects.

The various non-Buddhist views concerning matter and constituents were summed up in a refutation of them contained within the Buddhist text *Dharmagraha*. These are summarized as follows:

SAMKHYA: That there are three "qualities" (named *Tamas, Rajas, Sattva*) inherent in all matter and that these qualities constitute the human Self and all other things.

VAISHESHIKA: That all elements are real and eternal because they possess an eternal "nature" (termed the *Dravya*).

LOKATIKYA: That the atoms of the elements are eternal.

NIGRANTH (Jains): That the existence of elements and the nature of their existence is identical.

AHJIVIKA: That elements are not identical with their nature but each is different.

MAHESVARA: That there is an all-powerful God who makes elements, and he is all present and all eternal. He is the cause of all elements.

MIMAMSA: One branch holds that the sound of the Vedas is eternal and manifests all dharma (including elements). The other school also holds that the sound of the Veda is eternal, but that the production of dharmas (elements) depends upon various conditions.

The Cheng Wei Shi Lun concludes that elements should not only be considered by their purely substantial qualities (*Dravyas*) alone, for—although they are touchable by the body and can be experienced in this manner—their other qualities, such as heat, motion, or humidity, are also bases of experiential qualities. This view agrees with that of the *Abhidharmakosa*, which says Arahants can empower substances and seems to suggest some extra qualities above the merely physical lie inherent in matter. Such a view is not explicated further in the Theravada teachings.

Space was recognized as an entity within the Theravada and Mahasasaka Schools as being uncompounded and without a capacity to produce mental "moment events." Nagarjuna (see ref. 2a) and Vasubandhu (Anacker; op. cit. p. 81) held that Space is "an absence of impinging materiality." This "non-view" of Space made it possible for others to establish the element Ether as a cosmic (non-impinging) element which, though not directly connected to the human world, nevertheless could indirectly affect it (via the environment). Ether thus became something like a karmic pattern or underlay (*Vasana*) of the natural world, and somewhat similar in nature to the *Alaya vijnana* of the human realm.

From another point of view, Ether was the "substance" of which both Spirits and Gods were composed, and was therefore synonymous with the "element" of consciousness in the human realm. It was mainly considered when performing services of exorcism. Vasubandhu would have no doubt regarded such a categorization as irrelevant as his concern was predominantly directed toward human inner communication, clarity, and enlightenment.

Nearly 2000 years before Rutherford's Cambridge experiments, the early "elemental" Buddhists first asserted that atoms, being compound in their physical nature, could not be indivisible (and therefore could be "split"). The usage to which they put such knowledge was, of course, spiritual, and did not result in an ancient Indian Nuclear Physics.

See also: *Cheng Wei Shi Lun* (*Vijnaptimatrashastra of Hsuan Tsang*), translated by Wei Tat (Privately published, Hong Kong, 1973). In Japanese this is called the *Yuishikikyo*.

"A Discussion of the Five Aggregates" (*Pancaskandhaka prakarana*), contained within 7 *Works of Vasubandhu*, Translated by S. Anacker (Motilal Barnarsidass, 1984). This is the translation of Vasubandhu's works used throughout this book and is highly recommended to Kempo students, as it covers all sources, corrects many errors in translating Vasubandhu's writings, and uses a relevant form of English. This particular edition has some strange grammatical errors but these are no distraction. *Abhidharmakosa*, of Vasubandhu (Taisho Tripitaka No. 115).

Buddhist Thought in India, E. Conze (London: Allen & Unwin, Ltd. 1983). *The Opening of the Wisdom Eye*, The Dalai Lama. (Wheaton, IL: Theosophical, 1966). NB: This version is the original one by a Dalai Lama fresh from Tibet and without modernization or editing. It retains the original Gelugpa style of teaching and transmitting the doctrine, and is of more use than later versions.

Buddhist Logic (2 Vols.) by Th. Stcherbatsk (New York: Dover Publications, 1962). This work deals extensively with the processes and views of how "moment events" come into being. Its terminology should be compared with that given by Anacker (op. cit.).

San Kuo Shi, translated into Japanese as the *Sangoku Shi* by Goro Komiyanma (Tokyo: Kineiido , 1884). The text concerns the period A.D. 221–235.

Note 4: Visuddhi Magga: 11.2; 15. 17; Samyutta Nikaya: 14; Mahajima Nikaya: 115; Prakaranapada of Vasumitra; Prasna-Upanisad; Sathaphata-Brahmana; Vibhanga: 2.

Karmasiddhi Prakarana, translated by S. Anacker in 7 *Works* (supra). An English version of the pioneering French translation by E. Lamotte in 1936 has been done by Leo Pruden (Berkeley, CA: Asian Humanities Press, 1988). However, students should consult the Anacker text as this contains corrections to Lamotte's Sanskrit and draws from a wider range of modern resources. See also the *Dhamma Sangini* (circa 300 B.C.) which is contained within the *Abhidhamma Pitaka*. Also, *The Art of War*, by Sun Tzu, translated by S. Griffiths (Oxford: Oxford University Press, 1963, 9, 6: 27–31). Although this is one of the oldest military works, it is fairly certain that the Indians possessed similar texts before this. Vajramukti, one of the world's first martial systems had long been a prerequisite practice for the Ksatreya Caste, of which the Buddha was a member. It possessed a sophisticated strategic philosophy, utilizing all the symbols and philosophy of Indian spiritual systems. Its Buddhist form (*Bodhisattva Vajramukti*) being the progenitor of the exercises taught by Bodhidharma in China as part of his meditation trainings. Later generations of Hindus re-introduced Vedic weaponry and other similarly military equipped trainings into the art. These modern forms are usually devoid of Buddhist spiritual principles.

Also see *Siksa Sammuccaya* (The Collection of Trainings), by Shantideva, translated and edited by C. Bendall & W. Rouse (Delhi: Motilal Banarsidass, 1922, reprinted 1990); *Chandragomin's Cisya lekha dharma Kavya*, Ed: I. P. Minayeff (Zapriski. Vol 4. p. 414–452); *Maha Vyutpatti*, edited by Sakakai (Kyoto, 1928); *Avadana Sataka*, translated by J. S. Speyer (St. Petersburg: Bibliotheca Buddhica, 1906–9).

Note 5: The word *Karma* literally means "action" and gained much popularity in the 1960s flower power days. It is a spiritual term drawn from Hinduism and used to describe the causal force behind any, usually unfortunate, occurrence. Unfortunately many people who write about Buddhism seem to be still adhering (perhaps unknowingly) to this form of usage. In Hinduism, with its belief in immortal and unchanging qualities, the Self is held to be reborn after physical death. This process goes on and on until liberation (*Moksha*) is attained. In this type of belief it is fundamental that that which is re-incarnated each time remains essentially unchanged and/or retains its "identity." If it didn't, the thing reborn would not know who "it" was and spiritual lessons learned previously would be unavailable to help in its progression.

It is an image rather like that of going to school, where as one gets older, one does—or does not—pass various examinations, and progresses from class to class until graduation day. *Karma* is also often misquoted, in both popular Buddhism and Hinduism, to represent the inherited events which are endured as a result of actions performed in these previous lifetimes when what is meant is *Karma Vipaka* (the fruit of karmic action). In Hinduism this *Vipaka* can constitute physical or mental events. In Buddhism, *Vipaka* can only signify mental events. In Buddhism, *Karma* represents activities of the mind which modify its condition. It emphasizes the human, not supernatural, aspect of mentality, which is continually changing and modifying its nature and content according to circumstances both outward and inward. The resultant pattern is a continual and continuous one with each moment blending into the previous in an unending stream of consciousness. It is this stream of consciousness which, unaltered by physical death, continues in various manners and according to its inner quality. This quality is determined by the degree of liberating wisdom attained during its various previous periods of awareness.

The idea of a fixed or unchanging locus going to another locus is completely alien to Buddhist doctrine. One cannot properly speak of any "thing" being re-incarnated or re-born. In Buddhism there is simply a continuity of consciousness moments and nothing more is necessary. This is why it is possible to attain Supreme and Total Enlightenment within this lifetime. Because of the principle of change, it is possible to transform one's total being and attain Enlightenment in this very body. This theme is dealt with in the "Karma siddhi Prakarana" of Vasubandhu mentioned in the previous note.

Note 6: There are some, who, when they study Buddhism mistakenly, regard its conception of mind as if it were a map and the Skhanda as parts of the landscape. Such a view is but an erroneous substitute psychology in the Western mold which simply confers fixed attributes upon the consciousness and partitions the mind into supposed areas and functions. Viewing the Skhanda in such manner makes them into mere substitutes for neural functions. The purpose of describing the nature of mind is not simply to map it out, but to try to convey something of the manner in which it can be fully understood, experienced, and transcended. See Charts 1–4 which follow.

Note 6b. Also see "Slaves & Citizens," by S. Clarke in the *Journal of the Royal Institute of Philosophy*. Vol. 60, No.231 (London, Jan. 1985); and "The Definition of Person," J. Teichmann, in the *Journal of the Royal Institute of Philosophy*. Vol. 60, No.232. (London: Apr., 1985).

Note 6c. The schemata of Mind I have given here is simplified and I here expand on some of them. With regard to some of the categories mentioned, it should be pointed out that *Citta* represents a purely abstract (*Udgrahana*) condition of consciousness and that it is the associated, secondary activities of *Citta* (*Caitta*) which form what we experience as our "mind."

Buddhism has no term for what we would term the "individual." Instead, it refers to the *Citta Santana* or "continuity of consciousness." This *Santana* comprises all the mental and physical processes we think of as being "ourself." The purely abstract and subjective *Citta*, when it comes into contact with the *Mahabhuta*, becomes the objective *Caitta* and from this the *Skhanda* arise—they being particular aspects or patterns of its activities. All knowledge in Buddhism is derived from objective (*visaya*), material elements (*Mahabhuta*) or subjective (*indriya*) mental elements (*Mano Dharma*). When the *Mahabhuta* are regarded as sources for the knowledge of mind, it is their attributes as principles of activity which are considered foremost. When considered in such a manner, the *Mahabhuta* become *Mano Dharma*.

An important constituent of the *Samskara skhanda* is *Cetana* meaning "will" or the directed mental effort preceding actual mental volition. It is defined in exactly the same manner as *Samskara*, but whereas

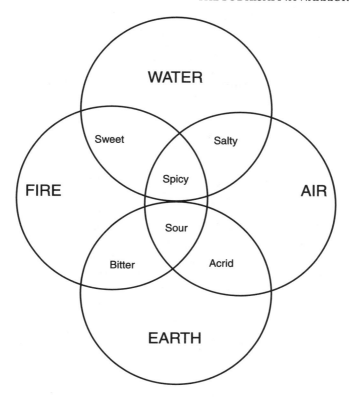

Chart 1. The six types of taste and their relation to the elements as defined in the Abhidharma Kosa *of Vasubandhu.*

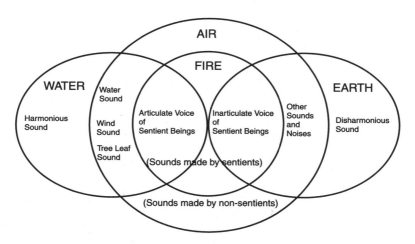

Chart 2. The five sounds and their respective elemental rulers and qualities.

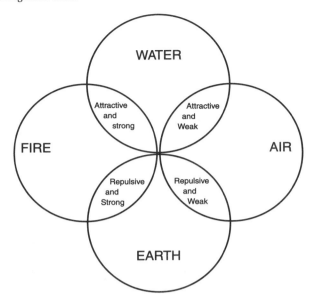

Chart 3. The four types of odor and their elemental rulers.

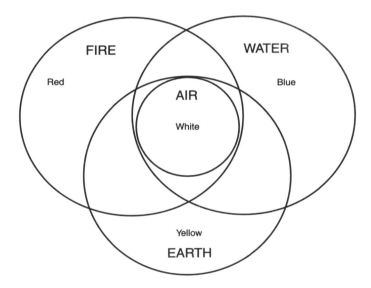

Chart 4. The four primary colors and the Maha Bhuta *according to the Chinese tradition. At least one school of the* Abhidharmakosa *ascribed the colors as follows: YELLOW = Fire and Air; BLUE = Earth and Air; RED = Fire and Earth; WHITE = Fire, Water, and Earth. In all the various traditions the color white always occupied the central position.*

Samskara also describes any concerted force in general, *Cetana* describes the personalized will (mental volition). *Cetana* precedes all *Samskara* as *Manas* precedes all *Mano Vijnana*. *Cetana* arranges the various elements of mind (perceived by *Samjna*) into their common grounds, thus permitting them to centralize around a specific goal or intent. They can then begin their specific activity (*Samskara*). We can see that for all intents and purposes our experience of mind is more or less restricted to the experience of *Samskara* and / or *Cetana*.

Note 7: See *Chinese Alchemy and the Manipulation Of Time*, N. Sivin. Technology Studies (Cambridge, MA: M.I.T., 1976); *Chinese Alchemy: Preliminary Studies*. N. Sivin (Cambridge, MA: Harvard University Press, 1968); *Science & Civilization* (series), J. Needham (Cambridge, England: Cambridge University Press, 1978).

Note 8: All the persons mentioned suggested or taught doctrines similar in nature to Buddhist principles. Pelagius was foolish enough to suggest that individuals were responsible for their own destinies. Origen (once dubbed the "wisest man in Christendom") said that there were two or three levels of truth inherent in all teaching. Basilides spoke of the "holy emptiness" of the human heart and mind in a manner reminiscent of the Buddhist Heart Sutra. Docetists said there were "emanation bodies" of Jesus. Patripassans said that the Church's doctrine of the Trinity as it was then held, must indicate that God would have suffered and died on the cross as well as Jesus. They were declared heretical for their attempts to redefine doctrine. That the Gnostics knew of India can be seen in the fact that the teacher Bardiesenes mentioned the Buddha; St. Jerome also spoke of the Virgin Birth and the Buddha (quoted from *Intercourse between India & the Western World*, by G. Rawlinson (Cambridge, 1910, pp. 142,174, 340–420.)

A quick and useful reference source to such views can be found in *The Concise Dictionary of the Christian Church*, edited by E. A. Livingstone (Oxford: Oxford University Press, 1977); and also *The Penguin Dictionary of Religions*, edited by J. R. Hinnells (1984). An alternative and magical view of the New Testament can be found in *King Jesus*, by R. Graves (London: Cassell, 1946, 1987). Especially recommended are *The Gnostic Gospels*, by E. Pagels (New York: Random House, 1979; London: Weidenfield & Nicholson, 1979; London: Penguin Books, 1982).

Note 8a: The simile of Indra's Net envisages an enormous net cast around the world. At each intersection of this net lies a mirror, and when gazing into any one of these mirrors there lies reflected all the images in the other mirrors. Thus, when you look into one, you cannot help seeing all the others ad infinitum. In such a way to see one is to see the all.

Note 8b: Various authorities interpret the word *Hatha* in different ways. Some say it represents two particles indicating the Sun and Moon. Others say it represents the sound of the in and outbreaths. All explanations interpret it as indicating two contrary polarities of some type. The basic system of Hatha Yoga has 8 "limbs" consisting of *Yama* (abstentions), *Niyama* (observances), *Asana* (postures), *Pranayama* (breath control), *Pratyahara* (sense withdrawals), *Dharana* (basic meditations), *Dhyana* (concentration), and *Samadhi* (spiritual awakenings). The term "Yoga" is used pejoratively in both the Theravada Pali *Mahvastu* 3:384–10 and the Mahayana Sanskrit *Cata hasrika Prajnaparamita*, p.438. Edited by P. Ghosa Calcutta, 1902–1903).

That the system of Hatha Yoga developed after Buddhism can be seen in the fact that the commentator of the Yoga Sutra, Vyasu, utilized several unique Buddhist terms previously unknown in the Vedas: i.e., *Samsara, Moksa, Hetu*. He also bases his summary of the medical art as disease, its causes; health, and its cures, upon the format of the Four Noble Truths. As the Yoga system developed, it borrowed many Buddhist ideas and re-interpreted them to suit its own usages and doctrines. See also Z. F. Lansdowne, *The Chakras and Esoteric Healing*, (York Beach, ME: Samuel Weiser, 1986).

Note 8c: The Six Realms of Existence consist of the realms of 1) Hells, 2) Hungry Ghosts, 3) Animals, 4) Warring Titans, 5) Human Beings, 6) Radiant Gods. Of these, the human realm is the most important. These realms can equally be considered (according to Vasubandhu) as states of consciousness within this and/or other lifetimes. See R. R. Desjarlais, *Body and Emotion* (Delhi: Motilal Banarsidass, 1994).

Note 8d: The Yoga of Tumo consists of various practices designed to increase the autothermic capacity of the practitioner. In Tibet it was an environmental necessity for the practice of solitary meditation. One of the tests involved in demonstrating an adept's prowess in this was to sit naked in subzero temperatures and have water-soaked (and freezing) blankets thrown over one's body. It was then required that the practitioner be able to dry out at least 7-8 blankets using the Tumo autothermic technique.

Note 9: Traces of esoteric monuments and temples are found all over these areas. In the 1920s, the vast temple of Boroboudur was excavated, mainly by the British army, from within the Javan jungle. The whole construction is of cut stone with thousands of Buddha and Bodhisattva statues. It is laid out in the shape of an enormous esoteric mandala which is larger than the pyramids. It must have taken much dedication and many years to build. Despite the growing monopoly of the Theravada School of

Buddhism, esoteric texts were known and extant in Ceylon as late as A.D. 805. The King himself possessed a copy of at least one.

One art, perhaps from Ceylon, preserved in Thailand is recorded to have been followed by King Naratsuan and was called in Thai "Vijja Taeng Konghap." This was an esoteric discipline for warriors which involved practices designed to make one's skin impenetrable to weapons and blows.

Note 10: At various times Buddhism was subjected to purges by the Imperial House, and Taoists often conspired to have it ejected whole-sale from the Nation as a foreign religion, particularly when it became popular and their sources of income began to dwindle. The various leaders of the Buddhist temple often had to act as Diplomats for their cause at the Imperial Court and such a task was demanding. If such purges persisted for a long time, or succeeded against them, great upheavals would ensue. As the temples often provided localized food supplies for the peasants and medical facilities for the poor, many people other than the monks were disrupted by such intrigues.

Note 11: The Sutra of Vimalakirti (Chinese: *Leng Yen Ching*; Japanese: *Yuima Kyo*) gives an account of a lay student of Buddhism (Vimalakirti) showing himself to be wiser than the Buddha's immediate disciples. This Sutra was very influential in spreading the idea that monastic life was not the only manner in which one could understand or practice the Dharma effectively. The Mahayana schools in general replaced the monk ordination with that of the Bodhisattva ordination ceremony. Technically viewed, none of the Mahayana teachers are therefore monks (Bhikku) in the earliest traditional sense of the word. Later, in Tibet, a new form of teacher arose in the form of the *lama*. This particular native term literally means a "superior one" and is not a religious title. In fact, Tibet has many Lamas who are not even Buddhists. It has developed a religious connotation simply by virtue of its popular usage. China also had its own teacher titles, such as "Sifu," meaning literally a "Father Teacher," which was variously interpreted as indicating the Sanskrit *Upodhaya* (giver, or initiator) or *Acarya* (see Glossary). *Chaan Shi* (Japanese: *Zenji*) meaning "Dhyana Teacher" and "Fa Shih" (Dharma Teacher) were also titles innovated by the Chinese. In China each of the different sects tended to create their own forms of honorific address. See also *Monks and Magicians: Religious Biographies in Asia*, P. Granoff and Koichi Shinohara, eds. (Delhi: Motilal Banarsidass, 1994).

Note 12: The Yogacara School was one of the seminal trends of Chinese Buddhist thought dealing with the voidness of being. This trend began with the Satyasiddhi school. No school of this precise name is known as such in India. The "Satyasiddhisastra," was translated into Chinese around A.D. 411–412. Kumarajiva, an Indian teacher, who, while in China, brought with him and translated many famous Buddhist texts, mentions Hanivarman as a teacher.

The Satyasiddhi sect was regarded as being one of the 18 original Indian Buddhist sects of northern India. Chinese students of Kumarajiva considered its Sastra contradicted many aspects of the *Abhidharmakosa*—the commentaries upon the Sutras by the Theravadins. Kumarajiva also translated some texts by Nagarjuna, who is generally regarded as the originator of this whole stream of *Sunya* emphasis. These included his *Twelve Gates* (*Dvadasadvara Sastra*) and the *Satasutra* by Aryadeva, the pupil of Nagarjuna.

At this time there were other strands of teaching, some of which later crystallized into definite schools of teaching. The most well-known were the *Sautrantika*—a term deriving from *Sutrata* (those who study the Sutras). During the 1–4th centuries they were known also as the *Sankrantivada, Sutrasvadins, Saurodayaikas, Darsanatika* and the *Sutrapramanika*. At later times these names were also used by sects which debated with the then current Sautrantika sects. The Sautrantika teaching came from the *Sarvastivada*. These latter were termed "realists" in that they regarded elements as having a provisional reality, but the self as void. Vasubandhu regarded the Sarvastivada teachings as having descended from the Vaibhasika teachings. The Sautrantika School was developed and was termed the *Satyasiddhi* (completion of truth). The Satyasiddhi held that both Self and elements were void of any substance.

Vasubandhu utilized the Satyasiddhi concepts of time in his own writings. A key summary of this school says there is "No substance (*anatma*), no lasting quality (*anitya*) and no bliss—except Nirvana." This tenet manifested later as the Vijnaptimatra (consciousness only) and the Yogacara (unifying practice) Schools. The Yogacara School was based upon teachings given to Asanga by Maitreyanatha. Its philosophical foundation was created by Vasubandhu, the elder brother of Asanga, whose own ideas, set out in the *Yogacarabhumi Sastra*, were considerably revised by Vasubandhu. After compiling the great source book of the *Abhidharmakosa*, Vasubandhu was converted by his brother to the Mahayana and spent the rest of his life promulgating its teachings instead.

Vasubandhu also annotated and improved a work by his brother called *Mahayana-samparigraha* which sets out the basic trend of Sunya orientation. Yogacara both innovated many ideas which passed into other and later schools (including the notion of a Buddha's different bodies and the division of consciousness into eight levels and realities) and re-popularized the teachings of Nagarjuna, the originating impetus of the school. The *Sarvasunyavada* (All is Void teaching) was first shown by Nagarjuna in the 1–2nd century. Its method of teaching was termed the *Madhyamika* (middle path) and its followers based themselves on a previous Sutra of that name by Nagarjuna which had been translated by Kumarajiva. The Sunya orientation was the final development of Buddhist doctrine in that it reduced the basis of all things, be they mental or physical, to the condition of total vacuity.

The Madhyamika teaching was directed against overly intellectualized views and produced a refined, critical logic of discussion and argumentation which was intended to render logic itself meaningless. Utilizing the *Prajnaparamita, Lotus* and *Nirvana Sutras*, it became known as the "Three Treatise" school (San Lun). By using the *Prajnaparamita*, the Madhyamika attempted to overcome the intellectualist tendency it saw developing in the Yogacara School. The later Ch'aan (zen) practices, methods, and attitudes were based firmly upon both Yogacara and Madhyamika teaching which themselves descend directly from the insight (Vipassana) meditation of the earliest Indian traditions [See Note 28].

Note 13: An important emphasis which arose as a result of the need to both study and practice the profound principles discovered within the Yogacara Schools was that of solitary retreat. Many schools developed practices enabling monks to live alone for a number of years in small and restricted areas. The monk was, at such times, completely a-social.

Some practitioners were walled up in caves for a number of years and their food brought by acolytes weekly or monthly. The actual practice of the experience of self vacuity (*anatmabhavacarya*) was strongly emphasized. There was also a noticeably greater emphasis upon self-confession of fault and the transference of one's merit to others. Both these features were eventually incorporated into the liturgies of nearly all the different schools and sects.

Note 13a: *The Bodhisattva Doctrine in Buddhist Sanskrit Literature,* by H. Dayal (Delhi: Motilal Banarsidass, 1932. 1978). This work uses a rather old-fashioned terminological understanding but its scope of interest has not yet been bettered. It contains a well-referenced "outsiders" view of the development of the Bodhisattva ideal, and some useful précis of important points in the development of doctrines and terms. Using Indian and Tibetan sources, it shows that the component title particle *Sattva* stems from a Vedic term meaning "a strong and valiant man, hero or warrior" (pp. 8–9). It further shows that in India the idea of *Bhakti* (devotion) comes from Buddhism and not vice versa as was commonly believed (p. 31). It also contains several suggestions and examples of Pali terms being taken from Sanskrit, effectively precluding any claim that Pali was the "original language" of the Shakyamuni Buddha. (See also Note 2, last paragraph.)

Note 14: Bodhidharma is certainly a famous figure in Chinese Buddhist history and is often mistakenly credited with being the sole founder of Kempo. Such a view can only come about by ignoring the history and spiritual philosophies which he represented, and concentrating instead upon the outward physical sequences of the Vajramukti techniques he demonstrated. The system credited to him is generically called the Shaolin Szu School—after the temple at which Bodhidharma introduced these physical practices. Most modern competitive and sporting schools of Karate try to credit their origin to him, but even a superficial knowledge of Yogacara Buddhism demonstrates their intrinsic antagonism to Buddhist teaching. In modern times only the *Wu Hsin Tao* (*Mushindo*) School of *Chuan Fa*, or schools similar to it, admit and uphold the original non-commercial, non-sporting, non-competitive, predominately spiritually oriented principles. There are many imitators of the real *Shaolin Szu Chuan Fa*.

Innovations such as Bodhidharma's were not unique in China. Hui Neng, another famous Ch'aan teacher is credited with the invention of several important medicines (including the original Tiger Balm) and of introducing the practice of sedatory respiratory sequences for the psychologically disturbed. Innovatory techniques, such as the use of special (physical) Yogas and other forms of healing, were part of the reason Buddhism as a system was easily accepted within China. Yogic physical trainings were (and still are) used in Tibetan, Chinese, and Japanese esoteric monasteries.

The Wall: The remark that Bodhidharma spent nine years "facing the wall" has given rise to much speculation as to what this term "wall" indicated. Though in China it is usually taken to refer to the mountain face opposite the *Shaolin Szu*, it is equally likely to refer simply to the barrier reached in the practice of meditation when one has reached a point seemingly impassable. A similar term is used nowadays by long distance runners. *The Hsieh Mai Lun* clearly mentions such a "wall" and it is difficult to see why some modern Japanese professional scholars have indulged themselves in so much speculation concerning the meaning and usage of such an unremarkable term, particularly when they are ever trying to convince themselves that accounts of the teachings of Bodhidharma are "unattested elsewhere."

See also: *Karate Do and Buddhism*, Shifu Nagaboshi Tomio, lecture given in 1972, published by The Cambridge University Buddhist Society. Lecture reprinted 1974/5/6/7 by Hakurenji Temple (London), Kongoryuji Temple 1982/4/6.

"*Shingon* Buddhism and Kempo," lecture given to the Buddhist Society Summer School (GB) by Shifu Nagaboshi, 1978, published by Mushindokai, 1979/1980/1981.

"Daruma," by Soen Sasaki Roshi. Published in *The Cats Yawn*, a Journal of the First New York Zen Society (date unknown, circa 1960).

Chinese Yoga (Volumes 1 & 2) by T. Dukes. London: Chinese Yoga Federation & Mushindokai, 1975/6/7/8. 1981.

Buddhism in China, by K. Chen (Princeton, NJ: Princeton University Press, 1964).

Sourcebook of Shingon Buddhism (*Kongoraiden sect*), by Shifu Nagaboshi Tomio. Privately printed by the Cambridge University Buddhist Society in conjunction with the Cambridge University Mushindo Kempo Association and the British Shingon Buddhist Association, 1972-1973. Reprinted by Hakurenji Temple 1974,1975,1976,1978. Japanese title *Honbun no Kongoraidenha Shingon*. This was the first work upon Shingon Buddhism in the English language ever published in Britain.

The Buddhist Conquest of China (2 Vols.), by E. Zurcher (Leiden: Brill, 1972). Read the review of this work given by Conze in *Further Buddhist Studies*, B. Cassirer, Oxford, 1975.

The Secret and Central Philosophy of Karate Do Kempo, by Shifu N. Tomio (London: Hakurenji Temple, 1975).

"Fighting the Buddha—Preserving the Sangha." Shifu T. Dukes. Tokyo: Kosei, Kaisha, 1975 (Extract) included within *Dharma World*, Vol. 2 No. 9.

"The Kingdom Of Heaven and Hell," Shifu T. Dukes (Tokyo: Kosei, Kaisha, 1926, in *Dharma World*, Vol. 2, No. 4).

The Buddhist Warrior & Non Violence, by Shifu Nagaboshi/Dr. T. Dukes (Thailand: World Federation of Buddhists, 1983).

Exchanging Dhamma whilst Fighting. Buddhdhassa Bikkhu (Bangkok, Thailand, 1972).

Refer also to the works cited in Notes 20, 25, and 39.

Note 15: Many of the trends within China are summarized within *Buddhism in China*, by K. Ch'en. (Princeton, NJ: Princeton University Press, 1972). This has useful glossaries of Chinese terms/characters and many reference texts for further study. See also E. Zurcher, *The Buddhist Conquest of China* (Leiden, 1972); B. N. Puri, *Buddhism in Central Asia* (Delhi: Motilal Banarsidass, 1994).

Note 15a: The Four Noble Truths are as follows—

1) The Truth concerning the origin of Suffering is thus: Birth is characterized by suffering and dissatisfaction, Death is characterized by suffering and dissatisfaction, Being with the unpleasant is characterized by suffering and dissatisfaction, Being away from what is pleasant is characterized by suffering and dissatisfaction.

2) The truth concerning the cause of this suffering and dissatisfaction is that it arises from cravings, the craving not to be forgotten, craving for sense pleasures and craving sometimes, for death.

3) The truth concerning the way to overcome the suffering and dissatisfaction brought about by craving is to cause craving itself to cease, to withdraw from participating in it, to renounce it, to liberate oneself from it completely.

4) The truth concerning the way to cease craving is to follow The Noble Eightfold Path of Virtue which consists of right views, right intentions, right speech, right activities, right livelihood, right effort, right mindfulness, right concentration.

Note 16: In the accounts of Chinese monks visiting India we find descriptions of monasteries (such as Nalanda) hosting and practicing all the current Buddhist traditions. Monks started in the mornings with the teacher of one school, worshipped at the service of another and in the afternoons went to study under a different school's teacher. Such homogeneity has never been equaled in any subsequent nation—even in modern times. China, however, did produce several traditions which were deliberate syntheses of the elements of other traditions. Tien t'ai, for instance, included the Sutra studies of the Theravada along with the chanting of the Ching T'u (Sukhavati) School. It practiced the esoteric rites (*Mi Ching*) and the Ch'aan meditations of both the northern and southern schools. In many cases the Tien tai practices consisted of and preserved a more ancient or complete form of its various component traditions. See *The Buddhist Conquest of China*, by E. Zurcher (Leiden: E. J. Brill, 1976).

Note 17: Within the Theravada, the scriptures are interpreted to indicate that it is forbidden for monks to practice medicine. In fact, the teaching relating to this actually forbids a monk to earn his living by practicing medicine and simply seems to be a ruling designed to keep monks predominantly concerned with spiritual studies. (One should also recall that at that time it was common for the Hindu Brahmin priests to prescribe medicines or magical health cures to their laity.)

Despite the monastic prohibition, it was, and still is, not uncommon for monks to advise the population but this is done in an indirect manner. The patient will approach a monk and say words to the effect of, "If a person had these symptoms (here he mentions his own symptoms) what would a person advise him to do?" The monk would then reply, "If a person had such symptoms a Doctor would advise (here he would tell the patient the method or content of a cure); this is what a Doctor would say." The monk has thus, technically speaking, not "practiced" medicine, he has merely been speaking hypothetically. Such circumlocutory practices were necessitated by the *Patimokkha* (monastic rules) but were criticized by the Mahayana, who took the attitude that it was better to openly acknowledge and practice medicine for the benefit of others than to deviously walk around the rules. This principle—that it is better to obey the spirit of a teaching rather than strictly observe its outer rules to the letter—was one of the main differences in outlook between the Mahayana and Theravada schools. Refer also to:

La médicine Chinoise au Cour des Siècles P. Huard & Ming Wong (Paris, 1959, p. 173). A very comprehensive popular work which mentions Kempo and is worthy of study. An English edition has been published in 1968 by the World University Library (Weidenfeld & Nicholson) as *Chinese Medicine.*

The Healing Buddha, R. Birnbaum. London: Rider & Co., 1979.

Ancient Buddhism in Japan Vols. 1 & 2. M. Wde Visser (Leiden: E. J. Brill, 1935).

Bhaisajyaguru Vaidurya Prabhasa Tathagata Sutra, Ven. Shih Shing Yun (Taiwan: Buddhist Culture Service, 1962).

One of the most interesting collections of emergency first aid based upon the traditional Buddhist Kempo medical practices used by monks is the *Kokusai Kyuho*. This was written down by Gentoku Tamba (also known as Rankei Raki) in 1789 and published in Tokyo. This work utilized the living Chinese practices used by the Chinese medical monks. Here the techniques of revival (*Katsuho*) are clearly detailed along with other first aid emergency treatments. Another Chinese work relied upon by Chinese and Japanese Kempo doctors was the *Ch'ien Chin Fang* (known in Japanese as the *Sen Kin Ho*) by Sun Szu Mo. This Tang dynasty text in 31 rolls (Chuan) was written down in A.D. 652 and reprinted from the Chinese original within Japan around 1700.

A modern form of the Vajra Yoga was founded by the charismatic Japanese Sensei Masahiro Oki, a man very familiar with the principles of Kempo (he once refused an offer of an Okinawan Eighth Degree Black Belt). He has authored many works on the theme as a healing and remedial art, most being published by Japan Trading Publications, New York.

Note 18: The Sanskrit word used in Buddhism to describe health is *Dhatusamya*. This literally means "balanced" or "stabilized elements."

Note 19: See *The Essentials of Buddhist Philosophy*, J. Takakasu (Westport, CT: Greenwood Press, 1956).

Note 20: Despite the prohibition, many well-known monks did in fact associate themselves with military concerns. This was particularly evident in Japan. While Zen Monks such as Bankei merely utilized military terminology to emphasize points of doctrine (Bankei was famous for punching through wooden boards with his bare hands to "inspire" monks) others, such as Sessai, actively engaged in formulating military tactics. Takeda Harunobu (d. 1573)—who became a Zen Roshi— was renowned for boiling the heads of his enemies within an iron pot while they were still alive. At various times in Japanese history, monasteries of the Zen, Shingon, and Tendai sects had engaged in open warfare against each other and achieved great prowess in military arts. Even at its most degenerate times such warfare never occurred in Chinese Buddhism.

It is quite obvious and naturally follows from the Buddhist precept against weapons that there can be no Buddhist "school" of weaponry of any form whatsoever, and legends (or stories) concerning monks inventing such are totally spurious. Any monk who associated himself with any kind of weaponry could not truly call himself a Buddhist, or represent any known form of Buddhism. (See Note 60 regarding spurious monks.) See also:

Journal of Mushindo Studies, Vol. 8 (British edition). Also in Serbo Croat, German, Chinese and Russian editions. Some articles available only in French, Mongolian, Japanese or Swedish versions. Included in the Journal are the following: "Zen and Kempo?" by Shifu Nagaboshi. June 1988 (reprint of the original article published in 1964); "MKA Technical Study Papers," June 1988. British edition, includes "Refuting critics of the JuhachirakanshuKyo" (The real Shipalohanshou in China) by Shifu Nagaboshi Tomio; "The Astadasarahantapani Sutra." A re-rendering and summary of the *Juhachirakanshoukyoshi* of R. Otomo, by K. Yasuka & T. Murakami, Ryushinji Temple edition (1950), Kadena, Ryukyu Islands, Japan. Several extracts (in English language) from this have appeared in yearly editions of the Journal of Mushindo Studies.

Hui Lu. Translated into Japanese by Seishi Sawagishi as the *Heiheiki Hyakkinpo Tekikyo*. Volumes 1–4 in 'Chuan' manuscript. 1853 edition.

Karate History and Traditions, B. Haines (Boston: C. E. Tuttle, 1968). Written for the mass market, this work has inaccuracies and ignores or deals only superficially with vital spiritual issues. Although it does mention some Buddhist connections, its main object seems simply to maximize the achievements of the exoteric karate teachers and their students. Unfortunately this is one of the better "public" books on karate history.

Buddhist Yoga, Rev. Ijima (Tokyo: Japan Publications, 1973). The author correctly identifies and acknowledges the Kempo training of the Shakyamuni Buddha.

Zengaku Yokan, Segawa Shobo (Japan, 1907, p. 248b).

"Flowing Star" *Journal of the British Shingon Buddhist Association*, Vol. 8. No. 1, (1985).

"No Self No Being," T. Dukes (reprint of the original published at Hakurenji Temple London, 1977).

"The Buddhist Warrior," lecture given by Lama Trungpa Rinpoche and Shifu T. Dukes at Samye Ling Monastic Center during its residential Chuan Fa seminars (1967–1969).

Otomo Kohaiki 1: "The Flowering and Decline of the Otomo Family," compiled by I. Oita (Japan, 1936).

Buddhism in China, K. Chen (Princeton, NJ: Princeton University Press, 1964).

Note 21: Refer to *Chinese Hand Analysis* by T. Dukes (York Beach, ME: Samuel Weiser, 1988; English edition by Thorsons, 1988.) This contains descriptions of various Buddhist ascriptions to parts of the hand as well as their philosophical bases and implications in the fields of medicine and mental well being.

Note 21a: See *Biological Rhythms in Human and Animal Physiology*, G. G. Luce (New York: Dover, 1971). This edition has a very informative reference section listing medical research projects and papers in the field. See also *Body Time*, G. G. Luce (London: Paladin Books, 1968).

Note 22: The *Jatakamala* scripture recounts stories of the Buddha's previous births, and one of them, titled *Prince Five Weapons*, describes his combat with a forest demon. This description includes details of many of the different types of attack and defense used within Kempo. It is interesting also to note that this scripture—which belongs to the Theravada School—includes an account of the prince threatening to kill the

Figure 124. Acala Vidyaraja carrying the sword which destroys ignorance. (Kongo-ryuji Temple.)

demon through the use of a sword made from a Vajra. Such Vajra swords were only used within the rituals and exorcisms of the esoteric schools of Buddhism. This indirect reference seems to suggest that the Vajramukti existed in Sri Lanka before the systematization of the Theravada School.

Note 23: The British National Health tradition of Physiotherapy was founded mainly on the efforts of a Swedish teacher named Edith Prosser. She taught at St. Thomas' Hospital in London up to the beginning of World War II, and trained nurses in the art of Swedish Remedial Massage. Edith Prosser lived for a long time in China and mentions her studies in Buddhist massage techniques in some of her writings.

Note 23a: Most of the polemic against the opium trade in Canton specifically can be found in a reply to the Anglo-Oriental Society for the Suppression of the Opium Trade made by the Cantonese Keuen Keae Shay in 1877. The Society included several prominent Buddhist priests and Kempo Masters as its founders. This report, published later in English by the A.O.S.S.O.T. was influential in bringing the matter to the attention of the British public and government.

Note 24: An interesting example of this occurred in 1972 in Taiwan when a member of a Mushindo Kempo dojo in Israel sought and eventually found a monastery whose monks practiced Kempo. After requesting instruction and being refused, he climbed a nearby mountain and, using a long range cine camera, filmed the monks training at Kempo in the temple courtyard. In 1987, members of the Yugoslavian Kempo Association attending a Buddhist seminar in Italy came across a party of Shingon Monks training in Mushindo Kempo. True to tradition they refused to teach anything and could not be persuaded to reveal either their teachers or temple names.

Note 25: There are several notable recorded instances of formerly famous warriors being converted to Buddhism through the practice of Kempo and who spent the rest of their lives as monks teaching, practicing or training others. Even as early as A.D. 750, the esoteric Master Amoghavajra is recorded as staying for five years with a group of military leaders in order to teach them esoteric Buddhist techniques and doctrines. Around 1430, 700 years later, Chan Sen Fong (Japanese: *Chosanho*) became a monk and after studying with temple masters is said to have originated a form of therapeutic Kempo based directly upon Bodhidharma's health teachings. He called this the *Jou Chuan* (softly clasped hand) School.

In the period 1560–1566 two monks, former Taoist Kioh Yuan Shang Jen (Japanese: *Kakuen Shonin*) and the Venerable Mikkyo Master Li Lao Shih (Japanese: *Riroshi*) refounded the *Shaolin Chuan Fa* system in a temple at the Omei Shan in Szechwan province. The practices were based upon the original form of Bodhidharma, but also included adaptations (simplifications) suited to the local trainee monks. Li himself maintained, and continued to train, the fully ordained and suitably initiated monks in the ancient and traditional esoteric forms school based directly upon the forms and the esoteric methods taught by Amoghavajra around 750. It is also said that at a later time a Buddhist Nun called Wing Shih did the same among women followers of the Buddha.

Li's school had branches at the Kuan-hsien szu, the Ma-Chou Szu and Kung-Hsien Szu near Chungking. Both the *Wu Hsin Tao Li* and the *Kempo Hishu* record that it was around the time of Li and Kakuen that Japan began to send troops of the Satsuma clan to occupy the Ryukyu Islands and, as a result of this, many Ryukyuan islanders went to China to escape and / or seek both religious and Imperial help.

Several, after studying martial arts with Li Fa and Kioh Yuan in China, returned to organize a secret resistance movement against the Japanese armies. Some of the fame of Li's school stemmed from the fact that two of his students, Te Chu To and Sekeko, taught and trained the personal bodyguard of Sho Gen—the Islands' hereditary monarch. The Li School tradition was firmly wedded to the esoteric school, and via its system of lineage teachers, continues to preserve the ancient tradition. The present master of the Southern Chen Yen esoteric Buddhism is of this school.

See: *Gedatsu* (The journal of the Ryukyu Tatekai) No. 6. 1947–1948. Article titled "The Ryukyuan's Struggle against Japanese Oppression, " by K. Obata, 1949; "Freedom for the Ryukyus," by M. Shimabukuro. Both articles were privately published by Kadena-Yonaburo Tatekai Renmei, and are also in a shortened edition by the Ryukyukoku Dokuritsu Koshirenmei (Okinawa, Japan, 1967);

Kempo Hisho (Secret Writings of the Art of Kempo) published (Naha) 1672 by students of Chen Gen Pin and in Japan circa 1682 (private edition);

Chi Hsia Hsin Shu, by Ch'i Chi Kuang, gives interesting accounts of the attitudes and tactics of the native Chinese against Japanese coastal invasions and raids during the 16th to 18th centuries. This work was translated into Japanese in 1856 (Tokyo) as *Kiko Shinso Shisan Teihon*; *Otomo Kohaiki 1*: "The Flowering and decline of the Otomo Family," compiled by I. Oita (Japan, 1936).

See also: *Higunkashi* (Hidden Army Records), by various authors—unpublished records, reports and manuscripts of the Japanese military forces in Okinawa during the period 1689–1740 and 1799–1850, held by the Otomo and Yasuka families (Ryukyus Archive). Copies were loaned to me in 1965. These have been supplemented by World War II research reports concerning the history of the Ryukyus Islands made by the Japanese forces and *Kenpotai* (Prefectural Secret Police) seized from the Japanese forces by American Intelligence Officers. The whereabouts of many of the traditional sites of the Chinese Temples, including those which practiced Kempo, can be found in the *Ta Ching I T'ung Chih*, first published in 1744 and reprinted last around 1920. Its 124 volumes detail the whereabouts of many now forgotten cities and temples.

In the preface to the *Cheng Wei Shi Lun*, translated by Professor Wei Tat (see Note 3) he gives an account of his witnessing a practical demonstration of unarmed combat, performed only with an act of mind, by a Tibetan Lama. Several accounts of similar methods can be found within *Mushindo Advanced Manual of Training*, by Shifu T. Dukes (Cambridge University Mushindo Kempo Assoc., 1971. Reprinted by Kongoryuji Temple, Cambridge, 1974/75/77/79; Kongoryuji Temple, Norfolk, 1980 (enlarged edition), 1981/86/89).

Note 26: Edward Conze has rightly pointed out that in Buddhism the prefix *Vajra* correctly refers to a description of the experience of individual enlightenment in its profound and revolutionary aspect. The earth shattering totality of self-revelation is well-described by the analogous term "Thunderbolt." In the Buddhist sense, it does NOT literally mean "Diamond" (as countless authors insist on translating it) although the attributes of, or associated with, a diamond could be used as a symbolic description conveying one facet of a quality inherent within the experience of total clarity—which arises only after the "Thunderbolt" experience.

Note 26a: See also, *The Secret and Central Philosophy of Karate Do Kempo*, by N. Tomio (London: Hakurenji Temple. 1977, 1978).

Note 27: The ability to read or write Chinese is not sufficient in itself to correctly translate Buddhist *Chuan Fa* or religious texts. Some Chinese sutras are translated from the original Sanskrit phonetically and require a thorough knowledge of Sanskrit, as well as a familiarity with the Buddhist philosophical terminology, in order to understand them in the manner intended by the authors. To attempt to translate a technical term literally (if it is phonetically rendered) results in something far from its meaning. Even native Chinese do not always realize this. A good example of this can be seen in the case of one of my own teachers Ryoshu Otomo. The surname "Otomo" is a transliteration of the Sanskrit Buddhist term "Kalyana Mitra" (a "spiritual good friend"). When studying in China, his name was written into an introductory letter to various temples by a Chinese monk who knew some Japanese. However the monk used the wrong characters and wrote down ones that meant "wild, fierce liberated" (*Fa Tao Meng*). These characters in Japanese are pronounced as O-To-Mo. I can well understand how this name may have been appropriate to my teacher when he was younger—but it is wrong! As a result of this error he bore the name *Fa Tao Meng* equally with the correct translation of his name (*Ta Pei*). Stefan Anacker has pointed out how various scholars have attempted to make one Vasubandhu into two different persons and several Vasumitras into one.

It is simply not sufficient, as unfortunately some writers in the Martial Arts field have done, to dismiss Chinese manuscripts as "forgeries" or "unsupported," simply because one either has never actually seen a copy—a very common but often unsuspected fact—or one doesn't fully understand either what they mean or signify. There seems to be a great fear among some writers that the general public might realize that the Martial Arts are not simply concerned with fighting, sport, or similar vested interests, but instead, espouse the eminently sensible Oriental viewpoint, that humankind is more than brute force and ignorance. A prime example of such pseudo research lies in the way some people deal with the historical figures of Bodhidharma and Leung Wu Ti by reiterating material copied from long out-of-date books saying that the traditional meeting between the two is apocryphal, or assert that the Ryukyuan peoples' struggle against the Japanese army invasion of 1609 onward is unattested. No current or past work on Okinawan Karate, including texts by native contemporary "Masters," evidences any knowledge or acknowledgment of the role of Chinese and Okinawan Buddhism and/or Shamanism in preserving certain of the martial traditions, nor of the close connections between the native Royal family and their monk teachers and guides.

Note 28: See: "Zen is the Theravada Branch of Buddhism in Mahayana Countries," by S. Ratnayaka, an essay in *Buddhist Studies in Honour of Walpola Rahula* (London & Vimamsa. Sri Lanka: Gordon Fraser). See also the references in Note 26b.

Note 28a: There are several versions of this text; most are based upon the Sanskrit/Tibetan forms preserved within the Peking tripitaka collection. The most useful source for English speakers is by Alex Wayman, *Chanting the Names of Manjusri* (Boston: Shambhala Press, 1985). A critical review of this translation appeared in the *Tibetan Review* (Dharamsala, India) of that year and should also be read if possible.

Note 29: The Chinese ideograph for element (*Hsing*) means "actions" or "activities" and denotes particular types of change which occur in time, especially in reference to material substances (i.e., changes caused by heat, cold or erosion). It was used to represent and translate the Buddhist Sanskrit term *Samskara*. The word *Hsing* also came to represent certain times as those qualities (i.e., the Chinese would speak of "cold" time or "hot" time). These terms indicated that the usual methods of judging time were to be accelerated or decreased by specific amounts or that a measurement of time was to be made by reference to some method other than the normal (i.e., the time it took a bird to fly from point A to point B, etc.). Such techniques upset our modern ideas built upon a sense of exactness or precision, but were very common in China. The Chinese "Elastic Ruler" was another such device and was stretched if necessary to measure the distance between points upon a patient's body. A detailed study of this term is outlined in the works mentioned within Note 7.

Note 30: See *Ancient Indian Medicine,* by Dr. P. Kutumbiah, FRCP (Bombay: Orient Longmans, 1969); *Indian Medicine,* by Dr. J. Jolly (India: Manishirum Manoharlal, 1977, 2nd edition. This has a very useful list of important sources and references.)

Note 30a: For types of sick people, nurses, and patients, etc., see *Anguttara Nikaya* 1:120. For visiting the sick, etc., see *Samyutta Nikaya* 3:120.

Note 31: These "limbs" classically are Mindfulness, Investigation of the Dharma, Energy, Joy, Tranquillity, Concentration, and Equanimity.

Note 32: It is hard to understand the position of students practicing Karate who hold that "Karate is Zen" and then proceed to totally ignore Buddhism and its teachings. Any reasonably intelligent person who practices such arts would be struck by the fact that modern Karate, or similar martial arts, are not taught with any serious reliance upon the Buddhist philosophical and historical precedents, principles, and goals that martial arts were clearly founded to achieve. In all traditional schools, especially of Karate, the concept of sport or competition is unknown and/or expressly denied. (The word "sport," itself, is a French 18th century invention meaning "to play" or "relax.") The term "serious sport" is a self-evident contradiction.

As a general rule when considering books concerning unarmed martial arts, such as Karate, should note especially how much space is dedicated to a) the history of Buddhism and b) the amount allocated to an exposition of its spiritual teachings and principles, particularly in relation to the art's moral implications in areas such as self-defense, the taking of life, etc.

Note 32a: Manuscript notes and diagrams of Ankoh Itosu while in China, translated and arranged by K. Obata & Z. Seionna. English translations of parts by N. Tomio (1967). Privately produced and circulated by the Ryukyu Tatekai. *Itosuka Shi* (Itosu family records/letters), translated by R. Otomo & T. Spearman (1958) Paris. Privately printed in a limited edition of 25 copies by the Dokuritsu Kempokoshikai, Naha, Japan. See References in Note 26b.

Note 33: See: *Patanjali and Yoga,* by M. Eliade (New York: Schocken Books, 1975). The sections upon Buddhism show misunderstanding of some principles and terms but give a balanced presentation of Yoga history and philosophies. The work has a useful bibliography. Also see *Chinese Yoga* (Two volumes) by T. Dukes (London: Chinese Yoga Federation, 1977). Volume 2 details the therapeutic and physiological aspects of spiritual practice in Buddhist esoteric Yoga.

Note 34: Apart from proper Kempo, modern derivatives of ancient Buddhist Nata movement forms are seen in Thai and Burmese boxing, Balinese and Malaysian Penjak Silat, and the Laku-Laku dances of Tonga. Even modern India has a form of Vajramukti (which has succumbed to Hindu influences and utilizes ancient weaponry). Several famous Hindu Dance forms commence with moves identical in stance and arm posture to that found in the classical Kempo preset sequences of movement.

Note 34 b: Vajramukti formed part of a holistic approach to spiritual and physical being and was not simply a martial art. Much of its tradition was based upon ancient Indian medical tradition. This particular aspect is said to have been developed by Shakyamuni's disciple and Doctor Jivaka. Jivaka was a famous pediatrician and herbalist and is included as one of the founding fathers of the then contemporary Hindu medical tradition. The Muslim "Hakkim" doctors are said to have developed from the *Ka-Chun* School of Indian Buddhist Vajramukti/Nata. Among contemporary exponents of Vajra medicine and boxing, the masters Otomo Ryushu (of Okinawa), Masahiro Oki and Shuzo Okada (Japan), Hyun-Ho (Korea) and Doshin So (Japan), are outstanding. All of these were trained in Chinese traditions stemming from the lineage culminating in Kempo. Several of these persons are active monks of esoteric or Chaan schools. Such persons and their successors form the living tradition of Nata/Vajramukti/Kempo in present times. In Tibet, Vajramukti trainings are evident in the Szechin-Po dances of the Lamas. These dances are ancient and are said to have been introduced into Tibet by the Buddhist esoteric teacher Padmasambhava during the early eighth century A.D.

Note 34c: China has many dialects, most being mutually uncommunicable even among the Chinese. It is for this reason that Chinese traveling in other parts of their country usually resort to writing down their queries in order to communicate with each other (written Chinese characters are mostly identical in all areas). One finds many source terms under many different Romanized (phonetic) spellings dependent upon which dialect is being used. Couple this with the fact that many eminent teachers used two or three names during their lifetime and one can see the difficulties facing all researchers!

Note 34d: The epithet "lion" occurs in many contexts throughout Buddhism. Shakyamuni sat on a Lion's Throne and proclaimed his teaching with a Lion's Roar. Such usage shows it as synonymous with "royal," "Sun-like," or "majestic." Shakyamuni's grandfather bore the word as part of his personal name. Lion (Sanskrit: *Simha*; Pali: *Simmha*) also occurs in other names, particularly of those belonging to the esoteric sects. One of Kukai's teachers was Shan-Wu-Wei = Subhakarasimha. The Lion Dance is still performed at Chinese New Year Festivals and was traditionally done by Kempo masters and their students. One offshoot of Buddhist Nata in Afghanistan and Iran was the school termed in China *Ka-Chun*. This art still exists and was demonstrated before Mao Tse Tung in the 1953 all Chinese Boxing Championship held at Peking.

Note 34e: At least one tradition ascribes the inspiration of Japanese Sumo (or its revival) to a Chinese Kempo master named Chen Yuan Pin (Japanese: *Chin Gen Pin*—in the Ryukyus he was known in their own pronunciation as *Chim Gen Ping*) who visited the Islands on the way to and from Japan. His story is interesting because it represents one of the few occasions that the Japanese have openly acknowledged their debt to a Chinese Master. Briefly his story goes thus:

> Ch'en Yuan Pin (1587–1671) was born in Hangchow (Chekiang). In the spring of 1621 he accompanied Shan Feng Hsiang as a bodyguard on a mission to Japan to lodge an official complaint against Japanese and other pirate raiders on the Chinese coastal areas. While there, he befriended the poet Nobukatsu Hayashi (1583–1657). In 1638 he again went to Japan but fell ill. He was nursed back to health at the Shikokuji (Kokusai In) monastery where was tended by Gensei Hoshi (1623–68) reputed to be a fellow Kempo Master. Later, through the offices of a temple, he secured a job with the Lord of Owari. He wrote poetry and historical commentaries for the Lord's library. He was also an expert potter (a profession

exported to the Ryukyus) and designed kilns for Lord Owari in the Chinese style. While in Japan, he taught three ronin (who had sought him out in order to learn from him) named Isokai Jirosaemon, Fukuno Masakatsu, and Miura Yoshitatsu (aka Yoshitoki). Through them he introduced the seminal art of Kempo to Japan. They in turn began the schools which led later to the development of Jujitsu and Aikijitsu. Miura, a doctor, is said to have later traveled to a Buddhist temple in China to learn more deeply and, after a hundred-day meditation practice, he was inspired to realize the spirit of the art through observing a Willow tree waving in a storm. He returned to Japan and was reputed to have become the main propagator of the art of Ju Jitsu in several of its schools. No doubt these three included some of their native techniques of semi-armed combat (sometimes called *Yawara*) into what they taught, but the basic impetus for the study of a purely unarmed combat clearly came directly from Chin Gen Pin. Chin Gen Pin's gravestone lies within the Kenchuji Temple at Nagoya (Japan).

Sources—Some information concerning Ch'en Yuan Pin can be found in the following texts: *Gen Gen Showa Shu* (Imperial Ancient Records of Japan); *Sentetsu Sodan 2*, by Z. Tsuji; *Kaigai Kotsu Shiwa*, S. Ushio, pp. 660–680; *Chin Gen Pin to Judo no Shiso*, Shirijin Co., No. 6/2, 1935; *Rekidai Hoan* (a collection of medieval documents and poetry relating to the Ryukyu Islands and their development); *Zuko Shinseki Shuran*, No. 6. Section entitled "Furoka zassho senja shoden." Also see: *Owari Meika Shiru* (1st roll, Owari family writings); *Otomo Kohaiki 1*: "The Flowering and decline of the Otomo Family," compiled by I. Oita, Japan, 1936; *Koko Ruisan. 3* (with portrait): *Owari Meisho Zuye*, No. 2. Tokyo: Owari Kei-Ko p. 99, and in the famous *Kempo Hisho* (Esoteric Teachings of Kempo) produced first in manuscript form (Chuan) by Chin Gen Pin's students and taken to Naha (1679), then published in an abbreviated version within Japan in 1681. See also the references given in Notes 26b (last paragraph) and Note 25 (first paragraph); *In the Path*, by Master Ri Jun Ji, translation of the *Tai Cheng Ju* made by Senda Ajari of Okinawa, translated into English by Y. Shimabukuro (1950) and T. Dukes (1968). British edition by Mushindokai, 1970.

It should be noted by students that the early Ju Jitsu schools contain many teachings of the original Chinese *Chuan Fa* traditions. Much later in Japan, a Jujitsu teacher named Okayama Hochiroji was credited with re-introducing the Vajaramukti method of Vyugaha—which he called simply *Atemi* (point striking). This does not seem to have been very popular. In 1850, a German doctor named Baeltz studied the art with Totsuka Senyu—one of the few contemporary masters then living. As

Figure 125. Enryakuji, head temple of the Tendai sect in Japan. (Author's collection.)

Baeltz was a Professor of Medicine at Tokyo University, he was in a position to rekindle popular interest in the art, and its continued existence in Japan at this period was due to his efforts. By 1882 there were over fifty separate and distinct schools of Ju Jitsu in Tokyo alone, and in this year Jigaro Kano formulated the art of Judo from his study of Jujitsu.

Note 34f: In Japan there are several ancient traditional lineages of Kuden: those received via the Tendai Shingon (*Tai-Mitsu Kuden*) and those received via the Koyasan Shingon (*To Mitsu-Kuden*). Both come from the Chinese lineage directly. In addition to these there are Kuden conferred within Temples unaffiliated with the previous two schools. Such Kuden are practiced by many of the Buddhist *Yamabushi* (mountain ascetics) sects of Mikkyo Buddhism. Some of these come directly from China, others are descended from independent teachers initially of the Taimitsu or Tomitsu traditions. There are a great number of such Kuden styles in Japan, but all resemble each other closely in content and form. The most important can only be conferred by an empowered master together with *Kanjo* (ritual unction). These usually take three forms and are concerned with (a) a pupil's acceptance into the lineage, (b) conferring of authority, and (c) the receipt of the Dharma spirit.

Note 34g: Indian Buddhist Sutras inscribed in Aramaic—the language of Jesus—have been unearthed as far west as Iran, Afghanistan, and Southern Russia. The interconnection between Palestine and India is thus clearly established. There is an ancient tradition of the disciple Thomas coming to Northern India and dying there after founding a church of what are now called Malabar Christians. On this note, see also *Jesus in Rome*, R. Graves (London: Cassell, n.d.) which includes an account of the discovery in India by General Gordon of a first century tomb ascribed to Jesus by the local Muslims. This tomb is extremely well-documented for the simple reason that, since the time of Mohammed, Islamic saints were buried around its precincts because of this association.

Note 34h: In relatively modern times, Dr. Sun Yat Sen revived a martial arts training center called the Li-Shang-Po Arena. Chang-kai-shek knew and approved this.

Note 34i: In the latter two accounts it is said that the inhabitants of Kapilivastu were *Upasikas* (10 precept upholders) and that only one Shakyan named Sabaka, or Sama (Chinese: *She Mo*, or *She Ma*) attacked the army of Virudaka on his own, putting them to flight. As in the previous story, he was refused entry on the same grounds, and, forced into exile he went, along with some relics of the Buddha, to a region named Bakuda (Chinese: *P'o Chu Ch'a*) where the inhabitants immediately made him a king, no doubt because of his great military prowess. The oral tradition of Nepal and Uddiyana as recorded by Hsuann Tsang states there were indeed four Shakyan heroes who drove out Virudhaka and these were banished to the North of India. One became the King of Wu Ch'ang Na (Uddiyana), another the King of Fan Yen Na (Bamyan), the third King of Hsi Mo Che Lo (Himatala in Kashmir) and the fourth became King of Shang Mi (Sambi).

Note 35: See the following publications:

The Brahmajala Sutta, translated by Bhikku Bodhi (Ceylon: Buddhist Publication Society, 1978).

Bodhicaryavatara, translated as *Entering the Path of Enlightenment*, by M. L. Matics (London: G. Allen & Allen, Ltd., 1971).

Myohorenge Kyo, translated by B. Kato, revised by W. Southill and W. Schiffer (Tokyo, 1971).

The Shorter Prajnaparamita Texts, translated by E. Conze (London: Luzac, 1973).

The Large Sutra on Perfect Wisdom, translated by E. Conze (Berkeley, CA: University of California, 1975).

The Jataka Mala Tales, translated by T. Francis and E. J. Thomas (Bombay: Jaico Publishing Co., 1970).

Jatakamala of Aryasura, J. S. Speyer (London, 1895).

Busho Gyosan (1) circa A.D. 420–500. Busho Kaisetsu. Japan.

Busho Gyosan (2) *Taisho Issaikyo* (Tokyo: National Collection of Combined Buddhist Sutras, 1924–1932). (Busho Gyo San = Buddhacaritakarya.)

Daijiten, Tokyo: Japanese Dictionary of Writings and Treatises on Buddhism.

Note 36: See the following publications:

Note 36a: *Visuddhimagga*, translated by Nanamoli Bikkhu (Ceylon: Buddhist Publication Society, 1972).

Note 36b: *A Dictionary of Chinese Buddhist Terms*, by W. E. Soothill & L. Houdous (Taipei, Taiwan: Cheng Wen Co., 1970).

Note 36c: *Sanskrit–Chinese Dictionary*, by E. J. Eitel (Tokyo: Sankusha Publishing Co., 1904; reprinted San Francisco: Chinese Materials Center, 1976).

Note 36d: *Buddha Caritakarya*, by Asvaghosa, edited by E. H. Johnson (New Delhi: Oriental Books Co., 1972). This details all extant alternative versions and dates the origins to the second century A.D.

Note 36e: *The Buddhist Attitude*, by F. Storey (Ceylon: Buddhist Publication Soc., 1973).

Note 36f: *Kukai: Major Works*, by Y. Hakada (New York: Columbia University Press, 1972).

Note 36g: *Lalita Vistara*, S. Lefmann (Halle, Germany: 1902–08).

Note 36h: *The Lion's Roar of Queen Srimala* (*Srimalsimhanada*) translated by A. and H. Wayman (New Delhi: Motilal Banarsidass, 1990).

Note 36i: *Siksasammuccaya of Shantideva*. Editor: P. L. Vaidya (Durbhanaga India, 1961).

Note 36j: *Bodhisattvabhumisastra* Editor: U. Wogihara (Tokyo, 1936).

Note 36k: *Mahavastu*, translated by R. Basak (Calcutta, 1963).

Note 36l: One should also not confuse the word *nata* used here with a much later term *natha* used to describe practitioners of Tantric Hinduism.

Note 36m: The term *nata* has varied meanings within Hinduism—in both its ancient and more modern forms. In Vedic times, under the title *Naatya*, it indicated a person who "enacted" something, usually before onlookers. It was thus intimately associated with the performance of early religious rituals of many kinds, and, over the years, this developed into lay drama. In Hindu writings, a *Nata* practitioner may be a singer, reciter of texts, actor, mime artist, or a combination of all these. Subtle differences in the spelling of the word indicate the differing roles (or arts) of their enactor. Hindu (dramatic) *nata* principles were first outlined in the South Indian *Naatyasastra* of Bharatamuni.

This treatise dates from the second century A.D. and is steeped in religious principles stressing the holiness and sanctity of the art. It describes how Brahma, in a state of meditation, drew from the four Vedas each of the constituent parts of the art. From the Rig Veda, he took its intellectuality, from the Ajurveda its music, from the Arthava Veda its emotion, and from the Sama Veda it's mime. The school which developed from this (*Bharatnatyam*) is the oldest in India. In this legend, however, we can see that nata art (or natya) was already developed and the sastra merely codifies, orients, and preserves already existing principles, perhaps because of the power of Buddhism at this time (and its espousal of its own more austere form of nata). Some of the earliest records show that those who practiced the Hindu nata were women—termed *Devadasi* (Servants of the Gods). Most areas of India subsequently developed their own dancing styles and theory, many acquiring a later reputation for debauchery which, quite unjustifiedly, lasted until modern times. There is also evidence to show that Buddhist dramatic *nata* existed around the second century A.D. and that Asvaghosa wrote at least one play for performance. This type of *nata* is mentioned in the *Vidurapandita Jataka* and the *Udaya Jataka*. See:

The Theatres of the Buddhists. H. V. Sharma (Delhi: Rajalakshimi, 1987).

Invitation to Indian Dances. Susheela Misra (Liverpool: Lucas Books, 1989).

Towards Performance, C. Choondal (Keralam, South India: Kerala Folklore Academy, 1988).

Indigenous Games and Martial Arts of India, edited by M. de Mellow (New Delhi: Sports Authority of India, 1987).

Visions of the Sacred Dance. K. C. Kamaliah (Madras: 1987).

Defensive Art of India. Dr. A. P. Singh (Delhi: Agam Kala Prakashan, 1990). This work has a useful short summary of the military history before and after the time of the Buddha.

Note 36n: Quoted in the *Indigenous Games and Martial Arts of India,* edited by M. de Mellow (New Delhi: Sports Authority of India, 1987), pp. 2–5, 2–6.

Note 36o: This shape is found in the oldest form of the Viking rune named *Ing*, which is the sixth in the series of eight attributed to the deity Tir who is the tutelary of the art of battle. The meaning of *Ing* is "renewal and transformation of one's being."

Note 36p: Nagarjuna was one of the first to focus attention upon the principles of bodily movement and elaborated descriptive terminologies which served to clarify the thinking about the theme. Some of these descriptions occurred when he came to expound upon the elements, particularly that of Space, as a physical entity (*Mahabhuta*). Briefly, he showed that there were several ways of considering Space in relation to bodily movement (*Gati*).

He distinguished generally between physical Space which had just been traversed, Space which was currently being traversed and Space about to be occupied. In terms of consciousness, movement itself was described as being of three stages—the generative (*utpada*), the continuation (*thiti*) and the fading away (*bhanga*). The manner of describing motion of the body triggered many later debates upon the notion of motion itself and several famous masters held varying views upon it.

Vasubandhu taught that all descriptions of bodily motion were in fact really descriptions of the motion of consciousness, itself, and that without an inner volition being present, an outer motion could not occur. He consequently spent many years clarifying also the "motion" of mind and all it implied. These views are summarized in his work *Karma Siddhi Prakarana*, and were re-expressed by Bodhidharma some 300 years later as the Zen doctrine. One result of Vasubandhu's teachings was that the current Abidharma-based ideas of motion were revised.

What took place when we spoke of bodily motion was shown by Vasubandhu to be a series of very fast, successive, and distinctly separate, moments of consciousness, the totality of which was perceived (incorrectly) as be a complete whole. Such a description had many philosophical implications; it showed that at any particular point in the series of mind/body movements the consciousness was amenable to change, and could potentially transform its intentions or patterns in the twinkling of an eye. It was not committed irrevocably to the end result of a series it had initiated. The work done on this theme led to many revisions in descriptions of other categories, such as those forming distinctive qualities, comparisons, intentions, motivations, colors, the nature of Citta, the three time periods, the nature of physical existence, and the capacities or descriptions of perception itself.

Given such a complexity in what appears initially to be but a simple description of visible movement, it is no surprise to realize that a bodily position or pose exhibiting physical stillness, itself, is far from being a "motionless" state of being. Even at the crude organic level, the body performs innumerable physical actions and processes, none of which are usually outwardly visible. To attain a real physical stillness is then a multi-dimensional undertaking and far from simple.

Chuan Fa's concepts of motion are expressed in many ways, the most common being that it corresponds to six elemental stages:

Earth = Resistance and Stability motion.
This is considered in several aspects (A) as adherence to bodily stances or positions, and (B) as relating to physical contact or impact;

Water = Inertia motion (i.e., a resistance to alterations);

Fire = Activating motion, which initiates (and re-initiates) activity;

Air = Momentum motion (which bears its pattern);

Ether = The gradual dissolution of physical motion.

Each of these stages has its patterning counterpart within the consciousness.

Important references to the various concepts of motion can be found within: *Karma Siddhi Prakarana* of Vasubandhu, in *Anacker 7 Works of Vasubandhu* (See Note 3); *Shoji Jisso Gi*, of Kobo Daishi, translated in *Kukai Major Works*, by Y. S. Hakeda (New York & London: Columbia University Press, 1972), and the appropriate chapter of the *Hsieh Mai Lun* (translated in the Appendices in this volume).

Note 36q: The Bodhisattva Vow can only be understood in terms of the Mahayana doctrine of immanent Buddhahood. Without this, it can seem to be simply promising something one doesn't have to give, rather like someone saying, "If I had a million dollars I would give you 3/4 of it." Until the person actually had such a sum, any promises about what he really would do with it are justifiably subject to skepticism. However the Vow is not simply a statement of intention alone . It rests upon the concept that all beings already possess the Buddha nature and can realize it within this lifetime. It is not something that is far away from the "now." Seen in this way, every person actually has the possibility of realizing it and attaining fully the Bodhisattva state.

This condition is pictured within the Lotus Sutra where there is a colorful story of a formerly rich heir to a kingdom who wanders the world living in poverty, forgetting his origins. He doesn't know that sewn in his jacket is a valuable jewel placed there secretly by his father, a jewel worth more than he can imagine. Certain authorities suggest that this parable was the real basis for the Christian parable of the "Prodigal Son." (See Note 29 of "Entering the Path" for the wording of the Vows.)

Note 37: We can see an example of this in action in some English translations of the Sutra. Starting with the incorrect assumption that the
word *nata* indicates "dancing" the Chinese terms meaning "moving
arms" are interpreted as indicating "juggling" when they actually refer
to the practice of the arm blocks and striking techniques of *nata/narya*.
The actual term used in the Lotus Sutra is *nataka* (or *naraka*), meaning
one or more who practice the *nata* (or *narya*) The Chinese characters
for the Sanskrit title *Natavajra* mentioned in the text can equally represent the term *Naryavajra*.

Note 37b: The early scriptures show many different ways of representing the titles of Buddha and his monks. He is called variously "Son of
the Shakya's," "Buddha," "Son of the Lion," "He who has arrived,"
"Son of the Arya's," "The Noble One," etc. Such diversity in title
(which exists in the original Sanskrit sutras) equally reflects in the
many titles for monks and their arts. The common Chinese compound
term *Seng* used to describe monks actually equally represents the lay
follower. Monks were also called the "Sons of the Buddha" (*Fo Tzu*),
"Sons of the Dharma" (*Fa Tzu*), "Teachers of the Dharma" (*Fa Shih*). In
addition to these, there were also titles special to a certain sect or teaching, as well as name particles which indicated the monks' national origins. (See the year 200–300 in the chronology.)

The early scriptures representing the title "Lion" (Sanskrit: *Simha*) in
Chinese used the phonetic characters *Seng* plus *Chia*. At that time these
must have sounded closest to the Sanskrit original. This particle *Seng* was
similar in form to that used to represent the Sanskrit term *Sangha* (order
of monks). Later the phonetic character for "Lion" (*Seng*) was replaced by
"Shih" meaning (in Chinese) "Lion." The earliest character for "Shih"
(Lion) was formed from the root radical for "Wild" plus a particle representing "military." These two perhaps suggested the nature of the wild
Lion. In medieval times, the character for *Shih* was replaced by another
particle *Shih*, literally meaning "teacher," with a different radical but pronounced the same. This latter term is commonly used nowadays.

Just to make things confusing, the common word for "Lion" in
Chinese and Japanese is no longer represented by a single character, but
instead by the two characters *Shih Tzu* (Japanese: *Shishi*) meaning a
"child" or "person" of a *Shih*. It seems that the suffix *Tzu*—originally
added to designate a "child" or "person" of the Buddha, i.e., a monk—
came to be understood (or misunderstood) as literally indicating the
Lion cub and was applied to describe a breed of small dogs!

Some of the Chinese title names used to designate the Lion's art
were as follows: *Seng Cha Hsiu* (Lion art), *Shih Hsing Hsiu Hsing* (Lion's
practice), *Tung Shih Hsiu Hsing* (Eastern Lion's practice), *Tung Shih
Chuan* (Eastern Lion's closed hand), *Tung Shih Shou* (Eastern Lion's

hand), *Seng Shih Fu* (Sangha Lion protector), *Shih Ch'ih Fo Fa* (holder of the Lion's protecting Dharma) and *Fa Huo* (Dharma protector). All of these terms indicate a practice coming directly from the Lion art of India. Later there were many other names and titles but it should be borne in mind that no proper Buddhist teacher would ever name the teaching or a school or group practicing it after his own name (i.e., make any attempt to personalize it).

The "Lion art" was designated in many different ways, in various parts and at different times within India. In common with Hinduism, its inner principles were termed (in Sanskrit) *Viddhi*. This word indicates the practices of a *Vidya* or esoteric art. Literally the term *Vidya* means "light" and is a synonym for many different metaphysical principles. In Chinese it was translated literally (as "light") and titled *Ming* and transliterated as *Hsiu*. This latter term was (in Japan) pronounced *Jitsu* and was the suffix added to many prefixes describing the method of a martial art. i.e., *Ju* (or *Yawara*) *Jitsu*. In the earliest times, when Japan first learned these arts from China, they were probably conveyed complete with their esoteric content intact—hence the nomenclature—however, later this was lost, or ignored, and the suffix *Jitsu* to most Japanese nowadays merely means an "art," "trick," or "method" of achieving something.

Note 38: These two terms are very similar to a pair first encountered in the Avatamsaka Sutra (*Kegon Kyo*—translated into Chinese in 643). In this there are mentioned *Hsiang Chi* and *Hsiang Ju*. The first describes the interaction and relations toward the self identity. The second describes the interaction with the sense of fusion or penetration of this identity. The two terms together describe the action of breaking down the identity of Self and Other into oneness—technically termed the *Abhisanditakayacitta* (dissolving mind and body into a unity of being). In Japanese, this is usually termed *Shinshinfuni* (Mind and Body are One) and is a famous saying attributed to Bodhidharma. In the Kegon School, *Hsiang Chi* is related to the spatial and static while *Hsiang Ju* is related to the temporal and dynamic aspects of experience.

Note 38a: The 18 Arahants of China are as follows:

1 Pin to lo pa lo to	10 P'an t'o chia
2 Chia no chia fa ts'o	11 Lo ku lo
3 Chia no chia po li to	12 Lo ch'ieh hsi na
4 Su p'in rt'o	13 Yin chieh t'o
5 No chu lo	14 Fa lo p'o ssu
6 Po t'o Lo	15 O shih to
7 Chia li chia	16 Ch t'u pan t'o chia
8 Fa she lo fu to lo	17 Ch'ing yu
9 Shu po chia	18 Pin t'ou lu

Note 38b: It is a measure of the depth of understanding prevalent within popular British and authoritative karate publications and magazines that some still express the opinion "because there were only 16 Arahants the story of the 18 Arahants must be a Chinese forgery." This opinion, blissfully ignorant of Chinese history, obviously develops from reading the Theravada scriptures (in which the 16 Arahant tradition is common). The 18 Arahants (and more) appear in the earliest Chinese histories of Buddhism. (See the year 217 B.C. in the chronology and the reference under *Fa Yuan Chu Lin* in Note 39.) Even the ordinary court records of the *Han Shu* and *Shi Chi* (circa A.D. 90) list groups of "18 Nobles." Such numerical nomenclatures were common to ancient China [Note 77].

Note 38c: The Tibetan Buddhist Professor Guiseppi Tucci in his *Minor Buddhist Texts* (See reference in Note 42c) mentions attempts to discredit even the Tibetan 18 Arahant tradition by proponents of the Theravada School in an effort to oust the Dhyana School teaching from Tibet. It seems the misunderstanding is a very old one.

The names *I-Chin Ching* and *Hsen Zui* are titles often misrepresented as being the Chinese for the *Asthimajja parisudhhi* and *Snavasjala nidana vijnapti* scriptures [see Notes 38c and 74c] and are used in many Chinese manuscripts claiming to represent (usually in a pictorial form) the physical practices taught by Bodhidharma. However, most currently available editions, although sometimes very old, are usually Taoist or folk compositions containing sequences different from those really taught and lack any spiritual doctrines of Indian origin. To those who know the original, they are easily recognizable as imitations. Such imitations often utilize Taoist terms such as *Tien Chi* (heaven and earth) which are never found in Buddhist works of any kind. Imitative versions are often the forms quoted or criticized in modern Western texts about the martial art by both native Chinese and other "experts" who should know better. Copies of the real manuscript concerning these teachings can only be found now within certain Mikkyo Temples. It is unlikely that any person except a practicing monk would get to see them. So far, reliable translations of parts of the pristine texts have only appeared within publications by branches of the Kongoryuji and Ryushinji Temples mentioned elsewhere.

It is significant that "schools" claiming to be of the original *Shaolin* (Japanese: *Shorin*) School of Tamo, whether in China, Okinawa, or elsewhere, never mention, or even seem to know of, the existence of Bodhidharma's other, and equally famous, texts concerning the *Nata* and *Pratima*. It should be obvious that there is no original Shorin School on the island of Okinawa, because all of the (many) traditions attributed to that school came from China, and all the Chinese traditions came from one Temple. (On modern claims to the contrary see the Introduction to this book.)

We should also be wary of more modern Chinese accounts emanating from Communist sources. These often present varying stories concerning *Tamo* and the *Shao Lin* which alter according to the current political thought. If the religious aspect of Buddhism seems too popular among tourists, accounts are produced in Chinese sports magazines asserting that persons other than Tamo "really" founded the *Shaolin Chuan Fa*. Sometimes these accounts name other monks prior to Tamo who—not being known so well to tourists—are "safe" and will not give rise to increased interest in spiritual studies or practices. Other accounts pretend that many different, and unknown, persons created the Shaolin tradition. Usually in such accounts, any monks mentioned are either wrongly named, of the wrong period or of sects completely unconnected with that area of China. A collection of such contradictory or misleading accounts issued in China over the period 1964–1990 is held by the author. It should be borne in mind that the present Shaolin Temple is considered a valued overseas tourist attraction by the present government.

No doubt many monks or laymen subsequent to Tamo added to or modified his teachings; indeed the surfeit of spurious schools demonstrates this, but this should not let us lose sight of the fact that *Chuan Fa* was based firmly on the early Madhyamika, Yogacara and Esoteric philosophical traditions, and only teachers of those traditions could properly understand and teach it to others. (See also Note 40a.)

Note 39: *Precedents to Bodhidharma's Dhyana Method*: Hui Yuan (334–416) and Tao-an (312–385) both actively sponsored and promoted an emphasis upon Dhyana. Tao-an collected many volumes and treatises upon the theme and wrote commentaries and explanations of them. Hui Yuan once commented that he much regretted the fact that since Buddhism had been introduced into China, there was so little emphasis upon the practice of Dhyana. He said the basis of the whole teaching needed to be firmly anchored in its practice, and that without such a foundation, the Dharma stood in danger of collapse. Buddhabhadra and Buddhasanta were both renowned teachers of Dhyana and the latter's most prominent disciple was Seng Ch'ou (d. 560).

Fo Shuo Fo Chih' Hsin Ching (Busetsubuchishin kyo). This is a sutra spoken by the Buddha upon Buddha's keeping the body in good order. It was translated (author unknown) during the Western Tsin Dynasty A.D. 265–316 (fascicle no. 31 in 2 leaves). Mentioned in the *Kai Yuen Lu* (compiled by Chi Shan in A.D. 730). The *Kai Yuen Lu* mentions this and the *Nai Shan* (infra) as Hinayana sutras.

Nai Shan Kuan Kan Ku Ching (Sutra on meditating upon the inner body): unknown translator, circa A.D. 25–220 (Han Dynasty). The Ken

Dynasty (A.D. 557–589) record at Nanking records the *Mahaparinirvana sutra* being translated by a *Tamo Pu Tai* (Dharmabodhi)—whose name is translated as Fa Chi (law intelligence). Contained in the *Chaio Yen Lu* and the *Nien Tien Lu* of A.D. 664.

Ta Mo Ta Lo Chan Ching (*Dharmottara Chaan kyo*), translated by Buddhabhadra (A.D. 308–422) of the Eastern Tsin Dynasty (317–420).

Significant Chinese Accounts relating to Bodhidharma's History

Fu Fa Tsang Yin Yuan Chih: Circa 472, this is the earliest literal Account of the 23 Patriarchs and their transmission of the Dhyana Meditation method. (See note on *Chuan Fa Chan Tsang Lun* compiled by Tao Yuan circa 1044 A.D., Kongoryuji Temple manuscript.)

Loyang Chile Lan Chi: written by Yang Hsuan Chih and completed in 547. In this text, he describes a Persian monk named Bodhidharma commenting upon the beauty of the Yung Ning Temple. This temple was built in 516, but in 526 it was damaged in a storm, and in 528 was used as an army barracks. In 534, it was destroyed in a fire. To have commented on it thus meant that Bodhidharma must have been viewing it in the period prior to 526. This indicates that the story of his first arriving in Canton in 526 as stated in the later *Ching Te Chuan Teng Lu* (*Dentoroku*) must be in error.

Shi Men Cheng Tung: this text, written by a Tien Tai School disciple of Ta'i Chi Che Ta'i Shih, circa 531–537 (aka Chih I) criticizes the followers of the Chaan sect as "ignorant of the scriptures they pretend to understand," and characterizes them as "lazy and improper followers of the Buddha's way."

Li Tai Fa Pao Chi (*Ridaihoboki*) [Taisho No. 2076] A Record of the Great Jewel of the Law: this is probably one of the texts used by the Tibetan Chaan Schools, and was found in the Tung Huang cave temples. It asserts that Gunabhadra, rather than Bodhidharma, was the first Chinese Chaan patriarch.

Nen Tien Lu (*Nentenroku*) A.D. 664.

Hsu Kao Seng Chuan (*Kosoden*) [Records of the High Sangha]: composed by Tao Hsuan, a scholar monk of the Vinaya School (circa A.D. 645). It records the existent teachers at that time and stories or details connected to them. This is often quoted in the West as if an "authoritative" source, but in fact, it is a compilation of already existent tales, stories, and legends for most of which there exists no other account. It states that Bodhidharma first entered Sung territory and then went to the northern Wei kingdom. The Liu Sung dynasty lasted from 420 until 479 which corroborates the earlier date of his arrival mentioned in the Loyang records. The record relating to the monk Sung Fu—a native of Tai Yuan in the North—says that he was a disciple and ordinee of Bodhidharma. Seng Fu left the north in 494 and traveled in the south until he died at age 61 in 524. As he was probably at least in his teens when he was ordained, this again suggests an earlier date for Bodhidharma's arrival in northern China or, alternatively (but unlikely) an earlier visit prior to his becoming a Chaan Master. It also contains accounts of the recorded sayings of both Bodhidharma and of Hui K'o mentioning that these texts were well known and used. These include accounts of the miraculous powers of the Sutra, itself, as well as the collection of his teachings known as *On calming the Mind* and *Entering the Path*, aka *Meditation of the Four Activities*. The advantage of this account is that it was not written by a Chaan partisan adherent and that it was written only 100 years or so after Bodhidharma's death. It deals with Bodhidharma as just one of many other monks of the period.

Fa Yuan Chu Lin (Japanese: *Hoenjurin*) [A Dharma Garden of Jewelled Trees] by Tao Shih, circa A.D. 668. This contains the first Chinese account of the 18 Arahants nomenclature utilized by Bodhidharma and records the arrival in Hsian Fu of Acarya Li Feng and 17 other Arahants around 217 B.C. They were imprisoned as "foreigners," but a "Golden Man" appeared outside their cell and freed them. Although we do not have any other record of this event, it is interesting to see an account of 18 Arahants, rather than the usual Theravadin 16, although an 18 nomenclature is equally ancient. Bodhidharma used exercises for monks named after the 18 Arahants. This account seems to have been either not known, or deliberately ignored by the historian Szu Ma Chien (c. 145–180) in his accounts of the period, as also by Pan Kuo in his *History of the Western Han Dynasty*, however this is not an uncommon occurrence in early Taoist historical records and texts.

Liang Su (753–793): one of the great and conservative literary figures of his time. Recorded many comments concerning the practitioners of the Chaan method. He said they taught that there is neither Buddha nor Dharma, that sin and goodness have no meaning, also that people of material desires and worldly pursuits support their aims avidly. People of weak disposition are attracted to the Chaan School because of such popular sayings and accounts, and this is why the school is gaining in popularity in China. He categorized such teachings as unskillful and dangerous for the public, as well as being heretical.

Chiao Yu Lu Written down by Chi Shan in A.D. 770.

Pu T'ai Ta Mo Nan Tsung Ting Shi Fei Lun [Treatise upon why the Southern school of Bodhidharma is Evil] by Shen Hui (700-762).

Cheng Teng Lu (*Dentoroku*) contains 1004 accounts of 28 patriarchs together with their "enlightenment verses." These are said by some to have been originally written by Chi Chang Lu of the Northern Wei Dynasty (384–534) and also by Na Lien Ya She—a foreign monk of the

Eastern Wei Dynasty (534–550). It includes both Indian and Chinese Patriarchs.

Tang Pao Lin Chuan (Horinden): written by Chi Chu (circa 801) and discovered in the Tung Huang caves. This lists 28 Patriarchs and the Enlightenment Verses. It is referred to in the Dentoroku (mentioned above) and records the handing over of the Lankavatara sutra to Hui K'o by Bodhidharma.

Sheng Chou Chi: Referred to in the *Dentoroku* (*Cheng Teng Lu*).

Li Tsu Tai Shi Fa Pao Tan Ching (*Rokudendaishihobodenkyo*), compiled by Tun Pao during the Tang dynasty (618–907). The Chinese Chaan Master Hui Neng (*Eno*) is recorded in this and gives a list of patriarchs in which he is the 33rd of a list which includes six previous Buddhas. The older Tun Huang Caves version of this scripture (*Tun Huang Li Tsu Tan Ching*) [Taisho 48] has some differences of text. Hui Neng states clearly that Bodhidharma used the Vajrasamadhisutra in his teachings. This Sutra contains the popular account of *Eno* being summoned secretly to the Patriarch's room and passed on his robe and bowl as a sign of being acknowledged his successor.

Leng Yen Chia Jen Fa Chih (*Rogakaninhoki*) [A Record of the Lanka-vatara Law Masters] circa A.D. 700. This Tung Huang manuscript by Husan Tse (Ching Chieh) has no story of Hui Neng succeeding Hung Jen, no passing of robes or of composing poems, etc. (vide: *Litsutaishi-fapaotan ching*). It considers Gunabhadra as the founder of the Chaan teaching in China. It also mentions that Hung Jen has 11 students, among them were Shen Hsiu and Hui Neng—who are both called "intelligent." This seems to disprove the oft-repeated story of Hui Neng being an illiterate, ignorant peasant.

Shizenmonku-Ki: an oral account of the transmission of the Chaan doctrine of the Tien Tai School by Chi Ko Daishi, circa A.D. 950–1127 (Sun dynasty).

Chuan Fa Chen Tsung Lun (*Denposhoshuron*) (Record of the Trans-mission of the Law in the Orthodox Sects) circa 1061 (Taisho No. 2078 p. 74) by Ch'i Sung (Ki Sun) of the Sui dynasty (960–1127). Translated circa 1064, it refers to the story of Mahakasyapa acknowl-edging a special teaching of the Buddha as being probably unfounded. It also asserts that Bodhidharma was an orthodox patri-arch and refutes the words of Shan-Ki, a sramana of the Tang dynasty (618–907), as well as the text known as *Fu Fa Tsan Yu Yuen Ching* (a history of the Indian Patriarchs) written in A.D. 472 by Tan Yao. This records the history of 23 patriarchs from Mahakasyapa to Simhanada. Bodhidharma is not mentioned here. It utilizes the Enlightenment Verses of the *Dentoroku*. Also by Ch'i Sung: *Chuan Fa Chen Tsung Chi* (*Denboshoshuki*): a history of the patriarchs and emi-nent priests of the Dhyana School.

Jen Tien Yen Mu (*Nintengenmoku*) Circa 985–1061: this "Heavenly and Human vision" by Ta Kuan T'ang Ying asserts that Bodhidharma did not use the Lankavatara Sutra at all, and that the person who translated the version by Bodhiruci was the same person who later poisoned Bodhidharma (see the Tibetan accounts for variant details).

Chen Teng Chih (*Shintoki*) [*Record of the Spread of the Lamp*] by Li Tsun Hsu, 1029.

Fu Fa Tsang Yin Yuan Chuan (*Fohozoinnendan*) circa 1004: said to have been based upon manuscripts compiled by Chi Cha Ye (circa 472) and Tang Yao of the Northern Wei Dynasty (388–534). It lists patriarchs 1–23—excluding Bodhidharma—plus the 7th, 25th, 26th, 27th and 28th of the Cheng Teng Lu. This account is used by the Tien Tai (Tendai) Chaan Sect.

Ching Te Chuan Teng Lu (*Keitokudentoroku*): compiled and recorded by Tao Yuan, a Chaan monk, in the Sung Dynasty (circa A.D. 1044), lists 28 patriarchs including Bodhidharma. It also contains the account of the "transmitting" of the doctrine by Shakyamuni to Kasyapa. The Chaan sect uses only 24 of these in its orthodox list of founders. This is the most common source of the story of Bodhidharma's meeting with the Emperor Wu, his practice of nine years meditation, and of his introduction to his succeeding disciple Hui K'o (formerly known as Shen Kuang). It also includes mention of Bodhidharma's teachings being written down and collected and an account of his *Meditation on the Four Activities*. This is recounted along with an introduction by Tan Lin.

The 5 Lamps meeting at the Source, by Ling Yen Ta Chih of the Sung Dynasty (960–1229).

Shih Men Ch'eng T'ung (*Rightful Lineage of the Shakya Dynasty*), a Tien Tai School historical work of 1237, by Tsung Chien.

Right Transmission of the Law, by Hsieh Sung, asserts that Bodhidharma took his famous "Blood, Flesh and Marrow" saying from the Vahrasamadhi sutra of Nagarjuna. In this sutra, Nagarjuna has a line thus: "Moral conduct is the skin, Meditation is the flesh and Right understanding is the bone."

Patriarchs: the Zen sect of Japan names 28 patriarchs up to and including Bodhidharma. The Tendai sect names 24, using a different list. Both lists borrow names from common Chinese sources. Most Chinese versions of the *Hsieh Mai Lun* in Japan date from the 14th century, and are said to be copies of Tang Dynasty originals. In such copies, 28 patriarchs are given; however, the Tung Huang cave excavations have yielded much earlier copies, and in most of these, 27 patriarchs only are common (as in this manuscript).

A useful catalog of all the Chinese works of the Buddhist Canon together with translations of their titles and variant editions can be found in *A Catalogue of the Chinese Translation of the Buddhist Tradition*, compiled by Bunyu Nanjio, and published by Classics India Publications, Delhi, India. 1989.

Note 40: The best and least expensive summary of the teachings of Zen can be found in *The Essence of Zen*, by Ven. Sangharakshita (London: Windhorse Publications, 1983). The history of Bodhidharma is also dealt with very thoroughly and critically in *Zen and Zen Classics*, Vol. .1, by R. H. Blyth (Japan: Hokuseido Press, 1964). The history of all the major Buddhist teachings is amply covered in *Fundamentals of Buddhist Philosophy*, by J. Takakasu (Westport, CT: Greenwood Press, 1975). Descriptions of the connections between Bodhidharma and esoteric physical trainings can be found within the references at Notes 25 (last paragraph) and 26b.

Note 40a: Other sources for Bodhidharma—as suggested in the Introduction, many modern works concerning Bodhidharma deal with him only superficially or as a legendary figure, completely missing the spiritual meanings his words record. This orientation, under the guise of textual criticism, is all too common and is an attitude copied by those in the field of Chinese studies in order to gain academic respectability or keep either their grants or tenures intact. Such attitudes are often used to promote external and materialistic concepts of Buddhism which, in turn, produce "blind spots."

One newer study of Chaan, *The Northern School and the Formation of Early Chaan Buddhism*, by J. Macrae (University of Hawaii, 1886) is a good example of this. The work is a very thorough study of texts but has relatively little concerning Bodhidharma, quoting only three Tun Huang manuscripts as its main authoritative sources, and is based upon the teachings of a Humanist professor, Seizen Yanagida. Already it has been quoted as a source to disprove Bodhidharma (see *The Eastern Buddhist*, Vol. 23, No. 1, 1990, review by W. J. Tanabe). No doubt it will be further quoted by materialistic karate teachers who are eager to discount any spiritual implications in the origins of their art.

The Chaan book mentioned above omits any mention of the influence and extent of Yogacara teaching upon Chaan, even though its lists of Chaan lineages specifically mention the famous Yogacara teacher Vasumitra. In its rare mentions, it erroneously attributes theories to the Yogacara School (page 66). Chaan can, of course, only be really understood through the medium of Yogacara teachings. In this text, the early influences of its schools are consistently ignored. The foreword (by P. Yampolsky) calls Northern Chaan "an unknown and forgotten school" (despite its tenets being taught and practiced continually within Chinese *Chuan Fa* for nearly 2000 years). Its mention of the Chaan Tibetan sources ignores all of G. Tucci's work in the field, and its dealing with the Eastern schools of Chaan omit any mention of the Korean sources so vital to understanding them. It goes without saying that all *Chuan Fa* traditions and sources are totally ignored. While the work is a good and thorough source of references regarding Chaan texts and writings, the opinions it draws from such a survey display all the shortcomings of an "outsider" to their spirit. The result is that we know little more than we did before of Bodhidharma, but a great deal of later, inter-school rivalries, all of which (as Edward Conze never tired of saying) are totally irrelevant to Buddhists. If this is the new trend in histories of Bodhidharma, be thankful we still have living monks as teachers.

Note 41: The Chaan teaching is usually summed up in 4 lines, attributed to Bodhidharma, which express the heart of the teaching as "a special transmission outside of the Scriptures; A direct pointing to the Human heart; Non-reliance upon words or letters; Seeing into one's nature and realizing Buddhahood."

Note 42: Quoted in the *Hsi Keng Chih Yu Li* (*The Records of old Hsu Tang Chih Yu*). Hsi Keng was a nickname used by Hsu Tang (1185–1226). In Japan he is known by the name Kido Chigu, which is the Japanese pronunciation of Hsi Keng Yu Li.

Note 42a: Tibet, Bodhidharma, and Chaan: It seems that both Chinese and Indian forms of Buddhism had penetrated Tibet equally by the eighth century. Indian Buddhism had come to Tibet in the form of Indian missionaries since the mid-fifth century. Two important influences were Padmasambhava, who introduced the esoteric school and was the guiding impulse for the later developing Nyingmapa sect; and Santiraksita, the teacher who organized practice of the more orthodox and Vinaya based type. He acted as a founding "Father" and advisor to the Tibetan monarchs. He came from an orthodox and impeccable lineage of teachers that included Sariputra, Rahula, Nagarjuna, Bhaviveka, Srigupta and Jnanagarbha. He consolidated the Buddhist teachings throughout the land, and later sent three of his Tibetan monks to the Vikramasila Monastery in India to bring back more. They returned with twelve Sarvastivada-trained monks who helped spread the Dharma. However, in addition to the Indian forms of Dharma, the Chinese Chaan (meditation) School seems to have been equally popular. There are many records of ordinations in this school taking place at the same time as Santarakshita's pupils. Its main teacher was known as "Hva san Mahayana."

Figure 126. A Tibetan Lama watching the practice of Chuan Fa in 1965.

Figure 127. The author teaching students at a Tibetan Monastery, circa 1968 (Kongo-ryuji Library).

The Great Debate: In common with the Chinese court of that time, Santiraksita was alarmed at the spread of the Chaan School in Tibet, as he considered it heretical. China had already taken steps to control the appearance of what it regarded as radical deviations from the scholastic forms of Chaan it sponsored, and had exiled several prominent members of its ranks. Perhaps because of such news, shortly before he died Santirakshita sent word to his pupil, the Indian master Kamalasila (circa 794) that he should come to Tibet and engage the main Chaan teacher there (Hva San) in open debate. The winner of this debate would decide which form of Buddhism would be officially sponsored, and therefore take root, in Tibet for the future.

The two schools at this time were accordingly classified into the "sudden path" (*Tun men p'ai*, Sanskrit: *Yugapad*), and the "gradual path" (*Tsien men pai*, Sanskrit: *Karamavrittya*). Kamalasila's school was the "gradual," and Hva san's, the "sudden." Both sides agreed to the debate, and so confident were they at this time that their respective schools would win, they willingly agreed to the condition that the loser should acknowledge his errors of view and present to the victor a garland of flowers and depart in peace.

As it turned out, proponents of both sides seem to have been much alarmed at the other's teachings, and after the debate, students of both parties are recorded as having committed suicide in protest at the verdicts reached. One named Nan sa mi cut his flesh into pieces. Two Tibetans crushed their genitals, and one of the Chinese teachers, called Mem go, set his head alight and died. Some of the Chinese party are said to have decided to assassinate members of the Indian. Chinese members claimed the Indians had already made a similar plan. In the *dPao gtsug p'ren ba* manuscript, it was recorded that the Chinese Chaan teacher hid some of his school's texts in a rock lest they all be killed and the teachings forgotten. It is said that three of these texts were the Lankavatara Sutra, The Bodhidharma Meditation Sutra, and The Prajna Paramita.

The records of this period are very fragmented, and we don't know for sure if the head teacher of Chaan within Tibet was actually a Chinese person or a Tibetan who had trained in China, but was known by his Chinese title. There were certainly both Chinese and Tibetan teachers of this school in Tibet at the time of Kamalasila. There also appear to be two different Tibetan noble families aspiring for a monarchical position, each supporting either side. Later accounts of these events vary according to which side's account you read, and in them each side claims to have won the debate. The later arising school of the *Gelug-Pa* (the Dalai Lama's sect) is said to have considerably edited the various (official) accounts of these events, but several alternative records exist still.

It is significant to note that from the various arguments and ideas used in the debate that the contemporary Chinese Chaan School was not like any present-day Japanese Chaan (Zen) Schools. This Chaan School used many rituals, mandalas, and other ceremonies in addition to its strict meditation practice. In this respect, it seems similar to the Chinese Chen-Yen (Shingon) and Tien tai (Tendai) Schools. Perhaps the Tibetan Chaan adherents preserved the ancient original tradition that was later lost or forgotten in China.

The founding lineage teacher of the Tibetan Chaan sect was named Akasagarbha (in Tibetan he was known as N'am m'ka Sbin Po). He claimed direct descent from Bodhidharma and was considered a legitimate successor of the Chinese Chaan Patriarch Hui Neng. That the Tibetans recorded his name in Sanskrit suggests he was an Indian rather than a native Chinese. Akasagarbha made many translations of Chinese and other sutras which are recorded in the *rNinma rgyud sbum*). In Tibet he is claimed also as a patriarch of the Ningma-pa sect. Another well-known personage of this period was called *San Si*, a Tibetan version of the Chinese term *Chaan Shi* = Chaan teacher.

Unfortunately for us, in most Tibetan accounts they refer to all the Chaan teachers as *San Si* indiscriminately, and it is not always possible to tell which *San Si* is being referred to at any particular point. This *San Si* is said to have been sent from China as part of an ambassadorial party to deliver Buddhist scriptures but never returned to China. He is said to have been a "dancer" or "movement specialist" (*nata*), who stayed on as a companion and teacher to the Monarch's son. The term *nata* was, of course, also used to represent those who practiced the Vajramukti, the original Buddhist form of Kempo. In some Tibetan accounts he was said to be the son of a Chinese princess who had married the Tibetan monarch at that period.

The Tibetan manuscripts call many teachers by the title *Hva san*, which is their Tibetan equivalent term for the Chinese *Ho Shang* or Dharma Master. Again this is a title used indiscriminately and usually without further description.

Later in Tibetan history the orthodox and the esoteric schools existed side by side along with many other sub-sects and factions, but the Chaan sect as a distinct and separate group gradually faded away, lacking as it did imperial patronage and support. A form of Tibetan Chaan was, however, preserved as a teaching within a sub-sect of the Nyingmapa School, and was known as the *Dzog Chen* method. This name is usually translated as meaning the "Infinite All-Embracing." It possessed an elaborate metaphysics and philosophy alongside its meditation trainings. It was very similar to the Chinese Chen Yen methods. According to the teachings, the world had been formed from five distinct "lights" and from these came all matter. An elaborate system of associated analogy gave birth to many of the symbols used within its ceremonies.

Color of the Five Lights	Negative Emotion	Material Element
White	Anger	Earth
Red	Attachment	Fire
Blue	Ignorance	Water
Green	Pride	Air
Yellow	Jealousy	Ether

This system of analogies seems quite distinct to the sect and doesn't correspond to lists given by Subhakarasimha drawn from the Vajrasekhara Sutra, or that of Vajrabodhi, each of whom drew, as the Tibetans, ostensibly from a common central source of esoteric writings. However, in common with the Southern Chinese sects of Chen Yen, the Dzog Chen also used mandalas of pure colors alone (i.e., without Buddha figures or symbols).

Note 42b: *Teachers mentioned in the Nyingmapa scriptures as being of the Chaan line*: Akasagarbha (Nam Ka Shin Po), Hva San Mahayana, aJug du, A dhan her, Ke hun, Dsin, sBab, Deu An, Tan bzan, Han ze, A rya rag, Bu c'un, K'a, Dsan, Len, Han, Kan, Dsi, Kam, Hyau agyeu, Gyi, Ci, P'og rtog, Jo, Yan, Han, Si, La, Ma, A mo gzon (Amogha?), Kri sron ldeu btsan, Ar na mt'ar p'yin, aDsae mgo rgyan, Li zu snin po, Yeses gyalpo, Koncog abyun gnas, Li tsu dri med grags pau ndo, dPal sbas, Nes adsum, Kar rgal, blo gros, bDos mos, dPal dhyana.

Various Lineages of Bodhidharma's students (according to Tao Hsuan)
(* = Contemporary to Tao Hsuan)

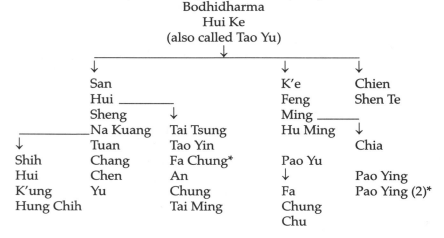

Texts recorded as being used by the above:

Form of Lankavatara Sutra used in number of books

Feng: 5
Ming: 5
Hu Ming: 5
Tai Tsung: 5
Tao Yin: 4
Fa Chung: 5 Regarded the Lankavatara as a fundamental study.
An: 5
Chung: 8
Tai Ming: 10
Hui K'e: Utilized the Vajrasamadhi, Lankavatara, and Srotthapada
          Sutras.
Chien: Interpreted the Lankavatara differently than Fa Chung.
Shen Te: Used Asanga's *Mahayana Samgraha*.

After Hung Jen, the Vajracheddika (thunderbolt slicing) Sutra was mainly used and replaced the Lankavatara. The Lankavatara sutra (*Ryogaabattarahokyo*. Taisho 16 No. 670) existed in three forms within China, these being translations from Sanskrit made by Gunabhadra, another by Bodhiruci, and one by Sikshanada. The Chinese translations appear to differ widely from that Sanskrit version used by Suzuki for his English language translation, and include mention of the mandalas and other esoteric teachings in a manner similar to the Tibetan accounts. In them, Shakyamuni speaks a prophesy that Nagarjuna will discover the "Iron Stupa" and learn the teaching of the Matrix and Diamond Mandalas, which he will then teach. It is more than likely that Bodhidharma would have used one of these Chinese translations in his teaching.

Note 42c: Tibetan Accounts of Bodhidharma's History and Teachings: A précis and new rendering of an entry found in the Potala edition of the *bKa" t'an sde lna*. (p. 19, a 1.2.3.4). Based upon a translation made by G. Tucci in his *Minor Buddhist Texts*, Pt. 2. (Serie Orientale) Vol IX. 2. Rome. 1958, pp. 375–376, 391–398. In these accounts Bodhidharma, Dharmotara, Bodhidhamala, and Dharmottara, etc., all refer to the same person.

(19,a): The teaching came to the Hva San (teacher) Mahayana, the last of the sevenfold lineage emanations which began in the person of the mKanpo (master teacher) Dharmottarala, who taught the school of "immediate entrance" to Enlightenment. Having crossed the eastern ocean he reached a country called Li Kun which is in China. Then he met the Chinese Emperor Sau Yuan. The mKanpo knew that the Emperor did not understand the true meaning. He then went to a castle called C'u. Some monks grew jealous of him and tried to poison him on six occasions but each time he was not harmed.

At last finding no place where he could deliver the teaching properly, he showed the way of dangerously entering the body. He left China for the upper land. A merchant named Bun met the mKanpo on a mountain pass called Karamatin. The Master was holding a boot in his hand.

There he (Bun?) accurately gave him back his teaching. The merchant called Bun returned to China and told the story to the Emperor, who then opened the tomb and found one of the shoes missing. All the people in China said he was a saint. . . .

(21,b) . . . The great Master Dharmottara said, "Really wide, unrelated to space, wide. When one stays in clarity there is neither self nor other. Consider the lowest ones and the noble ones as being equal; beyond the state of an unchangeable concentration.

Do not tread on the steps of the written teaching.

This we call abiding in a place which is the perfect foundation, the perfect meaning. No subjective representation, quietude, inactivity.

This is the immediate entrance into the meaning. . . . Moral conduct is No Mind, concentration is No Recollection. Non Organization of an illusory mind—this is Gnosis.

(24,a) . . . The Master of Dhyana Bodhidharmottara said, "That stillness, when the 6 vijnana move is the Dharma of the Buddha. The vijnana forms of men are illusion. (Note: This is a direct reference to a section of Bodhidharma's *Hsieh Mai Lun* preserved in Korea and China. No other trace of quotations from it are, as yet, known.)

[About Hva San]

The last successor of Bodhidharmottara is Hva San Mahayana. The main substance of his teaching is the method of Instantaneous Entrance. Having perfected this one knows many exemplary meanings, the kernel of the sutras; the kernel aiming at those meanings which are extant in writings. The extensive Chinese instructions of Dharmottara represent the authoritative tradition, the secret instructions and practices with no recourse to activity whatsoever. The Indian Kamalasila did not fully realize the meanings, the sense of which is to be determined. He (Hva San) solved the doubts of learning methods. He established the practice of reciting mantras and formulae, he laid out bridges to the Void and eliminated the narrow paths.

He erected many stupas and established great communities of ordained monks; he determined the rituals for reading and reciting the great sutras. He settled the explanations and meanings of texts during religious assemblies and the methods of aiding those in grief and the treatment of the diseased, whether close or far away. He strove for great liberality and blessings. Hva San practiced the twelve methods of the practice in the secret mantras of the great vehicle.

He received many methods of initiation. He opened many Mandalas of the esoteric realization. The method of tasting medicines, of accumulating offerings, of submitting Fire; building meditation Colleges. For all this he strove. To pay no homage to ordained monks, to communities and places of worship, to view things rejecting all traditional rules and tenets.

Such are the 12 methods of practicing the secret mantras. Kamalasila of the gradual school taught meditation on the three stages, namely learning, reflection and meditation. Hva San teaches Dhyana, the deep dhyana of inner yoga, the superior yoga.

The breathing up of the 4 Winds, the six deep Tantras concerned with reality. The 20 difficulties of Mind and the 18 states of No Mind.

Note 43: From the Esoteric point of view, the representation of Dharma in a symbolic form is, itself, an affirmation and participation within the Esoteric Path. In the esoteric branch of Tendai Buddhism (the *Taimitsu*), the Maha Mandala is the only form considered original and significant.

Note 44: See *Mudra*, by E. Dale Saunders (London: Routledge & Kegan Paul, 1960), pp. 184–191, for a brief history of this symbol. Be sure to consult E. Conze's corrections of this work as noted in *Further Buddhist Studies* (London: B. Cassirer, 1975). Conze's work contains excellent corrections and comments on many other works also cited in the notes.

Note 45: A useful discussion of this feature and its origins in Buddhist doctrine is found within *Skillful Means*, by M. Pye (London: G. Duckworth, 1978).

Note 46: The Japanese school of Shingon, founded by Kukai (Kobo Daishi) "is dedicated to support the principles that Kukai conceived" (Chapter 2, p. 27, in *Shingon Buddhism*, by M. Kiyota (Los Angeles and Tokyo: Buddhist Books International, 1978). This work is a good source for all the main Japanese Shingon traditions, doctrines, and doctrinal evaluations. See also Snodgrass (Note 56). There is, of course, also the Shingon Mikkyo tradition found within Tendai Buddhism. Founded by Saicho (Dengyo Daishi). Tendai often uses different sources than the former and includes both esoteric and exoteric teachings. The Tendai Mikkyo is referred to as *Taimitsu* while the Shingon Mikkyo is called

Tomitsu. The doctrinal rites of Tendai are described within *Homa Rites & Mandala Meditation in Tendai Buddhism,* by M. Saso (New Delhi: International Academy of Indian Culture, 1991). In addition to both of these there is also an ongoing Mikkyo tradition preserved by the Yamabushi (mountain ascetics) which, although sometimes stemming from or being connected to one or other of these two, also possesses its own quite distinct lineages of teachers and teaching. The esoteric tradition found in the Ryukyu Islands above Taiwan stems directly from China, and despite some connections with various Japanese *Acaryas,* does not fall into either the *To* or *Tai-Mitsu* classification, being more akin to the Japanese Yamabushi teachings.

At present there are some thirty plus different sects of Shingon registered with the Government of Japan as religious organizations in Japan. Others which, for various reasons choose not to register, bring this total to many more. Since 1972, many temples in the Ryukyus have been placed under control of the Japanese, and having lost their autonomy, are now counted as "branches" of mainland Japanese temples. Chinese schools of the Mi Chiao are, in present times, practiced underground.

Note 47a: If one observes the two Acaryas color order, it becomes obvious that they are the same but reversed. This directs our attention to the fact that in Subhakarasimha's source, humanity has to aspire upward toward Mahavairocana (from yellow to blue in his list), and while Amoghavajra's regards Mahavairocana in a revelatory aspect—coming downward from blue to yellow. These two different ways of regarding the nature and "work" of Mahavairocana are an important basis of the Southern Chinese esoteric traditions. Japanese schools often have different understandings of these two themes, reflecting perhaps their various sources and scriptures.

Note 47b: The *Abhidharmakosa 3,* p. 145–146 records the shapes of the "Four Continents" as being the square, circle, triangle and half-moon.

Note 48: This is recorded in the *Digha Nikaya* 2: v 99+.

Note 49: See *The Marathon Monks of Mt. Hiei,* J. Stevens (Boston: Shambhalla, 1988). Other ascetic practices are described within *Homa Rites & Mandala Meditation in Tendai Buddhism,* by M. Saso (New Delhi: International Academy of Indian Culture, 1991).

Note 50: In the Pali scriptures, the clasped hand of a teacher was termed *Acarya Mutthi.* The title *Acarya* (Chinese: *Achali*; Japanese: *Ajari*) is used today to indicate the masters of the esoteric Buddhist sects.

Whereas in Japan there are considered to be levels of *Ajari*, in China the title is used only to designate a master, and carries a meaning similar to the Theravada term, *Arahat*. It always indicates a teacher who actively pursues, by continual teaching and practice, the path he is dedicated to. It is never used to describe philosophical, purely doctrinal, or exclusively meditational teachers. The status of *Ajari* is conferred only personally by means of special rites by a suitably qualified master.

Note 51: If one is cognizant of the traditions and practices of the martial arts, a new and reoriented understanding of certain Buddhist writings can be reached. Such realization was displayed by the Mikkyo Master Kukai [Note 36f] who studied Sanskrit in China, and was the founder of Japanese Shingon. He pointed out in several of his writings that certain passages and terms in what were usually regarded as straightforward literal texts were, in fact, esoteric teachings, and that such teachings could not be understood without a "key." That key was correct revelation of the doctrine by an esoteric master (an *Ajari*). Such revelation was received at *Kuden* (oral transmission) [see Note 34f].The very same principle holds true today. Without a proper master to guide and reveal true meanings, it is possible to blunder through studies and practices blindly [see Note 32]. Such labors bring forth no fruits in the minds of practitioners. In southern China, a distinction was often made by means of name between those teachers, or teachings which lacked a spiritual teacher (these were often little groups founded by a non-Buddhist who was paid by a Warlord to train his mercenary troops) and the proper Buddhist ones. These non-spiritual schools were termed "half empty" (Chinese: *Pan-Gai*; Japanese: *Han-ko*) while the correct ones were called "perfectly full" (Chinese: *Ch'uan-Gai*; Japanese: *Zen-ko*). The *Pan Gai* term was also a pun on the Chinese word *Pan*, as it could also be understood as meaning "rice," "bread," or "meal"—a reference to those who taught anyone who paid for their meals. The terms "half" and "full" were common as descriptors in Buddhist schools of both China and Tibet. Such a description is found in the diary and notebooks of Ankoh Itosu—a Chinese-trained Kempo teacher who taught in Okinawa at the turn of the century [Note 32b]. At least one modern school in Okinawa proudly, but unknowingly, announces in its literature that it is descended from a Chinese school whose name contains the *Pan-Gai* characters! It is a sad truism that modern karate practitioners are usually the least capable of understanding their art. This is why it is vital that they are reminded of its noble and holy origins.

Note 52: Many students come to practice the *Chuan Fa* method because of injuries—to mind or body—received while practicing in despiritualized or "sport" karate. Such schools having incomplete understandings of both the nature of Kempo and the movements of the *Kata* (forms) cannot help but be what they are. Unfortunately for its students, such schools have no realization of this. The large drop out rate due to injuries or disillusionment experienced by karate clubs in many countries does not occur in a proper school—that is, one which has, and upholds, a spiritual tradition.

Many well-known Japanese and other karate teachers have abandoned teaching and taken up Chinese (Taoist) inspired exercises, such as Tai Chi Chuan, after a few years. This is usually due, not to any spiritual perception or aspiration, but simply because of joint damage, etc., stemming from the imbalanced and injurious manner of teaching movement which has been current in the karate schools of Okinawa and Japan for many years. Unfortunately, the Taoist movement methods and defense exercises are usually physically imbalanced (even in Tai Chi the body balance is maintained on only one leg) and often tactically less useful than karate. Their spiritual values, if known or taught, are inferior to those of Buddhism and have lesser, more "personal" goals, often inimical to the spirit of the Buddhadharma.

We can see that karate schools which purport to be schools of a "way" (i.e., a Karate *Do*) are usually simply ones which follow, not Buddhist teachings, but a mish-mash of allegedly Taoist principles. The basis for terming the path of karate a way at all, is itself dubious, seeing the widespread ignorance of the history of Kempo usual to karate practitioners. While there is some evidence that Chinese Buddhists spoke of a way, this was always in specific contexts and environments, none of them applicable to ordinary martial arts practitioners. As a result of my own studies, I have come across only one genuinely scriptural instance which could be cited for the application of the term *Do* to the Ryukyuan or Chinese art of karate (or *Tang Shu*, *To-De*, etc.). I will leave it for some future karate practitioner to tell me where and what this is. I am quite certain it will be many years before I am told.

Note 53: Although it is popularly understood as meaning "vapor," this ideograph in fact represents not an actual substance at all, but the relationship between two manifestations (the most and the least solid) of mundane existence. In popular understanding, a vapor of substances, like the steam from water, indicates a process of departure from one form of manifestation to another, and subtle form. As steam is the essence of water, so *chi* is the essence of the physical organism. In actuality, *chi* indicates the relationship between the different forms of animate, inanimate, and spiritual life. Healing was, in fact, a study and application of this relationship, rather than being simply a physical art. Although such subtleties were often lost on the ordinary practitioners, with the arrival of Buddhist methods, they were highlighted and examined far more closely.

Note 54: We can see that within India the two systems of energy and points co-existed. The *Prana-Chakra* pair were used in describing spiritual evolution, and the *Jivat-Marma* pair related to the therapeutic evolution. Although these two systems are quite clearly distinguished from each other, later—and also more modern Western works—often fail to recognize it. We can find books telling us that "prana energy is for healing," or that "the marma points can be used to manipulate pranic force."

Note 55: Most of the quotations indicated, or points discussed, can be found within the following selection of significant works and resources.

Chandyoga Upanishad. Ananadasrama Series Vol. 14. Poona, 1902.

"Vajra in the Rig Veda" by V. M. Apte, in *Annals of the Bhandarkar Oriental Research Institute*, Vol. 37, 1956, pp. 292–295.

Vinaya Pitaka. 5 Vols. Ed. H. Oldenburg, London, 1879–1883.

Mahajima Nikaya. 3 Vols. Ed. V. Trenckner & Lord Chambers, PTS, London 1889–1899.

Samyutta Nikaya. 6 Vols. Ed. L. Feer. Pali Text Soc., London, 1884–1904.

Satapatha Brahmana. Ed. A. Weber, Berlin-London, 1855.

Atharva Veda. Translated by Dr. M. Lindenau, Berlin, 1924.

Aranyaka Parva. Ed. V. S Sukthankur. Poona, 1942.

The Mahabharata (contains all the "Parvans"), available in a number of editions.

Rig Veda [*Hymns of the ancient Rig Veda*], translated by R. H. Griffiths, Benares, 1916–1917.

Vedic India. G. S. Ghurye, Bombay, 1979.

War in Ancient India. V. R. Dikshitar, Madras, 1948.

The Art of War in Ancient India. G. Date, Bombay, 1929.

Ancient Indian Warfare. S. D. Singh, Leiden, 1965.

Wu Ching Tsung Yao [Essentials of the Military Classics], Tseng Kung Liang, Sou K'u Ch'uan Shu, China.

Si Yu Ki [A Buddhist Record of the Western Kingdoms], Hsuen Tsang. This covers the period A.D. 629–645. Translated by S. Beal, Trubner & Co., London, 1884.

Nan Hai Chi Kuei Nai Fa Chuan [A Record of the Buddhist Religion], I. Tsing. This covers a period from A.D. 670–695. Translated by J. Takakasu, Clarendon Press, Oxford, 1896.

Fa Kue Ki [A Record of Buddhistic Kingdoms], Fa Hien. This covers a period of Indian/Chinese history from A.D. 399–414. Translated by J. Legge, Clarendon Press, Oxford, 1886.

Note 56: A useful account of the development and changes made to the early tradition of Buddhism by the Theravada School can be found within *The Ideas and Meditative Practices of Early Buddhism*, by Tilmann Vetter (Leiden: E. J. Brill, 1988).

Two very interesting and thought-provoking works, each taking a somewhat different view of the mind/body realm, can be found in the following: *The function of the Orgasm* by W. Reich (London: Panther Books, 1968); and *The Body*, by Yuasa Yasuo (State University of New York Press, 1987).

By far the best visual references in English concerning the mandala structure and contents is *The Matrix and Diamond World Mandalas in Shingon Buddhism*, by Prof. A. Snodgrass (New Delhi: Aditya Prakashan, 1988/1989). The author has several other informative works upon esoteric architecture and ritual—all recommended. Tendai sect mandala are discussed in the work listed in Note 49.

Note 56a: The equivalent of this term in Chinese is *Chih Yu Chieh Yuan* and in Japanese *Chigu Ketsuen*. These two terms mean "a fortuitous meeting or opportunity" with the Dharma.

Note 57: Mentioned in the article by Tskumoto Zenryu within the Journal *Tohogakuho* No. 3, 1941.

Note 58: "Selfless" expression is on the whole accomplished in Buddhism by working for others without reward, but this category can also indicate situational encounters within which only a selfless response is adequate. Such situational expressions occurred in both Chaan Buddhist encounters and in the application of Kempo. These were the main reasons for the introduction of sparring practices between fellow students.

"Self" expression usually indicates the fulfillment of duties and responsibilities toward others, such as is incurred, for example, in teaching or in being a healer of body and mind. Kempo tradition also has a unique practice of dramatic mime (called in Japanese *Kagejitsu*) in which participants have to enact certain set situations. These methods are very old and predate certain very modern forms of psychology which are now beginning to use similar methods called "psychodrama."

The formal movement sequences of Kempo known in Okinawa as *Kata*, based upon the four elements, are another method oriented toward self-revealing (Sanskrit: *Pratyanubhavati*) internal environments [see also Note 68].

Note 59: Mandala Paradigms: The ancient Chinese masters spent much time analyzing the various interconnections between different areas of activity, seeing each as a reflection of the other in another form. Chinese healers also used lists of paradigms called *Ping Li Hsing* (Correspondent activity) to diagnose the causes of disease, epidemics, or sudden death. These charts were highly secret, each teacher devising his own, but we can see traces of them in some of the esoteric Buddhist works pertaining to the mandalas in which the various Buddha knowledges are related to colors and mantras, etc. This chart outlines the fruits of some sixteen plus years of inter-relating such accounts into various other forms and manifestations, and by its use you will be able to see the same activities in other forms and understand how they relate to your own condition or state of being. Some of these are listed in the appendix of Mandala paradigms (page 391).

If you consult this, some simple examples as to personal temperament can be drawn, i.e., if you are highly flexible in body you will also incline to be mentally adaptable, you would value your family and friends, be inclined to jealousy and sorrows. You could naturally attain expertise in blocking techniques of *Chuan Fa* and become a capable defensive fighter. The meditations of compassion or visualizations would appeal most to you. Another and different example: if you suffer from frequent accidents or illnesses to your arms, you would also have disorders of the teeth, your thoughts would be easily disturbed and your usually keen concentrative skills would suffer. In overcoming personal problems you would tend to ignore any minor illnesses or discomforts, and try instead to be of service to others. Your best meditation would be either the development of the supernormal mental faculties or those involving study and learning. The practice of mantras would bring you better health and resistance. In *Chuan Fa*, hard training would bring you joy and you would incline to practice the *Hsings* involving clever tactics, jumping kicks, and close in fightings.

Note 60: In Japan the title *So Hei*—the transliteration of *Seng Ping*—was unfortunately appropriated and used incorrectly during medieval times to describe the warring groups of (nominally) Tendai and Shingon sect monks of Mount Hiei.

Note 61: There are many stories of how the Ryukyus developed its interest in the seminal disciplines that culminated in the art of karate. A native art called *Te* (hand) is popularly said to have been the earliest, but this sounds like an over-simplification. From the 12th century onward, China has had various interests in the islands, including the right to approve its monarchs, so it is likely that various forms of weaponless art came from there along with traders and missionaries. Japanese Buddhist monks in the 15th century acted as spies for the occupying Shoguns, so they are an unlikely source. In certain Ryukyuan family histories there are records of Chinese monks coming to teach and these monks knew Chuan Fa, but such teachings were only personally delivered, and to the majority of Islanders they were unknown. The manuscripts of the Itosu, Otomo and Kin families show that there was regular travel to and from the Chinese mainland for purposes of study and some Ryukyuan islanders were members of Chinese Buddhist temples that practiced *Chuan Fa*. The family of Otomo has been connected with the Okinawan Monarchy since the time of Sho En (15th century) and descendants served as personal bodyguards to subsequent monarchs, residing and teaching at the Sogenji Temple. It is said that an Otomo was responsible for introducing the Chinese design that became the Ryukuan national and monarchical flag (*Ryukyu kokki*).

In modern times, the Ryukyuan art of *To De* (karate) has mostly succumbed to commercialism and foreign influences, differing markedly from what it was even prior to World War II. Certain religious and semi-nationalist factions exist to offset this state but, being uncommercial, are largely unknown to the present generation of Ryukyuans who seem more concerned with getting visas to work abroad than studying their own culture. Unhappily this situation is likely to continue for some time. It is a fact that certain forms of older Ryukyuan Karate are found better preserved in Japan and the West than in their homeland. Some now only exist in Taiwan with emigrant Mikkyo monks.

Note 62: For some interesting modern discussions concerning the implications of defense, retribution and/or revenge, see the following works:

a: *The Morality of Terrorism*, by C. A .J. Cody. *Royal Institute of Philosophy Journal* (RIPJ), Vol. 60 No. 231. Jan. 1985.

b: *The Purposes of Retribution*. A. Manner. *R.I.P.J.* Vol. 60, No. 232, 1985.

c: *Relativism & Moral Complacency*, H. Unwine (R.I.P.J.).

d: *Liberty, Benificence and Involuntary Confinement*. J. C. Callahan. (*RIPJ*).

e: A useful statement of the Buddhist principles and concepts regarding the governing of a nation, its peoples, and its laws in relation to them can be found in Note 72m.

f: *Early Buddhism & the taking of Life.* I. B. Horner (Kandy, Ceylon: Wheel Publication No. 104, Buddhist Publication Society, 1967).

g: *Aspects of Buddhist Social Philosophy,* Prof. K. N. Jayatilleke (Kandy, Ceylon: Wheel Publication No. 128/9; Buddhist Publication Society, 1969).

Note 63: See "The Definition of Person" (Note 6c) and also "Mind Reactive & Creative," a lecture delivered by Ven. Sangharakshita to the Reading University Buddhist Society, circa 1967/8, published subsequently by the Friends of the Western Buddhist Order, Surlingham, England.

Note 64: "The Concept Of Eternity." J. Zeis in *International Journal for the Philosophy of Religion* (Leiden: M. Nijhoff Vol. 16, 1984).

Note 65: "Two Pathologies," A. Hawkins in *The Journal of Medicine & Philosophy,* Vol. 9, No. 3.

Note 66: A useful and inexpensive overall survey of the development of Chinese medicine and is found within *Chinese Medicine,* by P. Huard & M. Wong (World University Library-Wiedenfield & Nicholson, 1968). See also the Japanese work, *Ishinpo,* created by Tamba Yasunori in 982. A copy was printed by Taki Genkin in 1854. and is an interesting collection of mainly pre-tenth century medical texts from China. An English translation is available by E. Hsia, I. Veith & R. Geertsma under the title *Essentials of Medicine in Ancient China & Japan.* 2 Vols (Leiden: E. J. Brill, 1986). Near death experiences are considered within "Self, Near Death and Death," C. Cherry. *International Journal for the Philosophy of Religion,* Leiden: M. Nijhoff, Vol. 16, 1984.

Note 67: See *Chaos & Cosmos,* H. E. Plutschow (Leiden: E. J. Brill, 1990).

Note 68: The significance of the Two Truths drawn from within experience was first clarified by Nagarjuna, who sought to explain, as did Origen, why things appear to be other than they are, especially with reference to certain doctrines. He termed these two aspects of reality *Laukika* (worldly) and *Paramartha* (ultimate) *Satya* (truth). The *Laukikya* is also known as *Samvritisatya* (conventional truth). Their representation in the Mikkyo scriptures required special forms of symbolism, for here they are presented as experiential situations rather than dry doctrine. These situational presentations necessitate and acknowledge an awareness of simultaneity of multilevel being within a moment of consciousness. To express such moments is difficult (and unnecessary) for their realization is built upon inner experiences and peripheral forces or factors irrelevant to anyone else but their experiencer. Instead of attempting to describe such inner states, the Mikkyo Schools sought to recognize the situational environment in which such moments could reoccur in order to overcome and integrate any aspect of them which could be attributable to unskillful states of mind. A practical path of self de-illusioning arose as a result of this approach which used various means of symbolic and/or cathartic mind and body activities to pierce the fog of *Samsara* into which we are all born. This path was, in fact, the original impetus for the Bodhisattva Vajramukti.

Note 68b: These principles are dealt with thoroughly within the first book ever published in the English language in Europe about Japanese and Chinese esoteric Buddhism. *The Sourcebook of Shingon Buddhism*, by Shifu Nagaboshi Tomio. Cambridge: Kongoryuji Temple, 1973; reprinted Hakurenji (1975) Kongoryuji (Norfolk) 1980; British Shingon Buddhist Association 1989–1990.

Note 69: It should be borne in mind that the "King" (*Rajah*) Asanga mentions, may actually refer to one's own mind. The designation of mind by such a title is common to many of the esoteric texts (i.e., the Samadhiraja Sutra. Kukai, the Shingon master, often wrote of "the King of my mind" when referring to his own nature. In such a case the "government" could be understood as the associated mental *Klesa* of that individual and the "revolution," *Paravritti*.

Note 70: The best current study of the Warrior Emperor Asoka and his life is *The Legend of King Asoka*, by J. S. Strong (Delhi: Motilal Banarsidass, 1989).

Note 70a: In Ksatreya terminology, this Sutra name means "Queen Srimala's Warrior Lion's Battle Scream." Note also the earlier paragraphs in this section mentioning the translation of the word *mala* or *malla* as "wrestler."

Note 70b: Recent (1989–1990) archaeological discoveries in Korea have unearthed a previously unknown temple of an Eastern Mountain sect, and this could be one connected to *Chuan Fa* practice. It should be noted that Korea's close proximity to Northern China meant that many teachings which died out in Hopei and other Northern areas—such as Sung Shan—were preserved unchanged in Korea. This is one of the reasons that Chaan Buddhism (known in Korea as *Son*) grew so dominant there. I am certain that, as years go by, we shall find traces of many *Chuan Fa* practices and doctrines preserved in its temple records and monuments, which have been ignored by most researchers in the field.

Note 71: In the 1930s, perhaps sensing the coming danger to their art, masters in the Ryukyu Islands founded a semi-secret organization known as the *Ryukyu Koshirenmei* (Federation of Masters of the Old Tradition) sometimes called the *Tatekai* (Protecting Shield). This sought to preserve and record much of the ancient language, doctrines and ways of practice. During World War II it organized anti-conscription movements and was persecuted by the Japanese. After the war, it was accused of being communistic (because of its connections with mainland Chinese teachers and monks) by the governing authorities and was banned. Its members subsequently refused to participate in what it viewed as the "westernization" of Ryukyuan Karate and cultural tradition. Some members later helped organize the anti-Japanese and anti-American riots staged during the 1972 political and military "takeover" of Okinawa by Japan. Fundamentally nationalistic, royalist, and anti-Japanese, it includes the post-war survivors and representatives of the oldest families and their *Chuan Fa* schools, serving as the silent conscience of an independent and traditionally based Okinawan nation. It functions somewhat like a beneficent freemasonry. Many members of this organization furnished valuable sources to me in my researches and studies, but even nowadays they wish not to be acknowledged by name.

Note 72: Other references and sources of information used are:

a: References within *The History of the Dharma in Tibet*, by Ven. Lama L. Gya (Dharamsala, India, 1970). This manuscript was prepared especially at the request of the author. These were supplemented by information and comments given in the notes taken by R. H. Brunton during his tour of the Ryukyus and given in Vol. 4 of the *Transactions of the Royal Asiatic Society*, London, 1876.

b: Teachings and conversations received/recorded in 1965 by the author from Ven. Dragpa Dorje (State Oracle of Tibet). Translations by other lamas.

c: Interviews and discussions with Ven. Trungpa Rinpoche and other Lama teachers during 1967–1968 *Chuan Fa* seminars at Samye Ling. See also Note 20e).

d: Discussions with Ven. Vorasak Candamitto concerning his Thai boxing skills and studies, Buddhapadipa Temple, circa 1969–1971. Discussions with Phra Imm Sumangalo at Buddhapadipa Temple, circa 1972, and at Kongoryuji Temple, 1974.

e: Authors interviews: 1) with Sensei M. Oki and colleagues while resident teacher at the Hakurenji Temple, 1976–1977 concerning the origins of the Uechi, Shorin, and other schools of Karate in Okinawa; 2) while representing the Chinese Yoga Federation and teaching at the Zinal (Switzerland) conference of the European Yoga Federation. 1975. Also discussions with Master Z. Shimabukuro and colleagues, Naha, Okinawa, June, 1966; written communications with Professor Lokesh Chandra (India), 1990–1991; written communications with Dr. N. Varandani concerning the native martial traditions of Kerala, India, 1990–1991.

f: Discussions with Senseis, T. Hironishi, K. Yamanishi, M. Obata, T. Marushima and H. Kimura while resident at Hakurenji Temple. 1976–1978.

g: Lecture/discussion to members of the Naha Dojo by Ven. Shingon Kyoshi J. Tanaka, Myoshinji Temple, 1986–1988.

h: Discussions with Ven. Hyun Ho (Korea), Ven. Abbess Kuang Wu Li of Jong Kak Sa Temple (Korea), and Ven. J. Myung Soong of Unmunsa Temple (Korea), 1976–1977, while guests at Hakurenji Temple.

i: Teachings, discussions, classes and written communications with Sensei Shuzo Okada, Japan and Great Britain, 1965–1979.

j: Documents and other materials either copied, donated or loaned me by members of the Ryukyu Tatekai at Ryushinji Temple, Okinawa, 1965–1967, and elsewhere by the Dokuritsu Ryukyukoku Renmei.

k: Informal discussions with Sensei Dokyu Nakagawa at Jerusalem Mushindo Kempo Dojo, and Jerusalem Center for Zen Studies, Israel, 1972.

l: Discussions with Kyudo Roshi of Ryutakuji at Hakurenji Temple, 1976, 1977.

m: Article titled "The Social & Political Strata in Buddhist Thought," by Ven. Dr. S. Rinpoche in the *Maha Bodhi* (India) October, 1974, discussing the "Sarthavaha Jataka," "The 7 Evil Deeds of Body and Voice Permitted the Bodhisattva," the "Dasdachakra Kshitigarbha nama Mahayana Sutra," the "Nagaraja BheriGatha" and the "Arya Bodhisattvacharya-gocharaopaya Vishaya Vikurvana Nirdeshanama Mahayana Sutra."

n: Discussions with K. Nagamoto of Rishokoseikai (Japan) at Hakurenji, 1975.

o: Discussions with K. Kinowaki, leader of Koyasan University Students Union at Hakurenji, circa 1975–1976.

p: Discussions with Sensei Ozawa (Kochi University) at residential seminars of Cambridge University Mushindo Kempo Association and at Hakurenji, 1973–1976.

q: Discussions with Ven. Terasawa (Nichiren Shu) (Japan), at Hakurenji, 1977.

r: "Woman and Religion in the Ryukyu Islands," Rosamund J. Bell, unpublished M.L. Thesis, 1984, for Oxford University.

s: Rekidai Hoan records of ancient diplomatic and other relations of the Ryukyu Islands and its monarchs. See also A. Kobata, *Concerning the Rekidai Hoan*, Kyoto, 1963, and *Ryukuan Relations with Korea & South Sea Countries*, Kyoto, 1969; T. Miyata, "Tarosai Gosai," The Shimazu Clans' 1609 expedition to the Ryukyus (regarding the Rekidai Hoan account), undated typescript.

t: Nakajima Ankoh. *Okinawa Issennen Shi*, Tokyo, 1923.

u: R. S. Spencer. *The Noro or Priestesses of Loo Chu*, Tokyo, 1931.

v: S. Sakamaki, "Ryukyuan Names," monographs on and lists of personal and place names of the Ryukyus, Honolulu, 1964. See also *Ryukyu*, a bibliographical guide to Okinawan studies; P. Beillevaire, *Le Sutsu Upunaka de Tarama Jima*, description d'un rite saisonner et analyze du symbolisme spatial sur une Ile des Ryukyu, Japan, 1982.

w: W. P. Lebra. *Okinawan Religion, Belief, Ritual and Social Structure*, Honolulu, 1966. One of the few sympathetic accounts of the Ryukyus and their peoples. The author properly distinguishes the Ryukyuan form of Chinese/Japanese dialect and highlights the growing subservience of the islanders to the all intrusive Japanese culture.

x: Li Hsieng Chang. The Faith in Mat Tsu—tutelary goddess of navigation in the Ryukyus, 1961 (typescript photocopy, no ref.).

y: *Ta Pei Chugoku Nen Bu*. Notes, accounts and collected manuscripts of Master Otomo Yuta and others (Ching and Ming Dynasties) Otomo Family Archive. These include excerpted copies from the Ryukyuan temple records called *Urasoeki* and *Sogenjiki*, and the Imperial Guard Record (the *Sho Go Ki*).

z: *Wu Hsin Tao Lu (Mushindoroku)*, a manuscript collection and compilation of ancient records and contemporary annotations originally brought together by Otomo Nogunto in China around 1580 and added to by his family and students subsequently. It includes his travel documents and notes titled *Chang Tang Lu* ("the Longer Chinese records," Japanese: *Chotoroku*). This constitutes the basic and most authoritative record of the Chinese and Ryukyuan spiritual *Chuan Fa* and associated traditions, and includes Chinese family accounts of Shuri and other areas along with records and documents of the Sogenji royal temple in Naha secreted away prior to World War II: Ryushinji Temple Organization Archives (Okinawa). The original manuscript was taken to Taiwan for safety in 1972 and stored away. Certain sections have been copied and published.

Note 73: It is not generally known that one of the important examination requirements undertaken by an aspirant Dalai Lama to ascertain he really is an "emanation" of previous ones is the precise and accurate performance of the traditional sequences of the Lama movement sequences and dances. These clearly exhibit a variety of classical *Chuan Fa* maneuvers. The same is true of the traditional Japanese *Gagaku* dramas. Taken from Tang Dynasty Chinese traditions, they also preserve ancient movements of hand and leg which any person familiar with *Chuan Fa* would instantly recognize.

Note 74: Drums or bells were often used in religious services to indicate the ending of certain periods or activities. The drum was especially useful outdoors and where a large number of people needed to be able to hear directions clearly.

Note 74b: It is important to understand the differences between the many ways of translating *pratima* or its equivalents in Chinese. As was common with many Sanskrit terms introduced into China, the linguistic representation for *pratima* underwent several changes and variations. Initially it was simply phonetically represented, but later the word *Hsiang* was chosen to represent it. *Hsiang* indicates an image, shape, sign or picture of something. In Japanese *Hsiang* is pronounced *So*. It is also used occasionally to represent a Buddha image; the usual term for an image being *hsing* (Japanese: *Kata*).

    Later Chinese translated the Sanskrit term *rupa*—also used to represent an image or form of something in general—by the character meaning color (Chinese: *se*; Japanese: *shiki*). This character seems to have conveyed much more then than it does now and such usage of the character *se* to represent "form" can cause confusion. Such interchangeability also occurs in the various different Chinese translations of Sanskrit texts, and one may find many different combinations of characters used in the same text for the same thing. What is not so obvious is that the words *hsiang* (*zo*), *Hsing* (*kata*) and *se* (*shiki*) refer to different aspects of the creative process involved in forming "shapes." The word *rupa* in Sanskrit refers to an "image" formed through the assemblage of a number of previous components into a contemporaneous common characteristic, hence its use to describe the component and fixed factors or attributes of human consciousness. Inanimate things can also have a *rupa* in that their actual physical shape can represent, or call to mind, an image of something else. In this sense, a Buddha statue has, or is, a *rupa* for it acts as a static mnemonical of the Buddha's attributes. The term *pratima* refers to a form or image produced only or mainly by a dynamic interplay between its component factors, hence usage of the term in Chinese and Japanese words such as *Hsiang Hsiang* (Japanese: *sozo*) meaning "imagination" or visualization. It refers to a shape created by actual involvement of the onlooker in its creation. Though the result may be the same (e.g., one may build a religious image both physically or mentally), the process involved is different. The form indicated by *rupa* is, as it were, inherited or previously existing, whereas the "form" indicated by *pratima* is actually initiated by those involved with creating its result. In *Chuan Fa* one can have the "karma (activity) form" (Japanese: *jozo*) of a *pratima* and a *rupa* (static) form (Chinese: *pu tung hsiang*; Japanese: *fudozo*) of a *pratima*. This latter represents the total "image" or mnemonic the *pratima* embodies—such as the symbols found in the mandala—and was also called its *Li* or Principle. The "activity form" of a *pratima* indicates the actual movements themselves which form the *pratima*, in much the same way as various colors form a painting. I suspect that familiarity with such a distinction was the reason the ancient translators used this unlikely character indicating "color" to approximate the meaning of *rupa*. Such subtleties, which can be conveyed in Sanskrit, are not always so obvious in Chinese.

Note 74c: The two *pratima* mentioned are therapeutic (*Kriya*) yogas which each approach the practice of inner purification in the different manners indicated in their descriptive title. These are also used in traditional (Vedic) medicine and were employed by the famous Doctors Susruta and Charaka. These *pratima* names embody many principles of Ksatreya medicine and healing, which, at first sight are not obvious, and in order to make them clear I shall discuss these names and their various levels of meaning as they are taught within the *Wu Hsin Tao Lu* [Note 72z]. I give here, also, the Chinese and Japanese terms for the meanings of these names. (There are several other titles for these based upon phonetic representations.)

Snavasjala-nidana-vijnapti (Chinese: Shao-wang-pen-yuan-chihshih; Japanese: Sho-O-honyen-chishiki)

Snavas is a term of ancient (pre 500 B.C.) Indian healing and refers to the finest of the three forms of *Nadi* (channels, flows or veins) in the

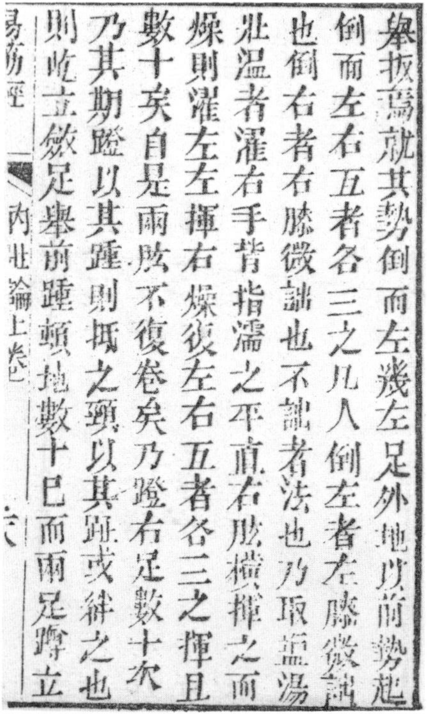

舉扳爲就其勢倒而左殘左足外地以前勢起
倒而左右五者各三之凡八倒左者左膝微誦
也倒右者右膝微誦也不誦者法也乃取鹽湯
壯溫者濯右手背指濡之平直右肱橫揮之而
燥則濯左左揮右燥復左右五者各三之揮且
數十矣自是兩肱不復卷矣乃蹬右足數十次
乃其期蹬以其踵則抵之頸以其趾或絆之也
則屹立斂足舉前踵頓地數十已而兩足齊立
易筋經 內壯論上卷

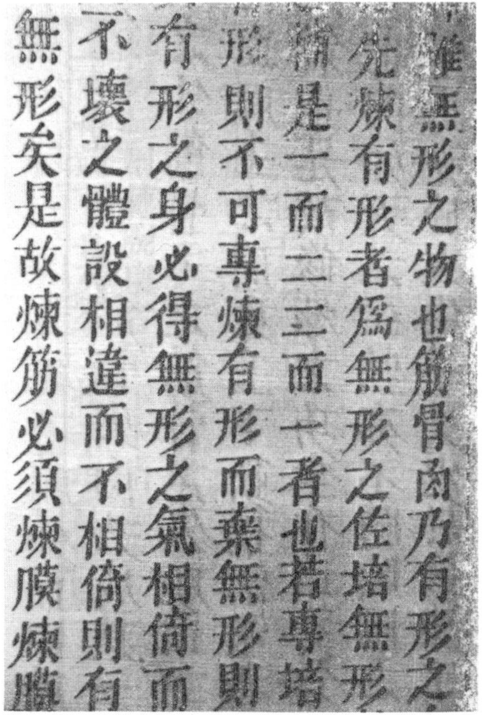

雖無形之物也筋骨肉乃有形之
先煉有形者爲無形之佐培無形
精是一而二二而一者也若專培
形則不可專煉有形而棄無形則
有形之身必得無形之氣相倚而
不壞之體設相違而不相倚則有
無形矣是故煉筋必須煉膜煉膜

Figure 128. Left: a 19th century Taoist forgery of Bodhidharma's Astimajja Parisuddhi *(Kuzui Chin Ching). Right: a page from a copy of a temple original, brought into the Ryukyu Islands during the 1490's. (Kongoryuji Temple.)*

human body. There are three forms of *Nadi*: the thick (*Dharmanis*), the fine (*Sira*) and the very finest (*Snavas*) and each deals with a different aspect of bodily harmony, and interconnection or communication. The term *Jala* means a net or, in this case, a "network" (The "Brahmajala Sutra). *Nidana* is a medical term meaning "causes" or "connected events." *Vijnapti* means "knowing" or "correctly discerning and determining." This Yoga refers to the development of a subtle perception of the body in which its currents and networks of energy are recognized and can be utilized in diagnosis (also *Nidana*) and treatment (*Kriya*). Such treatment is also applied to non-human entities (i.e., ghosts and spirits), and was employed in metaphysical rites resembling exorcism. One of Bodhidharma's reasons for teaching this Yoga is clearly to encourage the monks to become aware of the physical condition of their bodies in such a way that they would no longer mistreat them.

In addition to the therapeutic sense of the *pratima*, there exists also its paradigm or parallel meaning as a metaphysical doctrine. In its Buddhist doctrinal explication, the Yoga is concerned equally with developing an acute awareness of the cause and effect of personal events, as was taught in the doctrine of *Pratitya Samutpada*. The particle *Jala* refers to the "Net of Views"—the mind obsessed with questions, answers, opinions, and intellectuality. The particle *Snavas* represents the *Vasana* (subtle scent-like influences) of mental *Klesa* which lie dormant, but potentially active, in the deepest levels of consciousness. *Vijnapti* means "perceptible" or "recognizable" to consciousness.

Asthimajja parisuddhi (or Visuddhi)
(Chinese: Kuzui-Ching-Ching; Japanese: Honesui-Sei (or 'sho')-Jo)

This title literally means "Bone (*asthu*) marrow (*majja*) cleansing and purification" (*parisuddhi*). Long before Western medicine had arisen, the Ksatreya Vaidya (healers) taught that the elements of Fire and Air combined in the marrow to create, or revitalize, the blood. The marrow was therefore considered to be an important source of life energy.

If the marrow became imbalanced, the balance of the body's elements (*dhatu*) would be thrown out of order and, in turn, all the bodily functions suffered. In addition to the blood, the physical vital energies also were held to "mature" within the marrow, and thus the marrow was a point of contact between the different energy systems of this, and other, worlds. To "purify the marrow" indicated participation in a regime of balancing therapies designed to renew and rebuild the physical and mental well-being. Due to the metaphysical view of energy (Ether) it also indicated a spiritual catharsis or rebirth. In the Buddhist sense, this Yoga indicated the "evolution at source" of the subject which constituted the basis of spiritual progression and knowledge. For nonbelievers, it meant recognition of the Buddha's teaching and conversion to it. To a monk, it indicated an overcoming of the mental barriers and impurities (*Klesa*) which obscure wisdom. It is in this sense that the categories of "blood" and "marrow" etc. are also mentioned in Shantideva's *Siksa Sammuccaya* [see Note 4], a work completed around 691–700. (Nagarjuna's *Vajrasamadhi Sutra,* being written in the first century A.D.) Bodhidharma's usage of this practice seems to have been his way of teaching the Shao Lin monks that a basic re-appraisal of how they implemented their trainings should be undertaken. First the primal basis (marrow) had to be established clearly and then its concomitants (*Jala*) maintained correctly.

A proper appreciation and understanding of these teachings seems to have been preserved only within the *Chuan Fa* healers and practitioners. At a much later date, probably around the 12th century and thereafter, Taoists produced manuscripts of this esoteric training under various names and titles, the most common being crude mis-translations of *Asthimajja parisuddhi Kriya* as "Bone Washing" (*Hsien Zui Ching*) and the *Snavasjala-nidana-vijnapti Kriya* as "Prognosing the Veins" (*I Ching Ching*), this latter using such an obviously Taoist term (vide the I-Ching divination text) it is astounding that anyone with a knowledge of Buddhism could ever pretend it was Buddhist.

These names are probably attempts to represent the meanings of the original Sanskrit into Chinese, not after being taught them, but after hearing them spoken of. Given this context, they represent a very rough approximation of the original, although the rendering of *vijnapti* as "I" is misleadingly incorrect. The suffix *ching* (scripture) in the Taoist inspired names refers to the manuscript containing details of the practices. Both the Chinese translations of the originals have associated texts but these are properly titled *Lun* (discourse) and *Shih* (writings). Whoever thought up these titles obviously wished to enhance their status by calling them a *sutra* (*ching*). (See also Note 91 on *Visuddhi*.) Explanations of the significance of the movements in both these *pratima* can be found in references found in Notes 25,26, and 20.

Note 74d: *Pseudo schools*: In later times, parts of the monastic training system were plagiarized by Taoists and others who formed "schools" based on their own personalized ideas. As such groups possessed no Acarya lineage (*Gotra*) or spiritual family (*Kula*) they had no means of accessing either its inner teachings or its vast experience. As a consequence, such groups could only develop versions of the physical techniques involved in the *pratima* and nothing else. As the number of such variations is strictly limited after one or two generations, every school could do nothing better than imitate its contemporaries. Such obvious facts are the main reason the Taoist "schools" failed to develop any unique and evolutionary spiritual system.

Ranks: It is not generally realized that the system of according colored belt ranks to differentiate between various levels of skill stems directly from *Chuan Fa's* Buddhist practices. Originally Chinese monks wore different forms of ritual stoles (*Kasaya*; Japanese: *Kesa*) to signify their temple rank or duties at various times. This practice was adopted by the monastic *Chuan Fa* practitioners to indicate the special forms of training each student was undergoing. Modern Japan uses a system of six levels (now reflected in the training suit belt forms or colors) to designate various levels of student, and this number is based upon the Mahayana Buddhist doctrine of the six spiritually "perfecting practices" (*paramita*) outlined in the *Bodhicaryavatara* of Shantideva. (The colored belt system of designating ranks is also nominally used in Japan within mundane skills such as flower arranging, driving a car, swimming, etc.)

Chuan Fa uses the older system of ten levels, relating to the ten "stages of the Bodhisattva Path" described in the *Dhasabhumi Sutra* and the *Avatamsaka Sutra*. Kukai—the founder of Japanese Shingon—based his *Jujiron* (ten stages treatise) upon this idea, as did the Japanese Kegon sect and its derivatives. Unfortunately for many modern practitioners, the "rank" system has lost all its spiritual meaning and has developed merely into a form of proclaiming a practitioner's competitive achievement and/or a means of legitimizing either "authority," exhibitionist tendencies, or financial ambitions. This is, of course, far from the original purpose of the art. It is well to remember that no master in either modern secular Okinawa or ancient Buddhist China ever achieved a high ranking because of fighting skills, physical prowess, or financial expertise.

Note 75: It seems obvious that even at its crudest level the art of self defense requires the application of many different movement possibilities, and that no one animal can be used as a basis for this. Even the powerful tiger can only bite and claw its victim. Claims that this or that method is based upon the movements of any particular animal should therefore be treated with extreme caution. It was for this reason that the Vajramukti utilized the Satyasiddhi tenet of recognizing the principle embodied by many different animals. The misunderstandings common to those who sought to comprehend the meanings of the elemental and/or animal symbols of the original Vajramukti can still be seen in present times. One current Taoist school claims to have been founded by a Buddhist monk who based its movements on a fight he observed between an ape and a praying mantis! Another that its tenets stem from observing the movements of ants. Even the more serious Taoist schools often claim to be descended from Buddhist monk teachings and use Chinese names such as *Lohan Shu* (Arahant hands), *Dot Mor Chuan* (Bodhidharma fist), etc. Such claims beg the question as to how such Taoists can claim to be practicing a Buddhist art and still be Taoists as there are fundamental differences that cannot be reconciled, in both aim and viewpoint, between the two great traditions. It is very important for potential students of *Chuan Fa* (*Kempo*) to ask themselves such questions and be clear about the proper aims of both Buddhist *Chuan Fa* and Taoist philosophy.

Note 76: I have made extensive researches into this title in a search for possible alternative translations but it does not appear to be a Sanskrit or Tibetan title of any traceable Buddhist sutra. However, if a pure phonetic, it could represent Sanskrit words meaning either places, activities, or birds equally. Other possible alternatives seem to be that it represents either *Thathagati* (*Ta Ta Ga Ta Ga Ti*) or *Thatha-Gati*.

The first term means "the goings—or activities—of a Buddha(s)." The particle "Gati" indicates the goings in/arriving or goings out/departing of someone. In Vasubandhu's texts, it is used frequently to indicate activities of movement in both body or mind. The word Thathagata, used as a synonym for the Shakyamuni Buddha literally means "He who has arrived," or "He who has just gone," and is explained as referring to the coming into enlightenment or the departing from ignorance of a Buddha. The second possibility of *Thatha-gati* means "essence" or "spirit of" (*thatha*) + *gati* (as before). The two deities mentioned are equally untraceable. In the Chinese *tripitaka* (scripture collection) there are some similar titles for sutras (i.e., *Katurdaraka samadhi* (Meditation of [or for] the Childish), translated by both Dharmaraksha in the Western Tsin Dynasty (265–316) and Gnanaprabha. There is also the *Kutushka nirhara* (Sutra of the Four Dharmas) of Siksananda, but neither is relevant here. Both these works are known in Tibet. Two other similarly named works are simply mantras for relieving afflictions of the eyes. Some other possibilities for these names in Sanskrit are:

Ka-chu-ri: "dakini" (female celestial being); the female form of *Catura* (below).

Ka-shi-ma: *Catura*—one of the twelve spirits of the Buddha of Medicine; *kasina*—a colored device used for meditation; *Garjita* (thunderbolt); *Simha* (Lion).

The two titles could have originally been one long term thus: *Ka-chu-ri-ka-shi-ma-* Acaryasimha (Acarya's Lion).

Often in Sanskrit, the endings "i" and "a" refer to a male and female pair of things/qualities, or deities, so in this they appear to accord with Sanskrit grammar. Warring and fighting deities are known in Sanskrit as *Asura* and inhabit one of the six realms of existence.

Note 77: *Han Shu* of Pan Ku (c. A.D. 90) Published as *Han Shu Pu Chu*, Ch'ang Sha, 1900; reprinted I Wen Co., Taiwan, 1965. See also *Shi Chi*, a study of K. Takigawa (*Shi Ki Kaichu Kosho*), Tokyo, 1934. A study of these classic accounts and their eighteen noblemen, etc., is included in *Tung Pao* Vol XXV, LIVR 1–3 (Leiden: E. J. Brill, 1989).

Note 78: "Bhagwan Bhaisajyaguru Vaiduryaprabhasa purvapranidhana visevavistara." Translated by Hsuang Tsang (*Taisho* 14: Vol. 450). Other translations have been done by Chi Yu (A.D. 317), Hui Chian (420), Fa Hang (c. 580), and Yi Ching (690). Translation by Chow Su Chia, Taiwan: Buddhist Cultural Service, 1962. See also: *Li Fa Hu Fa* (Treatise on according with the Principle) by Ching la Shih. MSS. Translated from Chinese into English by K. Yasuka, 1950. Partially reprinted in the *Journal of Mushindo Studies* (Naha), 1967, Mushindokai, 1970.

Note 79: One famous Japanese practitioner of the "Five Element" healing system was Sogen Ishizuka, who studied with Chinese monks in the 1880s. He is credited with first discovering the significance of sodium and potassium in the human diet. His teachings were followed by a number of contemporaries and a modern offshoot of his teaching was followed by Sakurazwa Nyoti—better known in Europe as Georges Ohsawa, the founder of the Macrobiotic system of dietary regulation. Ohsawa introduced the arts of both Judo and Aikido into France in the 1920s and regarded them as essential complementary disciples to the study of healing arts. The Macrobiotic system is, however, not a purely Buddhistic one, but includes many Taoist features and principles. Much of the European literature produced by Ohsawa and currently available is "missionary like" in its polemic and zeal, and easily misinterpreted. The contemporary Master of the earlier system was my own teacher, Shuzo Okada. His form of macrobiotics is followed by practicing Kempo students in modern times. See *Ryorido—Buddhist Dietary Healing*, by N. Tomio (Cambridge: Kongoryuji Temple, 1973; reprinted London: Mushindokai, 1987, 1988).

Note 80: In our modern times of iatrogenic disease, environmental, dietary, and mental pollution, such life styles assume even greater significance and meaning.

Note 81: Modern China has devised a synthetic practice based upon various aspects of Buddhist Shugyo and Yoga practices allied with Taoist life-prolonging exercises which it calls *Chi Kung*. This art is now promoted and popularized to Westerners as an ancient practice. It is mainly ignored by most of the population who insist on doing their "primitive" *Tai Chi Chuan* and *Pa Kua*. Needless to say, *Chi Kung* lacks any spiritual basis—whether Taoist or Buddhist—and is but one more in a long line of modern "health exercises" produced by the current Chinese authorities.

Note 82: This situation is but a microcosm of the confrontation taking place every moment within the mind, which is assailed by stimuli from the senses, each clamoring for pre-eminence and attention. The multiple levels of consciousness have to make thousands of immediate decisions and resolve intercommunicative conflicts throughout its existence.

Note 83: See *Art and Ritual in Ancient Greece*, by Jane Harrison (London: Book Club Associates, circa 1985). This contains some very interesting descriptions of practices, and the reader will be able to see just what the "chorus," "orchestra," and "actor," really indicated to their originators.

Note 84a: Contained in the *Kongokai hachijuichisan daimandara* of Ennin (792–862) and brought by him from China. This is the form of the Mahamandala used in the Tendai sect. Animals are also described in the *Kongocho Giketsu*, quoted in Toganoo (infra) p. 199.

Note 84b: Other references and texts mentioned are as follows.

All references "T" indicate the *Taisho shinshudaizokyo* collection of the Chinese Buddhist Sutras held in Japan, edited by Takakasu, Ono & Watanabe (100 volumes), Tokyo: Taisho Issaikyo Kankokai, 1924–1932.

Mikkyo Daijiten, Vols. 1–3, Ed. S. Matsunaga (Kyoto: Naigai Press, 1931–1953).

Mandara no Kenkyu, Toganoo Shoun, Japan: Koyasan University Press, 1937.

Kongochokyoyuga Juhachieshiki (A short explanation of the 18 sections of the Kongochokyo), Taisho 18, No. 869, p. 284ff. [*Kongochokyo = Tattva samgraha Sutra*].

Gobushinkan (Meditation upon the five assemblies of Buddhas), a description with illustrations of the *Sarva thathagata tattva samgraha*. See

A 9th Century Roll of the Vajradhatu Mandala, by Lokesh Chandra (New Delhi: Aditya Prakashan & Indian Institute of World Culture, 1986).

The *Dainichikyo* is found as Taisho 18, No. 848, under the title *Mahavairocanabhisambodhi vikurvit adhistana vayipulya sutrendra rajanamadharmapayaya.* The last, though not very satisfactory, version in the English language is *The Mahavairocana Sutra,* by Chikyo Yamamoto (New Delhi: International Academy of Indian Culture, 1990). This is based on the A.D. 725 version of *Subhakarasimha & I-hsing* taken from the Chinese. This version contains a useful summary of other editions in Japan by Lokesh Chandra. A more recent study of texts by A. Wayman compares an English translation by A. Chakravarti of the first chapter of R. Tajima's Japanese translation of the *Dainichikyo,* and a summary of the remainder, with a Tibetan equivalent scripture. Published as *The Enlightenment of Vairocana,* by MLBD, Buddhist Tradition Series Vol. 18, Delhi, 1992. An excellent translation into English of Vol. 3, together with I Tsing's commentary, has been made by Hiroshi Murakami in *Tantric Poetry of Kukai Japan's Buddhist Saint,* by H. Murakami & Morgan Gibson (Thailand: Mahachulalongkorn University, 1982). Available from PO Box 212, Frankfurt, MI 49735, USA.

Tai Tsung tseng ssu K'ung Ta Pien Cheng Kuang Shih [T:52].

San tsung Shih Chuan La [T:55].

Note 84c: *Tsu Chih T'ung Chian* of Szu ma Kuang (Hong Kong: Chung Hua Shi Chi, 1971).

Note 85: One should recall the point made previously about the common misinterpretation of the term *nata* as "dance" (Japanese: *bu*) instead of "ritual movement." In Japanese Shingon texts, the character for "dance" was often used to represent the Chinese for *nata* even though the context suggests that this rendering was inappropriate.

Note 85a: The term *Sthana* has many and complex interpretations; however, I here briefly show the various ways in which it is employed within *Chuan Fa.*

A *Sthana* represents the sum total of the physical and mental effects of the *Klesa* (See Note 2g) in terms of an individual's understanding of consciousness. It is an instinctive pre-conscious "stance" vis-à-vis an individual's inner and outer realms of being. It is not, therefore, a viewpoint emanating from a "viewer." It is, instead, the result of a dynamic interplay between the mental and physical *Klesa* of any given moment. There are several forms of the term used in *Chuan Fa:* 1) *Citta Sthana* or *Pudgala Sthana* are terms that refer to the orientations assumed by a person's mind, and which create the means or method by, or through, which the person prefers to be known or approached. Although a person may create an image or, as the Ancient Greeks termed it, a persona, of him/herself to him/herself and/or to the world at large, such an image is the result of a conscious act of will. This very "will" and the persona itself have already been "filtered" by the pre-existent *Klesa*. It is by coming to recognize the constituents of this form of the *Sthana* that one can become aware of the nature, influence and extent of the *Klesa*. 2) *Kaya Sthana*: The physical reflections of the *Citta Sthana* modify the actual posture and kinesis of the body, itself, as well as its current forms of muscular and metabolic homeostasis. These, in turn, create the distinctive individual physical *Sthana*. The "way" in which a person moves his or her body is in accordance with both the body's inherited and created capacities and capabilities. These in turn derive, and are modified by, the qualities of the mental stimuli the person initiates toward them.

The qualities of those stimuli are reflected in the patterns of an individual's movements, and these, in turn, modify the appearance and tone of the physical shape and growth. If a negative *Klesa* predominates in the present consciousness, so the mental *Sthana* will modify to reflect it, and this, in turn, will reflect within the physical *Sthana*. Physical and mental illness is one obvious result of this.

Kaya Sthana is also of a latent, inherited form in that the term abstractly describes the "seeds" of physical *karmas* held in the *alaya* of the individual.

All *Sthana* are subject to the normal Buddhist distinction as being comprised of two aspects: 1) *Visaya* (as perceived by others), and 2) *Alambana* (one's own internal image of one's *Sthana*).

Note 86: This technical term had also been adopted by the Vaibhasika sect to represent and describe the apparent and dynamic "shape" of a visible entity.

Samasthana as Tactic: Such was the nature and structure of the balancing forces inherent within the *pratima* that certain external manifestations of their *samasthana* experience could, albeit momentarily, be expressed in actions. Such manifestations could often appear in the midst of complex situations created especially by the teacher for that very purpose. Typically these would be situations involving a simultaneous set, or sets, of problems, which required immediate but opposite actions on the part of the student. The student's response to such situations revealed what degree of attainment he or she had reached. Such "tests" were a common feature applied later in *Chuan Fa* history. The only equivalent in the non-physical Buddhist arts was the doctrinal debate in which eminent teachers engaged to mutually criticize each other's tenets for edificatory purposes. Such debates still continue in many traditions. Within *Chuan Fa* such test encounters were most easily created by placing students within a situation of self defense involving multiple and simultaneous attacks upon him (her) and for him (her) to successfully defend him- herself against all of them without mistake. (We should also bear in mind that this was not by any means the only type of environment suitable for such tests.) Such encounters could appear impossible to solve, or could involve multiple decisions for which there simply wasn't enough time for them even to be held "in mind." The "ordinary" consciousness could not adequately deal with this situation.

At a certain level, it was possible to solve these quandaries, but only by engaging a form of consciousness very different in nature from the ordinary, and one emanating directly from what was termed, among other things, the "unborn mind" (Chinese: *fusheng hsin*; Sanskrit: *anutpada citta*). The awareness developed through the attainment of the *samasthana* was held to be conducive to the "unborn mind." The whole situation is one very similar in nature to that involved in the Chaan sect's *Kung An* practice, where a student is set a theme to "solve" and reports the "solutions" to the Master. Like the *Kung An*, the *Samasthana* is not an answer, it is the process of wholeheartedly engaging in the demands of the search, itself, which often encourages the breakthrough in consciousness.

Note 86a: By way of a very basic and hypothetical example, we could consider the progression of new students as encompassing the following progressions. When first practicing the *pratima*, ordinary students would first view the movements as purely physical techniques. Later they would think about what they were doing—that is, what kind of attack they were a defense to. Even later they may come to learn of the movements as ritual gestures (*mudra*) and ponder their meanings and explanations. Eventually they would consider the idea of a "self" defense and thus consider the role of the "self," both in the actual process and as an entity in its own right. They would then consider the patterns of self within their life experiences, etc., and perhaps the causes for the life experiences being where and how they were. Later the students may begin to ponder the actual causes of their own existence. This may lead to a stage where former mental habits and activities have begun to change and more usual conceptual activity begun to display a more calm and insightful condition. Within such a condition students could experience *Samasthana*.

Note 86b: In the Buddhist meditation tradition, each of the many themes involving mind or body was the subject of a special meditation practice of its own, such as the mindfulness of the body, etc. In such meditative practices, the themes were usually dealt with in successive stages, progressing from basic to more complicated themes. In the case of *Samasthana*, the process was simultaneous but progressive, i.e., both mind and body were considered simultaneously, but at various levels or depths of completeness. These stages were gradually deepened as the practice was perfected. Such a method is not new, for it is implied in all the meditations without specific themes—that is, general awareness practices which, by their nature, can encompass many different things in succession. In the case of *Samasthana* it is simply a more precise generality.

Note 87: We should always be very wary of those who dwell in that dualistic mentality obsessed with the idea of the "rightness" or "wrongness" of things. Buddhism does not use such concepts. Throughout its history there have been many different canons of teaching drawn up by the various sects, and (in most cases) these were done simply to accredit works to the correct authors—which is what is literally meant by "authentic." This process still continues in present times. Shakyamuni Buddha in the *Kalama sutra* had long taught followers that they should accept no written word, saying, or tradition simply because it was so, but should, instead, test out a teaching in the light of their personal experience. That which could not be understood was therefore replaced by that which could.

In such a sense, the teachings are made real (realized). This has nothing to do with whether a written teaching is authentic or not, or whether it was included in any "official" canon. In general each sect developed and used its own canon, and this altered over the years to accord with the various practices which grew current within the sect, itself. No doubt there were some works which were produced exclusively within China, but this does not mean that they were "wrong" or had no value. To those who know, the Sutra's teachings that have no place in Buddhism are easily discernible, and history has shown over and over again that Buddhists are seldom hoodwinked. The tolerance of Buddhism to "newer" scriptures is but a reflection of the earliest attitudes where certain teachings were held to be universally true, but others required interpretation. It was commonly held that anything which was well-spoken was the word of the Buddha. Such a concept may bewilder those familiar with the Christian and other Semitic theological values embodied in such concepts as heresy. Useful references are as follows:

Chinese Buddhist Apocrypha. Ed. R. C. Buswell, Jr., University of Hawaii Press. 1990. Contains many useful bibliographies and critical evaluations of Chinese Buddhist sutras and catalogs of the scriptures, and suggests the sometimes ad hoc, or political reasons, for the classification of a Sutra as official or not. It also suggests that many of the texts in the Taisho Tripitaka collection are wrongly attributed.

The Eternal Legacy, by Sangharakshita (London: Tharpa Publications, 1985). A masterful work and highly recommended to those new to the field of study. The author shows clearly that Pali is not a language at all, and dispels many other myths concerning the teaching. Contains a useful bibliography.

Buddhist Sutras, by Kogen Mizuno (Tokyo: Kosei Publishing Co., 1982). A useful and detailed introduction to the wide variety and range of Sutras. Useful Bibliography of Chinese and Japanese Sutras.

3 Unknown Buddhist Stories in an Arabic Version, by S. M. Stern & S. Walzer. Oxford: Cassirer, 1971.

See also Elaine Pagel's work (Note 8) for a similar situation in the development of the various Christian "canons" within the Gnostic, unorthodox, orthodox and heterodox sects, and Conze's essay "Buddhism and Gnosis," in *Further Buddhist Studies* (Oxford: Cassirer, 1975).

Buddhist Thought in India, Edward Conze (London: Allen & Unwin, 1962). Reprinted with corrections 1983. All and any work by Conze is recommended.

A History of Buddhist Philosophy, by D. J. (Kalupahana, Delhi: Motilal Banarsidass, 1994).

Moral Dilemmas in the Mahabharata, B. K. Matilal, ed. (Delhi: Motilal Banarsidass, 1994).

Note 88: Several modern *To De* (Chinese Boxing) schools of the Okinawa Island in the Ryukyu Islands use a form (*Kata*) they call the *Sanchin*, although it is, in some cases, entirely unrecognizable as the original. Nor is it taught in such schools as a spiritual practice. The Shaolin (Shorin) *Chuan Fa* was supervised by the monk brothers Li Tsun San and Li Tsun Yi, both students of the Lineage Master Ching Fa Shih in southern China. Their tradition was studied, via students, in part by Itosu and Miyagi—both well-known pre-World War II teachers.

Li Tsun Yi's student Chang Shi Pai was sponsored by several local Buddhist supporters (including English Tea importers) and he taught many foreigners and non-local residents including Cho Tzu Ho, who is claimed to be a teacher of the founder of the Okinawan School now called Uechi (high ground). From observation of their movement patterns, it is fairly simple to see that Miyagi's practice derives from a fire/water orientation, and Uechi's from an earth/air teaching. Both

Miyagi and Uechi would have been shown something of Sanchin's correct form, but neither seems to have taught it to others, and instead, presented a hybrid and simplified version to their fellow Okinawans. Such simple versions were also used by the Ryukyuan teacher Kenwa Mabuni in the Japanese school he founded, and in several other schools founded by similarly expatriate Okinawans.

Neither Miyagi nor Uechi was granted the *Kuden* (see Note 34f) connected with performance of the Sanchin or its associated practices, due probably to the short time they studied, and the fact that they did not enroll as monks. Within a generation, even the form of the movements they taught were changed by subsequent teachers of their school. (Both these teachers' histories are detailed in the *International Journal of Mushindo Studies* for 1962 and 1965). It is interesting to note that the public school in Okinawa, which claims to be a direct descendant of the Chinese Shaolin (Shorin) style does not even know or teach the *Sanchin Hsing* or its associated studies. Another more modern school in Okinawa is also known as Shorin, but its name is spelled in different Chinese characters to that of the Shao Lin. It is also pronounced as Matsubayashi. This school claims to be based upon the teachings of one Matsumura, said to have been one of the bodyguards to the Ryukyuan Monarch in the 1700s and presumably familiar with the Chinese tradition of *Chuan Fa*. The Otomo records of the Monarch's bodyguards for this period never mention him in such a status, nor does the *Itosushi*, *Kempohishu*, or the *Mushindoroku* (see Notes 25,34b,e). There is no *Sanchin hsing* in this school. As stated elsewhere, there are private Shorin (Shaolin Szu) schools in the Ryukyus, which take great care to both preserve the Chinese proper forms and to keep separate from commercial or foreign-oriented organizations. Prior to World War II no Okinawan *To De* teachers were permitted to teach adults until they had attained a grade of at least 5th *Dan* or higher. Many of the emigrants who set themselves up as teachers outside of the islands had not reached such a grade, nor indeed had the many "masters" who appeared in Okinawa after World War II and were eagerly followed by the foreign troops stationed in the islands. See "Okinawa in New Hands," London: *The Guardian Newspaper*, June 23, 1972 for a Ryukyuan public expression of this attitude. "Politics in Okinawa since the Reversion of Sovereignty from the U.S. to Japan in 1972," a lecture by Prof. T. Egami (Ryukyu University), presented at Nissan Institute of Japanese Studies, Oxford, Great Britain, February 18, 1994.

Although modern Okinawans find it embarrassing to discuss, we should bear in mind that the traditional, royalist, and nationalist Ryukyuans regarded all such emigrants to Japan as traitors, who by their very actions, proved themselves unworthy and unqualified to be teachers. An interesting study of the mentality of karate practitioners can be found within *Martial Arts and Psychological Health,* J. R. Fuller, *British Journal of Medical Psychology,* No. 61, 1988, pp. 317–328. The author—needless to say—is an Aikido practitioner. He notes a report stating that few teachers take on the burden of helping their students outside of the *dojo.* This study, which quotes US and British written and film sources equally, unfortunately does not know of the existence of Mushindo Kempo, nor of the famous BBC2 TV documentary concerning it. One cannot help but feel that if he had, he would have been a little more optimistic concerning therapeutic benefits. The book includes a useful list of contemporary sources.

Note 89: The *Sanchin Hsing* is said to "work" at the physical level by intensifying the energy body of its practitioner. It draws in power from the surrounding environment which can then be redirected. It is said that perfection of this practice enables the practitioner to speak with animals, to make the body become lighter in weight, and to emit bright light. Another side effect, and one also mentioned in the Theravada scriptures, is that it enables a practitioner to create a *Manokaya* (mental body). This "body" is able to be sent outward and oversee events occurring a long distance away. In some circumstances, it is able to manifest itself to onlookers (as in the case of the Vemacitra story mentioned earlier). Such a "body" is not the "astral body" of psychic literature, and its usage is not regarded as a supernatural power, but simply as an advanced attribute of the properly developed spiritual consciousness. Such abilities, generally termed *Siddhi* in Sanskrit (Pali: *Iddhi*), are well-attested all through Buddhist scriptures, and in other religious literature (see Notes 64, 65, 66). The main purpose of the "energy body" lies within the field of the healing arts where its force is passed on, or in, to those suffering serious illness. It can achieve results similar to Acupuncture, but without any needles, and from a long distance away.

Note 90: In esoteric Buddhism each Buddha of the Mandala is accorded a tutelary color, and such colors often serve as a reference to the type of qualities or orientations being described or considered. White is the color ruling the Buddha Amoghasiddhi, who in turn represents the Buddha most skilled in Enlightened action. It is no surprise that it is this Buddha's color which occurs frequently in the descriptions of the arts and practices of both Buddhist *Chuan Fa* and healing. The presence of this term often serves as a clue to a researcher that what is being taught refers to physical matters or activities which have evolved from, or are based upon, a study of the esoteric mandalas.

Note 91: The Sanskrit word *Parivritti,* used to describe the processes of inner revolution and change of consciousness, literally means "turning," "completing," "complete(d)," "all including," or "round." *Vritti* (or *Vartana*) means "transforming," "evolving," or "changing." It was transcribed at first phonetically as *Pa-Li-Fa-Li* but wasn't really accurate enough, and later a proper transliteration was made, which in Japanese became the term *Rinhen.* The particle *Rin* (Chinese: *Lun*) means "revolving around like a wheel," and was also used to describe the Wheel of Dharma (*Dharmacakra*). The particle *Hen,* meaning "transmutation," or "transformation," is used in descriptions of the transformation body of a Buddha. This being the third of the esoteric sect's "Four Bodies of Mahavairocana."

A key to understanding what this term conveyed in the original Sanskrit lies in its earliest meaning as indicating "complete," for this conveys the idea of fulfilling a task or course of action. This is how it was understood in early Buddhism. The "turning around and transforming" of the consciousness enabled it to fulfill its task of attaining or realizing its intrinsic and original enlightened condition, a state seen in the esoteric teachings as underlying all humanity.

Most uses of the prefix *Pari-* in a Sanskrit Buddhist technical term refer in some manner to this principle of "returning to the natural condition of enlightenment." We should also recall when seeing such terms that often they refer only to a certain stage of a process or evolution. If we think in terms of the three "times" (past, present, and future), we see that any state of change undergoes at least an initial preparatory stage, a transitory stage and a completion stage. In such an example, the *Parivritti* used within *Chuan Fa* describes the middle stage of this process. The term as used within the *Yogacara Sutra* describes the last stage.

The term *Visuddhi* is used to describe the attainment of, or active involvement within a process to attain a state of "purity," i.e., a liberation from the causal forces or habits creating suffering. It can refer to a physical or mental stage. It does not mean free from "sin" or "evil," in the sense implied in theistic systems of belief. It is really a synonym for the initial process or stages of the *Parivritti* mentioned in the previous note.

Note 92: *Kayaka Manas* (Chinese: *Shen Hsin*; Japanese: *Shinshin*) is a general, overall term describing the effects of the various bodily generated stimuli that serve to perpetuate the continuity (*Kayasantana*) and homogeneity (*Kayasambhava*) of the physical being and life force (*Jivat*).

Note 93: According to Vasubandhu in his *Abhidharmakosa 9,* a manifest bodily action contains the following processes—impulse (*Chanda*) followed by initial mental application toward an effort (*Vitarka*), which produces a series (symbolized by the air element), which in turn sets the body into motion. This evolution is summarized and revised within his later work titled the *Karma siddhi prakarana* (Discussion of the Demonstration of Activity). This work of his amends the view of motion as being the "meaning" or "principle" of the air element, and the idea that motion, itself, is a "real" distinct event in its own right. For Vasubandhu, air can only be "responsible" for making a fresh event arise in another locus if it represents an event occurring immediately subsequent to a previous event, which itself is related to the fresh event by constituting its homogenous cause. Thus what actually takes place when we speak of "motion" is a continuous series of mental perceptions which have as their focus a series of visual changes taking place elsewhere, each of which is entirely separate from the other. For Vasubandhu, motion begins and ends within the *Manas* alone. The term "motion" simply and loosely summarizes the visual perceptions of the end results of this *Manas* process. This is exactly the view taken by Bodhidharma in his *Hsieh Mai Lun*.

Note 94: Genetic codes, however, are only descriptions of certain physical results of the patternings, and not the patterning tendency, itself, nor its source.

Note 95: Certain observable patterns of the body give obvious clues as to their source—i.e., a scar tells of an injury, a developed musculature "tells" of physical practice—other more subtle patterns do not. Some physical abilities, or inabilities, come about as a direct result of mental states and forces. By removing the mental sources of such states, a corresponding physical liberation from the impairment occurs. This is how the practice of meditation can heal or improve the physical body. The subtle body patternings correspond to the Skhanda of Consciousness, forming its totality and character. However, unlike Skhanda they are not created by conscious volitions (See Note 93 on the air element.)

Note 96: Vasubandhu applied an "Ockam's razor" technique to all the spiritual terminology he encountered in a manner similar to Nagarjuna. In discussion with his colleagues, he posed the question, "In that meditational attainment characterized by the total and complete cessation of all feelings and all consciousness, what is it that reasserts consciousness after the practice?" "As there is no mental basis or object for consciousness to arise dependent upon, why is it not the case then, when all forms of mental activity totally cease [which is what this actual meditation consists of] the practitioner does not cease to live?" This query was posed, not to find out the "answer," but to highlight popular misunderstandings of the descriptive factors involved. The subsequent replies in the records of such dialogues demonstrate the various contemporary ideas concerning the bases and supports of consciousness bereft of its usual stimuli. Some of these descriptions involve a "body (or organic) consciousness" as the support for its reawakening after such an attainment.

Vasumitra, in his *Pariprccha*, held that materiality moments could also serve as such a stimulus, and a similar position was noted by Asanga in his *Mahayanasamgraha*. The principle of a vicarious functioning of the body for the mind in such cases seems well established although often ignored (see the following notes). Anacker's perceptive translation of Vasubandhu's *Karmasiddhi Prakarana* details the various interesting and complex ideas about this question.

Note 97: Vasubandhu accepted the body/mind patterning occurring as a result of "professional or artistic activity" but does not explain this further. This category covers the bodily and mental skills developed as a result of the continued physical demands of an art. Such a category includes the art of *Chuan Fa* and highlights a certain type of description little used within most forms of Buddhism (see next note). The movement patterns of the organs simply functioning in their own right (such as eye movements, etc.) were regarded as being of an indeterminate karmic quality.

Note 98: If the reader refers to Table 7 (page 292) laid out in the first section of this work it will be seen that I have deliberately sectioned consciousness into three forms, namely: b) Body-to-Mind; c) Mind and Body; and d) Mind-to-Body. To be complete (but not shown in the chart) there should also be the category of a) Body-to-Body preceding it; and e) Mind-to-Mind succeeding it. Ordinary Buddhism tended to view the body from a passive, recipient position and emphasized explanations of how the Mind views itself, and how it then interacts with the experience of the body (categories e, d and c). All these views begin *from* the Mind and orient *to* the body. *Chuan Fa* deals also in category a and b.

Category a covers the autonomous activities of the body toward itself and cannot be known by our *manas* consciousness. It cannot, therefore, be an object for meditative awareness. Category b is that producing the "professional activities" mentioned by Vasubandhu, and includes the attributes of instinctive skills and judgment incurred in the performance of an art or practice. Such skills and judgments are karmically neutral, as they are not he result of *manas* and all that *manas* is subject to (i.e., the *Klesa*). One of the goals of *Chuan Fa* is to develop all activities of body and mind to be of this nature by overcoming the basis upon which it rests, namely the *Klesa*.

Note 99: We can see traces of *Chuan Fa's* teaching of body-mind in the early Theravada texts, where what it represents is included in terms like *Bhavangasrota* (being-limb-stream). This term is usually understood by Pali scholars as indicating "the undercurrent forming the condition for existence" (*Nyanitiloka's Pali Dictionary*). In the same vein, the term *Bhavanga Citta* is often interpreted as the subconscious. These two renderings of the term accord with the attitude mentioned in Note 98. However, it seems likely that *Bhavangasrota* equally indicates that part of physical "being" which inherits and carries the various physical karmas of their initiator, functioning as if a metaphysical genetic chromosome. It would thus, to use Vasubandhu's terms, be something like a physical *Alaya* acting to receive imprints (*Vasana*) or conditioning "seeds" and then modifying and transforming them to later manifest within the various bodily structures or modes of being.

What was termed *Rupaprasada* (bodily elemental harmony) in the Sarvastivada and Vaibhasika teaching could also serve as the active substratum for such an *Alaya* patterning. By virtue of the fact that it is a dynamic ever-changing underlay of elemental forces which, through asserting their intrinsic harmony, in turn give rise to the distinctive and individualized patterns of balance and expression particular to their bearer, it seems particularly appropriate as an agent of Vasubandhu's *Transformation of the Mind* series (*Parivarta*) within the *Alaya*.

The *Rupaprasada* does not seem to have been mentioned in such a context by Vasubandhu, although in his discussions with the Vaibhasikas (who used Vasubandhu's own *Abhidharma Kosa* as their authority), he refutes his earlier concept of "unmanifest action" (see Note 2) upon which the concept of *prasada* is based. Later, after some criticism, Vasubandhu modified his refutation of Avijnapti, accepting it as a "provisional" entity if it formed an object of consciousness.

Modern Theravada teachers often discuss the *prasada* as if it was an actual entity in its own right. One famous teacher spoke of it sending out rays of energy from the body and forming a means for the announcement of a person's imminent death. In such a view, the *prasada* seems to be considered as having a capability—under certain conditions—to interconnect sentient or insentient life forms, rather like the "life force" in the Hollywood film *Star Wars*. Certainly in my own experience, the ether of the *Chuan Fa* five elements tradition is regarded in this way, and forms the agent in the practice of healing energies.

Note 100: By way of example of what a body-based mental "moment" consists of, we can find in the Pali *Abhidhamma* the following description of the arising of a visual moment (*Cakku Citta Utpada*):

> The Eye Organ (*Cakkh Ayatana*)
> Object of the Eye (*Cakku Prasada*)
> Agitation arises in the *Bhavangasrota.*
> Consciousness activates and adverts to the object (*Aviajjna*).
> Organic consciousness's arise (*Cakku vinnana*),
> Organic "seeing" (*Dasana*) arises.
> Mind arises and receives the initial object impulse (*Sampaticchana*).
> Mental consciousness investigates it (*Santirana*) accompanied by
>   Indifference.
> Mental determination arises (*Votthapana*).

If the object seen is small or the impression is weak, only the impulsion or determining stages are reached. If the object is large, there flash up six or seven impulse moments (*Javanapana*). These consist of either:

1) One of the 8 karmic roots of the sense sphere. These are associated with either 8 wholesome consciousnesses (*Kusalamula*), 12 Unwholesome consciousnesses (*Akusalamula*) or 9 Functional consciousnesses (*Kryiyamula*); or:

2) If the object is very large there flash up one or two of the eight root-accompanied karma-produced classes of consciousness, or one of the three rootless karmic consciousnesses arises; or:

3) Consciousness registers what is seen (*Tadamannu*). If the object or sense impulse is very weak, only this Registering stage is reached.

4) The object is seen and recognized.

Note 101: Vasubandhu would possibly explain this occurrence as being due to emergent, previously latent "seeds" within the *Alaya* of the individual. If this was indeed the case, how much more useful (and less harmful) it would be to draw out such seeds within an enlightened and enlightening environment as occurs within *Chuan Fa* and help people contribute toward the development of spiritual insight within both their bearer and others around them.

Note 102: The "new" self syndrome often occurs in cases where people have decided to "turn over a new leaf," "start afresh," change professions, move house or meet strangers. It is very common among those who have convinced themselves they have found a new religious belief or political system. It is well to remind oneself that the pains, be they physical or mental, of the old selves are rarely experienced any differently by such new selves. The patterns which created them in the first place will eventually reassert, and any change that seems to have taken place is usually only cosmetic.

The idea of *Sthana* may be useful in that the spiritual aspiration, itself, can be understood as giving rise to a "new" *Sthana*. This *Sthana* is different in that its arising comes about through the study and application of the Buddhist teachings and it requires the practice of its various traditional disciplines and meditation themes. It is not simply a new "face" chosen purely for personal reasons (which is what the term *Sthana* usually indicates).

Note 103: Fifteen years may seem a long time, but the study of *Hsing* such as the *Ping An* lies not simply in its physical practice, nor only in meditation, but rather in a complex combination of Bodhisattva studies and practices all of which must be mastered. Every *Ping An* has five elemental levels, and each concerns a special theme and / or its principles and practices. A brief example is as follows.

In the first *Ping An*, study is divided into two strata concerned with the physical being and its concomitant principles. The physical theme includes the study of bodily balance and homeostasis, shape, internal physiology, kinesis and positionings. A student must learn how to analyze, assess, and correct imbalances in all these areas—both in himself and in others and by means of the five senses. This also involves study and practice of many of the natural healing arts, such as herbalism, bone manipulation, first aid and revival techniques. The second *Ping An* concerns the mind based "emotions," their origin and genesis, the nature of the self, its prolongation and eventual disintegration. It covers the physical, psychological, and doctrinal themes of stability, fear, friendship, change and death. It also covers various forms of healing and therapy. It rules the "flow" of movement itself, and what movement consists of. The Bodhisattva vows are associated with this *Hsing*. Each of the twenty-five constituent layers of the *Ping An* constitute a study in their own right and fifteen years, in fact, is a very brief and minimum time to cover them.

Note 104: See for instance, Ch. 5 v 30, *Bodhicaryavatara* (Entering the Path of Wisdom) by Shantideva. "For those who are fortunate enough to be able to exert themselves, even if only out of fear of being punished, mindfulness is more easily generated by living with one's Master."

Note 105: "If the self is to be protected it ought not to be concerned with its protection" Ch. 8 v 173, *Bodhicaryavatara* (Entering into the Path of Wisdom) by Shantideva.

Note 106: I have dealt with fear under the general title here of *Dausthulya*, but more accurately Buddhism distinguishes at least three important forms of the condition usually described in English by just the word "fear." It distinguishes the first type of fear as a presage to a higher state of human consciousness; that is, as a categorical and ultimately spiritual condition of consciousness arising from both its capacity and inclination to intimately link with states of suffering within others and the "self." Such a category is known as *Bhaya*. It develops as a result of intense spiritual training, usually within a monastic environment, and serves to highlight what are perceived as insufficiencies or vulnerabilities within the practitioner in his or her practices. One result of this is that the practitioner fears that his or her capacities may be inadequate or unable not to be overwhelmed with the results of past deeds.

The term is most often encountered in Buddhist writings in the form of its negative *Abhaya*, a term usually mis-translated in an oversimplified manner as meaning "fearlessness" when what is really being indicated by this term is an exalted attainment of a form of equanimitous wisdom within which those constituent factors which, in the past, gave rise to actual and dynamic causes of suffering within consciousness, have been completely overcome.

Buddhist doctrine then distinguishes a state of consciousness arising directly from a sudden and dynamic realization that it is within an acute or intense condition, the result of which will, by its very nature, render it susceptible (and likely) to immanently experience harmful suffering. This realization, in turn, creates the mental situation we term "fear." This type of fear is said to take two different forms, the first being that which renders one susceptible solely through the orientational and other activities of consciousness itself. This means the acute sense of vulnerability which arises as a direct result of the manner in which we know and apply our consciousness to things (i.e., our motivations—or lack of them—ideologies, attitudes or situations).

The second, and perhaps more refined, form arises within those actively engaged in following the spiritual path and refers to obstructions we create within our knowledge which hinder or restrict our actual capacity to overcome such sufferings as would be overcome by the development of wisdom. This form of self-induced suffering indicates self-defeating strategies, willful ignorance, the avoidance of wise teachers and situations, and destructive attitudes (i.e., engaging in spiritual endeavors half-heartedly, bearing grudges or hatreds, being intolerant, etc.). It also covers maintaining fixed, unyielding views of things and being unable to realize some essential spiritual truths because of such fixity. Both of these forms of obstructed consciousness entail the experience of situations within which there is a realization of the direct relation between our past acts and suffering. Such an immediate and experiential condition of realizing this situational susceptibility is what is termed *Dausthulya*.

The third type of suffering is that which we usually intend to convey by the word "fear" and is the body trembling, bowel-wrenching condition that categorizes its most obvious and physical symptoms, and is familiar to us all. This is termed *trasa*. Each of these three fear forms may assume great or small significance, be real or imaginary and may concern probable of improbable situations. We may think of fear as a useful defensive mental state of mind when faced with immanent dangers to life or limb, but it is never just this alone. The states of mind intimately associated with fearfulness (which is the state of fear projected over a period of time) may equally manifest as either seemingly simple mild stresses, "reasonable" worries, or wild obsessions. Such states, in turn, contribute toward other conditions linked with health imbalances and/or life threatening illnesses, such as cancer or ulcers. It is a sad fact of our modern times that even a simple activity, such as shopping for essentials, can be a cause for the arising of fears, depending upon where we live. Such connections and ramifications make it essential that we come to understand something of what constitutes the causal forces of fear.

The most meaningful descriptions of fear and its associated states occur in the works of Yogacara Acarya Vasubandhu, especially in his *Pancaskhandaka Prakarana 4*, and the *Madhyantavibhaga Bhasya 2*: v9;5: v12–15.

Note 107: A modern example of the potential inter-disciplinary value of Buddhist teachings can be seen within *Gentle Bridges*, by J. W. Hayward & F. J. Varela. Boston: Shambala, 1992. In this work, the Dalai Lama discusses and debates, from the point of view of Tibetan Buddhism, the subjects of neuroscience and physiology, cognitive and information processing psychology, artificial intelligence, computer science and programming, molecular science and nuclear physics—with leading exponents of these sciences. Although the Dalai Lama seems to base his views of the Yogacara path upon the interpretations of Dignaga rather than Vasubandhu himself, the possibilities inherent in the Buddhist worldview are amply exhibited in this excellent and interesting book.

GLOSSARY OF TERMS

Common alternative titles are noted where significant. Transliterations are enclosed in square brackets.

AJARI (Japanese); ACARYA (Sanskrit); ACHALI (Chinese)

One who practices and teaches the esoteric teachings as a way of life. The term is normally reserved for Master teachers of the Mikkyo sects.

BODHI MANDALA (Sanskrit); TAO CHANG (Chinese); DOJO (Japanese)

A term used in the Buddha's time to describe a place where martial arts are practiced solely for the pursuit of spiritual wisdom. It also described the actual site where the Buddha Shakyamuni attained Supreme Enlightenment.

BODHISATTVA (Sanskrit); PU SA (Chinese); BOSATSU (Japanese)

A Buddhist term meaning "wisdom" (*bodhi*) "essence" (*sattva*) indicating either the exalted spiritual condition of Shakyamuni before he was incarnated into this realm, or (in the Mahayana) someone who has undertaken the vow to renounce Enlightenment until all others are able to be enlightened.

BUDDHA (Sanskrit); FO (Chinese); BUTSU (Japanese)

A title literally meaning "one who has awoken," used to describe those who have attained complete and perfect Enlightenment. Often used to describe the last historical Buddha who was born as Gautama of the Shakya clan, but equally to other Buddhas before him and for those to come, i.e., Maitreya.

CHEN-YEN (Chinese); MANTRAYANA (Sanskrit); SHINGON (Japanese)

The title of the sect devoted to the practice and perpetuation of Mikkyo (qv) and literally meaning "word of truth / reality." One of the three component practices of the school, the other two being *Mudra* and *Mandala*.

DHARMA (Sanskrit); FA (Chinese); HO (Japanese)

The "law" or totality of the principles realized by Buddhas and taught to mankind. The Buddha Dharma is formed from many lesser dharmas. The second of the "Triratna" (qv).

HSING (Chinese); KATA (Japanese); PRATIMA [= Kayasamasthana-gatikriya] (Sanskrit)

1) Sequences of preset, patterned movements originally drawn from ancient Indian (Hindu) warrior techniques, but here involving particular attitudes and orientations of mind, breath and body based upon Buddhist principles. Used in Chuan Fa as a means of neutralizing attacks without harm to those involved, and as a "self unraveling" movement meditation capable of being explicated at many different levels of understanding. 2) A term for the Bodhisattva Nata. 3) A dynamic mimesis of a mind and body series performed to enact or illuminate cogent experiential patterns in order for these to serve as a basis for specific meditative concentrations.

KARATE/TO DE (Japanese); TANG SHOU (Chinese); SUNYATAPANI (Sanskrit)

The ancient traditional name of the Ryukyuan islanders form of Chinese *Chuan Fa*. The particle *tang* (Japanese: *to*) meaning "China.". Often shortened by them to simply *te* (hand). The Sanskrit equivalent (only utilized by Buddhist monks) means "hand of voidness."

KARATE (Japanese); KUNG SHOU (Chinese)

A term literally meaning "empty hand" innovated in the 1930s by certain Okinawans desirous of popularizing the native art with the Japanese authorities by obscuring its Chinese origins. Such a name change was not wholly agreed to by all the island's teachers. The particle *kara* means "empty," and is mentioned in the Prajna Paramita Sutra. It was not chosen for this spiritual implication. In Korean, this name is pronounced "Kuk Sul" and was also used there until its national government decided to amalgamate all its different Chinese schools under one synthetic name of *Tae Kwon Do*, meaning "Foot Fist Way." This term succeeded in dissuading many people from studying it.

KEMPO (Japanese); CHUAN FA (Chinese); DHARMAHASTA (Sanskrit)

The "Clasped Hand Dharma" Chinese monastic tradition that was based upon the Indian Vajramukti teachings of non-violent self defense, healing, health nourishing, and spiritual discipline. Utilized by ancient monks for religious purposes and based predominantly upon the Yogacara Buddhist philosophical doctrines. The word *Fa* ("law") was also used in Taoism to represent its inner principles and the laws of nature.

KUNG FU (Chinese); KOFU (Japanese); SUDRA (Sanskrit)

A Chinese term literally meaning "a workman" (syn., coolie) used also to describe their activities. Mistakenly applied to *Chuan Fa*. Use of this term was popularized by the Victorian British Traders in China who, when enquiring about demonstrations by persons doing Chinese Boxing were told that this is what it was (i.e., hard work). The humor was unrealized. Appropriated by

Hong Kong film actors in an attempt to legitimize their commercial popularization of emotionally turbulent violence. This term is correctly ignored by all mainland Chinese sources and Masters.

MAHAYANA (Sanskrit); TAI CHENG (Chinese); DAIJO (Japanese)

A title meaning "the great, all inclusive path" describing the Northern forms of Dharma existing in China, Japan, Korea, Tibet, etc., which soon developed from the early 18 Indian sects. It is distinguished by its usage of scriptures in the Sanskrit language as well as those of the countries into which it spread. It incorporates a teaching that people can realize the Bodhisattva ideal within their present existence, and holds distinctive doctrines concerning the Sunyata of self and of Dharmas.

MANDALA (Sanskrit); MANTOLO (Chinese); MANDARA (Dojo) (Japanese)

A special zone, area, or place delineated by line, color or other device representing the realm, peripheries, or relationships between various aspects of Perfect Wisdom (which may be presented in many different ways).

MARGA (Sanskrit); TAO (Chinese); DO (Japanese)

In India and Japan, a Buddhist term summarizing the particular method or tradition indicated by an enlightened being (usually Shakyamuni Buddha) to be followed as a way of life. In China the term for *Yana* (qv) was preferred in order to distinguish Buddhism clearly from Taoism.

MIKKYO (Japanese); MI-CHING or MI-CHIAO (Chinese); GUHYA-SUTRA (Sanskrit)

The Buddhist scriptures of the esoteric schools which are concerned with doctrines and practices of mind, speech and body conducive of enlightenment in this lifetime; the sects founded upon their study or practices.

MUDRA (Sanskrit); YIN (Chinese); IN (Japanese)

A ritual gesture or pose assumed by a part or all of the body in order to invite, evoke, express, sanctify, or convey a principle or power of the forces involved in Enlightenment. Mudra may be performed singly or in sequences.

NAGARJUNA (Sanskrit); RYUJU/RYUSHO/RYUMYO (Japanese); LUNG SHU (Chinese)

A second century Indian teacher who formulated the philosophy of the Madhyamika (middle way), the basis for the Vijnaptimatra (Mind Only) School of the Sunyavada. This influenced all later schools of Buddhist teaching within China and had many derivative forms. Also the fifth or sixth century Chinese Master of Esoteric (Mikkyo) Buddhism.

NARYA (Sanskrit); NA-LI (Chinese); NARA (Naha) (Japanese)

Ancient Indian term meaning "strong" or "manly" and used in combination with the term *Vajra* to describe the practitioners and practices of Vajramukti. Often used interchangeably to represent the Vajranata and prefixed by the term *Vajra*. Narya (or Narayana) was, in Hinduism, the name given to the first man created at the beginning of the world by the omnipotent deity Brahma.

NATA (Sanskrit); NA-PA, NA-RA (Chinese); NARA, NAPA, NAFA (Japanese)

Ancient Indian Buddhist term describing the earliest form of the art of ritual movement practiced for spiritual purposes, and used by the Vajramukti practitioners in India. Practitioners of early esoteric *Chuan Fa* were called *Vajranata*. The winner of its annual exhibitions was termed the *Nataraja* ("Monarch of the Nata"). In the mandala often replaced by the tern *Nrita*. A later offshoot of *Nata* was called *Caryagita* ("singing with the body"). The term *Nata* was later re-adopted by Hinduism to represent the secular art of dance, mime and movement used especially to enact legendary Vedic religious themes or dramas.

PI MI (Chinese); HIMITSU (Japanese); GUHYA VADA (Sanskrit)

Literally "secret words" or "oral teachings." A title used to describe the eso-teric method in general. An alternative designation for the Mi Chiao or Vajrayana.

SANGHA (Sanskrit); SENG (Chinese); SO (Japanese)

Sanskrit term meaning the "congregation" or "group of followers" and used in Buddhism to describe the Order of Monks. In the Mahayana, it is also applied to describe the Buddhist community in general and forms the third of the Three Jewels (qv).

SOTOBA (Gorinto/To) (Japanese); TOPA (Chinese); STUPA (Sanskrit)

The pagoda of five shapes, each representing one of the elements. In Mikkyo, it represents the perfect and ultimate body of Mahavairocana Buddha.

THERAVADA (Sanskrit); SHAO CHENG (Chinese); SHOJO (Japanese)

A title meaning "words (teaching) of the elders" and referring to one of the 18 early sects of the teachings. It now exists mainly in Sri Lanka, Thailand, and Burma, and is distinguished by its usage of scriptures in the Pali language, and its dedication to the Arahant ideal. In the Mahayana (Great Path), it is usu-ally referred to as the Hinayana (Smaller Path).

TRIRATNA (Sanskrit); SAN PAO (Chinese); SANBO (Japanese)

The Three Precious Things, comprising the Buddha, His Teachings (Dharma) and the Community of Monks (Sangha).

VAJRAMUKTI (Sanskrit); KONGOGEDATSU (Japanese); CHING KANG CHIEH T'O (Chinese)

The name given in India to the early tradition of *Chuan Fa* (*Kempo*) utilizing the Mikkyo philosophical tradition and Bodhisattva orientation.

VAJRAYANA (Sanskrit); KONGOJO (Japanese); CHING KANG CHENG (Chinese)

Term describing the esoteric teachings and paths used in China and Tibet and indicating a method or training as powerful in its revolutionary effect as the Thunderbolt. Together with the Mahayana and the Hinayana (Theravada) it forms the third "vehicle" (*Yana*) of Buddhism by means of which one crosses to the "other shore" of wisdom.

YANA (Sanskrit); CHENG (Chinese); JO (Japanese)

A term literally meaning a "carrying vehicle" or "ferry," and used to describe a Buddhist spiritual path or method(s), through which one is carried across the "sea of suffering." Inherently transient in nature, it is discarded when the journey has been completed. Also the Chinese Buddhist equivalent to Tao, often used as a synonym for Dharma (qv).

YOGA (Sanskrit); YUI CHA (Chinese); YU GA (Japanese)

A term meaning to "yoke" or "join" together, and used to indicate a wide range of mind/body practices or applications in both Buddhism and Hinduism. In Hinduism, it indicates practices designed to unify with Brahma—the all pervading God of the Universe. In Buddhism, it indicates only special methods of meditative or physical training oriented toward Enlightenment.

BUDDHIST AND OTHER REFERENCES

Alternative versions of some of these works are detailed in the Notes section.

Abbreviations used in the Sources Section

A: *Anguttara-nikaya*, 5 volumes, R. Morris and E. Hardy, eds. London: PTS, 1885–1900.

AA: *Manorathapurani*, (*Anguttara-atthakatha*), M. Walleser, ed. London: PTS, 1973.

ABORI: *Annals of the Bhandarkar Research Institute.*

AD: *Adhidharmadipa*, see Adv.

Adv: *Adhidharmadipa with Vibhasaprabhavrtti*, P. S. Jaini, ed. Patna: K. P. Jayaswal Research Institute, 1967.

Akv: *Abhidharmakosa-bhasa*, Pralhad Pradhan, ed. Patna: K. P. Jayaswal Research Institute, 1967.

BCA: *Bodhicaryavatara*, Santideva (Bib. Ind.).

BCAP: *Bodhicaryavatarapanjika*, Prajnakaramati (Bid. Ind.).

BEFEO: *Bulletin de l'Ecole Française d'Extrème Orient.*

BSOAS: *Bulletin of the School of Oriental Studies.*

Chung: *Ch'ang A-han Ching (Dirghagama)*, Buddhayasas, tr. Taisho No. 1; *Ch'ang Chung A-han Ching (Madhyamagama)*, Gautama Samghadeva and Samgharaksa, tr. Taisho No. 26.

CPB: *The Central Philosophy of Buddhism*, Prof. T. R. V. Mutti, London: Allen & Unwin, 1955.

D: *Digha-nikaya*, 3 volumes, T. W. Rhys Davids and J. E. Carpenter, eds. London: PTS, 1890–1911.

DHSA: *Atthasalini, Dhammasangani-atthakatha*, E. Muller, ed. London: PTS, 1897.

DHST: *Abhidhammamulatika (Tika on Dhammasangani-atthakatha)*, D. Pannasara and P. Wimaladhamma, eds. Colombo, Ceylon: Mahabodhi Press, 1938.

DMP: *Saddharmapundarika-sutra*, H. Kern and B. Nanjio, eds. St. Petersburg: The Imperial Academy of Sciences, 1921-S.

ERE: *Encyclopaedia of Religion and Ethics.*

HB: *Buston's History of Buddhism*, Obermiller, tr. Heidelberg, 1931.

HIL: *History of Indian Literature*, Vol. II, Winternitz. Calcutta: Calcutta University Press, 1933.

HOS: *Harvard Oriental Series*.

IHQ: *Indian Historical Quarterly*.

JMS: *Journal of Mushindo Studies*.

JPTS: *Journal of the Pali Text Society*.

JRAS: *Journal of the Royal Asiatic Society*.

JRMKA: *Journal of the Ryukyu Mushindokai*.

KP: *Kaiyapaparivarta of the Ratnakuta-sutra*, A. Stael-Holstein, ed. Shanghai: Commercial Press, 1926.

LAS: *Lankavatarasutra*, B. Nanjio, ed. Kyoto, 1923.

M: *Mahajima Nikaya*.

MA: *Madhyamakavatara*, Candrakirti. Chapter VI (incomplete), restored by Aiyaswami Sastri (*Journal of Oriental Research*, Madras, 1929ff.).

MKV: *Madhyamikakarikavrtti*, Candrakirti (Bib.Bud.IV).

MKV(V): *Madhyamakasastra of Nagarjuna with the commentary; Prasannapada*, by Candrakirti, P. L. Vaidya, ed. Darbhanga: The Mithila Institute, 1960.

MVSBT: *Madyhantavibhaga-sutrabhasyatika*, by Sthiramati, Part I, V. Bhattacharya and G. Tucci, eds. Luzac & Co., 1932.

NB: *Nyayasutrabhasya*, by Vatsyayana (Vizianagaram Sanskrit Series).

NK: *Nyayakandali*, by Sridhara (Vizianagaram Sanskrit Series).

NV: *Nyayavarttika*, by Udyotakara (Vizianagaram Sanskrit Series).

PEW: *Philosophy East and West*, Eliot Deutsch, ed. Honolulu: University Press of Hawaii.

PIPC: *Proceedings of the Indian Philosophical Congress*.

PTS: *The Pali Text Society*, London.

PU: *Kausitaki Upanisad*.

PU: *Kena Upanisad*.

PU: *Upanisads*, S. Radhakrishnan, ed. and tr. *The Principal Upanisads*, London, 1953; *The Upanishads*, Part I, SBE., Vol. I, tr. F. Max Muller (Oxford, 1879); *The Thirteen Principal Upanishads*, tr. R. E. Hume, second edition. Oxford University Press, 1934. *Sechzig Upanisad's des Veda*, tr. P. Deussen. Leipzig, 1921.

PV: "Pramanavarttika, by Dharmakirti," R. Sankrtyayana, ed. *Journal of Bihar and Orissa Research Society*, Patna, XXIV–XXV.

S: *Samutta-nikaya*, L. Feer, ed. 5 volumes. London: PTS, 1884–1904.

SAKV: *Sphutarthabhidharmakosa-vyakhya*, U. Wogihara, ed. Tokyo: The Publication Association of Abhidharmakosavyakhya, 1932–1936.

SN: *Sutta-nipata*, D. Anderson and H. Smith, eds. London: PTS, 1913.

SV: *Slokavarttika*, by Kumarila, Chowkhamba Sanskrit Series.

T: *Taisho Shinshu Daizokyo*, J. Takakusu and K. Watanabe, eds. Tokyo: Diazo Shuppan Company, 1924–1934.

THAG: *Thera-theri-gatha*, H. Oldenberg and R. Pischel, eds. London: PTS, 1883.

TS: *Tattvasangrana*, by Santaraksita, 2 volumes, Gaekwad Oriental Series.

TSENG: *Tseng-i A-han Ching (Ekottaragama)*, Gautama Samghadeva, tr. Taisho No.125.

TSN: *Trisvabhavanirdesa*, by Vasubandhu, S. Mukhopadhyaya, ed. Visvabharati.

TSP: *Tattvasangrahapanjika*, by Kamalasila, Gaekwad Oriental Series.

Ud: *Udana*, P. Steinthal, ed. London: PTS, 1948.

VbhA: *Sammohavinodani, Vibhangatthakatha*, A. P. Buddhadatta, ed. London: PTS, 1923.

Vin: *Vinaya Pitaka*, 5 volumes, H. Oldenberg, ed. London: PTS, 1879–1883.

Vism: *The Vissuddhi-magga of Buddhaghosa*, C. A. F. Rhys Davids, ed. London: PTS, 1975.

VMS: *Vijnaptimatratasiddhi*, by Vasubandhu, S. Levi, ed. Paris.

VMS(JBORS): *Vijnaptimatratasiddhi*, by Hsuan Tsang, partially reconstructed by R. Sankrtyayana, *Journal of Bihar and Orissa Research Society*, XIX–XX, Patna.

VSM: *Vedantasiddhantamuktavali*, by Prakasananda, Benaras.

Pali Sources

"*Abhidhammatthasangaha*," S. Z. Aung and C. A. F. Rhys Davids, trs.

Compendium of Philosophy, London, 1910.

Abhidhammavatara, A. P. Buddhadatta Thera, ed. London: PTS, 1915.

Anguttara Nikaya, 5 volumes, R. Morris and E. Hardy, eds. London: PTS, 1885–1900; F. L. Woodward and E. M. Hare, trs. *The Book of the Gradual Sayings*, 5 volumes, London: PTS, 1932–1936.

Aryapratityasamutpada Sutra, Printed in *Aryasalistamba Sutra*, q.v.

Aryasalistamba Sutra, N. A. Sastri, ed. Adyar, 1950.

Atthasalini, by Buddhaghosa, E. Muller, ed. London: PTS, 1897.

Dhammapada, S. Sumangala Thera, ed. London: PTS, 1914.

Dhammasangani, E. Muller, ed. London, 1885.

Digha Nikaya, T. W. Rhys Davids and J. E. Carpenter, eds. 3 volumes, London: PTS, 1890–1911. T. W. and C. A. F. Rhys Davids, trs., *Dialogues of the Buddha*, SBB, Vols. 2, 3 and 4, London: Oxford University Press, 1899–1921.

Itivuttaka, E. Windisch, ed. London: PTS, 1889.

Jataka, 6 volumes and index, V. Fausboll, ed. London, 1895–1907.

Kathavatthu, 2 volumes, A. C. Taylor, ed. London: PTS, 1894–1897.

"Kathavatthuppakarana, Atthakatha, Comy to Kathavatthu," JPTS, 1889, pp. 1–199.

Khuddakapatha, H. Smith, ed. London: PTS, 1915.

Mahaniddesa, V. Niddesa.

Mahavyutpatti, I. P. Minaev, ed. Bibliotheca Buddhica, Vol. 13, 1911.

Majihima Nikaya, 3 volumes, V. Trenkner and R. Chalmers, eds. London: PTS, 1948–1951; I. B. Horner, tr. *Middle Length Sayings*, 3 volumes, London: PTS, 1954–1959; R. Chalmers, tr. *Further Dialogues of the Buddha*, 2 volumes, London: PTS, 1888. K. E. Neumann, tr. *Die Reden Gotamo Buddho's aus der mittleren Samm-lung Majjhimanikayo*, Bande I und II, Leipzig, 1896–1900.

Manorathapurani, Commentary to Anguttara Nikaya, 5 volumes, M. Walleser and H. Kopp, eds. London: PTS, 1924–1956.

Milindapanha, V. Trenkner, ed. London, 1928.

Nettippakarana, E. Hardy, ed. London: PTS, 1902.

Niddesa, I-Mahaniddesa, 2 volumes, L. de la V. Poussin and E. J. Thomas, eds.; II-Cullaniddesa, W. Stede, ed. London: PTS, 1916–1918.

Papancasudanio, Commentary to Majihima Nikaya, 5 volumes, J. H. Woods, D. Kosambi, and I. B. Horner, eds. London: PTS, 1922–1938.

Paramtatthadipani, Commentary to Khuddaka Nikaya, Part III (to Petavatthu), E. Hardy, ed. London: PTS, 1894; *Commentary to Udana*, F. L. Woodward, ed. London: PTS, 1926.

Paramatthajotika II, Commentary to Suttanipata, 3 volumes, H. Smith, ed. London: PTS, 1916–1918.

Patisambhidamagga, 2 volumes, A. C. Taylor, ed. London: PTS, 1905–1907.

Puggalapannatti, R. Morris, ed. London, 1883.

Puggalapannatti Atthakatha, Commentary to Puggalapannatti, G. Landsberg and C. A. F. Rhys Davids, eds. JPTS, 1914, pp. 170–254.

Saddaniti, H. Smith, ed. London: La Grammaire Palie D'Aggavamsa, 1928.

Sammohavinodani, Commentary to Vibhanga, A. P. Buddhadetta Thera, ed. London: PTS, 1923.

Samyutta Nikaya, 6 volumes, L. Feer, ed. London: PTS, 1884–1904; C. A. F. Rhys-Davids and F. L. Woodward, eds. *The Book of the Kindred Sayings,* 5 volumes, London: PTS, 1917–1930.

Saratthappakasini, Commentary to Samyutta Nikaya, 3 volumes, F. L. Woodward, ed. London: PTS, 1929–1937.

Sumangalavilasini, Commentary to Digha Nikaya, 3 volumes, T. W. Rhys Davids, E. Carpenter, and W. Stede, eds. London: PTS, 1948.

Suttanipata, D. Anderson and H. Smith, eds. London: PTS, 1948; V. Fausboll, tr. SBE, Vol. 10, Part 2. Oxford, 1881.

Thera- and Therigatha, H. Oldenberg and R. Pischel, eds. London: PTS, 1883; C. A. F. Rhys Davids, tr. *Psalms of the Early Buddhists,* 2 volumes, London: PTS, 1903–1913.

Udana, P. Steinthal, ed. London: PTS, 1948.

Vibhanga, C. A. F. Rhys Davids and H. Oldenberg, eds. SBE, Vols. 13, 17, 20, Oxford, 1881–1885.

Visuddhimagga, by Buddhaghosa, 2 volumes, C. A. F. Rhys Davids, ed. London, 1920–1921.

Yamaka, 2 volumes, C. A. F. Rhys Davids, M. C. Foley, M. Hunt, and M. Smith, eds. London: PTS, 1911–1913.

Sanskrit, Tibetan, and Chinese Reference Texts and Translations Upon the *Yogacara* and Its Teachings

Abhidharmakosa. (a) Louis de la Vallée Poussin, ed. and tr. *L'Abhidharmakosa de Vasubandhu.* 6 volumes. Louvain: Museon, 1923–1931; (b) Louis de La Vallée Poussin, *L'Abhidharmakosa de Vasubandhu: Introduction, Fragment des Karikas, Index, Additions.* Paris: Geuthner, 1931; (c) *Abhidharmakosa,* R. Sankrtyayana, ed. Benares, 1955.

Abhisamayalankara. (a) E. Obermiller and Th. Stcherbatsky, eds., *Abhisamayalankaraprajnaparamitopadesasastra.* Leningrad: Bibliotheca Buddhica, No. 23, 1929; (b) Edward Conze, tr. *Abhisamayalarikara.* Rome: Serie Orientale Roma, No. 6, 1954.

Astasahasrika Prajnaparamita. (a) Edward Conze, ed. *Astasahasrika Prajnaparamita.* Calcutta: Asiatic Society, 1958; (b) Edward Conze, tr. *The Astasahasrika Prajnaparamita; Perfection of Wisdom in Eight Thousand Slokas.* Bibliotheca Indica, 1970. Reprinted as *The Perfection of Wisdom in Eight Thousand Lines.* Bolinas, CA: Four Seasons Foundation, 1973.

Adhidharmasamuccaya. (a) Pralhad Pradhan, ed. *Abhidharma Samuccaya of Asanga.* Santiniketan: Visva-Bharati, 1950; (b) Walpola Rahula, tr. *Le compendium de la super-doctrine (Abhidharmasamuccaya) d'Asanga.* Paris: Ecole française d'Extrème-Orient, 1971.

Bodhisatvabhumi, Vol. 1, Tokyo, 1930. Romanized text, pp. 37–57. Tibetan Tripitaka Peking edition (the PTT); D. T. Suzuki, ed. rpt. ed. Kyoto: Otani University, 1957. Vol. 110 (bstan-gyur, sems-tsam, Shi, folio sides 24b–37b), pp. 142–147; Gunaprabha's commentary on the chapter, "The Bodhisattvabhumivrtti," in PTT, Vol. 112 (bstan gyur, sems-tsam Yi, folio sides 196b–203b), pp. 9–12; Sagara-megha's commentary, *The Yogacaryabhumau bodhisattvabhumi vyakhya,* PTT, Vol. 112 (bstan-'gyur, sems-tsam Ri, folio sides 63b–91b), pp. 69–80; *Bodhisattvabhumi,* U. Wogihara, ed. 2 volumes. Tokyo, 1930–1936; *Bodhisattvabhumi.* Nalinaksha Dutt, ed. Tibetan Sanskrit Works Series, No. 7. Patna: K. P. Jayaswal Research Institute, 1966.

Buddhacarita, E. H. Johnston, ed. Punjab University Publications, No. 31. Calcutta; Part I, Calcutta, 1935. No 32. 1936.

Bu-ston. Chos-byung. E. Obermiller, tr. *History of Buddhism* by Buston. 2 volumes. Heidelberg, 1931.

Dasabhumikasutra (a) J. Rahder, ed. *Dasabhumikasutra et Bodhisattvavbhumi: Chapitres Vihara et Bhumi.* Paris and Louvain, 1926; (b) Megumu Honda and J. Rahder, trs. *Annotated Translation of the Dasabhumika-Sutra.* Satapitaka Series, No. 74. New Delhi: International Academy of Indian Culture, 1968.

History of Buddhism in India, by Tarantha. Translated from Tibetan by A. Chattopadhyaya and Lama Chimpa. Simla: Indian Institute of Advanced Study, 1970.

Jnanaprasthanasastra, by Katyayaniputra, S. B. Sastri, ed. and tr. Vol. I, Santiniketan, 1955.

Karmasiddhiprakarana of Vasubandhu. Translated (into English from the French of E. Lamotte) by Leo Pruden. Berkeley, CA: Asian Humanities Press, 1988. "Karmasiddhiprakarana of Vasubandu," translated by Stefan Anacker in *7 Works of Vasubandhu.* Delhi: Motilal Banarsidass. Religions of Asia Series, Vol. 4, 1984.

Lankavatarasutra, Vol. I. (1) Bunyiu Nanjio, ed. Kyoto: Biblioteca Otaniensis, 1923; *Lankavatara-sutra.* Tokyo, 1923; (b) D. T. Suzuki, tr., *Lankavatarasutra.* London, 1932; (c) D. T. Suzuki. *Studies in the Lankavatara Sutra.* London: George Routledge & Sons, 1930.

Las grub pa'i rab tu byed pa (Karmasiddhiprakarama) of Vasubandhu, Visuddhisimha, tr. devenddraksita and dPal-brtsegs. Peking/Tokyo edition. Tibetan Canon Vol. 113 pp. 295ff.

MadhyantavibhagaZ. (a) Ramchandra Pandeya, ed. *Madhyanta-Vibhaga-Sastra.* Delhi: Motilal Banarsidass, 1971; (b) Chandradhar Sharma, ed. *Arya Maitreya's Madhyanta-Vibhaga-Shastra.* Jabalpur: Shrimate Shanti Sharma, 1963; (c) S. Yamaguchi, ed. Nagoya, 1934; *Madhyantavibhanga.* 2 volumes. Nagoya, 1934; (d)

Th. Stcherbatsky, tr. *The Madhyanta-vibhanga*. Leningrad: Bibliotheca Buddhica, No. 30. 1936; (e) Paul O'Brien, tr., "A Chapter on Reality from the Madhyantavibhagaastra," *Monumenta Nipponica*. Vols. IX and X. Tokyo: Sophia University, 1953–1954; (f) Gadjin M. Nagao, ed. *Madhyantavibhaga-Bhasya*. Tokyo: Suzuki Research Foundation, 1964; *Madhyantavibhagatika*, by Sthiramati, S. Yamaguchi, ed. Nagoya, 1934; (g) "Madhantavighaga," Stefan Anacker, tr. *7 Works of Vasubandhu*. Delhi: Motilal Banarsidass. Religions of Asia Series Vol. 4. 1984; (h) N. Tata and A. Thukur, eds. *Tibetan Sanskrit Works Series*, Vol. 7. Patna: K. P. Jayaswal Research Institute, 1966, Devanagarai text, pp. 25–39.

"Madhyamakavrtti (Mulamadhyamakakarikas), by Nagarjuna," L. de la V. Poussin, ed. *Bibliotheca Buddhisca*, Vol. 4, St. Petersburg: Bibliotheca Buddhica, 1903–1913; (b) Kenneth Inada, ed. and tr. *(Nagarjuna's) Mulamadhyamakakarika*. Tokyo: Hokuseido Press, 1970.

Madhyamakavrtti. Chapter 17. Translated into English from the French of E. Lamotte by Leo Pruden in *Karmasiddhiprakarana*. Berkeley, CA: Asian Humanities Press, 1988.

"Mahayanasamgraha." Etienne Lamotte, ed. (Tibetan ed.) and tr. *La Somme du Grand Vehicule d'Asanga (Mahayanasamgraha)*. Louvain: Museon, 1938–1939. *Tattvartha-patala*. Sanskrit edition N. Dutt, ed. Bodhisattvabhumi.

"Mahayanasutralankara." (a) S. Bagchi, ed. *Mahayana-Sutralankara of Asanga*. Buddhist Sanskrit Texts, No. 13. Darbhanga: Mithila Institute of Post-Graduate Studies and Research in Sanskrit Learning, 1970; (b) Sylvain Levi, ed. and tr. *Mahayana-Sutralamkara*. Paris: Champion, 1907, 1911; (c) Gadjin M. Nagao. *Index to the Mahayana-Sutralamkara* (Levi edition). Parts I and II. Tokyo: Nippon Gakujutsu Shinko-Kai, 1958, 1961.

Mahavyutpatti, 2 volumes. Sakaki, ed. Kyoto, 1916–1925, 1928.

Nyayabindu, by Dharmottara. T. L. Stcherbatsky, ed. Petrograd: Bibliotheca Buddhisca, 1918.

"Pancaskandaka Prakarana of Vasubandhu." Translated by Stefan Anacker in *7 Works of Vasubandhu*. Delhi: Motilal Banarsidass. Religions of Asia Series, Vol. 4. 1984.

"Vimsatika Karika of Vasubandhu." Translated by Stefan Anacker in *7 Works of Vasubandhu*. Delhi: Motilal Banarsidass. Religions of Asia Series Vol. 4. 1984.

Ratnagotravibhaga. (1) E. Johnston, Skt. ed. Patna: Bihar Research Society, 1950; (b) E. Obermiller, tr. (from Tibetan). "The Sublime Science of the Great Vehicle to Salvataon," *Acta Orientalia*, No. 9, 1931; (c) Jikido Takasaki. *A Study on the Ratnagotravibhaga (Uttaratnatra)*. Rome: Serie Orientale Roma, No. 33. 1966.

"Ratnavali," by Nagarjuna, G. Tucci, ed. and tr. *The Ratnavali of Nagarjuna* in JRAS, April 1934, pp. 307–325.

Saddharmapundarika sutra. (a) H. Kern, tr. *The Saddharma-Pundarika or The Lotus Blossom of the Fine Dharma (The Lotus Sutra)*. Translations from the Oriental Classics series. New York: Columbia University Press, 1976.

Samdhinirmocanasutra, Etienne Lamotte, ed. and tr. (from Tibetan); *Samdhinir-mocana Sutra: L'explication des Mystères.* Publication, No. 34. Louvain and Paris: Université de Louvain, 1935.

Snags rim chen mo, by Tson-kha-pa, Jeffrey Hopkins, ed. and tr.; *Tantra in Tibet: The Great Exposition of Secret Mantra by Tson-ka-pa.* The Wisdom of Tibet Series, No. 3. London: George Allen & Unwin, 1977.

Sphutarthabhidharmakosavyakhya, U. Wogihara, ed. 2 Parts. Tokyo, 1932–1936.

Ta cheng ch'eng-yeh lun (Mahayana Karmasiddhiprakarana of Vasubandhu), translated by Hsuan Tsang (circa 651). Taisho Vol. 31 No. 1608, pp. 77 b16–781 a21.

Tattvartha-viniscaya samgrahani. Tibetan edition only. PTT, Vol. III (bstan-'gyur, sems-tsam Hi, folio sides 19b–29b), pp. 72–76.

"Trimsika Karika of Vasubandhu." Translated by Stefan Anacker in *7 Works of Vasubandhu* Delhi: Motilal Banarsidass, Religions of Asia Series, Vol. 4, 1984.

"Trisvabhavanirdesa of Vasubandhu." (a) Translated by Stefan Anacker in *7 Works of Vasubandhu.* Delhi: Motilal Banarsidass, Religions of Asia Series, Vol. 4, 1984; (b) *Trisvabhavanirdesa by Vasubandhu, S. Mukhopadhyaya, ed.* Visvabharati.

Vajracchedikaprajnaparamitasutraastrakarika and *Trisatikavah Prajnaparamiatayah* (Karikasaptathi) by Asanga. Guiseppe Tucci, ed. and tr. in *Minor Buddhist Texts.* Part I, Vol. 9. Rome: Serie Orientale Roma, 1956, pp. 1–128.

Vijnaptimatratasiddhi. (a) Louis de La Vallee Poussin, ed. and tr. *Vijnaptimatratasiddhi-La Siddhi de Hiuan-tsang,* 2 vols. Paris, 1925–1928; (b) La Vallee Poussin. *Vinjaptimatratasiddhi: La Siddhi de Hiuan-tsang, index to.* Paris, 1948; (c) Clarence Hamilton, tr. *Wei Shih Er Shih Lun: The Treatise in Twenty Stanzas on Representation Only.* New Haven: American Oriental Society, 1938; (d) *Cheng Wei Shih Er Shih Lun,* trans., Wei Tat. Hong Kong: Wei Shih Er Shih Lun Publication Committee, 1973; (e) *Vijnaptimatratasiddhi by Vasubandhu,* S. Levi, ed. Paris; (f) *Vijnaptimatratasiddhi by Husan Tsang,* partially reconstructed by R. Sankrtyayana, Patna: *Journal of Bihar and Orissa Research Society,* XIX–XX.

"Vadaviddhi of Vasubandhu." Translated by Stefan Anacker in *7 Works of Vasubandhu* Delhi: Motilal Banarsidass, Religions of Asia Series, Vol. 4, 1984.

Yeh ch'eng chiu lun, by Pi mu chih hsien (circa 541). Taisho Vol. 31 No. 1608, pp. 77b 16–786 a21.

"Yogacarabhumisastra." V. Bhattacharya, ed. *The Yogacarabhumi of Acarya Asanga: Part I* (bhumis 1–5 of the Bahubhumikavastu). Calcutta: University of Calcutta, 1954.

Yogacarabhumi'Z of Sangharaksa. Paul Demieville, tr. "La Yogacarabhumi de Sangharaksa." Hanoi: *Bulletin de Pecole française d'extrème Orient,* No. 44, 1954.

Non-Buddhist Sanskrit Sources

Aitareya Aranyaka, A. B. Keith, ed. F. Max Muller, tr. Oxford, 1909; *The Upanisads,* Part I, SBE, Vol. I, 1879.

Aitareya Brahmana, 4 volumes, Pandit S. Samasrami, ed. Calcutta: Bibliotheca Indica, 1894–1906.

Arthasastra of Kautalya, 3 volumes, T. G. Sastri, ed. Trivandrum, 1924–1925.

Astadhyayi of Panini, V. O. Bohtlinck, Panini's acht Bücher grammatischer Regeln, Bande I und II, Bonn, 1839–1840.

Atharvaveda Sanhita, R. Roth and W. D. Whitney, eds. Berlin, 1924.

Ayaramga Sutta, Part I (text), H. Jacobi, ed. London, 1882; H. Jacobi, tr. *Jaina Sutras, Part I—Acaranga and Kalpa,* SBE, Vol. 22, Oxford, 1884.

Bhagavati Sutra, with the Commentary (vrtti) of Abhayadeva, 2 volumes, S. C. P. Jhaveri and S. Kesarimalaji, eds. Vol. I, Surat, 1937; Vol. II, Jamnagar, 1940.

Brhaqdaranyaka Upanisad, v. PU. With Commentary of Sankara, K. S. Agase, ed. A.A.S., No. 15, 1914.

Caraka Samhita, with Ayurvedadipika of Cakrapanidatta, 2 volumes, N. N. Sastri, ed. Lahore, 1929.

Chandogya Upanisad, PU. With Commentary of Sankara, K. S. Agase, ed. A.A.S., No. 14, 1913.

Gopatha Brahmana, R. Mitra and H. Vidyabhushana, eds. Calcudtta: Bibliotheca Indica, New Series No. 251, 252, 1872.

Harivamsaparvan, R. Kinjawadekar, ed. Poona, 1936.

Katha Upanisad, J. N. Rawson, ed. and tr., *The Kasha Upanisad,* O.U.P., 1934.

Kausitaki Brahmana-Sankhayana Brahmana, G. R. V. Chaya, ed. A.A.S., No. 65, Rajkot, 1911; A. B. Keith, tr. *Rgveda Brahmanas Translated,* HOS, Vol. 25, Cambridge, MA, 1920.

Mahabharatam, 18 volumes, T. R. Krishnacharya and T. R. Vyasacharya, eds. Bombay, 1906–1910.

Maitri Upanisad (PU).

Manusmrti, with Commentary of Kulluka Bhatta, Pandit G. S. Nene, ed. Benares, 1935; With Commentary of Medhatithi, 3 volumes, G. Jha, ed. Calcutta, 1932–1939.

Mimamsa Sutras, by Jaimini, G. Jha, tr. SBH, Vol. 10, Allahabad, 1916; Pandit M. L. Sandal, tr. SBH, Vol. 27, Part I, Allahabad, 1923–1925.

Mundaka Upanisad (MU).

Nandi Sutra, by Devavacaka (Devarddhi Gani), with Curni of Jinadasa Gani and Vrtti of Haribhadra, Vijayadana Suri, ed. Indore, 1931–1932.

Nighantu and the Nirukta, text, L. Sarup, ed. University of Panjab, 1927; L. Sarup, tr. *The Nighantu and the Nirukta,* O.U.P., 1921.

Nyaya Sutra, with Nyayabhasya of Vatsyayana, D. N. Josi, ed. A.A.S., No. 91, 1922; *Nyayabhasya; Nyaya Sutra.*

Nyaya Sutras of Gotama, S. C. Vidyabhusana, ed. and tr. SBH, vol. 8, Allahabad, 1913.

Nyayamanjari, by Jayanta Bhatta, Pandit S. S. NH. Sukla, ed. Kasi Sanskrit Series, Benares, 1936.

Prasna Upanisad, v.

Raghuvamsa, by Kalidasa, M. A. Karandikar and S. Karandikar, eds. Bombay, 1953.

Ramayana, by Valmiki, Vol. 2, *Ayodhyakanda*, S. S. Katti, ed. Bombay, n.d.

Rgarthadipika, on Rgvedasamhita, by Madhava, 2 volumes, L. Sarup, ed. Lahore, 1939.

Rigvedasamhita, With Commentary of Sayana, 6 volumes, F. Max Muller, ed. London, 1849–1874; R. T. H. Griffith, tr. *The Hymns of the Rigveda*, 4 volumes, Benares, 1889–1892; K. F. Geldner, tr. *Der Rigveda*, Vol. I, Gottingen, 1923; H. H. Wilson, tr. *Rigveda Sanhita*, Vol. 2. Poona, 1925.

Samavayanga Sutra, with the Commentary (vivarana) of Abhayadeva, N. Nemachanda, ed. Ahmedabad, 1938.

Sankhya Karika, by Isvarakrsna, S. S. S. Sastri, ed. University of Madras, 1948.

Sankhya Pravacana Bhasya, R. Garbe, ed. HOS, Vol. 2, Harvard University, 1895.

Sankhya Pravacana Sutra, Sankhya Pravacana Bhasya.

Sarvadarsanasamgraha, by Sayana Madhava, V. S. Abhyankar, ed. Second Edition, Poona, 1951; E. B. Cowell, tr. *The Sarvadarsanasamgraha*. London, 1882.

Sarvasiddhantasamgraha, by Samkara, M. Rangacarya, ed. Madras, 1909.

Sathapatha Brahmana, 2 volumes, V. S. Gauda, C. Sarma and S. V. Sastri, eds. Kasi, 1922–1937; J. Eggeling, tr. *The Sathapatha Brahmana*, 5 Parts, SBE, Vol. 12, 26, 41, 43, 44. Oxford, 1882–1900.

Srimanmahabharatam, Mahabharatam.

Srimanmahabharatam Harivamsaparvan, Harivamsaparvan.

Sthananga Sutra, 2 volumes, V. Suracandra, ed. Bombay, 1918–1920.

Sutrakrtanga, with the Commentary (vivarana) of Silanka, 2 volumes, A. S. Suri and C. Ganindra, eds. Bhavangara, 1950–1953; H. Jacobi, tr. *Jaina Sutras, Part II, Uttaradhyayana and Sutrakrtanga*, SBE, Vol. 45. Oxford, 1895.

Svetasvatara Upanisad, with Commentary of Sankara, A.A.S., No. 17, 1905.

Taittriya Aranyaka, 2 volumes, B. S. Phadake, ed. Second Edition, A.A.S., No. 36, 1926–1927.

Taittiriya Brahama, 2 volumes, N. S. Godabole, ed. A.A.S., No. 37, 1898–1938.

Taittirya Upanisad.

Tandyamahabrahmana, A. C. Sastri and P. Sastri, eds. 2 Parts, Kaisi Sanskrit Series No. 105, Benares, 1935–1936.

Tattvasamgraha, with Tattvasamgrahapanjika of Kamalasila, 2 volumes, E. Krishnamacharya, ed. Gaekwad Oriental Series Nos. 30 and 31, Baroda, 1926.

Tattvapaplavasimha, by Jayarasi Bhatti, S. Sanghavi and R. C. Parikh, eds. Gaekwad Oriental Series No. 87, Baroda, 1940.

Uttaradhyayana Sutra, R. D. Vadekar and N. V. Vaidya, eds. Poona, 1954; H. Jacobi, tr. *Jaina Sutras*, Part II, "Uttaradhyayana and Sutrakrtanga," SBE, vol. 45, Oxford, 1895.

Vaisesika Sutras, by Kanada, N. Sinha, tr. SBH, Vol. 6, Allahabad, 1911.

Vajrasucika Upanisad.

Yogabhasya, P. S. R. Sastri and S. R. K. Sastri, eds. Madras Oriental Series No. 94, Madras, 1952.

Yogasutras, R. Prasada, ed. and tr. Third Edition, SBH, Vol. 4, Allahabad, 1924.

Reference Works, Essays and Monographs

(See also the works mentioned in the Reference Notes of the main text.)

Ayer, A. J., *Language, Truth and Logic*, London, 1958.

———, *The Problem of Knowledge*, New York & London: Penguin Books, 1957.

Bagchi, S., *Inductive Reasoning: A Study of Tarka and its Role in Indian Logic*, Calcutta, 1953.

Bareau, A., *Les Sectes Bouddhiques du Petit Véhicule*, Saigon, 1955.

Barua, B. M., *A History of Pre-Buddhistic Indian Philosophy*, Calcutta: University of Calcutta, 1921.

Basham, A. L., *History and Doctrines of the Ajtvikas*, London, 1951.

Beckh, H., *Buddhismus, Vol. I*, Berlin und Leipzig, 1919.

Bhattacharya, V., *The Basic Conception of Buddhism*, Calcutta, 1934.

Bloomfield, M., *Religion of the Veda*, New York and London, 1908.

Bradley, F. H., *Appearance and Reality*, London, 1906.

Broad, C. D., *Mind and its Place in Nature*, London, 1937.

Brough, J., *The Early Brahmanical System of Gotra and Pravara*, Cambridge: Cambridge University Press, 1953.

Burnet, J., *Early Greek Philosophy*, London and Edinburgh, 1892.

————, *Greek Philosophy: Thales to Plato*, London, 1943.

Chatterjee, S. P. (trans.) "Les Missions de Wang Hsien-ti dans l'Inde." Paris: *Journal Asiatique*. 1900. R/P with notes by B. C. Law. Delhi: Srisatguru Pub. 1987.

Chattopadhyaya, B., *Lokayata, A Study on Ancient Indian Materialism*, New Delhi, 1959.

Colebrook, H. T., *Miscellaneous Essays, Vol. I*, London, 1873.

Das Gupta, S. N., *A History of Indian Philosophy, Vol. I*, Cambridge: Cambridge University Press, 1922; Vol. III, Cambridge University Press, 1940.

Deussen, P., *The Philosophy of the Upanishads*. A. S. Gedden, tr. Edinburgh, 1906.

Ducasse, C. J., *The Belief in a Life after Death*, Illinois, 1961.

Dukes, T. J. D. *Okinawan Magic*, Naha, Japan: Mikkyo Kyokai 1966.

————, *Chinese Hand Analysis*, York Beach, ME: Samuel Weiser, 1989.

————, *A Sourcebook of Shingon Buddhism*, London: Cambridge University Buddhist Group & Mushindokai, 1972.

————, *Mushindo Kempo*, London: Lexington Press, 1972, distributed privately.

————, *Mushindo Kempo Advanced Manual*, Cambridge University Karate Club, 1971–1972; R/P Hakurenji Temple 1972–1979; Mushindokai, 1980–1982 (reprinted annually).

————, *Chinese Yoga, Vols. 1 & 2*. Peking/London: Chinese Yoga Federation 1970. R/P 1972–1992.

Dutt, N., *Early Monastic Buddhism*, Second Edition (Revised), Calcutta, 1960.

Ewing, A. C., *The Fundamental Questions of Philosophy*, London, 1958.

Flew, A. G. N. (ed.), *Essays on Logic and Language*, Second Series, Oxford, 1953.

Garbe, R., *Philosophy of Ancient India*, Chicago, 1899.

Geiger, W., *Pali Literatur und Sprache*, Strassburg, 1916.

Glasenapp, H. von, *Der Jainismus*, Berlin, 1925.

Hiriyanna, M., *Outlines of India Philosophy*, London, 1951.

Hopkins, E. W., *Ethics of India*, New Haven, 1924.

Hume, David, *A Treatise of Human Nature*, 2 volumes, London and New York: Everyman's Library No's. 548, 549, 1949.

Hume, R. E., *The Thirteen Principal Upanishads*, v. Upanishads.

Itosushi, The Itosu family records, Ryushinjikai. Naha, Japan, 1951

Jayatilleke, K. N. and Malalasakera, G. P., "Buddhism and the Race Question," *UNESCO*, 1958.

Jennings, J. G., *The Vedantic Buddhism of the Buddha*, London: Oxford University Press, 1947.

Kant, Immanuel, *Critique of Pure Reason*, N. K. Smith, tr. London, 1933.

Kaufmann, W., *Critique of Religion and Philosophy*, London, 1958.

Keith, A. B., *Buddhist Philosophy in India and Ceylon*, Oxford, 1923.

———, *Indian Logic and Atomism*, Oxford, 1921.

———, *Religion and Philosophy of the Vedas*, 2 volumes, HOS, Vols. 31 and 32, 1925.

Kern, H., *Manual of Indian Buddhism*, Strassburg, 1896.

Kirk, G. S. and Raven, J. E., *The Presocratic Philosophers*, Cambridge, 1960.

Konow, S., *Corpus Inscriptionum Indicarum*, Vol. 2, Part I, Calcutta, 1929.

Linquist, S., *Die Methoden des Yoga*, Lund, 1932.

———, *Siddhi und Abhinna*, Lund, 1935.

Luders, H., *Varuna*, 2 volumes, Göttingen, 1951–1959.

Ludwig, A., *Der Rigveda oder die heiligen Hymnen der Brahmana*, Band III, Prague, 1878.

Malalasekera, G. P., *Buddhism and the Race Question*, V. K. N. Jayatilleke.

MacDonell, A., *A Vedic Grammar for Students*, Oxford, 1916.

McKenzie, J., *Hindu Ethics*, O.U.P., 1922.

McCrindle, J. W., *Ancient India*, Westminster, 1901.

Mill, J. S., *A System of Logic*, London, New York, Toronto, 1941.

Mishra, U., *History of Indian Philosophy, Vol. I*, Allahabad, 1957.

Moore, C. A. and Radhakrishnan, S., *A Source Book of Indian Philosophy*, Princeton: Princeton University Press, 1957.

Muir, J., *Original Sanskrit Texts*, 5 volumes, London, 1872–1874.

Murti, T. R. V., *The Central Philosophy of Buddhism*, London, 1955.

Nyanatiloka, *A Guide Through the Abhidhamma Pitaka*, Colombo, 1957.

Ogden, C. K. and Richards, I. A., *The Meaning of Meaning*, London, 1923.

Oldenberg, *Buddha*, Hoey, tr. London and Edinburgh, 1882; Calcutta, 1927.

———, *Buddha, Sein Leben, Seine Lehre, Seine Gemeinde*, 13 Auflage, Stuttgart, 1959.

———, *Die Lehre der Upanishaden und die Anfange des Buddhismus*, Göttingen, 1915.

———, *Religion des Veda*, Stuttgart und Berlin, 1917.

Oltramare, P., *La Formule Bouddhique des douze Causes*, Geneva, 1909.

———, *L'Histoire des Idées Théosophiques dans l'Inde—La Théosophie Bouddhique*, Paris, 1923.

Otomo, R., tr. *Kempo Hishu*. A translation of the Chinese text of the "Chuan Fa Mi Shu" manuscript (held in the Lung Hsing Temple of China) into Japanese. Subsequently translated from Japanese to English by T. Spearman under the title *Esoteric Sourcebook of Kempo*. Both translations were published privately by the Naha Dojo, Okinawa, Japan in 1958.

Pande, G. C., *Studies in the Origin of Buddhism*, University of Allahabad, 1957.

Poussin, L. de la V., *L'Abhidharmakosa De Vasubandhu*, Paris, 1923–1925.

———, *Bouddhisme*, Third Edition, Paris, 1925.

———, *Théorie des Douze Causes*, Gand, 1913.

———, *The Way to Nirvana*, Cambridge University Press, 1917.

Prasad, J., *History of Indian Epistemology*, Second Edition, Delhi, 1958.

Radhakrishnan, S. and Moore, C. A., *A Source Book of Indian Philosophy*, v. C. A. Moore.

———, *The Principal Upanisads*, v. Upanisads. *Indian Philosophy*, Vol. I, London, 1941; Vol. II, London and New York, 1931.

Ranade, R. D., *A Constructive Survey of Upanishadic Philosophy*, Poona, 1926.

Ranade, R. D. and Belvalkar, S. K., *History of Indian Philosophy*, Vol. 2, v. S. K. Belvalkar.

Randle, H. N., *Fragments from Dinnaga*, London, 1926.

———, *Indian Logic in the Early Schools*, O.U.P., 1930.

Rapson, E. J. (ed.), *The Cambridge History of India, Vol. I*, Cambridge, 1922.

Rhine, J. B., *The New Frontiers of the Mind*, Penguin Books, 1950.

———, *The Reach of the Mind*, London, 1958.

Rhys Davids, T. W., *Buddhism*, London, 1917.

Ruben, W., *Die Philosophen der Upanishaden*, Bern, 1947.

———, *Geschichte der indischen Philosophie*, Bern, 1954.

Russell, B. A. W., *A History of Western Philosophy*, 3rd Impression, London, 1948.

———, *Human Knowledge*, London, 1948.

———, *The Philosophy of Leibniz*, 4th Impression, Second Edition, London, 1951.

Ryle, G., *The Concept of Mind*, London, 1950.

Sarathchandra, E. R. *Buddhist Psychology of Perception*, Colombo, Ceylon, 1958.

Saw, R. L., *Leibniz*, New York & London: Penguin Books, 1954.

Schayer, St., *Vorarbeiten zur Geschichte der Mahayanistischen Erlosungslehren*, München, 1921.

Sharma, C. D., *A Critical Survey of Indian Philosophy*, London, 1960.

Sinha, J., *A History of Indian Philosophy*, 2 volumes, Calcutta, 1952–1956.

Slater, R. L. *Paradox and Nirvana*, Chicago, 1950.

Smart, N., *A Dialogue of Religions*, London, 1960.

Stace, W. T., *A Critical History of Greek Philosophy*, London, 1950.

Stebbing, L. S., *A Modern Introduction to Logic*, London, 1945.

Stevenson, Ian, *The Evidence for Survival from Claimed Memories of Former Incarnations*, Essex: Thamesmouth Printing Co. Ltd., 1961.

Tatia, *Studies in Jaina Philosophy*, Banaras, 1951.

Thomas, E. J., *The History of Buddhist Thought*, London, 1953.

————, *The Life of the Buddha*, New York, 1927.

Tischner, R., *Telepathy and Clairvoyance*, London, 1925.

Toynbee, A., *An Historian's Approach to Religion*, O.U.P., 1956.

Ui, H., *The Vaisesika Philosophy*, London, 1917.

Weber, A., *History of Indian Literature*, London, 1878.

————, *Indische Studien*, Bande 18, Berlin und Leipzig, 1850–1898.

Wijesekera, O. H. de A., *The Three Signata*, Kandy, 1960.

Wintnernitz, M., *A History of Indian Literature, Vol. 2*, University of Calcutta, 1933.

————, *Geschichte der indischen Literatur*, 3 volumes, Leipzig, 1909–1920.

Wittgenstein, L., *Tractatus Logico-Philosophicus*, London, 1933.

————, *Philosophische Untersuchungen* [*Philosophical Investigations*], 2 volumes. Oxford, 1953.

Articles

Bahm, A. J., "Soes Seven-Fold Predication Equals Four-Cornered Negation Reversed," *Philosophy East and West*, Vol. 7, pp. 127–130.

Barua, B. M., "*Ajivika—What it means*," ABORI, Vol. 8, 1927, pp. 183–188.

————, "Faith in Buddhism," *Buddhistic Studies*, ed. B. C. Law, Calcutta, 1931, pp. 329–349.

Bevan, E. R., "India in Early Greek and Latin Literature," *The Cambridge History of India*, ed. E. J. Rapson, Vol. I, pp. 391–425.

Bloomfield, M., "The Marriage of Saranyu, Tvastar's Daughter," JAOS, Vol. 15, pp. 172–188.

Burnet, J., "Sceptics," ERE, Vol. II, pp. 228–231.

Chalmers, R., "Tathagata," JRAS, 1898, pp. 103–115.

Charpentier, J., "The Kathaka Upanisad," *Indian Antiquary*, November 1928, pp. 201–207.

Cory, C. A., "A Divided Self," *Journal of Abnormal Psychology*, Vol. 14, Boston, 1919–1920, pp. 281–291.

Das Gupta, M., "Sraddha and Bhakti in the Vedic Literature," IHQ, Vol. 6, pp. 315–335.

Demieville, P., "Le Mémoire des Existences Antérieures," BEFEO, Vol. 27, pp. 283–298.

Dutt, N., "Place of Faith in Buddhism," IHQ, Vol. 16, pp. 639–646.

———, "Popular Buddhism," IHQ, Vol. 21, pp. 251–256.

Dukes, T. J. D., "Exorcism in Esoteric Buddhism." Lecture delivered to the Society for Psychical Research & College of Psychic Studies, London, 1975.

———, "Shingon Buddhism," *The Middle Way*. London. May, 1978.

———, "Shingon Buddhism & Kempo Karate—The Buddhist Warrior Art." Lecture delivered to the Buddhist Society & Buddhist Society Summer School. Reprinted in various editions by the Buddhapadipa Temple, Oxford, Cambridge, Lancaster, Essex & Sussex University Buddhist Societies, 1969–1977. Reprinted London: Mushindokai, 1970–1980, 1987, 1992.

———, *Fighting the Buddha*, Tokyo: Rishokoseikai, 1977.

———, *Fighting the Dharma*, Tokyo: Rishokoseikai, 1977.

———, *Fighting the Sangha*, Tokyo: Kosei Pub., 1978.

———, *The Kingdom of Heaven & Hell*, Tokyo: Kosei Pub., 1978.

———, "The Purposes of Mushindo Kempo," Israel Mushindo Kempo Association Journal, 1974.

———, "The Buddhist Warrior," Bangkok: *Journal of the World Federation of Buddhists*, 1979.

———, "The Hsieh Mai Lun of Bodhidharma" (translation). *Journal of the World Federation of Buddhists*. Bangkok, 1990–1991.

———, "The 6 Gates of Bodhidharma" (translation). Bangkok: *Journal of the World Federation of Buddhists*, 1991.

————, "Entering the Path of Bodhidharma" (translation). *Journal of the World Federation of Buddhists*. Bangkok, 1990–1991.

————, "Mushindo Karate Do," in *Action Karate*. Los Angeles, 1974.

————, "Karate Teachers and Schools in Great Britain—The real story," *Journal of Mushindoka Studies* (JMS), 1969.

————, "The history of Karate Do Kempo in China & Okinawa," JMS, 1975.

————, "Kempo Kata and the Sephiroth of the Kabbalah," JMS, June, 1977.

————, "Early Gnostic Christianity and Buddhism (Pt. 1)," JMS, September, 1977.

————, "Basilides and the Heart Sutra—a Study of Emptiness (Pt 2)," JMS, January, 1978.

Ewing, A. C., "Meaninglessness," in *Mind*, 1937, pp. 347–364.

Faddegon, B., "The Catalogue of the Sciences in the Chandogyopanisad," *A. O.*, Vol. 4, pp. 42–54.

Foley, C. A., "The Vedalla Sutta as Illustrating the Psychological Basis of Buddhist Ethics," JRAS, 1894, pp. 321–333.

Glasenapp, H. von, "Vedanta und Buddhismus" *Abhandlungen der Geistes und Socialwissenschaftlichen Klasse*, 1950, pp. 1013ff.

Hume, R. E., "Miracles in the Canonical Scriptures in Buddhism," JAOS, Vol. 44, p. 162.

Jayatilleke, K. N., "A Recent Criticism of Buddhism," UCR, Vol. 15, pp. 135–150.

————, "Factual Meaning and Verification," UCR, Vol. 13, pp. 1–16.

————, "Some Problems of Translation and Interpretation, I," UCR, Vol. 7, pp. 212–223.

————, "Some Problems of Translation and Interpretation, II," UCR, Vol. 8, pp. 45–55.

Jacobi, H., "Der Ursprung des Buddhismus aus dem Sankhya-Yoga," *Nachrichten von der Königliche Gesellschaft der Wissenschaften tu Göttingen, philologisch-historische Klasse*. Göttingen, 1896, pp. 43–58.

————, "Zur Fruhgeschichte der indischen Philosophie," *Sitzungberichte der Preussische Akademie der Wissenschaften*, Berlin, 1911, pp. 733ff.

Jaini, P. S., "The Vaibhasika Theory of Words," BSOAS, Vol. 22, Part I, 1959, pp. 97–107.

Law, B. C., "The Formulation of the Pratitya-samutpada," JRAS, 1937, pp. 287–292.

Niyamoto, S., "The Logic of Relativity as the Common Ground for the Development of the Middle Way," *Buddhism and Culture*, S. Yamaguchi, ed. Kyoto, 1960, pp. 67–88.

Przyluski, J., "Dastantika, Sautrantika and Sarvastivadin," IHQ, Vol. 16, pp. 246–254.

Poussin, L. de la V., "Dogmatique Bouddhique," JA, Tome 20, 1092, pp. 237–306.

————, "Documents D'Abhidarma—les Deux, les Quatres, les Troit Vérités, Extraites de la Vibhasa et du Kosa de Samghabhadra," *Mélanges Chinois et Bouddhique*, Vol. 5, pp. 159–187.

————, "Faith and Reason in Buddhism," *Transactions of the Third International Congress for the History of Religions*, Vol. II, 1908, pp. 32–43.

————, "Le Bouddha et les Abhinna," in *Museon*, 1931, pp. 335–342.

————, "On the Authority (Pramanya) of the Buddhist Agamas," in JRAS, 1902, pp. 363–76.

Radhakrishnan, S., "The Teaching of Buddha by Speech and by Silence," in *The Hibbert Journal*, Vol. XXXII, pp. 342–356.

Raju, P. T., "The Principle of Four-Cornered Negation in Indian Philosophy," *Review of Metaphysics*, Vol. 7, pp. 694–713.

Ryle, G., "Categories," *Logic and Language*, A. G. N. Flew, ed., Second Series, pp. 65–81.

Rhys Davids, C. A. F., "Logic" (Buddhist), ERE, Vol. 8, pp. 132–133.

————, "Paticcasamuppada," ERE, Vol. 9, pp. 672–674.

Robinson, R. H., "Some Logical Aspects of Nagarjuna's System," *Philosophy East and West*, Vol. 6, pp. 291–308.

Ruben, W., "Uber den Tattvopaplavasimha des Jayarasi Bhatta eine Agnostizistische Erkenntnis kritik," in *Wiener Zeitschrift fur die Kunde Sud und Ostasiens und Archiv fur indische Philosophie*, Band II, 1958, pp. 140–153.

Sadaw, L., "Some Points in Buddhist Doctrine," in JPTS, 1914, pp. 115–163.

Thomas, E. J., "Buddhism in Modern Times," UCR, Vol. 9, pp. 215–225.

Tucci, G., "A Sketch of Indian Materialism," in PIPC, 1925, pp. 34–43.

Warder, A. K., "Early Buddhism and Other Contemporary Systems," BSOAS, Vol. 18, 1956, pp. 43–63.

Wijesekera, O. H. de A., "A Pali Reference to Brahmana Caran-s," *Adyar Library Bulletin*, Vol. 20, pp. 294–309.

————, "Upanishadic Terms for Sense Functions," UCR, Vol. 2, pp. 14–24.

————, "Vedic Gandharva and Pali Gandhabba," UCR, Vol. 3, pp. 73–95.

Other Useful Texts

Bapat, P. V., ed. *2500 Years of Buddhism*. New Delhi: Publications Division, Ministry of Information, 1956.

Bareau, André. *Les Sectes Bouddhiques du Petit Véhicule*. Saigon, 1955.

Beyer, Stephan. *The Cult of Tara: Magic and Ritual in Tibet*. Berkeley: University of California Press, 1973.

Bharati, Agehananda. *The Tantric Tradition*. London: Rider, 1965.

Bhattacharyya, Benoytosh. *An Introduction to Buddhist Esoterism*. Mysore: (Humphrey Milford) Oxford University Press, 1932.

Bhattacharyya, K. *Studies in Philosophy. Vol. I*. Calcutta: Progressive Publishers, 1956.

Bradley, F. H. *Appearance and Reality: A Metaphysical Essay*. Oxford: Oxford University Press, 1969.

Chatterjee, A. K. *The Yogacara Idealism*. Varanasi: Banaras Hindu University Press, 1962.

Conze, Edward. *Buddhist Thought in India*. Ann Arbor: The University of Michigan Press, 1967.

———. *Materials for a Dictionary of the Prajnaparamita Literature*. Tokyo: Suzuki Research Foundation, 1967.

———. "The Ontology of the Prajna-Paramita," *Philosophy East and West*, 3, No. 2 (1953), pp. 117–129.

———. *The Prajnaparamita Literature*. The Hague: Mouton, 1960.

———. "The Yogacarin Treatment of Prajnaparamita Texts," *Proceedings of the 23rd Congress of Orientalists*. Cambridge, 1959, pp. 230–231.

———. *30 years of Buddhist Studies*. Oxford: B. Cassirer, 1968.

———. *Further Buddhist Studies*. Oxford: B. Cassirer, 1975.

———. *Buddhist Texts Through the Ages*. Oxford: B. Cassirer, 1952.

———. *Buddhist Scriptures*, London: Penguin, r/p 1969.

———. *Memoirs of a Modern Gnostic* (Parts 1–2). Sherborne, England: Samizdat Pub. Co., 1979.

Coomaraswamy, Ananda K. *Buddha and the Gospel of Buddhism*. London: George G. Harrap, 1916. Rpt., New York: Harper and Row (Torchbook edition), 1964.

Dasgupta, Shashi Bhushan. *An Introduction to Tantric Buddhism*. Calcutta: Calcutta University Press, 1958.

———. *Obscure Religious Cults*. Calcutta: K. L. Mukhopadhyay, 1962.

Dasgupta, Surendranath. *Indian Idealism*. Cambridge: Cambridge University Press, 1969.

Datta, D. M. *The Six Ways of Knowing: A Critical Study of the Advaita Theory of Knowledge*. Calcutta: University of Calcutta, 1972.

Dayal, Har. *The Bodhisattva Doctrine in Buddhist Sanskrit Literature*. London: Routledge & Kegan Paul, 1932.

Dutt, Nalinaksha. *Aspects of Mahayana Buddhism and Its Relation to Hinayana*. London: Luzac, 1930.

———. *Buddhist Sects in India*. Calcutta: K. L. Mukhopadhyay, 1970.

———. *Early Monastic Buddhism*. Calcutta: K. L. Mukhopadhyay, 1971.

Dutt, Sukumar. *Buddhist Monks and Monasteries of India*. London: George Allen & Unwin, 1962.

Frauwallner, E. "On the Date of the Buddhist Master of the Law, Vasubandhu." *Serie Orientale Roma*, 3, 1951.

Govinda, Anagarika. *The Psychological Attitude of Early Buddhist Philosophy*. New York: Samuel Weiser, 1974.

Guenther, Herbert V., and Leslie S. Kawamura. *Mind in Buddhist Psychology*. Emeryville, CA: Dharma, 1975.

Guenther, H. V., and Chogyam Trungpa. *The Dawn of Tantra*. Berkeley: Shambala, 1975.

Hakeda, Yoshito S. *The Awakening of Faith*. New York: Columbia University Press, 1967.

Hamilton, Clarence H. *Buddhism, a Religion of Infinite Compassion: Selections from Buddhist Literature*. New York: Liberal Arts Press, 1952.

"K'uei Chi's Commentary on Wei-Shih-Er-Shih-Lun," *Journal of the American Oriental Society*. 53, 1933, pp. 144–151.

Horner, I. B. *Women under Primitive Buddhism*. London: Routledge & Kegan Paul, 1930; Rpt., Delhi: Motilal Banarsidass, 1975.

Jaini, Padmanabh. "Origin and Development of the Theory of Viprayuktasamskaras," *Bulletin of the School of Oriental and African Studies (University of London)*, 23, Part 3, 1959, pp. 531–547.

Jayatilleke, K. N. *Early Buddhist Theory of Knowledge*. London: Allen & Unwin, 1963.

Kalupahana, David J. *Buddhist Philosophy: A Historical Analysis*. Honolulu: The University Press of Hawaii, 1976.

Keith, Arthur B. *Buddhist Philosophy in India and Ceylon*. Oxford: Clarendon Press, 1923.

Lamotte, Etienne. *Histoire de Bouddhisme Indien*. Louvain: Museon, 1958.

MacDonell, Arthur. *A History of Sanskrit Literature*. New York: Appleton, 1900; Rpt., Delhi: Motilal Banarsidass, 1971.

————. *India's Past: A Survey of Her Literature, Religions, Languages, and Antiquities*. Oxford: Clarendon Press, 1927.

McGovern, W. M. *A Manual of Buddhist Philosophy*. New York: E. P. Dutton, 1923.

Mahathera, Praavahera Vajiranana. *Buddhist Meditation in Theory and Practice*. Colombo, Ceylon: M. D. Gunasena, 1962.

Majumdar, R. C. *Ancient India*. Delhi: Motilal Banarsidass, 1971.

Malalasekera, G. P. *Dictionary of Pali Proper Names*. Indian Texts Series. 2 volumes. London: Murray, 1937–1938.

————. ed. *Encyclopaedia of Buddhism*. Vol. 1. Part I: A–Aca. Colombo, Ceylon: The Government Press, 1961.

Matilal, Bimal Krishna. "A Critique of Buddhist Idealism," L. Cousins et al., eds., *Buddhist Studies in Honour of I. B. Horner*. Dordrecht, Holland: Reidel, 1974.

————. "Indian Theories of Knowledge and Truty" (review article), *Philosophy East and West*, 18, No. 4, 1968, 321–333.

————. *The Navya-Nyaya Doctrine of Negation*. Harvard Oriental Series, Vol. 46. Cambridge: Harvard University Press, 1968.

Murti, T. R. V. *The Central Philosophy of Buddhism*. London: Allen & Unwin, 1955.

Nagao, Gadjin. "President's Address to the International Association of Buddhist Studies," First Conference, New York, September 15, 1978.

Nariman, J. K. *Literary History of Sanskrit Buddhism*. Delhi: Motilal Banarsidass, 1972.

Obermiller, E. *Analysis of the Abhisamayalamkara*. Gaekwad Oriental Series, No. 27. Baroda: University of Baroda, 1933–1939.

————. "A Study of the Twenty Aspects of Sunyata (Based on Haribhadra's Abhisamayalamkaraloka and the Pancavimsatisahasirkaprajnaparamitasutra," *Indian Historical Quarterly*, 9, 1933, pp. 170–187.

————. "The Doctrine of Prajnaparamita as exposed in the Abhisamayalamkara of Maitreya," *Acta Orientalia*, 11, 1932, 1–133.

————. "The Term Sunyata in its Different Interpretations," *Journal of Greater India Society*, 1, 1934, 105–117.

Potter, Karl, *Presuppositions of India's Philosophies*. Englewood Cliffs, NJ: Prentice-Hall, 1963.

Rahula, Walpola. "Vijnaptimatrata Philosophy in the Yogacara System and Some Wrong Notions," *The Middle Way: Journal of the Buddhist Society*, 47, No. 3, 1972.

————. *What the Buddha Taught*. New York: Grove Press, 1959.

Raju, P. T. *Idealistic Thought of India*. Cambridge: Harvard University Press, 1953.

Ramanan, K. Ventaka. *Nagarjuna's Philosophy*. Rutland, VT: Charles E. Tuttle, 1966.

Robinson, Richard H. *Early Madhyamika in India and China*. Delhi: Motilal Banarsidass, 1976.

————. *The Buddhist Religion*. Belmont, CA: Dickenson, 1970.

Schmithausen, Lambert. "On the Problem of the Relation of Spiritual Practice and Philosophical Theory in Buddhism," *German Scholars on India. Contributions to Indian Studies, Vol. II*. Bombay: Nachiketa Publications, 1976.

Sharma, Dhirendra. *The Negative Dialectics of India*. Leiden: E. J. Brill, 1970.

Sopa, Geshe Lhundup, and Jeffrey Hopkins. *Practice and Theory of Tibetan Buddhism*. New York: Grove Press, 1976.

Speyer, J. S., tr. *Jatakamala: Garland of Birth Stories*. Sacred Books of the Buddhists, No. 1. London, 1895.

Stcherbatsky, Th. *Soul Theory of the Buddhists*. Varanasi: Bharatiya Vidya Prakasan, 1970.

————. *The Central Conception of Buddhism*. Calcutta: Susil Gupta, 1932.

————. *The Conception of Buddhist Nirvana*. Leningrad: Academy of Sciences of the USSR, 1927.

————. *Buddhist Logic, Vol. I*. Leningrad. 1930; New York: Dover, 1962.

————. *The Central Conception of Buddhism and the Meaning of the Word "Dharma."* London, 1923.

Strawson, P. F. *Individuals: An Essay in Descriptive Metaphysics*. London: Methuen, 1961.

Streng, Frederick J. *Emptiness: A Study in Religious Meaning*. New York: Abingdon Press, 1967.

Suzuki, D. T. *On Indian Mahayana Buddhism*. New York: Harper & Row, 1968.

————. *Outlines of Mahayana Buddhism*. New York: Schocken, 1963.

Swartz, Robert J., ed. *Perceiving, Sensing and Knowing*. New York: Doubleday, 1965.

Takakusu, Junjiro. *The Essentials of Buddhist Philosophy*. 1947; Rpt., Honolulu: University of Hawaii Press, 1956.

————. "The Life of Vasu-bandhu by Paramartha (A.D. 499–569)," *T'oung Pao*, Ser. II, 5, 1904, 269–296.

Thomas, Edward J. *The History of Buddhist Thought*. London: Routledge & Kegan Paul, 1951.

Tripathi, C. L. *The Problems of Knowledge in Yogacara Buddhism*. Varanasi: Bharat-Bharati, 1972.

Thurman, Robert A. F. "Buddhist Hermeneutics," *Journal of the American Academy of Religion*, 46, No. 1, 1978.

Tucci, G. *On Some Aspects of the Doctrines of Maitreya (natha) and Asanga*. Calcutta: University of Calcutta, 1930.

Ueda, Yoshifumi. "Two Main Streams of Thought in Yogacara Philosophy," *Philosophy East and West*, 17, January–October, 1967, pp. 155–165.

Ui, H. "Maitreya as a Historical Personage," *Indian Studies in Honor of Charles Rockwell Lanman*. Cambridge: Harvard University Press, 1929.

Warder, A. K. *Indian Buddhism*. Delhi: Motilal Banarsidass, 1970.

Warren, Henry Clarke. *Buddhism in Translations*. Cambridge: Harvard University Press, 1896; Rpt., New York: Atheneum, 1963.

Wayman, Alex. "Buddhism," *Historia Religionum*, Vol. II. Religions of the Present. Leiden: E. J. Brill, 1971.

———. "The Buddhism and the Sanskrit of Buddhist Hybrid Sanskrit," *Journal of the American Oriental Society*. 85, No. 1, 1965, pp. 111–115.

———. "The Meanings of the Term Cittamatra," Paper delivered at the Association of Asian Studies Meeting, 1972.

———. "Nescience and Insight According to Asanga's Yogacarabhumi, " Unpublished manuscript.

———. "The Yogacara Idealism" (review article), *Philosophy East and West*, 15, No. 1, 1965, pp. 65–73.

White, Nicholas P. "Aristotle on Sameness and Oneness," *The Philosophical Review*, 80, No. 2, 1971, 177–197.

Wittgenstein, Ludwig. *The Blue and Brown Books*. New York: Harper Torchbooks, 1965.

Yamakami, Sogen. *Systems of Buddhistic Thought*. Calcutta: University of Calcutta, 1912.

Yampolsky, Philip B. *The Platform Sutra of the Sixth Patriarch*. New York: Columbia University Press, 1967.

Zeyst, H. G. A. "Abhinna," *Encyclopaedia of Buddhism*. Vol. I, Part I. Colombo, Ceylon: The Government Press, 1967.

Zimmer, Heinrich. *Philosophies of India*. Bollingen Series, No. 26. London: Routledge & Kegan Paul, 1951; Princeton University Press.

Reference Books and Dictionaries

A Dictionary of Japanese Buddhist Terms, H. Inagaki. Kyoto: Nagata Bunshodo, 1985.

A Dictionary of Chinese Buddhist Terms. W. E. Soothill & L. Houdous. r/p Taipei: Cheng Wen Pub. Co., 1970.

A Sanscrit and Chinese Dictionary (Handbook of Chinese Buddhism), E. J. Eitel & K. Takakawa. r/p San Francisco: Chinese Materials Centre, 1976.

A Tibetan-English Dictionary, Dass, Sarat Chandra. Rev. ed. Delhi: Motilal Banarsidass, 1970.

A Sanskrit-English Dictionary, Monier-Williams, Sir Monier. Rpt., Oxford: Clarendon Press, 1964.

Abhidhanappadipika, M. Jinavijaya, ed. Ahmedabad, 1923.

Buddhist Hybrid Sanskrit Dictionary, F. Edgerton, ed. New Haven and London, 1953.

Chambers 20th Century Dictionary, E. A. Mcdonald, OBE, BA (Oxon). Chambers, 1978.

Critical Pali Dictionary, Vol. I, V. Trenckner, D. Anderson, H. Smith and H. Hendriksen, eds. Copenhagen, 1924–1948.

Concise Oxford Dictionary, H. W. Fowler and F. G. Fowler, eds. Fourth Edition revised by E. McIntosh, Oxford, 1959.

Concordance to the Principal Upanisads, G. A. Jacob, Bombay, 1891.

Dictionary of Pali Proper Names, 2 volumes, G. P. Malalasekera, ed. London, 1937–1938.

Dictionary of Philosophy, D. Runes, ed. London, 1945.

Dictionary of Philosophy, P. A. Angeles. New York: Harper & Row, 1981.

Encyclopaedia of Religion and Ethics, 12 volumes, J. Hastings, ed. Edinburgh, 1908–1926.

Pali Text Society's Pali-English Dictionary, T. W. Rhys Davids and W. Stede, eds., London, 1921.

The Mushindo Dictionary of Sanscrit, Chinese, Tibetan & Japanese Buddhist Terms, S. Ataie, C. Davis, N. Hammes & T. Dukes, eds. London: Hakurenji Temple, 1976.

Sanskrit-Worterbuch, 7 volumes, O. Bohtlinck and R. Roth, eds. St. Petersburg, 1855–1875.

Vedic Concordance, M. Bloomfield. Cambridge, MA, 1906.
(Works and sources upon Esoteric Buddhism are given in either the main text or within the Notes and Reference section.)

INDEX

A

Abhidhamma, 136, 482
Abhidharma, 111
Abhidharmakosa, 97, 105, 111, 139, 410
Abhimukkya avastha, 269
Abhisanditakayacitta, 48, 263
Acarya, 71, 84, 166, 181, 276, 450
Acarya Mutthi, 450
accomplishment, 250
Achali, 74
acupuncture, 146, 242
Adi-Buddha, 64, 74
Agadakayasiksa, 220
agata, 73
aggression, 264
Agni, 158
Ahjatasattu, 198
Ahjivika, 401
Aikijitsu, 426
air, 13, 50, 51, 52, 92, 250, 251
Ajari, 74, 451
Ajurveda, 430
Akasagarbha, 48
alambana, 15, 472
Alaya consciousness, 139
alchemy, 406
alloisus, 21
Amitabha, 274
Amoghavajra, 87, 88, 214, 215, 263, 420
An Shih Kuo, 242
Anagarika, 32
Ananda, 192
Anatma, 41
Anaxamines, 6
Angulimala, 182, 191
animal rulers, 273
Annica, 41
anti-logic, 111
Anupassanasti, 197
apana, 139
apratigaha, 133

arahant, 231
Arata, 168
Ardhacandra, 163
Arjuna, 163, 165, 170
Arthava Veda, 429
Aryadeva, 111, 410
asana, 103
Asanga, 200, 289, 458
Asantana, 290
Asibhandhakaputta, 160
Asoka, 165, 172, 173, 193, 277
Asphanaka, 105
Astadasajacan, 228, 230, 233
Astadasarahantapani, 228, 231
Astadasavijaya, 228
Asthimajja Parisuddhi, 230
Asvaghosa, 192
asvakaya, 161
Arthava Veda, 123
Avasavidya, 147
awakening, 356
awareness, 225
Ayamtamsaka Sutra, 75
Ayas, 162
Ayur, 7, 123

B

Balam, 159
Bankei, *416*
Bardiesenes, 407
Basilides, 40, 407
bells, 462
Bhagavad Gita, 170
Bhikku ceremony, 107
Bhikku Khantipalo, 397
Bhikshu Angapala, 243
Bhikshu Rakshana, 243
Bhima, 169, 170
Bhutadhata, 51
blocking

defensive, 178
Bodhidharma, 229, 267, 295ff, 412
Bodhiruci, 229
Bodhisattva ordination, 107
Bodhisattva Vajramukti, 243
Bodhisattva Vajramukti, defense
    sequences, 220
Bodhisattva Vow, 38, 262, 432
body, mystical, 66
body/mind, 258, 481
body/mind dissolving, 263
Body of Compassionate Anger, 201
bone splint, 142
Book of Han, 206
Book of War, 25, 205
Boroboudur Temple, 408
Brahma, 101, 430
breath, 125
Buddha Heart, 100
Buddha Akshobhya, 253
Buddha Amoghasiddhi, 178, 209
Buddha Mahavairocana, 63, 179
Buddha Ratnasambhava, 272
Buddha Shakyamuni, 35, 56, 63, 67, 89, 98,
    105, 116, 134, 168, 184, 191, 192, 197,
    198, 237, 265
Buddhaghosa, 197
Buddhi, 45
Buddhism, 6, 7, 8, 17, 24, 25, 28, 78, 362,
    393
Buddhist sects, 283
Butler, Bishop, 19
Byo O, 158

C

Caitya, 68
Cakku Citta Utpada, 482
cakra, 163
Cakravartin, 35
Chaan-Na, 202, 296
Chaan school, 182, 215
Chaan shi, 409
Chan Sen Fong, 419
Chang Chung Ching, 121
Charaka, 125
cheirology, 100
Chen Yen, 69
Ch'en Yuan Pin, 425
Chi, 67, 120, 125, 128, 129, 133, 452
Chi Chi Wang, 243

Chi Kung, 470
Chi Yu, 205
Chiao Ti Tsi, 205
chi chi hsiu, 206
Chih I, 147, 398
Chinese Buddhist Dynasties, 282
Ching Kang, 65
chronological records, 362
chronology, 284
Chuan Fa, 3, 4, 22, 49, 65, 104, 134, 137, 146,
    147, 184, 194, 202, 269, 458
Chuan Fa Mikkyo Acaryas, 86
citta, 287, 288, 289, 404
Clausewitz, 157
Collection of Essences, 87
collection beyond birth and death, 291
colors, four, 406
confrontation, 269
confusion, 47, 53, 253
consciousness, 11, 12, 22, 136, 230, 258,
    284, 285, 286, 289, 473, 479
    eighteen factors of, 16
    root, 291
    stream of, 292
consciousness only, 266
contemplation of five ways of moving,
    197
Conze, Edward, 266, 395
curse, 239

D

Dainichi, 64
Dainichikyo, 87
Danapala, 88
dances, 209
Darsatantika School, 396
dausthalya, 262
Dausthulya, 484
death, 238, 239
    imminent, 481
    personal, 269
defensive arts, 181
Dengyo Daishi, 88, 90
dependent origination, 253
destruction, 238
Devadasi, 430
Devadatta, 192, 194
devas, sensual, 198
Dharanimdhara, 48

Dharma, 15, 24, 28, 37, 40, 60, 68, 83, 110, 185, 196, 197, 393, 449
  closed hand of, 185
  teacher, 408
Dharmabhadra, 88
Dharmalaksana School, 396
dharmamukti, 185
Dharmanis, 465
Dharmapala, 194
Dharmavijaya, 158
Dharmic Chi, 67
Dharmic Ri, 67
Dhatusmriti, 26
Dhyana teacher, 409
diamond, 421
diamond steps, 235
dietary therapy, 148
dik, 71
directions, six, 71
doctrine of elements, 3, 8
doctrine of physical and mental energy, 136
dog syndrome, 352, 353
Dosa, 45
dragon, 16
dragon flow, 240
drums, 462
dualism, 78
Dukkha, 41, 250
dullness, 45
Duryodhana, 169
Dvasatya, 183
Dvadasadvara Sastra, 410

E

earth, 13, 50, 51, 52, 92, 250, 251
effort, 250
ego, 20, 356
eight limbs, 102, 408
eighteen arahants, 434, 435
Eighteen Assemblies, 88
eighteen classical sets of mudra, 231
eighteen entrances, 136, 258
eighteen levels of *prajna* wisdom, 230
eighteen moves of the *Arahants*, 231
eighteen original Indian Buddhist sects, 410
eighteen *paramitas*, 228
eighteen subdwings, 228, 229
eighteen victors, 228

eighteen Voidnesses of Wisdom, 228
eightfold nature of consciousness, 292
Eightfold Path, 82
Ekalavya, 163
elemental door to consciousness, 3
elemental mind, 17
elements, 13, 277, 395, 396, 432
elements
  eighteen, 17
elements of mind, 10, 13
Emperor Su Tsung, 215
Emperor Wu, 205
Emulating the Profected, 269
emulative conduct, 269
Enchin, 88
encounter, situational, 269, 270
energy, 453
enlightenment, 74, 393
enlightenment of the Buddha, 26
Entering the Buddha's Path, 309
esoteric schools, 60, 63, 89, 179, 477
ether, 50, 69, 92, 250, 251, 401
exercises, health giving, 220
experience, 353
  unreal, 359
expression, 454

F

Fa Hsien, 176
Fa Shih, 408
faith, 45, 53
fear, 484
feelings, 11
Fei Hsu, 215
feinting maneuvers, 208
field of experience, 258
fighting, 163
fire, 13, 50, 51, 52, 92, 250, 251
Fist of Wrathful Anger, 214
Five Animals Play, 123
Five Elements of Nature, 183
Five Essences, 252
Five Great Elements, 252
Five Natures, 252
Five Sections Mind Meditation, 87
five winds, 139
form, 11, 13
Four *Dharma* Gifts, 52
four elements, 138
Four Foundations of Mindfulness, 248

Four Noble Truths, 82, 96, 393, 414
Four Sons of *Shakya*, 193
free will, 86
Four Wisdoms, 249
Fukujoju, 178
Funnu Ken In, 214

G

Gaganaganja Parippccha, 51
gamyamana, 73
Gandhara, 156
gata, 71
Gautama Siddhartha, 393
genetic codes, 479
geographical considerations, 106
Gigekishu, 206
giver, 409
Gnanagupta, 193
Go Ti Ta, 205
Gobushinkan, 87
Gorin Hishaku, 69
Gramani, 160
Gomutraka, 169
gradual path, 444
Great Bliss, 204
Great White Shattering, 238
greed, 45, 46, 53
guna, 123
Gyo, 398

H

hand
    clasped, 166, 179, 184
    closed, 166, 178, 184
    extending, 208
    lightning, 162
    open, 184, 185
    thunderbolt, 162, 166, 186
Hangyo Hanza, 398
Hanivarman, 410
Harsha, 173
hastakaya, 161
Hastatigarta, 169
Hatha Yoga, 408
hatred, 45, 46, 53
healing, 119, 134, 140, 398, 463, 465, 466, 469, 477
healing conversation, 149
Heart Sutra, 59

Hinayana, 25
Hinduism, 6
history, 172
Hoben, 82
Hsen Zui, 435
Hsieh Mai Lun, 318, 347
Hsiang, 45, 462
Hsien Hsiu, 202
Hsing, 225, 231, 248, 249, 270, 423, 483
Hsiu Hsing, 75
Hua To, 121, 242
Hua Yen, 75
Huan Ting, 398
Hui Yuan, 436
Huo fa, 147
Huo Ming, 147

I

I-Chin Ching, 435
Ida, 129
ignorance, 53
illness, 129
inaction, 200
Indian Buddhist Sects, 294
Indo-Aryans, 155
Indra, 158, 166
Indra's net, 75, 407
Indrajala, 75
Indriya dhatu, 14
Ing, 431
initiator, 409
injuries, 451
inner cleansing, 4
intelligence, 45, 53
intention, 250
Ipponken, 209
Iryapatha, 197
I Sheng lau Li, 136
Ishinpo, 147
Ishoryu Ri, 136
I Tsing, 139, 208, 240

J

Jainism, 6
Jarasandha, 170
Jen Hsiang, 45
Jetavana, 237
Jigaro Kano, 427
jiva, 138

Jivaka, 139, 239
Jivat, 50, 129, 242
Jnana marga, 170
joge, 250
Jogenshinjoshakkyumokuroku, 88
Jojin, 88
Jou Chuan School, 419
Judo, 427
Juhachieshiki, 88
Ju Jitsu Schools, 427

K

Kaji, 214
Kaku shoku uchi, 205
Kalama, 168
Kalari, 174
Kalpa, 128
Kalyana mitra, 398
Kanjo, 427
Kan-Ku, 51
karate, 218, 423, 451, 456
Karma, 76, 249, 250, 358, 399, 403
Karma Siddhi Prrakrama, 254
Karmaphala, 250
Karma vipaka, 403
Kasina, 68, 73
Kasyapa Matanga, 206
Kausika, 169
Kaya, 13
Kayaka, 134
Kayaka manas, 137
kayakajiva, 138
Kayasmriti, 26
Kempo, 184, 425, 454, 455
Kenchuji Temple, 426
Kikatsuryu Ri, 136
King Asoka, 35
King Indrabhuti, 203
King Naratsuan, 409
King Pi Liu Li, 193
King Pradyota, 235
King Prasenadi, 197
Kioh Yuan Shang Jen, 420
Klesa, 53, 97, 201, 250, 255, 271, 399, 471
Kobo Daishi, 59, 88, 89, 90
Kongo, 64, 65
Kongobu Bodhisattva, 214
Kongochoyugakyo, 87, 88
Kongokai Mandara, 87
Kri, 76

Krisna, 163, 169, 170
Kriya, 261
Krtsna, 68
Ksatreya, 145, 146, 158, 161, 163, 165, 166, 167, 173, 176, 179, 192, 211, 228, 276
Ksatreya Devadatta, 191
Ksatreya Vajra mukti, 220
Kshantideva, 168
Ksurapra, 163
Kuan Kung, 51
Kuden, 427
Kukai, 88, 458
Kumarajiva, 410
Kundalini, 129
Kung, 24
Kung Fu Tzu, 121
Kuo Chi Yi, 242, 243

L

Laksana, 45
Laksya, 224
Lama dances, 203, 204, 462
Lao Tze, 121
Laukika, 82, 457
Leung Wu Ti, 277
Li Lao Shih, 420
life energy, 50
lightning, 162
lions, 168, 169, 425, 433
    Eastern Art Closed Hand, 207
    play, 197, 228, 239, 242
    skill, 207
logos, 21
Lokasema, 111
Lokatikya, 400
Lu Pu Wei, 121

M

mace, 162
macrobiotics, 469
Madhyamika School, 199, 411
Madhyanta Vibhaga Bhasya, 254
magic carpet, 65
magicians, stage, 65
Maha-Bhuta, 13, 14, 51, 138, 183
Maha Suklaja, 238
Mahabhuta Nata, 251
Mahajima Nikaya, 198
Maha Katyana, 235

Mahakasyapa, 139
Mahasanghika School, 291
Mahasasaka School, 401
Mahasisaka, 291
Mahasukha, 204
Maha Sukkha, 99
Mahavairocana, 69, 74, 209
Mahavairocana Buddha, 84, 86, 211
Mahavairocana Sutra, 52, 67, 69, 73, 87
Mahavastu, 105
Maha Vyutpatti, 69, 70
Mahayana School, 10, 21, 23, 25, 26, 35, 38,
    71, 83, 106, 112, 174, 175, 194, 197, 261,
    277, 284, 399, 409
Mahesvara, 401
maithuna, 204
Maitreyanatha, 410
manas, 23, 50, 137, 258, 259, 284, 285, 287,
    289
mandala,
    body, 99
    Buddhas, 211, 249, 477
    development, 84
    dharma, 84, 86
    esoteric, 391
    fivefold, 54
    Genzu, 85
    Karma, 84, 85, 86, 187, 235
    Kongokai Maha, 235
    maha, 84, 85, 87, 88, 89
    Nine Assemblies, 87
    of eighty-one *Bhagavats,* 87
    of elements, 6
    of experience, 95
    of healing, 119
    of human characteristics, 45, 97
    of *Mahavairocana,* 64
    of movement, 155
    of symbolism, 56
    paradigms, 455
    pictures, 273
    samaya, 84, 86
    sixfold, 54
    vajra, 87
    walking, 235
    woven, 65
Mandala Temple of *Borobodur,* 104
mano, 23, 50, 284, 285, 286, 287, 289
Mano Dhatu, 13, 14, 15, 17, 23, 285
Mano-Kaya, 13, 14, 15
mandalas, 3, 80, 91, 209, 271

Mano Vijnana, 22, 23, 287
Manovijnana dhatu, 15, 16, 285
manovinnanadhatu, 285
Mano visaya dhatu, 15
mantras, 147, 230
maranasmriti, 269
marma, 129, 240, 242
martial arts, 452
massage, 242
Matreyanatha, 69
medicine, 100, 119, 132, 140, 230, 398
meditation, 147, 230, 348, 473, 479
    Bodhidharma method, 319
    Brahmavihara, 105
    five sections mind, 87
    insight, 411
    Kuan Kung, 253
    perpetually moving, 398
    physical, 172
    solitary, 408
Mei Ching, 205
mental,
    drama, 223
    purification, 77
    stain, 250
    volitions, 11
Mi Chiao, 75, 151, 179, 194, 231
Mikkyo, 3, 66, 67, 75, 87, 151, 188, 194,
    204
Mikkyo School, 63, 65, 73, 74, 77, 83, 89,
    215, 427, 458
military, 160
military arts, 205
Mimamsa, 401
mind, 19, 261, 285, 287
mind moment, 400
mind/body, 132
mind/body complex, 11
mindfullness, 26, 248, 254
mindfullness of breath, 197
Mi-Shu sect, 89
Mi Tsung sect, 89
Moha, 45
Moksha, 181, 403
monastic traditions, 30
monasteries in China, 107
Monastic Body protecting form, 243
monk warriors, 182, 194
monuments, esoteric, 408
mudra
    abhaya, 191, 192

knowledge fist, 209
fearlessness, 188
vara, 192
vajra, 65, 179
mudras, 187, 188, 208, 221

N

Na Lo Yen Tien, 174
Naatyasastra, 430
nadi, 129, 240, 242, 463, 465
naga spirits, 30, 32
naganadi, 240
Nagarjuna, 71, 87, 110, 111, 139, 178, 199,
    237, 242, 263, 401, 410, 411, 431, 457
Nairatmyacitta, 263
Nama-Rupa, 22, 23
nama, 134
Namo, 13
Namo Kaya, 15
narasimha, 176
narya, 175, 176, 178, 214
Nar(y)ayana Deva, 174
narya-nata vajramukti, 196
Nasatya, 159
nata, 166, 167, 173, 174, 175, 178, 181, 203,
    219, 231, 425, 429, 471
Natabhata Monastery, 175
Nataraja, 173, 174
natavajra, 175
nature of the self, 10
Naya Vipassana, 56
near death experience, 457
new self syndrome, 483
Ni Wan Ti, 243
Nidana, 465
Nigranth, 401
Ninso, 45
Nirvana, 393
nispati, 250
Noble EIghtfold Path, 394
Non-Self Being, 263
nrita, 214
Nyingma-Pa, 106, 204

O

object, 250
Ockam's razor, 479
odor, four types, 406
Ohsawa, Georges, 469

Okayama Hochiroji, 426
opiates, 142
opium trade, 151
origen, 40, 407

P

Padmasambhava, 202, 204, 442
Palagius, 40
Pan Kuo, 206
Paramarthasatya, 37, 82, 457
paramitas, 51, 200
paratantra, 269
Parinirvana, 26, 102
Parjanya, 162
Patanjali, 424
Path of Inner Emptiness, 110
Patripassans, 407
patti, 160
patti kaya, 161
Parivritti, 478
Peking Tripitaka, 51
Pelagius, 407
perception, 11, 287
perfection, 16 stages, 211
physical language, 134, 135
physiognomy, 45, 100
Pi Mi, 179
Ping An, 252
Ping An Hsing, 270, 483
Ping Li Hsing, 455
Ping Wang, 158
Pingala, 129
Plato, 6
Po Fu technique, 208
prajapala, 243
Prajnaparamita Sutra, 71
Prajnatara, 229
prana, 125, 129, 133, 139
prasada, 133, 137, 252
Prasna-Upanisad, 7
Pratima, 220, 221, 223, 248, 252, 254, 262,
    462, 463, 473
Pratipatti, 169
pratyanubhavati avastha, 269
prayoga, 250
precept, 409
predestination, 170
Prince Five Weapons, 191
Prince *Siddartha*, 37
Prodigal Son, 432

Prosser, Edith, 419
Protectors of the Doctrine, 186
pseudo schools, 466
psyche, 21
psychotherapy, 398
Pu Kung Chin Fang, 87
Pudgala, 45

Q

Queen *Srimala*, 201, 242

R

Raga, 45
Rajah, 168
Rajanga, 158
rathakaya, 160
reality, two aspects, 457
realm,
    diamond, 64
    matrix, 64, 86
    Thunderbolt, 85, 87
Rig Veda, 123
Right Transmission of the Law, 440
ritual, 77
    empowerment, 214
    gestures, 188
    unction, 426
Rudrakarama, 168
rumination, 46
Rupa, 11, 134, 396, 462, 463
Rupa-Kaya, 13
Rupaprasada, 133
Ryukyu Koshirenmei, 459

S

sacred places, thirty-two, 193
Saddha, 45
safety, 191
Sahaja Sukkha, 99
St. John of the Cross, 262
sakti, 163
Sakurazwa Nyoti, 469
Sama Veda, 123, 429
Samadhi, 105
Samana, 139
Samasthana, 222, 225
Samatha, 224
Samjna, 11, 250

Samkhya, 6, 400
Sammitya School, 396
Samskara, 11, 250
Sanchin, 235
Sanchin Hsing, 209, 233, 235, 477
Sangha, 30
Santiraksita, 442
Sarakupa, 169
Sarana, 235
Sarvastivada tradition, 67, 133, 136, 196,
    202, 207, 238, 243, 250, 267, 284, 396
Sataghni, 163
Satapatha Brahmana, 7
Satasutra, 410
Satyasiddhi School, 396, 410
schools, 226, 290
sekeko, 420
self-deceit, 266, 269
selfhood belief, 47, 53
self-purification rites, 75, 79
Senani, 160
Seng I Shih, 26
Seng Yi, 119
Sensei, 160
Senjutsu, 178
Setsuri, 158
sexual intercourse, ritual, 204
Shan Wu Wei, 87
Shang, 24
Shantideva, 199
Shaolin Monastery, 216, 229
Shaolin School, 435
Shaolin Wu I Method, 216
shih, 24
Shingon, 69, 88, 449
Shipalohanshou, 231
Shu, 141
Shugyo, 75, 76, 77, 78, 269
Shuzo Okada, 469
Siddhi, 69
Siksa, 169
Silamegha, 88
Simha, 168
Simhahanu, 168
Simhavikridita, 169
simultaneous being, 75
sira, 465
sistrum, 216
Six Gates, 306
Six Realms of Existence, 408
Skandha

consciousness, 479
form, 395
Skhandas, 11, 20, 21, 23, 50, 404
skillfull means, 82, 449
skillfull striking, 206
sloth, 46
smriti, 355
snavas, 463, 465
Softly Clasped Hand School, 419
Sogen Ishizuka, 469
somatypes, 48, 97
Sotoba, 64, 66
sounds, five, 405
space, 13, 69, 250, 401
space meditation, 51
sparring, 264, 269
spiritual friend, 398
spiritual liberation, 181
spiritual lineage, 226
spiritual path of action, 270
Sri Lanka, 28
stance, 221
Sthana, 221, 225, 269, 270, 471
stupa, 64, 66
stupidity, 45, 46
Subhakarasimha, 69, 87
sudden path, 444
suffering, 79, 250
Sugata, 30
Suklavijaya, 239
sumo, 178
sun, 168
Sun Ssu Miao, 123
Sun Tzu, 25, 157, 205
Sung Tai Jo, 243
Sunyavada School, 110
Surangama Sutra, 48, 103
Surya, 168
Suspala, 163
Susruta, 125
Susumna, 129
Sutra, Abhaya Rajakumara, 198
Sutra, Astahasrika Prajnaparamita, 202
Sutra, Brahmajala, 197, 199
Sutra, Catasahasrika Prajna Paramita, 197
Sutra, Dhasabhumi, 467
Sutra, Lankavatara, 262, 447
Sutra, Large Sutra on Perfect Wisdom, 263
Sutra, Lotus, 47, 176
Sutra, Maha-Prajnaparamita, 139
Sutra, Mahavairocana, 214, 218

Sutra, of 42 Sections, 206
Sutra of Trapusa and Bhalika, 71
Sutra, Srimalasimhanada, 201, 242
Sutra, Surangama, 103, 198, 243
Sutra, Suvarnaprabhasa, 200
Sutra, Vajrasamadhi, 230
Sutra, Vajrasekhara, 183
Sutra, Vajrausnisa, 201
Sutra, Virmalakirti, 409
Sutra, White Lotus, 174, 206
Sutra, Yogacara, 254
Sutras, 32
sword, sacred, 161
symbols, 65
systems,
three, 53
five, 53
six, 53
Sze Hung Pei, 208
Szechinpo Lama dances, 243

T

Tai Chi Chuan, 452
Tai Tsung, 215
Taizokai, 86
Taimitsu, 76
Ta Jih, 63
Takeda Harunobu, 416
tantra, 204
left-hand, 203, 204
right-hand, 203
Tao-an, 436
Tao Yi, 119
Taoism, 120, 128, 216
taste, six types, 405
Tatvasamgraha, 69
Te Chu To, 420
teaching, open-handed, 185
temperaments, four elements, 198
Temple sleep, 398
ten stages of *Bodhisattva* path, 467
Tendai sect, 88
Tenketsuho, 146
Theravada, 13, 21, 28, 29, 104
Theravada Arahants, 25, 107
Theraveda monastic code, 77, 106
Theravada School, 14, 23, 25, 33, 35, 56, 71,
110, 136, 175, 193, 196, 199, 202, 248,
292, 396, 398, 401, 419
Theravada Vipassana, 224

Thor, 162
thought, 287
Three Jewels, 56, 80, 399
Three Seals, 41
thunderbolt, 162, 181, 233, 235, 421
Thunderbolt Body, 204
Thunderbolt Path, 202
Thunderbolt Suei, 145
Tibetan School, 106
Tien Hsueh Fa, 146
Tien T'ai, 75, 182, 252, 397
Tiger Striking, 169, 208, 239, 242
time, 356
timelessness, 357
Tirthantika School, 396
To De, 456, 475
topa, 65, 66, 67, 68, 73, 82
training, dangers, 100
Trican, 233
Trilokavijayakayasthana, 235
Triple Battle, 233
Trisatyabhumi, 233
Tsou Yen, 121
tumo, 106
Tung Chuan, 243
Tvastr, 162
Twelve Gates, 410
Two Truths, 183, 457

U

Ucchumsa, 48
udana, 139
unimanifest action, 481
Upanisads, 6
Upaya, 82
Usnisa, 165
Utpadajiva Srotasiddhanta, 136

V

Vaibhasika, 207, 259, 267, 396, 397, 410
Vaibhasya School, 202
Vaisya, 159
vajra, 64, 65, 162, 163, 166, 233, 419, 421
Vajra Kings, 186
vajra maces, 166
Vajra World Mandala, 87
Vajradhara, 182, 186
Vajrahasta, 162

Vajradhatu Mahamandala, 209
Vajramukti, 166, 167, 168, 169, 179, 184, 197, 207, 208, 228, 235, 239, 261, 269, 272, 425
Vajramukti nata, 181, 219, 220
Vajramusti Bodhisattva, 178
Vajranrita, 214
Vajrapani, 182, 186
Vajrasandhi Bodhisattva, 178, 211
Vajrasattva, 186
Vajrasekhara Sutra, 69, 87
Vajrasekharayoga Sutra, 88
Vajrayaksa, 209
Vajrayana, 202, 204
Varamudra, 188
Varuna, 48
Vasana, 249
Vasheshika, 400
vastu, 250
Vasubhandu, 139, 193, 197, 200, 236, 250, 252, 254, 256, 258, 263, 266, 267, 276, 286, 289, 400, 401, 410, 480
Vasumitra, 7, 480
Vedana, 11
Vedanta, 6
Vedas, 6, 25, 123, 156
Vetali method, 239
Vibharva, 138
Vidyuthasta, 162
Vijnapti, 465
Vijnaptikayakrita, 179
Vijnaptimatra School, 199, 207
Vimoksaprajna, 193
Vinaya, 30
Vijnana, 11, 12, 16
Vijnana dhatu, 14, 17
Vinaya, 77
Vis, 159
visah, 160
Visaya, 15
Visaya dhatu, 14
visual moment, 482
Visuddhi, 76, 262
Visuddhikriya, 75
Visuddhi Magga, 45, 51, 53, 56, 68, 69
Visvabhi, 48
Vitakka, 46
Vodana, 76
Vyaghraja, 239, 243
Vyana, 139
Vyasu, 408

W

Wang, 24
war hammer, 162
warriors, 419
water, 13, 50, 51, 52, 92, 250, 251
Way of Wisdom, 170
wheel, 35
    eight-spoked, 56
Wheel-turning King, 35
white, 237
White Heron Grove, 237
White Heron Lake, 237
winds, five, 139
Wing Shih, 420
wordless doctrine, 266
wrestling, 178
Wu I, 216
Wu Shu, 205
Wu Ti, 295

Y

Yajur Veda, 123
Yaksa, 170
Yamaka, 169
Yamaka Patihariya, 98

yang, 121
yantra, 163
yeh hua, 250
Yellow Emperor's Book of Internal Medicine,
    119
Yi Yen, 149
yin, 121, 179
yoga, 125
    Buddhist, 101
    Great Bliss, 99
    Hatha, 101, 125, 408
    Kriya, 463
    of inner fire, 106
    respiratory, 230
    Tantric, 99
    Tumo, 408
    Vajra, 220, 415
Yogacara School, 108, 111, 202, 207, 215,
    229, 409, 410, 411
Yuan Hua, 121

Z

Za, 398
zombies, 239

THE MUSHINDOKAI

The Mushindokai (MKA) is an ancient organization brought to Britain by two Okinawan masters of *Kempo* (Chinese: *Chuan Fa*) in 1958. It teaches and organizes physical and spiritual studies in many different subjects, all of which share a common goal. It has little in common with sporting Karate. MKA studies cover a wide range of oriental medical and spiritual practices and its Kempo is an unmodified and original form of the Chinese Shorin School (the style of Itosu and Sakugawa). The British branch has since 1960 published a quarterly Journal of Advanced Studies (J.A.S.) which contains articles, anecdotes, ancient legends, and other information regarding the history, formation, practice, and spiritual principles of *Kempo* along with its allied arts stemming from India, China, and the Ryukyu Islands. Despite the rarity and relevance of such "source" information to the more serious student, much of the Journal's content is unknown to mainstream Karate proponents. Its inclusions are often revolutionary and do not shrink from representing little known views and historical details concerning the genesis and development of the different schools and teachers of Karate, etc., in Okinawa at variance with many of the published accounts as found within commercial publications. In such endeavors it acts as the conscience of the silent majority of the traditional Masters. The journal is non-commercial; it deliberately makes no profit, and is funded by subscriptions and donations.

The head teachers of MKA are leading members of the Independent Ryukyu Kempo Federation, a traditional group composed of pre-WWII graduate masters and their disciples unwilling to compromise their principles or cooperate in either Westernization (or Japanization) of the traditional Sino-Ryukyuan Buddhist Kempo.

In Britain, as in other nations, our group has its own residential Buddhist Temple, clubs, and study groups, to which students may come to study and practice for periods of up to several years. Such training is felt to be the only way one can seriously study or perfect the original *Kempo* as it is its original environment. This Temple, the first of its kind in Europe, has been active since 1974, and forms part of the European Buddhist Community. It has an extensive library and research facilities devoted to oriental projects and holds many study seminars throughout the year for both native and overseas students. It also has meditation, ritual and retreat facilities for both monks and lay persons. Currently it is in the process of building up a Buddhist medical dispensary. The Mushindo School of *Kempo* is firmly committed to the preservation, propagation, practice, and study of the ancient Buddhist spiritual values within traditional Kempo, and has no time for competition or commercialism. All its teachers give their services voluntarily.

If you would like to avail yourself of more information you are invited to become a member of the GB branch by writing to the Secretary enclosing a SSAE. Membership is selective and requires certain commitment. Overseas students should enclose an I.M.O.

Kongoryuji
London Road
East Dereham NR191AS
England

Shifu Nagaboshi Tomio has studied with Buddhist teachers from Japan, Korea, Thailand, Ceylon, and Tibet, learning about oriental medicine, cheirology, the art of Kempo, and Shingon ritual. He is an ordained teacher and initiate of the Ryushinji Temple in Okinawa, Japan and has practiced as a *Yamabushi* (mountain ascetic). In 1974, he received his 4th degree Black Belt in Mushindo Kempo Karate Do while serving as head Kempo teacher at Cambridge University. He currently teaches a the Kongoryuji Temple in Norfolk, England, which he founded in 1978 after establishing the Hakurenji Temple in London. Shifu Nagaboshi Tomio is the author of *Chinese Hand Analysis*, also published by Samuel Weiser.